DICTIONARY
of Daily Life
IN BIBLICAL & POST-BIBLICAL ANTIQUITY

Volume IV
O-Z

Edwin M. Yamauchi & Marvin R. Wilson

HENDRICKSON PUBLISHERS

Dictionary of Daily Life in Biblical and Post-Biblical Antiquity
Volume IV, O-Z
© 2016 by Hendrickson Publishers Marketing, LLC
P. O. Box 3473
Peabody, Massachusetts 01961-3473
www.hendrickson.com

ISBN 978-1-61970-728-3

Printed in the United States of America

Second Printing — February 2017

Library of Congress Cataloging-in-Publication Data

Yamauchi, Edwin M.
    Dictionary of daily life in biblical and post-biblical antiquity /
Edwin M. Yamauchi and Marvin R. Wilson.
        volumes cm
    Includes bibliographical references.
    Contents: Volume I. A-Da.
    ISBN 978-1-61970-460-2 (v. 1)
    1. Bible—Dictionaries. 1. Title.
    BS440.Y37 2014
    220.95—dc23
                        2014017152

Dedicated to our esteemed colleague,

the eminent Old Testament scholar

Roland K. Harrison

1920–1993

TABLE OF CONTENTS

CONTRIBUTORS

RB-L BAILLEUL-LESUER, Rozenn. ABD, University of Chicago.

ALB BEAN, Adam L. PhD, Johns Hopkins University.

RGB BRANCH, Robin G. PhD, Adjunct Professor, Christian Brothers University, Memphis, Tennessee; Extraordinary Associate Professor, Faculty of Theology, North-West University, Potchefstroom, South Africa.

STC CARROLL, Scott T. PhD, Director, Manuscript Research Group.

ACC CHAMBERS, Adam C. PhD.

JJD DAVIS, John J. ThD, Professor of Old Testament and Hebrew emeritus, Grace Theological Seminary.

JFD DEFELICE, John F., Jr. PhD, Associate Professor of History, University of Maine Presque Isle.

LMF FIELDS, Lee M. PhD, Professor of Biblical Studies, Mid-Atlantic Christian University.

LPG GRIMSLEY, Lucas P. ABD, Southwestern Baptist Theological Seminary.

RKH *HARRISON, Roland K. PhD, Professor of Old Testament, Wycliffe College, University of Toronto. *Deceased.

RSH HESS, Richard S. PhD, Professor of Old Testament, Denver Seminary.

DLH HOFFMAN, Daniel L. PhD, Senior Adjunct Professor of History, Lee University.

CSK KEENER, Craig S. PhD, Professor of New Testament, Asbury Theological Seminary.

GLL LINTON, Gregory L. PhD, Professor of New Testament, Johnson University.

PLM MAIER, Paul L. PhD, Russell H. Seibert Professor of Ancient History emeritus, Western Michigan University.

GLM MATTINGLY, Gerald L. PhD, Professor of Biblical Studies, Johnson University.

LJN NESS, Lester J. PhD, Foreign Expert, Yunnan University, China.

JAP PATTENGALE, Jerry A. PhD, University Professor, Indiana Wesleyan University, and Distinguished Professor, Excelsia College.

HP PEHLKE, Helmuth. ThD, Professor of Old Testament, Southwestern Baptist Theological Seminary, and Professor of Old Testament, Bibelseminar Bonn, Germany.

EBP POWERY, Emerson B. PhD, Associate Professor of New Testament, Lee University.

TR RATA, Tiberius. PhD, Professor of Old Testament, Grace College and Seminary.

WJR REED, William J. ABD, Johns Hopkins University.

SMR RODRIQUEZ, Seth M. PhD, Adjunct Professor of Old Testament Interpretation, The Southern Baptist Theological Seminary.

FDS SCALF, Foy D. PhD, Head of Research Archives, The Oriental Institute, University of Chicago.

KNS SCHOVILLE, Keith N. PhD, Professor of Hebrew and Semitic Studies emeritus, University of Wisconsin.

BVS SEEVERS, Boyd V. PhD, Professor of Old Testament Studies, University of Northwestern – St. Paul.

TMS SIGLER, Tim M. PhD, Professor of Hebrew and Biblical Studies, Moody Bible Institute.

RWS SMITH, Robert W. PhD, Professor of Bible and History, Mid-Atlantic Christian University.

PS SPRINKLE, Preston. PhD, Vice President, Eternity Bible College, Boise Extension.

GCT TUCKER, Gordon C. Professor of Biological Sciences, Eastern Illinois University.

MRW WILSON, Marvin R. PhD, Harold J. Ockenga Professor of Biblical and Theological Studies, Gordon College.

EMY YAMAUCHI, Edwin M. PhD, Professor of History emeritus, Miami University.

MSZ ZIESE, Mark S. PhD, Professor of Old Testament, Johnson University.

ABBREVIATIONS

GENERAL

#(#)	number(s)
||	parallel to
AD	*anno domini*, in the year of the Lord
Akk.	Akkadian
Arab.	Arabic
Aram.	Aramaic
ASV	American Standard Version
AV	Authorized Version (i.e., KJV = King James Version)
b.	*ben,* Hebrew "son"; born
b.	Babylonian Talmud
BC	before Christ
c.	century
C	centigrade
ca.	*circa*, about
CE	Codex Eshnunna
CEB	Common English Bible
cf.	*confer*, compare
ch(s).	chapter(s)
CH	Code of Hammurabi
CJB	Complete Jewish Bible
cm.	centimeter
col(s).	column(s)
d.	died
Dyn.	Dynasty
EA	El Amarna (designation of texts from)
ed.	editor(s), edition
e.g.	*exempli gratia*, for example

Egy.	Egyptian
Elam.	Elamite
Eng.	English
Ep.	epistle, letter
esp.	especially
ESV	English Standard Version
et al.	*et alia*, and others
Eth.	Ethiopic
F	Fahrenheit
fig.	figure
fl.	*floruit*, flourished
frag.	fragment
ft.	foot, feet
gal.	gallon(s)
Gk.	Greek
ha.	hectare (about 2.5 acres)
Heb.	Hebrew
i.e.	*id est*, that is
ibid.	*ibidem*, in the same place
in.	inch(es)
JB	Jerusalem Bible
JPS	*The Holy Scriptures according to the Masoretic Text: A New Translation* (Jewish Publication Society)
kg	kilogram(s)
KJV	King James Version
km.	kilometer
Lat.	Latin
lb(s).	pound(s)
LCL	Loeb Classical Library
lit.	literally
LL	Laws of Lipit-Ishtar
LXX	Septuagint
m.	meter(s)
m.	Mishnah
MAL	Middle Assyrian Law Code
MASCA	Museum Applied Science Center for Archaeology
MFA	Museum of Fine Arts (Boston)
mi.	mile(s)
MK	Middle Kingdom (of Egypt)
Mt.	mount, mountain
MT	Masoretic Text
n.	(foot/end)note

NAB	New American Bible
NASB	New American Standard Bible
NEB	New English Bible
NET	New English Translation
NEV	New English Version
NHC	Nag Hammadi codices
NIV	New International Version
NJPS	*Tanakh: The Holy Scriptures: The New JPS Translation according to the Traditional Hebrew Text*
NK	New Kingdom (of Egypt)
no(s).	number(s)
NRSV	New Revised Standard Version
n.s.	new series (of journals)
NT	New Testament
OB	Old Babylonian
OK	Old Kingdom (Egypt)
Old Pers.	Old Persian
OT	Old Testament
Oxy.	Oxyrhynchus
oz.	ounce(s)
Pap.	Papyrus
Phoen.	Phoenician
pl.	plate
pl.	plural
R.	rabbi
r.	reigned
REB	Revised English Bible
repr.	reprint(ed)
rev.	revised
RSV	Revised Standard Version
RV	Revised Version
sing.	singular
sq.	square
St.	saint
Sum.	Sumerian
Suppl.	Supplement
t.	Tosefta
tr.	translated
trans.	translator(s)
Ugar.	Ugaritic
vol(s).	volume(s)
vs(s).	verse(s)

Vulg	Vulgate
y.	Jerusalem (*Yerushalmi*) Talmud
YLT	Young's Literal Translation

ANCIENT SOURCES

Hebrew Bible/Old Testament

Gen	Genesis
Exod	Exodus
Lev	Leviticus
Num	Numbers
Deut	Deuteronomy
Josh	Joshua
Judg	Judges
Ruth	Ruth
1–2 Sam	1–2 Samuel
1–2 Kgs	1–2 Kings
1–2 Chr	1–2 Chronicles
Ezra	Ezra
Neh	Nehemiah
Esth	Esther
Job	Job
Ps(s)	Psalm(s)
Prov	Proverbs
Eccl	Ecclesiastes
Song	Song of Songs
Isa	Isaiah
Jer	Jeremiah
Lam	Lamentations
Ezek	Ezekiel
Dan	Daniel
Hos	Hosea
Joel	Joel
Amos	Amos
Obad	Obadiah
Jonah	Jonah
Mic	Micah
Nah	Nahum
Hab	Habakkuk
Zeph	Zephaniah

Hag	Haggai
Zech	Zechariah
Mal	Malachi

New Testament

Matt	Matthew
Mark	Mark
Luke	Luke
John	John
Acts	Acts
Rom	Romans
1–2 Cor	1–2 Corinthians
Gal	Galatians
Eph	Ephesians
Phil	Philippians
Col	Colossians
1–2 Thess	1–2 Thessalonians
1–2 Tim	1–Timothy
Titus	Titus
Phlm	Philemon
Heb	Hebrews
Jas	James
1–2 Pet	1–2 Peter
1–3 John	1–3 John
Jude	Jude
Rev	Revelation

Apocrypha and Septuagint

1–2 Esd	1–2 Esdras
1–4 Macc	1–4 Maccabees
Add Esth	Addition to Esther
Bar	Baruch
Bel	Bel and the Dragon
Ep Jer	Epistle of Jeremiah
Jdt	Judith
Pr Azar	Prayer of Azariah
Pr Man	Prayer of Manasseh
Sg Three	Song of the Three Young Men
Sir	Sirach/Ecclesiasticus

Sus	Susanna
Tob	Tobias
Wis	Wisdom of Solomon

Old Testament Pseudepigrapha

2 Bar.	*2 Baruch*
1 En.	*1 Enoch*
2 En.	*2 Enoch*
4 Ezra	*4 Ezra*
Jos. Asen.	*Joseph and Aseneth*
Jub.	*Jubilees*
Lad. Jac.	*Ladder of Jacob*
Let. Aris.	*Letter of Aristeas*
Odes Sol.	*Odes of Solomon*
Ps.-Phoc.	*Pseudo-Phocylides*
Pss. Sol.	*Psalms of Solomon*
Sib. Or.	*Sibylline Oracles*
T. Ash.	*Testament of Asher*
T. Benj.	*Testament of Benjamin*
T. Isaac	*Testament of Isaac*
T. Jac.	*Testament of Jacob*
T. Jos.	*Testament of Joseph*
T. Levi	*Testament of Levi*
T. Naph.	*Testament of Naphtali*
T. Zeb.	*Testament of Zebulun*
Vis. Ezra	*Vision of Ezra*

New Testament Apocrypha and Pseudepigrapha

Acts John	*Acts of John*
Acts Thom.	*Acts of Thomas*
Apoc. Paul	*Apocalypse of Paul*
Apoc. Pet.	*Apocalypse of Peter*
Prot. Jas.	*Protevangelium of James*

Dead Sea Scrolls and Cairo Geniza

CD	*Damascus Document*
1QHᵃ·ᵇ (=1Q35)	*Hodayot* (Thanksgiving Hymns)
1QS	*Serek Hayaḥad* (Rule of the Community)

1QSa	1Q28a (Rule of the Congregation)

4QMMT (=4Q394–399) (*Miqṣat Maʿaśê ha-Torah*)

11QTemple^a,b	11Q19–20 (Temple Scroll)

Judaica

ʿAbod. Zar.	ʿAbodah Zarah
ʾAbot	ʾAbot
ʾAbot R. Nat.	ʾAbot de Rabbi Nathan
ʿArak.	ʿArakin
B. Bat.	Baba Batra
B. Meṣ.	Baba Meṣiʿa
B. Qam.	Baba Qamma
Bek.	Bekorot
Ber.	Berakot
Beṣah	Beṣah (Yom Ṭob)
Deut. Rab.	Deuteronomy Rabbah
Eccl. Rab.	Ecclesiastes Rabbah
ʿEd.	ʿEduyyot
ʿErub.	ʿErubin
Exod. Rab.	Exodus Rabbah
Gen. Rab.	Genesis Rabbah
Giṭ.	Giṭṭin
Ḥag.	Ḥagigah
Ḥul.	Ḥullin
Kelim	Kelim
Ker.	Keritot
Ketub.	Ketubbot
Kil.	Kilʾayim
Maʿaś.	Maʿaśerot
Maʿaś. Š.	Maʿaśer Šeni
Mak.	Makkot
Makš.	Makširin
Meg.	Megillah
Mek.	Mekilta
Menaḥ.	Menaḥot
Mid.	Middot
Miqw.	Miqwaʾot
Moʿed Qaṭ.	Moʿed Qaṭan
Naz.	Nazir
Ned.	Nedarim
Neg.	Negaʿim

Nez.	Neziqin
Nid.	Niddah
Num. Rab.	Numbers Rabbah
ʾOhol.	ʾOholot
Parah	Parah
Peʾah	Peʾah
Pesaḥ.	Pesaḥim
Qidd.	Qidduśin
Qod.	Qodaśim
Roš Haš.	Roš Haššanah
Šabb.	Šabbat
Sanh.	Sanhedrin
Šeb.	Šebiʿit
Šebu.	Šebuʿot
Sem.	Semaḥot
Šeqal.	Šeqalim
Sifre Num	Sifre (to Numbers)
Sifre Deut	Sifre (to Deuteronomy)
Song Rab.	Song of Songs Rabbah
Soṭah	Soṭah
Sukkah	Sukkah
Ṭ. Yom	Ṭebul Yom
Taʿan.	Taʿanit
Tamid	Tamid
Ṭehar.	Ṭeharot
Tem.	Temurah
Ter.	Terumot
ʿUq.	Uqṣin
Yad.	Yadayim
Yebam.	Yebamot
Yoma	Yoma (=Kippurim)
Zebaḥ.	Zebaḥim

Apostolic Fathers

1–2 Clem.	1–2 Clement
Barn.	Barnabas
Did.	Didache
Herm. Mand.	Shepherd of Hermas, Mandate(s)
Herm. Simil.	Shepherd of Hermas, Similitude(s)
Herm. Vis.	Shepherd of Hermas, Vision(s)
Ign. Eph.	Ignatius, To the Ephesians

Ign. *Magn.*	Ignatius, *To the Magnesians*
Ign. *Phld.*	Ignatius, *To the Philadelphians*
Ign. *Pol.*	Ignatius, *To Polycarp*
Ign. *Rom.*	Ignatius, *To the Romans*
Ign. *Smyrn.*	Ignatius, *To the Smyrnaeans*
Mart. Pol.	*Martyrdom of Polycarp*
Pol. *Phil.*	Polycarp, *To the Philippians*

Ancient Authors

Achilles Tatius (ca. 3rd c. AD)
  Leuc. Clit.   *Leucippe et Clitophon (The Adventures of Leucippe and Cleitophon)*
Aelian (ca. AD 170–235)
  Nat. an.   *De natura animalium (Nature of Animals)*
  Var. hist.   *Varia historia*
Aeschines (ca. 397–ca. 322 BC)
  Tim.   *In Timarchum (Against Timarchus)*
Aeschylus (ca. 525–455 BC)
  Ag.   *Agamemnon*
  Cho.   *Cheophori (Libation-Bearers)*
  Eum.   *Eumenides (Eumenides)*
  Suppl.   *Supplices (Suppliant Women)*
Ambrose (AD 339–397)
  Exp. Ps.   *Expositiones in Psalmos*
  Hex.   *Hexaemeron libri sex (Six Days of Creation)*
  Virg.   *De virginibus (On Virgins)*
Ammianus Marcellinus (ca. AD 330–395)
  Res G.   *Res Gestae (Roman History)*
Anonymous
  Cod. Theod.   *Codex Theodosianus (Theodosian Code)*
  Dig. Just.   *Digest of Justinian*
  H.A.   *Historia Augusta*
Appian (ca. AD 95–ca. 165)
  Bell. civ.   *Bella civilia (Civil Wars)*
Apuleius (fl. ca. AD 155)
  Apol.   *Apologia (Pro se de magia) (Apology)*
  Metam.   *Metamorphoses (The Golden Ass)*
Aristophanes [Aristoph.] (ca. 446–ca. 386 BC)
  Ach.   *Acharnenses (Acharnians)*
  Eccl.   *Ecclesiazusae (Women of the Assembly)*
  Eq.   *Equites (Knights)*

Lys.	*Lysistrata*
Nub.	*Nubes (Clouds)*
Plut.	*Plutus (The Rich Man)*
Ran.	*Ranae (Frogs)*
Thesm.	*Thesmophoriazusae*
Vesp.	*Vespae (Wasps)*

Aristotle [Arist.] (384–322 BC)

Ath. pol.	*Athēnaiōn politeia (Constitution of Athens)*
Div. somn.	*De divination per somnum (Prophesying by Dreams)*
Eth. Nic.	*Ethica Nichomachea (Nichomachean Ethics)*
Gen. an.	*De generatione animalium (Generation of Animals)*
Hist. an.	*Historia animalium (History of Animals)*
Mete.	*Meteorologica (Meteorology)*
Part. an.	*De partibus animalium (Parts of Animals)*
Pol.	*Politics*
Rhet.	*Rhetorica (Rhetoric)*
Somn.	*De somniis (Dreams)*

Arrian (ca. AD 86–160)

Anab.	*Anabasis*

Artemidorus Daldianus (mid/late 2nd c. AD)

Oneir.	*Oneirocritica*

Athanasius (ca. AD 295–373)

C. Gent.	*Contra gentes (Against the Pagans)*
H. Ar.	*Historia Arianorum (History of the Arians)*
Vit. Ant.	*Vita Antonii (Life of Antony)*

Athenaeus (fl. ca. AD 200)

Deipn.	*Deipnosophistae (The Learned Banqueters)*

Athenagoras (fl. ca. AD 180)

Leg.	*Legatio pro Christianis (Embassy for the Christians)*

Augustine (AD 354–430)

Bon. conj.	*De bono conjugali (The Good of Marriage)*
Civ.	*De civitate Dei (The City of God)*
Conf.	*Confessionum (Confessions)*
Cons.	*De consensu evangelistarum (Harmony of the Gospels)*
De mend.	*De mendacio (On Lying)*
Doctr. chr.	*De doctrina christiana (Christian Instruction)*
Ennarat. Ps.	*Ennarationes in Psalmos (Expositions of the Psalms)*
Ep.	*Epistulae (Letters)*
Faust.	*Contra Faustum Manichaeum (Against Faustus the Manichaean)*
Haer.	*De haeresibus (Heresies)*
Incomp. nupt.	*Incompetentibus nuptiis (Adulterous Marriages)*

Man.	*De moribus Manichaeorum (On the Morals of the Manichaeans)*
Nupt.	*De nuptiis et concupiscentia ad Valerium comitem (Marriage and Concupiscence)*
Op. mon.	*De opere monachorum (On the Work of Monks)*
Quaest. ev.	*Quaestionum evangelicarum*
Tract. Ev. Jo.	*In Evangelium Johannis tractatus (Tractates on the Gospel of John)*
Virginit.	*De sancta virginitate (Holy Virginity)*

Aulus Cornelius Celsus (fl. ca. AD 25)

Med.	*De medicina*

Aulus Gellius

Noct. Att.	*Noctes atticae (Attic Nights)*

Basil (AD 330–379)

Ep.	*Epistulae*
Hex.	*Hexaemeron*
Hom. in Ps.	*Homiliae in Psalmos*

Caesar, Julius (100–44 BC)

Bell. gall.	*Bellum gallicum (Gallic War)*

Cassius Dio (ca. AD 155–235)

Hist. rom.	*Historia romana (Roman History)*

Cato (234–149 BC)

Agr.	*De agricultura (Agriculture)*

Cicero [Cic.] (106–43 BC)

Att.	*Epistulae ad Atticum*
Cael.	*Pro Caelio*
De or.	*De oratore*
Div.	*De divinatione*
Dom.	*De domo suo*
Fam.	*Epistulae ad familiares (Letters to His Friends)*
Flac.	*Pro Flacco*
Font.	*Pro Fonteio*
Inv.	*De inventione rhetorica*
Leg.	*De Legibus*
Mur.	*Pro Murena*
Off.	*De officiis*
Parad.	*Paradoxa Stoicorum*
Rep.	*De republica*
Verr.	*In Verrem*

Clement of Alexandria [Clem.] (d. ca. AD 214)

Paed.	*Paedagogus (Christ the Educator)*
Protr.	*Protrepticus (Exhortation to the Greeks)*

Quis div.   Quis dives salvetur (Salvation of the Rich)
Strom.   Stromateis (Miscellanies)
Clement of Rome (fl. ca. 96) (see 1–2 Clement)
Columella (fl. AD 60–65)
  Arb.   De arboribus
  Rust.   De re rustica (On Farming)
Cyprian (ca. AD 200–258)
  Ep.   Epistulae (Letters)
  Hab. virg.   De habitu virginum (The Dress of Virgins)
  Laps.   De lapsis (The Lapsed)
  Unit. eccl.   De catholicae ecclesiae unitate (The Unity of the
                   Catholic Church)
Demosthenes [Dem.] (384–322 BC)
  1 Boeot.   Contra Boeotum i (1 Against Boeotos)
  1–3 Olynth.   Olynthiaca i–iii (1–3 Olynthiac)
  Cor.   De corona (On the Crown)
  Ep.   Epistulae (Letters)
  Eub.   Contra Eubulidem (Against Eubulides)
  Pant.   Contra Pantaenetum (Against Pantaenetus)
  Timocr.   In Timocratem (Against Timocrates)
Dio Chrysostom (ca. AD 40–after 110)
  2 Fort.   De fortuna ii (Fortune 2)
  Rhod.   Rhodiaca (To the People of Rhodes)
Diodorus Siculus [Diod. Sic.] (fl. ca. 60–39 BC)
  Bib. hist.   Bibliotheca historica (Library of History)
Dionysius of Halicarnassus (ca. 60–7 BC)
  Ant. rom.   Antiquitates romanae
Dioscorides Pedanius (fl. ca. AD 40–80)
  Mat. med.   De materia medica
Epictetus
  Disc.   Dissertationes (Discourses)
Epiphanius (ca. AD 315–403)
  Pan.   Panarion (Adversus haereses) (Refutation of All Heresies)
Euripides (ca. 485–406 BC)
  Bacch.   Bacchae (Bacchanals)
  Hipp.   Hippolytus
  Med.   Medea
Eusebius of Caesarea [Eus.] (AD ca. 260–ca. 339)
  Coet. sanct.   Ad coetum sanctorum (Oration of the Emperor Con-
                   stantine to the Assembly of the Saints)
  Comm. Ps.   Commentarius in Psalmos (Commentary on the Psalms)
  Ecl. proph.   Eclogae propheticae (Extracts from the Prophets)

Hist. eccl.	*Historia ecclesiastica (Ecclesiastical History)*
Mart. Pal.	*De martyribus Palaestinae (The Martyrs of Palestine)*
Prep. ev.	*Praeparatio evangelica (Preparation for the Gospel)*
Vit. Const.	*Vita Constantini (Life of Constantine)*

Gaius (ca. AD 130–180)

| *Dig.* | *Digest* |

Gregory of Nazianzus

| *Ep.* | *Epistulae (Letters)* |
| *Or. Bas.* | *Oratio in laudem Basilii* |

Herodotus [Her.] (ca. 484–ca. 425 BC)

| *Hist.* | *Historiae* |

Hesiod [Hes.] (ca. 700 BC)

| *Op.* | *Opera et dies (Works and Days)* |
| *Theog.* | *Theogonia (Theogony)* |

Hippocrates (ca. 460–ca. 370 BC)

Aph.	*Aphorismata (Aphorisms)*
Artic.	*De articulis reponendis (Joints)*
Carn.	*De carne (Fleshes)*
Epid.	*Epidemiae (Epidemics)*
Jusj.	*Jus jurandum (The Oath)*
Med.	*De medico (The Physician)*
Morb.	*De morbis (Diseases)*
Nat. hom.	*De natura hominis (Nature of Man)*

Hippolytus (ca. AD 160–235)

Comm. Dan.	*Commentarium in Danielem*
Haer.	*Refutatio omnium haeresium (Refutation of All Heresies)*
Trad. ap.	*Traditio apostolica (The Apostolic Tradition)*

Homer [Hom.] (8th c. BC)

| *Il.* | *Ilias (Iliad)* |
| *Od.* | *Odyssea (Odyssey)* |

Horace (65–8 BC)

Carm.	*Carmina (Odes)*
Ep.	*Epistulae (Epistles)*
Sat.	*Satirae (Satires)*

Ignatius of Antioch (d. ca. AD 115) (see under *Apostolic Fathers*)

Irenaeus (ca. AD 130–ca. 200)

| *Epid.* | *Epideixis tou apostolikou kērygmatos (Demonstration of Apostolic Preaching)* |
| *Haer.* | *Adversus haereses (Against Heresies)* |

Jerome (ca. AD 347–ca. 420)

| *Comm. Ezech.* | *Commentariorum in Ezechielem* |
| *Epist.* | *Epistulae* |

Jov.	*Adversus Jovinianum*
Qu. hebr. Gen.	*Liber Quaestionum hebraicarum in Genesim*
Vigil.	*Adversus Vigilantium*
Vir. ill.	*De viris illustribus (On Illustrious Men)*
Vit. Malch.	*Vita Malchi monachi* ("The Life of Malchus the Monk")

John Chrysostom (AD 347–407)

Exp. Ps.	*Expositiones in Psalmos*
Hom. Act.	*Homiliae in Acta apostolorum*
Hom. Col.	*Homiliae in epistulam ad Colossenses*
Hom. 1 Cor.	*Homiliae in epistulam i ad Corinthios*
Hom. 2 Cor.	*Homiliae in epistulam ii ad Corinthios*
Hom. Eph.	*Homiliae in epistulam ad Ephesios*
Hom. Heb.	*Homiliae in epistulam ad Hebraeos*
Hom. Jo.	*Homiliae in Joannem*
Hom. Matt.	*Homiliae in Mattaeum*
Hom. Rom.	*Homiliae in epistulam ad Romanos*
Hom. 1 Tim.	*Homiliae in epistulam i ad Timotheum*
Hom. Tit.	*Homiliae in epistulam ad Titum*
Inan. glor.	*De inani gloria (On Vainglory)*
Laz.	*De Lazaro*

Josephus [Jos.] (AD 37–after 93)

Ag. Ap.	*Against Apion*
Ant.	*Jewish Antiquities*
J.W.	*Jewish War*
Life	*Life*

Justin Martyr (d. AD 165)

1 Apol.	*Apologia 1 (First Apology)*
2 Apol.	*Apologia 2 (Second Apology)*
Dial.	*Dialoges cum Tryphone (Dialogue with Trypho)*

Justinian (ca. AD 463–565)

Corp.	*Corpus Iuris (Codex of Justinian)*
Nov.	*Novellae*

Juvenal [Juv.] (fl. 2nd c. AD)

Sat.	*Satirae (Satires)*

Lactantius [Lac.] (ca. AD 240–ca. 320)

Inst.	*Divinarum Institutionum Libri VII (The Divine Institutes)*
Mort.	*De morte persecutorum (The Death of the Persecutors)*
Opif.	*De opificio Dei (The Workmanship of God)*

Livy (59 BC–AD 17)

Ira	*De ira*
Rom. Hist.	*Ab urbe condita libri (Books from the Foundation of the City)*

Lucian of Samosata (ca. AD 120–180)

Alex.	*Alexander (Pseudomantis) (Alexander the False Prophet)*
Dial. meretr.	*Dialogi meretricii (Dialogues of the Courtesans)*
Luct.	*De luctu (Funerals)*
Nav.	*Navigium (The Ship or The Wishes)*
Nigr.	*Nigrinus*
Peregr.	*De morte Peregrini (The Passing of Peregrinus)*
Philops.	*Philopseudes (The Lover of Lies)*
Salt.	*De saltatione (The Dance)*

Macrobius (fl. early 5th c. AD)

Sat.	*Saturnalia*

Martial (ca. AD 40–103)

Ep.	*Epigrammaton*

Methodius (d. ca. AD 311)

Symp.	*Symposium (Convivium decem virginum) (Banquet of the Ten Virgins)*

Minucius Felix (fl. ca. AD 200)

Oct.	*Octavius*

Musonius Rufus (ca. AD 30–100)

Lec.	*Lectures*

Origen [Orig.] (ca. AD 185–254)

Cels.	*Contra Celsum (Against Celsus)*
Comm. Matt.	*Commentarium in evangelium Matthaei*
Ep. Afr.	*Epistula ad Africanum*
Hom. Luc.	*Homiliae in Lucam*
Hom. Num.	*Homiliae in Numeros*
Prin.	*De principiis (First Principles)*

Ovid [Ov.] (43 BC–AD 14)

Ars	*Ars amatoria (The Art of Love)*
Med.	*Medicamina faciei femineae (Drugs for the Female Face, i.e., Cosmetics)*
Metam.	*Metamorphoses*
Rem. am.	*Remedia amoris (Remedies of Love)*

Palladius (fl. 4th c. AD)

Hist. Laus.	*Historia Lausiaca (Lausiac History)*
Rust.	*De re rustica (On Farming)*

Pausanias (fl. ca. AD 160)

Descr.	*Graeciae descriptio (Description of Greece)*

Pedanius

Mat. med.	*De materia medica*

Persius (AD 34–62)

Sat.	*Satirae (Satires)*

Petronius (d. AD 66)
    Sat.   *Satyricon*
Philo (ca. 20 BC–ca. AD 50)
    Abr.   *De Abrahamo (On the Life of Abraham)*
    Agr.   *De agricultura (On Agriculture)*
    Cher.   *De cherubim (On the Cherubim)*
    Congr.   *De congressu eruditionis gratia (On the Preliminary Studies)*
    Contempl.   *De vita contemplativa (On the Contemplative Life)*
    Decal.   *De decalogo (On the Decalogue)*
    Ebr.   *De ebrietate (On Drunkenness)*
    Flacc.   *In Flaccum (Against Flaccus)*
    Gig.   *De gigantibus (On Giants)*
    Her.   *Quis rerum divinarum heres sit (Who Is the Heir of Divine Things?)*
    Hypoth.   *Hypothetica (Apology for the Jews)*
    Ios.   *De Iosepho (On the Life of Joseph)*
    Leg. 1–3   *Legum allegoriae 1–3 (Allegorical Interpretation 1–3)*
    Legat.   *Legatio ad Gaium (On the Embassy to Gaius)*
    Migr.   *De migratione Abrahami (On the Migration of Abraham)*
    Mos. 1, 2   *De vita Mosis I, II (On the Life of Moses 1, 2)*
    Mut.   *De mutatione nominum (On the Change of Names)*
    Opif.   *De opificio mundi (On the Creation of the World)*
    Plant.   *De plantatione*
    Post.   *De posteritate Caini (On the Posterity of Cain)*
    Prob.   *Quod omnis probus liber sit (That Every Good Person Is Free)*
    QG   *Quaestiones et solutiones in Genesim (Questions and Answers on Genesis)*
    Somn.   *De somniis (On Dreams 1–2)*
    Spec.   *De specialibus legibus (On the Special Laws)*
    Virt.   *De virtutibus (On the Virtues)*
Philostratus (fl. 3rd c. AD)
    Vit. Apoll.   *Vita Apollonii (The Life of Apollonius [of Tyana])*
Pindar
    Pyth.   *Pythionikai (Pythian Odes)*
Plato (ca. 429–347 BC)
    Apol.   *Apologia (Apology of Socrates)*
    Ep.   *Epistulae (Letters)*
    Gorg.   *Gorgias*
    Leg.   *Leges (Laws)*
    Parm.   *Parmenides*

Phaed.	*Phaedo*
Phaedr.	*Phaedrus*
Resp.	*Respublica (Republic)*
Symp.	*Symposium*
Theaet.	*Theaetetus*
Tim.	*Timaeus*

Plautus (ca. 250–184 BC)

Amph.	*Amphitruo*
Aul.	*Aulularia (The Pot of Gold)*
Cas.	*Casina*
Curc.	*Curculio*
Trin.	*Trinimmus (Three-Dollar Day)*

Pliny the Elder [Pliny] (AD 23–79)

Nat.	*Naturalis historia (Natural History)*

Pliny the Younger (AD 61–113)

Ep.	*Epistulae*
Ep. Tra.	*Epistulae ad Trajanum*
Pan.	*Panegyricus Traiani (Praise of Trajan)*

Plutarch [Plu.] (ca. AD 50–129)

Aem.	*Aemilius Paulus*
Alc.	*Alcibiades*
Alex.	*Alexander*
Ant.	*Antony*
Arist.	*Aristides*
Caes.	*Caesar*
Cat. Maj.	*Cato Major (Cato the Elder)*
Crass.	*Crassus*
Def. orac.	*De defectu oraculorum (Obsolence of Oracles)*
Luc.	*Lucullus*
Lyc.	*Lycurgus*
Lys.	*Lysander*
Mor.	*Moralia*
Mulier. virt.	*Mulierum virtutes (Bravery of Women)*
Num.	*Numa*
Per.	*Pericles*
Pomp.	*Pompeius*
Quaest. conv.	*Quaestiones convivialum (Table Talk)*
Quaest. rom.	*Quaestiones romanae et graecae (Roman and Greek Questions)*
Rom.	*Romulus*
Sol.	*Solon*
Sull.	*Sulla*

Tim.   *Timoleon*
Polybius [Polyb.] (ca. 200–118 BC)
 Hist.   *Historiae (Histories)*
Polycarp (ca. AD 69–155) (see under *Apostolic Fathers*)
Possidius (ca. AD 370–ca. 440)
 Vita Aug.   *Vita Augustini*
Quintilian (ca. AD 35–ca. 90s)
 Inst.   *Institutio oratoria (The Orator's Education)*
Sallust (86 BC–ca. 35 BC)
 Bell. Cat.   *Bellum catalinae*
Seneca (ca. 4 BC–AD 65)
 Apoc.   *Apocolocyntosis*
 Ben.   *De beneficiis (Benefits)*
 Clem.   *De clementia*
 Ep.   *Epistulae morales (Moral Essays)*
 Helv.   *Consolationem ad Helviam Matrem (Consolation to*
      His Mother Helvia)
 Ira   *De ira (On Anger)*
 Tranq.   *De tranquillitate animi*
 Vit. beat.   *De vita beata*
Servius (Maurus Servius Honoratus)
 Aen.   commentary on Virgil's *Aeneid*
Sextus Empiricus
 Pyr.   *Pyrrhoniae hypotyposes (Outlines of Pyrrhonism)*
 Math.   *Adversus mathematicos (Against the Mathematicians)*
Socrates Scholasticus (ca. AD 379–ca. 450)
 Eccl. Hist.   *Ecclesiastical History*
Sophocles (ca. 496–406 BC)
 Aj.   *Ajax*
 El.   *Elektra*
Soranus (fl. 2nd c. AD)
 Gyn.   *Gynaecology*
Sozomen (ca. AD 375–ca. 447)
 Eccl. Hist.   *Ecclesiastical History*
Strabo [Str.] (64 BC–ca. AD 24)
 Geogr.   *Geographica (Geography)*
Suetonius [Suet.] (ca. AD 75–ca. 140)
 Aug.   *Divus Augustus*
 Cal.   *Gaius Caligula*
 Claud.   *Claudius*
 Dom.   *Domitianus*
 Gramm.   *De grammaticis*

Jul.	*Divus Julius*
Nero	*Nero*
Tib.	*Tiberius*
Vesp.	*Vespasian*
Vit.	*Vitellius*

Tacitus [Tac.] (AD 56–ca. 117)

Agr.	*Agricola*
Ann.	*Annales*
Germ.	*Germania*
Hist.	*Historiae*

Tatian

Or.	*Oratio ad Graecos*

Tertullian (ca. AD 160–200)

Adv. Jud.	*Adversus Judaeos (Against the Jews)*
An.	*De anima (The Soul)*
Apol.	*Apologeticus (Apology)*
Bapt.	*De baptismo (On Baptism)*
Carn.	*De carne Christi (The Flesh of Christ)*
Cor.	*De corona militis (The Crown)*
Cult. fem.	*De cultu feminarum (The Apparel of Women)*
Exh. cast.	*De exhortatione castitatis (Exhortation to Chastity)*
Fug.	*De fuga in persecution (Flight in Persecution)*
Idol.	*De idololatria (Idolatry)*
Jejun.	*De jejunio, adversus Psychicos (On Fasting, against the Psychics)*
Marc.	*Adversus Marcionem (Against Marcion)*
Mart.	*Ad martyras (To the Martyrs)*
Mon.	*De monogamia (Monogamy)*
Nat.	*Ad nationes (To the Heathen)*
Or.	*De oratione (On Prayer)*
Paen.	*De paenitentia (Repentance)*
Pall.	*De pallio (The Pallium)*
Praescr.	*De praescriptione haereticorum (Prescription against Heretics)*
Res.	*De resurrectione carnis (The Resurrection of the Flesh)*
Scap.	*Ad Scapulam (To Scapula)*
Scorp.	*Scorpiace (Against the Scorpion's Sting)*
Spec.	*De spectaculis (The Shows)*
Ux.	*Ad uxorem (To His Wife)*
Virg.	*De virginibus velandis (The Veiling of Virgins)*

Theocritus (fl. early 3rd c. BC)

Id.	*Idylls*

Theodoret (ca. AD 393–ca. 460)
   Hist. eccl.   *Historia ecclesiastica (Ecclesiastical History)*
Theodosius II (ca. AD 408–450)
   Sirm.   *Sirmondian Constitutions*
Theophilus (fl. late 2nd c. AD)
   Autol.   *Ad Autolycum (To Autolycus)*
Theophrastus (ca. 370–ca. 285 BC)
   Char.   *Characteres (Characters)*
   Hist. plant.   *Historia plantarum (History of Plants)*
   Sens.   *De sensu*
Thucydides (ca. 455–400 BC)
   Hist.   *History of the Peloponnesian War*
Varro (116–27 BC)
   Rust.   *De re rustica (On Farming)*
Virgil (70–19 BC)
   Aen.   *Aeneid*
   Georg.   *Georgica (Georgics)*
Xenophon (ca. 428–354 BC)
   Anab.   *Anabasis*
   Cyr.   *Cyropaedia*
   Mem.   *Memorabilia*
   Oec.   *Oeconomicus*
   Symp.   *Symposium*

JOURNALS AND REFERENCE WORKS

ABD   *Anchor Bible Dictionary.* Edited by D. N. Freedman. 6 vols. New York: Doubleday, 1992
ABR   *Australian Biblical Review*
AcOr   *Acta Orientalia*
ADAJ   *Annual of the Department of Antiquities of Jordan*
AEL   *Ancient Egyptian Literature.* M. Lichtheim. 3 vols. Berkeley: University of California, 1971–1980
AER   *American Ecclesiastical Review*
AF   *Altorientalische Forschungen*
AfO   *Archiv für Orientforschung*
AHB   *Ancient History Bulletin*
AJA   *American Journal of Archaeology*
AJAH   *American Journal of Ancient History*
AJBA   *Australian Journal of Biblical Archaeology*
AJP   *American Journal of Philology*

ANEP	*The Ancient Near East in Pictures Relating to the Old Testament.* Edited by J. B. Pritchard. Princeton: Princeton University, 1954
ANES	*Ancient Near Eastern Studies*
ANESTP	*The Ancient Near East: Supplementary Texts and Pictures Relating to the Old Testament.* Edited by J. B. Pritchard. Princeton: Princeton University, 1969
ANET	*Ancient Near Eastern Texts Relating to the Old Testament.* Edited by J. B. Pritchard. Princeton: Princeton University, Princeton: Princeton University, 1955
ANRW	*Aufstieg und Niedergang der römischen Welt: Geschichte und Kultur Roms im Spiegel der neueren Forschung.* Edited by H. Temporini and W. Haase. Berlin: W. de Gruyter, 1972–
AnSt	*Anatolian Studies*
AntCl	*Antiquité Classique*
Antiq	*Antiquity*
AR	*Archiv für Religionswissenschaft*
ARAB	*Ancient Records of Assyria and Babylonia.* Edited by D. D. Luckenbill. 2 vols. Chicago: University of Chicago, 1926–1927
Arch	*Archaeology*
ArchOd	*Archaeology Odyssey*
ARE	*Ancient Records of Egypt.* Edited by J. H. Breasted. 5 vols. Chicago, 1905–1907. Reprint, New York, 1962
ARM(T)	Archives royales de Mari, transcrite et traduite
AThR	*Anglican Theological Review*
Aug	*Augustinianum*
AUSS	*Andrews University Seminary Studies*
AW	*Ancient World*
BA	*Biblical Archaeologist*
BAR	*Biblical Archaeology Review*
Barrett	*The New Testament Background: Selected Documents.* Edited by C. K. Barrett. Rev. ed. San Francisco: Harper & Row, 1987
BASOR	*Bulletin of the American Schools of Oriental Research*
BASP	*Bulletin of the American Society of Papyrologists*
BBR	*Bulletin for Biblical Research*
Ber	*Berytus*
BETS	*Bulletin of the Evangelical Theological Society*
BHM	*Bulletin of the History of Medicine*
BI	*Biblical Illustrator*
Bib	*Biblica*
BibInt	*Biblical Interpretation*

BICS	*Bulletin of the Institute of Classical Studies*
BN	*Biblische Notizen*
BO	*Bibliotheca Orientalis*
BRev	*Bible Review*
BRM	Babylonian Records in the Library of J. Pierpont Morgan
BSac	*Bibliotheca Sacra*
BSOAS	*Bulletin of the School of Oriental and African Studies*
BT	*The Bible Translator*
BTB	*Biblical Theology Bulletin*
BurH	*Buried History*
BWL	*Babylonian Wisdom Literature.* Edited by W. G. Lambert. Oxford: Clarendon Press, 1960
BZ	*Biblische Zeitschrift*
CAD	*The Assyrian Dictionary of the Oriental Institute of the University of Chicago.* Edited by I. J. Gelb et al. 1956–2010
CAM	*Civilization of the Ancient Mediterranean: Greece and Rome.* Edited by M. Grant and R. Kitzinger. 3 vols. New York, 1988
CANE	*Civilizations of the Ancient Near East.* Edited by J. Sasson. 4 vols. New York: Scribners, 1995. Repr., Peabody, MA: Hendrickson, 2000
CBQ	*Catholic Biblical Quarterly*
CCSL	*Corpus Christianorum Series Latina*
CH	*Church History*
ChrÉg	*Chronique d'Égypte*
CIG	*Corpus inscriptionum graecarum.* Edited by A. Boechth. 4 vols. Berlin, 1828–1877
CIL	*Corpus inscriptionum latinarum*
CJ	*Classical Journal*
CML	*Canaanite Myths and Legends.* Edited by G. R. Driver. Edinburgh: T&T Clark, 1956
COS	*The Context of Scripture: Canonical Compositions from the Biblical World.* 3 vols. Edited by W. W. Hallo and K. L. Younger Jr. Leiden: Brill, 1997–2002, 2003
CP	*Classical Philology*
CQ	*Classical Quarterly*
CSR	*Christian Scholar's Review*
CT	*Christianity Today*
CTA	*Corpus des tablettes en cunéiformes alphabétiques découvertes à Ras Shamra-Ugarit de 1929 à 1939.* Edited by A. Herdner. Mission de Ras Shamra 10. Paris: P. Geuthner, 1963
CTBM	*Cuneiform Texts from Babylonian Tablets in the British Museum*

CurTM	*Currents in Theology and Mission*
DANE	*Dictionary of the Ancient Near East.* Edited by P. Bienkowski and A. Millard. Philadelphia: University of Pennsylvania, 2000
DDD	*Dictionary of Deities and Demons in the Bible.* Edited by K. van der Toorn, B. Becking, and P. W. van der Horst. 2nd rev. ed. Leiden: Brill, 1999
DJBA	*A Dictionary of Jewish Babylonian Aramaic.* Edited by M. Sokoloff. Ramat-Gan: Bar Ilan University / Baltimore: Johns Hopkins University, 2002
DNTB	*Dictionary of New Testament Background.* Edited by C. A. Evans and S. E. Porter. Downers Grove, IL: InterVarsity, 2000
DOP	*Dumbarton Oaks Papers*
DOTHB	*Dictionary of the Old Testament: Historical Books.* Edited by B. T. Arnold and H. G. M. Williamson. Downers Grove, IL: InterVarsity, 2003
DOTP	*Dictionary of the Old Testament: Pentateuch.* Edited by T. D. Alexander and D. W. Baker. Downers Grove, IL: InterVarsity, 2003
DPL	*Dictionary of Paul and His Letters.* Edited by G. F. Hawthorne, R. P. Martin, and D. G. Reid. Downers Grove, IL: InterVarsity, 1993
DRev	*Downside Review*
DSD	*Dead Sea Discoveries*
EAC	*Encyclopedia of Ancient Christianity.* Edited by A. Di Berardino. 3 vols. Downers Grove, IL: IVP Academic, 2014
EAEHL	*Encyclopedia of Archaeological Excavations in the Holy Land.* Edited by M. Avi-Yonah. 4 vols. London: Oxford University Press, 1975
EDB	*Eerdmans Dictionary of the Bible.* Edited by D. N. Freedman, A. C. Myers, and A. B. Beck. Grand Rapids: Eerdmans, 2000
EDEJ	*The Eerdmans Dictionary of Early Judaism.* Edited by J. J. Collins and D. C. Harlow. Grand Rapids: Eerdmans, 2010
EGA	*Egypt's Golden Age: The Art of Living in the New Kingdom, 1558–1085 B.C.* Edited by E. Brovarski, S. K. Doll, and R. Freed. Boston: Museum of Fine Arts, 1982
EGL & MWBS	*Eastern Great Lakes and Midwest Biblical Societies*
EncJud	*Encyclopaedia Judaica.* Edited by F. Skolnik. 22 vols. Detroit: Macmillan Reference, 2007

EMQ	*Evangelical Missions Quarterly*
ErIsr	*Eretz-Israel*
ETCSL	*The Electronic Text Corpus of Sumerian Literature.* J. A. Black, G. Cunningham, J. Ebeling, E. Flückiger-Hawker, E. Robson, J. Taylor, and G. Zólyomi. Oxford: 1998–2006. Online at http://etcsl.orinst.ox.ac.uk/
ETL	*Ephemerides theologicae lovanienses*
EvQ	*Evangelical Quarterly*
Exped	*Expedition*
ExpTim	*Expository Times*
FGrH	*Die Fragmente der griechischen Historiker.* Edited by F. Jacoby. Berlin: Weidmann, 1923
FiHi	*Fides et Historia*
GCS	Die griechische christliche Schriftsteller der ersten [drei] Jahrhunderte
Gibson	John C. L. Gibson. *Canaanite Myths and Legends.* 2nd ed. London: T&T Clark, 2004
GOTR	*Greek Orthodox Theological Review*
GR	*Greece and Rome*
Grant	Galen. *Galen on Food and Diet.* Translated by M. Grant. London: Routledge, 2000
GRBS	*Greek, Roman, and Byzantine Studies*
HAR	*Hebrew Annual Review*
HR	*History of Religions*
HSS	*Harvard Semitic Studies*
HTR	*Harvard Theological Review*
HUCA	*Hebrew Union College Annual*
IBD	*The Illustrated Bible Dictionary.* Edited by J. D. Douglas. 3 vols. Leicester, England: Inter-Varsity, 1980
IDB	*The Interpreter's Dictionary of the Bible.* Edited by G. A. Buttrick. 4 vols. New York: Abingdon, 1962
IEJ	*Israel Exploration Journal*
IJNA	*International Journal of Nautical Archaeology and Underwater Exploration*
Int	*Interpretation*
IOS	*Israel Oriental Studies*
ISBE	*The International Standard Bible Encyclopedia.* Edited by G. W. Bromiley et al. 4 vols. Grand Rapids: Eerdmans, 1979–1988
ITT	Ismaili Texts and Translations
JAC	Jahrbuch für Antike und Christentum

JANESCU	*Journal of the Ancient Near Eastern Society of Columbia University*
JAOS	*Journal of the American Oriental Society*
JARCE	*Journal of the American Research Center in Egypt*
JASA	*Journal of the American Scientific Affiliation*
JATS	*Journal of the Adventist Theological Society*
JBL	*Journal of Biblical Literature*
JBQ	*Jewish Bible Quarterly*
JCS	*Journal of Cuneiform Studies*
JE	*The Jewish Encyclopedia*. Edited by I. Singer. 12 vols. New York: Funk & Wagnalls, 1907
JEA	*Journal of Egyptian Archaeology*
JECS	*Journal of Early Christian Studies*
JEgH	*Journal of Egyptian History*
JEH	*Journal of Ecclesiastical History*
JESHO	*Journal of the Economic and Social History of the Orient*
JETS	*Journal of the Evangelical Theological Society*
JFA	*Journal of Field Archaeology*
JHI	*Journal of the History of Ideas*
JHIL	*Journal of the History of International Law*
JHS	*Journal of Hellenic Studies*
JJP	*Journal of Juristic Papyrology*
JJS	*Journal of Jewish Studies*
JLH	*Journal of Library History*
JMA	*Journal of Mediterranean Archaeology*
JNES	*Journal of Near Eastern Studies*
JNSL	*Journal of Northwest Semitic Languages*
JQR	*Jewish Quarterly Review*
JR	*Journal of Religion*
JRA	*Journal of Roman Archaeology*
JRE	*Journal of Religious Ethics*
JRS	*Journal of Roman Studies*
JSJ	*Journal for the Study of Judaism in the Persian, Hellenistic, and Roman Period*
JSNT	*Journal for the Study of the New Testament*
JSOT	*Journal for the Study of the Old Testament*
JSP	*Journal for the Study of the Pseudepigrapha*
JSS	*Journal of Semitic Studies*
JSSEA	*Journal of the Society for the Study of Egyptian Antiquities*
JTS	*Journal of Theological Studies*
King	*Musonius Rufus: Lectures and Sayings*, rev. ed. Translated by C. King. Createspace, 2011

LAE	*Literature of Ancient Egypt.* W. K. Simpson. New Haven: Yale University, 1972
LS	*Louvain Studies*
MARI	*Mari: Annales de recherches interdisciplinaires*
MDOG	Mitteilungen der Deutschen Orient-Gesellschaft
Meyer	*The Nag Hammadi Scriptures.* Edited by M. Meyer. New York: HarperOne, 2007
MGWJ	*Monatsschrift für Geschichte und Wissenschaft des Judentums*
MVN	Materiali per il Vocabulario Neo-Sumerico
NEA	*Near Eastern Archaeology*
NEASB	*Near East Archaeological Society Bulletin*
Neot	*Neotestamentica*
Neusner-T	*The Tosefta.* Translated by Jacob Neusner. 2 vols. Peabody: Hendrickson, 2002
Neusner-Y	*The Jerusalem Talmud.* Translated by Jacob Neusner. CD. Peabody: Hendrickson, 2009
NewDocs	*New Documents Illustrating Early Christianity.* Edited by Greg H. R. Horsley and Stephen Llewelyn. North Ryde, NSW: The Ancient History Documentary Research Centre, Macquarie University, 1981–
NG	Neosumerischen Gerichtsurkunden
NIDNTT	*New International Dictionary of New Testament Theology.* Edited by C. Brown. 4 vols. Grand Rapids: Zondervan, 1975–1985
NIDOTTE	*New International Dictionary of Old Testament Theology & Exegesis.* Edited by W. A. VanGemeren. 5 vols. Grand Rapids: Zondervan, 1997
NovT	*Novum Testamentum*
NRVN	Neusumerische Rechts- und Verwaltungsurkunden aus Nippur
NTA	E. Hennecke. *New Testament Apocrypha.* Edited by W. Schneemelcher and R. McL. Wilson. Translated by E. Best et al. 2 vols. Philadelphia: Westminster Press, 1965
NTS	*New Testament Studies*
OCCC	*The Oxford Companion to Classical Civilization.* Edited by S. Hornblower and A. Spawforth. Oxford: Oxford University Press, 1998
OCD	*The Oxford Classical Dictionary.* Edited by S. Hornblower and A. Spawforth. 3rd ed. Oxford: Oxford University, 1996
ODCC	*The Oxford Dictionary of the Christian Church.* Edited by F. L. Cross and E. A. Livingstone. 3rd ed. Oxford: Oxford University, 1997

OEANE	*The Oxford Encyclopedia of Archaeology in the Near East.* Edited by E. M. Meyers. New York: Oxford University, 1997
OEBA	*The Oxford Encyclopedia of the Bible and Archaeology.* Edited by D. M. Master. 2 vols. Oxford: Oxford University, 2013
OHJDL	*The Oxford Handbook of Jewish Daily Life in Roman Palestine.* Edited by C. Hezser. Oxford: Oxford University, 2010
Or	*Orientalia* (NS)
OrAnt	*Oriens antiquus*
OTP	*Old Testament Pseudepigrapha.* Edited by J. H. Charlesworth. 2 vols. New York, 1983, 1985
PAAJR	*Proceedings of the American Academy of Jewish Research*
PAPS	*Proceedings of the American Philosophical Society*
PEQ	*Palestine Exploration Quarterly*
PGM	*Papyri graecae magicae: Die griechischen Zauberpapyri.* Edited by K. Preisendanz. Berlin, 1928
PloS ONE	Public Library of Science One (http://www.plosone.org/)
PRSt	*Perspectives in Religious Studies*
PSBA	*Proceedings of the Society of Biblical Archaeology*
PSCF	*Perspectives on Science and Christian Faith*
PSTJ	*Perkins School of Theology Journal*
PTS	Patristische Texte und Studien
RA	*Revue d'assyriologie et d'archéologie orientale*
RB	*Revue biblique*
REAug	*Revue des études augustiniennes*
REJ	*Revue des études juives*
RelSRev	*Religious Studies Review*
ResQ	*Restoration Quarterly*
RevExp	*Review and Expositor*
RevQ	*Revue de Qumran* (DC Qumrân)
RHPR	*Revue d'histoire et de philosophie religieuses*
RHR	*Revue de l'histoire des religions*
RIDA	*Revue internationale des droits de l'antiquité*
SciAmer	*Scientific American*
SCJ	*Stone-Campbell Journal*
SecCent	*Second Century*
S.H.A.	*Scriptores Historiae Augustae* (Augustan History)
SJOT	*Scandinavian Journal of the Old Testament*
SJT	*Scottish Journal of Theology*
SPhilo	*Studia Philonica*
SR	*Studies in Religion*

ST	*Studia Theologica*
StPatr	Studia patristica
STRev	*Sewanee Theological Review*
TA	*Tel Aviv*
TAPA	*Transactions of the American Philological Association*
TDNT	*Theological Dictionary of the New Testament.* Edited by G. Kittel and G. Friedrich. Translated by G. W. Bromiley. 10 vols. Grand Rapids: Eerdmans, 1964–1976
TDOT	*Theological Dictionary of the Old Testament.* Edited by G. J. Botterweck and H. Ringgren. Translated by J. T. Willis, G. W. Bromiley, and D. E. Green. 15 vols. Grand Rapids: Eerdmans, 1974–2006
Them	*Themelios*
TJ	*Trinity Journal*
TS	*Theological Studies*
TSFB	*Theological Students Fellowship Bulletin*
TWOT	*Theological Wordbook of the Old Testament.* Edited by R. L. Harris, G. L. Archer Jr., and B. K. Waltke. 2 vols. Chicago: Moody Press, 1980
TynBul	*Tyndale Bulletin*
TZ	*Theologische Zeitschrift*
UF	*Ugarit-Forschungen*
USQR	*Union Seminary Quarterly Review*
UET	Ur Excavations: Texts
UT	*Ugaritic Textbook.* Cyrus H. Gordon. AnOr 38. Rome: Pontifical Biblical Institute, 1965
VC	*Vigiliae Christianae*
VT	*Vetus Testamentum*
WO	*Die Welt des Orients*
WTJ	*Westminster Theological Journal*
YBC	Yale Babylonian Collection
YOS	Yale Oriental Series
ZA	*Zeitschrift für Assyriologie*
ZABR	*Zeitschrift für altorientalische und biblische Rechtsgeschichte*
ZÄS	*Zeitschrift für ägyptische Sprache und Altertumskunde*
ZAW	*Zeitschrift für die alttestamentliche Wissenschaft*
ZDMG	*Zeitschrift der deutschen morgenländischen Gesellschaft*
ZDPV	*Zeitschrift des deutschen Palästina-Vereins*
ZNW	*Zeitschrift für die neutestamentliche Wissenschaft und die Kunde der älteren Kirche*
ZPE	*Zeitschrift für Papyrologie und Epigraphik*

PERIODS, AGES, AND DATES

Aside from a few passages that deal with "beginnings" or "origins" (e.g., Genesis 1–11; Psalm 104; John 1:1–5), the Bible, as received, recounts events in the lives of individuals, tribes, and nations located primarily in the ancient Near East that appear to have occurred over a period of approximately 1800 years, that is, from about 1700 BC to AD 100. The events portrayed in the Bible span a period that saw the development of technology from the use of bronze to the use of iron in the ancient Near East from Anatolia to Mesopotamia to Egypt. This same period saw political development from tribal cultures to the rise (and fall) of major empires—Egypt, Assyria, Babylon, Persia, Greece, and Rome, among others that figure less prominently in the biblical text. Numerous major religions flourished (and many fell out of use) during this same period (e.g., Egyptian, Assyrian, Babylonian, Persian, Greek, and Roman religions as well as Judaism and Christianity), not to mention other religions more local or tribal in character (e.g., Philistine, Aramean, Edomite, and Ammonite).

There is little evidence of how the passage of extended periods of time was marked in pre-history. With the advent of major empires, the reigns of kings and dynasties and the rule of nations began to be used to mark the passage of extended periods of time. Modern convention, of course, marks the passage of time using calendrical dates, which in the Western world are marked as BC (or BCE) and AD (or CE) surrounding the approximate date of the birth of Jesus of Nazareth during the period of the Roman Empire. But it is also a modern convention to use the development of technology to mark long periods of time, e.g., the various Stone Ages, the Copper or Chalcolithic Age, the Bronze Ages, and the Iron Ages. And, further, it remains a convention to mark some periods of time by the rule of political leaders, dynasties, and nations.

The various terms used for periods of time found in this Dictionary are often defined by approximate dates within the articles where they are used and, in the case of periods that covered millennia, closer approximations of the dates of events within a given period are provided. For convenience, however, the following tables provide a list of these periods and ages, as well as the durations of major empires (or dynasties within an empire) marking significant time periods in the ancient Near East, accompanied by their approximate and commonly associated dates.

Technological Ages

Technological ages vary widely from place to place, even within the ancient Near East. The following dates encompassing a given technology should be seen as highly approximate, as representing the ancient Near East generally, and as subject to ongoing scholarly debate. The dates below are intended to provide a general sense of time and are not to be used as a precise guide, simply because technological development is seldom linear.

Neolithic (Late Stone Age)	8500–4500 BC
Chalcolithic (Copper Age)	4500–3500 BC
Early Bronze Age	3500–2250 BC
Intermediate Bronze Age	2250–1950 BC
Middle Bronze Age	1950–1550 BC
Late Bronze Age	1550–1200 BC
Iron Age I (Early Iron Age)	1200–985 BC
Iron Age II (Late Iron Age)	985–586 BC

Political Ages

The dates of empires and dynasties are likewise subject to scholarly debate, which not infrequently includes proposals of "high chronologies" and "low chronologies" or sometimes even of "middle chronologies." Moreover, there was significant overlap among the various empires and dynasties, some of which rose in place of or fell to another, but which more often contested various geographic areas with varying degrees of hegemony at any given time as the politics of a given moment were usually in flux.

Egypt

Predynastic	4000–3150 BC
Early Dynastic (1st to 2nd Dynasties)	3150–2545 BC
Old Kingdom (3rd to 8th Dynasties)	2545–2120 BC
First Intermediate (9th to 10th Dynasties)	2120–1980 BC
Middle Kingdom (11th to 12th Dynasties)	1980–1760 BC

Second Intermediate (13th to 17th Dynasties)	1760–1540 BC
New Kingdom (18th to 20th Dynasties)	1540–1075 BC
Third Intermediate (21st to 24th Dynasties)	1075–722 BC
Late Period (25th to 30th Dynasties)	722–332 BC
Ptolemaic Dynasty	332–30 BC
Roman Period	30 BC–AD 395

Assyria

Old Assyrian Period	1850–1700 BC
Middle Assyrian Period	1360–1060 BC
Neo-Assyrian Period	910–612 BC

Babylon

Old Babylonian Period	1900–1590 BC
Middle Babylonian Period	1590–1100 BC
Neo-Babylonian Period	605–539 BC

Persia   550–331 BC

Greece

Minoan Era	2000–1500 BC
Mycenaean Era	1500–1200 BC
Dark Age	1200–800 BC
Archaic Age	800–500 BC
Classical Era	500–338 BC
Philip II & Alexander of Macedon	338–323 BC

Rome

Founding of Rome	753 BC
Etruscan kings of Rome	753–510 BC
Roman Republic	509–27 BC
Roman Empire	27 BC–AD 476
Roman control of Palestine	63 BC–AD 337

Biblical Chronology

There are two competing chronologies for the period before the monarchy, which are based upon a choice of either an early date for the Exodus of ca. 1450 BC, or a late date for the Exodus of ca. 1250 BC.

	Early Dates	Late Dates
Patriarchs (Abraham–Joseph)	ca. 2150–1850 BC	ca. 1950–1700 BC
Sojourn in Egypt	ca. 1850–1450 BC	ca. 1650–1250 BC
Conquest of Canaan	ca. 1400 BC	ca. 1200 BC
Period of the Judges	1400–1050 BC	1200–1050 BC

The United Monarchy
    Saul   1050–1010 BC
    David   1010–970 BC
    Solomon   970–930 BC

The Divided Kingdoms
    Northern   930–722 BC
    Southern   930–586 BC

The Exilic Period
    Restoration of Jews from Mesopotamia   537 BC
    Rebuilding of the Temple   515 BC
    Return of Ezra   458 BC
    Return of Nehemiah   445 BC
    Malachi, the last prophet   ca. 400 BC

Birth of Jesus   ca. 5 BC

Crucifixion of Jesus   AD 30 or 33

Execution of Paul and Peter   AD 64

Destruction of Jerusalem temple by Rome   AD 70

For the early dates for OT chronology, see G. L. Archer Jr., "The Chronology of the Old Testament," in *The Expositor's Bible Commentary* (ed. F. Gaebelein. Grand Rapids: Zondervan, 1979), 359–74. For the late dates, see K. A. Kitchen, *On the Reliability of the Old Testament* (Grand Rapids: Eerdmans, 2003). For a summary of the arguments, see E. M. Yamauchi, *The Stones and the Scriptures* (Philadelphia: J. B. Lippincott, 1972), 46–50. For more recent bibliography on the ongoing debate, see E. M. Yamauchi, "Akhenaten, Moses, and Monotheism," *NEASB* 55 (2010): 1–15.

For NT chronology, see H. Hoehner, "The Chronology of the New Testament," in *The Expositor's Bible Commentary* (ed. F. Gaebelein. Grand Rapids: Zondervan, 1979), 593–607 and H. Hoehner, *Chronological Aspects of the Life of Christ* (Grand Rapids: Zondervan, 1977). See also J. M. Vardaman and E. M. Yamauchi, eds., *Chronos, Kairos, Christos: Nativity and Chronological Studies Presented to Jack Finegan* (Winona Lake: Eisenbrauns, 1989).

For a detailed general reference see J. Finegan, *Handbook of Biblical Chronology* (rev. ed.; Peabody: Hendrickson, 1998).

INTRODUCTION

The *Dictionary of Daily Life in Biblical and Post-Biblical Antiquity* (*DDL*), of which this is the fourth and final volume, was a project begun 30 years ago with the collaboration of the distinguished Old Testament scholar Roland K. Harrison (1920–1993), to whom Marvin Wilson and I dedicate this reference work. In the original conception of the project, Harrison, Wilson, and I were to write all the articles for a work entitled *Dictionary of Bible Manners and Customs*. It subsequently became expedient to engage the research and writing skills of other select scholars of the ancient world.

While there are many excellent Bible dictionaries and encyclopedias, and popular books on biblical backgrounds available, I had noticed a serious deficiency. I noted that while every one of these had an entry on "Abomination," none (with the exception of the six-volume *Anchor Bible Dictionary*) had an entry on "Abortion." Why was this the case? It was because these references were keyed to the words which occurred in the Bible.

From my 40 years of teaching the history of ancient Mesopotamia, Egypt, Greece, Rome, early Judaism, and early Christianity, I was well aware of the widespread practice of abortion, contraception, and infanticide in these societies and epochs. I therefore proposed a new framework for the *DDL*, one based on the Human Relations Area Files, an anthropological grid of human society, which would systematically and comparatively survey different aspects of culture, whether they were highlighted in the Bible or not.

The biblical texts were not intended to give us a complete representation of their worlds. In fact, they take for granted what was well known to both the writers and readers, but of which we are not aware. It is as though we hear the vocalization of an operatic libretto, but do not see the scenery and the costumes of the singers. Thanks, however, to extra-biblical texts and archaeology, we are able to recreate much of the background for the Bible.

For example, what did ancient people eat and drink? In the essay on FOOD PRODUCTION, one will learn that before the introduction of rotary mills, housewives had to labor on hands and knees about four hours a day to grind wheat and barley for their daily bread. Most of the bread in the ancient world was flat (unleavened) bread, because the predominant emmer wheat and the barley in Mesopotamia, Egypt, and Greece did not have the gluten necessary to cause bread to rise.

From the articles on CLOTHING, DYEING, LAUNDRY & FULLERS, and TEXTILES, one would learn that white linen was the preferred textile in Egypt, and was worn by Israelite priests and New Testament angels. How was Jesus dressed? Jesus's sole garments, except for his burial shroud, were woolen. As wool was not easily laundered, his clothes would have been dirty except for the moment of his transfiguration.

How did Jesus appear? From the article on BARBERS & BEARDS, we can conclude with near certainty that Jesus had a beard. Why? Men in antiquity could not shave themselves. They had to resort either to slaves or to barbers for a shave. Moreover, beards were a symbol of masculinity and seniority. The Old Testament word for "elders" is literally "bearded ones."

Where did people live? This would have varied from place to place and from one time period to another. From the article on DWELLINGS, one would learn that in the Old Testament era in Palestine most would have lived in houses with flat roofs and courtyards full of animals. In Rome, 95% of the people would have lived in *insulae*, crowded tenements without kitchens or bathrooms.

What about the relations between men and women? From the articles on EDUCATION and MARRIAGE, one would learn a striking fact, which is missing from both the Old and the New Testaments—the average age of spouses. We learn from our extra-biblical evidence that the bride would have certainly been a young teenager, and the groom several years her senior. The early marriage of girls, to preserve their purity, meant that they had only at best a primary education, with the exception of those from wealthy Roman families, which could afford private tutors for their daughters.

The *DDL* is also quite unique in attempting to trace the developments of the features of the biblical world along what the French historians of the Annales School have called the *longue durée*, that is, over the centuries *after* the New Testament era. It is instructive to understand how the Jewish rabbis, in following the traditions of the Pharisees, debated over the application of biblical laws in changing circumstances, and how the Church Fathers also responded to these same developments.

Rather than attempting to cover all possible topics, we have chosen to concentrate on 120 subjects, not because of their prominence in the biblical text but because of their significant roles in the ancient world. For example, ASTROLOGY, DREAMS, MAGIC, and DIVINATION & SORTITION (i.e., the casting of lots) are mentioned sparingly in the biblical texts themselves but they were dominant facets of life in antiquity.

The outline each contributor has followed is to briefly summarize references to his or her subject in: (1) the Old Testament and (2) the New Testament; followed by (3) the Near Eastern world, primarily Mesopotamia and Egypt, with some references to Anatolia and Persia; (4) the Greco-Roman world, from the Minoans and Mycenaeans, Homer, through the Hellenistic era, the Roman Republic, and the Roman Empire; (5) the Jewish world, including the Old Testament Apocrypha, Pseudepigrapha, Philo, Josephus, the Dead Sea Scrolls, the Mishnah, and the Talmuds (Babylonian and Jerusalem); and (6) the Christian world, including the church fathers up to Chrysostom and Augustine, as well as the early Byzantine empire to Justinian. Each article closes with a bibliography providing both source material for the article and material for further study. Further, the articles are carefully cross-referenced with other articles in print or planned.

The citations from the Old Testament and the New Testament, unless otherwise marked, are from the New International Version. Citations from the Septuagint (LXX) are taken from A. Pietersma and B. G. Wright, trans., *A New English Translation of the Septuagint* (New York: Oxford University Press, 2007). Citations from the Tosefta are taken from J. Neusner, *The Tosefta* (2 vols.; Peabody, MA: Hendrickson, 2013 repr.). Citations from the Midrashim are from the *Soncino Midrash Rabba for Macintosh* (Copyright Institute for Computers in Jewish Life and Davka Corporation, 2008). Citations from the Old Testament Apocrypha are from the Revised Standard Version; those from the Old Testament Pseudepigrapha are from James H. Charlesworth, ed., *The Old Testament Pseudepigrapha* (2 vols.; Garden City, NY: Doubleday, 1983, 1985). The classical citations (including Philo and Josephus) are from the Loeb Classical Library. References to the Dead Sea Scrolls are from *The Dead Sea Scrolls: A New Translation* by Michael Wise, Martin Abegg Jr., and Edward Cook (rev. ed.; New York: HarperSanFrancisco, 2005). Citations from the Mishnah are from Herbert Danby, trans., *The Mishnah* (Oxford: Oxford University Press, 1933). Citations from the Babylonian Talmud are from *The Soncino Talmud* (Institute for Computers in Jewish Life and Davka Corporation, 2007); those from the Jerusalem Talmud are from *The Jerusalem Talmud, A Translation and Commentary*, ed. Jacob Neusner (Peabody, MA: Hendrickson Publishers, 2009). With the exception of citations from Michael W. Holmes, *The Apostolic Fathers: Greek Texts and English Translations* (3rd. ed.; Grand Rapids: Baker Academic, 2007), patristic references are from the New Advent, *Fathers of the Church* (www. NewAdvent.org; 2007; © Kevin Knight). Citations from the Nag Hammadi texts are cited from Marvin Meyer, ed., *The Nag Hammadi Scriptures* (New York: HarperOne, 2007).

My deepest gratitude is first of all to Marvin R. Wilson, who has carefully examined all the essays and provided innumerable edits and corrections. I thank Graham Harrison for allowing us to update and expand his late father's excellent entries. I wish to express my appreciation to all of the contributors, many of whom were my history PhD students at Miami University. My thanks go also to my wife, Kimi, who spent countless hours photocopying pages from books and journals. I am also grateful to Sue Cameron, who has checked the biblical and apocryphal references for me.

Marvin and I express our profound thanks to Allan Emery, senior editor at Hendrickson, for spending much of the final two years before his retirement overseeing the first volume of this project, and also to Carl Nellis for his work on that volume. We are also deeply grateful to Jonathan Kline, our new editor at Hendrickson, for his painstaking and meticulous supervision of the work on Volumes 2, 3, and 4, and to Hannah Brown for her assistance with all four volumes. Our appreciation also goes to John F. Kutsko, who assisted with some of the research in the earliest stages of this dictionary project. Special thanks are also due to Foy D. Scalf, Chief Archivist of the Oriental Institute of the University of Chicago, for supplying us with the sources of many Near Eastern quotations.

For their assistance in providing some of the photographs for this dictionary, we are grateful to Rami Arav (University of Nebraska at Omaha), Michal Artzy (University of Haifa), Rozenn Bailleul-LeSuer (University of Chicago), Thomas E. Levy (University of California at San Diego), Daniel Master (Wheaton College), Amihai Mazar (Hebrew University), Foy D. Scalf (University of Chicago), Steven L. Tuck (Miami University), and Alain Zivie (Centre national de la recherche scientifique).

Finally, our profound gratitude goes to Andrew Pottorf for his valuable assistance with this project. A very gifted young scholar with unusual talent for writing and editing, Andrew is currently pursuing his doctorate in the department of Near Eastern Languages and Civilizations at Harvard University. The authors of this dictionary and the editors at Hendrickson Publishers appreciate Andrew's superb scholarship, dedicated work ethic, and great flexibility.

Edwin M. Yamauchi
April 2016

OATHS & VOWS

Oaths and vows were formal statements made with divine sanction to give them added force. Oaths were commonly used in personal, legal, and political settings. The speaker called on his or her god or gods to attest to the truth of the speaker's statement or to hold the speaker accountable to keep a promise of some future action. Vows, by contrast, were conditional promises in which the speaker promised to give something to the god if the god would provide something the speaker needed. Vows were usually made during a time of great need.

The making of both oaths and vows was widely practiced throughout the ancient world. This resulted in part from a general understanding that the gods saw and judged human beings and worked along with them to maintain justice and order. The gods held people accountable for their words and actions, thus helping to ensure truth in people's words and fidelity in their deeds.

A. THE OLD TESTAMENT

Oaths (Heb. sing. *šĕbûʿâ*, *ʾālâ*) appear often in all genres of the OT. Two of the Ten Commandments helped regulate oaths: the third commandment forbids vain oaths (Exod 20:7) and the ninth forbids false oaths (Exod 20:16). Oaths were sworn in private conversations and at formal public events by all types of people, from commoners to kings. Oaths were often used in legal proceedings, especially when adequate evidence or testimony was unavailable to establish guilt or innocence (e.g., when goods had been stolen or destroyed, Exod 22:10–11; when lost goods were found, Lev 6:3; or when a witness failed to come forth, Lev 5:1). Oaths were also used to guard against perjury, since swearing falsely in God's name would profane it (Lev 19:12). An oath could also be used to compel a response (1 Sam 3:17). Oaths were sometimes combined with an ordeal in which

God demonstrated the speaker's guilt or innocence by the result of the ordeal (e.g., in the case of a wife suspected of adultery, Num 5:11–31; cf. Daniel in the lions' den, Dan 6).

When they swore oaths, Israelites were to call on their God as a witness to the truth of an assertion (1 Kgs 18:10) or to strengthen their promise to complete some act (1 Sam 14:44). Such oaths commonly included the swearer calling divine curses on him- or herself if the oath was not ful-filled. The curses might be spelled out (Num 5:19–28; Job 31), but often they were implied (Ruth 1:17; 2 Sam 3:35). The Israelites were expected to honor their oaths, even to their disadvantage (Josh 9:18–19; Ps 15:4). God himself swore oaths as well (usually by himself), despite the fact that his character and word could not be challenged. God's oaths usually affirmed a promise to his people in order to give them greater confidence that he would fulfill the promise (Gen 22:16).

Sometimes swearing an oath was accompanied by an authenticating action. Raising one's hand while swearing an oath (Deut 32:40–41; Dan 12:7) was so common that simply naming the action was enough to signify an oath (Gen 14:22–23). Oaths often included invoking witnesses (1 Sam 12:5, the Lord; Gen 31:52, inanimate objects) who were to watch and thus motivate the parties to keep the oath. Sometimes animals were slaughtered in connection with oaths. Parties to treaties that were sealed with oaths might unite in a ceremonial meal and then slaughter one or more animals, thereby threatening such a fate on either party should they break the oath (Gen 15). Sacrificing seven animals may have been the original and fullest expression of this concept and may be the reason that the verb "to swear" (*š-b-ʿ*) has the same root as the number "seven" (Gen 21:28–32).

Along with actions, particular expressions could signify oaths. The most common was "As (surely as the Lord) lives . . ." or "By the life of (the Lord) . . ." (1 Sam 19:6). Also common was "May God deal with (the speaker), be it ever so severely, if . . ." (1 Sam 25:22; cf. 1 Kgs 19:2). Al-though oaths were used extensively, they were not always uttered in earnest or with integrity (Jer 5:2).

Vows (Heb. sing. *nēder*) appear less commonly in the OT than oaths. We see Jacob vowing allegiance and a tithe after a safe return (Gen 28:20–22), the Israelites vowing to utterly destroy their enemies if they are victori-ous (Num 21:2), Jephthah promising to sacrifice the first thing that greets him after military victory (Judg 11:30–31), Hannah offering the service of a requested son (1 Sam 1:11), and Absalom vowing worship in exchange for a safe return (2 Sam 15:8). Vows also appear frequently in psalms of lament, where the distressed supplicant makes a vow so that God will give desired aid. In response, the supplicant might promise a sacrifice, service, or public praise—the last apparently reflecting the ancient belief that gods desired praise as well as sacrifice.

Israelites were not required to make vows, but once made, a vow was irrevocable (Num 30:2), even if it was an unwise one (like Jephthah's). Females, like males, could make vows, although husbands or fathers had the power to nullify the vow of a wife or daughter if they did so promptly (Num 30). Vows could be made anywhere but apparently had to be paid at a religious center. Prompt payment was an indication of piety (Deut 23:21–23; Eccl 5:4–5). A Nazirite vow set aside a person in devotion to Yahweh temporarily (Num 6:1–21), though occasionally for life (Samson).

Elkanah had two wives, Peninnah and Hannah. Since the latter was barren, she made a vow to the Lord: "Lord Almighty, if you will only look on your servant's misery and remember me, and not forget your servant but give her a son, then I will give him to the Lord for all the days of his life, and no razor will ever be used on his head" (1 Sam 1:11). After Samuel was weaned, Hannah presented him to serve in the Lord's sanctuary (1 Sam 1:28).

B. THE NEW TESTAMENT

Oaths (Gk. sing. *horkos*) and vows (Gk. sing. *euchē*) also appear in the NT, but less frequently than in the OT. In the NT, oaths are still used to reinforce human (Matt 14:7, 9) and divine (Heb 6:17) promises as well as statements presented as truth (Matt 26:72; Heb 6:16). An oath can still compel a response (Matt 26:63), but it cannot force a desired action from a supernatural being (Mark 5:7, Jesus; Acts 19:13–16, evil spirits).

Apparently, the overuse and misuse of oaths and vows (Matt 15:3–6; Mark 7:9–13) led to commands by Jesus (Matt 5:33–37) and James (Jas 5:12) for God's people to avoid oaths as a guarantee of truth. Instead, this was to be provided by one's own character and integrity. However, we see that Paul still used oaths (Rom 1:9; 2 Cor 1:23) and that he took a temporary Nazirite vow (Acts 18:18; cf. Acts 21:23–24). This mixed picture may suggest that the commands to avoid oaths were considered to be applicable for most situations, but with an allowance for exceptions.

When Peter denied Jesus three times, he strengthened his denial with an oath: "Then he began to call down curses, and he swore to them, 'I don't know the man!'" (Matt 26:74; cf. Mark 14:71). When Peter "cursed," he was not using profanity, nor was he cursing anyone else; he was drawing down upon himself the implied curses that were thought to come upon one who was not telling the truth.

According to the author of Hebrews, God confirmed his promise to Abraham by swearing an oath by himself:

> When God made his promise to Abraham, since there was no one greater for him to swear by, he swore by himself. . . . People swear by someone greater than themselves, and the oath confirms what is said and puts an end to all argument. Because God wanted to make the unchanging nature of his purpose very clear to the heirs of what was promised, he confirmed it with an oath.
> (Heb 6:13, 16–17)

C. THE NEAR EASTERN WORLD

Mesopotamia

Records from ancient Mesopotamia attest to the widespread use of oaths and vows. Oaths were often sworn in the name of the god of a city (e.g., "by the life of Marduk my lord"). They could be used in legal contexts as a substitute when physical evidence or witness statements were unavailable. In such cases, the party could be charged to swear before their god the truth of their position or else drop their case. However, by the Neo-Babylonian period, courts showed a marked preference for more tangible proofs. Oaths of innocence could be enhanced by an ordeal by which the gods were believed to demonstrate guilt or innocence. Ordeals could involve casting the accused into a river, such as the Euphrates (CH 132), or fire (cf. Dan 6) to test the person, or giving them consecrated food to cause illness if guilty (cf. Num 5:11–31).

Treaties between nations often included oaths sworn by both parties, invoking the gods of both nations and calling on them to serve as witnesses who would take the life of an animal that was sacrificed. These oaths were also made by touching one's throat (ARMT II, 77.2–8), perhaps in a slashing gesture to signify the god potentially taking one's life. The oath that Hammurabi swore to Zimri-Lim of Mari reads as follows:

> Swear by Šamaš of heaven! Swear by Addu of heaven! These are the gods that Hammurabi, son of Sin-muballiṭ, king of Babylon, invoked (when taking this oath), From now on, as long as I live, I shall indeed be enemy of Ṣiwa-palar-ḫuḫpak. I shall not let my servants or my messengers mingle with his servants, and I shall not dispatch them to him. . . . I shall certainly consult with Zimri-Lim, son of Yaḫdun-Lim, king of Mari and the Tribal-land. (Sasson, 99)

Later, as Hammurabi expanded his empire, he destroyed the city of Mari.

In 1955, in the excavations under Max Mallowan at Nimrud (ancient Kalḫu, biblical Calah), more than 350 fragments of cuneiform tablets were discovered in the throne room of the Assyrian palace. When scholars were able to reassemble some of these, they discovered that when the Medians attacked and conquered Nimrud in 612 BC, they deliberately destroyed a vassal treaty that their ancestors had signed with Esarhaddon sixty years before. (See Wiseman.)

Esarhaddon had made the Median vassals swear before a host of gods that they would respect the succession of his son Ashurbanipal upon the threat of a long list of dreadful curses:

> If you try to reverse the curse, to avert the consequences of the oath . . .
>
> May Ashur, king of the gods, who determines the fates, decree for you an evil, unpropitious fate, and not grant you fatherhood, old age, . . . ripe old age.
>
> May Shamash, the light of heaven and earth, not give you a fair and equitable judgment, may he take away your eyesight; walk about in darkness!
>
> Just as lead does not resist fire, so may you not resist your enemies, but take your sons and daughters by the hand (and flee).
>
> Just as a mule has no offspring, may your name, offspring and descendants disappear from the land. (*ANESTP*, 538–39)

Vows also appear extensively in Assyrian and Babylonian literature, in which they are offered by kings and commoners. They often include requests such as healing or protection from a flood that was threatening crops or a city. In exchange, vows promised gifts, sacrifices, or perhaps even praise, since praise was also considered food for the gods. Prompt payment of vows was expected, and problems such as illness could be attributed to unpaid vows. If desperate, one might acquire the money to pay a vow through prostitution. Votive gifts known from Mari include silver items (such as pouches and a statue of Ishtar), a daughter dedicated to serve a deity, and sheep.

A letter from Eidem to Till-abnu refers to a certain Mutiya who made vows but did not keep them:

> In the past, before he could ascend his throne, Mutiya kept on making the following vow, "If I were to ascend to my throne, I shall donate silver, gold, cups of silver, cups of gold, and skillful maids to Belet-Nagar, my Lady!" This is what he kept on vowing. (Yet) when this man did ascend his throne, he totally ignored the goddess and did not even visit her once! (Sasson, 240)

Vows were apparently also common among the Hittites, who would make them when asking for divine aid for problems like illness or impotence. Hittite commoners promised gifts such as cattle, a shrine, or sons or daughters as servants at a temple (cf. Hannah and Samuel). Hittite royalty are known to have promised golden shields or a life-size silver statue of the king.

Egypt

In Egypt, oaths were often sworn in the name of a god such as Ptah, the "Lord of Truth," or in the name of the pharaoh (in the "Oath of the Lord"), who was also considered a god. Common oaths might assert the truth of something said ("I speak in truth"), the truth of a fact ("I did it myself"), some statement of emotion ("This is grievous in my heart"), or the truth of a statement in a judicial setting ("The Oath of the Lord was given to her not to speak falsely") (see Wilson). Oaths might include penalties for false statements (e.g., beatings, the cutting off of the ears or nose, exile, payment of a fee, or loss of property). Oaths often accompanied promises of some future act (e.g., the pharaoh taking vengeance on rebels) or statements of loyalty to an overlord. Although the Egyptians generally respected oaths because they called on divine power, oaths did not have absolute force.

D. THE GRECO-ROMAN WORLD

Greece

Early Greek society did not use written contracts, so oaths were used to seal agreements in private life, commerce, and the political realm, including treaties between cities. Parties swore by gods as witnesses and called on them to punish oath breakers. People typically swore by one to three gods (especially Zeus, Poseidon, Demeter, Helios, and Ge) but occasionally by as many as sixteen, reflecting the number and variety of Greek gods. Women swore by Artemis. The gods themselves swore by the Styx. Solemn oaths were sometimes sealed with the sacrifice of an animal (Hom. *Il.* 2.124; 3.73).

When Agamemnon signs a (temporary) truce with Priam, the king of Troy, he slits the throat of sacrificial lambs, pours a libation of wine on the ground, and declares: "Zeus, most glorious, most great, and ye other immortal gods, which host soever of the twain shall be first to work harm in defiance of the oaths, may their brains be thus poured forth upon the ground even as this wine, theirs and their children's; and may their wives be made slaves to others" (Hom. *Il.* 3.298–301). Elsewhere in the *Iliad*, Achilles vows to avenge his friend Patroclus's death at the hands of Hector (*Il.* 18.333–337), a vow that he duly fulfills.

Oaths were used in many parts of Greek society. The king swore oaths to benefit the political and economic life of the kingdom. Judges swore oaths when taking office, and jurors swore oaths when assuming their duties. Oaths were considered a vital part of holding society together (Lycurgus, *Against Leocrates* 79), and piety was measured by one's respect for oaths and vows as well as for the gods (Isocrates, *To Demonicus* 1.12–13). In literature, "Oath" (*horkos*) even became a personified figure who punished those who committed perjury and broke their oaths (Hes. *Op.* 219, 804) by wiping out their family line (Her. *Hist.* 6.86).

Before the crucial battle of Plataea, which took place in 479 BC between the Persians and their allies (including Thebes) and the Greek city-states led by Athens and Sparta, the Greeks took an oath (Her. *Hist.* 7.132). Such an oath was published in 1938. It reads in part:

> I will fight to the death, and I will not count my life more precious than freedom. I will not leave my officer, the commander of my Regiment or Company, either alive or dead. . . . I will bury the dead of those who have fought as my allies, on the field, and will not leave one of them unburied. After defeating the barbarians in battle, I will tithe the city of the Thebans; and I will never destroy Athens or Sparta or Plataia . . . nor cut them off from running water, whether we be friends or at war.
>
> And if I keep well the oath, as it is written, may my city have good health; but if not, may it have sickness; and may my city never be sacked; but if not, may it be sacked; and may my land give increase; but if not, may it be barren; and may the women bring forth children like their fathers; but if not, monsters. (cited by Burn, 513; cf. Yamauchi 1990, 219–20)

The most famous Greek oath is "The Hippocratic Oath," which is still sworn in a modified form by medical students today. It reads in part:

> I swear by Apollo Physician, by Asclepius, by Health, by Panacea and by all the gods and goddesses, making them my witnesses, that I will carry out, according to my ability and judgment, this oath and this indenture. . . . Neither will I administer a poison [*pharmakon*] to anybody when asked to do so, nor will I suggest such a course. Similarly I will not give a woman a pessary [*pesson phthorion*] to cause abortion. But I will keep pure and holy both my life and my art. (*Jusj.* 1–5, 18–22)

The oath seems to have been influenced by Pythagorean ideas, which included the condemnation of suicide and abortion. (See Edelstein.)

Over time, oaths became so abused that their force dwindled dramatically. Some Greeks banned from common usage oaths invoking the gods in order to give them more force. Out of religious respect, Socrates chose to swear by trivial things rather than by the gods.

Because of the widespread practice of perjury both by plaintiffs and defendants, Plato proposed that while judges should take oaths, this should not be the case with litigants: "And in general, during a trial, the presidents of the court shall not permit a man to speak under oath for the sake of gaining credence, or to imprecate curses upon himself and his family" (*Leg.* 12.949b).

Individuals made vows to request divine aid when facing dangers such as poor health, childbirth, crop failure, or peril at sea. Votive offerings often consisted of votive tablets made of precious metals. Individuals also gave suitable voluntary gifts to their god(s) following a time of transition or achievement, such as tools when a craftsman retired, or trophies from competitions (Hes. *Op.* 659) or from victory in battle (Hom. *Il.* 7.83). Civic and religious officials led public ceremonies asking for a god's help when their communities or regions were threatened by war, epidemic, or drought. Afterward, the community might give to the god a gift such as an altar, an arch, or a temple, or they might hold athletic games in the god's honor.

Many votive gifts were sent to be placed in small treasuries that surrounded the temple of Apollo at Delphi. The gifts were sent not only by various Greek city-states but even by Croesus, the king of Lydia in western Anatolia.

In thanksgiving for healing, many grateful patients dedicated replicas of body parts that had been healed (Gk. *anathēmata*; Lat. *simulacra*) at the shrines of the deity Aesclepius (Lat. Aesculapius) at Epidaurus and Pergamon.

Rome

In the early history of Rome, during the seventh century BC, a notable treaty was made between the Romans and the Albans by which they agreed to abide by the outcome of a combat of their respective champions. According to Livy, Spurius Fusus served as the *pater patratus*, the priest who pronounced the oath that solemnized the pact. He declared:

> "The Roman People will not be the first to depart. If it shall first depart from them, by general consent, with malice aforethought then on that day do thou, great Diespiter [i.e., Jupiter], so smite the Roman People as I shall here to-day smite this pig . . ." When Spurius had said these words, he struck the pig with a flint. (Livy, *Rom. Hist.* 1.24.8–9)

Later, during the Empire, the Romans added the genius of the emperor to the gods in their oaths. They used oaths in legal proceedings, calling on defendants and sometimes also plaintiffs to swear oaths in order to strengthen a judgment if no witnesses were available. Romans also used oaths in civil, tax, and public documents, often stating that the penalty for perjury would be the swearer's honor, possessions, or even life. Client kings or provincial governors would swear an oath of allegiance to the emperor, sometimes along with their subjects, when Rome absorbed a new realm into the empire (Jos. *Ant.* 17.42). Soldiers swore an oath (Lat. *sacramentum*) when they joined the army, from which only death or the end of the war could grant release. Members of the military would also take an oath of loyalty at the accession of a new emperor, and then annually on the anniversary of his accession.

One unusual vow (*votum*) was the act of *devotio* in which the Roman general Publius Decius Mus offered his own life to the gods for a victory for his army in a battle against the Latins in the fourth century BC near Mount Vesuvius. Decius called out to Marcus Valerius, the pontiff (priest), in desperation. He was instructed to wear a purple bordered toga, veil his head, thrust out one hand and touch his chin, stand on a spear, invoke Janus Jupiter, Mars, and other gods, and say: "I devote the legions and auxiliaries of the enemy, together with myself, to the divine Manes and to Earth" (Livy, *Rom. Hist.* 8.9.8). A generation later, his son made a similar *devotio* of himself against the invading Gauls (Livy, *Rom. Hist.* 10.28.13).

Punic inscriptions reveal that some babies in Carthage, Rome's enemy in North Africa, were sacrificed to fulfill vows that their parents had made (see Brown).

E. THE JEWISH WORLD

Jewish literature reflects a general reluctance to use oaths and vows, although Nazirite vows continued (Jos. *Ant.* 19.292–293; *J.W.* 2.313). Sirach advises: "Do not accustom your mouth to oaths, and do not habitually utter the name of the Holy One" (Sir 23:9). He adds: "A man who swears many oaths will be filled with iniquity, and the scourge will not leave his house" (Sir 23:11). Philo also writes extensively on oaths and vows, arguing that it is best to avoid them whenever possible, since swearing falsely profanes the name of God (*Spec.* 2:1–38; *Decal.* 82–95). According to Josephus, the Essenes avoided oaths altogether (*J.W.* 2.135; *Ant.* 15.368–371), although he also states that converts to their teachings had to swear "tremendous oaths" during their initiation.

The Dead Sea Scrolls include extensive teaching on oaths and vows. The Temple Scroll combines the instructions on oaths and vows from Num 30 and Deut 23:22–24, occasionally making subtle alterations to the biblical material (11Q19 LIII, 11–LIV, 5). 4QInstruction goes beyond the teaching in Num 30 to suggest that husbands annul all the oaths and vows of their wives (4Q416 2 IV, 10; 4Q418 10 8–10). Like the Essenes, the authors of the Scrolls discouraged the general use of oaths and vows but required oaths of their initiates:

> Every initiate into the party of the *Yahad* is to enter the covenant in full view of all the volunteers. He shall take upon himself a binding oath to return to the Law of Moses . . . with all his heart and with all his mind, to all that has been revealed from it to the Sons of Zadok . . . Each one who thus enters the Covenant by oath is to separate himself from all of the perverse men, they who walk in the wicked way, for such are not reckoned a part of His Covenant. (1QS V, 7–11; cf. *CD* XV, 5–6, 12–13)

The Mishnah includes entire sections entitled "Vows" (*Nedarim*) and "Oaths" (*Šebuʿot*) that seek to clarify and regulate their use. Issues include when a vow is in force, at what age a speaker's vow is considered valid (a boy—thirteen years plus a day; a girl—twelve years plus a day), and what types of vows are not binding (those of incitement, exaggeration, those made in error, and those that cannot be fulfilled by reason of constraint; *Ned.* 3:1–3). Likewise, swearing an oath that one cannot possibly fulfill makes it a vain oath (*Šebu.* 3:8). Much of the discussion on vows focuses on prohibitive vows that likened one's property to temple property. Such vows consecrated the item as *qorban* and prevented anyone from using it. Vows of this kind were forbidden in the Dead Sea Scrolls (*CD* XVI, 13–20) and condemned by Jesus (Mark 7:9–13). The Mishnaic tractate *Nazir* gives regulations for Nazirite vows, which later rabbis debated in the Talmud.

F. THE CHRISTIAN WORLD

The early church seems to have largely followed the teaching from the NT to avoid oaths and vows, especially in regard to the Roman emperor. Perhaps as early as the late first century, Christians refused to swear the common oath by the genius or fortune of the emperor, to say "Caesar is Lord," or to offer sacrifices to him. They refused, thinking that these actions amounted to idolatry; on the other hand, Christians were willing to pray *for* the emperor.

In the early second century, Pliny the Younger, the governor of Bithynia in northwestern Asia Minor, tested Christian recanters by having them invoke Roman gods, offer incense and wine to the emperor, or curse Christ. He recounted this to the emperor Trajan. Pliny tortured Christian slave women who were *ministrae* and discovered that

> they had met regularly before dawn on a fixed day to chant verses alternately among themselves in honour of Christ as if to a god [*quasi deo*], and also to

bind themselves by oath [*sacramento*] not for any criminal purpose, but to abstain from theft, robbery and adultery, to commit no breach of trust and not to deny a deposit when called upon to restore. (*Ep.* 10.967–968)

The Roman government continued to put pressure on Christians. Nearly a half century after Pliny, Polycarp, the bishop of Smyrna, was urged to say "Caesar is Lord" or offer sacrifice, but though excused from this requirement, he was eventually martyred. A decade later, Justin Martyr and six other Roman Christians were brought before Junius Rusticus, prefect of Rome, who had them beaten and sentenced to death for refusing to sacrifice to the gods. In the early third century, Tertullian noted that although Christians did not swear by the genius of the Caesars, they swore by a more significant oath, "by their salvation."

In the account of the martyrs of Scilli in North Africa in 180, the proconsul Saturninus demanded of the Christian Speratus, "If you begin to malign our sacred rites, I shall not listen to you. But swear rather by the Genius of our lord the emperor." Speratus responded, "I do not recognize the empire of this world. . . . I acknowledge my lord who is the emperor of kings and of all nations." He and eleven others were beheaded. (See Musurillo, 87–89.)

By the fourth century, in the context of an increasingly formal church, Gregory of Nazianzus, who later would become the archbishop of Constantinople, wrote an oath to attest to his fidelity as a bishop. He swore by "the very Logos, who for me is greatest God," not to speak or think heretically, and included curses that should fall on him should he fail (*Poemata de seipso* 2.1.2; Rebillard, 180). Thus Gregory did not prohibit swearing oaths altogether, but he did warn elsewhere against excessive swearing and stressed the importance of avoiding perjury. The church of Gregory's time seems to have accepted some oaths, such as the Hippocratic Oath, oaths sworn by bishops when taking office, oaths guaranteeing the truth of documents submitted to authorities, and oaths taken by judges when assuming office or by parties when in court.

According to the Theodosian Code: "We have previously commanded that before they give their testimony, witnesses shall be bound by the sanctity of an oath" (*Cod. Theod.* 11.39.3). Military service also required an oath, as we learn from another law: "If any person should be found to have caused damage to his body by cutting off his fingers to avoid the oaths of military service, he shall be consumed in avenging flames" (*Cod. Theod.* 7.12.5).

BIBLIOGRAPHY: L. Adkins and R. A. Adkins, *Dictionary of Roman Religion* (2001); L. Adkins and R. A. Adkins, *Handbook to Life in Ancient Rome*

(1998); J. K. Aitken, *The Semantics of Blessing and Cursing in Ancient Hebrew* (2007); A. A. Bell, Jr., *Exploring the New Testament World* (1998); J. Ben-Dov and E. Ratzon, "The Oath and the Name in 1 Enoch 69," *JSS* 60 (2015), 19–51; M. Benovitz, *Kol Nidre: Studies in the Development of Rabbinic Votive Institutions* (1998); J. Berlinerblau, *The Vow and the "Popular Religious Groups" of Ancient Israel* (1996); S. Brown, *Late Carthaginian Child Sacrifice and Sacrificial Monuments in Their Mediterranean Context* (1991); A. R. Burn, *Persia and the Greeks* (1962); T. W. Cartledge, *Vows in the Hebrew Bible and the Ancient Near East* (1992); B. Conklin, *Oath Formulas in Biblical Hebrew* (2011); L. Edelstein, trans., *The Hippocratic Oath* (1979); M. H. Floyd, "Vow," in *The New Interpreter's Dictionary of the Bible*, ed. K. D. Sakenfeld (2009), V.793–94; G. Frank, "Pilgrimage," in *The Oxford Handbook of Early Christian Studies* (2008), 826–41; R. M. Grant, "Sacrifices and Oaths as Required of Early Christians," in *Kyriakon: Festschrift Johannes Quasten*, ed. P. Granfield and J. A. Jungmann (1970), 1.12–17; T. M. Gregory, "Oath," in *The Zondervan Encyclopedia of the Bible*, ed. M. C. Tenney and M. Silva (Rev. ed., 2009), IV.526–29; A. M. Kitz, "An Oath, Its Curse and Anointing Ritual," *JAOS* 124 (2004), 315–21; M. R. Lehmann, "Biblical Oaths," *ZAW* 81 (1969), 74–92; N. Lewis and M. Reinhold, ed., *Roman Civilization: Selected Readings* II: *The Empire* (3rd ed., 1990); D. Marcus, *Jephthah and His Vow* (1986); J. M. Munn-Rankin, "Diplomacy in Western Asia in the Early Second Millennium B.C.," *Iraq* 18 (1956), 68–110; H. Musurillo, trans., *The Acts of the Christian Martyrs* (1972); A. Pagolu, *The Religion of the Patriarchs* (1998); J. Priest, "Ὅρκια in the *Iliad* and Consideration of a Recent Theory," *JNES* 23 (1964), 48–56; S. A. Rebillard, "The Speech Act of Swearing: Gregory of Nazianzus's Oath in *Poema* 2.1.2 in Context," *JECS* 21 (2013), 177–207; J. M. Sasson, trans. and ed., *From the Mari Archives: An Anthology of Old Babylonian Letters* (2015); A. J. Spalinger, *Aspects of the Military Documents of the Ancient Egyptians* (1982); G. Stob, "Vow," in *The Zondervan Encyclopedia of the Bible,* ed. M. C. Tenney and M. Silva (Rev. ed., 2009), 1033–34; B. Studevent-Hickman, S. C. Melville, and S. Noegel, "Neo-Babylonian Period Texts from Babylonia and Syro-Palestine," in *The Ancient Near East: Historical Sources in Translation*, ed. M. W. Chavalas (2006), 382–406; A. C. Thiselton, "Oath," in *The New Interpreter's Dictionary of the Bible*, ed. K. D. Sakenfeld (2009), IV.309–12; H. G. White, "The Divine Oath in Genesis," *JBL* 92 (1973), 165–79; J. Wilson, "The Oath in Ancient Egypt," *JNES* 7 (1948), 129–56; M. O. Wise, M. G. Abegg, Jr., and E. M. Cook, *The Dead Sea Scrolls: A New Translation* (rev. ed., 2005); D. J. Wiseman, *The Vassal Treaties of Esarhaddon* (1958); E. M. Yamauchi, "Oaths," in *The New International Dictionary of Biblical Archaeology*, ed. E. M. Blaiklock and R. K. Harrison (1983), 343–44; E. M. Yamauchi, *Persia and the Bible* (1990); Y. Ziegler, "'As the Lord Lives and as

Your Soul Lives': An Oath of Conscious Deference," *VT* 58 (2008), 117–30; Y. Ziegler, *Promises to Keep: The Oath in Biblical Narrative* (2008) Y. Ziegler, "'So Shall God Do ... ': Variations of an Oath Formula and Its Literary Meaning," *JBL* 126 (2007), 59–81.

BVS

See also HUMAN SACRIFICE and LAWS & CRIMES.

PALACES

Grand buildings or complexes of buildings for a ruler usually had a public or official area, including a throne room and reception hall, as well as private quarters for the ruler and his family, and at times quarters for his harem.

A. THE OLD TESTAMENT

The Hebrew word *hêkāl* (derived from Akk. *ēkallu*) usually designates the temple, but it is used eleven times for a palace, as in 1 Kgs 21:1 and 2 Kgs 20:18. The phrase *bêt hammelek*, "house of the king," is sometimes used as a synonym for "palace" (Jer 39:8; cf. 1 Kgs 7:1). The word *'armôn*, which denotes a "fortified palace," is found frequently in the prophets—for example, in Isa 32:14, Jer 30:18, Hos 8:14, and, most notably, in Amos 1:4–2:5. *Bîrâ* (from Akk. *birtu*), "citadel," is used in the postexilic books, ten times out of eighteen in the book of Esther. *Bîtān* (from Akk. *bîtānu*) occurs only three times in the Bible (Esth 1:5; 7:7–8), always in reference to the palace at Susa. *Appeden* (from Old Pers. *apadâna*, "audience hall") occurs but once, at Dan 11:45, in the phrase "tents of his palace," which indicates royal quarters.

Saul, the first king of Israel, rebuilt a fortress-palace at his home in Gibeah (Tell el-Fûl) three miles north of Jerusalem (1 Sam 15:34). As reconstructed from the preserved corner, the crudely constructed fortress would have measured 52 x 35 meters (171 x 115 ft.), with rooms around a courtyard and with an upper story.

All that we know about David's palace is that it was constructed using cedar beams and with the aid of carpenters and stonemasons sent to him by Hiram, king of Tyre (2 Sam 5:11; 7:2; 1 Chr 14:1). Eilat Mazar believes that a "large stone structure" dating to the tenth century BC that she has uncovered in Jerusalem and a Proto-Aeolic column found in the area were part of David's palace.

Hiram later sent similar supplies and workmen to aid Solomon in his construction of the temple (1 Kgs 5:1–18), and presumably also for the building of his palace. A detailed description is given of the construction of Solomon's palace in 1 Kgs 7:1–12. Whereas Solomon spent seven years building the temple (1 Kgs 6:38), he spent thirteen years building his palace (1 Kgs 7:1).

The Bible describes several distinctive structures related to Solomon's building activities. The Palace of the Forest of Lebanon (1 Kgs 7:2–5) was a great hall, 100 cubits long, 50 broad, and 30 high (46 x 23 x 13.5 m. [150 x 75 x 45 ft.]), which received its name from its forty-five cedar columns. There is some uncertainty as to whether these were arranged in four rows (MT) or in three (LXX, Vulg). This building evidently served as an armory for the storage of weapons (1 Kgs 10:17, 21; Isa 22:8) and as a treasury for precious objects (2 Chr 9:20).

A colonnade that measured 50 x 30 cubits (75 x 45 ft.) and that had a porch may have served as a waiting room (1 Kgs 7:6). The throne room served as the "hall of judgment" (1 Kgs 7:7). It was paneled from the floor to the ceiling with cedar. The interspersing of timber courses among the courses of stone (1 Kgs 7:9–11) was designed as protection against earthquakes. Solomon's throne was inlaid with ivory and gold (1 Kgs 10:18–20). Of the residences themselves it is simply stated that he built a similar palace for himself and a separate one for the pharaoh's daughter (1 Kgs 7:8; 9:24). Josephus, in his expanded description of Solomon's palaces, speaks of a "very splendid hall for feasts and banquets, filled with gold" (*Ant.* 8.137–138).

Archaeologists have not been able to recover any of Solomon's buildings at Jerusalem, with the possible exception of a fragmentary wall. But two palaces attributed to Solomon have been identified at Megiddo. The southern palace, Building 1723, measuring 23 x 21 meters (75 x 69 ft.), was surrounded by a large court with a plastered floor. The outer walls were made of finely drafted ashlars in alternating headers and stretchers. Two Proto-Aeolic capitals were recovered. The northern palace, Building 6000, resembled the *bīt ḫilāni* palaces of Neo-Hittite Syria.

Ahab's palace (1 Kgs 22:39) has been excavated at Samaria. This was made with superbly drafted header and stretcher ashlars, which were no doubt the work of Phoenician masons that Jezebel, Ahab's queen, employed from her homeland. The podium of the palace is the largest pre-Roman structure to have been found in Palestine. The northern section was residential. A long colonnaded structure contained storerooms. An archive of sixty-three ostraca (8th c. BC) records the shipment of oil and wine sent to the palace. A large courtyard (100 x 72 m. [328 x 235 ft.]) may have been a parade ground for chariots. About two hundred ivory plaques illustrate the ostentatious luxury denounced by Amos (Amos 3:15; 6:4; cf. Ps. 45:8).

Jeremiah (22:13–19) upbraided Jehoiakim for exploiting his people to build a great palace with spacious upper rooms. Yohanan Aharoni has uncovered this palace at Beth-Haccherem (Ramat Raḥel), just south of Jerusalem. The inner citadel covered an area 90 x 50 meters (295 x 164 ft.). Aharoni recovered four Proto-Aeolic capitals, some imported Assyrian palace ware, a painting of a bearded king on a sherd, and decorations from windows that correspond to those described in Jeremiah's diatribe (Jer 22:14).

B. THE NEW TESTAMENT

The word *aulē*, literally, "court," is used of the residence of the high priest, as in Matt 26:3, 58, 69, which English versions translate as "court" or "palace." The word *basileios*, "palace" (derived from Gk. *basileus*, "king"), is used but once, at Luke 7:25. The word *praitōrion* (from Lat. *praetorium*, originally "the praetor's court") refers to the residence of the Roman governor where Jesus was tried (Mark 15:16; John 18:28, 33). Though some scholars have favored the Fortress Antonia as the site of Jesus's trial before Pilate, the more probable site is Herod's palace in the citadel area, as this would have served as the Roman governor's residence when he was in Jerusalem.

The word *praitōrion* in Phil 1:13 should not be translated "palace" (as in the KJV) but rather as "palace guard" (NIV). The Praetorian Guard in Rome was the emperor's special legion of bodyguards.

C. THE NEAR EASTERN WORLD

Mesopotamia

The Sumerian word É.GAL (lit., "big house") is found with the meaning "palace" in archaic texts from Ur. The word was borrowed by the Akkadian language as *ēkallu*. Palace A from Kish, which was built for Mesilim (2600 BC), is the earliest example of a palace from Sumer. It has a monumental entrance and rooms arranged around a square courtyard. At Eshnunna, the small palace for the governor (23rd c. BC) is a long rectangular complex arranged around a courtyard. The placement of the audience chamber between a forecourt and an inner court anticipates the layout of later Assyrian palaces.

The classic layout of Mesopotamian palaces had two courtyards connected by a throne room, which served as an audience hall. The *bābānû*, or outer courtyard, was used for public ceremonies. Surrounding this courtyard were offices, workshops, and storage areas. The *bītānu*, or inner courtyard, was used for private ceremonies and was surrounded by the residential quarters of the royal family.

Italian excavations at Tell Mardikh (ancient Ebla) uncovered a palace that was destroyed around 2250 BC by Naram-Sin. The audience room had a dais of mud-brick covered with plaster. It faced a public square, 52 x 32 meters (171 x 105 ft.) in area. Nearby were a monumental gateway and a ceremonial stairway. A scepter of wood and gold was also found in the palace. The most spectacular discovery in the remains of this building was the more than sixteen thousand tablets found in the archives.

The great palace of Zimri-Lim at Mari on the Euphrates River was excavated by André Parrot beginning in 1933. Covering over five acres and measuring 200 x 120 meters (656 x 394 ft.), the Mari palace is the largest royal residence of the second millennium BC thus far uncovered. It was made with sun-dried bricks, with timbers used for the ceilings and roofs. Mainly one story in height, it contained about three hundred rooms. There was but one main entrance to the building, located in the north. The complex contained two large courtyards, numerous storerooms, servants' quarters, and even a schoolroom with brick benches. One courtyard was a fifth of an acre in size, measuring 48 x 32.5 meters (158 x 56 ft.). The archive of some twenty thousand tablets found in the palace casts invaluable light on the patriarchal period.

Near the entrance of the palace, a suite of twelve rooms with a kitchen and bathroom may have been used for the reception of visiting dignitaries. The main hall measured 26 x 12 meters (85 x 40 ft.), with walls about nine meters (30 ft.) high. The court of the throne room was provided with a podium of limestone painted to imitate marble for the throne, and was richly decorated with wall frescoes. The bathroom in the royal suite had two terra-cotta bathtubs. The lower part of the walls in the bathrooms was made of baked brick set in bitumen. Rainwater was dispersed into underground drains some ten meters (33 ft.) below the surface. The palace at Mari was regarded as a marvel, as indicated by a letter that reads: "The king of Ugarit has written me as follows: 'Show me the palace of Zimri-Lim! I wish to see it'" (Gates, 70). Mari was destroyed by Hammurabi in 1757 BC.

Leonard Woolley discovered the important city of Alalakh at Tell Atchana in the Orontes River Valley of Syria. Two palaces were uncovered: the first was that of Yarim-Lim (17th c. BC) and the second was that of Niqmepa (16th/15th c. BC). The earlier palace was a narrow rectangle, measuring 95 x 30 meters (312 x 98 ft.), that was subdivided into three areas, each with its own court: (1) the audience chamber and ceremonial apartments (in the north); (2) the central court; and (3) the residential apartments (in the south). Especially significant is that this palace contains the first known use of painted orthostats in a decorative dado (that is, the lower section of a wall), a practice that was later used by the Assyrians. The later palace of Niqmepa features the oldest known example of the *ḫilāni* plan, that is, a rectangular building with a pillared forehall, the entrance to which was on one of its long sides.

From the Middle Babylonian era (1590–1100 BC) has survived a palace at Dur Kurigalzu, which has been partially excavated. The rooms were arranged on three sides of a large court measuring sixty-four meters (210 ft.) square, which was bordered by a portico with square pillars. The most striking features are the doorways, which were decorated with frescoes of figures in a procession. Fragments of glass, gold, and jewelry were found in the remains of the palace.

During the Neo-Assyrian period—that is, from the ninth century BC until the fall of Nineveh in 612 BC—the Assyrians became the dominant power in the Near East. About twenty Neo-Assyrian palaces have been found, of which only about a third have been excavated with any degree of completion.

In the ninth century BC, the Assyrians moved their capital from Aššur to Calah (Nimrud), which is located eight kilometers (5 mi.) from the confluence of the Tigris with the Great Zab. Calah became the main military capital of the Assyrians. The huge northwest palace of Assurnasirpal II (883–850 BC), which measured 200 x 130 meters (656 x 427 ft.) and which sprawled over six acres, is the earliest of the classical type of the Neo-Assyrian palaces. The king's throne was placed before a relief that depicts the king standing beside a sacred tree. For the first time in Assyrian art, the king is portrayed in a narrative relief fighting enemies and hunting lions. The gateways are guarded by colossal *lamassū*, or *šēdū*, human-headed lions or winged bulls, often with five legs. At a feast to inaugurate his new palace, Assurnasirpal boasted that he fed 69,574 people for ten days.

Other palaces were located on the fortified acropolis in the southwest of Calah. Outside the citadel is "Fort Shalmaneser," built by Shalmaneser III (859–824 BC) to serve as a combination of palace, barracks, and arsenal. In its vast throne room, Max Mallowan found a throne base decorated with scenes in relief.

Two provincial palaces from the reign of Tiglath-pileser III (745–727 BC) near the section of the Euphrates in the northwest were excavated by Paul Thureau-Dangin. The first, at Tell Ahmar (ancient Til Barsip), was located twenty-five miles south of Carchemish. The palace was centered around a trapezoidal court measuring 65 x 25 meters (213 x 82 ft.) and had a throne room measuring 27 x 9 meters (89 x 30 ft.). The outstanding feature is the most extensive display of Assyrian wall painting ever recovered, extending over 120 meters (394 ft.). The second palace excavated by Thureau-Dangin was twenty miles to the northeast, at the site of Arslan Tash (ancient Hadatu). The palace, which was 150 meters long (492 ft.), was centered around a court about 39 meters (128 ft.) square. A polychrome frieze decorated the palace. Outstanding ivories were also recovered from the site.

In 717 BC Sargon II built a new capital on an unprecedented scale, locating it fifteen miles northeast of Nineveh at Dur-Sharrukin (Khorsabad). His palace, which covered twenty-four acres, was erected on a huge brick platform. It contained over two hundred rooms. An inscription proclaims: "Sargon, King of the World, has built a city. Dur Sharrukin ['Sargon's Fortress'] he has named it. A peerless palace he has built within it" (Kleiner, 28).

First discovered by Paul Émile Botta in 1843, the palace at Khorsabad has been the most thoroughly investigated of all the Assyrian palaces. The ceremonial court covered a quarter of an acre; the throne room measured 49 x 11 meters (161 x 36 ft.). From the throne room a spiral staircase led up to the roof, where celestial omens were observed. The palace was equipped with granaries, kitchens, bakeries, and wine cellars. Water was dispersed through terra-cotta pipes into large drains of burnt brick underground. On the floor were stone tracks to guide the wheels of a portable brazier to provide heat. The walls were decorated by some five thousand square meters (six thousand square yards) of stone reliefs. Unfortunately, some 150 cases of these slabs sank in the Tigris River in 1855 as they were being transported on rafts.

Nineveh was the great Assyrian capital to which Jonah was sent. Though it was one of the earliest sites to attract archaeological attention, only one of its two great mounds, Kuyunjik, has been excavated; a village rests atop the other mound, Nebi Yunus ("Prophet Jonah"), which probably covers the palace of Esarhaddon. Over a dozen Assyrian kings built at the site, but the two principal palaces at Kuyunjik are those of Sennacherib (704–681 BC) in the southwest and Ashurbanipal (662–628 BC) in the north. Sennacherib's "Palace without a Rival" (*ēkallu ša šānina lā īšû*) covered five acres and contained seventy halls. It was built on a terrace measuring 500 x 240 meters (1640 x 787 ft.). There are both texts and reliefs describing its construction. Sennacherib proclaimed that "for the construction of my palace, the people of enemy towns and the men of remote (*lit.*, hidden) mountain (districts), the conquest of my hands, with iron picks and pickaxes quarried, and I turned it (the limestone) into mighty protecting bull-colossi, for the gates of my palace" (*ARAB* 2.178). Sennacherib himself supervised the removal of a colossal statue, twenty feet tall and weighing about fifty tons, as it was dragged on a large sledge. The reliefs depict captive Philistines, Tyrians, Cilicians, and Arameans carrying baskets on their backs and pulling on ropes.

The materials used in the palace included gold, silver, copper, sandstone, breccia, marble, ivory, cedar, sandalwood, and ebony.

The halls of Sennacherib's palace were adorned with more than 3011 meters (9880 ft.) of sculptured stone slabs, which were originally painted in bright colors. Military campaigns were the subject of the wall reliefs in all but three of the thirty-eight rooms. Of particular interest are the reliefs of room XXXVI, now in the British Museum, as they depict the king's conquest of the Judean city of Lachish (2 Kgs 18:13–17). Depicted in vivid detail is the assault of the double-walled city by battering rams and by attackers ascending siege ramps—details that have been confirmed by excavations. The king is seated on a throne reviewing the booty from the city, while a forlorn group of women and children are marched into exile.

Only a fraction of Nineveh's north palace of Ashurbanipal, originally 135 x 120 meters (443 x 294 ft.), has been uncovered. The outer court, the throne room, and the inner court (which included a reception suite) were cleared by Hormuzd Rassam. Room C is adorned with magnificent reliefs of a royal lion hunt. Other reliefs depict the king's campaigns against Elam. One celebrated scene depicts the king and queen banqueting while nearby the decapitated head of the Elamite king Teuman hangs as a trophy from a tree. This is the first known depiction of the custom of reclining at a meal, a tradition that spread through the Near East and eventually to Rome. The most significant discovery was the famous library of Ashurbanipal, a scholar-king who collected all of the literature of previous generations, including the Gilgamesh Epic.

The site of Babylon was excavated by Robert Koldewey between 1899 and 1913. Because of groundwater, the lower levels, in which the palace of Hammurabi (18th c. BC) is located, could not be excavated. In the Neo-Babylonian era, Nebuchadnezzar II (605–562 BC) made Babylon the largest city in the ancient world.

As described by Herodotus (*Hist.* 1.178–187), the city was bisected by the Euphrates River and surrounded by walls and canals. The major palace was located on the east bank of the river at the northern edge of the city, next to the Ishtar Gate. When excavated, the gate was found to have been preserved to a height of fifteen to eighteen meters (50 to 60 ft.), and it was decorated in blue, yellow, red, and white molded glazed bricks depicting 120 lions, which were sacred to Ishtar. The gate has been reconstructed in the "Pergamon" Museum in Berlin. A smaller-scale replica was rebuilt at the site of Babylon by Saddam Hussein.

The main palace occupied a trapezoidal area measuring 300 meters (984 ft.) west to east and between 120 and 200 meters (between 394 and 656 ft.) north to south; this area enclosed five major blocks, each arranged around a central courtyard. The central court, which measured 42 x 17 meters (138 x 56 ft.), was the most important, as the king's throne room was located at its southern end. This room was decorated with enameled bricks with a frieze of lions, above which were Proto-Aeolic palm columns, probably inspired by Greek artisans. This court was the setting for Belshazzar's feast (Dan 5).

In the northeast corner of the palace area was an unusual structure with two rows of seven chambers with barrel vaults. Koldewey believed that the famous Hanging Gardens, one of the Seven Wonders of the Ancient World, were located here. As Donald Wiseman has proposed, however, the correct location of this fabled five-stage garden would have been by the banks of the Euphrates River. The location that Koldewey had identified as the site of the Garden turned out to be an archive room, where the famous Jehoiachin (*Ya-u-kin*) ration tablets were found (cf. 2 Kgs 25:27–30).

Nebuchadnezzar boasted that he replaced the crude bricks of the palace of Nabopolassar, his father, with burnt brick. He boasted: "Mighty cedars I caused to be laid down at length for its roofing. Door leaves of cedar overlaid with copper, thresholds and sockets of bronze I placed in its doorways. Silver and gold and precious stones, all that can be imagined of costliness, . . . I heaped up within it" (Koldewey, 113; cf. Dan 4:30). He further boasted that the palace was "the marvel of mankind, the centre of the land, the shining residence, the dwelling of Majesty" (Koldewey, 113).

Just to the north of the main palace area was the "northern" palace. Nearby was an area that functioned, down to the Persian era, as a kind of museum. At the northernmost edge of the ruins of Babylon lie the scanty remains of the "summer palace." It was equipped with ventilation shafts to cool the building.

Nabonidus (555–539 BC), the last Neo-Babylonian king, built a large palace at Ur, perhaps for his daughter, whom he had dedicated to the service of the moon god Sin. It was built on a trapezoidal plan measuring about 90 x 47 meters (295 x 154 ft.) and had eighty rooms. The Persian Verse Account tells us that Nabonidus also built a palace in Tema in Arabia, his place of self-imposed exile.

Persia

The Persian Empire had several major capitals. Susa is the site of the story of Esther, which takes place in the days of Ahasuerus, i.e., Xerxes (485–465 BC). The author of Esther refers to the gate of the king (Esth 2:19), the outer court (Esth 6:4), the inner court (Esth 4:11), the house of the women (Esth 2:9), and a second area for concubines (Esth 2:14). Striking is the author's use of the word *bîtān*, which in the context (Esth 1:5; 7:7–8) may mean "pavilion."

Darius made Susa the administrative capital of the Persian Empire in 522 BC. The Apadana, or "Audience Hall," mound at Susa was a quadrilateral terrace that measured 250 meters (820 ft.) along each side. A detailed inscription reveals that from 518 to 512 BC Darius built a palace on the Apadana mound by employing materials and workmen from every part of his realm:

> This palace which I built at Susa, from afar its ornamentation was brought. . . . And that the earth was dug downward, and that the rubble was packed down, and that the sun-dried brick was molded, the Babylonian people—it did (these tasks). . . . The gold was brought from Sardis and from Bactria, which here was wrought. . . . The ivory which was wrought here, was brought from Ethiopia. (Kent, 144)

In 1970 French excavators discovered a monumental gate eighty meters (260 ft.) east of the palace. This gate measured 40 x 28 meters (131 x 92 ft.) and had a central square room measuring twenty-one meters (69 ft.) on a side. This may have been the gate where Mordecai sat (Esth 2:19). In 1972 the excavators discovered a larger-than-life-size statue of Darius, minus its head, near this gate.

In the reign of Artaxerxes I (464–424 BC), the palace of Darius burned to the ground. Artaxerxes may have begun the small palace in the Donjon area of the Ville Royale. From this small hypostyle hall have come all the fragments of stone bas-relief recovered from Susa.

The remains of the Apadana palace as seen today belong to the reconstruction of Artaxerxes II (404–359 BC). The building included a square central hall measuring 59 m. (194 ft.) with six rows of six columns and porticoes on three sides, each with two rows of six columns. The columns were twenty meters (65 ft.) high and were capped by double bull protomes. Colored decorations in molded enameled brick depicting the archers of the Ten Thousand Immortals covered the walls.

Pasargadae was the capital of Cyrus the Great (550–530 BC). It was excavated by David Stronach from 1961 to 1963. The Residential Palace (Palace P) is a structure measuring 78 x 44 meters (256 x 144 ft.) with six rows of five columns.

The Palace of Audience (Palace S) was a hypostyle hall measuring 45 x 56 meters (148 x 184 ft.) with black stone bases and white columns. Fragmentary jambs depict a man clad in a fish garment of an Assyrian type. Some of these jambs, which also have Urartian elements, may iconographically represent Cyrus's religious toleration.

The Gatehouse (Palace R) was the monumental entrance to the palace area. It measured 22 x 27 meters (72 x 89 ft.). The main doorways were flanked by colossal winged bulls, not a trace of which remains today. One white limestone jamb bears a figure with four wings who wears a triple Egyptian Atef crown and an Elamite garment.

About fifty miles south of Pasargadae lies the new capital established by Darius, namely, Persepolis, a site that contains some of the most impressive remains from antiquity. The buildings were completed after sixty years of labor during the reigns of Darius, Xerxes, and Artaxerxes I. They were built upon a huge artificial terrace that was twelve meters (39 ft.) high and that covered thirty-three acres. Access to the terrace was gained by a magnificent double stairway.

The Apadana, Darius's great audience hall, was without doubt the most impressive building on the site, with its tall columns that were nearly twenty meters (66 ft.) high and that were capped by double bull protomes. Of the original seventy-two columns, thirteen have been reerected. The main hall was square, 60.5 meters (198 ft.) on a side. The Apadana could have accommodated a crowd of ten thousand. The stairways have reliefs that depict representatives bearing tribute from twenty-three satrapies.

Darius's Tachara, or palace proper, is located just south of the Apadana. Outstanding features of this structure include cavetto (i.e., concave) cornices derived from Egyptian prototypes and masonry polished like mirrors.

The palace of Xerxes is in the southwest area of the terrace. Considerably larger than that of Darius, its central hall had six rows of six columns. Xerxes's Hall of One Hundred Columns to the east of Darius's Apadana is, next to the latter, the largest single structure on the terrace. The hundred columns (which were arrayed in ten rows of ten columns each) may have been about eleven to thirteen meters (36 to 43 ft.) high; none of them is still standing.

Though the superstructures of all the buildings at Persepolis have been destroyed, some features can be reconstructed from the debris and from written sources. It is known from an analysis of the ashes that the roof of the Apadana was made with cedar beams. No doubt there were elaborate curtains decorating the walls (Esth 1:6). Wooden doors covered with gold are also mentioned. Gold-plated bronze nails have been recovered from Xerxes's throne hall. Traces of color indicate that the Persian reliefs were originally painted in bright colors.

Egypt

The Egyptian word for palace, *pr-ʿ3* (*per aa*, lit., "big house"), became the name for the king by the New Kingdom; as borrowed by the Hebrew language and transliterated into English, it became the word "pharaoh." There are almost no remains of palaces from the early eras of Egyptian history. A large fortified enclosure at Hierapolis from the 2nd Dynasty may have enclosed a palace. From the New Kingdom there are two types: residential palaces and smaller "temple" palaces used by the pharaohs as they participated in religious festivals.

One of the best examples of a residential palace is that built by Amenhotep III (1417–1379 BC) at "Malqata" on the west bank of the Nile at the city of Thebes. The huge enclosure (350 x 270 m. [1148 x 886 ft.]), which covered eighty acres, contained four palatial buildings and a huge "pleasure" lake. The buildings were made of mud-brick with wooden columns on stone bases. The main palace was known as the "House of Rejoicing." There were reception rooms, columned audience halls, and a throne room made of a brick core sheathed with sandstone. Queen Tiy and other minor wives had their own apartments. Two long rectangular halls with rows of columns have been identified as dining halls.

Amenhotep IV (1379–1362 BC) changed his name to Akhenaten and established a new capital at Akhetaten (Amarna) to promote the sole worship of the god Aten. Amarna, which was occupied only briefly and then abandoned, has yielded remains of several palaces. The West or Great Palace, which was also known as "The House of the Rejoicing of the Aten," contained pillared audience halls and a courtyard with colossal statues of Akhenaten. It was here that foreign dignitaries from Palestine, Lebanon, Syria, Mitanni, Assyria, Babylonia, and Anatolia were received. There were also servants' quarters, a harem, and store rooms, which were colorfully painted.

A triple-arched bridge over the hundred-foot Royal Road connected the "House of Rejoicing" with the "King's House," a small private palace in the east. Here the royal apartments were painted with murals depicting intimate family scenes. The *sšd n ḫ'*, or "Window of Appearance," from which Akhenaten showered gifts, was located on the bridge or at a corner of this building.

To the south there was Meruaten, the "pleasure" palace, which had an open air temple, a garden, a lake, stables for horses, and kennels for dogs. The North Palace contained stalls for antelopes and gazelles and cages for birds.

It is known that Ramesses II (1279–1213 BC) had a residential palace at Qantir in the Delta and a temple palace at the Ramesseum in western Thebes. His son Merneptah (1213–1204 BC) built a large palatial enclosure at Memphis that measured 30 x 105 meters (98 x 328 ft.) and that had a huge audience hall. He also built a residential palace at Thebes.

The palace of Ramesses III (1185–1154 BC) was dedicated to the god Amun: "I made for thee an august royal palace within it, like the palace of Atum which is in heaven, the columns, the doorjambs, and the doors of *ḏ'm*-gold [electrum, a naturally occuring alloy of gold and silver] and the great window of appearance of fine gold" (Hölscher, 2–3). His beautiful

harem was a hall thirty meters (98 ft.) long with a ceiling that was decorated with figures of the vulture goddess.

D. THE GRECO-ROMAN WORLD

Greece

Four Minoan palaces have been found on the island of Crete: in the
south at Phaistos, in the north at Knossos and Mallia, and in the east at
Zakro. These palaces were built in the Middle Minoan IB period (1900–
1800 BC), were destroyed by earthquakes ca. 1700 BC, were then rebuilt,
and were destroyed again by the cataclysmic eruption of the island of Thera
(Santorini), some seventy miles to the north, ca. 1600 BC.

The palaces at Knossos, Phaistos, and Mallia each have a central court
that measures about 24 x 52 meters (78 x 171 ft.), whereas the court at Zakro
is smaller, measuring 12 x 30 meters (39 x 98 ft.). These may have been
used for the famous bull-leaping games in which young men and women
somersaulted over the backs of rampaging bulls. The Minoan palaces were
unwalled. They evidently depended for protection upon their navy.

Legend ascribed the building of the Labyrinth (from *labrys*, "double
axe") to Daedalus, the architect of King Minos of Crete. This may have
referred to the enormous palace at Knossos, extending over four acres,
which was uncovered and partially reconstructed by Arthur Evans from
1900 on. The rooms were arranged around the central court, with store
rooms on the west, archives on the north, and private rooms for the royal
family on the east. A grand staircase at the east of the court led to the Hall
of the Double Axes, which was the king's room. Nearby was the Queen's
Room. The queen's apartment was provided with a bathroom that included a clay bathtub. The red columns that tapered from top to bottom
were made of cypress. The walls were covered with magnificent frescoes of
plants, marine life, and women with uncovered bosoms.

The northeast wing contained the artisans' quarter and the palace laundry. To the northwest was a so-called theatral area, with stepped seats, perhaps for the viewing of ceremonial dances. To the west of the court were a
series of fifteen long, narrow storerooms, which held tributes of oil, wine,
and grain, as well as treasures of copper, bronze, silver, and gold.

The French excavated a Minoan palace at Mallia, eighteen miles east
of Knossos, a site nine thousand square meters in area. Fabulous treasures
were discovered in the cemetery to the north of the palace. The Italians
excavated a similar-sized Minoan palace at Phaistos, thirty-six miles south
of Knossos.

At the eastern end of Crete, at Zakro, a small Minoan palace (6,000 sq. m.) was excavated by N. Platon between 1963 and 1968. A treasury of nine chests of mud-brick contained a rock crystal rhyton, Egyptian stone vases, and marble amphoras. Other treasures of elephant tusks and copper ingots bear testimony to the importance of Zakro as the nearest port for trade with the East. The west wing contained a cult shrine and a lustral basin. The east wing contained the living quarters and a banquet hall. The bedrooms were upstairs, with balconies jutting over the court. A large kitchen, measuring 9 x 12 meters (30 x 39 ft.), which also functioned as a dining area, was strewn with animal bones.

Homer mentions in his epics the palaces of Menelaus at Sparta, of Odysseus at Ithaca, and of Nestor at Pylos. The features of the fabulous palace Odysseus visits at Phaeacia (*Od.* 6.303–309) can be illustrated by the remains of actual (14th–13th c. BC) palaces excavated at Mycenae, Tiryns, and Pylos. Strongly fortified, these palaces are about 50 x 32 meters (164 x 105 ft.) in size and were very similar in plan. The megaron, or throne room, was characterized by a great central hearth surrounded by four columns, with the throne to one side.

The megaron at Mycenae measured 13 x 12 meters (43 x 39 ft.) and was decorated with a painted stucco floor. Its walls were covered with frescoes depicting chariots and warriors. North of the megaron was a bathroom that had walls painted a blood-red color. There was an upper floor above the throne room. The so-called "House of Columns" at Mycenae closely matches the two-storied palace of Odysseus at Ithaca described by Homer.

Some eight miles southeast of Mycenae lies Tiryns, the legendary home of Heracles. Like Mycenae, it was excavated by Heinrich Schliemann. The palace measured 70 by 60 meters (230 x 197 ft.). The megaron and other buildings had both painted floors and walls decorated with frescoes of octopi, dolphins, and a boar hunt. The bathrooms were floored with limestone slabs.

In the southwest Peloponnesus, Carl Blegen discovered the "Palace of Nestor" at Pylos. He uncovered forty-six rooms in an area measuring 110 x 60 meters (361 x 197 ft.); a similar number of rooms would have existed on the second floor. There was a room with a built-in bath. Visitors entered through an anteroom that was provided with benches. The megaron was 13 x 11 meters (43 x 36 ft.), with a central hearth 4 meters (13 ft.) in diameter. Pantries with over eight thousand whole pots were uncovered. The greatest prize of all was a cache of six hundred tablets inscribed in Linear B, including a text that led to Michael Ventris's decipherment of Linear B, the earliest Greek dialect, in 1952.

The capital of Macedonia was established at Pella by Archelaus I (413–399 BC). He invited the Athenian tragedian Euripides, who presented his play *The Bacchae* here. The palace was located on a hill and covered an area of sixty thousand square meters (14 acres). There were several complexes of rooms and porticoes arranged around square courtyards. The south portico, which was 153 meters (502 ft.) long, overlooked the city below.

Macedonian kings had another early capital north of Greece at the site of Aigai (present-day Vergina). The main palace was arranged around a large peristyle court with rooms on its four sides. It was built on a terrace with a commanding view. A *tholos* (circular structure) on the eastern wing served as the throne room. An important feature of the palace was rooms with *klinai*, couches, for banquets. Below the palace was a small theater, perhaps the site where Philip, the father of Alexander, was assassinated in 336 BC. At Vergina a tomb was discovered that had not been looted. It contained the cremated remains of a royal individual who has been identified as Philip.

The *basileion*, or palace complex, established by the Ptolemies in Alexandria became the most elaborate in the world. Built on the Lochias peninsula, it covered two hundred hectares (approximately 500 acres; almost a square mile). There was a monumental portal before a large forecourt, which could accommodate a great crowd. Each of the Ptolemies built his own addition, so that by the Roman era the palace occupied at least a quarter of the city.

Ptolemy II built a huge, tent-like pavilion with twenty columns twenty-six meters (85 ft.) high to house a symposium in honor of Dionysus. There were *katalymata* (guest quarters), *diaitai* (pavilions), a *peripatos* (covered portico), and a *paradeisos* (garden/zoo), an institution borrowed from the Persians. Most notable were the beautiful gymnasium, the greatest library in the world, and the *mouseion*, which attracted the leading scholars of the Greek world. The *sēma* held the body of Alexander.

Rome

The last Etruscan king, Tarquin the Proud, was overthrown by the Romans in 509 BC when they established the Republic. A relic of the monarchy was the *Regia*, a structure on a small plot between the Forum Necropolis and Vesta's shrine. This area became the traditional home of the *pontifex maximus*, the supervisor of religion.

Augustus (27 BC–AD 14), the first emperor, purchased the "House of Livia," a building on the Palatine located on two terraces. (The English word "palace" is derived from the building of the emperors' homes on the *Palatinus collis*, "the Palatine Hill.") This had three large reception rooms opening onto a peristyle court. There was also a second floor. Augustus made his libraries of Greek and Latin scrolls available to some of his friends. In keeping with his nature, the house was modestly decorated. Suetonius expressed surprise that the emperor used the same bedroom in both summer and winter.

To Augustus's home Tiberius (AD 14–37) added a new wing, the *Domus Tiberiana*, a structure about 160 x 120 meters (525 x 394 ft.) in size that was located on the northwestern part of the Palatine. This was ten times larger than Augustus's palace. In AD 26, Tiberius retired to the beautiful island of Capri in the Bay of Naples, where he built the *Villa Jovis* in the northeast extremity of the island. This was provided with large vaulted cisterns, baths, and ambulatories with spectacular views. A staircase led up to a *specularium*, or observatory, for Tiberius, who was devoted to astrology. According to Suetonius (*Tib.* 62), the sadistic emperor delighted in having his victims hurled off the steep cliffs to the sea about three hundred meters (almost 1000 ft.) below.

Nero (AD 54–68) erected the *Domus Transitoria*, "House of Passage," which linked his townhouse on the Palatine Hill with the imperial gardens on the Esquiline Hill. The destruction of much of Rome in the great fire of AD 64 enabled Nero to carry out a grandiose reconstruction project, including the erection of the famous *Domus Aurea*, "Golden House," so called because the façade of the palace was gilded. Nero's new estate extended over a vast area of 80 hectares (200 acres) and encompassed an artificial lake, woods, and even a zoo. A triple colonnade extended a mile.

Of the remains of the *Domus Aurea* in the Esquiline wing, the most innovative structure was an octagonal reception room that opened out into five antechambers. It was provided with an *oculus*, or opening, in the ceiling that was 6 meters (20 ft.) wide. A small waterfall cooled the air. Suetonius relates:

> There were dining-rooms with fretted ceilings of ivory, whose panels could turn and shower down flowers and were fitted with pipes for sprinkling the guest with perfumes. The main banquet hall [*cenationum rotunda*] was circular and constantly revolved day and night, like the heavens. (*Nero* 31)

There were also seawater baths and baths of sulfur-water. In Nero's bedroom were displayed 1,808 gold crowns, which he had "won" in artistic and athletic "competitions" in Greece. A gilt bronze statue of Nero stood 37 meters (120 ft.) high. After completing this extraordinary edifice, Nero remarked that at last he was beginning to be housed *quasi hominem*, "like a human being."

This extravagant palace was destroyed by Vespasian, who erected the Flavian amphitheater, better known as the Colosseum, on the site of Nero's lake. Remains of Nero's palace can be seen embedded in the cellars of Trajan's bath, two hundred meters (656 ft.) northeast of the Colosseum, and beneath the terrace of Hadrian's temple of Venus and Rome. The Colosseum was so called after the site of Nero's colossal statue.

The lifestyle of the emperor Vespasian (AD 69–79) was in sharp contrast to Nero's. According to Cassius Dio,

> The general routine of life that he followed was as follows. He lived but little in the palace, spending most of his time in the Gardens of Sallust. There he received anybody who desired to see him, not only senators but also people in general. With his intimate friends he would hold converse even before dawn while lying in bed; and others would greet him on the streets. The doors of the palace stood open all day long and no guard was stationed at them.
> (*Hist. rom.* 65.10.4–5)

The greatest Roman palace after Nero's was built by Domitian (AD 81–96) on the eastern half of the Palatine. This palace consisted of two levels. The *Domus Augustana* was the lower and private level. The stairways that led down to the private rooms were arranged around an octagonal pool lined with colored mosaic. The pool was surrounded by an arcade with arches 12 meters (39 ft.) high. The *Domus Flavia* was the upper and public level. There were three large peristyles surrounded by porticoes of Egyptian granite and Numidian and Phrygian marble. The *Aula Regia*, or Throne Hall, was an enormous room, measuring 30 x 40 meters (99 x 131 ft.). Its walls, which were made of Cappadocian gypsum, acted like mirrors and would therefore warn of any potential assassins. The *Basilica* was a hall with an apse for the emperor's tribunal. The so-called "hippodrome," which was shaped like a race track and which measured 184 x 50 meters (604 x 164 ft.), was a secluded garden situated on the brow of the hill. A broad exedra provided the imperial household with a clear view of the chariot races in the Circus Maximus at the base of the Palatine. The gigantic scale of the palace reflected the megalomania of the emperor, who demanded that his subjects address him as *dominus et deus*, "lord and god." Domitian's palace remained the residence of the Roman emperors throughout the Late Roman Empire.

The peripatetic emperor Hadrian (AD 117–138), who spent half of his twenty-one-year reign touring the provinces, never lived on the Palatine Hill but built a remarkable palatial villa at Tibur (Tivoli), eighteen miles east of Rome. The varied architectural styles reflected the emperor's travels in Greece and in Egypt. It covered an area of 250 acres. The many buildings included guest quarters, dining rooms, baths, porticoes, pools, a library, a stadium, and a *palaestra* (i.e., an area for wrestling). He provided a mile of cryptoporticoes, covered galleries that were partly subterranean, where one could walk in the shade. Many beautiful statues, frescoed walls, and mosaics adorned the buildings.

The most important palace at Tivoli is known today as the Piazza d'Oro, "The Golden Square." Its circular vestibule with a hole in the roof resembled a miniature Pantheon. The central room is in the shape of a four-leaf clover with a fountain in the middle. Another structure is the Maritime Theater, a round portico with a barrel vault supported by pillars. Inside the portico was a pool with a central island, which would provide privacy for dining and sleeping. The island was connected to the portico by two drawbridges.

One of the best preserved areas is a pool named the *Canopus*, after the site in Egypt where Hadrian's companion, Antionous, drowned himself. This was a long, narrow pool, measuring 119 x 18 meters (390 x 60 ft.). At the south end was an outdoor dining area with a fountain that has been called the Serapeum, as it honored the Egyptian god Serapis. At the north end were several statues, including copies of the Athenian Caryatids, an Amazon, a Hermes, and the deified Nile. There was also a large (232 x 97 m. [761 x 318 ft.]) artificial lake called the *Poecile* (from the Gk. *poikilē*, "a multicolored embroidery").

The Piazza Armerina in central Sicily was probably the hunting villa of the emperor Maximian, who was the joint Augustus with Diocletian (AD 284–305) during the Tetrarchy. The villa's architectural plan is elaborate and unique. The entrance is a polygonal porticoed atrium, which leads to a set of baths that feature apses, clover-leaf designs, and an octagonal *frigidarium*. A huge *basilica* measuring 30 x 14 meters (99 x 46 ft.) served as an audience hall. Outstanding are the forty-two polychrome mosaic pavements; these covered 2,926 square meters (31,500 sq. ft.) and were composed from thirty million tesserae. A mosaic in the bath area depicts cupids fishing from boats. Another mosaic depicts the chariot races in the Circus Maximus at Rome. The transverse corridor was seventy meters (230 ft.) long and was probably used for dining. It has a mosaic floor that depicts a great hunt of forty-five animals. The most sensational mosaics are of young women running, tossing a ball, throwing a discus, and lifting weights while clad in "bikinis"!

Upon his voluntary retirement from the Tetrarchy, Diocletian returned to his native Dalmatia (Croatia) on the Adriatic coast and built a monumental palace on a promontory at modern-day Split. Considerable remains of the palace and auxiliary buildings may be seen within the rectangular fortress measuring 190 x 160 meters (623 x 525 ft.) and covering 3.8 hectares (9.5 acres). The southern façade, which faced the sea, was unfortified; the other three facades had towers and each had a single gate: the *porta ferrea*, "Iron Gate," in the west; the *porta argentea*, "Silver Gate," in the east; and the *porta aurea*, "Golden Gate," in the north. The gates could be closed by a portcullis.

The *decumanus*, or transverse road, connected the western and eastern gates. The southern half of the fortress contained the imperial halls, private residence, and temples. The northern half housed officials, soldiers, and servants. The palace was built of local limestone and tufa (soft volcanic stone). Egyptian granite and fine imported marble were used for columns, capitals, and wall veneer. A domed vestibule led into a basilican reception hall. As the last great pagan emperor, Diocletian had temples erected to Jupiter and to Aesculapius. Ironically, the octagonal mausoleum of Diocletian was transformed into the Church of St. Domnius.

E. THE JEWISH WORLD

After their successful revolt against the Seleucids in 165 BC, the Jews established an independent monarchy under the Hasmoneans that lasted for a little more than a century. John Hyrcanus (134–104 BC), Alexander Jannaeus (104–76 BC), and the latter's widow, Alexandra Salome (76–67 BC), built a set of identical twin palaces at Jericho, each with a small swimming pool that was surrounded by a garden. In addition, there were two large swimming pools, in one of which Herod had Aristobulus III, the high priest and brother of his wife Mariamne, drowned in 36 BC (Jos. *Ant.* 10.53–56).

Herod the Great (37–4 BC), who served as a client king of the Jews under the Romans, was a prodigious builder of numerous palaces. Though these were built in Roman style and served to express his fealty to the emperor, Herod respected his subjects' sensitivities in avoiding human and animal figures in his artistic decorations.

Herod built three "winter" palaces at the Wadi Qelt at Jericho. The first was built in 35 BC south of the Wadi Qelt. This palace, which was primarily residential, was rectangular in shape (87 x 46 m. [285 x 151 ft.]). One entered from the north through a large entrance hall into a peristyle that surrounded a central courtyard with a garden. In addition to a Roman bathhouse, Herod also installed a *miqwê*, a stepped Jewish ritual bath.

The second palace, built in 25 BC north of the Wadi Qelt, was primarily recreational. It was built on two levels. The upper level featured a large peristyle garden and a banqueting hall with a view of the Wadi Qelt. On the lower level was a large swimming pool.

The third and largest palace, which covered three hectares (7 acres), was built on both banks of the Wadi Qelt, with a bridge spanning the wadi. To the north was the main palace (84 x 37 m. [276 x 121 ft.]), which contained reception rooms, two peristyle courtyards, and a Roman bathhouse. The largest and most impressive room was the *triclinium* (28.9 x 18.9 m. [95 x 62 ft.]), which was located in the western wing and surrounded on three sides by colonnades. Next to it was a large hall leading to the throne room, which was found to have four impressions in the floor where posts once rested for a canopy.

South of the wadi was a large sunken garden (140 x 40 m. [460 x 131 ft.]) and a huge pool (92 x 40 m. [302 x 131 ft.]), which was used for boating and swimming. On a large artificial mound was a reception hall with a clear view of the surrounding countryside, and also a bathhouse. The use of Pompeian-type frescoes, concrete, and *opus reticulatum* (netlike) brickwork indicate the employment of Roman craftsmen.

In Jerusalem, near the present site of the Jaffa Gate, Herod erected in 24–23 BC three magnificent towers called Hippicus, Phasael, and Mariamme (Jos. *J.W.* 5.161–169). The base of Phasael is still preserved in the so-called "David's Tower." It was just south of these towers that Herod erected his palace, which according to Josephus defied description (*J.W.* 5.176–181). It "contained immense banqueting-halls and bedchambers for a hundred guests" (*J.W.* 5.177–178). There were also groves of trees, canals, and ponds. Excavations in the area of the Armenian Gardens by M. Broshi and D. Bahat have revealed that the palace was erected on a podium measuring about 350 x 130 meters (1150 x 427 ft.). Corinthian and Ionic capitals were recovered, but only a few rooms in the northwest were preserved.

According to Josephus, at Caesarea on the coast Herod built "the most magnificent palaces, displaying here, as nowhere else, the innate grandeur of his character" (*J.W.* 1.408). Archaeologists have discovered the remains of a palace on a long, narrow promontory jutting out into the sea. It was a luxurious two-story building, measuring 80 x 55 meters (262 x 180 ft.). The upper story probably contained a reception hall, a dining room, and bedrooms. The central feature was a large swimming pool cut into the rock; this pool measured 35 x 18 meters (115 x 60 ft.) and was two meters (6.5 ft.) deep. There was also a *miqwê*.

At the rock fortress of Masada west of the Dead Sea, Herod built two palaces. According to Josephus, "The fittings of the interior—apartments, colonnades, and baths—were of manifold variety and sumptuous" (*J.W.* 7.290). The Northern Palace was built on three terraces at the northern (which was the coolest) edge of the plateau with a spectacular view of the Dead Sea. The lowest terrace, which was built on supporting walls and surrounded by a covered portico, was designed for leisure. The central terrace was provided with a rotunda, which may have served as a dining area. The upper terrace had four living rooms for Herod and one of his nine wives.

Not mentioned by Josephus is the large Western Palace, which covered four thousand square meters (43,056 sq. ft.). Its southern wing contained a large audience hall, a banquet room, a throne room, and a private bath, which was fed hot water from an oven behind a wall. The floors were decorated with colorful aniconic mosaics. The northern wing contained service and administrative quarters.

At the artificially heightened hill of Herodium, located nine miles south of Bethlehem, Herod began a palace in 23 BC. According to Josephus, "the enclosure was filled with gorgeous palaces, the magnificent appearance of which was not confined to the interior of the apartments, but outer walls, battlements, and roofs, all had wealth lavished upon them in profusion" (*J.W.* 1.420).

At the top of the hill, three hundred feet above the level of the plain, was a ring-shaped fortress with three semi-circular towers and one elevated circular tower in the east. Excavations by Virgilio Corbo in the interior floor below these towers uncovered remains of a *triclinium*, or dining hall (15 x 11 m. [49 x 36 ft.]), which was later transformed into a synagogue by the Zealots, who occupied Herodium during their revolt against the Romans in AD 66.

Excavations by Ehud Netzer of Lower Herodium at the base of the steep hill revealed that these lower structures covered fifteen hectares (37 acres). On the lower slope of the hill, a large palace with an audience hall that measured 130 x 55 meters (427 x 180 ft.) overlooked a hippodrome. Also revealed was a large formal garden surrounding a huge central pool (92 x 40 m. [302 x 131 ft.]) with a depth of 2.5–3.0 meters (8–10 ft.).

Herod the Great, who died in 4 BC shortly after the birth of Jesus in nearby Bethlehem, was buried at Herodium. In 2007, after a thirty-five-year search, Netzer discovered the site of the king's burial on the northeastern slope of Herodium. This contained the remains of a highly ornamented limestone sarcophagus, which had apparently been deliberately shattered by the Jewish Zealots, who regarded Herod as a puppet ruler for the Romans.

Herod Agrippa II, who made additions to the Hasmonean palace in Jerusalem in the reign of Nero (AD 54–68), enjoyed viewing the proceedings in the temple from this palace. This provoked the priests, who built a wall to block his view (Jos. *Ant.* 20.189–193). During the siege of Jerusalem by the Romans in AD 70, the Jewish insurgents burned down the palace, as they resented Agrippa II's collaboration with the Romans (Jos. *J.W.* 2.426).

F. THE CHRISTIAN WORLD

For the first three centuries AD until the Roman empire adopted Christianity under Constantine, no palaces were built by Christians. After his conversion and victory at the Milvian Bridge in AD 312, Constantine became sole emperor in AD 324. He decided to move the capital of the

Empire from pagan Rome to a New Rome on the site of Byzantium, which he dedicated in AD 330, naming it after himself, "Constantinople." He built his new palace on the peninsula of the Golden Horn, with his *kathisma*, or imperial box, looking over the new hippodrome that he had established to the west. The palace included a vast complex of reception halls, government offices, domestic apartments, and baths.

In his hagiographical biography of the emperor, the church historian Eusebius observes that Constantine made "his very palace into a church of God" (*Vit. Const.* 4.17). The emperor "set up in the front of the portico of his palace" a depiction of the cross over a dragon (i.e., the devil) stricken through with a dart (*Vit. Const.* 3.3). In the principal apartment of the palace, in the center of its gold-covered paneled ceiling, Constantine "caused the symbol of our Saviour's Passion to be fixed, composed of a variety of precious stones richly inwrought with gold. This symbol he seemed to have intended to be as it were the safeguard of the empire itself" (*Vit. Const.* 3.49).

Constantine had numerous palaces, none more significant than the one at the site of Nicaea, forty-three miles from Constantinople, where the emperor convened the first ecumenical council in AD 325 to resolve the divisions in Christendom caused by the teachings of Arius, who denied the deity of Christ. Constantine provided transportation to the council for nearly three hundred bishops. The emperor himself, "clothed in raiment which glittered as it were with rays of light, reflecting the glowing radiance of a purple robe, and adorned with the brilliant splendor of gold and precious stones" (*Vit. Const.* 3.10), presided over the council, which condemned Arius.

One of Constantine's palaces, the *Aula Palatina*, located at Trier in northern Germany, is nearly perfectly preserved as the largest building from Roman antiquity. The *aula*, or "hall," which was built in AD 310, measures 67 x 26 meters (220 x 85 ft.) and has towers that are 33 meters (108 ft.) high. The building was originally embellished with marble inlay and golden mosaics. It was also equipped with hypocaust heating in the floor and walls, such as was employed in Roman hot baths. During the Middle Ages, this palace was used as the residence of the Bishop of Trier. In 1856 it became a Protestant church named St. Saviour.

BIBLIOGRAPHY: Y. Aharoni, "Ramat Raḥel," *EAEHL* IV.1000–9; P. Albenda, *The Palace of Sargon, King of Assyria* (1986); D. Bahat and M. Broshi, "Excavations in the Armenian Garden," *Qadmoniot* 5 (1972), 102–3; J. Baines, "Palaces and Temples of Ancient Egypt," *CANE* 1.303–17; R. D. Barnett, *Assyrian Palace Reliefs in the British Museum* (1970); R. D. Barnett et al., *Sculptures from the Southwest Palace of Sennacherib at Nineveh* (1998);

C. W. Blegen and M. Rawson, ed., *The Palace of Nestor at Pylos in Western Messenia* (3 vols., 1966, 1969, 1973); A. Boëthius, *The Golden House of Nero* (1960); G. Cadogan, *Palaces of Minoan Crete* (1976); V. Corbo, *Herodion I: Gli Edifici della Reggia Fortezza* (1989); W. G. Dever, "Palaces and Temples in Canaan and Ancient Israel," *CANE* 1.605–14; M. K. Devitt, "Knossos Revisited: An Architectural Analysis of the Palace of Minos," Ph.D. diss., Saint Louis University (1982); H. Frankfort, *The Art and Architecture of the Ancient Orient* (2nd rev. ed., 1958); M.-H. Gates, "The Palace of Zimri-Lim at Mari" *BA* 47 (1984), 70–87; K. L. Gleason, "Ruler and Spectacle: The Promontory Palace," in *Caesarea Maritima*, ed. A. Raban and K. G. Holum (1996), 208–27; F. Gurgone, "Golden House of an Emperor," *Arch* 68.5 (2015), 37–43; W. Hoepfner and G. Brands, ed., *Basileia: Die Paläste der hellenistischen Könige* (1996); U. Hölscher, *The Excavation of Medinet Habu III; The Mortuary Temple of Ramses III, Part I*, trans. K. C. Seele (1941); R. G. Kent, *Old Persian* (2nd ed.; 1953); K. Kenyon, *Royal Cities of the Old Testament* (1971); F. S. Kleiner, *Gardner's Art through the Ages: A Concise Western History* (3rd ed., 2014); R. Koldewey, *The Excavations at Babylon*, trans. A. S. Johns (1914); S. Lackenbacher, *Le palais sans rival: Le récit de construction en Assyrie* (1990); E. Lévy, *Le système palatial en Orient, en Grèce et à Rome* (1987); D. D. Luckenbill, *Ancient Records of Assyria and Babylonia II: Historical Records of Assyria: From Sargon to the End* (1927); P. MacKendrick, *The Greek Stones Speak* (1962); P. MacKendrick, *The Mute Stones Speak: The Story of Archaeology in Italy* (1960); M. E. L. Mallowan, *Nimrud and Its Remains* (3 vols., 1966); E. Mazar, *The Palace of King David: Excavations at the Summit of the City of David: Preliminary Report of Seasons 2005–2007* (2009); C. M. McCormick, *Palace and Temple: A Study of Architectural and Verbal Icons* (2002); A. G. McKay, *Houses, Villas, and Palaces in the Roman World* (1975); E. Netzer, *The Architecture of Herod, the Great Builder* (2008); E. Netzer, *Hasmonean and Herodian Palaces at Jericho I: Stratigraphy and Architecture* (2001); I. Nielsen, *Hellenistic Palaces: Tradition and Renewal* (1999); A. Parrot, *Mari, capitale fabuleuse* (1974); N. Platon, *Zakros: The Discovery of a Lost Palace of Ancient Crete* (1971); H. Rassam, *Asshur and the Land of Nimrod* (1897; repr. 1971); R. Reich, "Palaces and Residencies in the Iron Age," in *The Architecture of Ancient Israel From the Prehistoric to the Persian Period*, ed. A. Kempinski and R. Reich (1992), 202–22; M. Roaf, "Palaces and Temples in Ancient Mesopotamia," *CANE* 1.423–41; J. M. Russell, *Sennacherib's Palace without a Rival at Nineveh* (1991); D. Stronach, *Pasargadae: A Report on the Excavations Conducted by the British Institute of Persian Studies from 1961 to 1963* (1978); B. Tamm, *Auditorium and Palatium: A Study on Assembly-Rooms in Roman Palaces During the 1st Century B.C. and the 1st Century A.D.*, ed. P. Hort (1963); D. Ussishkin, "King Solomon's Palaces," *BA* 36

(1973), 78–105; J. J. Wilkes, *Diocletian's Palace, Split* (1986); R. J. A. Wilson, *Piazza Armerina* (1983); D. J. Wiseman, *Nebuchadrezzar and Babylon* (1985); Y. Yadin, *Masada*, trans. M. Pearlman (1966); E. Yamauchi, "Palaces in the Biblical World," *NEASB* 23 (1984), 35–67; E. Yamauchi, *Persia and the Bible* (1990).

EMY

See also ARCHIVES, CITIES, DOORS & KEYS, DWELLINGS, EUNUCHS, and IVORY.

PERFUMES

The word "perfume" comes from the Latin phrase *per fumum*, which means "through smoke." Perfumes are substances that produce a pleasing odor. The simplest of such odors are emitted by plants and vegetables themselves, such as by the leaves of the lavender plant or the petals of roses and violets. Scents also can come from glucose, as is the case with jasmine and iris. Additionally, scents can be extracted from bark, as in the case of cinnamon; from roots, which yield mandrake and nard; or from fruit, including oranges, lemons, and peaches. Seeds like anise and almonds give aromas, as do some resins. Tapping trees produced frankincense and myrrh, two resin compounds that did not require refining. Trees deposited resin on their bark in little globules, which are called "tears."

The aromatic compounds that are prepared from such naturally aromatic substances are generally termed perfumes. Perfumes come in various forms; for example, they can be liquid, jelly-like, or dry. Gradually, perfumes came to be classified, for example, as costly aromatic oils and spice compounds.

Those who made perfumes were called perfumers. Their wares were used for both religious and secular uses. Perfumers processed oils from plants and fruits and then mixed them with gums, resins, spices, and animal parts in various combinations. Perfumers needed to know what odorless fats and oils would absorb fragrances. Perfumes had to be packaged and kept safe and sealed to keep their scent from dissipating and to keep them from being stolen. Packaging and storing could be done in a cloth or in more elaborate objects like an alabastron or a perfume box. Over the centuries, perfumery became a specialized trade, and guilds were organized to guard against counterfeiting the product. Perfumery required great skill. Many guilds represented families, and recipes were closely guarded and passed down from generation to generation. (See Dayagi-Mendels; Fletcher; Green.)

The rarity and value of such products as myrrh and frankincense created a high demand for costly aromatics, which in turn made those who produced and traded them quite wealthy. Along with the trade of other luxury items (like silk and spices), the trading of perfumes and ingredients opened up the world, for it established commerce between Greece and Rome and Arabia, Egypt, the Persian Gulf, Sri Lanka, and India.

Because the pleasant scents emitted by perfumes counteracted odors from putrid or dead organic matter and from spoiled, soiled, or unclean materials, perfumes quickly began to play an important part in the economic, religious, and social lives of many peoples. Their scents were used to enhance sexual appeal. Perfumes are frequently associated with incense, but incense was used primarily for religious purposes. The fragrance of perfumes adorned the marriage bed and enhanced household furniture.

A. THE OLD TESTAMENT

The Hebrew verb *rāqaḥ* refers to the mixing or blending of perfume, incense, ointment, or oil. Ointments and perfumes were produced from various spices. These included aloes, balsam, galbanum, henna, saffron, frankincense, labdanum, myrrh, stacte, gum, nard, balm, cassia, cane, calamus, and cinnamon. Some of these spices were local, such as henna from En Gedi (Song 1:14), and others were traded, as evidenced by Ishmaelite traders passing through Canaan to Egypt with spices (Gen 37:25).

The base oil for perfume in Palestine was olive oil (*šemen zayit*), while in Mesopotamia it was sesame oil or castor oil. Exodus 30:23–25 indicates that holy anointing oil (*šemen mišḥat-qōdeš*) was made from liquid myrrh (*mor-dĕrôr*), cinnamon (*qinnāmôn*), sweet cane (*qānê*), and cassia (*qiddâ*). The text continues with a description for making holy incense (*qĕṭōret*), which consisted of four ingredients (Exod 30:34–35): stacte (*nāṭāp*, a type of gum resin), onycha (*šĕḥēlet*), galbanum (*ḥelbĕnâ*), and frankincense (*lĕbōnâ*). The text omits the instructions for combining these ingredients, perhaps because whoever tried to copy these recipes for personal use would be cut off from the people (vss. 33, 38). The anointing oil was used for anointing the ark of the covenant, sacred objects in the tent of meeting, and Aaron and his sons (Exod 30:26–30). The sweet-smelling incense was only for use in the tent of meeting (Exod 30:36). Proverbs 27:9 states that "scented oil (*šemen*) and incense (*qĕṭōret*) make the heart glad" (King and Stager, 280).

Perfumery became a specialized task during Israel's wilderness experience (Exod 37:29) as well as in the monarchic (1 Sam 8:13) and postexilic periods (Neh 3:8). Bezalel, Oholiab, and other skilled craftsmen commissioned to make furnishings for the tent of meeting also worked as perfumers, which required great skill. They made the sacred anointing oil and pure incense (Exod 37:29). The temple utilized large quantities of perfumes and "some of the priests took care of mixing the spices" (1 Chr 9:30). It is possible that En Gedi was a perfume-producing region, as the many vessels and decanters found there that date from the First Temple period (1000–586 BC) attest.

A typical vessel for perfume was a jug-like container with a carinated shoulder and a ridged neck. Perfumes were also kept in bottles (see Isa 3:20). Archaeologists have found poor-quality bottles, which indicate a somewhat careless manufacturing standard, in Israelite tombs dating from before the First Temple period. Toward the close of the First Temple period, alabastra (see the section on Egypt below) appear along with carrot-shaped and pear-shaped bottles. The alabastron bottles imitate the alabastron bottles of Egypt, and the carrot-shaped bottles imitate an Assyrian model.

Perfumes were used in burials. According to Egyptian practice, Jacob and Joseph were embalmed, which included adding spices to their bodies (Gen 50:2, 26). King Asa of Judah was buried in a "tomb that he had cut out for himself in the City of David. They laid him on a bier covered with spices and various blended perfumes" (2 Chr 16:14). Perfume was often used before special events, such as a wedding (Ezek 16:9).

Several notable women in the OT are associated with pleasant scents and sensuality. Naomi tells Ruth to bathe, put oil on herself (*sûk*), and dress in her best attire (Ruth 3:3) before going to Boaz. Esther and the other young women in the contest to be King Ahasuerus's queen engage in twelve months of cosmetic treatment, "six months with oil of myrrh [*šemen hammōr*] and six with perfumes [*běśāmîm*] and cosmetics [*tamrûqîm*]" (Esth 2:12).

The Song of Solomon contains many references to kinds of perfumes, for good smells are associated with love and springtime (2:13). The woman says of her beloved, "While the king was at his table, my perfume spread its fragrance. My beloved is to me a sachet of myrrh resting between my breasts. My beloved is to me a cluster of henna blossoms from the vineyards of En Gedi" (Song 1:13). The daughters of Jerusalem exclaim over the woman borne in Solomon's carriage: "Who is this coming up from the wilderness like a column of smoke, perfumed with myrrh and incense made from all the spices of the merchant?" (Song 3:6; see Garrett and House, 176–77.) The man compares his beloved to sweet spices, including nard, saffron, and aloes (Song 4:10–14). The woman dips her hands in myrrh before meeting her lover (Song 5:5). The vines spread their good fragrance (Song 2:13) and the man flees "to the mountain of myrrh and to the hill of frankincense" (Song 4:6, ESV). The woman describes her beloved's cheeks as being "like beds of spice yielding perfume" and his lips as being "like lilies dripping with myrrh" (Song 5:13). The woman notes that the name of her lover "is like perfume poured out" and likens his presence to the fragrance of perfumes (Song 1:3).

Perfumes were highly valued. Jacob sent his sons with gifts, including balm, spices, and myrrh, on their second trip to Egypt for food (Gen 43:11). Perfumes rank alongside gold and silver in lists of wealth. For example, Hezekiah displayed his spices, fine oils, and precious metals to the envoys from Babylon (2 Kgs 20:13). Excess or extravagance in wine and fragrant lotions showed wealth (Amos 6:6). Proverbs 7:17 mentions a sweet-smelling bed-freshener of myrrh, aloes, and cinnamon. An ancient dry-cleaning method, surely a sign of wealth, called for making one's garments fragrant with myrrh, aloes, and cassia (Ps 45:8).

Incense and perfume played an important role in worship. God is said to be pleased by the aroma of burnt sacrifices (Gen 8:21; Exod 29:25; Lev 26:31), and he tells the exiles that he will accept them "as fragrant incense" (Ezek 20:41). On the other hand, God is not pleased when his people offer incense and perfume to other deities, or when they offer it to him but disobey his law. For example, God indicts Judah for bringing olive oil and perfume to Molech (Isa 57:9), and Jer 6:20 records the Lord's disdain at the use of these products in the context of his people's disobeying the law: "What do I care about incense from Sheba or sweet calamus from a distant land? Your burnt offerings are not acceptable; your sacrifices do not please me."

The OT also includes references to oil and perfume in connection with curses. The curse for Israel's covenant disobedience involves a lack of ripe olives for olive oil (Deut 28:40). Similarly, a punishment Judah would face for apostasy would be pressing olives but being denied the use of oil (Mic 6:15). Isaiah tells the women of Jerusalem who fancy perfume bottles that instead of wearing a fragrance they will wear a stench (Isa 3:20, 24).

B. THE NEW TESTAMENT

Oil appears in several episodes of Jesus's ministry. Early in his ministry, while Jesus is at a Pharisee's house, a woman described as sinful (Mary Magdalene, according to tradition) pours perfumed oil on his feet from an alabastron (Luke 7:36–38, 46). Later, at Simon the Leper's house in Bethany, another woman anoints Jesus's head with perfume, also from an alabastron. Jesus says that the woman has done this to prepare him for burial (Matt 26:6–12; Mark 14:3–9; John 12:1–8). Since Matthew and John note the expense of the perfume (which is sometimes translated "nard" or "spikenard"), scholars think that it was imported from Kashmir and Nepal at the base of the Himalayas.

Nicodemus anoints Jesus's body for burial with a mixture of myrrh and aloes weighing seventy-five pounds (John 19:39). The women surrounding Jesus go home after the crucifixion and prepare spices and perfumes (Luke

23:56). Mary and Salome attempt to anoint the body of Jesus with spices and perfumes, but they discover that he has risen from the dead (Mark 16:1–6).

Paul uses perfume as an image in various places in his writings. In 2 Cor 2:14–16, he writes:

> But thanks be to God, who always leads us as captives in Christ's triumphal procession and uses us to spread the aroma of the knowledge of him everywhere. For we are to God the pleasing aroma of Christ among those who are being saved and those who are perishing. To the one we are an aroma that brings death; to the other, an aroma that brings life.

Ephesians states that Christ offered himself as a fragrant offering to God (5:2), and according to Philippians, believers' monetary gifts are a fragrant offering before the Lord (Phil 4:18).

Archaeological evidence indicates that during NT times perfume was packaged and stored in ivory containers, alabastra (see Matt 26:7), terracotta jars, and perfume boxes. In 2008, Italian archaeologists found vases containing perfumed ointment in Magada, a town outside Jerusalem. The vases, which remained unopened until their discovery, date from the first century AD and were preserved in mud at the bottom of a swimming pool. They contained greasy substances that might have been similar to those used by the woman whose anointing of Jesus's feet is recorded in Luke 7:36–50.

C. THE NEAR EASTERN WORLD

Mesopotamia

From the palace archives of Mari (18th c. BC) we have a letter from one official to another, requesting scented oil: "I am herewith having a *ḥatrum*-flask sent to you. If truly you are my brother, and if you do care for me, send me some scented oil for my trip. Do not withhold it from me" (ARM(T) 18.36; Sasson, 157).

Cuneiform tablets dealing with the processes of making perfume were discovered in the Temple of Ashur, dating from the reigns of Tukulti-Ninurti I (ca. 1244–1208 BC) and Tiglath-pileser I (1115–1077 BC). These were published by E. Ebeling in 1950–1952. These texts list ingredients used in making perfume as well as the formulas and equipment required. They mention that materials selected for the perfume were steeped in hot water during the day. Spices were added at night, and the next day the entire mixture was reheated. Only at the end of the process was oil added. The mixture was left in a covered vessel, stirred, and then probably re-strained, if need be. From there it was poured carefully into flasks. Some of the processes were repeated up to forty times (Levey, 385).

At Mari, perfume-makers combined resins of fragrant woods like cedar, cypress, juniper, myrtle, and storax, some of which quite likely had to be imported. Most perfume makers were men, but women manufactured perfumes as well, especially in the Neo-Assyrian (910–612 BC) and Neo-Babylonian (605–539 BC) periods.

Aromatic fragrances were used in cosmetics, medicines, and perfumes, and for ritual and and magical purposes. Oils applied to the skin and scalp helped replenish the natural oils created by the body that were depleted by exposure to the sun. Many sources attest to the popularity, prevalence, and economic importance of perfumes in the ancient Near East. When his sister Kilu-Hepa became one of Pharaoh Amenhotep III's wives, king Tushratta of Mitanni sent her perfume as a gift (EA 17). Herodotus, who visited Mesopotamia in the fifth century BC, states that Babylonian men used perfumes (*Hist.* 1.195).

Egypt

Castor oil was the most widely used oil in Egypt, where it was half the price of sesame oil. Castor oil, which must be handled with care because of its high toxicity, proved a popular base for perfumes because it was slow to spoil. Castor oil also was used as lamp oil, for massages, and for treating skin diseases and lice. Sesame oil, a pale-colored oil made from the tiny seeds of a plant native to Egypt, was used in the preparation of perfumes and unguents for massage. During the New Kingdom, tomb workers in the Valley of the Kings received sesame oil for their cooking and their lamps.

Other oils used in Egypt included almond, moringa, balanos, safflower, olive, and linseed. Less frequently used oils also included extractions from such sources as radish, tiger nut, lettuce, poppy, and colocynth. Almond oil was probably imported from Greece, but local almonds may also have been used, because some were found at the New Kingdom workmen's village at Amarna and also in Tutankhamun's tomb. Almonds were used in the production of Metopion perfume and aromatic unguents as well as for therapeutic massages and for the treatment of bad skin and facial spots. Balanos oil, because it was both odorless and tasteless, was used widely in cosmetic preparation, though it was also used in perfume production. Balanos served as a base for the Megaleion and Mendesian perfumes. These perfumes were named after their places of origin. Additions that were made in the production of perfumes included varying amounts of myrrh, cinnamon, and resin. Tiger nut oil, which is extracted from the edible tubers of the cyperus plant, was also a popular oil for perfumes because it did not go rancid quickly. Susinon, a strongly fragrant lily oil, was reportedly used by Cleopatra to scent the sails of her royal barge. Late Period reliefs show susinon being produced only by women.

Egyptians used a variety of flowers, plants, and woods in their perfume-making. Chamomile, a yellow flowering plant, was found in garlands on Tutankhamun's mummy, and traces of the plant were found on the body of Ramesses II. The lily, known for its heavy scent, was popular in perfume-making. Late Period tomb scenes show women collecting lilies for the Susinon perfume. Both the seeds and sweet-smelling flowers of henna were used to produce Cyprinum perfume. Egyptians believed that the heavy perfume of the lotus improved moods, and lotus oil, a favorite of priestesses, served as an aphrodisiac. Both the white lotus and the aromatic blue lotus were native varieties of water lily. Juniper, a wood with a clear, resiny, peppery fragrance, was used as one of many ingredients for the perfume kyphi.

Kyphi was useful as a fragrant air freshener. According to a recipe found on the walls of the temples at Edfu and Philae, kyphi contained wine, raisins, and aromatic herbs, as well as myrrh, broom, frankincense, buckshorn, and other plant ingredients. These substances were pounded together, mixed, and then put on the fire, with the result that the house and clothes smelled pleasant. The Egyptians stressed the importance of having an agreeable body odor and often relied on kyphi for this purpose. The Egyptians also favored adding honey to this mixture, which made a kind of chewing gum or pill; women in particular chewed this mixture to sweeten their breath.

The ingredients for kyphi were first listed in the Ebers Papyrus (ca. 1500 BC). It is remarkable that this mix of ingredients was maintained down through the Roman era, as shown in the discussion of perfumes in Book One of Dioscorides's *Materia medica*. (See Riddle, 89–93.)

The Megaleion perfume had the reputation of being incredibly difficult to create. Its base, balanos oil, had to be boiled for ten days and nights to remove impurities from it. After this was done, burnt resin and cinnamon mixed with myrrh, which had to be pressed for a few days, were added.

The Mendesian perfume was known throughout the world as "the Egyptian (perfume)," and was considered by many to be the best (Pliny, *Nat.* 13.2.4). Cleopatra was reported to have used the oil on her feet. Mendesian perfume was initially made from balanos oil, but beginning in Ptolemaic times, almond oil became the norm.

Dioscorides writes that the root of the iris was known as a perfume by the Egyptians (*Mat. med.* 1.1). He also discusses the balsam tree, which produced a resinous exudate. This was primarily used medicinally, but as it was fragrant, it could also be used as a perfume. He mentions the Metopion perfume, which contained bitter almond oil (*Mat. med.* 1.39).

While the Egyptians used many local and imported plants and materials to produce their perfumes and oils, it has proved difficult to identify all the specific ingredients. Moreover, while historians know that Egypt must have been a major center for perfume production, no production centers have been found by archaeologists. Representations of how Egyptians made perfumes have been found on the walls of tombs and in special temple chambers that housed ointments and perfumes. One example comes from a tomb at Beni Hasan; although it is now destroyed, a representation of the making of perfumes on the tomb wall was copied by Frederic Cailliaud, a French naturalist, in 1831. Of great interest is a painting in a tomb from the fourteenth century BC showing a perfumer's workshop and the craft in progress. A painting from a tomb of the 18th Dynasty seems to illustrate in detail the preparation of perfumes for cosmetics. There are also Late Period (722–332 BC) reliefs in the Turin Museum and in the Louvre, as well as a Ptolemaic period (332–30 BC) relief in the Museum Scheurleer in Holland. The perfumes depicted in each case were extracted from lilies.

The Ptolemaic temple of Edfu provides details of perfume preparation. Preparation may have been labor- and time-intensive, perhaps even lasting a year or two. The primary ingredient was oil or fat, to which herbs and spices were added. Perhaps this was born of necessity, for if left alone oils and fats may become rancid and produce a disagreeable odor. Floral scents might need to be macerated (i.e., to undergo hot steeping) several times. The materials were then squeezed in a cloth in the same way grape stalks and skins were squeezed. Dioscorides mentions macerating a thousand lilies for twenty-four hours in spiced balanos oil (*Mat. med.* 1.62).

Another technique employed by the Egyptians was cold steeping (*enfleurage* in French), which was suitable for some cosmetics that were scented with flowers. This method involved smearing a layer of animal fat on a board and placing flower petals on top of the substance. The sticky substance was then topped by another board and left for a day or so. Then the petals were removed and replaced with new ones until the scent was completely transferred to the fat. The result was perfumed pomade. Cold steeping proved effective with jasmine and roses.

The Egyptians were the first to design alabastra, which are containers for oil made from either a soft, white marble known as alabaster or from glass. They were adapted with a narrow neck and opening to prevent the evaporation of the odor of the perfumed substance they carried. Alabastra came in various shapes and sizes, but most seem to have been able to be held easily in the hand. One jar of perfume dating from the Middle Kingdom (1980–1760 BC) contained a gum resin similar to myrrh and splinters of aromatic wood. Another jar contained pure resin that resembled copal, the amber-like resin from the copal tree used as incense in Mesoamerica.

An artifact of particular note dating from the Late Bronze Age (1550–1200 BC), when the Egyptians had control in Palestine, was found in the Fosse Temple at Lachish. It is an ivory tusk carved into a vessel with a narrow neck and decorated with a female figure holding out a spoon. Once tilted, a few drops of liquid from inside would fall into the spoon (see *ANEP*, fig. 69). Bottles shaped like women were popular in the ancient Near East between the seventh and fifth centuries BC.

Perfume was exported from Egypt in exquisite glass bottles manufactured in Alexandria. These have been found all over the Mediterranean world. From the first century BC until the present, glass has been the preferred container for unguents and perfumes. A typical bottle had a rounded bottom and a somewhat narrow lip. Its mouth or tail would be broken off and its contents poured into toilette vases.

Frankincense trees were brought to Egypt in 1490 BC by Queen Hatshepsut, and small balls of frankincense were buried in Tutankhamun's tomb. Embalmers used unguents in burial practices, for they helped preserve the remains. Egyptian women used fragrant unguents in the form of cones placed on the head. As the cones melted from the body's natural heat, the fragrant oil spread through the hair and down the neck and arms. The scent produced was intense and inviting. There is evidence in the love poetry of Egypt that a man and a woman might be attracted by each other's scent. Known from Egyptian iconography from the eighteenth dynasty, the "nose kiss" included breathing or sniffing around the nose area of the partner.

Theophrastus (*De sensu* 6.30–31; 9.38; 10.42, 44; 11.55) and Pliny (*Nat.* 13.2, 6) both describe Egyptian perfumes. Theophrastus mentions a perfume made from ingredients that included myrrh and cinnamon (*De sensu* 6.28). According to Athenaeus, Egypt was the country most well known for sweet-smelling unguents among the Romans, and perfumed oils from Egypt were the best (*Deipn.* 3.124b). The Greeks and Egyptians competed to find the best scent, and Egypt was thought to excel in this regard by the Greco-Roman world.

D. THE GRECO-ROMAN WORLD

Greece

The Greeks believed that the goddess Aphrodite taught the man Phaon and Oenone, the first wife of Paris, the secrets of self-beautification. Early records of perfume-making from a Mycenaean palace at Pylos in Greece date from the second millennium BC. The Pylos tablets indicate the use of wool in the straining process.

Perfumes required a base. In ancient Greece most perfumers, or "brewers," as they were called, used the natural fat of sheep's wool (*oisypē*, i.e., lanolin) as a base, but this decomposed quickly and therefore had to be both manufactured and used locally. Olive oil was also used as a base (see below).

Maceration, that is, the soaking of petals and leaves in liquids, was evidently one of the most common ways to make perfumes in the ancient world. Theophrastus writes that perfumes were set in oil and then became ready for use. First, the ingredients of the perfumes would thicken the oils. The order in which the ingredients were added was important, for the last ingredient added would give the perfume its dominant scent (*De sensu* 4.14–19). The oil was also pre-treated in a solution of astringent materials that were mixed with wine and water. Theophrastus writes of the essential nature of this stage, especially when the base was olive oil or when an aromatic material had a volatile nature (*De sensu* 4.14, 17; 11.55). Something like a double boiler was used, for jars containing oil were heated in larger containers of boiling water so that the heat could be controlled (*De sensu* 5.21–22). The heated mixture was allowed to cool, was stirred every now and then, and was left standing for a few days. If desired, the perfumer added dyes. Straining the perfume and pouring it into lead containers constituted the last stages of the process. Perfume made with this method was stored in a cool place.

Dioscorides records that a pleasant-smelling perfume can be made by combining spiced wine with the fat of bulls and calves, plus their marrow. After melting and heating, the mixture is skimmed and the following ingredients are added: palma, cassia, calamus, aspalathus, xylobalsamum, cinnamon, cardamomum, and nard (*Mat. med.* 2.91).

Modern perfumery consists of distillation by alcohol, a process that was unknown to the ancients. Aristotle (*Mete.* 1.9, 11; 2.3), Theophrastus (*Hist. plant.* 9.3.1–3), and Pliny (*Nat.* 15.7; 16.21–22) all mention distillation, but scholars think this was a primitive method. It included boiling the plants, steeping them in oil, and pressing them.

The Greeks first used perfumes made in Syria, but perfume-making then spread to Rhodes and Corinth. Corinthian trade routes for perfumes and unguents copied the successful and well-worn routes of the earlier Phoenicians. Corinth became a center for the manufacture of the iris perfume, which became a staple of its trade. In Athens, an entire section of the agora was occupied by the perfume market.

The perfume flask industry developed in Athens and in Corinth in the Archaic Age (8th–6th c. BC). Many decorated vessels were produced, including some with animal heads and others with female heads. Because of its beauty and lightness, glass soon became the preferred material for these flasks, replacing pottery, especially in Alexandria. Like the pottery flask, the glass flask had a long neck, a feature that reduced evaporation (see *m. Parah* 12:2). Perfumes were sold in attractive vases, such as alabastra, aryballi, and pyxides.

Like the Egyptians, the Greeks used perfumes a great deal. Greek corpses were covered in perfume in preparation for burial. The flasks that held the scented oils were left in the tombs. Perfumes, oils, and scents were also commonly used during bathing rituals and in preparation for athletic contests. Perfumes counteracted body odors and the unpleasant smells that were prevalent in city life. When going about town, people carried sachets whose fragrances they would inhale in order to overcome unpleasant scents and odors. In addition, fragrant-tasting gum mixtures were chewed to counteract these odors and to sweeten one's breath.

According to Xenophon, Socrates taught that perfumes were only for women (Xenophon, *Symp.* 2.3–4). The plays of Aristophanes depict women perfuming themselves, especially before making love: for example, Praxagora in *Ecclesiazusae* (524–526) and Myrrhina in *Lysistrata* (938–949). Athenaeus (fl. AD 200), the Greek grammarian and author, writes of a woman remembered by her faint scent of crocus oil, by the fragrance of the myrrh anointing her arms, and by the aroma of flowers sprinkled on her hair (see Giordano and Casale).

Greek perfumes were smeared on as they were more like a lotion or a paste than a liquid. In ancient Greece perfume was a luxury item, available only to the upper class. Greek perfumers were known for producing cheap concoctions and smells that did not last. One way to tell a good-quality item was to expose it to heat and to cold. If the smell held up over time, the unguent was worth a high price.

Rome

In the imperial period, aromatic substances became the focus of a major industry in the Mediterranean world. Perfumes and spices were valued as highly as gold and silver by the Romans, according to Pliny the Elder, writing in the first century AD. From Illyria (western Balkan Peninsula) the Romans gathered the iris plant, from which the orris root and a high-quality pungent perfume were made. Perfumes favored by the kings of Parthia incorporated myrrh. Pliny gives the Persians credit for the invention of perfumes (*Nat.* 13.1–3), but this is erroneous. Perfumes or their plants came to the Mediterranean world from as far away as Nepal and India. Frankincense and myrrh came from Arabia, nard from Nepal, saffron and aloes from India, cinnamon from Sri Lanka, and onycha from a mollusk harvested from the Red Sea.

By the first century AD, the civil wars in the Roman world had come to an end, and Augustus (27 BC–AD 14) and succeeding emperors established a *Pax Romana*, a Roman peace, which enabled trade to flourish. (See Hopkins; McLaughlin.) The senatorial class obtained enormous wealth from serving in overseas provinces. This concentration of new wealth created a taste for luxuries. As a consequence, the demand for perfumes grew and became increasingly profitable. Important trading centers developed at Alexandria and Mendes in Egypt and in Palestine. From the first decades of the Roman Empire, Egypt's perfume industry also faced competition because of excellent flower crops in Capua, Neapolis, and Paestum in Italy.

In his *Natural History*, the Roman author Pliny gives an account of plants and perfumes and the regions in which they grow, along with meticulous details relating to their production and prices. Grapes and olive oil were pressed to form liquid bases in Roman perfumery (*Nat.* 12.60). Grape juice was favored because it does not alter aromas and is suitable for every pigmentation. Pliny also praises unguents from Egypt, which were heavily used in the Roman world. Unguents from Mendes were known to contain complex mixtures that included oil of balanus, resin, myrrh, bitter almonds, unripe olives, cardamon, sweet rush, honey, and wine, as well as galbanum and turpentine resin (*Nat.* 12.2). Pliny goes on to describe how balsam sap, a viscous and sweet-smelling resin, was obtained. Incisions were made in the shrub from which drops of sap were collected in earthenware containers (*Nat.* 12.54).

Pliny states that the Roman perfumers of his day (and quite likely this refers to the Egyptian perfumers, too) believed that mixing gum resin with a perfumed substance set the perfume. He also notes that at Alexandria workers were forced to remove their clothes before leaving the premises in order to prevent theft (*Nat.* 12.32).

An unguent found at Pompeii included rose, fennel, myrrh, and lily—a combination of the many fruits, vegetables, and flowers in the land. Honey and saffron may have been added as well. Shells of the *Pecten* mollusk, some of which contained makeup powder and colored unguents, were also found at Pompeii, in a villa that was probably owned by the banker Caecilius Iucundus. These and other artifacts are housed in the Villa of the Silverware Treasure at Boscoreale. Pompeii, however, could not compete in terms of perfume production with Naples, which manufactured lavender and rose perfumes, and Capua, which was famous for a scent called *Seplasium*. However, Pompeii is thought to have had its own *officinae* for the production of aromatic substances. Support for this belief includes inscriptions that document the presence of *unguentarii* (perfume-makers) who formed a corporation in the town and murals that depict garland- and perfume-making.

Some Roman coins depict the goddess Pietas, who personified the attitude of honoring the gods, the nation, and the ancestors, holding a perfume box. For example, a gold aureus of Hadrian shows Pietas holding a perfume box and standing beside an altar (Noreña, 76), perhaps indicating that the perfume would be used in a religious ritual. Perfumes and other costly aromatics were also added to Roman funeral pyres as a way of honoring the deceased. On the other hand, using perfume was commonly associated with *luxus*, which was contrary to *pietas*. In fact, Roman perfume shops became known as haunts of prostitution.

During performances in Roman theaters and amphitheaters, a large canopy was spread over the participants to protect them from the sun. The audience was sprinkled with water mixed with perfume to give them respite from the heat. Similarly, guests at Roman dinner parties received a foot washing with perfumed water.

There are texts that mention that nard and saffron scents were used by women as perfumes (Martial, *Ep.* 3.65.8; Pliny, *Nat.* 13.5.9; cf. Olson, 76–78). Women on occasion carried lumps of amber in their hands to give off a sweet aroma. The most popular amber used in this way by Roman women came from Germany. In Pompeii, women used *lomentum*, a cream based on broadbean flour that resembled a modern-day face lotion. Martial speaks of its use to hide wrinkles (*Ep.* 3.42) and Caelius Rufus mentions its cleansing properties in a letter to Cicero (*Epistulae ad familiares* 97.4).

Perfume, like dress, could indicate a woman's status. Roman matrons enjoyed expensive perfumes, evidently to such an extent that it jeopardized public finances. A law called the *Lex Oppia* limiting the purchase of perfume failed to curtail their tastes for luxury. Cato commented that the law was abolished because "all other [non-Roman] men rule their wives; we rule all other men, and our wives rule us" (Plu. *Cat. Maj.* 8).

Pliny comments that the first thing to know about perfumes is that fashionable scents change frequently. In addition, the fashion might vary in each region of the empire. At one time, the most praised perfume came from Delos (Greece); at another time, from Mendes (Egypt). Later, the iris perfume from Corinth was greatly favored (*Nat.* 13.2). Pliny was also a vocal critic regarding the extravagant use of perfumes in Rome (*Nat.* 13). Likewise, the emperor Tiberius later complained, though without effect, that the Romans' spending on perfumes, estimated at one hundred million sesterces a year, went straight to the pockets of foreign peoples. Pliny points out that perfume, which he regarded as a useless luxury item, was of less value than pearls, for at least pearls could be passed down to heirs and even clothing could have more than one wearer. Unguents, however, die out after an hour (*Nat.* 13.4). Martial advises: "Never leave unguent or wine to your heir. Let him have the money, but give these all to yourself" (*Ep.* 13.126).

E. THE JEWISH WORLD

The Jewish writer Philo links perfume to the four elements from which "the whole world was brought to completion" (*Her.* 197). The oil drop is likened to water, the cloves to land, the galbanum to air, and the frankincense (which can be pure and transparent) to fire. He also posits that the harmonious composition and mixture of perfume is symbolic of God's perfect and holy work of creating the world, commending the work of the apothecary who, in effect, mirrors the wisdom with which the world was created (*Her.* 198–199).

Josephus mentions the economic importance of balsam and notes that Antony gave Cleopatra a palm grove at Jericho that produced balsam (*J.W.* 1.361). Pliny also elaborates on the economic importance of balsam in Judea (*Nat.* 12.54). Evidently, in AD 70, when the army of Titus was approaching Jerusalem, the Jews wanted to chop down the ancient balsam orchards to prevent their falling into Roman hands (Jos. *J.W.* 4.402–403). But the Romans prevailed, and Titus even displayed balsam trees as part of his triumphal procession (*Nat.* 12.54).

The Mishnah states that, as a portion of the dowry, a husband must pay his wife ten *denar*s for her *kuppa*, the perfume basket (*qûppâ šel běśāmîm*). Rabbi Simeon b. Gamaliel supplied the restriction, however, that the husband must pay her only the normal cost of the cosmetics in the city in which they live (*y. Ketub.* 6:4).

A Mishnaic prohibition reads, "No benediction may be said over . . . spices of gentiles, . . . or spices used for the dead, . . . or spices used for idolatry" (*m. Ber.* 8:6). The Talmud mentions that spices eliminate the bad odors of the dead and of privies (*b. Ber.* 53a). The spices used for the dead included some of the most well-known fragrances of the ancient world: balsam and nard.

The Talmud contains many references to scents and perfumes and their uses. Even in a place known for refuse, it is said, the fragrance from a vial of nard gives off a good scent (*b. Sanh.* 108a). Oil of nard, which was quite expensive and much sought after, was kept in a bottle of transparent glass called a *šělôḥît*. Once the bottle was opened or broken, the aroma escaped (*b. ʿAbod. Zar.* 35b). The Babylonian Talmud states that there were balsam gatherers from En-Gedi to Ramtha (*b. Šabb.* 26a).

The Talmud notes that perfumers perform their craft happily and their trade is blessed. The rabbis taught that the world cannot exist without a perfume-maker and without a tanner, but that the perfume-maker has a blessed trade whereas the tanner has a woeful one (*b. Qidd.* 82b).

The rabbis taught that water may be conducted into a garden on the eve of the Sabbath, just before dark, and that the garden may go on being filled the whole day. Similarly, they taught that a perfume brazier may be placed under clothes that would continue to absorb the perfume throughout the Sabbath day (*b. Šabb.* 18a).

Perfume was only for women, and it was offensive for a man, particularly for a learned man, to stroll around perfumed, according to Talmudic teaching (*b. Ber.* 43b). However, in some regions, men used perfumes and wore beautiful clothes on the Sabbath (*Soperim* 20:1). A teaching from *Gen. Rab.* 17:8 explains the need for women to use perfume. The reasoning given is that man was created from the earth, which never putrefies, but woman was created from bone (from Adam's rib), which putrefies quickly, just like unpreserved meat. After the destruction of Jerusalem, however, women were no longer, according to R. Judah b. Baba, to use an expensive perfume like nard (*t. Soṭah* 15:9).

The sages were concerned about the effects of perfume on the populace. Evidently, some women in Jerusalem put myrrh and balsam in their shoes and walked the marketplaces of the city, enticing young men by kicking their feet at them and spreading the perfume scents (*b. Šabb.* 62b).

F. THE CHRISTIAN WORLD

Christian leaders did not condone the use of perfumes since it was associated with prostitutes (cf. Juv. *Sat.* 6.130–132; Humphreys) and actresses in the Roman world. When Margarito (later St. Pelagia), a beautiful mime actress who was also known as a courtesan, came into the city of Antioch, Bishop Nonnus and his colleagues watched her procession. She was bejeweled and richly costumed. The deacon who wrote about her conversion by Nonnus recalled: "As this prostitute passed in front of us, the scent of perfumes and the reek of her cosmetics hit everyone in the vicinity" (Brock and Harvey, 43).

Though Tertullian, who inveighs against the use of cosmetics and jewelry, does not direct his denunciations against perfumes, Clement of Alexandria does have extensive comments on perfumes in his *Paedagogus* ("The Instructor"). Clement denounces effeminate men who pluck their bodily hair, adorn their hair like women, and apply perfume (*Paed.* 3.3).

He criticizes women who use perfume not only on themselves but also on their clothes:

> They use, too, the ointment made from lilies, and that from the cypress. Nard is in high estimation with them, and the ointment prepared from roses and the others which women use besides, both moist and dry, scents for rubbing and for fumigating; for day by day their thoughts are directed to the gratification of insatiable desire, to the exhaustless variety of fragrance. Wherefore also they are redolent of an excessive luxuriousness. And they fumigate and sprinkle their clothes, their bed-clothes, and their houses. Luxury all but compels vessels for the meanest uses to smell of perfume. (*Paed.* 2.8)

On the other hand, Clement utilizes the imagery of ointments and perfumes in a positive fashion. He exhorts:

> Let woman [*sic*] breathe the odour of the true royal ointment, that of Christ, not of ointments and scented powders; and let her always be anointed with the ambrosial chrism of modesty, and find delight in the holy ointment, the Spirit. This ointment of pleasant fragrance Christ prepares for His disciples, compounding the ointment of celestial aromatic ingredients. (*Paed.* 2.8)

Polycarp, the bishop of Smyrna, was martyred ca. AD 155–160 by being burned at the stake. Christians who witnessed it likened it to a sacrifice aromatically pleasing to God: "For we also perceived a very fragrant aroma [*euōdias*], as if it were the scent of incense [*libanōtou*] or some other precious spice [*timiōn arōmatōn*]" (*Mart. Pol.* 15).

A number of Christians were martyred in AD 177 at Lyons, France. In Blandina's account, Christians like herself who did not deny their faith wore their chains like some lovely ornament, "exhaling at the same time the *sweet odour* [*euōdian*] *of Christ*, so that some thought they had anointed themselves with a perfume [*myrō*] of this world" (cited in Musurillo, 72–73). (See Lallemand.)

BIBLIOGRAPHY: L. Adkins and R. A. Adkins, *Handbook to Life in Ancient Greece* (1997); S. Bertman, *Handbook to Life in Ancient Mesopotamia* (2003); S. P. Brock and S. A. Harvey, trans. and ed., *Holy Women of the Syrian Orient* (1987); J. A. Coray, "Perfume," *EDB* 1029; R. David, *Handbook to Life in Ancient Egypt* (1998); M. Dayagi-Mendels, *Perfumes and Cosmetics in the Ancient World*, trans. I. Pommerantz (1989); E. Ebeling, "Parfümrezepte und kultische Texte aus Assur," *Or* 17 (1950), 129–45; 18 (1951), 404–18; 19 (1952), 265–78; A. Erman, *Life in Ancient Egypt* (repr. of 1894 edition, 1971); R. Flacelière, "Perfume," in *The Praeger Encyclopedia of Ancient Greek Civilization*, ed. P. Devambez (1966), 354; J. Fletcher, *Oils and Perfumes of Ancient Egypt* (1998); D. Garrett and P. R. House, *Song of Songs/Lamentations* (2004); C. Giordano and A. Casale, *Perfumes, Unguents, and Hairstyles in Pompeii*, trans. F. Poole (2007); D. A. Green, *The Aroma of Righteousness: Scent and Seduction in Rabbinic Life and Literature* (2011); K. Hopkins, "Roman Trade, Industry, and Labor," *CAM* II.753–77; J. W. Humphrey, J. P. Oleson, and A. N. Sherwood, *Greek and Roman Technology: A Sourcebook* (1998); R. Humphreys, trans., *The Satires of Juvenal* (1958); P. J. King and L. E. Stager, *Life in Biblical Israel* (2001); A. Lallemand, "Le parfum des martyrs dans les Actes des martyrs de Lyon et le Martyre de Polycarpe," StPatr 16 (1985), 186–92; A. Lehnardt, "The Scent of Women: Incense and Perfume in Talmud *Yerushalmi Sheqalim* 5:2," in *A Feminist Commentary on the Babylonian Talmud V: Introduction to Seder*, ed. T. Ilan, M. Brockhaus, and T. Hidde (2012), 23–31; M. Levey, "Babylonian Chemistry: A Study of Arabic and Second Millennium B.C. Perfumery," *Osiris* 12 (1956), 376–89; A. Lucas and J. R. Harris, *Ancient Egyptian Materials and Industries* (1999); L. Manniche, "Perfume," in *UCLA Encyclopedia of Egyptology* (2009), 1–7; L. Manniche, *Sacred Luxuries: Fragrance, Aromatherapy and Cosmetics in Ancient Egypt* (1999); R. McLaughlin, *Rome and the Distant East: Trade Routes to the Ancient Lands of Arabia, India and China* (2010); H. Musurillo, trans., *The Acts of the Christian Martyrs* (1972); K. R. Nemet-Nejat, *Daily Life in Ancient Mesopotamia* (1998); C. F. Noreño, *Imperial Ideals in the Roman West* (2011); G. Ohloff, W. Pickenhagen, and P. Kraft, *Scent and Chemistry: The Molecular World of Odors* (2012); K. Olson, *Dress and the Roman Woman: Self-presentation and Society* (2008); J. M. Riddle, *Dioscorides on Pharmacy and Medicine* (1985); F. Rosner, trans. and ed., *Biblical and Talmudic Medicine* (2004); H. W. F. Saggs, *Everyday Life in Babylonia and Assyria* (1965); J. M. Sasson, *From the Archives of Mari: An Anthology of Old Babylonian Letters* (2015); J. Scarborough, *Facets of Hellenic Life* (1976); M. Serpico and R. White, "Oil, fat and wax," in *Ancient Egyptian Materials and Technology*, ed. P. T. Nicholson and I. Shaw (2000), 390–429; M. Serpico and R. White, "Resins, amber and bitumen," in Nicholson and Shaw, ed. (2000), 430–74; S. Stewart, *Cosmetics and Perfumes in the Roman World* (2007); J. B. White, *A Study of the Language of Love in the Song of Songs and Ancient Egyptian Poetry* (1978).

RGB

See also BOTTLES & GLASS, COSMETICS, INCENSE, JEWELRY, PROSTITUTION, and SANITATION.

PLANTS & FLOWERS

Plants include medicinal herbs, grasses, and sedges. The Mediterranean region is characterized by a high level of plant diversity. This is especially true of the land of Palestine, whose natural diversity is enhanced due to its geographic location near the meeting point of two continents. This small land area supports about twenty-seven hundred plant species, of which 150 (5.5 percent) are found nowhere else. Scientific studies continue to add to our understanding of this diversity, as overlooked species are identifed for the first time in a scientific manner. Our modern system of classification of plants and animals includes numerous Greek and Latin names for plants that were adopted by Linnaeus in his 1753 work *Species Plantarum*.

In ancient times, plants were valued as food and as medicinal ingredients, and flowers were prized for their beauty and scent. Grains and vegetables are discussed more fully under FOOD PRODUCTION. See DYEING for plants used in this process.

A. THE OLD TESTAMENT

Grains and legumes are mentioned frequently in the OT. Millet, originating from China, had made its way to the Middle East during the OT period and is mentioned in Ezekiel (4:9). The earliest archeological evidence for broad beans comes from sites in Israel.

The account of the rivalry between Jacob's two wives, Leah and Rachel (Gen 30:14–16), mentions that Reuben obtained an aphrodisiac plant at the request of his mother, Leah. It was a mandrake (*Mandragora officinarum*; Heb. *dûdā'îm*), a member of the nightshade family. The plant has large oval leaves, purple flowers, and yellow fruit the size of the plum. What must have struck the ancients were its roots, which appear to have the shape of a man's body.

An important plant for ritual use was hyssop (*Origanum maru*), which was used, for example, in the cleansing of a person (Exod 14:4). This is a shrub with stems that are stiff, strong, and aromatic. It grows to a height of about a meter. Its hairy branches can be used for sprinkling.

The popularity of onions, leeks, and garlic is evidenced by the Israelites' pining for these and other choice foods of Egypt during their desert wanderings (Num 11:5). Cucumbers and melons, which are mentioned in the same verse, were first domesticated in India and Africa, respectively.

The setting of the romantic encounters between a royal lover and his beloved in the Song of Solomon is a garden (Song 4:12, 15; 5:1; 6:2; 7:12; 8:13). The lyrical dialogue is filled with floral imagery. She declares: "I am a rose of Sharon, a lily of the valleys" (Song 2:1). The rare word translated here as "rose" occurs elsewhere only in Isa 35:1, where the NIV translates it "crocus." Others would render it "asphodel." The Hebrew word for "lily" is *šôšān*, which is derived from Egyptian, in which it designated a lotus. Scholars have identified this flower variously as a hyacinth, anemone, narcissus, or crocus. Elsewhere in the book, the beloved declares, "His lips are like lilies" (Song 5:13), referring perhaps to the red lily (*Lilium chalcedonicum*).

The caper plant (Heb. *ʾăbiyyônâ*; LXX *kapparis*) is referred to only once in the OT, in the allegorical description of old age in the book of Ecclesiastes (12:5). This is a widespread shrub with large white flowers that bloom only for one night. As it was widely considered an aphrodisiac, both the KJV and the NIV render it "desire."

Flax (*Linum usitatissimum*) provided the basis for linen. Its importance in Jericho is obvious, as is reflected by the drying stems on Rahab's rooftop, which provided concealment for the spies (Josh 2:2–7). The Gezer Calendar offers an independent confirmation of the cultivation of flax in Palestine in the tenth century BC.

The existence of royal gardens is attested at the time of Nebuchadnezzar's attack on Jerusalem (2 Kgs 25:4; Jer 39:4). Jeremiah counseled the exiles who were carried off by this king to Babylonia: "Build houses and settle down; plant gardens and eat what they produce" (Jer 29:5).

Esther's Hebrew name, Hadassah, is derived from Hebrew *hădas*, "myrtle" (*Myrtus communis*), a fragrant evergreen that was used in the Feast of Tabernacles (Neh 8:15). The one occurrence of "cotton" (Heb. *karpas*) in the OT appears in a description of the royal garden at Susa (Esth 1:6); the word is translated as "white" by the NIV. Cotton (*Gossypium herbaceum*), which was native to India, was known to the Assyrians.

Isaiah denounced the pagan sacrifices that some Judeans were offering in gardens (Isa 1:29; 65:3; 66:17). But the prophet also promised that the Lord would transform Zion's wastelands so that they would become "like the garden of the LORD" (Isa 51:3). He also declared: "You will be like a well-watered garden, like a spring whose waters never fail" (Isa 58:11).

B. THE NEW TESTAMENT

The NT has fewer references to plants (about thirty distinct names used) than the OT (about seventy-five), which reflects the latter's greater length and its more agricultural setting.

Nonetheless, numerous well-known verses in the NT mention plants, flowers, and herbs. In the Sermon on the Mount, Jesus declared: "And why do you worry about clothes? See how the flowers [Gk. sing. *krinon*] of the field grow. They do not labor or spin. Yet I tell you that not even Solomon in all his splendor was dressed like one of these" (Matt 6:28–29). Many commentators believe that Jesus may have been referring to the brightly colored anemone (*Anemone coronaria*).

Jesus used many images from plant life in his parables, such as in the Parable of the Sower (Matt 13:3–23||Mark 4:3–20||Luke 8:5–15); the Parable of the Tares (Gk. sing. *zizanion*; *Lolium temulentum*; Matt 13:24–43); the Parable of the Mustard Seed (Gk. *sinapi*; *Brassica nigra*; Matt 13:31–32||Mark 4:30–32||Luke 13:18–19); the Parable of the Laborers in the Vineyard (Matt 20:1–16); the Parable of the Wicked Tenants (Matt 21:33–45||Mark 12:1–12||Luke 20:9–19); and the Parable of the Seed Growing Secretly (Mark 4:26–29).

Jesus declared: "I am the true vine, and my Father is the gardener. He cuts off every branch in me that bears no fruit, while every branch that does bear fruit he prunes so that it will be even more fruitful" (John 15:1–2). Jesus condemned the Pharisees for assiduously paying tithes of mint, dill, and cumin (Matt 23:23) while ignoring other laws less to their liking.

Jesus was arrested in the Garden of Gethsemane. The Roman soldiers mocked him by plaiting a crown of thorns, perhaps from the jujube (*Ziziphus spina-christi*). When he hung on the cross, a soldier offered him wine mixed with gall (Gk. *cholē*) as a kind of sedative (Matt 27:34); the parallel passage in Mark 15:23 indicates that the wine was mixed with myrrh. After tasting it, Jesus declined to drink the pain-killing solution.

James warns the wealthy that they will pass away like a wildflower (Jas 1:10). Peter notes that, like flowers, all of our lives are transient: "All people are like grass, and all their glory is like the flowers of the field; the grass withers and the flowers fall, but the word of the Lord endures forever" (1 Pet 1:24–25; cf. Isa 40:6–8).

C. THE NEAR EASTERN WORLD

Mesopotamia

Soon after the invention of their cuneiform writing system (3rd millenium BC), the Sumerians began to compile word lists for various categories, including plants and animals. The glossary list URU.AN.NA lists the names of plants in Sumerian and Akkadian.

Among the earliest Mesopotamian texts is the *Šammu šikinšu* ("the nature of plants"). This important pharmacological series gives the names of plants and describes their appearance and primary uses. Examples from this list include:

> Kamantu seed is a plant to have seed. It is to be ground (and) given to drink (mixed) with first quality beer.

> Atkam seed is a plant to have seed. It is to be ground, mixed with roasted grain flour in beer dregs (and) placed in her vagina.

> Nuḫurtu [asafoetida] resin is a plant for constriction of the urethra. It is to be given to drink (mixed) with beer, rubbed gently on (mixed) with oil (and) blown into his penis (via) a tube. (Scurlock, 277)

Wheat and barley were the most widely cultivated grains in the ancient world. Both were domesticated ca. 6000 BC in the Fertile Crescent. Legumes, which include three of the world's most ancient crops—lentils, peas, and broad beans—were domesticated contemporaneously with wheat and barley in the Fertile Crescent. Other important vegetables included onions, garlic, lettuce, cabbage, cucumbers, carrots, and radishes.

Since olive trees did not grow in Mesopotamia, the sesame was an important plant (Akk. *šamaššammū; Sesamum indicum*), whose seeds provided oil for cooking.

It was the imperialistic Neo-Assyrian kings who began the practice of cultivating foreign plants in their royal gardens, beginning with Ashurnasirpal II (9th c. BC). Sargon II was the first to use the term *kirimaḫḫu*, "pleasure garden," as opposed to simply speaking of a botanical garden, or *kirû*. The gardens of Ashurbanipal are depicted on reliefs from his North Palace at Nineveh.

The Chaldean king Merodach-Baladan II (721–710 BC) had a royal garden that included vegetables and such herbs as mint, basil, saffron, coriander, rue, thyme, and *asafoetida*.

In the second millennium BC, cotton (domesticated in India) reached Mesopotamia. Sennacherib described "trees bearing wool." Cotton cultivation is attested in the Persian Gulf at Qal'at al-Bahrain (ca. 600–400 BC), and in North Africa between the first and fourth centuries BC.

Egypt

The Egyptian water plant called papyrus (*Cyperus papyrus*) is perhaps the best known plant of antiquity. It is a tall (10–15 ft.), leafless sedge that once grew abundantly in the marshes of the Delta. It became the symbol of Lower (i.e., Northern) Egypt. Papyrus flowers were used as decorations and as offerings to the goddess Hathor. The stalks could be chewed for their sweet, sap-like sugar.

Papyrus was of great economic and cultural importance. In Egypt, small boats, baskets, and sandals were made from its culms (triangular-to-rounded stems). However, its major cultural impact was in the manufacture of papyrus (pl. papyri), for thousands of years the main writing material in Egypt. The manufacture of papyrus involved the pressing and drying of alternately layered strips of pith (soft inner stem tissue), and was thus labor intensive. Papyrus was exported all over the ancient world. As the Greeks obtained Egyptian papyrus from the Phoenician port of Byblos, they called a book or papyrus roll *biblos*. By about the third century AD, parchment had replaced papyrus as the preferred writing material in the Roman Empire.

The marshes also supported such plants as reeds (*Phragmites australis*) and cattail (*Typha domingensis*). Rushes (*Juncus acutus*, *Juncus rigidus*) were very useful for wickerwork.

The name lotus (Gk. *lōtos*) has been applied to several plants from classical times. The white lotus (*Nymphaea lotus*), which blooms at night, was less popular than the Egyptian blue lotus (Egy. *sšn*; *Nymphaea caerulea*). This is a water lily with circular, notched leaves and striking blue flowers supported on stalks well above the water's surface. The flowers, which bloom in the morning and then close, have a brilliant yellow center and a pleasant aroma. The lotus was prominent in love songs, as in the following stanza: "Distracting are the plants of her rush. The sister is a lotus bud. Her breasts are of perfume" (Papyrus Harris 2.10–12; White, 114).

The lotus plant was featured in ancient Egyptian art and was part of the mythology surrounding the sun god Re and Egyptian cosmogony. A spell of *The Book of the Dead* entitled "Chapter for being transformed into a lotus" reads: "I am the pure lotus which went forth from the sunshine, which is at the nose of Re, I have descended that I may seek it for Horus, for I am the pure one who issued from the fen" (Faulkner and Goelet, ch. 81A, plate 28-B).

Also indigenous to Egypt was the narcissus (*Narcissus tazetta*). With the expansion of the Egyptian empire during the 18th and 19th Dynasties, all kinds of flowers were imported, including the field poppy (*Papaver rhoeas*), the oriental cornflower (*Centaurea depressa*), the hollyhock (*Alcea ficifolia*), the lily (*Lilium candidum*), the delphinium (*Delphinium orientale*), and the safflower (*Carthamus tinctorius*).

The Egyptians cultivated a diverse array of plants. Chufa, or tiger nuts (*Cyperus esculentus*), were domesticated by the ancient Egyptians after they had been gathered for millennia in the Nile Valley. The ground tubers were mixed with honey and baked to make bread.

Lettuce (*Lactuca sativa*) was domesticated by the Egyptians ca. 4500 BC. The early varieties were used for medicine and seed oil; later cultivars were less bitter and were used as a vegetable. Lettuce, which was considered an aphrodisiac, was sacred to the fertility god Min. Onions (*Allium cepa*) were known in Egypt from ca. 3200 BC. Leeks (*Allium porrum*) were known only from the time of the New Kingdom. Garlic (*Allium sativum*) was found in the tomb of Tutankhamun (1350 BC).

Many plants of the Cucurbitaceae family flourished in Egypt. Cucumber was domesticated in India and arrived in Egypt by 1000 BC. The honey melon (*Cucumis melo*) has only been found in tombs. Only the seeds and not the flesh of the watermelon (*Citrullus lanatus*) found in Egypt could be eaten.

Many different plant products were used in medical and magical solutions. The Ebers Papyrus is sixty-eight feet long and contains over eighty prescriptions that utilize plant sources, such as mint, myrrh, frankincense, poppy, castor oil, onion, saffron, aloe, mandrake, cedar wood, gum, and henbane. An analysis of the substances used as laxatives or antidiarrheal agents indicates that the most used ingredient (14.6 percent) was a substance called *djaret* in Egyptian; this may have been the opium poppy (*Papaver somniferum*), which was introduced into Egypt after the New Kingdom (Estes, 101). A remedy that Isis prepared for Re's headache reads: "Take equal parts of the following: berry of the coriander, berry of the poppy plant, wormwood, berry of the *sames*-plant, berry of the juniper-plant, honey. Mix the ingredients together and a paste will form. Smear the afflicted person with the paste and he will instantly become well" (Brier, 282–83).

We have numerous depictions of gardens from ancient Egypt, including a Middle Kingdom model of a garden (now at the Metropolitan Museum of Art). The gardens are walled and have a pool in the center that is bordered by trees and plants. In a scene of the garden of Ipy (ca. 1500 BC), we see gardeners using a *shaduf*, a weighted lever, to lift buckets of water to irrigate his garden. Gardens were also placed in palaces, temples, and tombs. Khem was the god of gardens.

The Papyrus Harris, the longest papyrus preserved (133 ft.), enumer-
ates the gifts that Ramesses III (d. 1198 BC) presented to the temples at
Memphis, Heliopolis, and Thebes during his thirty-year reign. They include a staggering number of offerings, among them plants and flowers
such as:

cinnamon	155 measures
grapes	1,550 measures
papyrus sandals, pairs	15,110
pomegranates	15,500
blossoms, tall bouquets	3,100
blossoms, garden fragrance	15,500
flowers, garlands	60,450
lotus flowers for the hand	46,500
papyrus flowers, bouquets	68,200
vegetable bundles	770,200
blossoms, bouquets	1,975,800

(See *ARE* 5.87–156)

Inside the coffin of Tutankhamun were preserved floral decorations of
red poppies and blue cornflowers. Around the neck of Ramesses II were
found remains of narcissus bulbs.

D. THE GRECO-ROMAN WORLD

Greece

The earliest flowers depicted in the Aegean are sea daffodils (*Pancra-
tium maritimum*). These appear on the sixteenth-century BC frescoes
in the Room of the Ladies at Akrotiri on the island of Santorini (ancient
Thera), which were uncovered by Spyridon Marinatos from the ashes of a
volcanic explosion. Sea daffodils are fragrant white flowers that blossom
for one night only and are found on seashores. In another fresco, the red
lily (*Lilium martagon*) is depicted in a vase. Also depicted in the frescoes is
the crocus (*Crocus sativus*).

The Greek Linear B tablets from Knossos, Pylos, and Mycenae, which
date to the fourteenth and thirteenth centuries BC, indicate that Near Eastern spices were already reaching the Aegean at this time, probably by way
of Cyprus. These included: (1) sesame (Linear B *sa-sa-ma*; Gk. *sēsamē*;
Ugar. *ššmn*; Akk. *šamaššammū*); (2) coriander (Linear B *ko-ri-ja-do-no*; Gk.
koriandron; Akk. *kisibirru*); and (3) cumin (Linear B *ku-mi-no*; Gk. *kymi-
non*; Akk. *kamūnu*). (See Ventris and Chadwick, 105, 222.)

The lotus of Homer's *Odyssey* was a soporific plant eaten by the "Lotus Eaters" (Gk. *Lōtophagoi*), a people encountered by Odysseus on an island off the Libyan coast (cf. Her. *Hist.* 4.177). It has traditionally been identified as the woody plant *Ziziphus lotus*. Eating this plant caused Odysseus's companions to forget about going home to Ithaca.

Greeks in the Archaic and Classical Ages had vegetable and herb gardens but did not have room in their small homes for ornamental flower gardens. Pots found in homes in Olynthus may have held either herbs or flowers.

Grain was sacred to Demeter, and the vine to Dionysus. A festival in the month of Anthesteria, which was dedicated to Dionysus, involved flowers. The mugwort (*Artemisia*) plant, which had healing properties, was sacred to Artemis, the goddess of childbirth.

To commemorate the death of Adonis, the beloved of Aphrodite slain by a wild boar, the Greeks would plant quick-growing seedlings in pots and then place them on rooftops, where the plants would quickly die. A myth recounts that Aphrodite's tears turned into the anemone flower.

The Hellenistic philosopher Epicurus established a community, which included women and slaves, in a garden (Gk. *kēpos*) setting in Athens in 307 BC. According to Pliny (*Nat.* 19.19.51), such a garden in a Greek city was unprecedented. According to Diogenes Laertius, Epicurus's will stipulated: "And I entrust to my School in perpetuity the task of aiding Amynomachus and Timocrates and their heirs to preserve to the best of their power the common life in the garden" (Diogenes Laertius, *Lives of Eminent Philosophers* 10.17).

The Greeks became acquainted with new flora through the conquests of the Near East by Alexander. According to Quintus Curtius (*Life of Alexander the Great*, 5.1.17–23), when Alexander entered Babylon the road before him was strewn with flowers. Harpalus, the governor Alexander set up in Babylon, tried to transplant Greek plants in Mesopotamia, but he failed in his attempt to grow ivy there (Plu. *Alex.* 35.15).

The Ptolemies gathered not only books for their great library but also plants and flowers for their gardens in Alexandria. A reception given by Ptolemy II in 279 BC for foreign visitors was quite memorable:

> The entire floor had been strewn with flowers of every kind; for the fact that the air in Egypt is temperate, and the gardeners there cultivate plants that grow elsewhere only in limited quantities and in particular seasons, means that the country produces enormous quantitites of flowers at every time of year, and the general rule is that no flower, including roses, snowdrops, or anything else, ever completely stops blooming. (Athen. *Deipn.* 5.196d)

Theophrastus, a student of Plato and Aristotle, is regarded as the founder of botany. He was lured from Athens to Alexandria by the offer of financial support from the Ptolemaic court. He evidently received reports of exotic plants such as cotton, pepper, cinnamon, and the banyan tree from Alexander, who had been a student of Aristotle during his youth. Rice, which was domesticated in China, is believed to have been brought west in 300 BC by Alexander the Great's armies. The English word "rice" is derived from Greek *oryza*, via the Latin, which is spelled the same (cf. Italian *riso*).

Theophrastus wrote two major works: *Enquiry into Plants* (Gk. *Peri phytōn historia*; Lat. *Historia plantarum*) and *On the Causes of Plants* (Gk. *Peri phytōn aitiōn*; Lat. *De causis plantarum*). The first discusses the structure, reproduction, and growth of plants, and their uses. Book 9 is devoted to the medicinal use of plants. The second work deals with the growth and fertilization of plants. Theophrastus knew the mandrake (Gk. *mandragoras*) not only as an aphrodisiac but also as a soporific. Sage (*Salvia officinalis*), another plant described by Theophrastus, was used in medicine from classical Greek times through the Middle Ages.

Rome

Pliny the Elder lists numerous plants that were used in his day, including rocket, parsnip, mallow, carrot, nettles, chervil, and thistle. Pliny advises students to crown themselves with peppermint to sharpen their wits, and to moisten their throats with peppermint juice before engaging in lengthy speech. Ovid's poem *Metamorphoses* relates several Greek and Roman myths about plants and trees. Romans and Greeks associated celery seed with funerals and considered it an omen of bad luck. Columella's treatise on farming discusses sixty plants, twenty-three of which are herbs that were used as condiments.

The Latin word for "flower" is *flos* (pl. *flores*); Latin has two words for "plant," *herba* and *planta*. The Latin word for "garden" is *hortus*, and for "gardener," *topiarius*. The Romans invented the art of topiary, shaping bushes (such as the *Anthyllis barba-jovis*) into the form of animals.

Our best evidence of Roman gardens comes from Pompeii, which was buried by the eruption of Vesuvius in AD 79. Over six hundred gardens have been counted there, half of them in the peristyle courts of wealthy homes, where they provided private space for families. Frescoes often depict gardens; one of the most beautiful of these was found in the House of the Wedding of Alexander (VI.17), excavated in 1984. Some of the Pompeiian gardens were evidently used for mystery religions. The garden of the House of the Golden Bracelet (VI.17.42) has scenes celebrating Dionysus. The House of Julia Felix had a long pool with a niche for a statue of Isis.

Roman gardens had pools and statues, evergreen plants (laurel, myrtle, oleander, box, ivy, and rosemary), and flowers (daisy, lily, oleander, rose, and violet). There were three varieties of violet, which were valued for their scent. Of the three varieties—the purple (*Viola odorata*), the white (*Matthiola incana*), and the yellow (*Cheiranthus cheiri*)—the most highly esteemed was the yellow variety (Pliny, *Nat.* 21.14.27). Pliny commented: "Our countrymen know among garden plants very few kinds of chaplet flowers, practically violets [*violas*] only and roses [*rosas*]" (*Nat.* 21.10.14).

The Romans knew many varieties of rose: *Rosa phoenicia*, *Rosa gallica*, *Rosa damascena*, *Rosa canina*, and *Rosa alba*. Rose petals were used for perfumes along with marjoram, narcissus, saffron, spikenard, and styrax.

A primary purpose for which flowers were grown and gathered was to weave them into chaplets (*coronae*), which were used for both secular celebrations and religious rites. Garlands of flowers and ivy were draped on altars and sacrificial animals.

The use of honorary chaplets was at first limited by law. The earliest set of Roman laws, the Twelve Tables (ca. 450 BC), stipulated the following for the dead: "Let there be no costly sprinkling . . . no long garlands. . . . When a man wins a crown himself or through a chattel or by dint of valor, the crown bestowed on him . . . [may be laid in the grave] with impunity [on the man who won it] or on his father" (Table X; Meyer and Reinhold, 115). Pliny reports that "in the second Punic War [218–201 BC] L. Fulvius, a banker, who was said to have walked out into the Forum from his veranda wearing in the daytime a chaplet of roses, was on the authority of the senate led away to prison, not being released before the end of the war" (*Nat.* 21.6.8). He also notes: "Already by that time chaplets were used to honour the gods, the lares [guardian spirits] public and private, tombs and spirits of the dead; the highest distinction was the plaited chaplet" (*Nat.* 21.8.11).

Flora, the goddess of flowers, was honored with a temple on the Quirinal Hill and a second temple close to the Circus Maximus. The festival of Floralia was celebrated in April, and the *ludi Florales*, which included games and contests, were celebrated annually from 173 BC. People paraded in bright clothing. Beans and lupines were scattered as emblems of fertility. In time, the celebration took on a character of indecent merriment and was regarded by prostitutes as their festival.

The greatest Roman writer on plants and medicines was Dioscorides, who came from Anazarbus near Tarsus. He served as a physician in Nero's army. His great compilation was written in Greek (Gk. *Peri hylēs iatrikēs*) but is known today by its Latin title, *De materia medica*, "The Materials of Medicine." He comments on about a thousand products, mainly made from plants, that were used in drugs. He not only names plants and describes their characteristics but also provides drawings of them.

Unlike his contemporary Pliny the Elder (d. AD 79), who includes all kinds of fantastic details in his encyclopedic *Natural History*, Dioscorides includes only a few strange data in *De materia medica*, which he qualifies as hearsay. For example, he writes, "They say [*phasi*] . . . of gladiolus that the upper part of the root stimulates sexual drive, the lower part represses it, and the middle part can be given to children" (*Mat. med.* IV.20; Riddle, 84), and "It is said [*legeitai*] . . . that Christ's thorn placed before doors and windows keeps away *pharmaka* [i.e., 'bad drugs'—poisons, spells, or enchantments]" (*Mat. med.* 1.90; Riddle, 84). Dioscorides's compilation was translated into Latin and Arabic, and it was the authoritative pharmacopeia until the Renaissance.

E. THE JEWISH WORLD

Herod the Great built two winter palaces at Jericho. The first was built south of the Wadi Qelt. In this palace, a peristyle surrounded a central courtyard with a garden. The second palace also featured a large peristyle garden and a banqueting hall with a view of the Wadi Qelt. South of the wadi was a large sunken garden (140 x 40 m. = 460 x 131 ft.).

The Wisdom of Solomon appears to convey a negative attitude toward medicines, including those consisting or made of plants, when it says, "For neither herb nor poultice cured them, but it was thy word, O Lord, which heals all men" (Wis 16:12). On the other hand, Ecclesiasticus, one of the very few ancient texts with a highly positive view of medicine, states: "The Lord created medicines from the earth, and a sensible man will not despise them" (Sir 38:4).

First Enoch states that the fallen angels were the ones who gave men "magical medicine, incantations, the cutting of roots, and taught them (about) plants" (*1 En.* 7:1; cf. 8:3). According to the book of *Jubilees*, the angel Raphael revealed to Noah the various remedies obtained from the fallen angels, and Noah recorded them in a book that he gave to his son Shem: "And the healing of all their illnesses together with their seductions we [the angels] told Noah so that he might heal by means of herbs of the earth. And Noah wrote everything in a book just as we taught him according to every kind of healing" (*Jub.* 10:12–13).

Both *1 Enoch* and *Jubilees* were highly regarded by the community of Qumran, which most scholars have identified with the Essenes. Based on statements by Josephus, J. E. Taylor has discussed in a recent article (Taylor 2009) the idea that the community at Qumran had an interest in medicinal plants and healing. According to Josephus, "They have an extraordinary enthusiasm concerning the works of the ancients, especially selecting those for the benefit of soul and body; thus with these they search out roots, remedies, and properties of stones for treatment of diseases" (*J.W.* 2.136).

The prohibition in Lev 19:19 against mixing species of seed ("Do not plant your field with two kinds of seed") is explained in the Mishnah (*m. Kil.* 8:1) along with similar kinds of prohibitions. This explanation is accompanied, however, by the statement that diverse kinds of seeds may be eaten together and that other benefits may be derived from them.

The Talmud declares: "One should not live in a town where vegetables are unobtainable" (*b. ʿErub.* 55b). For the Passover meal, "Bitter herbs [*mārôr*] can include lettuce, endives, leeks, coriander, mustard, gourd, and horseradish" (*b. Pesaḥ.* 39a). The Talmud states that in the city of Jerusalem "neither gardens nor orchards should be cultivated . . . , with the exception, however, of the garden of roses which existed from the days of the former prophets" (*b. B. Qam.* 82b). The reason given for this is the possibility of bad odor from the decaying vegetation.

In the Talmud, nearly seventy plants are mentioned as having medicinal properties, including both food plants (e.g., olives, dates, and pomegranates) and seasonings (e.g., cumin, fennel, and garlic). The following are some examples of herbaceous plants mentioned: *yôʿezer*, "maidenhair fern" (*Adiantum capillus-veneris*), for liver ailment (*b. Šabb.* 109b); *ʾabbûbrôʿê*, "knotweed" (*Polygonum aviculare*), as an antidote for snake poison; *ʾēzôb*, "hyssop" (*Origanum syriacum*), for intestinal worms (*b. Šabb.* 109b); and *tārād*, "spinach beet" (*Beta vulgaris var. cicla*), for skin disease (*b. Šabb.* 133b.)—"a broth of beet is beneficial for the heart, good for the eyes, and needless to say for the bowels" (*b. Ber.* 39a).

Cabbage was believed to help the sick recover from illness (*b. Ber.* 44b). As cress was considered an aphrodisiac, the high priest was not supposed to eat it on the Day of Atonement (*b. Yoma* 2a). Cumin, which was to be tithed, was applied to a circumcision wound (*b. Šabb.* 133a). It was believed that if one ate fenugreek on an empty stomach and then drank water, intestinal worms might develop (*b. Šabb.* 109b). Eating mustard once in thirty days was thought to keep sickness away, but it was not to be eaten every day lest it weaken one's heart (*b. Ber.* 40a).

Ground garlic was believed to be good for a toothache (*b. Giṭ.* 69a). The rabbis taught five things about garlic: "It satiates, it keeps the body warm, it brightens up the face, it increases semen, and it kills parasites in the bowels. Some say that it fosters love and removes jealousy" (*b. B. Qam.* 82c). Therefore husbands were to consume garlic before performing their marital duty on Friday nights.

As for fragrant flowers and herbs, blessings were to be said over jasmine, fragrant woods, and the narcissus. "Whence do we learn that a blessing should be said over sweet odours? Because it says, Let every soul praise the Lord. What is that which gives enjoyment to the soul and not to the body?—You must say that this is fragrant smell" (*b. Ber.* 43b).

F. THE CHRISTIAN WORLD

Very few references to plants can be found in the writings of the early church fathers. The Didache states, "Take, therefore, all the first fruits of the wine press and threshing floor, and of the cattle and sheep, and give these first fruits to the prophets, for they are your high priests" (*Did.* 13.3).

Origen maintained a positive attitude toward medicine. He maintained that all good knowledge comes from God. On the other hand, he stressed that "spiritual" Christians should rely only on God for healing.

Clement of Alexandria praised the beauty and the fragrance of flowers, while decrying the pagan custom of making chaplets of flowers:

> Such a use of crowns, also, has degenerated to scenes of revelry and intoxication. Do not encircle my head with a crown, for in the springtime it is delightful to while away the time on the dewy meads, while soft and many-coloured flowers are in bloom, and, like the bees, enjoy a natural and pure fragrance. But to adorn one's self with a crown woven from the fresh mead, and wear it at home, were unfit for a man of temperance. For it is not suitable to fill the wanton hair with rose-leaves, or violets, or lilies, or other such flowers, stripping the sward of its flowers. . . . Besides, those who crown themselves destroy the pleasure there is in flowers: for they enjoy neither the sight of them, since they wear the crown above their eyes; nor their fragrance, since they put the flowers away above the organs of respiration. . . . As beauty, so also the flower delights when looked at; and it is meet to glorify the Creator by the enjoyment of the sight of beautiful objects. (*Paed.* 2.8)

He also acknowledged the beneficial use of flowers in medicinal ointments:

> To resume, then: we have showed that in the department of medicine, for healing, and sometimes also for moderate recreation, the delight derived from flowers, and the benefit derived from ointments and perfumes, are not to be overlooked. And if some say, What pleasure, then, is there in flowers to those that do not use them? Let them know, then, that ointments are prepared from them, and are most useful. . . . We should have much to say respecting them, were we to speak of flowers and odours as made for necessary purposes, and not for the excesses of luxury. And if a concession must be made, it is enough for people to enjoy the fragrance of flowers; but let them not crown themselves with them. (*Paed.* 2.8)

The learned Jerome, who was the only church father who knew Hebrew well, produced a new Latin translation of the Bible, which eventually became known as the Vulgate. He translated the plant God created to shade Jonah by the Latin *hedera*, "ivy," in place of the Old Latin *cucurbita*, "gourd" (Jonah 4:6). In a letter written in 403, Augustine informed Jerome that when a bishop of Oea (Tripolis) in Libya read Jerome's new translation, the congregation nearly rioted. A scholar in Rome also criticized the translation. It appears from Jerome's commentary that he was inclined to identify the "ivy" with the castor bean plant, a view that some scholars today favor. In his letter written in 405, Jerome responded to Augustine: "If you have read my commentary on Jonah, I think you will not recur to the ridiculous gourd-debate" (*Ep.* 115). (See Rebenich, 58–60; cf. Robinson.)

BIBLIOGRAPHY: G. Bare, *Plants and Animals of the Bible* (1969); L. Boulos, *Medicinal Plants of North Africa* (1983); B. Brier, *Ancient Egyptian Magic* (1980); E. B. Brite and J. M. Marston, "Environmental Change, Agricultural Innovation, and the Spread of Cotton Agriculture in the Old World," *Journal of Anthropological Archaeology* 32 (2013), 39–53; C. P. Bryan, trans., *Ancient Egyptian Medicine: The Papyrus Ebers* (1974); M. Ciaraldi, *People and Plants in Ancient Pompeii* (2007); G. Contenau, *Everyday Life in Babylon and Assyria* (1959); S. Dalley, *The Mystery of the Hanging Garden of Babylon* (2013); P. H. Davis, P. C. Harper, and I. C. Hedge, ed., *Plant Life of South-West Asia* (1971); J. W. Estes, *The Medical Skills of Ancient Egypt* (rev. ed., 1993); L. Farrar, *Ancient Roman Gardens* (1998); R. O. Faulkner and O. Goelet, Jr., trans., *The Egyptian Book of the Dead, The Book of Going Forth by Day*, ed. J. Wasserman (rev. ed., 2015); G. B. Ferngren, *Medicine & Health Care in Early Christianity* (2009); L. M. Gallery, "The Garden of Ancient Egypt," in *Immortal Egypt: Invited Lectures on the Middle East at the University of Texas at Austin*, ed. D. Schmandt-Besserat (1978), 43–49; D. Garrett, *Song of Songs* (2004); R. Germer, "Flora," trans. J. Harvey, in *The Oxford Encyclopedia of Ancient Egypt*, ed. D. B. Redford (2001), I.535–44; A. L. Giesecke, *The Epic City: Urbanism, Utopia, and the Garden in Ancient Greece and Rome* (2007); A. L. Giesecke, *The Mythology of Plants: Botanical Lore from Ancient Greece and Rome* (2014); A. S. Gilbert, "The Flora and Fauna of the Ancient Near East," *CANE* 1.153–74; K. L. Gleason, "Gardens: Gardens in Preclassical Times," *OEANE* II.383–85; K. L. Gleason, "Gardens: Gardens of the Hellenistic and Roman Periods," *OEANE* II.385–87; W. B. Harer, Jr., "Pharmacological and Biological Properties of the Egyptian Lotus," *JARCE* 22 (1985), 49–54; N. Hareuveni, *Ecology in the Bible* (1974); R. K. Harrison, *Healing Herbs of the Bible* (1966); B. Herzhoff, "Lotos: Botanische Beobachtungen zu einem homerischen Pflanzennamen," *Hermes* 112.3 (1984), 257–71; P. R. House, *Lamentations* (2004); I. Jacob and W. Jacob, "Flora," *ABD* II.803–17; W. Jashemski, "Gardens," in *The World of Pompeii*, ed. J. J. Dobbins and P. W. Foss (2007), 487–98; W. Jashemski, *The Gardens of Pompeii* (1993); B. Leach and J. Tait, "Papyrus," in *Ancient Egyptian Materials and Technology*, ed. P. T. Nicholson and I. Shaw (2000), 227–53; E. Lev, "Reconstructed *materia medica* of the Medieval and Ottoman al-Sham," *Journal of Ethnopharmacology* 80 (2002), 167–79;

E. Lev and Z. Amar, *Ethnic Medicinal Substances of the Land of Israel* (2002) (in Hebrew); N. Lewis and M. Reinhold, ed., *Roman Civilization: Selected Readings I: The Republic and the Augustan Age* (3rd ed.; 1990); C. Linnaeus, *Genera Plantarum* (5th ed., 1753); G. P. Luttikhuizen, ed., *Paradise Interpreted* (1999); E. B. MacDougall, ed., *Ancient Roman Villa Gardens* (1987); E. MacDougall and W. Jashemski, ed., *Ancient Roman Gardens* (1981); S. Marinatos, *Excavations at Thera V (1971 Season)* (1972); H. N. Moldenke and A. L. Moldenke, *Plants of the Bible* (1952); E. Netzer, "The Winter Palaces of the Judean Kings at Jericho at the End of the Second Temple Period," *BASOR* 228 (1977), 1–13; A. L. Oppenheim, "On Royal Gardens in Mesopotamia," *JNES* 24 (1965), 328–33; S. A. Palmer, "Archaeogenomic Evidence of Punctuated Genome Evolution in *Gossypium*," *Molecular Biology and Evolution* 29.8 (2012), 2031–38; S. Rebenich, "Jerome: The 'Vir Trilinguis' and the 'Hebraica Veritas,'" *VC* 47 (1993), 50–77; J. M. Riddle, *Dioscorides on Pharmacy and Medicine* (1985); B. P. Robinson, "Jonah's Qiqayon Plant," *ZAW* 97 (1985), 390–403; F. Rosner, *Medicine in the Bible and the Talmud* (augmented ed., 1995); L. Ryken, J. C. Wilhoit, and T. Longman III, ed., *Dictionary of Biblical Imagery* (1998); R. Sallares, *The Ecology of the Ancient Greek World* (1991); S. R. Shimoff, "Gardens: From Eden to Jerusalem," *JSJ* 26 (1995), 145–55; V. Täckholm, *Students' Flora of Egypt* (2nd ed.; 1974); J. E. Taylor, "'Roots, Remedies and Properties of Stones': The Essenes, Qumran and Dead Sea Pharmacology," *JJS* 60 (2009), 226–44; R. C. Thompson, *A Dictionary of Assyrian Botany* (1949); United Bible Societies, *Fauna and Flora of the Bible* (1972); J. Scurlock, *Sourcebook for Ancient Mesopotamian Medicine* (2014); J. Van Ruiten, "Garden of Eden—Paradise," *EDEJ* 658–61; J. G. Vaughan and C. Geissler, *The New Oxford Book of Food Plants* (1997); M. Ventris and J. Chadwick, *Documents in Mycenaean Greek* (2nd ed., 1973); W. von Soden, *The Ancient Orient: An Introduction to the Study of the Ancient Near East* (1994); J. F. Wendel and R. C. Cronn, "Polyploidy and the Evolutionary History of Cotton," *Advances in Agronomy* 78 (2003), 139–86; J. B. White, *A Study of the Language of Love in the Song of Songs and Ancient Egyptian Poetry* (1978); D. J. Wiseman, "Mesopotamian Gardens," *AnSt* 33 (1983), 137–44; D. J. Wiseman, *Nebuchadrezzar and Babylon* (1985); D. Zohary and M. Hopf, *Domestication of Plants in the Old World* (1988); M. Zohary, *Plant Life of Palestine* (1962).

GCT

See also AGRICULTURE, ALCOHOLIC BEVERAGES, APHRODISIACS & EROTIC SPELLS, FOOD PRODUCTION, LIBRARIES & BOOKS, MEDICINE & PHYSICIANS, PERFUMES, TEXTILES, TREES, and VITICULTURE.

POLICE & PRISONS

A police force is a body of trained persons authorized to preserve civil order and well-being at all times by enforcing enacted laws. A corresponding organization exists also in military circles in order to ensure that wrongdoing in the armed forces will be minimal and that criminals will be apprehended and punished.

The term "police" is derived from the Greek *polis*, "city," which points to the urban origin of the concept. While the ancient world did not share the modern concept of a designated police force, there were officials who wielded authority in order to deter crime and keep the peace.

Prisons and jails are two very different places in the modern criminal justice system. Prisons are places of punishment where convicted felons are sentenced to more than two years of incarceration, while jails are places to hold those awaiting trial or transfer to prison or those who are sentenced to punishment of incarceration for two years or less for minor offenses. Although today such jails and prisons usually bring to mind structures built specifically to confine criminals for designated sentences of months or years, in the various civilizations of the ancient world they were primarily used to hold persons suspected, accused, or convicted of crimes temporarily, until further punishment was imposed or the prisoners were released. Also, while today some legal theorists emphasize a rehabilitative purpose for incarceration, justice was more retributive in antiquity.

A. THE OLD TESTAMENT

In the patriarchal period, the heads of tribes and elders administered customary law and punished those who committed crimes. The men of these households looked after the safety of those in the expanding spheres of family, clan, tribe, and the broader society. From the time of Moses such individuals exercised formal judicial power in the congregation and would have delegated any policing duties to others (Num 11:16; Deut 16:18; 29:10;

Josh 8:33). In the absence of public prosecutors, it was the duty of each individual to be on watch in the community and to bring charges against
evildoers when a crime was witnessed (Deut 17:2–7)—but investigations
and trials could also be manipulated (1 Kgs 21:9–13).

Several terms indicate a formal awareness of policing roles in Israelite
society. The *šōṭēr* was an "official" or "officer" who exercised civil, judicial,
or military authority (Num 11:16; Deut 1:13–18; Prov 6:7) or provided
supervision, as when Pharaoh's taskmasters appointed "foremen" to over-
see Israelite workers (Exod 5:14–26). In Modern Hebrew the word *šōṭēr*
means "policeman," and from the same verbal root comes *mišṭārâ*, "police."
In ancient Israel, the *šōmēr* was a "guard" or "watchman." Such individuals
functioned at times to patrol cities at night and to deter crime (Song 3:3;
5:7–8; Isa 21:11–12). The sometimes synonymous *mišmār*, "guard, watch,
guarding," is from the same root and can be used in parallel with *šōmēr* to
refer to those appointed to protect a city (Jer 51:12). The *ṣōpê* referred to
the "watchman" who teamed up with the *šōʿēr*, "gatekeeper," to cooperate
in the policing and protecting of walled cities (2 Sam 18:26). It is also possible that the *pāqîd*, a "deputy" (Judg 9:28) or "commissioner" (Esth 2:3),
acted as a policeman. Further, it is evident that the Levites would have arrested any person who was attempting to violate the sanctity of the tabernacle and later the temple, since it was their duty to protect these locations
(1 Chr 27:1; 2 Chr 19:11; 34:13). The *nĕgîd bêt hāʾĕlōhîm*, "captain of the
house of God" (1 Chr 9:11; 2 Chr 31:13; Neh 11:11), or *pāqîd nāgîd bĕbêt
yhwh*, "chief commissioner of the house of the LORD" (Jer 20:1), served
under the high priest with authority over the temple precincts and gates
(2 Chr 34:13; cf. Jos. *J.W.* 6.5.3).

The Torah does not impose terms of imprisonment as a penalty. Instead, crimes involving property were settled by restitution, usually of
at least double the amount stolen (Exod 22:1–15). The principle of just
(measure-for-measure) retaliation (Lat. *lex talionis*) is illustrated by the
biblical phrase "an eye for an eye." Laws based on this principle cover property and personal damage and were intended to restore the status quo; they
were so basic to Israelite jurisprudence that they appear in triplicate in the
Mosaic code (Exod 21:23–25; Lev 24:17–22; Deut 19:21). Property rights
violations did not incur the death penalty.

Although the Torah does not contain legislation regarding imprisonment, individuals were sometimes temporarily held against their will, especially those awaiting trial or sentencing (Lev 24:10–12; Num 15:34). A
number of the prophets became political prisoners for offending the kings
of Israel or Judah (e.g., Micaiah in 1 Kgs 22:26–27 and Hanani in 2 Chr
16:7–10). Most notably, Jeremiah experienced confinement in stocks and
flogging near the temple during his frequent imprisonments for warning

of God's judgment and the coming exile (Jer 20:1–2; 37:15–16). Jeremiah was thrown into a cistern, from which he was rescued by Ebed-Melech, a Cushite servant of the king (Jer 38:6–10).

In Ezekiel's lament for the princes of Israel, he poetically depicts the exile as a political imprisonment: "With hooks they pulled him into a cage and brought him to the king of Babylon. They put him in prison, so his roar was heard no longer on the mountains of Israel" (Ezek 19:9).

As the practices of other nations influenced postexilic Jewish communities, prisons came to be used for the punishment of various offenders. When King Artaxerxes granted permission for Ezra and the people of Israel to return in peace to Jerusalem, he expressly listed a number of punishments that might come upon those who would hinder the Jews. Failure to support his royal decree could lead to death, banishment, confiscation of goods, or imprisonment (Ezra 7:26).

In earlier periods of Israel's history, confinement was common only as punishment for involuntary manslaughter. But this confinement was only to a city of refuge, in order to protect the perpetrator from the avenger of blood (Num 35:6–34; Deut 4:41–43; 19:1–13; Josh 20:1–9). Confinement to cities of refuge does not necessarily suggest that they were viewed as prisons, though some interpreters stress a dual function for these sanctuaries: protection and punishment.

Dry cisterns (Gen 37:20), granaries (Judg 16:21), or even private homes (Jer 37:15) were used as early prisons. During the monarchy, special cells or dungeons connected with administrative buildings came to be used (Jer 32:2; 37:16; 2 Chr 16:10). The second word of the phrase *bêt (hak)kele*, "house of confinement" (e.g., 2 Kgs 17:4; 25:27; Isa 42:7; 44:22), derives from the root *kālāʾ*, meaning to "shut up" or "restrain." The verb *ʾāsar* means "to bind" and the noun *ʾāsîr*, which derives from the same root, means "prisoner." A prison could therefore be referred to as *bêt hāʾăsîrîm*, or "house of the prisoners" (Judg 16:21, 25).

Joseph's prison in Egypt is called *bêt hassōhar*, literally, "the round house" (Gen 39:20–23; 40:3, 5); this may refer to the shape of the prison, which was perhaps a cistern or hole in the ground. This prison was "in the vizier's house" (40:3–4); the vizier supervised nearly everything for the pharaoh, including security. When Joseph was imprisoned in Egypt, he gained the respect of the chief jailer and was made supervisor of prisoners (Gen 39:20–22). One of his responsibilities would have been to ensure that prisoners did not escape, since this was itself considered a very serious crime. The mention of Joseph's fetters, iron collar, and ultimate release in the poetic account of his imprisonment in Ps 105:16–22 recalls the great moral of his story, namely, that what others intend for evil God often intends for good (Gen 50:20).

The mental and physical anguish of prisoners is hinted at in numerous passages (Pss 79:11; 142:7; Isa 14:17; 42:22; Lam 3:34; Zech 9:11). For many prisoners, their only hope of relief was from God (Pss 69:33; 102:20; 107:10–16; 142:7; 146:7; Isa 42:7; 61:1). In contrast, according to certain texts the wicked should fear that God will be not only their judge but also their jailer (Job 11:10; 12:14; Isa 24:22; Lam 3:7).

B. THE NEW TESTAMENT

In the postexilic period, the ancient theocratic traditions of maintaining law and order were revived and guarded zealously by such groups as the "scribes" and Pharisees, whose position in this regard was even recognized by Pontius Pilate (John 18:31; 19:7), the Roman procurator of Judea. Their overall jurisdiction was rather circumscribed, however, since it was unlawful for them to impose capital punishment.

The Gospels and the book of Acts refer to numerous arrests and imprisonments as well as the activities of various types of policing authorities. The official known as the *hypēretēs* (Matt 5:25; Acts 5:22, 26) was an inferior court official such as a bailiff and therefore much like the Roman *lictor*. The *praktōr* (Luke 12:58) was likely the kind of court registrar found at Athens who would exact punishments.

Debtors were held in confinement to motivate family members to pay off their liabilities. Imprisonment for unpaid debts is illustrated in the Parable of the Unforgiving Servant (Matt 18:21–35), a story about a man who refused to wait patiently for his full payment but decided to have his counterpart "thrown into prison until he could pay the debt" (18:30).

Imprisonment for political reasons was common under the Romans. Such incarceration normally resulted in a trial that led either to release or punishment by death. Herod Antipas, tetrarch of Galilee and Peraea, imprisoned John the Baptist at the fortress city of Machaerus (Jos. *Ant.* 18.5.2) to stop the preacher's disapproving admonitions against Herod's illicit marriage to Herodias, the wife of his half-brother Herod Philip (Luke 3:19–20). In time, the prophet-turned-political-prisoner was beheaded, at the request of Herodias (Matt 14:1–12; Mark 6:16–17, 27).

What appears to have been an armed police unit was brought by Judas Iscariot to Gethsemane (John 18:3; Luke 22:4, 52) in order to arrest Jesus and bring him to trial. The company of men and officers had been recruited and dispatched by the chief priests and the Pharisees, and judging from their startled reaction to Jesus's use of the divine name (John 18:6) they were likely Jews rather than Romans. Perhaps these officers had been sent by the captain of the temple (*stratēgos tou hierou*), whose policing activities are also noted throughout Acts 3–5 in connection with the efforts to prohibit the apostles' preaching of the gospel. Peter and John were taken into custody (*eis tērēsin*) overnight (Acts 4:1–3) and released the next day after Peter's bold defense before the Sanhedrin (Acts 4:5–22). The moving account of the arrest of the apostles in Acts 5 illustrates both the authority of the Sanhedrin and the limitations of Jewish leadership in terms of policing the temple area and in terms of imprisonment and punishment. Motivated by jealousy over the favor the apostles' teaching had received in the temple, the Sadducees arrested Peter and the other apostles and placed them in custody (5:17–18). But after hearing the counsel of Gamaliel, the council decided to release the apostles after a beating and further warnings (5:33–40). This favorable outcome only strengthened the resolve of the apostles and promoted further boldness (5:41–42). The place of their detention is called a public jail (*tērēsis dēmosia*) in Acts 5:18 as well as a prison (*phylakē*) in Acts 5:19, suggesting that these terms were used interchangeably (akin to how the terms "jail" and "prison" are sometimes used interchangeably today, despite the distinctions these terms often carry).

Herod Agrippa I arrested James and Peter to ingratiate himself with the Jerusalem establishment. James was killed, but Peter miraculously escaped (Acts 12:1–19).

The nature of the frequent imprisonments of Paul, who was a Roman citizen, illustrates both Roman legal theory and actual practice (2 Cor 6:5; 11:23–27). He was falsely accused, severely beaten, and unlawfully imprisoned, along with Silas, by Roman magistrates in a secure inner cell in Philippi, with their feet placed "in the stocks" (Acts 16:24). When an earthquake shook the jail, the jailor, afraid that his prisoners had escaped, was about to commit suicide when Paul presented the good news of salvation to him. The Roman officials, when they learned that Paul and Silas were citizens, wished to have them leave quietly. But Paul responded, "They beat us publicly without a trial, even though we are Roman citizens, and threw us into prison. And now do they want to get rid of us quietly? No! Let them come themselves and escort us out" (Acts 16:37).

Later, when Paul visited Jerusalem, a group of fellow Jews from Asia Minor brought the false charge against him that he had brought a gentile into the inner area of the temple. A Greek inscription from the temple precincts carries the following warning: "No foreigner is to enter within the balustrade and enclosure around the temple area. Whoever is caught will have himself to blame for his death which will follow" (Finegan, 197). This matches the description in Josephus (*Ant.* 15.417; *J.W.* 6.125).

Paul was rescued from certain death by a military unit from the Fortress Antonia under the command of the chief captain responsible for maintaining civil order in the province (Acts 21:27–30). The crowd that seized Paul apparently had no status as law enforcement officials but acted spontaneously with vigilante mob violence when angered by his activities. Since Jewish authorities were not permitted to carry out capital punishment, their attempt to kill Paul was thwarted (Acts 21:31–33).

While Paul was under the protective custody of the Roman tribune, another plot against his life was foiled, and he was taken secretly by night under heavy guard to Caesarea (Acts 23:12–24). He was then held for over two years at the whim of the governor Felix, who "was hoping that Paul would offer him a bribe, so he sent for him frequently and talked with him" (Acts 24:26).

Paul presented his case before the new governor, Festus (Acts 25:1–12), and before Herod Agrippa II and his sister Berenice, who was later to become the mistress of Titus (Acts 25:13–22). But Paul used his right as a Roman citizen to appear before the emperor Nero himself (Acts 25:10). Thus, Paul and other prisoners were placed under the charge of Julius, a centurion, and put on board a ship to be transported to Rome. After surviving a shipwreck at Malta, Paul finally arrived at Puteoli in the Bay of Naples (Acts 28:13) before he was transferred to Rome.

The book of Acts ends with Paul meeting with fellow Jews and other friends in relative freedom for two years; during this time, while Paul awaited trial, he was guarded by a soldier and bound with a chain in his own rented apartment (Acts 28:16–30). Modern descriptions of the conditions of Paul's house arrest have erred toward both sides of the spectrum, some by minimizing and others by exaggerating his circumstances. While he was not in a dark, miserable dungeon at this time, he was nevertheless bound and not able to enjoy complete freedom of movement. Perhaps the confusion over his circumstances is due to a conflation of two separate Roman imprisonments—one that is recorded in the latter chapters of Acts, and one that occurred shortly thereafter.

The chronology of Paul's life is difficult here, and he may have been released or declared innocent at his first appearance before Nero. Brief statements from Clement of Rome (AD 95) and Eusebius (AD 325) suggest that Paul was released from his first Roman imprisonment and was able to preach "in the East and in the West" (*1 Clem.* 5.7; cf. Rom 15:28) but also that he was eventually rearrested, imprisoned in Rome a second time, and then executed under Nero (Eus. *Hist. eccl.* 2.22). Thus, during Paul's first Roman imprisonment (ca. AD 60–62), he had relative freedom to witness, and he received many guests (Acts 28:30).

It has traditionally been believed that Paul penned the Prison Epistles (Ephesians, Philippians, Colossians, and Philemon) during this time. Since this arrest was due to false accusations of heresy in Jerusalem and sedition against Rome (28:17–19), Paul was optimistic about his potential for acquittal and release (Phil 2:23–24).

Paul's second Roman imprisonment (ca. AD 64–68), traditionally associated with the persecution of Christians by Nero, was far more serious and formidable. Nero, attempting to deflect the widespread suspicion that he was responsible for the fire that devastated Rome in AD 64, blamed the Christians and had them martyred (Tac. *Ann.* 15.44; Suet. *Nero* 16).

It could be that during this time Paul wrote 2 Timothy, in which he states that he suffers as a bound criminal (2:9), anticipates being executed (4:6), and mentions that he has been deserted by many friends and that only Luke is with him (4:11). He also requests a cloak due to the cold, and he asks for "my scrolls, especially the parchments" (*ta biblia, malista tas membranas*) (4:13). The Latin loanword *membranas* used here refers to parchments, probably in a notebook form. We do not know whether these were copies of the OT Scriptures in Greek, his notes, or even copies of his own letters.

These real experiences of Paul in prison illuminate the metaphorical uses of prisoner language in his gospel proclamation (Gal 3:22; Rom 7:23) as well as the larger NT ethic of visiting those in prison (Matt 25:31–46; Heb 10:32–34; 13:3). Paul repeatedly calls himself a prisoner (*desmios*) of Christ (Eph 3:1; 4:1; 2 Tim 1:8; Phlm 1, 9), and refers to his chains (sing. *halysis*) in his letters (Eph 6:20; 2 Tim 1:16). Paul encourages the Philippians by reporting that while in Rome, as a result of his being chained to a member of the elite Praetorian Guard, the gospel spread through their barracks (Phil 1:13).

Prison language is also employed in the NT to illustrate divine judgment. *Hadēs*, where people may be "abandoned" in the world of the dead (Acts 2:31; cf. Ps 16:10), can refer to a prison-like place of torment and punishment (Luke 16:23). An abode of evil known as the abyss (*abyssos*, lit., "pit") is the home of the beast (Rev 11:7) as well as a very deep, even "bottomless" place that will serve as the devil's dungeon (Rev 20:3). Yet, "Satan will be released from his prison" prior to his final judgment (Rev 20:7). Like a maximum-security prison with "chains of darkness," *tartaros* appears to be the place where evil angels are "reserved for judgment" (2 Pet 2:4). Gehenna (Gk. *geenna*) is also comparable to a prison for the dead into which the disobedient will be "thrown" after the final judgment (Luke 12:5; cf. Rev 21:8). Jesus connects the imagery of prison and the final judgment when he asks, "How shall you escape the sentence of hell?" (Matt 23:33, NASB).

C. THE NEAR EASTERN WORLD

In general in the ancient Near East the responsibility for maintaining civic order rested with the military forces, who were periodically faced with revolts, riots, pillaging, and other acts of social disorder that needed to be controlled. Consequently, various types of guards and guardians functioned in a broad variety of capacities—and their actual military fierceness fueled numerous myths.

Mesopotamia

The *Gilgamesh Epic* describes terrifying "scorpion men" who guard the gate to the netherworld. The Akkadian "Epic of Creation" indicates that Marduk called for a total of six hundred guards to keep the instructions of Anu: three hundred in heaven and three hundred on earth (*COS* 1.111). Various legal texts, such as the Code of Hammurabi, refer to crimes and punishments and reflect the expectation that guards will arrest and punish offenders (*COS* 2.131). The Akkadian text "Punishment by Fire" relays the case of two men who have been accused of a serious offense. While the allegation is under investigation, the accuser is guarded in prison (*ANET*, 627–28).

The earliest form of policing arose among the Sumerians, who appointed soldiers to keep watch over their cities at night. Unfortunately, some of these men abused their duties by being delinquent and indulging in dishonest and illegal activities. When Sumerian laws were broken, the authorities endeavored to arrest the culprits, the warrant for such activity coming either from the ruler (LUGAL) or the executive priest (ENSI) of the city.

Cuneiform legal and administrative tablets from the Eanna temple in Uruk and the Ebabbar temple in Sippar suggest that among several new offices that arose in the Neo-Babylonian and Persian periods, the *paqūdu* was a type of policeman in cities and villages (Pirngruber, 1; British Museum, Museum no. 031041; University of Pennsylvania Museum of Archaeology and Anthropology, Museum no. CBS 05398). The *paqūdū* appear in these texts as low-level officials who investigate crimes, arrest criminals, and guard temples. Pirngruber comments as follows:

> The fact that law enforcement was entrusted to a permanent office marks a telling difference with the Old Babylonian period, when policing tasks were often conferred upon individuals with a background in the military or recruited from the retinue of imperial magnates. Instead it seems to be that Babylonia in the first millennium BC was closer to Roman Egypt as regards the organization of the maintenance of public order, where rather low-ranking civic officials such as the *nyktostrategoi* and the *eirenarchai* are found in capacities similar to the Babylonian *paqūdus*. (Pirngruber, 1)

Captured enemies, local thieves, and other criminals performed hard labor in state or temple "milling houses" (sing. *bīt ararri*). Such prisoners were routinely blinded and bound with bronze fetters, a fate recorded for

Samson in Gaza (Judg 16:21, 25) and the Judean king Zedekiah in Babylon (Jer 52:11). A pleading letter written in Old Babylonian attests to the prison conditions experienced by two women held for debt: "Come here before your wife and daughter die grinding (barley) in prison" (UET V 9, 17–22). Esarhaddon's letter to the god Aššur refers to the dramatic surrender of Rusa, who did so in order to avoid an otherwise certain death. He sent his envoys to the enemy carrying a statuette representing his likeness. The figure was covered in sackcloth and clasping a grinding stone, indicating his willingness to surrender as a prisoner of war to labor in the grinding mills (van der Toorn, 249).

The Sumerian hymn "Nungal in the Ekur" praises the goddess Nungal, queen of the underworld, as "The Warden of the Prison" and "The Lady of the Great House" (see Civil). The hymn proceeds to detail various miseries of incarceration in prison: it is a place to which a man goes when "his god disapproves" of him, where people are secluded in darkness and no one knows how to say "open up this door!" Prison is compared to a trap lying in wait for the enemy, fearsome waves, an angry storm, a flood, a house of sorrow, and a city in ruins. Such a place "gives rise to weeping, laments, and cries." Prisoners are said to be "listening for snakes and scorpions in the darkness of the House." At the other end of the spectrum of justice, Nungal also asserts, "I temper severe punishments, I am a compassionate mother." Miguel Civil suggests why "the Warden of Mesopotamian jails is a woman":

> A prison sentence is a compassionate alternative to the death penalty, and compassion in Mesopotamia is mainly a female attribute. . . . The metaphors of the text insist on the darkness of the jail and on its solid enclosure. The prison's gate is a source of light. All this points to the underlying metaphor of the jail as a womb from which a new, rehabilitated man will, after expiating his crime, emerge to the light of day. (Civil, 78)

As with Nungal, compassion was emphasized by the reformer king Uruinimgina (formerly known as Urukagina), who granted a general amnesty and pardon to serious criminals. He claims to have "swept their prisons clean" upon his ascension to power in Lagash. Such kindnesses were not always the way of kings, as seen from the royal archives at Mari (c. 1800–1750 BC). In one text from this archive, Šamši-Addu I writes to his son Yasmaḫ-Addu that a prisoner might be sentenced to "disappear":

> I am sending you Simti-Eraḫ. He should stay in jail. Whether he lives or dies, no news about him must come out. He should receive 1 liter of beer and 5 liters of bread per day, as well as scented and (regular) oil for (personal) care. Whether living or dead he should be (forgotten). (ARM(T) 1.57; Sasson, 228)

Egypt

The "Turin Judicial Papyrus" records the trials of those who plotted the assassination of Ramesses III and refers to the use of magical wax figurines to neutralize the pharaoh's guards via execration rituals (*COS* 3.8). In addition to these guards, the Egyptian policing personnel comprised various other gatekeepers, temple and palace guards, border patrolmen, and military officials.

For most offenses, penalties such as public beating and hard labor in the mines appear to have better served the Egyptian sense of justice and order (*maʿat*) than punishment by execution. In Egyptian prisons, all prisoners lived and labored together regardless of crime or social status. They usually worked at weaving or milling. The *ḥnrt wr*, "great prison," of Thebes was a granary, and Egyptian art from the Middle Kingdom era depicts prisoners laboriously hand-grinding grain on large stone slabs. Egypt, known as the land of the Israelites' bondage in which they were forced to make bricks without straw (Exod 5), had a reputation for sentencing prisoners to forced labor in miserable conditions, often mining metals and precious stones or milling grain. Mutilation of prisoners was common, as seen in the Greek designation for the Egyptian penal settlement Rhinocorurua, "the [place of] cut-off noses" (Str. *Geogr.* 16.2, 31–32; Diod. Sic. *Bib. hist.* 1.60).

D. THE GRECO-ROMAN WORLD

Greece

Greek city-states created public authorities to determine crimes and punish criminals. The most efficient police force of antiquity was found in Sparta, where young men between the ages of twenty and thirty served as enforcement officers, keeping the large population of helots (enslaved Messenians) in subjugation to their masters and generally enforcing the stern laws of Sparta. Spartan youths were enlisted in this force, known as the *krypteia* (perhaps "secret service"), and were given the freedom to kill helots in order to intimidate them (Plu. *Lyc.* 28.3–7).

Herodotus relates the escape of Hegesistratus, who was held in a Spartan prison with one of his legs in stocks: "He got an iron weapon that was brought in some wise into his prison ... he cut off his own foot at the instep. This done, he burrowed through the wall out of the way of the guards that kept ward over him, and so escaped to Tegea" (*Hist.* 9.37).

The Attic orator Andocides records that three hundred Scythian archers were imported as a type of police force for Athens ca. 477 BC (Andocides, *On the Peace with Sparta* 503.5). The size of this corps was later increased to twelve hundred. These *toxotai* ("archers") figure prominently in the comedies of Aristophanes (*Lys.* 433, 455; *Thesm.* 923, 940; *Eccl.* 143, 258). The Scythians with their colorful trousers and peaked hats are depicted on over four hundred Greek vases. (See Yamauchi, 104–7.)

According to Attic court documents, both public and private authorities maintained Athenian order. "Not only does policing appear to have been a collective enterprise, but its methods were embedded in a variety of social institutions, resulting in the blurring of the line between state and society"—often privileging the powerful, as in any age (see Hunter, back cover). Other forerunners of modern police forces are attested in numerous papyri regarding the predominantly privately organized Ptolemaic security personnel of Hellenistic Egypt.

For personal crimes such as adultery, homicide, and theft, the aggrieved victim would, with the help of family and friends, apprehend the criminal and bring him to court. The *Areiopagos* ("The Hill of Ares" = "Mars Hill") was one such court, composed of former magistrates that included a special group known as the Eleven, who were in charge of prisons and of executions. Only in the case of one who owed the state a sum of money were the slave assistants of the Eleven dispatched to arrest the delinquent debtor.

In Athens, many of those in the *desmōtērion*, "place of chains," were restricted by a wide variety of shackles and stocks, although some were permitted limited freedom of movement (Andocides, *On the Mysteries* 1.48). The city's prisoners of war were held in the *dēmosion*, "the public [place/thing]," near the Athenian Agora (Thucydides, *Hist.* 5.18.7).

According to Plato, Socrates reasoned that punishments including imprisonment could be both rehabilitative and retributive, as well as valuable for restraining evil in others who observed a criminal's incarceration: "And it is fitting that every one under punishment rightly inflicted on him by another should either be made better and profit thereby, or serve as an example to the rest, that others seeing the sufferings he endures may in fear amend themselves" (*Gorg.* 525b). Criminologists today refer to these outcomes as specific deterrence (deterring the offender from committing new offenses) and general deterrence (deterring the observing public from criminal activity).

On the common term *phylakē*, the lexicographers Louw and Nida observe, "Practically all languages have terms for a jail or a prison, though in some instances a descriptive phrase is employed, 'a place where people are tied up' or 'a place to be chained.' In some instances, highly idiomatic expressions are used, 'a place for eating iron' or 'a room with rats'" (Louw and Nida, 85). None of these enjoys positive connotations.

Prisoners in general received different treatment depending on their social status and the seriousness of their crimes; slaves and serious offenders were tortured. Debtors were imprisoned to coerce their family and friends to repay their debts. A certain Androtion remained in prison for five years (Dem. *Timocr.* 125).

Demosthenes himself was imprisoned for debt in 323 BC because he could not pay the enormous fine that had been imposed on him for accepting bribes from the Macedonian court. When he escaped, he wrote in exile to the Athenians, "And surely my departure from Athens would not afford you just grounds for resentment against me. . . . in the first place, I was pained at contemplating the disgrace of imprisonment, and in the second, on account of my age I was in no condition to endure the bodily discomforts" (Dem. *Ep.* 2.17).

Many in prison suffered from hunger and thirst (Thucydides, *Hist.* 7.87.1–3). Rather than the state, family and friends were expected to provide food to the prisoners.

Executions, including Socrates's sentence of compulsory suicide (as mandated by a jury of 501 Athenians), also took place within a prison (Plato, *Phaed.* 57–61). In the Platonic dialogue that bears his name, Crito, a good friend of Socrates, is able to have the guard open the gate of the prison so that he can arrive at the side of Socrates even before he awakes. Crito, who with other friends has the funds to bribe the guards, begs Socrates to escape, but the latter declines to do so (*Crito* 44b–c).

After the majority of 501 jurors condemned Socrates to death, he remained in prison for thirty days, awaiting the return of a ceremonial ship from the island of Delos. On the day the board of Eleven released him from his fetters and allowed his family and friends to say farewell to him, no fewer than twenty persons crowded in to see him. After a bath, he drank a cup of hemlock. His last words were, "Crito, we owe a cock to Aesculapius. Pay it, and do not neglect it" (Plato, *Phaed.* 118a).

A poros (coarse limestone) building uncovered by the Agora has been identified by E. Vanderpool as the prison of Socrates. It consists of a series of rooms on either side of a corridor, a courtyard on the south, and a semi-detached annex of four rooms, which probably had an upper story. Vanderpool suggests that the annex housed the Eleven. While his arguments have convinced some scholars (e.g., Wycherley, 46–47), others remain skeptical (e.g., Hunter 1997, 319–23).

Rome

Although later legislation from the time of Justinian (r. AD 527–565; *Dig. Just.* 48.18.9) indicates that Roman law did not authorize imprisonment itself as punishment, numerous statements in earlier literary works imply that actual practices frequently did not match that theory. For example, Julius Caesar, according to Cicero, considered life imprisonment an "exemplary punishment" for a "heinous crime" (*Cat. Maj.* 4.7). Plutarch also seems to find nothing unusual in the fact that the poet Sotades "rotted in prison for many years" (*Mor.* 11a) before being thrown into the sea wrapped in lead for composing an insulting verse about Ptolemy II. The island of Pandateria (modern Ventotene), off the west coast of Italy, served as a prison for several women of the Roman imperial family who were banished for various reasons, including Julia, the daughter of Augustus, whose crime was adultery (Tac. *Ann.* 1.53; 14.63–64). Finally, Suetonius says that when Tiberius was inspecting the prisons and a man begged him for a speedy death, he replied, "I have not yet become your friend" (*Tib.* 61.5).

Roman prisoners were usually chained or manacled during the day, fastened into painful leg stocks at night, and held in quarters so cramped that they sometimes trampled each other to death (Libanius, *Orations* 33.41; 45.11, 31). Extreme crowding resulted in lack of oxygen, intense heat, horrific filth, and the spread of disease and lice (Diod. Sic. *Bib. hist.* 34.2.22–23). Beating was commonplace. The worst inner part of some prisons was underground in perpetual darkness (Acts 16:24, 29; *Cod. Theod.* 9.3; Sallust, *Bel. Cat.* 55.3–4; *T. Jos.* 9.1). Roman slave farms (sing. *carcer rusticus*) had dungeons for dangerous, disobedient, or even displeasing slaves. Such a dungeon was known as an *ergastulum* and was often underground with narrow windows out of the reach of the slaves (Pliny, *Nat.* 18.7.4; Columella, *Rust.* 1.6.3). These abusive structures were outlawed by Hadrian by the second century AD: "Houses of hard labour for slaves and free he abolished" (*S.H.A.* 18.9–10; cf. Gaius, *Inst.* 1.53).

The Stoic philosopher Epictetus (AD 55–135) commented on his preference toward introversion and the fact that others like him find themselves forced into undesirable social scenarios. In this context, he concludes, "where a man is against his will, that for him is a prison" (*Disc.* 1.12.23).

For possibly a century, the Roman Republic witnessed numerous political crises before its demise. As the shared governance of the Republic ended and the Roman Empire emerged under the victories of Octavian and the senate's bestowal of his title Caesar Augustus in 27 BC, a new approach was necessary to maintain public order:

> The need for a city police force was glaringly apparent at the end of the Republic, but the establishment of such an organization was not really possible under the old system, when there was no tradition of standing army units and the scramble for personal power escalated to the point of civil war. Significantly, Augustus waited until probably 13 BC before creating the Urban Cohorts (*Cohortes Urbanae*), commanded by the city prefect (*Praefectus Urbi*).
> (Southern, 119)

Ranking below the Urban Cohorts in Rome were the *Vigiles*, "watchmen," who primarily served as a nighttime firefighting force but also guarded against petty crimes (*Dig. Just.* 1.15). The Urban Cohorts, as city police, offset the influence of the Praetorian Guard—the immediate household troops of the emperor. Other military and governmental personnel of various ranks and statuses also performed duties associated with police (e.g., enforcing the law, preserving public order, protecting property and citizens, assisting in emergencies, registering complaints, investigating crimes, arresting and transporting criminals, and administering punishments).

E. THE JEWISH WORLD

The Bible holds up many Jewish examples of unjust imprisonment (e.g., Joseph, Jeremiah, Daniel and his friends, John the Baptist, and Paul). Early sages comforted detainees by telling them that though they were incarcerated, godly wisdom provides hope:

> When a righteous man was sold, wisdom did not desert him, but delivered him from sin. She descended with him into the dungeon, and when he was in prison she did not leave him, until she brought him the scepter of a kingdom and authority over his masters. Those who accused him she showed to be false, and she gave him everlasting honor. (Wis 10:13–14)

Conversely, this wisdom text warns that the condemnation of a guilty conscience brings paralyzing fears that cause the wicked to feel "shut up in a prison not made of iron" (Wis 17:16).

Various crimes were grounds for imprisonment. During one of the battles of the Maccabees (162 BC), a traitor named Rhodocus "gave secret information to the enemy; he was sought for, caught, and put in prison" (2 Mac 13:21). In AD 52, the Roman leader Ummidius Quadratus, governor of Syria, arrested Ananias the high priest and Ananus, the captain of the temple, after accusing them of acts of violence against the Samaritans. He had them taken bound to Rome for trial under Emperor Claudius Caesar, who later acquitted them (Tac. *Ann.* 20.6.2).

When Jewish confidence in the high priest's presiding over the Sanhedrin waned in 191 BC, the position of Nasi was created to serve as its head. The officeholder was recognized as the Jewish Patriarch and eventually honored by the Romans as part of its hegemonic hierarchy to the extent that he ruled the land of Israel with "the knowledge of the Emperor" (Orig. *Ep. Afr.* 10). The Romans recognized the jurisdiction of R. Judah ha-Nasi, compiler of the Mishnah, and supported the authority of his court, which is described in the following text:

> When a person came before Rabbi [Judah ha-Nasi] for judgment, if he accepted his verdict, well and good; if not, he would say to a member of his household, 'Show him the left side,' and he would show him a chopping movement in that direction. (*Eccl. Rab.* 10:2; Oppenheimer, 186)

Oppenheimer concludes that "there was a sort of police force associated with the Patriarch which helped to carry out court orders" as well as "the involvement of the Roman authorities in the execution of the sentences of Jewish courts" (Oppenheimer, 185–86). This collaboration was not always admired, as a later Talmudic haggadah reports: R. Joshua b. Korah called Eleazar b. Simeon "vinegar son of wine" for his service to the Romans as a police officer (*y. Maʿaś.* 3:8, 50d; *b. B. Meṣ.* 83b).

Judges were appointed through *sĕmîkâ*, the "laying on of hands" (Num 27:23; *y. Sanh.* 4:13), and courts were set up to administer justice in Jewish communities since ancient times. The *bêt dîn*, "house of judgment," met as a court to address matters both civil and criminal. A court of three judges decided civil matters, while a court of twenty-three judges ruled in criminal matters (*y. Sanh.* 1:3–4). The rabbis traced the origins of the *bêt dîn* back to Moses but considered its formal establishment to have occurred under the ninth-century BC king Jehoshaphat of Judah (*Deut. Rab.* 19:8). Under Ezra, courts were established to determine sentences, including imprisonment (Ezra 7:25–26), and later tradition suggests that he established a schedule for hearings on Mondays and Thursdays (*b. B. Qam.* 82a). The institution of the *bêt dîn* remained active throughout the Second Temple period and possibly later.

A Talmudic discussion on reciting the Shema records the experiences and reflections of Rabbi Akiba (AD 50–137), who was imprisoned and eventually martyred. It begins, "Once the wicked Government issued a decree forbidding the Jews to study and practise the Torah" (*b. Ber.* 61b). A discussion among the early Amoraim centers on such suffering in spite of often-miraculous rabbinic powers:

> R. Johanan once fell ill and R. Hanina went in to visit him. He said to him: Are your sufferings welcome to you? He replied: Neither they nor their reward. He said to him: Give me your hand. He gave him his hand and he raised him. Why could not R. Johanan raise himself? They replied: The prisoner cannot free himself from jail. (*b. Ber.* 5a)

While punishment by incarceration is not prescribed in the Torah, such did occur in the biblical period, and later Jewish law rendered the sentence of imprisonment appropriate for certain crimes. *Seder Neziqin*, "the order of damages" (the fourth section in the Mishnah, Tosefta, and Talmud), addresses numerous civil and criminal issues. Specifically, tractates *Sanhedrin*, "sitting together" or "council," and *Makkot*, "stripes," rule on specific punishments for crimes. Debtors in default were not imprisoned nor deprived of their basic necessities (Exod 22:24–26; Deut 24:6, 10–12), but thieves who were unable to make restitution could be enslaved (Exod 22:2–3). A criminal who was condemned a third time for the same offense after being punished twice by flogging was placed by the *bêt dîn* "in a cell and fed with barley bread, until his stomach bursts" (*b. Sanh.* 81b). This was effectively equivalent to the death penalty. The same tractate indicates that imprisonment should occur when one deserves the death penalty but is unable to receive this sentence due to some technicality: "One who commits murder without witnesses is placed in a cell and [forcibly] fed with bread of adversity and water of affliction" (*b. Sanh.* 81b). Outright death sentences were so uncommon that the Mishnah states, "A Sanhedrin that effects an execution once in seven years is branded a destructive tribunal" (*b. Mak.* 7a).

Confinement in a cell, *haknasâ lakkîppâ*, enabled courts to avoid issuing the sentence of execution directly (*y. Sanh.* 9:5; *t. Sanh.* 12:7–8). In the event that a man was imprisoned (or if he was unable to hear or speak, or if he was insane) a rabbinical court had the authority to issue a warning to his wife if there was suspicion that she may have strayed from marital fidelity (denoted by the term *śōtâ*). The wife was subject to the ordeal of jealousy (Num 5:12) and could be formally accused of adultery upon her husband's release from prison (*y. Soṭah* 4:5). Jewish prisoners could be offered release from prison in connection with the celebration of Passover or other festivals (*y. Pesaḥ.* 8:6; *y. Mak.* 3:1). The above-mentioned adage "The prisoner cannot free himself from jail" (*b. Ber.* 5a; *b. Sanh.* 95a) suggests that imprisonment as a punishment was well known.

F. THE CHRISTIAN WORLD

Paul warned Christians in Rome not to rebel against the authorities that God has established (Rom 13:1–2). Peter concurred: "Submit yourselves for the Lord's sake to every human institution, whether to a king as the one in authority, or to governors as sent by him for the punishment of evildoers and the praise of those who do right" (1 Pet 2:13–14, NASB). This sentiment of submission extended to the police forces of the Roman Empire, who persecuted the early followers of Jesus.

Polycarp, the bishop of Smyrna and an early martyr, encountered the local police, who arrested him and delivered him to the proconsul for not offering incense to Caesar. The arresting officers "found him in bed in an upstairs room in a small cottage; and though he still could have escaped from there to another place, he refused, saying, 'May God's will be done.'"

He lavishly fed them and sought their permission to pray at length. His prayer was so convicting that "many regretted that they had come after such a godly old man" (*Mart. Pol.* 7). The irenarch Herod, who brought Polycarp to the location where his impending death sentence would be carried out, was a type of police chief. Herod and his father pled with Polycarp, "Why, what harm is there in saying, 'Caesar is Lord,' and offering incense . . . thereby saving yourself?'" (*Mart. Pol.* 8). Throughout these tragic injustices, Polycarp's civil obedience is remarkable in its similarity to the submission of Jesus and Paul to ungodly authorities (Matt 6:10; Acts 21:14).

The first believers in Jerusalem were so overtaken with the importance of continued worship and fellowship that they eagerly shared their possessions (Acts 2:44; 4:32), to the extent that "there were no needy persons among them" (Acts 4:34). This charity was extended to the poor (Gal 2:10; 1 Cor 16:1) and even to prisoners, as collections were taken for the brethren in prison.

Tertullian of Carthage wrote an extensive letter of encouragement to those imprisoned for their faith and facing martyrdom. He urged, "The prison, indeed, is the devil's house as well, wherein he keeps his family. But you have come within its walls for the very purpose of trampling the wicked one under foot in his chosen abode" (*Mart.* 1). This spiritual battle is illustrated in the prison diary of the young heroine Perpetua, who wrote of her spiritual victories during incarceration. She chronicled her spiritual journey throughout her arrest and imprisonment, until just before she was executed at the military games in Carthage in 203. She writes of a vision in which she perceived that "I was not to fight with beasts, but against the devil. Still I knew that the victory was awaiting me" (*Martyrdom of Perpetua and Felicity* 3).

Patristic sources distinguish martyrs (who died for their faith) and confessors (who were willing to die). Many confessors endured imprisonment and torture. In the ninth year of Diocletian's reign, he issued an edict demanding the destruction of churches, the burning of Scripture, and the deprivation of various rights from Christians. "Two more edicts followed soon after, one ordering the imprisonment of all the church's leaders across the empire, the next commanding that every available means be used to force them to sacrifice" in allegiance to the imperial cult (Litfin, 146). In the last great persecution, Diocletian issued four edicts, in 303 and 304. According to Eusebius:

> An imperial letter was everywhere promulgated, ordering the razing of the churches to the ground and the destruction by fire of the Scriptures, and proclaiming that those who held high positions would lose all civil rights, while those in households, if they persisted in their profession of Christianity, would

be deprived of their liberty. . . . But not long afterwards we were further visited with other letters, and in them the order was given that the presidents of
the churches should all, in every place, be first committed to prison, and then
afterwards compelled by every kind of device to sacrifice. (*Hist. eccl.* 8.2.4–5)

The Christianization of the Empire brought discernable change for
prisoners. The Edict of Toleration of 311 promulgated by Emperor Galerius
legalized Christianity and ended the Diocletian persecution. Then, in 313,
Emperor Constantine and Licinius, ruler of the Balkans, met in Milan and
determined to improve policies toward Christians. Ultimately, the Edict of
Thessalonica, promulgated in 380, made Christianity the official religion of
the Empire. The Roman Emperor Theodosius I, who ruled from 379 to 395,
established Nicene Christianity as the law of the land. His later namesake
Theodosius II, emperor of Byzantium from 401 to 450, published the vast
law code that bears his name in 438/439 as a compilation of the laws of
emperors and legal scholars. Just as the Passover occasioned the pardon of
Jewish prisoners, the Code's so-called Sirmondian Constitutions ruled that
prisoners be released as part of the celebration of the resurrection and be
"restored to their pristine status" (*Sirm.* 7). The Constitutions also state that
"with the exception of the five capital crimes, all accused persons whom
the celebration of Easter finds in prison shall be released, in accordance
with the joy and veneration of so great a festivity" (*Sirm.* 8). The five capital
crimes were homicide, adultery, high treason, astrology (including poison-
ing and practicing magic), and forgery—such, declares the Constitutions,
"are not worthy of the enjoyment of the festive day" (*Sirm.* 8). Immorality
was also taken seriously. "Clerics shall not live with extraneous women;
the ravishers of holy maidens shall be punished with exile by deporta-
tion" (*Sirm.* 10). Sadly, Jews and pagans were also deported or pressured
to convert: "We order all persons of such ill-omened false doctrine to be
banished, unless swift reform should come to their aid" (*Sirm.* 6).

The rhetorician Lucian of Samosata (ca. 125–180) recounts the philosophical career and misguided wanderings of Peregrinos Proteus (ca.
95–165). Through his travels, "he learned the wondrous lore of the Christians" and for a while became a leader in the believing community and was
imprisoned (*Peregr.* 11). Lucian recounts how the Christians "left nothing
undone in the effort to rescue him" and seems disgusted by the extravagance of Christian concern:

> From the very break of day aged widows and orphan children could be seen
> waiting near the prison, while their officials even slept inside with him after
> bribing the guards. Then elaborate meals were brought in, and sacred books
> of theirs were read aloud, and excellent Peregrinus—for he still went by that
> name—was called by them "the new Socrates." (*Peregr.* 12)

When Peregrinus was exposed as a charlatan, he was expelled by the Christians and became a wandering Cynic philosopher. He ended his life by theatrically hurling himself into a pyre at the Olympic Games in AD 165.

Despite Lucian's mocking the Christians as gullible dupes, his account demonstrates that they were practioners of the NT ethic: "Continue to remember those in prison as if you were together with them in prison, and those who are mistreated as if you yourselves were suffering" (Heb 13:3).

Traditions from the fourth and fifth century began to embellish the imprisonments of Peter and Paul, locating them at the Mamertine Prison in Rome. While Peter evangelized in the Tullianum below, these traditions recounted, water miraculously sprang forth, enabling him to baptize his jailers. Since the fifth century, a stone crypt by the forum at Philippi has been designated as Paul's prison (see McRay, 288–89).

BIBLIOGRAPHY: R. S. Bagnall, "Army and Police in Roman Upper Egypt," *JARCE* 14 (1977), 67–86; J. V. Bartlet, "Two New Testament Problems: 1. St. Paul's Fate at Rome," *Expositor* 8.5 (1913), 464–68; R. A. Bauman, *Crime and Punishment in Ancient Rome* (1996); J. Bauschatz, "Ptolemaic Prisons Reconsidered," *The Classical Bulletin* 83 (2007), 1–48; J. A. Black et al., trans., *The Literature of Ancient Sumer* (2006); R. E. Brown, *The Death of the Messiah* (2 vols., 1994); M. Civil, "On Mesopotamian Jails and Their Lady Warden," in *The Tablet and the Scroll: Near Eastern Studies in Honor of William W. Hallo*, ed. M. E. Cohen, D. C. Snell, and D. B. Weisberg (1993), 72–78; H. Dörries, *Constantine the Great*, trans. R. H. Bainton (1972); J. Finegan, *The Archeology of the New Testament* (rev. ed.; 1992); G. W. Forell, *History of Christian Ethics* (1979); I. J. Gelb, "Prisoners of War in Early Mesopotamia," *JNES* 32 (1973), 70–98; L. Griffith, "The Fall of the Prison: Some Biblical and Historical Perspectives," *Brethren Life and Thought* 29 (1984), 9–22; G. Grote, *A History of Greece: From the Time of Solon to 403 B.C.*, ed. J. M. Mitchell and M. O. B. Caspari (1907); W. W. Hallo, "Notes from the Babylonian Collection, I: Nungal in the Egal: An Introduction to Colloquial Sumerian?" *JCS* 31 (1979), 161–65; W. W. Hallo, "Back to the Big House: Colloquial Sumerian, Continued," *Or* 54 (1985), 56–64; C. Homoth-Kuhs, *Phylakes und Phylakon-Steuer im griechisch-römischen Ägypten: Ein Beitrag zur Geschichte des antiken Sicherheitswesen* (2005); V. J. Hunter, "Plato's Prisons," *GR* 55 (2008), 193–201; V. J. Hunter, *Policing Athens: Social Control in the Attic Lawsuits, 420–320 B.C.* (1994); V. J. Hunter, "The Prison of Athens: A Comparative Perspective," *Phoenix* 51 (1997), 296–326; B. Kinman, "Debtor's Prison and the Future of Israel (Luke 12:57–59)," *JETS* 42.3 (1999), 411–25; G. L. Knapp, "Prison," in *ISBE* III.973–75; S. N. Kramer, *The Sumerians: Their History, Culture, and*

Character (1963); R. Lanciani, *The Ruins and Excavations of Ancient Rome* (1967); B. M. Litfin, *Early Christian Martyr Stories: An Evangelical Introduction with New Translations* (2014); G. Lopuszanski, "La police romaine et les Chrétiens," *AntCl* 20 (1951), 5–46; D. Lorton, "The Treatment of Criminals in Ancient Egypt through the New Kingdom," *JESHO* 20 (1977), 2–64; J. P. Louw and E. A. Nida, ed., *Greek-English Lexicon of the New Testament: Based on Semantic Domains* (2nd ed., 1989); J. McRay, *Archaeology and the New Testament* (1991); M. Miguéns, "Pablo Prisionero," *Liber Annuus* 8 (1957–58), 5–112; F. Millar, "Condemnation to Hard Labour in the Roman Empire, from the Julio-Claudians to Constantine," *Papers of the British School at Rome* 52 (1984), 124–47; H. Musurillo, trans., *The Acts of the Christian Martyrs* (1972); A. Oppenheimer, "Jewish Penal Authority in Roman Judaea," in *Jews in a Graeco-Roman World*, ed. M. Goodman (1998), 181–91; T. S. Pattie, "The Creation of the Great Codices," *The Bible as Book: The Manuscript Tradition*, ed. J. L. Sharpe III and K. Van Kampen (1998), 61–72; E. M. Peters, "Prison before the Prison: The Ancient and Medieval Worlds," in *The Oxford History of the Prison: The Practice of Punishment in Western Society*, ed. N. Morris and D. J. Rothman (1995), 3–47; R. Pirngruber, "Policemen in 1st Millennium BC Babylonia," *The Ancient Near East Today* 3.9 (2015), 1; R. Pirngruber and S. Tost, "Police Forces in First Millennium BC Babylonia and Beyond," *Kaskal* 10 (2013), 69–87; W. M. Ramsay, "The Imprisonment and Supposed Trial of St. Paul in Rome," *Expositor* 8.5 (1913), 264–84; B. M. Rapske, *The Book of Acts and Paul in Roman Custody* (1994); B. M. Rapske, "The Importance of Helpers to the Imprisoned Paul in the Book of Acts," *TynBul* 42.1 (1991), 3–30; B. M. Rapske, "Prison, Prisoner," in *DNTB* 827–30; D. G. Reid, "Prison, Prisoner," *DPL* 752–54; O. F. Robinson, *Penal Practice and Penal Policy in Ancient Rome* (2007); H. W. F. Saggs, *Everyday Life in Babylonia & Assyria* (1965); J. M. Sasson, trans. and ed., *From the Mari Archives: An Anthology of Old Babylonian Letters* (2015); E. J. Schochet, *Animal Life in Jewish Tradition* (1984); A. Seri, *The House of Prisoners: Slavery and State in Uruk during the Revolt against Samsu-iluna* (2013); D. C. Snell, *Life in the Ancient Near East: 3100–332 B.C.E.* (1997); P. Southern, *The Roman Army: A Social and Institutional History* (2007); P. M. Steinkeller, "The Reforms of UruKAgina and an Early Sumerian Term for 'Prison,'" *Aula Orientalis* 9 (1991), 227–33; E. Vanderpool, "The Prison of Socrates," *Illustrated London News* 264.6 (1976), 87–88; E. Vanderpool, "The State Prison of Ancient Athens," in *From Athens to Gordion*, ed. K. DeVries (1980), 17–31; K. van der Toorn, "Judges XVI 21 in the Light of the Akkadian Sources," *VT* 36.2 (1986), 248–53; K. van der Toorn, "Prison," *ABD* 5.468–69; R. VerSteeg, *Law in the Ancient World* (2002); C. S. Wansink, *Chained in Christ: The Ex-*

perience and Rhetoric of Paul's Imprisonments (1996); R. E. Wycherley, *The Stones of Athens* (1978); E. M. Yamauchi, *Foes from the Northern Frontier: Invading Hordes from the Russian Steppes* (1982).

DLH and TMS

See also ARMIES, CITIES, LAWS & CRIMES, and MINING.

PROSTITUTION

Prostitution is the act of offering sexual services to another for payment. These services may include heterosexual or homosexual acts.

A. THE OLD TESTAMENT

There are several Hebrew words that are translated "prostitute," "whore," or "harlot" in modern versions. The most common word is *zōnâ*. The act of prostitution is denoted by the related words *zĕnûnîm*, *zĕnût*, and *taznût*. These words usually refer to a literal act of prostitution (Gen 38:15, 24; Judg 16:1), but they are also frequently used as a spiritual metaphor describing the fallen, rebellious, or compromised condition of Israel and Judah (Isa 1:21; Jer 2:20; Ezek 16:1–63; 23:1–49) or surrounding nations (Isa 23:15–16; Nah 3:1–7).

According to the Law of Moses, a woman who has been a prostitute may not marry a priest (Lev 21:14). The law also forbids parents from prostituting their daughters (Lev 19:29). Because prostitution is mentioned in almost every historical period, it must have been an ongoing profession, although women occasionally risked extreme penalties (Gen 38:15–24). Jephthah was the son of a prostitute (Judg 11:1), and Samson consorted at least once with a prostitute (Judg 16:1). Solomon judged between two prostitutes in a case that demonstrated his wisdom (1 Kgs 3:16). Proverbs advises men not to waste their goods upon prostitutes (7:10; 29:3), especially warning against "strange" or "foreign" women (2:16; 5:20; 22:14).

Another Hebrew word, *qĕdēšâ*, is usually translated as "hierodule" or "sacred prostitute." Deuteronomy 23:17 states that there should be no male *qādēš* or female *qĕdēšâ* from among the sons and daughters of Israel. In Hos 4:14 the terms *zōnâ* and *qĕdēšâ* seem to be used as synonyms. Another passage where both these words are used for the same person is the story of Tamar and Judah in Gen 38:15–24. The widow Tamar, after waiting a long time for her father-in-law Judah to provide her with a husband, disguises herself as a prostitute and has sexual relations with him. Judah has no money to pay, so he leaves his staff and his personal seal with her, thinking she is a *zōnâ* and promising to pay her later. The next day, when he sends his friend with a goat, she has disappeared. His friend inquires among the locals about where the *qĕdēšâ* who was by the road has gone, but he cannot find her. This oft-discussed passage offers several possibilities. The first is that *zōnâ* and *qĕdēšâ* are synonyms. The second is that these terms may represent different kinds of prostitutes, one secular and one sacred. The third is that Judah's friend may have desired to protect Judah's reputation by asking the locals for the location of a simple temple worker. Here, as in other places, the meaning of *qĕdēšâ* is unclear. Thus, while *zōnâ* clearly refers to a prostitute, *qĕdēšâ* may denote a prostitute, a female temple worker, a cult devotee, a sacred prostitute of a fertility cult, or a woman who dedicated the earning of prostitution to the temple or used such earnings to pay a vow. Part of the problem is that this word is infrequently used, appearing only four times in the Hebrew Bible (Gen 38:21, 22; Hos 4:14; Deut 23:17). In each case, the context indicates the possibility of sexual and religious activity.

The masculine form of the word, *qādēš*, is found in 1 Kgs 14:24; 15:12; 22:46; 2 Kgs 23:7; and Deut 23:17–19. Though *qādēš* has the literal meaning of one who is sacred or set apart, sexual overtones are attributed to it because Deut 23:17–18 [Heb. vss. 18–19] associates the *qādēš* with a term, *keleb*, that is usually translated "dog" but that in this context may refer to a homosexual male prostitute. While older scholarship associates *keleb* with one's fidelity to one's god or lord, there is presently little agreement as to whether *qādēš* and *qĕdēšâ* have a sacred as well as a sexual meaning in each OT context. Philological comparisons to related cultic words in other ancient Near Eastern cultures offer interesting suggestions but are inconclusive. It is possible that both the *qādēš* and the *qĕdēšâ* had a cultic and sexual function.

B. THE NEW TESTAMENT

In the NT, a common prostitute serves as a symbol of redemption in the case of Rahab the harlot (*pornē*), whose heroic faith in protecting the spies of Joshua is cited in Heb 11:31 and Jas 2:25. Rahab appears in Matthew's genealogy of Jesus (Matt 1:5), as does Tamar (Matt 1:3).

It is possible that the woman who anoints Jesus with perfume was a prostitute, based upon the Pharisee's reaction (Luke 7:37–39). In any case, Jesus speaks of prostitutes entering the kingdom of God as an example of how the humble repent and receive grace while the proud reject his message (Matt 21:31–32). Jesus's story of the prodigal son includes a description of how the young man wasted his inheritance with prostitutes (Luke 15:13, 30–32).

The word *porneia* is used in the Gospels, Acts, and the Epistles to denote the moral prohibition of any kind of sex outside of marriage. It is usually translated as "fornication" or "immorality" (Matt 5:32; Mark 7:21; Acts 15:20, 29; 21:25; 2 Cor 12:21; Gal 5:19; Eph 5:3; 1 Thess 4:3). This would include prostitution.

The most important text that concerns Christians and prostitutes is 1 Cor 6:15–20. It is here that prostitution itself is directly interdicted as an act that defiles the temple of one's body. According to the text, joining oneself to a prostitute, sacred or secular, defiles the body, the temple of the Holy Spirit. Thus prostitution is subject to the same kind of disapproval in the NT as it was in the OT. It is perhaps no accident that these verses are applied to the church in Corinth, a famous port city with a reputation for numerous brothels and taverns. Strabo mentions that Corinth had over one thousand temple prostitutes dedicated to Aphrodite (*Geogr.* 8.6.20). This is part of a long tradition of sacred prostitution that dates to the Classical period and earlier, when the prayers of Corinthian temple prostitutes were considered to have contributed to the defeat of the Persian army (Simonides, *Epigram* 14; *Deipn.* 13.575). Corinth was destroyed by the Romans in 146 BC and rebuilt by Caesar in 44 BC as a Roman colony. It is possible that by Paul's time sacred prostitution had been reestablished or that there was sexual activity associated with religious feasts, though no source confirms this.

Prostitution is also used metaphorically in the NT to depict spiritual unfaithfulness. Thus the words *pornē* and *porneia* are used to describe the great prostitute and her activities in the book of Revelation (Rev 17:1, 15–16; 19:2), and the word *pornos* describes those outside of grace at the final judgment (Rev 21:8; 22:15).

C. THE NEAR EASTERN WORLD

Mesopotamia

In the *Gilgamesh Epic*, the prostitute Shamhat (whose name means "luscious one") seduces the wild man Enkidu, who has been sent by the gods to tame Gilgamesh. In his deathbed curse, Enkidu implies that the normal venue for prostitutes was the tavern. The Sumerian Inanna (Akkadian Ishtar) was the goddess of prostitutes. Many scholars believe she had cultic personnel performing sacred prostitution in her temples. Clay and lead figurines depict sexual intercourse in possible religious contexts.

The point where religion, sexual activity, and prostitution intersect has been subject to new analyses on philological and historical grounds. It has long been assumed that the religious rituals of the ancient Near East contained sexual components involving prostitution, specifically in the form of (1) sexual activity associated with temple worship and (2) the rite of sacred marriage between the ruler of a city-state and the high priestess of a temple complex, representing the union of Dumuzi and Inanna (Ishtar). In scholarly literature the former is referred to as "cultic prostitution" and the latter as the rite of "sacred marriage" (*hieros gamos*). Both are usually considered fertility rituals. The evidence often cited is erotic artwork, erotic elements in hymns dedicated to Inanna/Ishtar, and lists of women who are associated with temples and who are assumed to have a sexual function.

A new generation of scholars has attempted to counter this evidence in a number of interesting ways. For example, some have revived older interpretations of sexual intercourse depicted in art as mere pornography with no ritual function. They also assert that female personnel in various Mesopotamian temples did not have a sexual role. This recent scholarship tends to dismiss what is referred to as "the myth and ritual school," popularized by Frazer's 1922 edition of *The Golden Bough*, which contributed to the concept that sexual motifs commemorated divine unions to establish fertility. Scholars of more recent revisionist position argue that Mesopotamian love songs, hymns involving Inanna and Dumuzi, and sexual images had popular as opposed to royal audiences and that these simply served to aid courtship, marriage, and sexual instruction to ease anxiety about sex.

One significant group of evidence supporting this new scholarly position comes from the numerous economic texts that have been recovered from temples in Mesopotamia. For example, about two thousand tablets from the Ur III period have been recovered from Inanna's temple in Nippur. Of these, 1163 are economic in nature. None of these economic texts list prostitution as a source of temple income.

In addition, words that older scholarship translated as "prostitute" may have other meanings. For example, the Sumerian term KAR.KID (and its Akkadian equivalent *harimtu*) had been defined as "prostitute." More recently, a reevaluation indicates that these may simply denote unmarried, independent women, some of whom were possibly prostitutes but others not so. A phrase that occurs in Akkakian sources that is usually translated as "the *harimtu* of the streets" has now been interpreted as merely referring to a single woman who lived independently of her father's authority (Assante, Budin). In several scribal legal exercises, as well as laws from the Code of Lipit Ishtar, the paternity of children born from a man's union with a KAR.KID, or *harimtu*, seems not to be in question, and under several circumstances a child of this union can be designated an heir. In addition, Ishtar, who is periodically referred to as a *harimtu*, is usually not designated as a prostitute in love poetry but as an independent, unmarried woman. However, there is one notable exception to this idea about Ishtar's status. In *A Balbale to Inanna as Nanaya*, this goddess names two different prices for two different sexual positions.

*Harimtu*s were possibly women who were sexually active outside of marriage as distinct from prostitutes, who demanded remuneration. But it is clear from the primary sources that in the ancient Near East a woman unconnected with husband or father had a social and legal status that did not differ very much from those of an actual prostitute. Sometimes terms used to describe other legal categories of women use *harimtu* as a synonym, or they are shown to be associated with *harimtu*s and thus are assumed to be prostitutes. Women categorized in texts as *kezretu*, *šamhatu*, or *qadištu*, terms that currently have no independent definitions, have been assumed by scholars to be prostitutes because they are associated with *harimtu*s in other texts. But the difference between a *harimtu* who is a prostitute and one who was promiscuous was possibly socially indistinct. These revisionist theories rejecting the concept of cultic prostitution in the ancient Near East, and by extension, ancient Israel, have convinced many but not all scholars.

Egypt

Evidence for prostitution in Egypt is very limited. Documents and graffiti from the New Kingdom workmen's village at Deir el-Medina seem to indicate that prostitutes were available. Female singers buried at Abydos had possibly served as prostitutes. The clearest evidence comes from Turin Papryus 55001, which was acquired in 1820 but not published until 1973. A woman who is possibly a prostitute is shown in twelve erotic scenes with a bald man. She is called a singing girl who serves Hathor, the goddess of love. Captions include the woman saying, "Let me make it nice for you" and "O you wicked man!" (Manniche, Omlin).

D. THE GRECO-ROMAN WORLD

Greece

Prostitution of various kinds was practiced in the Greek world. There are perhaps fifty Greek words that can be translated as "prostitute." Most of these are colloquial terms, such as *chamaitypē*, which literally means "ground-striker"; the most generic term is *porne*. Any Greek word containing the morpheme *porn-* can describe some aspect of prostitution. The word *porneuō* means "to prostitute oneself"; *porneion* means "brothel"; *porneia* may mean "adultery," "fornication," or "prostitution"; and *pornoboskeō* means "to maintain a brothel." Generally, these terms describe the activities of a variety of women. The basest would be the slave woman serving in a dingy brothel or walking the streets. Others possibly in view in such terms are women who served as prostitutes in or near the great temples of Greek cities.

Beside these, there was a class of prostitutes known as the *hetairai*. Although the *hetairai* belonged to a unique class of courtesans, the general term *porne* is often used to describe its members. The *hetairai* clearly existed for the pleasure of men (Pseudo-Demosthenes, *Against Neaera* 59.122). Ancient sources depict *hetairai* as witty, intelligent female companions to men who often attended the symposia, the famous male drinking banquets. They provided games, music, and companionship, as well as sexual pleasure (Athenaeus, *Deipn.* 13). Many *hetairai* had notorious reputations because of their great wealth. The Thracian Rhodophis, a contemporary of the poetess Sappho and the lover of her brother, Charaxus of Mytilene, was believed by Herodotus to have purchased her own pyramid from her earnings in Egypt (Sappho, fragments 5, 15V; Her. *Hist.* 2.134–135). While this is legendary, it is apparent that she offered iron spits, a rich offering, to the temple of Delphi. Other *hetairai* gained the property and money of their lovers (Xenophon, *Mem.* 3.11.4–15). Later traditions indicate that Aspasia, the *hetaira* lover of Pericles, was one of the most influential women of Classical Greece. According to Plutarch, she encouraged the 440 BC expedition against Samos (*Per.* 24–25). She also gained the respect of the Athenian philosophical circle and was a teacher of rhetoric (Plu. *Per.* 24.3; Xenophon, *Oec.* 3.15; Cic. *Inv.* 31.51). While much of the material about her is legendary or exaggerated, the fact that she was lampooned as the cause of the Peloponnesian War (431–404 BC) indicates her notoriety (Aristoph. *Ach.* 527–530).

No child born of a prostitute could inherit his or her father's property. Children of these unions were known as *nothoi*, "bastards," and could not vote in Greek assemblies as citizens (Isaios, *On the Estate of Philoctemon* 6; Arist. *Ath. pol.* 26.4). Indeed, a common tactic of a political enemy in court was to try to throw doubt on an opponent's paternity. Fear of this explains one reason why women in Classical Greece were kept in seclusion, with only limited access to the world outside their homes (Xenophon, *Oec.* VI-X; Arist. *Pol.* 1.13). In the ideology of Classical Athens, wives were considered the opposite of *hetairai* in most respects. Apollodorus declared, "We have courtesans [*hetairai*] for pleasure, concubines for the daily tending of the body, and wives to beget legitimate children and have a trustworthy guardian of what is at home" (Pseudo-Demosthenes, *Against Neaera* 59.122).

Rome

In Rome, prostitution was legal and tolerated (Cic. *Cael.* 48–50). Prostitutes even had a holiday (April 25–26) dedicated to them. The most common word in Latin for "prostitute" was *meretrix*, although in Roman literature there are at least fifty synonyms or euphemisms. In most cases, there was little or no stigma attached to any male who visited a brothel (Horace, *Sat.* 1.2.31–35). In fact, a number of prominent Romans ran brothels on property they owned, usually through the management of a slave or freedman client (*Dig. Just.* 5.3.27.1). It is also evident that men and women practiced prostitution not only in brothels but also in other settings, such as in taverns or at city entrances. Sometime they plied their trade in the tombs outside the city, or even the forum (*Dig. Just.* 23.2.43. pr.; Plautus, *Curc.* 461–485; Martial, *Ep.* 1.34; 3.82). Most legal and literary evidence in Roman sources involves female prostitutes.

Pompeii provides unique evidence of prostitution in the first century. Though the activity of prostitutes was not limited to specialized buildings or rooms, a number of these are preserved in the city as a result of its burial under volcanic ash by Mount Vesuvius in AD 79. In some cases, a room dedicated to sexual activity, known as a *cella meretricia*, can be recognized by the remains of a permanent concrete bed in a single room that is often associated with a private home or another business. This would have been covered by cushions when used. Sometimes sexual services were offered in inns and taverns, but fewer than half of the inns and taverns in Pompeii have nearby them any of the erotic graffiti associated with brothels. It is also possible that prostitutes may have worked in some of the baths at Pompeii.

Clients often left graffiti behind in the outside walls near an establishment; these graffiti usually contained their names and expressions of their satisfaction with the services offered. Often, in various places around the city, the name of a prostitute would be scratched into a wall with the price of her services. Most prostitutes cost not much more than the price of a glass of wine or a meal.

One specialized building in Pompeii was dedicated to prostitution. It has been designated the "Grand *Lupanar* [i.e., Brothel]" in most tour guides and is located at VII.xii.18–19. The building has an odd triangular shape and has two floors. Five rooms on the first floor, all *cellae meretricia*, were dedicated to the sex trade. The upstairs rooms apparently made up an apartment. At the entrance of each *cella meretricia* was a picture of a sexual act, possibly related to the specialty of the woman within. Outside this structure is the greatest concentration of erotic graffiti in the city. The word "pornography," which literally means "the writing of prostitutes," was coined to describe the graffiti of this kind from Pompeii.

In the Roman Empire, a number of social prohibitions were directed against prostitutes. The most important was the fact that a prostitute could never have *conubium*, the legal right to marriage, and thus she was free from the penalty of Augustan adultery laws (*Dig. Just.* 23.243.4). A prostitute's child in Rome could never be a legitimate heir to an estate due to questionable paternity. These prohibitions were extended periodically to severely limit marriage potential for women who probably were not prostitutes but who worked in public in lower-class jobs; this included cooks, waitresses, and even those who sold vegetables (*Dig. Just.* 48.5). According to Roman law, such women "made a living from their bodies" and took money from customer's hands. This is a metaphor of the prostitute's trade, and such women's status was equally low. This barred them from the traditional role of a Roman matron. Most women in these positions were slaves or freedwomen. Roman laws classified them as "infamous" (i.e., having the legal status of *infamia*).

Abandoned babies were often raised as prostitutes. Free (i.e., non-slave) prostitutes had to be registered. They were recognizable by their dress: women wore togas and not *stolae*; men wore loose girdles and left their shoulders exposed.

Roman men from a variety of classes would see prostitutes or frequent brothels. Roman males, like men in earlier Greek society, had a significant amount of sexual freedom, as opposed to the severe restrictions placed upon citizen women. Before marriage, it was common for young men to indulge themselves with prostitutes in the Suburra, the red-light district of Rome. A Roman male could have sex with most women who did not have *conubium* (the legal right to marry) without risking a charge of adultery or *stuprum* (illegal sex). This would include prostitutes, foreign women, slaves (of either sex), and women divorced due to adultery. Children born of these unions could receive gifts from their fathers but no inheritance. Besides marriage prohibitions and low social status, prostitutes had to pay a tax based upon the income of their trade (Suet. *Cal.* 40; Dio Cassius [in the Epitome of Xiphilinus 59.28.8]). Such a tax based upon income was a unique innovation attributed to Caligula.

Some Roman writers regarded prostitution as shameful and foolish. One author who attacked brothels on moral grounds was Dio Chrysostom (*The Euboean Discourse* 133–138).

E. THE JEWISH WORLD

Sirach warns: "Wine and women lead intelligent men astray, and the man who consorts with harlots is very reckless" (19:2). Commenting on Deut 23:18, Josephus remarks: "The Deity has pleasure in naught that proceeds from outrage, and no shame could be worse than the degradation of the body" (*Ant.* 4.206). Likewise, Philo declares: "The hire of a harlot should not be brought into the temple; the hire, that is, of one who has sold her personal charms and chosen a scandalous life for the sake of the wages of shame" (*Spec.* 1.280). He also observes, "The harlots' traffic indeed is often brought to a close by old age, since when the freshness of their charm is passed, all cease to seek them now that their bloom is faded like the bloom of flowers" (*Spec.* 1.282).

Antiochus IV defiled the temple of Jerusalem with prostitutes (2 Macc 6:3–4). The *Psalms of Solomon* warns that "They set up the sons of Jerusalem for derision because of her prostitutes" (2:11). This could be because holy places were being defiled with prostitution on the premises or it could be a metaphor for spiritual apostasy. The rabbis declared that *zĕnût* (which can refer to prostitution, fornication, or immorality) was one of the causes for the destruction of the temple in AD 70 (*m. Soṭah* 9:13). Rabbinic literature takes note of the fact that some Jewish captives were forced into prostitution, and that some women were driven to prostitution by poverty (*y. Taʿan.* 1:4, 64b).

F. THE CHRISTIAN WORLD

The Fourth Mandate of the *Shepherd of Hermas*, written in the first half of the second century, demands faithfulness in marriage and the avoidance of any desire toward another woman. Hippolytus, a Roman priest from the first quarter of the third century, refused to baptize people from a number of disreputable occupations, among them male and female prostitutes (Hippolytus, *Trad. ap.* 16).

Canons 12 and 44 of the Council of Elvira (early fourth century) also disciplined those involved with prostitution. Oddly, in Canon 12 parents who sell themselves or their children into prostitution are denied communion even at death, but in Canon 44 a prostitute who has repented and who has married may be immediately accepted into the church. Church laws from the time of Constantine onward seem to manifest a concerted effort to enforce morality upon the Christian population and in particular to regulate the sexuality of women of all classes, far more than pre-Christian Roman law.

According to Eusebius, Constantine destroyed a temple in Aphaca on Mt. Lebanon (Mt. Libanus) in Phoenicia where various kinds of sexual activity, including prostitution, took place (*Coet. sanct.* 8.5–7). Pope Leo I tried to ban prostitution in 460, but the tax on prostitution continued to be collected until 498.

Mary Magdalene, though not identified in the NT as a prostitute, was later identified by Christians with the unnamed "sinful woman" in Luke 7 and became a model of redemption for prostitutes-turned-saints, such as Mary of Egypt and Pelagia the Harlot. In many instances, there were special efforts to convert and reform prostitutes. In the sixth century, the Empress Theodora, herself a former tavern dancer and prostitute, established the monastery Metanoia ("Repentance") for the spiritual development of prostitutes (Procopius, *Buildings* 1.9.1–10). The emperor Justinian emancipated slaves who had been forced into prostitution by their masters. The next few centuries witnessed the efforts of monks, such as the Blessed Abramios and Saint Symeon Salos, to convert prostitutes to the faith and restore them to a holy life. "Holy fools" in the Byzantine tradition occasionally attempted to convert prostitutes back to their faith by unconventional means.

BIBLIOGRAPHY: J. N. Adams, "Words for 'Prostitute' in Latin," *Rheinisches Museum für Philologie* 126 (1983), 321–58; J. Assante, "From Whores to Hierodules: The Historiographic Invention of Mesopotamian Female Sex Professionals" in *Ancient Art and Its Historiography*, ed. A. A. Donohue and M. D. Fullerton (2003), 13–47; P. Bird, "'To Play the Harlot': An Inquiry into an Old Testament Metaphor," in *Gender and Difference in Ancient Israel*, ed. P. L. Day (1989), 75–94; G. Brunet, "L'hébreu kèlèb," *VT* 35 (1985), 485–88; S. L. Budin, *The Myth of Sacred Prostitution in Antiquity* (2008); J. B. Burns, "Qādēš and Qĕdēšā: Did They Live off Immoral Earnings?" *Proceedings: EGL & MWBS* 15 (1995), 157–68; J. Davidson, *Courtesans and Fishcakes: The Consuming Passions of Classical Athens* (1997); J. Day, "Does the Old Testament Refer to Sacred Prostitution and Did it Actually Exist in Ancient Israel?" in *Biblical and Near Eastern Essays: Studies in Honour of Kevin J. Cathcart*, ed. C. McCarthy and J. F. Healey (2004), 2–21; P. E. Dion, "Did Cultic Prostitution Fall into Oblivion during the Postexilic Era?" *CBQ* 43 (1981), 41–48; C. Edwards, *The Politics of Immorality in Ancient Rome* (1993); W. Fauth, "Sakrale Prostitution im Vorderen Orient und im Mittelmeerraum," *JAC* 31 (1988), 24–39; E. J. Fisher, "Cultic Prostitution in the Ancient Near East? A Reassessment," *BTB* 6 (1976), 225–36; J. M. Ford, "Bookshelf on Prostitution," *BTB* 23 (1993), 128–34; M. I. Gruber, "Hebrew qĕdēšāh and her Canaanite and Akkadian Cognates," *UF* 18 (1986), 133–48; I. Hamley, "What's Wrong with 'Playing the Harlot'? The Meaning of זנה in Judges 19:2," *TynBul* 66 (2015), 41–62; R. A.

Henshaw, *Male and Female: The Cultic Personnel: The Bible and the Rest of the Ancient Near* (1994); H. Herter, "Die Soziologie der antiken Prostitution im Lichte des heidnischen und christlichen Schrifttums," *JAC* 3 (1960), 70–111; E. Keuls, "The Hetaera and the Housewife: The Splitting of the Female Psyche in Greek Art," *Mededelingen van het Nederlands Historisch Instituut te Rome* 44–45 (1983), 23–40; W. G. Lambert, "Prostitution," in *Aussenseiter und Randgruppen: Beiträge zu einer Sozialgeschichte des Alten Orients*, ed. V. Haas (1992), 127–57; G. Leick, *Sex and Eroticism in Mesopotamian Literature* (1994); G. Lerner, "The Origin of Prostitution in Ancient Mesopotamia," *Signs: Journal of Women in Culture and Society* 11 (1986), 236–54; B. MacLachlan, "Sacred Prostitution and Aphrodite," *Studies in Religion* 21.2 (1992), 145–62; L. Manniche, *Sexual Life in Ancient Egypt* (1997); T. A. J. McGinn, *Prostitution, Sexuality, and the Law in Ancient Rome* (1998); T. A. J. McGinn, "The Taxation of Roman Prostitutes," *Helios* 16 (1989), 79–110; J. A. Omlin, *Der Papyrus 55001 und seine satirisch-erotischen Zeichnungen und Inschriften*, (1973); S. Pomeroy, *Goddesses, Whores, Wives, and Slaves* (1975); A. Richlin, ed., *Pornography and Representation in Greece and Rome* (1991); B. S. Rosner, "Temple Prostitution in 1 Corinthians 6:12–20," *NovT* 40 (1998), 336–51; A. Rousselle, *Porneia: On Desire and the Body in Antiquity*, trans. F. Pheasant (1988); T. Scheer and M. Lindner, ed., *Tempelprostitution im Altertum* (2009); K. van der Toorn, "Female Prostitution in Payment of Vows in Ancient Israel," *JBL* 108 (1989), 193–205; B. Ward, *Harlots of the Desert: A Study of Repentance in Early Monastic Sources* (1987); J. G. Westenholz, "Tamar, *Qĕdēšā, Qadištu*, and Sacred Prostitution in Mesopotamia," *HTR* 82 (1989), 245–65; E. Yamauchi, "Cultic Prostitution: A Case Study in Cultural Diffusion," in *Orient and Occident*, ed. H. A. Hoffner (1973), 213–22.

JFD

See also ADULTERY, BANQUETS, INFANTICIDE, KISSES & EMBRACES, and MARRIAGE.

PURITY & IMPURITY

Many societies in antiquity held concepts of purity and impurity, which maintained that certain actions could defile a person, such as contact with a corpse. Such defilement would require purification, usually by water, before the affected individual would be restored to a state of ritual purity, enabling him or her to participate in religious activities, such as entering a temple.

A. THE OLD TESTAMENT

Foundational to the idea of purity in the OT is the holiness of God. Israel was challenged to "be holy, because I am holy" (Lev 11:45; see also Lev 19:2; 20:7, 26; 21:8). The central idea of the root *qdš* ("holy" or "sacred") is best understood as "separateness" (Young 1965, 242). God's holiness separates him from human beings: "For I am God, and not a man—the Holy One among you" (Hos 11:9). He is also separate from sin and the mundane. Of the Lord, Habakkuk declares, "Your eyes are too pure to look on evil; you cannot tolerate wrongdoing" (Hab 1:13). The OT concept of purity refers to those who are free from any physical, ritual, or moral contamination.

The principal root for "pure" or "clean" in the Hebrew text is *thr*, which appears roughly two hundred times, with nearly half of the usages in Leviticus and Numbers. Cognate roots in Ugaritic and Arabic carry the same meaning. The LXX translates the Hebrew verb *ṭāhar* with *katharizō*, "to purify," and the related adjective and noun as *katharos*, "pure," and *katharismos*, "purity." Many of the uses of this Hebrew root are in connection with gold. The adjective *ṭāhôr* is frequently used to describe the equipment of the tabernacle (Exod 25:17) and the temple (1 Chr 28:17), as well as the throne of Solomon (2 Chr 9:17).

The Hebrew adjective *zak*, "pure, clean," is used in the Pentateuch only for oil (Exod 27:20; Lev 24:2) and frankincense (Exod 30:34; Lev 24:7), but elsewhere it is applied to people (Job 8:6; 33:9), doctrine (Job 11:4), and conduct (Prov 16:2; 20:11). The verb *bārar* means "to purify" or "to clean," while the adjective *bar* describes that which is "clean" or "pure." The latter is commonly employed to describe a human condition. For example, Ps 24:4 speaks of a "pure heart" and Song of Songs refers to the maiden as "pure" (6:10).

The idea of "uncleanness" is conveyed by the verb *ṭāmē²*, the essential meaning of which is "to be(come) unclean." It appears over 150 times in the Old Testament; the related adjective *ṭāmē²*, "unclean," occurs eighty-eight times and the related noun *ṭum²â* ("uncleanness") is employed thirty-six times. The LXX translates these terms with *miainō* ("to defile"), *akathartos* ("unclean"), and *akatharsia* ("uncleanness"). Also used to designate uncleanness is the verb *gā²al*, "to defile." One object of pollution or stain is human hands: "For your hands are stained [*něgō²ălû*] with blood" (Isa 59:3). The city of Jerusalem is called "the city of oppressors, rebellious and defiled [*nig²ālâ*]" (Zeph 3:1)!

Following scholarly convention, Jonathan Klawans argues that there are two categories of impurity in the OT, "ritual" and "moral." He readily acknowledges the problems of this terminology, which is not found in the biblical text, but still finds it the best (Klawans, 22). According to Klawans,

> there are two distinct conceptions of defilement articulated in the Hebrew Bible. The first, ritual impurity, concerns the impermanent contagion contracted by direct or indirect contact with a number of natural processes, such as birth, death, and sexual relations. The second kind of defilement, moral impurity, concerns the longer-lasting contagion conveyed to persons, the land, and the sanctuary, through the performance of three grave sins: idolatry, incest, and murder. (Klawans, 158)

To be ritually pure meant to be free of some flaw or uncleanness that would prevent one from coming in contact with holy objects or places, or standing in the presence of God in worship. All who were pure were permitted to eat the flesh of sacrifices, but whoever ate it while impure would be cut off from the community (Lev 7:19–21). Sources of ritual impurity included contact with human corpses (Num 19:11–22) or the carcasses of certain impure animals (Lev 11), various skin diseases and molds (Lev 13:1–46; 14:1–32), childbirth (Lev 12), and genital discharges (Lev 15). Impurity could also result from engaging in purificatory procedures (Lev 16:28; Num 19:8). On the other hand, moral impurity was the direct result of immoral behavior, including sexual sins (e.g., Lev 18:1–23), bloodshed (e.g., Num 35:33–34), and idolatry (e.g., Lev 19:31; 20:1–3).

The OT strictly forbids eating unclean animals. Hebrew dietary laws were very specific about what kinds of animals were clean and, therefore, allowed to be eaten. Some of these distinctions were revealed even before the time of Moses (Gen 7:2, 8; 8:20).

Genesis 1 divides the animal world into three spheres: creatures that fly, those that walk on the ground, and those that swim in the seas (Gen 1:20–30). Land animals that chew the cud and have divided hoofs were considered clean (Lev 11:3–8), whereas fish without fins and scales were unclean (Lev 11:10–12). As for insects, only those that fly and have "jointed legs for hopping on the ground" (Lev 11:21) were clean, but all other insects were unclean (Lev 11:20–23). Especially forbidden was the eating of blood, which was first forbidden for Noah and his sons (Gen 9:4) before it was forbidden for the tribes of Israel (Lev 17:10–16). With regard to this prohibition and its being based on the idea of the life-force residing in the blood (Lev 17:11), the Hebrew people were unique in the world of the ancient Near East.

Various views exist concerning the origin of these laws. A very popular view is that they were established for the purpose of good hygiene. While a case can be made that some animals that the OT calls unclean might be harmful to human health, it is far from clear that all unclean animals mentioned in Leviticus are harmful. For example, the Arabs have long enjoyed camel meat and milk without medical difficulties. Furthermore, the biblical text does not make specific mention of hygienic benefits associated with not eating certain foods. Finally, if hygiene was the motive underlying the OT regulations, why did the early church allow their abolition in the first century AD? What was harmful when Lev 11 was written that would have not been just as dangerous in the early days of the church?

It has been suggested that the unclean animals were forbidden because they were closely associated with pagan religions; it has been argued that such animals were used in sacrifices or that deities were believed to manifest themselves in animal form (Wenham 1981, 7). The pig was a sacrificial animal among the ancient Canaanites, and there is some evidence that pigs were eaten in Canaanite rituals (Isa 65:4). In addition, the pig was sacred in Babylon, Cyprus, and Syria. In Egypt the camel was a totem for the god Seth, and the dog was a representative of Anubis (Knapp, 105).

Since the unclean land animals were carnivorous and the unclean birds ate carrion, it has been suggested that this was the basis for Israel's unclean designations (Milgrom 1963, 288–301). This view has merit, but it is important to note that in the list of unclean land animals their carnivorous nature is not mentioned. Whatever the explanation may be for why the Israelites were prohibited from eating certain foods, what is most important is that the laws on this subject came from God, who gave them to Moses to deliver to Israel (Lev 11:1–2).

Legislation regarding the treatment of various skin diseases and molds is found in Lev 13–14. The severe nature of these diseases is illustrated by the careful provisions for priestly examination and for isolation. Those suspected of having such skin diseases could prove their health (Lev 14:1–3) and ultimately be restored through purification rituals (Lev 14:4–32). Molds that afflicted clothes (Lev 13:47–59) or houses (Lev 14:33–53) were treated similarly; the law includes provisions for isolation, inspection, and restoration, when possible.

Like a menstruating woman, a woman who bore a son was unclean for seven days. On the eighth day, the son was to be circumcised. After the circumcision, she continued to be unclean and was forbidden from touching or eating that which was holy for another thirty-three days (Lev 12:1–4). The reason for the numbers seven and forty (seven plus thirty-three) is not explained, but it is likely that seven symbolized "completeness" or "wholeness" (Terry, 385; Hartill, 121) while forty symbolized a long period of time (Drinkard, 712). Thus, the forty days represented the completion of her impurity. Procedures were legislated for the birth of daughters as for sons, except the mother would be unclean for twice as long, including fourteen days of being unclean with an additional sixty-sixty days of avoidance of holy objects and the sanctuary (Lev 12:5).

Genital discharges due to both disease and normal causes rendered the individual unclean. Leviticus 15:2–15 describes secretions related to some disease of the male sexual organs. When the man was healed, he was required to set aside seven days for his cleansing. This would include washing his body and his clothes (vs. 13). On the eighth day, he was to take two turtledoves or two young pigeons to the tabernacle and give them to the priest, who would, in turn, use them for a sin offering and a burnt offering (vs. 14). Seminal emissions, which are described in Lev 15:16–18, required that the man's body, as well as any clothing on which the emissions appeared, be purified by water. No sacrifice was required for this cleansing.

Natural menstrual discharges are treated in Lev 15:19–24, while secretions of blood that are not part of menstruation (vs. 25) and that indicate disease are treated in Lev 15:25–30. A woman was considered ritually impure for seven days from the beginning of her menstrual flow (Lev 15:19; cf. 12:2). Purification rites included the use of water and the presentation of two turtledoves and two young pigeons for a sin offering and a burnt offering (Lev 15:29–30).

Any contact with the dead would render one unclean. If one touched a dead animal, whether it was considered clean or unclean, that person would be unclean until his or her clothes were washed and the evening had passed (Lev 11:8, 11, 24–25, 27–28, 39). If an unclean animal, such as a lizard or rodent, died and fell on any furniture, the furniture had to be washed and was unclean until the evening (Lev 11:32). If such an animal fell on a pot, the pot had to be broken (Lev 11:33). Anyone who touched a human corpse was unclean for seven days (Num 19:11). Purification included washing with water on the third and seventh days (Num 19:12). Impurity would also be declared if anyone entered a tent in which another person had recently died; even open containers in the tent were considered unclean (Num 19:14–15). Those who performed purificatory procedures, such as burning contaminated materials, were regarded as unclean and were required to bathe their bodies and wash their clothes (Lev 16:28; Num 19:8).

B. THE NEW TESTAMENT

A constellation of terms appear in the NT that communicate the concept of purity and related ideas. These include the following (because specific verses are cited here, the specific forms attested in the text are given): *katharismou* ("purification rites," Luke 2:22), *hagnisthēti/hagnistheis* ("purification rites/purified," Acts 21:24, 26), *hagios*, "holy" (cf. *hēgiasmenē*, "sanctified," Rom 15:16), *amōmous* ("blameless," Eph 1:4), *anegklētous* ("blameless," 1 Cor 1:8), *anepilēmptoi* ("[so that no one may be] open to blame," 1 Tim 5:7), *amemptoi* ("blameless," Phil 2:15), and *athōon/athōos* ("innocent/innocent," Matt 27:4, 24). Terms for impurity or pollution include *memiammenois* ("corrupted," Titus 1:15), *emolunan* ("[they] soiled," Rev 3:4), *akatharsia* ("impurity," Rom 6:19), *spiloi* ("blots," 2 Pet 2:13), *mōmoi* ("blemishes," 2 Pet 2:13), and *alisgēmatōn* ("polluted," Acts 15:20).

The NT contains little in the way of reference to OT ritual practices, though there are a few references to the purification that the Mosaic law required after childbirth (Luke 2:22) and healing from skin disease (Matt 8:4||Mark 1:44||Luke 5:14). This was largely due to the transition among the followers of Jesus away from external ritual practices of purification to internal cleansing by means of faith in the redemptive work of Christ. Jesus said that he came to fulfill the law (Matt 5:17). The Apostle Paul states in Rom 6:14: "For sin shall no longer be your master, because you are not under the law, but under grace." A similar sentiment is offered in Gal 5:18: "But if you are led by the Spirit, you are not under the law."

When Jesus's disciples did not ceremonially wash their hands before eating food, the Pharisees wanted to know the reason (Mark 7:1–5). The issue here was that of ritual purity, not hygiene, though this practice of hand-washing before eating was not an OT ritual but rather one that had developed among the Pharisees during the Second Temple period. Jesus responded to the Pharisees by saying: "Nothing outside a person can defile them by going into them. Rather, it is what comes out of a person that defiles them" (Mark 7:15). Mark 7:19 states that "In saying this, Jesus declared all foods clean." There is considerable debate among scholars over the textual integrity of this statement, but evidence supports its reliability (Hendriksen, 281–83).

The fact that Jesus and his disciples ignored ritual washing before eating raises the question whether they ignored other ritual requirements, for example, those associated with entry into the temple at Passover. Jesus is recorded as having made a number of journeys to Jerusalem for the festivals. John mentions five journeys to Jerusalem: two for Passover (2:13; 11:55), one for Sukkot (7:10), one for an unnamed feast (5:1), and one for Hanukkah, the post-OT "Festival of Dedication" (10:22) during which the Jews remembered the rededication of the temple.

Special purification was required of anyone entering the temple at Passover. Such purification required an immersion of the entire body in water from a natural source.

In Jesus's day, such purification was usually carried out with the use of the ubiquitous *miqwā᾽ôt* (ritual baths) found throughout the land of Israel. The highest concentration of *miqwā᾽ôt* has been found in Jerusalem, but they were abundant in Judea and Galilee as well. They have also been discovered at Masada, Jericho, and Qumran (from the Hasmonean period), and they continued in use until the second century AD. Most *miqwā᾽ôt* were cut into bedrock and were rectangular with steps descending to a pool, which was to contain at least forty *sĕ᾽îm* (about sixty-six gallons) of water according to rabbinic standards (*b. ʿErub.* 4b; *b. Yoma* 31a). The steps were divided by a low parapet in the center. The unclean individual would descend on one side and ascend on the other side ritually clean. The divided staircase was necessary to prevent transmitted impurity by climbing steps that had been rendered impure. Though the early Christians abandoned the use of *miqwā᾽ôt* as the means of purifying those who had incurred some kind of impurity, they seem to have adapted the use of the *miqwā᾽ôt* for baptism as an initiation to the Christian faith, in the same way that they were used for the immersion of gentile converts to Judaism (see LaSor, 59).

It does not appear that the members of the early church practiced any purification rituals that were so common to the Jews. For these Christians, ceremonial defilement did not exist (Mark 7:6–23; Matt 15:3–20), hence there was no need for ritual washing. Jesus fulfilled this aspect of the law as well as others. "Baptism by whatever mode and feet washing whether viewed as a right or only as a Gospel incident have no connection with ritual uncleanness, hence no connection with OT ritual or interpretation" (Culver, 8).

The conversion of gentiles to faith in Jesus as their savior created a major conflict among the early disciples of Jesus as to requirements over maintaining Jewish purity laws. This is seen most dramatically in the development of Peter's attitudes, as witnessed by Acts 10, Acts 15, and Gal 2.

Before the conversion of the Roman centurion Cornelius, Peter was on the roof of Simon the Tanner's house at Joppa. He saw a vision of a large sheet with various animals, including four-footed animals, reptiles, and birds, and he heard a command to kill and eat (Acts 10:1–13). Shocked, Peter, responded, "Surely not, Lord!" (Acts 10:14). But he was told by the Lord, "Do not call anything impure [*koinou*] that God has made clean" (Acts 10:15). Sometime after this experience, Peter enjoyed table fellowship with gentile Christians in Antioch, but he later changed his behavior and separated himself from them, as recounted by Paul:

> When Cephas came to Antioch, I opposed him to his face, because he stood condemned. For before certain men came from James, he used to eat with the Gentiles. But when they arrived, he began to draw back and separated himself from the Gentiles because he was afraid of those who belonged to the circumcision group. The other Jews joined him in his hypocrisy, so that by their hypocrisy even Barnabas was led astray. (Gal 2:11–13)

It is likely that this incident at Antioch took place before the council at Jerusalem (see Longenecker, 71). At this council, presided over by James, Jewish Christians debated whether or not gentile Christians needed to be circumcised and keep Jewish purity laws. Peter agreed with Paul that gentile believers did not need to be circumcised (Acts 15:1–21). Gentile converts were asked, however, to observe four rules: "You are to abstain from food sacrificed to idols [*eidōlothytōn*], from blood [*haimatos*], from the meat of strangled animals [*pniktōn*] and from sexual immorality [*porneias*]. You will do well to avoid these things" (Acts 15:29).

C. THE NEAR EASTERN WORLD

Mesopotamia

Concepts of purity in Mesopotamia were reflected in the Akkadian words *ebbu* and *ellu*. While these two terms are similar in meaning, there are important distinctions or special nuances in their usage. *Ebbu* means "gleaming" (with respect to metals, gold, precious stones, wood), "clean" (for clothing), "sacred" or "pure" (for objects, materials, or animals for cultic use, as well as for rituals and divine beings), and "trustworthy" or "proper." *Ellu* can mean "gleaming" or "pure" but is never used in connection with physical cleanness. The verbs *ebēbu* and *elēlu* are generally synonymous (both can be translated "to be pure") and often occur together.

The Babylonians believed that the activity of demons and ghosts affected their well-being, but they believed that it was personal failures that brought impurity. A number of purity rituals existed that an individual could perform, many of which were practiced on the royal level. These rituals were markedly different in their purpose and setting. Of the royal rituals for which there is documentation, the most elaborate is known as *bīt rimki*, or "House of Ablution" (Farber, 1902). This ritual was an Assyrian adaptation of earlier Babylonian practices, and it contained elaborate purification rites for the king, normally performed outside the city in reed huts for several days (Farber, 1903). Personal sin, demonic activity, and natural calamities that signaled some failure on the part of the king required purification rituals.

Other purification rites were associated with the "House of Water Sprinkling" or "House of Detention." These rituals were concerned with cultic impurity brought about by contact with impure substances or people, by transgressing taboos, or by situations beyond human control, such as natural disasters or other signs of what were believed to be divine wrath. Most of these rituals made use of water, oil, and potash (Farber, 1903).

In the cultures of ancient Mesopotamia, the introduction of a new statue to a temple representing one of the deities required a special ceremony known as *pīt/mīs pî*, "Opening/Washing of the Mouth" (Farber, 1903). This ritual was thought to infuse the new statue with the spirit of the god. Two days were devoted to this ceremony, which included transportation of the statue from the workshop to a reed hut. It was in this hut that the statue was ritually purified and was believed to become a living god. After the ritual was complete, the god was transported and installed in its temple sanctuary. Additional applications of the *pīt/mīs pî* ritual included the purification of humans, animals, and sacred objects before coming into contact with the deity.

An important event in the annual Babylonian *akitu* festival was the purification of Marduk's temple with a censer, torch, and water from the Tigris and Euphrates Rivers. The censer and torch introduced an idea of cosmic destruction and fire, while the water symbolized purification, birth, and new creation (Sommer, 86).

Egypt

The Egyptians put a strong emphasis on purity as a requirement for all acceptable temple activity. Above many of the temple entrances, there was a sign that read, "Everybody who enters the temple, must be pure" (Bleeker, 86). The Egyptians believed that the well-being of the universe depended on the power of Osiris, who was pure and holy. Anyone associated with the god, the king, the priest, and the dead had to be purified.

The body of a dead person was purified by washing it with natron water (water mixed with various naturally occurring sodium compounds, such as sodium bicarbonate). The deceased is pictured in tomb paintings, as if alive, standing on a pedestal or in a basin while priests pour the water over him.

From the Middle Kingdom onward, the pharaoh underwent purification rites beginning in infancy. There was a pre-coronation ritual that consisted of sprinkling the child with water both to purify him and to endow him with vital force and divine qualities of power and wisdom. Just before he ascended to the throne, there was another purification ritual. Coronation scenes in tombs and palaces commonly portray the purification of the king and usually show Horus and Thoth purifying the king with libation flasks. The purification of the king not only removed impurities but endowed him with new strength to fulfill his monarchal responsibilities.

Purification rituals in ancient Egypt might involve the following five acts: pouring water over oneself, burning incense, using natron, changing one's clothes, and removing all body hair. The use of water in purification rites was critical because it represented ritual cleansing as well as the gift of good fortune. Most temples had a sacred pool or small pond from which purification water was drawn.

The third plague brought on Egypt in the biblical story of the exodus (Exod 8:16–19) takes on special significance in the light of the Egyptians' purity requirements for serving in a temple. When Aaron strikes the ground with a rod, the surface dust of the land is turned into gnats (Heb. *kinnîm*). Since everyone in Egypt, including all temple priests, who wished to approach a deity had to be pure, being infected with gnats would have disqualified them for temple service. Herodotus observed in this regard that, "Their priests shave the whole body every other day, that no lice or aught else that is foul may infest them in their service of the gods" (*Hist.* 2.37). Other ritual customs that were required of priests were cutting their nails short so dirt or other substances would not render them unclean, circumcision, and sexual abstinence.

D. THE GRECO-ROMAN WORLD

Greece

In Greek religious thought, impurity or defilement (*miasma*) could be the result of deviant actions, conscious wrongdoing, or departure from a recognized state of normality. It could affect people, families, cities, holy places and even the gods themselves (Vernant, 123). The various kinds of impurity can often be discerned by the means used to eliminate it. These included purification rites and legal procedures, such as purifying an entire city, depriving offenders of the rights of full citizenship, and secluding offenders from society (Regev, 394). The sacred remedy was purification (*katharismos*) by rituals that were established to deal with the failures of both social and cultic life. When these rituals were accomplished properly, an individual was regarded as "pure" (*hagnos*).

Mystery religions, which were cults dedicated to particular deities, became a dominant feature of Greek religious life during the Hellenistic and Roman periods (after 333 BC), and some of their practices are also attested in Greece before 600 BC. The mystery cults did not die out in Greece until ca. AD 500 (Brisco, 1991, 997). Greek purification rituals in the Classical period often employed effigies to purify the location of ghosts and hostile spirits (Johnson, 4n14). Such effigies were made of clay, bronze, and wax. Wax effigies were frequently used in purification rituals in order to banish harmful spirits. A "healer" would melt the wax effigies in order to drive the spirits from his patient (Johnson, 15).

Participation in these cults was established by elaborate initiation rituals and secret rites. The exact nature of many of the rites associated with these religions is largely unknown because the initiates were required to take vows of secrecy. However, we do know that initiation into the mystery religions included various rituals for purification that involved the use of water, fire, and sacrifices.

Greek society also observed distinctions between sacred space and common space: the former belonged to a particular deity while the latter was accessed by ordinary mortals. In order for a worshipper to enter sacred space, he or she had to be free from pollution contracted by childbirth, contact with the dead, recent sexual activity, murder, sacrilege, or madness. The practice of hand-washing or sprinkling oneself with water before pouring libations and sacrificing was a strict requirement in Greek rituals. The Athenian Assembly was required to be ritually purified before each meeting.

Rome

Religion in ancient Rome involved both practices and beliefs that the Romans considered their own and those from the many cults imported to Rome. Beliefs about most Roman gods and goddesses contained a blend of several religious influences. Many were introduced by way of the Greek colonies of southern Italy, and some had their roots in the religions of Etruscan tribes. As the Romans extended their dominance throughout the Mediterranean world, their general policy was to absorb the deities and cults of other peoples rather than try to eradicate them.

Although the concept of purity in ancient Rome generally did not have an ethical component, ethical obligations were promoted in the concept of *pietas*. This notion of proper behavior was at the foundation of Roman life. When announcing laws for a state religion, Cicero began, "They shall approach the gods in purity, bringing piety, and leaving riches behind" (*Leg.* 2.8.19). He also suggested that purity should include the mind as well as the body (*Leg.* 2.10.24–25).

Purification rites were included in Roman religious rituals. These often involved the sprinkling of water (Stukey, 286; Piscinus, 10). The ritual was only to use running water, which was regarded as pure and clean. As a sign of purity, both men and women often appeared in purification ritual barefoot. Some Roman purification rituals also required a fast. One interesting requirement for some purification rituals was that the worshipper was to remove any knots or bindings from his or her garments when performing them (Piscinus, 3).

The early Romans believed that participation in a funeral brought impurity, and therefore one had to engage in a purification ritual in order to remove those negative effects. Those who had taken part in a funeral had to purify themselves at home on the same day by means of the *suffitio*, a rite of purification by fire and water. By the end of the second century AD, however, such rituals had progressively fallen into disuse.

E. THE JEWISH WORLD

Ritual purity and impurity constitute one of the most frequently discussed topics in the literature of Qumran. Among the Jewish groups of the Second Temple period, the Qumran community was the most rigorous in their maintenance of priestly and personal purity. Their ideas can be discerned from the more than eight hundred fragmentary documents from Qumran that date from the third century BC to the first century AD. The members of the Qumran community were likely Essenes, an austere and extreme Jewish sect that settled in various locations. The Essenes are mentioned by Josephus (*J.W.* 2.119–161), Philo of Alexandria (*Prob.* 75), and Pliny the Elder (*Nat.* 5.15). They are never mentioned in the NT, however.

According to Ringgren,

> The statements concerning purification in the Dead Sea Scrolls can be divided into two groups. On the one hand, the Manual of Discipline and sometimes the Damascus Document speak of the "purity of the many" (*ṭohᵒraṯ hārabbîm*, 1QS 6:16,25; 7:3,16,19) or "the purity of the holy men" (*ṭohᵒraṯ ʾanšê haqqōḏeš*, 1QS 5:13; 8:17), or simply *ṭohᵒrâ* (1QS 6:22; 7:25; 8:24; CD 9:21,23) as something that outsiders are forbidden to touch. (Ringgren, 295)

He then adds,

> On the other hand, the Hodayoth contain several occurrences of the verb *ṭhr*,
> mostly in the piel, with reference to cleansing from sin and iniquity (*ʿāwôn*,
> 1QH 1:32; *pešaʿ*, 3:21; 7:30; 11:10; *ʾašmâ*, 4:37; 6:8). One passage (15:16) com-
> pares cleansing to the refining (*zqq*) of silver; another (6:8) uses *zqq* without
> mentioning silver. (Ringgren, 296)

For the Qumran community, possible sources of impurity included a
corpse, leprosy, sexual discharges, outsiders, and excrement. Purification
rites at Qumran were generally more stringent than those required by the
Torah. A minimum purification from any impurity involved laundering,
bathing, and waiting for sunset (4QMMT B 14–16; 11Q19 L, 8–9). Only
clean water could be used for purification, and it had to be deep enough to
make ripples, whether it was used in a *miqwê* or for washing dishes (*CD* X,
10–13). The more serious impurities would require animal sacrifices.

Qumranic regulations stipulated that corpse-contaminated individuals could not eat the communal meal and had to undergo a week-long purification process. Contamination could occur through direct contact with
the corpse or merely being in the same room with it.

An important text from Qumran that deals with disputed matters of
purity is *Miqṣat Maʿaśê ha-Torah* ("Some of the Works of the Law," 4Q394–
399, commonly abbreviated 4QMMT), which has been called "A Sectarian
Manifesto." As Martin Abegg points out, it is the sole Jewish text to refer,
as does the Apostle Paul, to "the works of the law" (Abegg, 53). It is a letter
that describes a score of issues that had caused a rift between the priestly
author and his former colleagues. As some of the material in 4QMMT (and
also in the Temple Scroll) reflects Sadducean as opposed to Pharisaic views
(cf. Baumgarten, 157–70), it has been proposed that the original founders
of the Qumran sect were dissident Zadokites (i.e., Sadducean) priests (see
Schiffman 1990, 69). Of special interest is a ruling on poured liquids:

> [Co]ncerning streams of liquid, we have determined that they are not intrin-
> sically [p]ure. Indeed, streams of liquid do not form a barrier between the
> impure and the pure. For the liquid of the stream and that in its receptacle
> become as one liquid. (B 55–58a; see also 4Q274, which deals with ritual pu-
> rity laws concerning liquids)

This is in striking contrast with the Pharisaic position, as enunciated in
the Mishnah: "The Sadducees say, We cry out against you, O ye Pharisees,
for ye declare clean an unbroken stream of liquid" (*m. Yad.* 4:7), meaning
that the Pharisees held that a stream of liquid did not convey uncleanness
backwards to the vessel from which it was poured.

The Qumran community was destroyed by the Romans in AD 68, and the temple was burned by Titus in AD 70, ending the sect of the Sadducees. Apart from the small remnant of the Samaritans, who survive to this day, the dominant form of Judaism became the Pharisaic tradition as preserved in the Mishnah and the Talmuds. The Pharisees sharply disagreed among themselves, most notably in the frequent disputes between the House of Shammai and the more liberal House of Hillel. Many of the disputes in rabbinic texts revolve around the details of how purity laws should be kept, how much contact was required for contamination, and the minimum amount of material that could convey uncleanness.

The Mishnah refers to several types of unclean objects. The first type includes "These Fathers of Uncleanness, [namely] a [dead] creeping thing, male semen, he that has contracted uncleanness from a corpse, a leper in his days of reckoning" (*m. Kelim* 1:1). The so-called "Fathers of Uncleanness" could convey uncleanness to people and vessels. The second type, "Offspring of Uncleanness," could convey uncleanness only to food and liquids. In another tractate in the Mishnah, we read:

> Food rendered unclean by a Father of Uncleanness and food rendered unclean by an Offspring of Uncleanness may be included together so as to convey uncleanness according to the lighter degree of uncleanness of the two. Thus if a half-egg's bulk of food suffering first-grade uncleanness and a half-egg's bulk of food suffering second-grade uncleanness were mixed together, they together count as suffering only second-grade uncleanness. (*m. Ṭehar.* 1:5)

Gentiles and women are assumed to convey uncleanness in the following ruling:

> If thieves entered a house, only that part is unclean that was trodden by the feet of the thieves. What do they render unclean? Foodstuffs and liquids and open earthenware vessels; but couches and seats and earthenware vessels having a tightly stopped-up cover remain clean. If a gentile or a woman was with them all becomes unclean. (*m. Ṭehar.* 7:6)

In the Babylonian Talmud, every possible source of uncleanness is debated. For example, if a weasel with a dead reptile in its mouth comes into contact with some loaves of bread, the loaves are still deemed clean if it is doubtful that the reptile came into contact with them. On the other hand, any uncovered water nearby is deemed unclean, presumably because the weasel may have drunk from it (*b. Ḥul.* 9b). Water, wine, and milk were to be kept covered at all times. To the question of how long it would take for uncovered liquids to become unclean, the answer is: "Such time as it would take a reptile to come forth from a place nearby and drink" (b. Ḥul. 10a). Shammai and Hillel at first disagreed about whether grapes gathered for the winepress were susceptible to uncleanness. Shammai held that they were; Hillel disagreed at first but later agreed with Shammai (b. Ḥul. 36b).

F. THE CHRISTIAN WORLD

The apostolic fathers, like the NT writers, were deeply Christocentric in their approach to the basic doctrines of the faith. Their hermeneutical approach was frequently allegorical with the goal of proving that OT narratives point to NT truths. Clement of Rome, for example, saw Rahab's scarlet thread (Josh 2:18) as prefiguring the blood of Christ (1 Clem. 12:7).

The second- and third-century apologists were noted for their vigorous defense of the Christian faith against the attacks of both Jewish and pagan thinkers. They often relied on Greek philosophy in their defense, but this was not to the exclusion of Scripture, which they regarded as the final authority in matters of truth. However, Justin's Dialogue with Trypho, for example, exhibits a rather consistent rejection of Jewish practices in Christianity based on his reading of the OT (Dial. 10, 18, 27). The fathers largely ignored the various purification rituals of Judaism or declared them void. When they do refer to "purity" or "impurity," it is usually in the context of moral or spiritual values.

In the second and third centuries, church writers tended to view Mosaic ritual legislation in a symbolic manner (Larin, 4). Justin Martyr and Origen both interpret the categories of "purity and "impurity" allegorically thereby making them symbols of virtue and sin (Wendebourg, 153–55). With the exception of Tertullian, the apologists were not primarily theologians. Since their main goal was "to exhibit Christianity to emperors and to the public as politically harmless and morally and culturally superior to paganism" (Cross and Livingstone, 87), their attention was focused on the existence and character of God and the divinity of Christ rather than on the details of purification rites.

BIBLIOGRAPHY: M. Abegg, "Paul, 'Works of the Law' and MMT," BAR 20.6 (1994), 52–55, 82; J. M. Baumgarten, "The Pharisaic-Sadducean Controversies about Purity and the Qumran Texts," JJS 31 (1980), 157–70; A. M. Blackman, "Purification (Egypt)," in Encyclopaedia of Religion and Ethics, ed. James Hastings (1919), X.476–82; C. J. Bleeker, "Guilt and Purification in Ancient Egypt," Numen 13 (1966), 81–87; G. Brin, "The Firstling of Unclean Animals," JQR 68 (1977), 1–15; T. Brisco, "Mystery/Mystery Religions," in Holman Bible Dictionary, ed. T. C. Butler (1991), 997–98;

A. H. Cadwallader, "The Hermeneutics of Purity in Mark's Gospel: Consideration for the AIDS Debate," *Pacifica: Australasian Theological Studies* 5 (1992), 145–69; P. R. Callaway, "Source Criticism of the Temple Scroll: The Purity Laws," *RevQ*, 12.2 (1986), 213–22; J. J. Collins and D. C. Harlow, ed., *The Eerdmans Dictionary of Early Judaism* (2010); F. L. Cross and E. A. Livingstone, ed., "Apologists," *ODCC*, 87; R. D. Culver, "Ablution," in *Wycliffe Bible Encyclopedia*, ed. C. F. Pfeiffer, H. F. Vos, and J. Rea (1975), I.7–8; D. Daube, "A Note on a Jewish Dietary Law," *JTS* 37 (1936), 289–91; M. L. Davies, "Levitical Leprosy: Uncleanness and the Psyche," *ExpTim* 99 (1988), 136–39; J. D. M. Derrett, "The Samaritan Woman's Purity (John 4:4–52)," *EvQ* 60 (1988), 291–98; M. Douglas, "The Forbidden Animals in Leviticus," *JSOT* 59 (1993), 3–23; J. F. Drinkard, "Numbers," in *Harper-Collins Bible Dictionary*, ed. P. J. Achtemeier (1985), 711–12; C.-M. Edsman, D. M., and M. Paul, "Fire," in *The Encyclopedia of Religion*, ed. M. Eliade (1987), V.340–46; J. H. Elliott, "Household and Meals vs. Temple Purity Replication Patterns in Luke-Acts," *BTB* 21 (1991), 102–8; W. Farber, "Witchcraft, Magic, and Divination in Ancient Mesopotamia," *CANE* 3.1895–1909; T. Finan and V. Twomey, ed., *Scripture Interpretation in the Fathers: Letter and Spirit* (1995); E. Firmage, "The Biblical Dietary Laws and the Concept of Holiness," in *Studies in the Pentateuch*, ed. J. A. Emerton (1990), 177–208; M. FitzPatrick, "From Ritual Observance to Ethics: The Argument of Mark 7:1–23," *ABR* 35 (1987), 22–27; S. Haber, *"They Shall Purify Themselves": Essays on Purity in Early Judaism*, ed. A. Reinhartz (2008); H. K. Harrington, *The Purity Texts* (2004); J. E. Hartill, *Biblical Hermeneutics* (1960); W. Hendriksen, *Mark* (1975); H. Hübner, "Mark VII. 1–23 und das 'Jüdisch-Hellenistische' Gesetzesverständnis," *NTS* 22 (1976), 319–45; R. Johnson, "Effigies and Exorcisms: Rituals to Purify Patients and Expel Hostile Spirits in Greece and the Near East," Master's Thesis, Brandeis University (2014); T. Kazen, *Issues of Impurity in Early Judaism* (2010); T. D. S. Key and R. M. Allen, "The Levitical Dietary Laws in the Light of Modern Science," *Journal of the American Scientific Affiliation* 26 (1974), 61–64; J. Klawans, *Impurity and Sin in Ancient Judaism* (2000); A. B. Knapp, *The History and Culture of Ancient Western Asia and Egypt* (1988); J. T. Koch, "*Interpretatio romana*," in *Celtic Culture: A Historical Encyclopedia* (2006), III.974–75; J. L. Kugel and R. A. Greer, *Early Biblical Interpretation* (1986); W. G. Kümmel, "Äußere und innere Reinheit des Menschen bei Jesus," in *Das Wort und die* Wörter, ed. H. Balz and S. Schulz (1973), 35–46; V. Larin, "What Is 'Ritual Purity' and Why?," *St. Vladimir's Theological Quarterly* 52 (2008), 3–4; W. S. La Sor, "Discovering What Jewish Miqva'ot Can Tell Us about Christian Baptism," *BAR* 13.1 (1987), 52–59; H. Lindsay, "Death-Pollution and Funerals in the City of Rome," in *Death and Disease in the Ancient City*, ed. V. M. Hope and E. Marshall (2000),

152–72; R. N. Longenecker, *Galatians* (1990); H. Maccoby, "The Washing of Cups," *JSNT* 14 (1982), 3–15; S. Meier, "House Fungus: Mesopotamia and Israel (Lev 14:33–53)," *RB* 96 (1989), 184–92; R. Meyer and F. Hauck, "καθαρός, καθαρίζω, καθαίρω, καθαρότης," *TDNT* III.413–31; J. Milgrom, "Ethics and Ritual: The Foundations of the Biblical Dietary Laws," in *Religion and Law: Biblical-Judaic and Islamic Perspectives*, ed. E. B. Firmage, B. G.Weiss, and J. W. Welch (1990), 159–91; J. Milgrom, "Food and Faith: The Ethical Foundations of the Biblical Diet Laws," *BRev* 8.6 (1992), 5, 10; J. Milgrom, "The Paradox of the Red Cow (Num. XIX)," *VT* 31 (1981), 62–72; J. Milgrom, "Seeing the Ethical Within the Ritual," *BRev* 8.4 (1992), 6, 13; J. Neusner, *The Idea of Purity in Ancient Judaism* (1973); H. Nibley, *The Message of the Joseph Smith Papyri* (1976); F. D. Nichol, ed., "Exodus," in *The Seventh Day Adventist Bible Commentary* (1953), 1.491–689; S. Niditch, "War, Women, and Defilement in Numbers 31," *Semeia* 61 (1993), 39–57; M. H. Piscinus, "Purification Rites," *Societas Via Roma* (2001), 1–10; Eyal Regev, "Moral Impurity and the Temple in Early Christianity in the Light of Ancient Greek Practice and Qumranic Ideology," *HTR* 97 (2004), 383–411; H. Ringgren, "טָהַר *tāhar*," *TDOT* V.287–96 (1986); J. W. Rogerson and W. G. Jeanrond, "History of Interpretation," *ABD* III.424–43; L. H. Schiffman, "The New Halakhic Letter (4QMMT) and the Origins of the Dead Sea Sect," *BA* 53.2 (1990), 64–73; L. H. Schiffman, "New Halakhic Texts from Qumran," *Hebrew Studies* 34 (1993), 21–33; J. Scurlock, *Magico-Medical Means of Treating Ghost-Induced Illnesses in Ancient Mesopotamia* (2006); B. D. Sommer, "The Babylonian Akitu Festival: Rectifying the King or Renewing the Cosmos," *JNES* 27 (2000), 81–95; H. J. Stukey, "Purity in Fifth and Fourth Century Religion," *TAPA* 67 (1936), 286–95; M. S. Terry, *Biblical Hermeneutics* (n.d.); J. M. C. Toynbee, *Death and Burial in the Roman World* (1971); G. J. Wenham, "The Theology of Unclean Food," *EvQ* 53.1 (1981), 6–15; G. J. Wenham, "Why Does Sexual Intercourse Defile (Lev 15 18)?" *ZAW* 95.3 (1983), 432–34; R. Whitekettle, "Levitical Thought and the Female Reproductive Cycle: Wombs, Wellsprings, and the Primeval World," *VT* 46 (1996), 376–91; D. P. Wright, "Purification from Corpse-Contamination in Numbers XXXI 19–24," *VT* 35 (1985), 213–23; D. Wendebourg, "Die alttestamentlichen Reinheitsgesetze in der frühen Kirche," *Zeitschrift für Kirchengeschichte* 95/2 (1984); J.-P. Vernant, *Myth and Society in Ancient Greece* (1988), 121–41. E. Yamauchi, "טָהֵר (*ṭāhēr*)," *TWOT* I.343–45; E. J. Young, *The Book of Isaiah* (3 vols., 1965–1972); R. F. Youngblood, "Pure; Purification; Purity," *ISBE* III.1054–56; N. Zohar, "Repentance and Purification: The Significance and Semantics of חטאת in the Pentateuch," *JBL* 107.4 (1988), 609–18.

JJD

See also BATHS & BATHING, BONES & OBJECTS OF BONE, BOTTLES & GLASS, BUTCHERS & MEAT, CHILDBIRTH & CHILDREN, DEATH & THE AFTERLIFE, DEMONS, DISEASES & PLAGUES, DOGS, FOOD CONSUMPTION, FOOD PRODUCTION, MENSTRUATION, and VIRGINS & VIRGINITY.

RAPE

Rape, which often involves force, is sexual intercourse without one's consent. Cultures throughout antiquity addressed sexual matters that affected individuals, families, and communities, including the punishment of rape.

A. THE OLD TESTAMENT

Death was the punishment for a number of sexual offenses in ancient Israel, including the rape of an engaged girl (Deut 22:25), various incestuous relationships (Lev 20:11–12), homosexuality (Lev 20:13), and bestiality (Exod 22:19; Lev 20:15–16). The fact that a conviction of rape carried the death penalty indicates the severity with which the Lord and the community judged this act of violence.

The law regarding rape in the OT was much more generous to the woman who was raped than were the laws in the surrounding cultures, especially the laws from the Middle Assyrian empire. In Israel, a man who raped a virgin had to marry her, and he could not divorce her. He had to support her for life, even if she did not fulfill her duty to have sex with him. In this way, she would be provided for and not become a burden to her family.

Being a patriarchal culture, ancient Israel regulated female sexuality in part for inheritance purposes and in part so that paternity could be determined in a reliable way (Day, 1358). The bride-price was called the *mōhar*. Once a young woman's bride-price had been negotiated, the young woman was expected to remain a virgin until marriage. A premarital consensual act of sexual intercourse was punishable by death—the deaths of the young woman and her illicit partner (Deut 22:13–21, 23–27) (Day, 1358–59).

There are, however, indications in the biblical text that girls and women were viewed as the property of their husbands or fathers "and it could be assumed that women had no rights of their own" (Evans, 898). Daughters could be sold as slaves (Exod 21:7), for example, though not as prostitutes (Lev 19:29) (Evans, 899). Another example of the view that women were property can be found in Exod 21:22, where it seems that an injury to a pregnant woman could result in payment to the woman's husband according to what the husband demanded.

On the other hand, assaults on female slaves were treated as seriously as assaults on male slaves (Exod 21:20, 26–32), and Deut 15:12–17 says that female slaves were to be freed after six years, as were male slaves. The apparent restriction of Exod 21:7 ("when a man sells his daughter as a slave, she shall not go out as the male slaves do") provides "protection for a woman who had been taken as a slave-wife, preventing her from being cast off after six years, rather than restricting the freedom of all bonded women" (Evans, 899).

A man who had intercourse with a young woman who was not pledged in marriage was obliged to marry her, but the woman's father had to give his consent for the marriage and the man had to pay the bride-price to the father (Exod 22:16–17). If on the battlefield Israelite soldiers captured virgins, these women could be forced to marry their captors. Should an Israelite soldier later decide that the conquered woman was not to his liking in some way, he could divorce her and "let her go wherever she wishes" (Deut 21:14a). She had some protection, however, in that he could not sell her as a slave (Deut 21:14b).

The inhabitants of Sodom are punished for their desire to rape the three visitors of Lot, the Hebrew verb "to know" here being a euphemism for "to have sex with" (see Gen 19:5, NIV). Later in Genesis comes the story of the rape of Lot by his own daughters: After the destruction of Sodom, Lot's daughters fear they will never have husbands or children. They decide to make their father drunk and to have sex with him. This happens on two consecutive nights (Gen 19:30, 36). The resulting children become the ancestors of the Moabites and Ammonites, who became the enemies of Israel.

Over many days Potiphar's wife persistently pursues Joseph, who is a slave in Potiphar's household. When Joseph consistently repels her advances, she seizes his garment and tells the servants of the household that it is proof that Joseph attempted to rape her (Gen 39:11–18).

Honor and shame figured in the biblical view of sexuality. "Sexual exclusivity was the primary location of honor," writes deSilva (434). One way to view the story of the rape of Dinah by Shechem (Gen 34:2) is through the lens of honor and shame. The honor of a family was tied to the honor of the women in the family; therefore, gaining improper or premature access to the "virtue" of a woman in a family structure might critically damage the family's status in the community. "Families tended to defend their honor vigorously" (deSilva, 434).

According to Frymer-Kensky, Dinah's virginity was an asset to her household to be protected by her father and her brothers. When Dinah "went out to visit the women of the land," apparently without male protection, her walking alone was provocative. According to Gen 34:2, "When Shechem son of Hamor the Hivite, the ruler of that area, saw her, he took her and raped her."

The rape of Dinah and the action taken by her brothers had dangerous implications for the relation of their family with the surrounding Canaanites (Gen 34:30). These events are mentioned by Judith in her prayer (Jdt 9:1–4). Dinah's sexual defilement by Shechem has repercussions for her father and her brothers. Like David in the case of Tamar, Jacob does not react to vindicate Dinah immediately (see Stiebert, 51). Although Shechem and his father, Hamor, attempt to rectify the situation by proposing marriage and even having the males in their city undergo circumcision, their efforts prove futile because Dinah's brothers, Simeon and Levi, murder the Hivites as they recover from the operation of circumcision. They shame the Hivites by taking as plunder the women and children of Hamor's community (Gen 34:29).

In the list of blessings Jacob gives to his sons (Gen 49), the best blessings go to Judah and Joseph; Reuben, the firstborn, is largely bypassed because he slept with his father's wife (49:3–4). Simeon, the second-born, is bypassed because of "his misconduct following the rape of Dinah," specifically the murder of the family of Shechem (Rigsby, 482), as is Levi, the third-born son (Gen 49:5–7).

Judges 19 tells the story of a Levite, his concubine, and his servant who undertake a journey from Bethlehem to a remote area in the hill country of Ephraim (Judg 19:18). They obtain lodging in Gibeah for a night with an old man. Some of the residents of Gibeah demand that the host give them the Levite for a night of revelry. The old man refuses. The Levite sends his concubine out to them instead. They abuse her throughout the night. She crawls to the door of the house and dies with her hands on the threshold (vv. 26–27). The Levite loads her body on a donkey, and when he gets home he cuts up the body and sends its parts throughout Israel. The gruesome parcels create outrage. Israelites from Dan to Beersheba assemble and decimate the offending Benjamites (Judg 20).

Scholars disagree about whether David raped Bathsheba or whether the liaison was consensual sexual intercourse (2 Sam 11–12). Abasili sums up the two sides of the argument as follows. Scholars such as G. G. Nicol, B. Randall, and H. W. Hertzberg believe that Bathsheba seduced David; one argument is that her action of bathing within viewing distance of the palace was deliberately provocative. On the other hand, scholars such as R. M. Davidson, L. W. Spielman, J. C. Exum, and David and Diana Garland see Bathsheba as the victim of rape and David's abuse of power (see Abasili, 1–2).

Abasili believes that the Hebrew Bible's definition of rape is much the same as the contemporary one, namely that rape is "the abuse of another by the use of intimidation, domination, subjugation and/or violence" (Abasili, 14). However, he notes that "David's lordship of the sexual encounter, which hinges on the power difference between him and Bathsheba," is not rape in the biblical understanding of the word (ibid.). The story contains no mention of the use of physical force. Abasili points out that there is no indication that David had had any social contact with Bathsheba prior to this event so that it was a premeditated action (Abasili, 8). Instead, the narrative indicates that as soon as David saw her bathing on the roof, "he became aroused and strongly desired her sexually. This is suggested by the increased pace of the narrative" (ibid).

Although there is no evidence that Bathsheba cried out during the sexual intercourse, as was required by Hebrew law (Deut 22:25–27), Abasili concludes that the fault lies with David as the powerful monarch who initiates the sexual encounter with a powerless woman. In the phrase, "and he lay with," David is the subject and Bathsheba is the object (Abasili, 12). The narrative of the incident closes with these ominous words: "But the thing David had done displeased the LORD" (2 Sam 11:27). Among the punishments the Lord decrees for David's sin is that "the sword will never depart from your house" (2 Sam 12:10). When confronted with his sin by Nathan the prophet, David admits his guilt. The child born of this union dies as a result of God's judgment (2 Sam 12:19–23), but the second son borne by Bathsheba is Solomon.

The superscription of Ps 51 reads: "For the director of music. A psalm of David. When the prophet Nathan came to him after David had committed adultery with Bathsheba." Although this comment may not have derived from the composition of the psalm, it is nonetheless quite ancient as it is already included in the version of the Psalms at Qumran (see Abegg, Flint, and Ulrich, 530).

David's punishment begins quickly. Tamar, David's beautiful daughter, is raped by her half-brother Amnon (2 Sam 13). Amnon commits several crimes against Tamar: not only does he rape her, he also sends her away and refuses to marry her. After the rape, Amnon "hated her with intense hatred. In fact, he hated her more than he had loved her. Amnon said to her, 'Get up and get out!'" (2 Sam 13:15). The verbs śānēʾ, "to hate" (2 Sam 13:15), and šālaḥ, "to send" (2 Sam 13:17), are paired in divorce contexts in the OT.

It is Absalom, not David, who takes in Tamar and who acts to respond to the shame that had come on the family. David, a king with unparalleled powers and the father of both Tamar and Amnon, says nothing and does little. He does not communicate with his daughter. David's silence and lack of action indicate he favors his firstborn son Amnon and totally disregards Tamar (Stiebert, 63). "David does not emerge well from this story" (Stiebert, 59). Tamar experiences rejection from her father and isolation from society; she never marries and remains childless.

B. THE NEW TESTAMENT

There are no accounts of rape in the NT. Though rape is not specifically addressed, Paul's condemnation of *porneia*, "sexual immorality," would certainly entail the condemnation of rape. Paul exhorts believers to consider their bodies the temple of the Holy Spirit and to flee all immorality (1 Cor 6:18–20).

C. THE NEAR EASTERN WORLD

Mesopotamia

A story from Sumer indirectly addresses the issue of illicit sexual encounters. A love poem recounts the meeting of the god Dumuzi and Inanna, a young goddess. Dumuzi desires Inanna; he puts his arm around her shoulders and tries to convince her with beguiling words. Inanna asks what she would tell her mother if such an encounter should take place. Dumuzi proposes that she tell her mother that she was in the square with a girlfriend listening to music. Meanwhile, says Dumuzi, she can engage with him in "dallying in the moonlight." Inanna, however, convinces Dumuzi that he must court her with propriety and invites him to come to see her mother, Ningal (Frymer-Kensky, 88).

A Sumerian liturgical text that concerns the journey of Enlil and Ninlil to the Tummal sanctuary just outside Nippur deals with the subject of rape. According to this text, Enlil, an adolescent boy, accosts Ninlil, an adolescent girl, on the banks of the Nunbirdu Canal. Enlil entreats Ninlil with beguiling words: "Let me copulate with you. . . . Let me kiss you." But she will not agree to have intercourse with him: "My vagina is young, and has never learned to stretch (?), My lips are young, and have never learned to kiss. My mother will learn of it, and will slap my hand (?), My father will learn of it, and will lay hold of me" (Cooper 1980, 185). But Enlil refuses to abide by her words. He pursues and impregnates her, and she gives birth to the moon god, Su'en (cf. Akk. Sin). Later, in disguise, Enlil impregnates her with three underworld gods. But that is not the end of the matter for Enlil. When he comes to Nippur, he is confronted by the gods:

> The very fifty great gods,
> The very seven gods who decide destinies,
>   Seized Enlil in Ki'ur,
> "Enlil, that violator, must leave the city!"
>   (Cooper, 186)

Enlil is banished, but Ninlil loves him and follows him. According to Frymer-Kensky, the story shows that Enlil's rape of Ninlil is too dangerous to the social order to allow him to stay in the community (Frymer-Kensky, 88). Scurlock, however, writes that what Enlil did to Ninlil was not rape, but seduction whereby he caused the "ruination of an unmarried woman," that is, her chances of marrying anyone else (Scurlock, 103). Therefore, Ninlil pursued him, and her society demanded that he marry her.

Rape is part of the plotline in "Enki and Ninhursag," a story in which Enki rapes three of his daughters. Enki was quite sexually active. After he has an encounter with the goddess Ninhursag, she becomes pregnant, and after nine days she gives birth to Nin-nisig. Nin-nisig later becomes the focus of Enki's sexual interest. When she goes to a marsh, Enki lusts after her and decides to seduce her. The encounter is described this way:

> He put one foot on the boat,
> He put the other (foot) on the dry land.
> He grasped her by the chest and kissed her.
> Enki ejaculated into her womb.
>   (Gadotti, 75)

In the story of Inanna and Šukaletuda, Inanna, disguised as a woman, is raped by a mortal man, Šukaletuda, while she is sleeping under a poplar tree. The poem is quite explicit: A cloth that indicates Inanna's deity covers her vulva. Šukaletuda, working on a plot of his land, sees her, comes near her, and rapes her. Inanna awakens and sees that Utu (the sun god) has been born. "Pure Inanna," as she is described in the poem, examines herself and wonders what she should do.

She decides to get revenge. She fills the wells of the land and the wells of the orchards with blood. Slaves and "black-headed people" (i.e., the Sumerians) alike drank the blood of the wells. "No one knew the end of it!" (Gadotti, 78). Demanding that the culprit be brought forth, Inanna decrees two more plagues. She sends a terrifying storm that sweeps through the land; the streets are blocked. The situation becomes a contest between deities. Enki eventually reveals the hiding place of Šukaletuda. Inanna sentences him to death. However, his name was preserved in songs and literature.

The poem shows that Šukaletuda is guilty of rape by stealth rather than rape by force. His crime is even more reprehensible because he knew the woman was a goddess. He recognized the significance of the cloth covering her and had seen "her coming clouded in a divine light" (Gadotti, 78).

Rape in cuneiform law is considered within the context of adultery. Ancient Mesopotamian laws covered women who were unattached, inchoately married (i.e., betrothed but not living together), or married. Rape "is considered by the cuneiform law codes in the context of a discussion of adultery. Two main aspects are treated: the status of the victim and her lack of consent" (Westbrook, 552).

The Ur-Nammu Laws, the oldest known law code that survives today, were written in the Sumerian language probably around 2100–2050 BC. Noticeable characteristics are that they protect the "reasonable expectations of persons of relative weakness" and "reflect a deep concern for the family" (VerSteeg, 8). The preserved text speaks about rape only in the case of a slave woman: "If a man proceeded by force, and deflowered the virgin (lit.: 'undeflowered') slave-woman of another man, he must pay five shekels of silver" (Law 5; *ANESTP*, 524).

The Laws of Eshnunna (18th c. BC) state: "If a man gives bride-money for a(nother) man's daughter, but another man seizes her forcibly without asking the permission of her father and her mother and deprives her of her virginity, it is a capital offence and he shall die" (CE 26; *ANET*, 162; cf. Yaron, 32–33). In this context, "betrothal is as sacrosanct as a marriage already consummated" (Finkelstein, 356). This law typifies many of the laws of the Near Eastern world in that the law does not compensate the woman for a major effect of rape, namely that the violated woman suffered because either she would remain unmarried, or her bride-price would be much reduced.

The Laws of Eshnunna also address the case of a man who rapes a slave girl (CE 31). His punishment is to pay one-third of a mina (twenty shekels) of silver, with the slave girl remaining the property of her master. The monetary payment here compensated the master for the reduction of the slave girl's value, should her master choose to sell her (Finkelstein, 356).

According to the Code of Hammurabi, CH 130: "If a man pins down [*ka-bil-ši-ma*] another man's virgin wife who is still residing in her father's house, and they seize him lying with her, that man shall be killed; that woman shall be released" (CH 130; *COS* 2.131:344). The Akkadian verb *kabālum* in the D stem means to "constrict," "paralyze," "bind," or "gag." This law refers to a case in which bride money has been paid, and thus the betrothed woman is inchoately married. (See Westbrook, 552; cf. VerSteeg, 65.)

The Middle Assyrian Laws (12th c. BC) address a case in which a woman is in the street on legitimate business—in other words, she is not a prostitute—and the following occurs:

If, as a seignior's wife passed along the street, a(nother) seignior has seized her, saying to her, 'Let me lie with you,' since she would not consent (and) kept defending herself, but he has taken her by force (and) lain with her, whether they found him on the seignior's wife or witnesses have charged him that he lay with the woman, they shall put the seignior to death, with no blame attaching to the woman. (MAL 12; *ANET*, 181)

MAL 55 addresses a situation in which an unattached girl is raped:

In the case of a seignior's daughter, a virgin who was living in her father's house . . . whose hymen had not been opened since she was not married, . . . if a seignior took the virgin by force and ravished her, either in the midst of the city or in the open country or at night in the street or in a granary or at a city festival, the father of the virgin shall take the wife of the virgin's ravisher and give her to be ravished; he shall not return her to her husband (but) take her; the father may give his daughter who was ravished to her ravisher in marriage. If he has no wife, the ravisher shall give the (extra) third in silver to her father as the value of a virgin (and) her ravisher shall marry her (and) not cast her off. (*ANET*, 185)

Anatolia

The Deuteronomic laws make a distinction between a sexual encounter in the city and out in the country. In the former case, the woman is liable because she did not scream, but in the latter case she is deemed innocent because her scream could not be heard (Deut 22:23–27). There is nothing comparable among the Mesopotamian laws. But the Hittite Law Code, which was in use from ca. 1600 to 1200 BC, does have a similar law (#197); it states: "If a man seizes a woman in the mountains, it is the man's crime and he will be killed. But if he seizes her in (her) house, it is the woman's crime and the woman shall be killed" (*ANET*, 196).

Egypt

The Kahun Medical Papyrus was found by Flinders Petrie in 1889. It is dated to between 2100 and 1900 BC. It records perhaps the first case of recorded rape in Egyptian history in this way: "INSTRUCTIONS for a woman suffering in her vagina and likewise in every limb: one who has been maltreated. YOU SHOULD DECLARE About Her, 'This has bound up her womb.' YOU SHOULD PRESCRIBE FOR IT: oil to be eaten until she is well" (K9; Stevens, 950).

In the *Tale of Two Brothers* (ca. 1100 BC), the wife of the older brother, Anubis, attempts to seduce the younger brother, Bata, who, like Joseph, indignantly resists her attempts at seduction. To avoid the harsh penalty for adultery, she falsely accuses Bata of raping her, and "she took fat and grease and made herself appear as if she had been beaten" (*AEL* 2.205).

A maxim of Ptah-hotep warns: "IF THOU DESIREST to make friendship last in a home to which thou hast access as master, as a brother, or as a friend, into any place where thou mightest enter, beware of approaching the women. It does not go well with the place where that is done" (*ANET*, 413).

Annette Depla comments on this text as follows: "Although many terms are known for sexual congress from ancient Egypt, the distinctions are not yet fully understood. At the present level of knowledge of the Egyptian language it is not possible to distinguish between accounts of rape and acts of intercourse with consent" (Depla, 36).

The *Instruction of Amenemope* (ch. 28) counsels: "Do not pounce on a widow when you find her in the fields, and then fail to be patient with her reply" (*AEL* 2.161). Ramesses III claimed that he ensured that women in Egypt could travel without being molested on the road (Eyre, 101).

The accusations of illicit sex that have been preserved in texts all deal with married women. These were considered criminal cases of adultery. C. J. Eyre comments: "It may thus be presumed that copulation with an unmarried and willing woman was of relatively neutral implication socially and legally, at least for the man. . . . In a general sociological context one may more often expect seduction, and even rape, to be the prelude to (perhaps forced) marriage than to a revenge-killing" (Eyre, 95). Janet Johnson observes that in ancient Egypt "the sexual activities of unmarried persons, whether they had never been married or were divorced or widowed, were not the subject of ethical or moral literature" (Johnson, 153).

The demotic *Instruction of Ankhsheshonq*, which dates to the Ptolemaic period, warns: "Do not violate a married woman. He who violates a married woman on the bed will have his wife violated on the ground" (22.18–19; *AEL* 3.176).

According to the Greek historian Diodorus (1st c. BC), Egyptian law punished a man convicted of the rape of a married woman with castration. In cases of adultery, the man received a thousand lashes and the woman had her nose cut off (Diod. Sic. *Bib. hist.* 1.78).

D. THE GRECO-ROMAN WORLD

Greece

The Greeks lacked a strict definition of sexual assault, but both Greek law and Greek custom included definite sanctions against rape. There is no single word in Greek to designate "rape." The use of *bia*, "force," and the verbs *biazō/biaō*, "to force," *harpazō*, "to abduct," *aischynō*, "to shame," and *hybrizō*, "to outrage," when used with women as the object, signified "rape."

Based on the literature and resources that have survived, we have no way of knowing how common rape was in ancient Greece. Women could not initiate the prosecution of a suit, but they could appear as witnesses (Cole, 105). According to Greek law, if a man forced a woman to have extramarital sexual intercourse against her will, the woman and her *kyrios*, that is, her male protector, were entitled to bring a private case against the rapist.

The Athenian lawmaker Solon (6th c. BC) set the compensation for rape at one hundred drachmas (a drachma was a day's wage). By the fourth century BC, the penalty for rape had acquired both civil and criminal aspects. If convicted, a rapist paid an equal amount to the victim for compensatory damages and to the state for a fine.

Athenian law allowed a victim's *kyrios* to kill a seducer or rapist who was caught in the act. Similarly, Plato stipulates in his dialogue *Laws*,

> The man who forcibly violates a free woman or boy shall be slain with impunity by the person thus violently outraged, or by his father or brother or sons. And should a man discover his wedded wife being violated, if he kills the violator he shall be guiltless before the law. (*Leg.* 874cC)

Plutarch believed that Solon's laws concerning women were absurd because the same crime was in some cases punished severely but in other cases leniently. Plutarch writes:

> For instance, he [Solon] permitted an adulterer caught in the act to be killed; but if a man committed rape upon a free woman, he was merely to be fined a hundred drachmas; and if he gained his end by persuasion, twenty drachmas, unless it were with one of those who sell themselves openly, meaning of course the courtesans. . . . Still further, no man is allowed to sell a daughter or a sister, unless he find that she is no longer a virgin. (Plu. *Sol.* 23.1)

The Athenian orator Lysias records a fine of fifty drachmas for a sexual assault on a slave (Cole, 113). In his celebrated speech *On the Murder of Eratosthenes*, he defends an aggrieved husband who has killed an adulterer whom he found in bed with his wife, citing the Athenian law to justify the killing (*On the Murder of Eratosthenes* 32).

Since respectable women are not named and only a few less reputable women are named in court cases from this time, it appears that cases of rape would not have been publicly prosecuted in Athens, as it would have brought too much shame on the families and especially on the women's *kyrioi* ("guardians"), whether fathers or husbands.

According to Plutarch, when Alexander the Great conquered the Greek city of Thebes in 335 BC, his Thracian allies entered the house of Timocleia, a woman of high repute. The commander raped her, and then asked her if she had concealed any gold or silver. She led him to a well, and as he was leaning over, she pushed him in and hurled many stones down the well, killing him. When she was brought before Alexander for punishment, he was impressed with her lineage and demeanor. According to Plutarch, "Amazed, therefore, at her reply and at what she had done, Alexander bade her depart in freedom with her children" (Plu. *Alex.* 12).

In a celebrated debate over various forms of government that Herodotus attributed to Persian officials, one of the criticisms by Otanes of a monarchy was that a single ruler "turns the laws of the land upside down, he rapes women, he puts high and low to death" (*Hist.* 3.80).

Rape is a theme in Greek mythology and drama. Zeus was known as the abuductor or seducer of Europa, Io, Ganymede (a handsome young male), Danaë (mother of Perseus), Alcmene (mother of Heracles), and Leda (mother of Helen and Clytemnestra). Hades abducted Persephone to the underworld.

According to legend, Auge, the virgin priestess of Athena at Tegea, was raped by Heracles. The son that she bore was the hero Telephus, who is depicted in one of the friezes on the great altar of Zeus at Pergamon (now housed in Berlin). Several of the tragic plays of Euripides also mention gods committing rape. For example, in *Ion*, Creusa reproaches Apollo for his treatment of her (*Ion* 891–901).

Rape plays a central role in Menander's comic play *Epitrepontes*, "The Arbitrants." After returning from a trip, Charisios is informed by his slave that his wife, Pamphile, has secretly given birth to a baby, which she exposed. The baby, however, is found and raised by a slave named Syros. As a result, Charisios refuses to sleep with his wife.

It turns out that Pamphile had been raped before her marriage, at the Tauropolia, an all-night festival for women (line 452). The word used for the rape in the play is *biasmos*. Abrotonon, a flute-girl living with Charisios, recalls the event:

> And of a sudden then she comes back on a run
> Alone, and bathed in tears, and tearing at her hair.
> Her silken Tarentine so very beautiful—
> Ye gods, diaphanous!—was ruined utterly,
> For it was all in tatters.
>   (*Epitrepontes* 270–273)

Charisios, who was drunk on that occasion, realizes that he was the rapist, that his wife is innocent of adultery, and that the baby was his. Charisios berates himself as follows: "Look at me, the villain. I myself commit a crime like this, and am the father of a bastard child. Yet I felt not a scrap of mercy, showed none to that woman in the same sad fortune. I'm a heartless brute" (lines 698–703).

Rome

The Latin word for "rape" is *raptus*, derived from the verb *rapere*; other terms are *flagitium*, "a disgraceful action," and *vitium*, "vice." Verbs used to indicate "to rape" included *comprimere*, "to embrace tightly," *stuprare*, "to ravish," and *vitiare*, "to corrupt."

Roman law had a special category called *vis*. The word can be translated "force" or "violence." *Vis* was a broad concept that included many categories of criminal conduct, but in particular it included "physical and sexual assault (including abduction)—motivated either by political advancement, sexual desire, or profit" (VerSteeg, 337). Romans used the word *stuprum* for conduct that would be classified today as seduction and rape (having sex without consent with an unmarried victim) (VerSteeg, 363).

In the *Controversiae* of the elder Seneca, debates take place over hypothetical laws. One hypothetical law gives a woman who was raped the chance to choose between death for her rapist or marrying him without paying a dowry. Another debate allows the rapist to win over the girl's father within thirty days—or die (Cole, 105).

Late Roman law recognized that a girl or woman who was abducted, and who may or may not have been raped as a result of the abduction, had lost her reputation. Her family often had no choice but to marry her off to her abductor; consequently, abduction with a view toward a forced marriage became somewhat common. The community's resultant anger was aroused not so much because of the violence done to a girl or woman but because a *raptus*, or an abduction leading to rape, denied a father the right to choose the man who would benefit from his daughter's inheritance. A rapist caught in the act could be killed by the woman's kin; or, if the victim was a slave, by her owner. A betrothed man who raped his intended wife was considered a rapist, for the society believed that "marriages must be properly made" (Clark, 36–37).

Rape was an important theme in the legendary stories of early Roman history. According to legend, Rhea Silvia, a Vestal Virgin, was found to be pregnant and claimed that she had been ravished by the god Mars. Since she was a Vestal Virgin, she was condemned to death, and her twin boys Romulus and Remus—the mythical founders of Rome—were exposed on the banks of the Tiber, where they were suckled by a she-wolf until they were found by Faustulus and Laurentia (Livy, *Rom. Hist.* 1.4.1–6).

The so-called "Rape of the Sabine Women" took place after Romulus became king of the new city. He invited the Sabines, a neighboring Italic tribe, to a feast. "At a given signal the young Romans darted this way and that, to seize and carry off the maidens" (Livy, *Rom. Hist.* 1.9.10–11). But after a while, the Sabine women became reconciled to their fate and intervened to prevent a war between their families and the Romans.

The overthrow of the last Roman king, Tarquin Superbus ("The Proud"), and the revolution that established the Roman Republic in 509 BC were initiated by the rape of a noble matron, Lucretia, by Sextus, the son of the king. After saying to her husband Collatinus, "Yet my body only has been violated; my heart is guiltless, as death shall be my witness," she killed herself with a knife (Livy, *Rom. Hist.* 1.58.7).

The rape of captured women by Roman soldiers was a frequent occurrence. One rare occasion of retribution for such violence is recorded by Plutarch. He writes that when a Galatian woman named Chiomara was captured in a battle in Asia Minor in 189 BC, "the officer who obtained possession of her used his good fortune as soldiers do, and dishonoured her" (Plut. *Mulier. virt.* 22.258e). When the Roman officer released her in exchange for a large sum of gold, Chiomara signaled a Galatian to decapitate the soldier. She picked up the head, wrapped it in her garment, and threw it at the feet of her husband, who exclaimed, "A noble thing, dear wife, is fidelity." She responded, "It is a nobler thing that only one man be alive who has been intimate with me" (ibid.).

Rape is a central theme in the Roman comedies of Plautus and Terence, which were adaptations of the Hellenistic plays of Menander and others. In Plautus's comedy *Aulularia*, "The Pot of Gold," the character Lyconides rapes the miser Euclio's daughter, Phaedria, while he is drunk at the festival of Ceres. When Lyconides discovers she is pregnant, he offers to marry her. The young man shows no remorse but blames the gods for his actions (*Aul.* 737–742).

In Plautus's play *Cistellaria*, a merchant from Lemnos rapes a maiden while he is drunk at a Dionysiac festival at Sicyon. He departs for his home in Lemnos, while the girl bears a daughter at Sicyon. Years later, the merchant returns and marries the woman he had wronged.

Rape is also featured as an important part of the plot in three of the six surviving comedies of Terence. In *Eunuchus* ("The Eunuch"), Terence's most popular comedy, Chaerea falls madly in love with Pamphila, a sixteen-year-old girl he sees on the street. His slave suggests that he disguise himself as a eunuch who is to be delivered to the house where the young girl lives with Thais, a courtesan. As a trusted eunuch, Chaerea is left alone with the young girl, whom he rapes. Later, he dismisses the rape as a *paulum quiddam*, "a mere trifle" (*Eun.* 856). But when the girl, who had been a foundling, is proven by her nurse to be the daughter of a citizen (*Eun.* 856–58), Chaerea marries her.

In *Hecyra* ("The Mother-in-Law"), the character Pamphilus rapes a girl named Philumena on the street while he is drunk. He also takes a ring from her finger and gives it to a courtesan, Bacchis. Later, he marries Philumena without recognizing that she is the woman he has raped. When after five months he discovers her to be pregnant, he puts her out of his home, though he professes his love for her. But the ring worn by Bacchis, Pamphilus's mistress, is recognized by Philumena's mother. Bacchis then realizes that the woman Pamphilus has raped is now his wife and that the child is his.

E. THE JEWISH WORLD

The Mishnah makes a distinction between the penalties imposed on a seducer and on a rapist: "The seducer must pay on three counts and the violator on four. The seducer must pay [compensation for] indignity and [for] blemish and the [prescribed] fine; the violator adds thereto in that he must pay [compensation for] the pain" (*m. Ketub.* 3:4).

The rabbis even debated whether a girl who had been raped before she was three would be eligible to marry a priest. They answered in the affirmative, because they believed that her hymen could be regenerated (*m. Nid.* 5:4; *b. Nid.* 44b–45a; Satlow, 284).

F. THE CHRISTIAN WORLD

During the persecution of Christians by Theotecnus, an official at Antioch under the emperor Maximian (r. AD 285–305), seven Christian women were condemned to be raped. But Tekousa, who was over seventy years old, tore off her veil, revealing her white hair, and pointed to her wasted body. This deterred the young men who were appointed to this task. Theotecnus then ordered the women to be ordained as priestesses of the goddesses Artemis and Athena. The women were stripped naked, placed on carts carrying the statues of the goddesses, and led through the city to the lake. But when these women refused to accept the white robes of the priestesses, they were drowned with stones tied around their necks (Elm, 54).

Some Christian women who chose an ascetic life faced the threat of rape because they lacked the protection of a father or husband. When they were attacked, some of these women chose to commit suicide. This created a theological problem, which was addressed by the church fathers. In his letter to the nun Eustochium, Jerome uses the example of Dinah (Gen 34) to urge Eustochium to remain indoors. John Chrysostom wrote that virgins who committed suicide to avoid rape had not sinned, but for Augustine "the flight from sin is not a sufficient motive for suicide" (Castelli, 87).

In his first Hymn on Virginity, Ephrem the Syrian (d. AD 373) refers to the situation of women who were raped:

> If a robber seizes you and you are raped in the field, the unclean man's force will be persuasive evidence that you are chaste—just as Sarah in the bosom of Pharaoh was chaste, for she did not commit adultery by her own will.
> (Hymn 1, 9; McVey, 263)

In a second hymn, Ephrem comments on the case of Tamar:

> Tamar tore her garments when she saw her pearl had perished. Instead of her tunic she could acquire another, but her virginity did not have a successor, because it is not able, if stolen, to be sought out again. (Hymn 2, 4; McVey, 267)

Eusebius of Emesa writes in his *Homilia* 6 of virgins who had gone to great lengths to escape rape; he mentions one Theodora, who traded clothes with Didymus, a fellow Christian who managed to get into her cell, help her to escape, and preserve her from rape. However, Castelli concludes that on the whole the church fathers concentrate less on the horrible consequences of violence and rape toward female ascetics and more on the view that if such women were raped, their bodies would be "damaged goods, no longer eligible for the celestial bridal chamber" (Castelli, 87).

After the emperor Constantine's conversion and promulgation of new laws, nobles were no longer free to have sexual license over servants or those of lesser status. Constantine decreed that if a person of noble rank should rape a maiden or commit other damnable crimes, he was to be punished by the judges in the place where he committed the crime; the accused rapist could not plead to go to a more favorable jurisdiction (*Cod. Theod.* 9.1). Constantine also declared that if a man should rape a maiden or a widow who was consecrated to God, that man would not "be able to delude himself by the later consent of the woman whom he ravished" (*Cod. Theod.* 9.25.1). The interpretation of this law elaborates: "If any man should perhaps rape a maiden or a widow consecrated to God, and if afterwards they should come to an agreement about the marriage, they shall be punished equally" (ibid.)

After the establishment of Christianity in the Roman Empire, there developed a custom of pardoning some offenders during the Easter season. However, Constantine stated, "We may not rashly permit to escape punishment the crime of homicide, the disgrace of adultery, the outrage of high treason, the evil of magic, the treachery of sorcerers, and the violence of rape" (*Cod. Theod.* 9.38.4).

A number of Constantine's laws shed light on relations between free women and slaves during his time. Constantine wrote that "if any free woman should suffer violence at the hands of a slave or of any other person whatsoever, and against her own will should be united to a man of servile status, she shall be avenged by the due severity of the law" (*Cod. Theod.* 4.12.1). However, if a free woman "was unmindful of her own honorable status" and cohabited with a slave voluntarily, she stood to forfeit her freedom and would become the slave of the master of the slave with whom she cohabited (*Cod. Theod.* 4.12.1). Furthermore, her children would become the slaves of this master.

A law of Constantine stipulates that a male guardian, who would serve as a tutor, should not have sex with the young virgin who was his ward (Clark, 74). Constantine declared that if a suitor approached and wanted to marry the girl, she should not be married until it was proved that her virginity had not been violated by her tutor. If the tutor had violated her virginity, he was to be "sentenced immediately to exile," and the fisc, the public treasury of Rome, was to take charge of his property (*Cod. Theod.* 9.8).

Under the emperor Justinian, the laws condeming rape covered the abduction, seduction, or rape of women of all classes and categories—virgins, dedicated virgins, married women, and free or slave women. Under his law, the penalties for rape depended not on the level of violence done to the victim but on her social status. Justinian's pronouncements about rape reflect a view that was balanced for his time. Although he states that existing laws "punish the detestable wickedness of women who prostitute their chastity to the lusts of others," in his view punishment was not to extend to women who were violated against their will. Furthermore, Justinian states that "it has been very properly decided" that the reputations of women who have been violated by force "are not lost and that their marriage with others should not be prohibited on this account" (*Codex* 9.9.20 L).

BIBLIOGRAPHY: A. I. Abasili, "Was it Rape? The David and Bathsheba Pericope Re-examined," *VT* 61 (2011), 1–15; M. Abegg, Jr., P. Flint, and E. Ulrich, trans., *The Dead Sea Scrolls Bible* (1999); E. Castelli, "Virginity and Its Meaning for Women's Sexuality in Early Christianity" *Journal of Feminist Studies in Religion* 2 (1986), 61–88; G. Clark, *Women in Late Antiquity: Pagan and Christian Life-styles* (1993); D. Cohen, *Law, Sexuality, and Society: The Enforcement of Morals in Classical Athens* (1991); S. G. Cole, "Greek Sanctions against Sexual Assault," *CP* 79 (1984), 97–113; J. S. Cooper, review of H. Behrens, *Enlil und Ninlil: Ein sumerischer Mythos aus Nippur*, *JCS* 32 (1980), 175–88; P. L. Day, "Virgin," *EDB*, 1358–59; S. Deacy and K. F. Pierce, ed., *Rape in Antiquity* (1997); A. Depla, "Women in Ancient Egyptian Wisdom Literature," in *Women in Ancient Societies*, ed. L. J. Archer, S.

Fischler, and M. Wyke (1994), 24–52; D. A. deSilva, "Honor and Shame," in *DOTP* 431–36; S. Elm, *"Virgins of God": The Making of Asceticism in Late Antiquity* (1994); L. M. Epstein, *Sex Laws and Customs in Judaism* (1967); M. J. Evans, "Women," in *DOTP* 897–904; C. J. Eyre, "Crime and Adultery in Ancient Egypt," *JEA* 70 (1984), 92–105; J. J. Finkelstein, "Sex Offenses in Sumerian Laws," *JAOS* 86 (1966), 355–72; T. Frymer-Kensky, "Virginity in the Bible," in *Gender and Law in the Hebrew Bible and the Ancient Near East*, ed. V. Matthews, B. Levinson, and T. Frymer-Kensky, (2004), 79–96; A. Gadotti, "Why It Was Rape: The Conceptualization of Rape in Sumerian Literature," *JAOS* 129 (2009), 73–82; E. Hamilton, *Mythology: Timeless Tales of Gods and Heroes* (1989); J. Jensen, "Does *Porneia* Mean Fornication? A Critique of Bruce Malina," *NovT* 20 (1978), 161–84; J. H. Johnson, "Sex and Marriage in Ancient Egypt," in *Hommages à Fayza Haikal*, ed. N. Grimal, A. Kamal, and C. May-Sheikholeslami (2003), 149–59; R. Langlands, *Sexual Morality in Ancient Rome* (2006); K. E. McVey, trans., *Ephrem the Syrian: Hymns* (1989); R. Omitowoju, *Rape and the Politics of Consent in Classical Athens* (2002); Z. M. Packman, "Call It Rape: A Motif in Roman Comedy and Its Suppression in English-Speaking Publications," *Helios* 20 (1993), 42–55; C. Pharr, trans., *The Theodosian Code and Novels and the Sirmondian Constitutions* (2012); R. O. Rigsby, "Judah," in *DOTP* 480–84; M. L. Satlow, "'Texts of Terror': Rabbinic Texts, Speech Acts, and the Control of Mores," *Association for Jewish Studies Review* 21 (1996), 273–97; J. Scurlock, "But was She Raped? A Verdict through Comparison," *NIN: Journal of Gender Studies in Antiquity* 4 (2003), 61–103; J. M. Stevens, "Gynaecology from Ancient Egypt: The Papyrus Kahun," *The Medical Journal of Australia* 2 (1975), 949–52; J. Stiebert, *The Construction of Shame in the Hebrew Bible* (2003); R. VerSteeg, *Law in the Ancient World* (2002); R. Westbrook, "Punishments and Crimes," *ABD* V.546–56; R. Yaron, *The Laws of Eshnunna* (1969).

RGB

See also ADULTERY, LAWS & CRIMES, MARRIAGE, PROSTITUTION, and VIRGINS & VIRGINITY.

SAME-SEX RELATIONS

Same-sex relations refer to sexual activity between persons of the same biological sex. While the word "homosexual" was first used in the nineteenth century, same-sex relations have existed throughout history. Even though the concept of same-sex *attraction* (or orientation) is explored in some ancient sources, the focus of this article will be on same-sex sexual *behavior*.

A. THE OLD TESTAMENT

The OT contains two clear prohibitions of same-sex sexual activity between males. Leviticus 18:22 states: "You shall not lie with a male as one lies with a female; it is an abomination" (NASB). Leviticus 20:13 reads: "If there is a man who lies with a male as those who lie with a woman, both of them have committed a detestable act; they shall surely be put to death" (NASB).

These two prohibitions should be interpreted within the context of Israel's Holiness Code, in which they are found, especially in relation to the other laws regarding sexual immorality in Lev 18:6–23, and also in the light of Near Eastern values. Some have suggested that the same-sex prohibitions target a particular form of same-sex activity, such as rape, pederasty, or a violation of social status (e.g., penetrating a social equal). While these acts would be included in the Levitical laws, both texts are "unqualified and absolute" (Gagnon, 115) in their prohibitions. There is nothing in the actual text that specifies a certain type of same-sex act, and reconstructing a specific background to these laws provides fragile conclusions, since we possess so little insight into the same-sex practices of the Near Eastern world. Furthermore, as will be shown, what we do know about same-sex behavior in the Near East yields some measure of diverse perspectives, which must make us resist neatly mapping a particular perspective onto the Levitical laws unless the text demands it. Moreover, in the case of Lev 20:13, both partners are equally condemned, which suggests some measure of consensual responsibility. The older view that these prohibitions should be limited to male cult prostitution has received much less support recently, since the existence of such an institution in the Near East rests on very little (if any) evidence. (See Budin.)

Many suggestions have been made regarding the "moral logic" (Brownson) of the prohibition. Lack of procreative potential (Milgrom), the feminization of the passive partner (Nissinen 1998), the impurity of mixing semen with feces (Olyan), and the confusion of mixing gender classes (a male acting as a female; Deut 22:5; cf. Gagnon) are all possible motivations behind the command. However, there is no clear indication from the text or the historical background that any one of these options should be promoted to the exclusion of the others. The seriousness of the prohibition, which refers to the act as "an abomination" and calls for the death penalty, suggests an act more serious in the lawgiver's eyes than a violation of purity or sex that cannot lead to procreation (Loader 2012, 22–27).

Other OT passages that have been used to argue against same-sex relations are at best inconclusive, since they have other concerns. Sodom is not condemned for homosexuality per se in Genesis (19:1–9), and Ezekiel refers to Sodom's sin as pride and selfish affluence (Ezek 16:49–50). When the Sodomites demanded that the men be brought out to them so that they might "know" them, they may have intended a sexual act, but this would have been homosexual rape, not consensual sex (see also Judg 19:1–30). Morschauser (482–85) argues that the story of Sodom should be interpreted in light of the ancient Near Eastern practice of hostage-exchange, and that there was no sexual intent on the part of the men of the city.

Some have argued that there was a sexual relationship between Ruth and Naomi (Ruth 1:16–18) and between Jonathan and David (1 Sam 18:1–4; 2 Sam 1:26). However, there is no substantial evidence to support this view. Even if these couples actually did engage in sexual relations with each other, the biblical writers would not have endorsed this behavior: the former would have been incest, and the latter would have involved an extramarital affair and would also have been a direct violation of the aforementioned Levitical laws.

B. THE NEW TESTAMENT

There are three passages in the NT that refer to same-sex relations. The most significant and extensive is Rom 1:26–27, which states:

For this reason God gave them over to degrading passions; for their women exchanged the natural function for that which is unnatural, and in the same way also the men abandoned the natural function of the woman and burned in their desire toward one another, men with men committing indecent acts and receiving in their own persons the due penalty of their error. (NASB)

The view that Paul's words are limited to pederasty (Scroggs) cannot be substantiated for two reasons. First, there were several Greek words used to describe those involved in pederasty (e.g., *paiderastēs*, "lover of boys"; *paidophthoros*, "corruptor of boys"; *paidophilēs*, "fond of boys"), and none of these is used here. Second, pederasty did not exist (as far as we know) between females, and yet Paul condemns female same-sex relations on the same grounds as male same-sex relations—they are "unnatural" (Gk. *para physin*, Rom 1:26). And since there is no mention of master-slave relations, rape, or prostitution in this context, Paul's words should not be limited to one of these particular forms of same-sex acts. Like Lev 18:22 and 20:13, Paul's words include all forms of same-sex relations, including consensual and marital unions—even though these were rare in Paul's day. It should be noted that Paul uses language of mutuality throughout the passage: "desire toward one another," "males with males" (not masters with slaves, or men with prostitutes), and "received in themselves the due penalty for their error." If Paul only had in mind same-sex sexual relations that were driven by power differentials and oppression, he certainly does not make this clear. Furthermore, female same-sex relations were largely consensual in Paul's world (see Brooten 1996), and yet Paul considers these to be "unnatural" (Rom 1:26) and parallels these (e.g., "in the same way," Rom 1:27) to male same-sex relations.

The view that Paul only has in mind same-sex relations that are driven by excessive lust (Brownson) does not make sense of the female-female relations referred to in Rom 1:26. While Greco-Roman writers often portrayed male same-sex behavior as the result of excessive lust, the same is not true of female same-sex relations, which, as stated above, were largely consensual. Furthermore, Paul's language of exchange (see Rom 1:23, 26, 28) provides an interpretive lens for how we are to understand his indictment. Paul does not say that people exchanged non-lustful sexual relations for lustful ones. Rather, he says that they exchanged opposite-sex relations for same-sex relations (see Sprinkle 2016). According to Paul, this is rooted in humanity's exchange of its Creator (Rom 1:19–24) and the Creator's intention for sexual relations. This is why Paul is not just singling out idolatrous forms of sex; rather, he is saying that all humanity *is* idolatrous based on how it has exchanged God's will for its own, including its desire for same-sex unions.

There are two other passages in the NT that have been traditionally understood to condemn same-sex relationships: 1 Cor 6:9–10 and 1 Tim 1:9–10. Both of these passages contain vice lists, a common genre in first-century Greco-Roman literature. In 1 Cor 6:9–10 we find the terms *arsenokoitai* and *malakos*, which have been subject to much debate. The term *arsenokoitai* also appears in 1 Tim 1:10.

Malakos literally means "soft, gentle, or tender," and was sometimes used to describe effeminate men. If a man dressed in soft clothes, shaved his chest hair, wore perfume, or did anything else that crossed gender boundaries, he would be labeled as a *malakos*. One of the clearest ways in which a man would be considered effeminate, or *malakos*, is if he played the passive role in intercourse with men. Given the fact that in 1 Cor 6:9 *malakos* occurs in the context of sexual immorality, it is most probable that Paul has this sexual meaning in mind here.

Arsenokoitai is a more difficult word to translate since it is rare in Greco-Roman literature. In fact, 1 Cor 6:9–10 is the first time the word occurs in all of Greek literature. *Arsenokoitai* is a compound word that combines *arsen* ("male") and *koitē* ("bed"); together, they mean "one who sleeps with a male." However, merely adding up the compound parts of a word does not necessarily provide the meaning of the word in context, as in the case of "butterfly," which has nothing to do with butter or flies, or in the case of the word "understand," which does not mean "to stand under." The interpreter must provide more evidence to interpret and understand the meaning of *arsenokoitai*.

Such evidence can be found in the Septuagint of Lev 20:13—one of the two verses in the OT that condemn same-sex relations. Here the Septuagint reads: *kai hos an koimēthē meta arsenos koitēn gynaikos* ("and whoever lies with a male as with the lying with a woman"). Given the fact that *arsen* and *koitē* occur side by side in this text, it is likely that Paul created the compound word *arsenokoitai* based on the words *arsenos* and *koitēn* in Lev 20:13. If this is the case—and it is very likely that it is—then Paul's intended meaning of *arsenokoitai* is rooted in the Levitical prohibition against all forms of same-sex relations. First Corinthians 6:9–10 and 1 Tim 1:9–10, therefore, do not merely prohibit a particular form of same-sex relations but include all forms of same-sex relations (contra Martin). This interpretation is confirmed by later Coptic, Syriac, and Latin translations, which all render the word as "those who sleep with males" (Sprinkle 2016).

C. THE NEAR EASTERN WORLD

Mesopotamia

Martti Nissinen rightly states: "Ancient Near Eastern sources document same-sex erotic interaction meagerly and ambiguously" (1998, 19). It is therefore with great caution that the modern interpreter must investigate this literature.

Homosexual themes might possibly be present in the famous *Gilgamesh Epic*, in which Gilgamesh and Enkidu have some sort of love-relationship. However, the line between homoeroticism and homosocialism is often blurred in this text, and it does not provide a window into the everyday practice of ancient Mesopotamian people (Nissinen 1998, 24).

The earliest explicit references to same-sex acts are found in the Middle Assyrian Law Code (MAL A 19 and 20), dating from around 1250 BC. In paragraph 19, it is implied that it is shameful to play the passive role in a same-sex act, and paragraph 20 states that it is criminal to have sex with a social equal (see Nissinen 1998, 25–26). However, the text is unclear as to whether the passive partner or the active partner is punished (Bottéro and Petschow).

There is also a group of four omens found in *Šumma ālu* (ca. 668–627 BC) that speak to same-sex relations (*CTBM* 39 44:13; 45:32, 33, 34). These omens emphasize the significance of the active and passive roles in a same-sex act. To be penetrated involves shame and suppression; to penetrate reflects power and superiority (Wold, 48; Nissinen 1998, 28). The first of these four omens (44:13), in which the active partner gains power over the passive partner who is a social equal, appears to sanction, even applaud, the active partner. This omen, therefore, lends credibility to the interpretation that Middle Assyrian Law paragraph 20 condemns the passive partner rather than the active partner.

Mesopotamian sources also speak of the *assinnū*, *kurgarrû*, and *kulu'ū*, devotees of Ishtar who are described as singers, dancers, and (possibly) actors. All three groups appear to display some sort of gender ambiguity (*Erra Myth* 4.55–57), which would be expected for devotees of Ishtar, who typically transgressed conventional gender boundaries (Nissinen 1998, 30). Some scholars argue that the *assinnū*, *kurgarrû*, and *kulu'ū* received sex from other men (Bottéro and Petschow), while others say that there is little clear evidence that their cultic roles were sexual in nature (Nissinen 2010). Budin goes so far as to say that there is no evidence that cultic prostitution existed in the ancient world and that the three aforementioned groups are never described as performing sexual services (Budin, 19–20).

Another Mesopotamian text (BRM 4 20:5–7), which is part of an almanac of incantations, discusses the effect of the stars on lovemaking. One incantation refers to the love of a man for a woman (Libra), one refers to the love of a woman for a man (Pisces), and the last speaks of the love of a man for a man (Scorpio). The parallel between male-female "love" (*râmu*) and male-male love is striking. One might interpret this incantation as evidence for (and an approval of) mutual same-sex love. However, "[w]hat this means in concrete terms is extremely difficult to determine" (Nissinen 1998, 35).

Egypt

In Egypt, as elsewhere in the ancient Near East, same-sex acts were generally viewed negatively, as seen in the *Book of the Dead* (125 A 20, B 27; Nissinen 1998, 19). However, one man could show domination over another if he played the active role in sexual intercourse with another man (e.g., Coffin Text 636). Pederasty appears to have been condemned (Ptahhotpe maxim 32; *Instructions of Ankhsheshonq*, col. 13, 24; see Manniche, 14), and female same-sex relations receive hardly any mention apart from a passage in a dream book that reads: "If a woman has intercourse with her, she will experience a bad fate" (Manniche, 14–15).

The famous story about Seth and Horus is retold with variation, especially as it pertains to the nature of their homosexual encounter. On the one hand, the Late Egyptian *Contendings of Horus and Seth* displays clear contours of power rape and domination, as Seth seeks to denigrate Horus through anal penetration. However, other retellings of their sexual encounter suggest more reciprocity, as in the Pyramid Texts: "Horus has insinuated his semen into the backside of Setekh; Setekh has insinuated his semen into the backside of Horus" (cited in Parkinson). The nature of such reciprocity is disputed. The story is also preserved on a late 12th Dynasty fragment from el-Lahun, in which the sexual act is again viewed as an attempted rape. However, in this later retelling, Seth's sexual advances appear to be driven by sexual desire and not just an attempt to shame Horus, for Seth declares: "How lovely is your backside!" Horus is told (by his mother, Isis) to reject Seth's advances by telling him that: "It is too painful for me entirely, as you are heavier than me. My strength shall not support your strength" (Parkinson, 70–71). Horus's words would be an odd way to reject Seth's advances, if Seth only intended to rape Horus; the victim's pain would be an irrelevant concern for the active partner and therefore an inadequate deterrent (Parkinson).

There are a few debated examples from Egypt of what may be considered consensual same-sex relations. The one that has received a good deal of attention is the depiction in the tomb of Niankhkhnum and Khnumhotep—two male Egyptian manicurists who lived during the 5th Dynasty of Egypt's Old Kingdom. Several depictions of these two men show them in an intimate pose. Some have argued that they were twin brothers or simply good friends; however, as Greg Reeder has argued, the iconography of these two men is similar to other depictions of married couples during the same era. Another possible example of a consensual same-sex couple comes in the tale of King Neferkare and his military commander Sasenet (ca. 1700 BC). Here, the king paid nightly visits to his military commander, which lasted four hours (probably ruling out power-rape, although the number "four" maybe be symbolic). Then, "after his Person had done what he desired with him he returned to his place" (cited in Parkinson, 72). The reference is clearly sexual, and the king's visits are described as being regular. The fact that it was at night suggests that the relationship violated social protocol and hence was kept secret.

The extant texts and inscriptions from Egypt reflect negative views about same-sex relations. However, as in the case of Niankhkhnum and Khnumhotep, there appear to be exceptions to the norm.

D. THE GRECO-ROMAN WORLD

Greece

The most well known and widely accepted—perhaps the *only* accepted— form of same-sex relations in Ancient Greece (primarily in Athens, Sparta, and Crete) was pederasty (Gk. *paiderastia*), or "love for boys" (Dover). Pederastic relations consisted of an adult male citizen (*erastēs*) and a free-born youth (*erōmenos*), who was usually twelve to eighteen years of age. The adult *erastēs* would educate and train his *erōmenos* in the ways of society and culture, and in return the *erōmenos* would reward his mentor with sexual pleasure by playing the passive role in sexual intercourse. This type of relationship was considered honorable when practiced within the boundaries of certain societal norms and legal restrictions (Plato, *Symp.* 183e-185b), although there were always protesting voices. Plato himself, who seems to speak positively of pederasty in the *Symposium*, later condemned all same-sex relations as "unnatural" in his *Laws* (*Leg.* 636b–d). One of the most famous examples of pederastic same-sex love is the abduction of Ganymede by the god Zeus. Homer states that Ganymede was taken because he was the most beautiful of mortal men (*Il.* 20.231–235). Although Homer does not speak of a physical relationship between the two, later sources make it clear that this was how it was interpreted by both Greeks and Romans.

In most cases, the pederastic relation would end once the *erōnemos* showed evidence of manhood (e.g., growing a beard or chest hair). In some cases, however, the relationship developed into a lifelong, consensual love affair (see Plato, *Symp.* 181–183), as in the cases of Agathon and Pausanias (Plato, *Symp.* 193b; cf. Aelian, *Var. hist.* 2.21) and Parmenides and Zenon (Plato, *Parm.* 127a). Therefore, strict pederasty, as a temporary relationship between an adult and a teenage boy, is not the only type of same-sex relation that existed in ancient Greece (contra Scroggs 1983). There is also evidence, both literary and visual, that teenagers of the same age would court one another and engage in same-sex sexual relations (Hubbard 2003, 5; Hubbard 2014). One writer (Xenophon, *Anab.* 2.6.28) even refers to an older youth with a beard playing the role of the passive partner, while a younger youth is the active partner (Scroggs, 34). The second-century AD novel *An Ephesian Tale* by a different individual named Xenophon depicts a young man named Hippothous who falls in love with another man of the same age named Hyperanthes (*Ephesian Tale* 3.2). Another novel, written around the third century AD by Achilles Tatius, depicts male lovers who are roughly the same age (*Leuc. Clit.* 1.7–8, 12–14; 2.33–38).

Consensual, same-sex love can be found among women in ancient Greece (and in Rome; see below), although these relations are rarely mentioned. Such silence is to be expected in a culture where elite males, who generally abhorred same-sex female relations, were the ones whose writings have been preserved. The existence of female homoerotic relations is reflected, however, in Plato's *Laws* (previously mentioned), where he considers them to be "unnatural" (*Leg.* 636b–d). Unlike male same-sex relations, female homoerotic relations were not pederastic, nor did they reflect the active (dominant) and passive (dominated) power differentials like most male relations in the ancient world (Nissinen 1998, 79; Brooten 1996). The most well-known (and earliest) example is the poet Sappho, who was born on the island of Lesbos (from which we get the term "lesbian") around 612 BC. She appears to have been the head of a community of women known as a *thiasos*. Most of her poetry has been lost, but what is extant reveals strong evidence of her same-sex desire for some of her students. Cantarella (78–82) argues that Greek culture accepted love relationships between women in the seventh and sixth centuries BC as normal and even formalized them in these communities. Cantarella may be assuming too much, but it is clear that Sappho does speak of a woman's desire for another woman (see also Plato, *Symp.* 191e; Ovid, *Metam.* 9.666–797). Other references to female homoerotic relations include those on vase paintings that depict two adult women engaging in sexual foreplay (see Brooten 1996).

Rome

In general, male same-sex relations in Rome exhibited strict power differentials between the active and passive partners. The active partner was associated with masculinity and strength, while the passive partner was viewed as feminine and weak. Therefore, as long as the active partner was a person of higher social standing than the passive partner, most Romans would have approved of the sexual relationship. For this reason, the modern concepts of "homosexual" and "homosexuality" do not capture the mindset of the ancient Roman person (nor other ancient cultures, for that matter), since the gender of the passive partner was largely irrelevant. A dominant man could penetrate a female or a male, and as long as the passive male was of a lower social status (slave, prostitute, boy, etc.), no one would have considered the active partner "gay" or "homosexual" by modern standards. Being active and therefore masculine was what mattered. The accepted Roman view thus rejected "Greek love" because it would have subjected a freeborn and therefore equal-status Roman youth to playing the passive part in a same-sex act, resulting in unmanliness, disgrace, and humiliation (Williams).

In actuality, there was much more diversity in the types of same-sex relations in the Roman world. While we have numerous examples that fit the active and passive paradigm, there were several exceptions to this norm. We know of at least two emperors who played the passive role in intercourse with other men. Nero dressed up as a bride when he married his "husband" Pythagoras (Tacitus, *Ann.* 15.36–37). In this second marriage to another man, Nero—obviously of high status—assumed the passive role. Elagabalus (AD 218–222) also "[indulged] in unnatural vice with men" (*S.H.A. Elagabalus* 5.1–2) and made a public bath in the palace that "by this means he might get a supply of men with unusually large organs" (*S.H.A. Elagabalus* 8.6–7). Finally, the emperor Hadrian, while maintaining the active role, had a public love affair with the Bithynian Antinoüs. According to Aelius Spartianus, Hadrian wept passionately for Antinoüs when he died, which suggests that Hadrian's love for Antinoüs was more than just an exploitative sexual outlet.

Although same-sex sexual relations were largely accepted (as long as they followed certain social mores), there were those who were critical. Most notably, the Stoics and other moral philosophers believed that all forms of same-sex relations were "against nature." Musonius Rufus (ca. AD 30–100), for instance, said: "Among other sexual relationships, the most illegitimate involve adultery, and the relationships in which males relate to males are no more tolerable than adulterous ones because this outrage is contrary to nature" (King, 55). Others who believed that same-sex relations were "contrary to nature" included Seneca (4 BC–AD 65), Plutarch (AD 50–129), and Dio Chrysostom (d. ca. AD 112).

As among the Greeks, female same-sex relations in the Roman world defied the dominant/dominated patterns of male-male sexual relations. Consensual, same-sex love—even marriages—can be found during the time of imperial Rome. A second-century AD writer named Iamblichos talks about a marriage between two women named Berenike and Mesopotamia (Photios, *Bibliothēkē* 94.77a–b), and Lucian of Samosata mentions the marriage of two wealthy women named Megilla and Demonassa (*Dial. meretr.* 5.1–3). Ptolemy of Alexandria, a famous second-century AD scholar, refers to women taking other women as "lawful wives" (*Tetrabiblos* 3.14 sect. 172). And several archaeological discoveries depict mutual love between women, including a funeral relief that dates to the time of Caesar Augustus in which two women are holding hands in a way that resembles "the classic gesture of ancient Roman married couples" (Brooten 1994, 59–60).

In both Republican and Imperial Rome, some laws were passed against same-sex relations, although the details are not entirely clear. It seems that during the Republican period sexual relations between men and freeborn youths were forbidden, but this does not address all forms of same-sex acts (e.g., male slaves were still used as sexual outlets). The *lex Scantinia*, which was in existence before 50 BC, seems to have been directed at males who played the passive role in same-sex relations. However, there are only scant references to this law, and its details are shrouded in mystery. It is clear, on the other hand, that during the reign of Justinian (AD 482–565) all forms of same-sex relations were deemed "against nature" and therefore considered unlawful (see Dunn 1998a).

E. THE JEWISH WORLD

The Jewish opinion of same-sex relations during the biblical and post-biblical period is unanimous, clear, and unequivocal: all types of homosexual relations were considered sinful. For the most part, Jewish writers condemned pederasty, which was the most common form of homoerotic behavior known to them (Jos. *Ant.* 1.200–201; *Ag. Ap.* 2.273–275; Philo, *Leg.* 3:37–42; *Contempl.* 59–60). However, Jewish writers also made mention of—and condemned—same-sex relations without reference to pederasty. Josephus, for instance, raises the question, "What are our laws about marriage?" His answer is that "the law owns no other mixture of sexes but that which [is] according to nature [*kata physin*]," and he cites Lev 18:22 and 20:13 in support (*Ag. Ap.* 2.199). Other Jewish writers condemned same-sex relations, or even same-sex passion, without mentioning age distinctions (*Ps.-Phoc.* 3, 190–191; *Let. Aris.* 152; *2 En.* 34:1–2 P).

The rabbis of the postbiblical period maintained this early Jewish view and sometimes applied Lev 18:22 and 20:13 to the question of same-sex marriages (*b. Sanh.* 58a; *Sipra Ahare* 9:8; and *Sipra* on Lev 18:3; Nissinen 1998, 99–101). The Mishnah calls for stoning if a man is caught lying with another man (*m. Sanh.* 7:4). Most scholars agree that rabbinic literature sees same-sex acts between men as wrong (Nissinen 1998, 98–101; Satlow, 23). Female same-sex acts were acknowledged (*b. Yebam.* 76a; *b. Šabb.* 65a–b; *b. Giṭ.* 49c), and although the rabbis did not denounce same-sex female relations as aggressively as they did male same-sex relations, they still considered the former to be sin.

While Lev 18:22 and 20:13 were the main biblical passages that Jewish writers drew upon to condemn same-sex relations, the story of Sodom (Gen 19) was sometimes used as well, but not until the first century AD. The OT frequently references the sin of Sodom without ever mentioning same-sex behavior (e.g., Isa 1:10–17; 3:9; Jer 23:14; Zeph 2:8–11), and this "non-homosexual" interpretation appears to have been adopted by Jesus and the NT writers (Matt 10:15; 11:23–24; though see Jude 7 for a disputed reference). Sirach 16:8 (180 BC) mentions the sin of Sodom but with no reference to same-sex behavior, and the Wisdom of Solomon (10:6–9; 19:13–17) specifies the sin of Sodom as pride with no mention of same-sex behavior. Likewise, the Pseudepigrapha contain many references to Sodom that do not identify a specific sin (*Jub.* 13:17; 16:5–6; 20:5–6; *T. Ash.* 7:1; *T. Benj.* 9:1; *T. Isaac* 5:27; *T. Levi* 14:6; *4 Ezra* 5:7; 7:106; cf. 3 Macc 2:4–5). It is in the writings of Philo that we first see same-sex behavior being listed as one of the sins of Sodom (Philo, e.g., *Abr.* 134–137), a tradition we also find in Josephus (Jos. *Ant.* 1.194–95, 200–201). As for the rabbis, the non-homosexual interpretation appears to be the most common (*b. Sanh.* 109a; *b. Ketub.* 103aa; *b. B. Bat.* 12b; 59a; 168a; *b. ʿErub.* 49a).

F. THE CHRISTIAN WORLD

Early Christianity maintained the universal prohibition against all forms of same-sex relations that we find in Judaism and in the Bible. In some cases, pederasty is singled out (*Did.* 2.2; *Barn.* 10:6–7; 19:4; Clem. *Protr.* 10.108.5). In other cases, however, same-sex acts are condemned without any reference to age distinctions or exploitation (*Apoc. Pet.* 10:4 [Eth.]/10:17 [Gk.]; *Apoc. Paul* 39; cf. *Acts Thom.* 6:55). The prohibition of consensual same-sex acts is most clear in prohibitions of female same-sex activity. Augustine, for instance, warns nuns of the temptation of engaging in sexual activity with each other:

> The love which you bear to each other must be not carnal . . . for those things which are practiced by immodest women in shameful frolic and sporting with one another ought not even to be done by . . . chaste virgins dedicated to be handmaids of Christ by a holy vow. (*Ep.* 211.15)

Clement of Alexandria states that not only sex between women but also marriage between women is unnatural (*Paed.* 3.3.21.3). Other references to "women who rub"—the term used for women who engage in same-sex acts—can be found in Tertullian (*Res.* 16.6; *Pall.* 4.9).

Although female homoeroticism is universally condemned in early Christianity (Brooten 1996), it is striking that Rom 1:26—the only biblical reference to female same-sex activity—was not universally interpreted this way. While John Chrysostom (*Hom. Rom.* 1:26–27), Clement of Alexandria (*Paed.* 2.10.86), and Ambrosiaster (Pseudo-Ambrose) (*Epistle to the Romans* on 1:26) interpret Rom 1:26 to refer to female homoerotic behavior, Augustine (*Bon. conj.* 10.11; *Nupt.* 20.35) and Anastasias (cited by Clement of Alexandria in his *Paedagogos*) understand the verse to prohibit "unnatural," non-procreative sex between man and woman (e.g., anal sex) (see Brooten 1985).

Early Christian writers give various reasons for condemning same-sex activity. First, many writers echo the belief we find in some Greco-Roman writings that same-sex acts are the byproduct of excessive lust and indulgence (or luxury) (Clem. *Paed.* 3.3; Lac. *Inst.* 6.23; John Chrysostom, *Hom. Rom.* 1:26–27). However, same-sex behavior does not appear to be critiqued simply because it was believed to result from excessive lust (as if non-lustful forms of same-sex behavior would have been applauded). Again, female homoerotic behavior is not described in terms of excessive lust, as male same-sex behavior is, and yet it is still condemned. Second, most writers believed that sex was designed for procreation (Clem. *Paed.* 2.10.92, 95; Lac. *Inst.* 5.9; *Opif.* ch. 12; Augustine, *Nupt.* 1.6.7; *Bon. conj.* 11, 13). Therefore all non-procreative forms are ruled out, and this would obviously include same-sex activity (Clem. *Paed.* 2.10.95; cf. Dunn, "Evolution"). Third, according to early Christian writers same-sex activity is prohibited because it confuses God-given gender roles. In the most explicit and lengthy denunciations of same-sex activity, it appears that gender confusion and violating God's order of nature are the main reasons why homoeroticism is condemned (Clem. *Paed.* 2.10; 3.3; John Chrysostom, *Hom. Rom.* 1:26–27), though not to the exclusion of the previous two reasons.

BIBLIOGRAPHY: D. S. Bailey, *Homosexuality and the Western Christian Tradition* (1975); J. A. Banister, "Ὁμοίως and the Use of Parallelism in Romans 1:26–27," *JBL* 128.3 (2009), 569–90; A. Birley, trans., *Lives of the Later Caesars: The First Part of the Augustan History: With Newly Compiled Lives of Nerva and Trajan* (1976); J. Boswell, *Christianity, Social Tolerance, and Homosexuality* (1980); J. Bottéro, *Mesopotamia: Writing, Reasoning, and the Gods*, trans. Z. Bahrani and M. Van De Mieroop (1992); J. Bottéro and H. Petschow, "Homosexualität," in *Reallexikon der Assyriologie und Vorderasiatischen Archäologie*, ed. D. O. Edzard (1972–1975), IV.459–68; D. Boyarin, "Are There any Jews in the 'History of Sexuality?'" *Journal of the History of Sexuality* 5.3 (1995), 333–55; B. J. Brooten, *Love Between Women: Early Christian Responses to Female Homoeroticism* (1996); B. J.

Brooten, "Patristic Interpretations of Romans 1:26," StPatr 18 (1985), 338–40; J. V. Brownson, *Bible, Gender, Sexuality* (2013); S. L. Budin, *The Myth of Sacred Prostitution in Antiquity* (2009); E. Cantarella, *Bisexuality in the Ancient World* (1992); P. Cartledge, "Alexander the Great: Hunting for a New Past?" *History Today* 54.7 (2004), 10–16; M. R. D'Angelo, "Sexuality," *EDEJ*, 1222–24; J. Davidson, *The Greeks and Greek Love* (2007); J. B. DeYoung, "The Meaning of 'Nature' in Romans 1 and Its Implications for Biblical Proscriptions of Homosexual Behavior," *JETS* 31 (1988), 429–41; J. B. DeYoung, "The Source and NT Meaning of *arsenokoitai*, with Implications for Christian Ethics and Ministry," *The Master's Seminary Journal* 3 (1992), 191–215; K. J. Dover, *Greek Homosexuality* (2nd ed., 1989); L. A. Dunn, "The Evolution of Imperial Roman Attitudes toward Same-Sex Acts," PhD diss., Miami University (1998); J. H. Elliott, "No Kingdom of God for Softies? Or, What Was Paul Really Saying? 1 Corinthians 6:9–10 in Context," *BTB* 34 (2004), 17–40; L. J. Eron, "Homosexuality and Judaism," in *Homosexuality and World Religions*, ed. A. Swidler, (1993), 103–34; P. F. Esler, "The Sodom Tradition in Romans 1:18–32," *BTB* 34.1 (2004), 4–16; V. P. Furnish, "The Bible and Homosexuality: Reading the Texts in Context," in *Homosexuality in the Church: Both Sides of the Debate*, ed. J. S. Siker (1994), 18–35; K. L. Gaca, "Philo's Principles of Sexual Conduct and Their Influence on Christian Platonist Sexual Principles," *SPhilo* 8 (1996), 21–39; R. A. J. Gagnon, *The Bible and Homosexual Practice: Texts and Hermeneutics* (2001); D. M. Halperin, *One Hundred Years of Homosexuality and Other Essays on Greek Love* (1990); R. B. Hays, *The Moral Vision of the New Testament* (1996); R. B. Hays, "Relations Natural and Unnatural: A Response to John Boswell's Exegesis of Romans 1," *JRE* 14 (1986), 184–215; C. Heard, "What does the Mob Want Lot to Do in Genesis 19:9?" *Hebrew Studies* 51(2010), 95–105; T. K. Hubbard, ed., *Homosexuality in Greece and Rome: A Sourcebook of Basic Documents* (2003); T. K. Hubbard, "Peer Homosexuality," in *A Companion to Greek and Roman Sexualities*, ed. T. K. Hubbard (2014), 128–49; C. King, trans., *Musonius Rufus: Lectures & Sayings*, ed. W. B. Irvine (rev. ed., 2011); W. R. G. Loader, *The Dead Sea Scrolls on Sexuality: Attitudes towards Sexuality in Sectarian and Related Literature at Qumran* (2009); W. R. G. Loader, *The New Testament on Sexuality* (2012); L. Manniche, "Some Aspects of Ancient Egyptian Sexual Life," *Acta Orientalia* 38 (1977), 11–23; D. B. Martin, "*Arsenokoitês* and *Malakos*: Meanings and Consequences," in *Biblical Ethics & Homosexuality*, ed. R. L. Brawley (1996), 117–136; J. Milgrom, *Leviticus 17–22: A New Translation with Introduction and Commentary* (2000); S. Morschauser, "'Hospitality,' Hostiles and Hostages: On the Legal Background to Genesis 19.1-9," *JSOT* 27.4 (2003), 461–85; J. Neusner, ed., "Homosexuality," in *Dictionary of Judaism in the Biblical Period* (1999), 299–300; M. Nissinen, "Are There

Homosexuals in Mesopotamian Literature?" *JAOS* 130.1 (2010), 73–77; M. Nissinen, *Homoeroticism in the Biblical World: A Historical Perspective*, trans. K. Stjerna (1998); S. M. Olyan, "'And With a Male You Shall Not Lie the Lying Down of a Woman': On the Meaning and Significance of Leviticus 18:22 and 20:13," *Journal of the History of Sexuality* 5 (1994), 179–206; R. B. Parkinson, "'Homosexual' Desire and Middle Kingdom Literature," *JEA* 81 (1995), 57–76; W. L. Petersen, "On the Study of 'Homosexuality' in Patristic Sources," StPatr 20 (1989), 283–88; B. N. Peterson, "The Sin of Sodom Revisited: Reading Genesis 19 in Light of Torah," *JETS* 59 (2016), 17–31; P. Ramsey, "Human Sexuality in the History of Redemption," *JRE* 16 (1988), 56–86; M. L. Satlow, "'They Abused Him Like a Woman': Homoeroticism, Gender Blurring, and the Rabbis in Late Antiquity," *Journal of the History of Sexuality* 5.1 (1994), 1–25; R. Scroggs, *The New Testament and Homosexuality* (1983); M. B. Skinner, *Sexuality in Greek and Roman Culture* (2005); H. F. D. Sparks, *The Apocryphal Old Testament* (1984); P. Sprinkle, "A Critical Evaluation of the Excessive-Lust Interpretation of Romans 1:26–27," *BBR* 25 (2015), 497–517; P. M. Sprinkle, *People to Be Loved: Why Homosexuality Is Not Just an Issue* (2016); P. M. Sprinkle, "Romans 1 and Homosexuality: A Critical Review of James Brownson's *Bible, Gender, Sexuality*," *BBR* 24 (2014), 515–28; H. J. Toensing, "Women of Sodom and Gomorrah: Collateral Damage in the War against Homosexuality?" *Journal of Feminist Studies in Religion* 21.2 (2005), 61–74; R. B. Ward, "Why Unnatural? The Tradition behind Romans 1:26–27," *HTR* 90 (1997), 263–84; C. A. Williams, *Roman Homosexuality* (2010); D. V. Wold, *Out of Order: Homosexuality in the Bible and the Ancient Near East* (1998); D. F. Wright, "Homosexuals or Prostitutes? The Meaning of ΑΡΣΕΝΟΚΟΙΤΑΙ (1 Cor. 6:9; 1 Tim. 1:10)," *VC* 38 (1984), 125–53.

PS

See also APHRODISIACS & EROTIC SPELLS, CELIBACY, EUNUCHS, MARRIAGE, RAPE, and VIRGINITY.

SANITATION

Sanitation, the application of principles promoting public health, was barely observed in antiquity. Ancient societies knew that diseases were contagious. They had to cope with the removal of human waste, especially from cities. But many of the key discoveries of hygiene were not made until the nineteenth century, such as the discovery of microscopic pathogens (bacteria, viruses) and the link between food and water contaminated with feces and cholera and typhoid fever.

Human urine breaks down through a bacterial process to produce ammonia, with its characteristic smell. It was used along with animal urine in the processes of laundering, dyeing, and tanning. Feces produces skatole (C^9H^9N), a compound that emits a pungent stench. Human and animal feces are rich in nitrates and phosphates and were widely used as fertilizer. But this practice involved the risk of the spread of disease.

A. THE OLD TESTAMENT

The Hebrew word "to urinate," *šîn*, occurs six times in the OT, always in the historical books (1 Sam 25:22, 34; 1 Kgs 14:10; 16:11; 21:21; 2 Kgs 9:8) and always in the phrase *maštîn běqîr*, which the KJV renders literally as "one that pisseth against a wall," an idiom that describes an adult male and that is found in threats of extermination. (See Smith.) The noun for "urine," *šayin*, appears only in two parallel passages (2 Kgs 18:27; Isa 36:12), in the Assyrian threat by Sennacherib's general that unless Jerusalem surrenders its inhabitants will be forced by the siege to "eat their own excrement and drink their own urine" (KJV, "eat their own dung, and drink their own piss"). A modern parallel of similar desperate measures sometimes occurs in mining disasters as trapped miners have used their own excrement and urine in final efforts to stave off dehydration and remain alive.

The only ordinance in the Torah concerning defecation comes in the context of a military campaign, during which the Lord commands:

"Designate a place outside the camp where you can go to relieve yourself. As part of your equipment have something to dig with, and when you relieve yourself, dig a hole and cover up your excrement" (Deut 23:12–13). Covering the feces would make it impossible for flies to alight on the waste matter and subsequently transmit various diseases, such as poliomyelitis, conjunctivitis, and trachoma, through contact with foodstuffs.

The Hebrew idiom for "defecate" was "to cover one's feet." Ehud assassinates Eglon, the king of Moab, while he is sitting on a toilet in the upper room of his palace. The king is not discovered for a time because his officials think he is relieving himself (Judg 3:24). When Saul goes into a cave to relieve himself, David, who is hiding in the interior, spares his life (1 Sam 24:3).

The Hebrew word for "dung," *gēl*, appears in only three verses. Zophar reminds Job that man "shall perish for ever like his own dung" (Job 20:7). It was a quite common practice to use dried animal dung as fuel to bake bread, but the Lord commands Ezekiel to bake bread with "human excrement" as a sign to disobedient Israel (Ezek 4:12). When the prophet protests, the Lord relents and allows him to use animal dung rather than human excrement (Ezek 4:15).

A related word appears in the Lord's threat to burn the house of Jeroboam like dung (*gālāl*) (1 Kgs 14:10). The Hebrew word *madmēnâ*, "manure," is used once, in a threat against Moab (Isa 25:10). The word *'ašpōt*, translated "dunghill," or place where dung is burned, designates the lowest level of humiliation from which the Lord raises up the beggar (1 Sam 2:8) and the poor (Lam 4:5). Earthly kings threatened to reduce the houses of rebels to "dunghills" (KJV, Dan 2:5; 3:29; Ezra 6:11).

The use of animal dung and possibly human excrement as fertilizer is alluded to in a number of passages that speak of the spreading of dung (2 Kgs 9:37; Ps 83:10; Jer 8:2; 9:22; 16:4; 25:33).

The only occurrence of the Hebrew word for latrine (*maḥărā'ôt*) occurs when Jehu kills Ahab's servants of Baal: "They demolished the sacred stone of Baal and tore down the temple of Baal, and people have used it for a latrine to this day" (2 Kgs 10:27).

Pigs, who are omnivorous, devoured garbage, sewage, and even corpses. The Hebrew prohibition against eating pork protected the Israelites from some parasites. The recent discovery of two stone toilet seats in Jerusalem (7th–6th c. BC) has revealed, however, that the Jews were subject to parasites. A microscopic analysis of the coprolites (dried fecal material) from a cesspit below one of the seats revealed that (possibly because of the siege of Nebuchadnezzar in 586 BC) the diet of the inhabitants was restricted to four types of vegetables and plants rather than wheat and barley. The analysis also revealed thousands of eggs of the tapeworm (*Taenia*) and whipworm (*Trichuris trichina*) from beef that had been inadequately cooked. (See Cahill et al.)

The streets of Palestine were unpaved and often covered with rubbish and mire (2 Sam 22:43; Ps 18:42; Isa 5:25; Mic 7:10; Zech 9:3; 10:5). As everyone wore sandals, the washing of the feet of guests before they entered a home was widely practiced (Gen 18:4; 19:2; Judg 19:21).

Garbage was taken out of Jerusalem from the "Dung Gate" (*ša'ar hā'ašpōt*; Neh 2:13; 3:13–14; 12:31), located at the southern end of the walled city of Jerusalem, and was deposited in the Hinnom Valley (2 Kgs 23:10; Jer 7:31; Neh 11:30) to the southwest of the city. This was where the wicked kings Ahaz and Manasseh performed human sacrifices (2 Kgs 16:3; 2 Chr 33:6). Its name in Hebrew was *gê'-hinnōm*, which is rendered in Greek by the LXX as *Gaienna*. Its Latin version, *Gehenna*, became the name for hell in the NT (Gk. *geenna*). (See Bailey.)

B. THE NEW TESTAMENT

In Jesus's parable about an unproductive fig tree, a servant responds: "Sir . . . leave it alone for one more year, and I'll dig around it and fertilize it" (Luke 13:8, NIV). In this case the KJV renders the Greek phrase *balō kopria* more accurately "I shall . . . dung it." Salt that has lost its savor, Jesus declares, is not fit for the *kopria* (KJV "dunghill"; NIV "manure pile"; Luke 14:35).

In order to provide an example of humble service, Jesus himself takes on the role of a servant in washing the feet of his disciples (John 13:1–11). Jesus is challenged by some Pharisees as to why he and his disciples eat food without washing their hands first (Matt 15:1–3; Mark 7:1–3). The earliest Jewish text that refers to this custom appears in the Mishnah, compiled ca. AD 200 (see Lachs, 246–47).

The Greek word for toilet, *aphedrōn*, appears in parallel passages (Matt 15:17; Mark 7:19) as Jesus explains to his disciples that people are defiled not by the food that is digested and goes into the "draught" (KJV) but by the words which come out of their mouths. The NIV chose not to translate the word in question, but other English versions do, such as the CEB ("sewer") and CJB ("latrine").

The KJV renders the phrase *katharizōn panta ta brōmata*, "purging all meats," in Mark 7:19, understanding it as applying to the process of digestion. But modern translations—e.g., the NIV, "Jesus declared all foods clean" (see Marcus, 455)—indicate that this is an important declaration, by which Jesus apparently does away with the distinction between kosher and nonkosher foods (see, however, Boyarin). This is also the message conveyed to Peter during the vision he has on the rooftop of the house of Simon the tanner at Joppa (Acts 10), signifying the acceptance of the Roman centurion among the people of God's covenant. This is also Paul's message in Rom 14 (cf. 1 Tim 4:1–5).

In contention with certain Judaizers at Philippi, Paul declares, after listing his own credentials as a member of the tribe of Benjamin and as a leading Pharisee, that he now counts all these as nothing more than *sky-bala* (KJV "dung"; NIV "garbage"; Phil 3:8). The etymology of the Greek word indicates that it originally referred to scraps of food thrown to the dogs who often lingered by tables during meals and served as convenient "garbage disposals" (cf. Matt 15:27||Mark 7:28).

C. THE NEAR EASTERN WORLD

The Indus River Valley

A most remarkable sewage system was discovered at the site of Mohenjo-Daro, "The Mound of the Dead," on the right bank of the Indus River, 250 miles north of Karachi. It was part of the Indus Valley Civilization, which flourished from 2500 to 1800 BC. The site was first discovered in 1922, and then excavated from 1924 to 1931 by John Marshall.

Mohenjo-Daro, which was built ca. 2450 BC, was a well-planned city. It was provided with three hundred wells, or one for every three houses. The "Great Bath," which measured 52 meters (170 ft.) by 32.4 meters (105 ft.), was used for communal bathing, and possibly for ritual purposes.

Houses were equipped with bathing platforms located near the wall closest to the street. These platforms measured about two square meters and were made of bricks with rims to form shallow basins. An outlet in the walls directed wastewater into the streets.

Nearby these platforms were toilets with brick supports that probably held wooden seats. Feces and urine would be directed through chutes into sewers built under the streets. In some cases, there is evidence of toilets on upper floors, whose contents were directed down by terra-cotta pipes set in the walls.

The sewage pipes, which were also made of terra-cotta, were placed eighteen to twenty-four inches (45–60 cm.) below the streets. They were covered with baked bricks. Settling pools were placed at intervals. These were covered with limestone blocks, which could be removed for the cleaning out of solid materials. The branches of the sewers fed into a large, corbelled vault sewer that directed the waste outside the city. (See M. Jansen.)

Mesopotamia

In Mesopotamia, garbage was thrown out into the streets, where wild dogs and feral pigs roamed. Some adoption contracts refer to babies who were abandoned on the streets and rescued from the mouths of dogs.

Large rubbish dumps (Akk. sing. *kiqillutu*) were formed outside the cities. At Tell Majnuna outside of Tell Brak a rubbish mound that formed over three centuries (3900–3600 BC) covered 7.5 acres to a depth of twenty-three feet (7 m.). At the Royal Cemetery of Ur, Leonard Woolley dug into a large rubbish mound measuring about 400 x 164 feet (120 x 50 m.), which was thirty-three feet (10 m.) deep. It is estimated that this dump contained about one hundred eighty thousand cubic meters of trash. An omen from the *šumma ālu* series predicts: "If a city's garbage pit is green—that city will be prosperous" (*COS* 1.120:424). Another omen predicts that if a dump grows too high, the city will be abandoned.

The Akkadian word for "urine" was *šīnātu*, and for "to urinate," *šânu*. Judging from the dream omen texts *Ziqīqu*, many urinated outdoors:

> If his urine flows in front of (his) penis (onto) a wall of a street, he will h[ave] sons. If his urine flows in front of (his) penis (onto) the streets, his property will be robb[ed] and given to the city. (Cited by Smith, 709)

> If he pours his [urine] into a river: his harvest will be bountiful. If he pours his urine into a well: he will lose his property.

> If he pours his urine into an irrigation-canal: Adad (the Weather-god) will flood his harvest. (Oppenheim, 265)

An Akkadian word for "to defecate" was *ezûm*; one of the words for excrement was *zû*. The phrase for a toilet was *bīt musâti*. There is considerable archaeological evidence for toilets, but rather scanty evidence for sewers. In "The Descent of Ishtar," Ereshkigal, the queen of the netherworld, threatens Isthar's envoy: "The food of the city's *gutters* shall be thy food: the *sewers* of the city shall be thy drink" (*ANET*, 108).

The most extensive evidence of a sewage system in Mesopotamia comes from a Sumerian colony (3300–3200 BC) located at Habuba Kabira (El-Kowm) in Syria. This site was originally fifty miles west of the Euphrates but is now under the waters of Lake Assad, created by the Tabaqah Dam on the Euphrates. The houses had drains that evacuated wastewater and sewage through fitted sections of two-foot-long clay pipes into an open gutter that ran along the streets.

Six toilets with baked-brick seats were found in the Northern Palace at ancient Eshnunna (modern Tell Asmar) (2300–2150 BC). The toilets were located in long, narrow rooms paved with baked brick. The toilets were provided with brick platforms supporting seats covered with bitumen. Vertical clay drains twenty-two inches in diameter drained the excrement. A sewer carried waste and water for a distance of 164 feet (50 m.).

Typical deep pit toilets from 2750–2500 BC were found at Eridu. A toilet, or at times nothing at all, was placed over a cylindrical pit. Such pits were formed by stacked perforated ceramic rings and were about fifteen feet (4.5 m.) deep.

Leonard Woolley found many houses northwest of the sacred area of Ur (ca. 2000 BC) that had small rooms, some under stairs, with toilets over deep drains. Thirty-six percent of homes in one district and 68 percent in another area had toilets. Three houses in district AH had two toilets each. The drains led the waste to containers outside the houses.

At Nippur (early 2nd millennium BC), 30 percent of the homes were provided with deep pit toilets. A. Parrot found two clay bathtubs from the same era at the palace at Mari. Beside them were simple "Turkish type" toilets, consisting of holes over narrow drains. Ceramic drains went deep below the palace.

The palace at Nuzi (ca. 15th c. BC) had baked-brick toilet seats, one of which had a marble slab "backsplash." Four systems of channels drained water from the toilets, kitchens, and courtyards. From the same era, the Syrian coastal site of Alalakh, which was excavated by Leonard Woolley, was found to have had sixteen "flush" toilets. They were placed in rooms with plastered floors and walls and were provided with brick foot-stands. The contents of the toilets were passed into drains that ran below the walls through interlocking pipes either into the streets or into cesspits.

The provincial Assyrian palace (9th c. BC) at Til Barsip (Tell Ahmar), located in northern Syria by the Euphrates River, was provided with two bathrooms and nine toilets. Their water and wastes were drained through a conduit for a distance of 260 feet (80 m.). In the major Neo-Assyrian palaces (8th–7th c. BC), a bathing room was included close to the throne-room. These bathing rooms had a wall that was pierced for the drainage of water. Turner concludes that these drain holes were too small to serve toilets, so chamber pots must have been used (Turner, 192).

The Babylonians feared a demon that was believed to lurk in latrines and cause epilepsy:

> If his right side is let down: stroke (inflicted by) a lurker; he will recover. If the right side of his body is in its entirety let down: stroke (inflicted) by a lurker; he has been hit at the rear. If his left side is let down: Hand of Šulak. If his left side is let down in its entirety: he has been hit at the front; Hand of Šulak, Lurker of the bathroom. A conjurer shall not make a prognosis for his recovery. (Stol, 76)

To protect themselves against such a *rābiṣ musâti*, "demon of the toilet," the Babylonians set up images of the protective lion-man *urmaḫlullû* outside their privies.

The sluggish flow of the Euphrates over a low gradient and the network of irrigation canals and marshes in southern Mesopotamia provided a breeding ground for diseases such as malaria and schistomiasis. Medical texts describe the emergence of the *urbatu* worm (Ascaris) from the anus, nose, or mouth of patients.

Egypt

In Egypt, communal dumps of rubbish and garbage were placed outside of villages at the edge of the desert, where they attracted scavengers such as rodents, dogs, hyenas, jackals, crows, and vultures. Unwanted babies were at times abandoned at these sites. The dumps were not as much of a problem in Upper (southern) Egypt as they were in Lower (northern) Egypt because of the former area's hot and dry climate.

The Egyptian word for "urine" was *wsšt*; its written form includes a depiction of a man's penis with drops of urine falling from it. The word for feces was *ḥw33t*, "putrefaction"; a euphemism was the phrase *ḥtp-k3*, "that which appeases the *ka* [i.e., a man's spirit]." The Egyptians believed that most disease was caused by a noxious substance called *wḥdw*, which they thought was formed from residues of undigested food. They believed this flowed backward from the large intestine to the heart and was eventually expelled through the anus. The Egyptians were therefore quite concerned about seeking remedies for a "warm anus" and a "hot anus." The *wḥdw* was also believed to turn into worms.

The Papyrus Ebers contains prescriptions for urinary and digestive problems; for example:

To Relieve Retention of Urine in a Child.

Cook an old papyrus in oil and smear on the body of the child.

Constipation.

Mix half an onion in the froth of beer. Drink it. This is also a delightful remedy against death. (cited in Brier, 284)

Most villagers relieved themselves outdoors. The earliest evidence of a toilet comes from a 2nd Dynasty (ca. 2700 BC) tomb (no. 2302) at Sakkara, where a dish filled with sand was placed below the hole of a seat held in place by brick supports.

At the Middle Kingdom (ca. 2000 BC) city of Lahun, a central gutter ran down the main street. Bathrooms and toilets placed in small rooms next to the bedrooms emptied out their waste and water into this gutter through holes in the house walls.

The tomb of Kha, a senior official (ca. 1350 BC) in the workmen's village of Deir el-Medina, had a toilet consisting of a wooden seat with a slot in its middle, which would have been used with a pottery vessel below it.

There were relatively few cities in ancient Egypt. The best archaeological evidence comes from the short-lived capital of the heretic pharaoh Akhenaten (r. 1352–1336 BC) at Akhetaten (Amarna). Several bathrooms with facilities for bathing and toilets have been identified at this site; these bathrooms were always next to the bedrooms. A rimmed limestone slab behind a low screen served as a place where the bather stood and either poured water over himself or had a servant do so. The water ran off through an outlet in the wall or into a receptacle that was emptied outside. Next to this was placed the toilet. The excavators recovered a seat of limestone with a keyhole opening, which would have been set on brick supports over a vessel filled with sand. This would be emptied into a cesspit. In one case, a vessel set in a wall may have served as a urinal.

The excavations indicate that luxurious homes and poorer homes were located in the same neighborhoods. The city had garbage dumps and open sewers, which must have emitted a noxious odor and attracted flies, which would have transmitted diseases (see *CANE*, 3.1791).

Herodotus, the Greek historian who visited Egypt in the fifth century BC, was a keen observer of foreign customs. He commented as follows on the odd postures of the Egyptians in relieving themselves: "Women make water standing, men sitting. They relieve nature indoors, and eat out of doors in the streets, giving the reason, that things unseemly but necessary should be done in secret, things not unseemly should be done openly" (*Hist.* 2.35).

The examination of scores of mummies has revealed that the Egyptians suffered from numerous diseases that were caused by unsanitary conditions such as the failure to properly dispose of human waste, the pestilence of flies, the eating of beef and pork infested with worms, the pollution of the Nile River, and the endemic existence of worms in the irrigation canals. Parasites that affected the Egyptians included *Trichinella*, which causes trichinosis; wire worms (*Strongyloides*); pork or beef tapeworms (*Taenia*); guinea worms (*Dracunculus*); and bilharzia, which causes *Schistosomiasis*.

D. THE GRECO-ROMAN WORLD

Crete

A highly developed system of bathrooms, toilets, and sewers was constructed by the Minoan civilization (2200–1600 BC) in their palaces (Knossos, Mallia, Phaistos) on the island of Crete and on their colony at Thera (Santorini).

The so-called "Palace of Minos" was discovered by Arthur Evans in north central Crete at the site of Knossos. Evans excavated the great site and also reconstructed some of its structures. All three of the great Minoan palaces have similar plans, with a large central court for the bull-jumping games and a residential quarter to one side of the court.

When the terrace for the palace at Knossos was built (ca. 2000 BC), a complete loop of drains extending at least 472 feet (150 m.) was built under the principal areas of the domestic quarter to evacuate water and sewage. Beginning from the Court of Distaffs, the northern branch went under a light-well, the Hall of the Colonnades, and the Hall of the Double Axes. The southern branch went under the Room of the Plaster Couch and south of the Queen's Megaron and joined the northern branch under the south light-well of the Hall of Double Axes, then exited out of the eastern wall of the palace.

The drains were provided with air vents and manhole covers and in places were large enough to permit men to descend and clear out any blockages. Water from the roof was used for the baths and to flush out the toilets. There was a private toilet room in the Queen's Hall, which could be closed with a door. Along the rear wall there was a hole about fourteen inches wide over a drain. The floor and walls were covered with gypsum for easier cleaning. A clay bathtub was found nearby. Another lavatory in the Room of the Plaster Couch was also faced with gypsum. Fittings for a seat were found over a hole leading to the drain below. (See MacDonald and Driessen.)

At the palace of Mallia to the east of Knossos, a tiny partition shielded a toilet next to the Queen's Hall. The toilet was connected to drains that exited from the west wall of the palace. There was also a bathing room and a toilet in the Men's Hall that was connected to drains there.

At Phaistos in south central Crete, there was a lavatory (5 ft. x 12 ft.) in the North Residential Quarter. This room, which was walled off with a thin brick partition, was lined with gypsum. In one corner, there was a gap in the floor over a drain where a wooden toilet seat was probably set up.

The Minoan colony on the volcanic island of Thera (modern Santorini) in the central Aegean Sea was destroyed by a cataclysmic eruption ca.

1600–1500 BC. The remains of the settlement of Akrotiri were excavated by the Greek archaeologist Spyridon Marinatos. He found interior lavatories, for example in the West House, that were connected to an extensive underground sewer system. (See Palyvou.)

Greece

The Greek word for "urine" was *ouron*. The word for animal dung was *onthos*. *Kopros* could indicate either animal or human excrement. A *kopria* or *koprōn* was a dunghill or cesspit. The verb meaning "to manure" was *koprizein*. An abandoned baby rescued from a cesspit could be given the name *Koprion*.

The Fifth Labor of Heracles (Hercules) was to clean out the stable of Augeas's three thousand oxen, which had not been cleaned out for thirty years. The hero accomplished the task by diverting the Alpheus River (Pausanias, *Descr.* 5.1.9).

There are two memorable scenes involving animal dung in the Homeric epics. During the contest between Ajax and Odysseus to see who will inherit Achilles's armor, the goddess Athena intervenes on behalf of her protégé and trips up Ajax so he slips on the offal from sacrificed bulls and "with the filth [*onthos*] of the bulls were his mouth and nostrils filled" (*Od.* 23.772).

Odysseus returns disguised as a beggar after twenty years of absence fighting the Trojans and enduring all kinds of adventures on his way back to Ithaca. No one recognizes him except for his nurse and his faithful dog Argos ("swift"), of whom it is said:

> But now he lay neglected, his master gone, in the deep dung of mules and cattle, which lay in heaps before the doors, till the slaves of Odysseus should take it away to dung his wide lands. There lay the hound Argos, full of vermin; yet even now, when he marked Odysseus standing near, he wagged his tail and dropped both his ears, but nearer to his master he had no longer strength to move. Then Odysseus looked aside and wiped away a tear. (*Od.* 17.296–304)

Greeks often relieved themselves outdoors, even on streets at night when they could not be seen. Hesiod (ca. 700 BC) advises:

> And do not urinate standing up facing the sun; but be mindful to do so after it sets, and before it rises, but even so do not completely bare yourself: for the nights belong to the blessed ones. And do not urinate while you are walking on the road or off the road: it is crouching that the god-fearing man, who knows wisdom, does it, or after he has approached towards the wall of a well-fenced courtyard. (*Op.* 727–733)

Theophrastus, in his sketch of the "Stupid Man," comments: "When after a hearty supper he has to get up in the night, he returns only half awake, and missing the right door is bitten by his neighbour's dog." In Aristophanes's comedy *The Wasps*, Philocleon prays to Lycus, the patron hero of jurors: "O save me and succour me, Power Divine! And never again will I do my needs [*apopardō*] by thy osier matting that guards thy shrine" (*Vesp.* 393–394).

Diogenes, the noted Cynic (from the Greek word *kynos*, "dog"), who delighted in defying conventions, squatted to defecate in public in daylight, to the disgust of his listeners (Dio Chrysostom, *Discourses* 8.36–37).

Athenian audiences enjoyed the numerous scatological references to urination and defecation in the comedies of Aristophanes. Even the god Dionysus was depicted as wiping himself with a sponge after he had soiled himself with feces because he had been afraid (*Ran.* 478–490). The eternal place of punishment is described as a place of "ever-rippling dung [*borboron*]" (*Ran.* 145). (See Henderson.)

As most houses during the Archaic and Classical eras (8th–5th c. BC) lacked toilets, Greeks used pots for urination and for defecation. These were emptied by servants into cesspits outside the house. A vase painting depicts a nude woman squatting over a krater to urinate; another painting shows a male urinating into a vessel held by a servant.

As early as the sixth century BC, the Greeks developed *koprodochoi*, ceramic commodes for children to sit in while they relieved themselves. Different chamber pots were used: the *amis* for men and the *skaphion* for women. The *lasana* were stands for the chamber pots. The *lasanophoros* was the slave charged with emptying chamber pots.

Archaeologists have found several examples of brick-lined cesspits in courtyards and on streets. These measured 1 meter in width, 2.5 meters in length, and 1 to 1.5 meters in depth. Some mortgage deeds list the sale of *koprones*, "cesspits," along with houses. The dung could be emptied onto wagons and sold for fertilizer to farmers. Contractors known as *koprologoi* were hired to remove the dung from cities. An inscription from Delos records payment to a certain Nicias for removing pigeon droppings from roofs and *kopros* from the agora.

The earliest Greek set of laws, the Gortyn Code from Crete, forbade the location of dung heaps within a certain distance of house walls. A law of 485 BC forbade the dumping of animal dung in the precincts of the Hecatompedon on the acropolis. According to Aristotle, the members of the city council were to "keep watch to prevent any scavenger [*koprologos*] from depositing ordure [*kopron*] within a mile and a quarter of the city" (*Ath. pol.* 50.2).

The Greek word for toilet was *aphedrōn*. Other words used for such a facility were *thakos*, "a seat," and *apopatos* ("going out of the way [to relieve oneself]"). Though toilets are mentioned in texts of the era, archaeologists have not been able to find any in Athens from the Archaic or Classical eras (8th–5th c. BC). Evidence from outside of Athens indicates that both private toilets in houses and public latrines in cities became common in the Hellenistic era (4th–2nd c. BC).

By the end of the fifth century BC, the island of Thera had the only publicly accessible latrines in the Hellenistic world. Placed near the agora and with direct access from the streets, one seated three persons, and another seated eight. Though they were paved with marble slabs, they would have been dark, as the only available light was from the doorway.

A latrine with four seats arranged around three walls was uncovered at the gymnasium of Minos on the island of Cos (mid-4th c. BC). The sewage was flushed through a large conduit that was provided with naturally flowing water. At the city of Olynthos, which was destroyed by Philip of Macedon in 348 BC, a terra-cotta toilet seat was discovered in an alcove in a room with a bathtub and a basin. A pipe found on the floor may have directed sewage out into the street.

The best evidence for private toilets and public latrines comes from the island of Delos, which flourished as an international trade center in the Hellenistic era. Of about one hundred houses, 70 percent were provided with toilets that emptied their contents into the extensive sewer system. The majority (fifty-four) of these toilets were placed in small rooms near the entrances of the homes, close to the streets. There were also public latrines. As Delos has no springs, water for flushing would have been quite scarce.

Rome

The Latin words for urine were *urina* and *lotium*. "To urinate" was *mingere*. *Stercus* was the word for human excrement and animal dung. The *stercorius* was one who removed the dung. "To defecate" was *cacare*. Various terms were used for toilets, including *necessaria*, "a necessary room," *secessus*, "privy," *cella*, "chair," and *latrina*, which was a contraction from *lavatrina* (from the word *lavare*, "to wash"; cf. "lavatory"). The *latrina* was a public toilet; the *forica* was a multi-seated public latrine.

Both animal dung and human excrement were collected in dung heaps to be used as manure. Columella gave the following advice for farmers: "Nor should he hesitate to bring as food for new-ploughed fallow-ground whatever stuff the privy vomits from its filthy sewers" (*Rust.* 10.84–86). Varro recommended building the latrine for slaves over the dung pit (*Rust.* 1.13.4). He reported: "Cassius states that next to pigeon dung human excrement is the best, and in the third place goat, sheep, and ass dung; that horse dung is least valuable, but good on grain land" (*Rust.* 1.38.2–3). Because of the stench of decomposing dung created by the formation of hydrogen sulphide (H2S) and methane (CH4), Columella instructed that beehives should be situated far "from the foul odours, which come from the latrines, the dunghill and the bathroom" (*Rust.* 9.5.1). Both human and animal urine, which contain nitrogen and phosphorus, were also used as fertilizer.

In his encyclopedic *Natural History*, Pliny the Elder lists a variety of kinds of animal dung that were used for cosmetic and for medical purposes. For alopecy (loss of hair), he noted the use of bull's urine and stale human urine (*Nat.* 28.46); to impart a rosy tint to cheeks, bull's dung (*Nat.* 28.50); and to ensure durable firmness of the breasts of a young girl, the drinking of nine pellets of hare's dung (*Nat.* 28.77). For the sting of a serpent, horse's dung (*Nat.* 28.42); for the bite of a mad dog, goat's dung (*Nat.* 28.43); and for hearing problems, ass's dung (*Nat.* 28.48).

Numerous cesspits for human waste have been found at Pompeii, some in the streets and others in gardens. Some could be as deep as thirty-six feet (11 m.). When full, they would have had to be emptied by a *stercorius*. At the military site of *Oppidum Batavorum* (Netherlands), eighty-four cesspits were excavated. The diameter of these barrel-shaped pits ranged from 0.9 to 2.4 meters. The pits were formed by multiple wooden barrels placed on top of one another.

Babies were sometimes abandoned in cesspits. Some of these would have been rescued as foundlings (*alumni*) and raised as slaves or prostitutes. Babies recovered from the cesspits sometimes were given the name *Stercorius* or *Stercorosus*. In some cases, wealthy women who did not wish to go through the ordeal of childbirth would secretly claim such a baby as their own, as Juvenal comments: "I won't mention spurious children and the joys and prayers so often cheated at the filthy latrines [*lacus*], the high priest and Salian priests so often acquired from there to bear the name of Scaurus in their false persons" (*Sat.* 6.602–604).

Farmers and villagers relieved themselves out in the fields. A number of inscriptions warned city dwellers of divine wrath for urinating and defecating in public spaces: "To the one defecating [*cacator*] here beware of the curse [*malum*]. If you scorn this curse you will have an angry Jupiter" (*CIL* IV.7716). "May he who pisses [*mixerit*] or shits [*cacarit*] here incur the wrath of the gods above and below" (*CIL* VI.13740). "Twelve gods and goddesses and Jupiter the biggest and best will be angry with whoever urinates or defecates here" (*CIL* VI.29848). (Hobson, 143.)

As human urine was used in dyeing, tanning, and especially in fullers' laundering of wool clothes, pottery jars were placed in alleys for men to urinate into them. Commenting on revelers, Macrobius remarks, "On their way there's not a single pot [*amphora*] in an alleyway that they don't fill, their bladders are so full of wine"(*Sat.* 3.16.16). When the emperor Vespasian imposed a tax on the collection of such urine, his son objected: "When Titus found fault with him for contriving a tax upon public conveniences, he held a piece of money from the first payment to his son's nose, asking whether its odour was offensive to him. When Titus said 'No,' he replied, 'Yet it comes from urine'" (Suet. *Vesp.* 23.3). The Celtiberians of Spain were known for using human urine to brush their teeth (Catullus 39.17–21).

Chamber pots (*lasanae*) were generally made of pottery. Some (*matellae*) were made of bronze. Two intact pottery chamber pots were recovered from a sewer at the military post of Carnuntum in Austria, along with fragments of numerous other pots. These intact examples, dated to the second to third centuries AD, measured twenty-six to forty centimeters (10.25 to 15.75 in.) in diameter and thirty-one centimeters (12.2 in.) in height, so they were quite capacious.

Some wealthy individuals even used chamber pots made of precious metals. Pliny the Elder reports: "The orator Messala has told us that the triumvir [Mark] Antony used vessels of gold in satisfying all the indecent necessities, an enormity that even Cleopatra would have been ashamed of" (*Nat.* 33.14.50). The despised emperor Elagabalus (d. AD 222), who was assassinated by soldiers in his toilet room, used gold chamber pots and urinals made of precious stones (*S.H.A.* 32.2).

It was expected that innkeepers would provide chamber pots for their guests. A graffito from Pompeii (VIII.7.6) reads: "Dear Host: We admit we've pissed in the bed. 'Why?' You ask. Because you didn't give us a chamber pot [*matella*]" (*CIL* IV.4957; Hobson, 134). Trimalchio provided chamber pots for his guests at his famous dinner recounted in the *Satyricon*. It was one of the more demeaning duties of slaves to hold the pisspots for their masters (see Arrian's *Discourse on Epictetus* 1.2.8–9). As Trimalchio was playing a ball game, he beckoned for a slave: "Menelaus had just finished when Trimalchio cracked his fingers. One eunuch came up at the signal and held the jordan [*matella*] for him as he played. He relieved his bladder and called for a basin to wash his hands and wiped them on a boy's head" (*Sat.* 27.3).

The overwhelming majority (perhaps 98 percent) of Rome's population of nearly a million in the early Empire lived in crowded, multi-storied tenements called *insulae*, "islands." These were limited by Augustus to a height of six stories. Water had to be collected from the public fountains and carried in buckets up the stairs. The apartment dwellers were supposed to empty their chamber pots into a bin located at the bottom of the steps. But many no doubt chose the easier method of throwing their contents out of the windows at night, as Juvenal warned:

You could be thought careless and unaware of what can suddenly befall if you go out to dinner without having made your will. As you pass by at night, there are precisely as many causes of death as there are open windows watching you. So make a wish and a pathetic prayer as you go that they'll be content with emptying their shallow basins on you. (*Sat.* 3.273–277)

The *Notitia Regionum*, a catalogue of buildings in Rome (AD 315), lists 144 *latrinae* and 254 *necessariae* in the city. But our archaeological evidence for such facilities from Rome itself is sparse. Our best archaeological evidence for latrines comes from Pompeii and Herculaneum, two cities that were buried by the eruption of Vesuvius in AD 79; from Ostia, a city by the mouth of the Tiber River that flourished under Trajan (AD 98–117; see Figure 1 on p. 471); and from Tibur (Tivoli), the expansive villa built by Hadrian (AD 118–138).

From Rome itself the remains of only twenty-three latrines have been identified, along with forty others from the rest of Italy. The latrine at the Domus Transitoria could seat sixty clients. The typical public latrine was a multi-seated facility attached to a bath, so that water from the *frigidarium* could be used to flush out the sewage under the seats [see Figure 2 on p. 471]. The seats would be placed about twelve inches (30 cm.) apart with no partitions in between. The early latrines were dimly lit with a single window high above the wall.

The satirist Martial describes the behavior of a social parasite who wanted to cadge a dinner invitation: "Vacerra spends hours in all the privies, sitting all day long. Vacerra doesn't want a shit [*cacaturit*], he wants a dinner" (*Ep.*11.77). About an annoying pest, Martial comments: "You read to me as I stand, you read to me as I sit, you read to me as I run, you read to me as I shit [*cacanti*]" (*Ep.* 3.44).

Though there were a few cases of separate baths for men and women, most public baths included mixed bathing of men and women. There were no separate toilet facilities for women. Though no text describes women using public latrines, scholars believe that women may well have used them.

Pompeii, a town of ten thousand inhabitants, was buried in a shower of volcanic ash when Vesuvius erupted. Archaeologists have been able to clear most of the city's buildings. Pompeii had a network of sewers, which drained mainly water and waste from the streets and not sewage from toilets. Public latrines were found in the Forum Baths, the Central Baths, and the Suburban Baths. Shops and bars had single toilets, which could be entered from the streets. Of the 195 toilets found at Pompeii, thirty-three of those found in private homes were located in the kitchen, eighteen near the kitchen, twenty-two in courtyards or gardens, and nine in upper floors. Only six houses had more than one toilet. Some had a hole under the seat to allow a bucket of water to flush the toilet into the cesspit below. In only two cases did thresholds suggest that a door closed the room. (See Jansen, "Private Toilets at Pompeii.")

The nearby city of Herculaneum, with a population of five thousand, was covered with a wave of volcanic mud, which hardened in place so that only a few blocks of the city have been cleared. The lava under the city was not suitable for cesspits, so the toilets emptied their contents into a sewer system that sloped toward the sea. Recently a vast section of the underground sewer, measuring some 10 feet (3 m.) high and almost 3 feet (1 m.) wide and extending 282 feet (86 m.) in length, has been explored. This retained a mound of all kinds of waste, including excrement, food waste, glass and pottery fragments, gaming counters, and even a gold ring (see Roberts, 265–68).

Ostia was a thriving port city of twenty thousand. The remains of its numerous buildings include multi-storied *insulae*. Evidence of human waste has been recovered from drain pipes of fifteen upper-story latrines, which were located in narrow rooms near the stairs. An examinaton of these drain pipes revealed the presence of the eggs of *Trichuris* and *Ascaris* parasites (Hobson, 77). There were three public latrines associated with three baths. A unique arrangement made it possible to deliver urine from the Mithras bath to a neighboring fullery by means of a lead pipe.

High up on the walls of the Bath of the Seven Sages at Ostia are the figures of three Greek philosophers giving advice to patrons of the adjoining latrine:

> Solon of Athens holds up a small rod in his right hand, as if to get our attention for his lesson. The inscription over his head reads, *ut bene cacaret ventrum palpavit Solon:* "In order that he would crap well, Solon shook (or rubbed) his stomach." Thales of Miletus, also holding a short rod, sits opposite him with this advice: *durum cacantes monuit ut nitant Thales,* "Thales advised those having a difficult shit (crapping hard) to push hard (strain)." Above the head of Chilon of Sparta on the next wall are the words, *vissire tacite Chilon docuit subdolus,* "Sneaky (sly?) Chilon taught [how] to fart silently."
>   (Koloski-Ostrow 2015, 115)

Ostia's sewage system drained away from the nearby Tiber River to prevent a backflow when the river flooded. All the toilets and latrines at Ostia emptied into its sewer system. There are fifty manhole openings, which would have allowed slaves to descend to clear out any blockages in the system. Prisoners were used to perform this loathsome function in Bithynia (Pliny the Younger, *Ep.* 10.32).

Hadrian built a lavish villa covering three hundred acres at Tivoli (ancient Tibur), which is located twenty miles from Rome. Forty-seven toilet facilities have been identified at the site. Multi-seat latrines with seats for as many fifteen persons were built for the servants. Single-seat toilets were built for the emperor, his entourage, and guests. The only known toilet room in the Roman world with a partition between seats was the one found above the Cryptoporticus. (See Jansen 2003.)

A similar hierarchy of toilet facilities can be observed in military installations, for example, at the fort of Housesteads at Hadrian's Wall in northern England. While the rank and file used a multi-seat latrine, the officers had private toilets. An inscription indicates that a soldier on latrine duty must clean out the *stercus* from a cesspit.

The second century AD saw the appearance of so-called "luxury" latrines, which had mosaic floors, marble paneling, and provision for air and light through an open ceiling or a line of columns in place of a wall [see Figure 3 on p. 472]. An example is the latrine by the Vedius Baths north of the Curetes Street at Ephesus, where the seats were arranged around three sides of a room. Another example was found at the site of Hierapolis in western Asia Minor. This spacious room, measuring 92 x 49 feet (28 x 15 m.), had about 160 seats. It was supplied with a continuous flow of water to flush the excrement out through a drain in a corner into the sewer under the town square. Other impressive examples of "luxury" latrines may be found at Lepcis Magna, Timgad, and Thugga, Roman sites in North Africa.

A narrow and shallow gutter filled with water was placed in a number of multi-seat public latrines. Scholars believe that this gutter was provided to rinse out the sponge on a stick that was used to clean the anus after defecation. There are a number of literary references to such a device. Martial refers to an *infelix damnatae spongea virgae*, "a luckless sponge on a doomed mop stick" (*Ep.* 12.48.7). Seneca recounts the dramatic suicide of a German gladiator:

> A German, who was making ready for the morning exhibition; he withdrew in order to relieve himself,—the only thing which he was allowed to do in secret and without the presence of a guard. While so engaged, he seized the stick of wood, tipped with a sponge, which was devoted to the vilest uses, and stuffed it, just as it was, down his throat; thus he blocked up his windpipe, and choked the breath from his body. (*Ep.* 70.20)

There is some evidence that basins of water were provided for the rinsing of hands after defecation. But as there was neither soap nor towels, and as the water was probably not replaced until the end of the day, this may have led to further contamination instead of improving sanitation. The same may also be observed of baths: physicians advised their sick patients to avail themselves of these facilities, which endangered bathers who were healthy.

To protect themselves from *malum*, which would have included the evil eye, Romans affixed various apotropaic symbols to their latrines, such as phalli and concentric circles. They also placed images of the goddess Fortuna in their latrines. There are seven depictions of this goddess in the latrines at Pompeii. The Romans also venerated Venus Cloacina, the goddess who presided over the sewers.

The *Cloaca Maxima*, the great sewer of Rome, whose opening can still be seen on the banks of the Tiber River, was a marvel of Roman engineering. It was begun by the last Etruscan king, Tarquin the Proud (6th c. BC), as an open channel. This was then enclosed by the Romans and improved by a number of emperors (Dionysius of Halicarnassus, *Ant. rom.* 3.67.5; Livy, *Rom. Hist.* 1.56.2; Strabo, *Geogr.* 5.3.8). In places, it was large enough for a wagon to pass through (Pliny, *Nat.* 36.24). As measured by archaeologists at its greatest dimensions, it is more than thirteen feet (4 m.) high and ten feet (3 m.) broad. The system of sewers under Rome served primarily to dispose of rainwater from streets and not sewage from toilets. A good reason not to connect latrines to the sewer system in Rome was the frequent flooding of the Tiber, which would have sent water and sewage back through such connections.

The maintenance of clean streets in Rome fell to the office of the *aedile*. During the reign of Caligula (AD 37–41), the emperor became displeased with the condition of the streets. He took out his displeasure on his *aedile*, Vespasian (the future emperor): "When Vespasian was aedile, Gaius Caesar, incensed at his neglect of his duty of cleaning the streets, ordered that he be covered with mud, which the soldiers accordingly heaped into the bosom of his purple-bordered toga" (Suet. *Vesp.* 5.3). Streets would be littered with mud, manure, excrement, and even corpses. Suetonius relates the following incident that occurred after Vespasian became the emperor: "Once when he was taking breakfast, a stray dog brought in a human hand from the cross-roads and dropped it under the table" (*Vesp.* 5.4).

The unsanitary conditions at Rome created breeding grounds for a multitude of diseases, including cholera, dysentery, gastroenteritis, infectious hepatitis, leptospirosis, tuberculosis, malaria, salmonella, and typhoid fever.

Alex Scobie's classic study on slums and sanitation in Rome concluded:

> It is clear that in Rome there was a very high risk of food and water contamination through direct or indirect contact with human or animal fecal matter which was inadequately dealt with by city authorities. Open cesspits in kitchens, a general lack of washing facilities in latrines, defecation and urination in the streets, the pollution of water basins with carrion and filth, lack of efficient fly control, and inadequate street cleaning, do not provide a basis for

health in an urban community, but do help to explain a very high mortality rate. (Scobie, 421)

After firsthand investigation of the numerous ancient toilets and latrines in Italy, Gemma Jansen came to these further conclusions:

> For instance, the Roman habit of using a sponge tied to a stick for the purpose of cleaning the body constitutes a tremendous health risk. Although the cleaning device could be rinsed in a water basin, which was usually installed in the toilet room, the sponge stick was used repeatedly by many different people. Further-more, toilets had no stench traps and the connection to sewers and cesspits was open, which allowed rats and insects easy access to the toilet room itself and to the rest of the house. To make matters worse, the toilet was often situated in the kitchen, which is where all the food was prepared. The emptying of household cesspits must also have involved a high health risk.
> (Jansen 2000, 277)

E. THE JEWISH WORLD

In describing the strict sect of the Essenes, The Jewish historian Josephus asserted that they chose not to "go to stool" on the Sabbath day. He then stated:

> On other days they dig a trench a foot deep with a mattock—such is the nature of the hatchet which they present to the neophytes—and wrapping their mantle about them, that they may not offend the rays of the deity, sit above it. They then replace the excavated soil in the trench. For this purpose they select the more retired spots. And though this discharge of the excrements is a natural function, they make it a rule to wash themselves after it, as if defiled.
> (J.W. 2.148–149)

Most scholars have accepted the identification of the Essenes with the Qumran community, which produced the Dead Sea Scrolls. Roland de Vaux, the excavator of Qumran, discovered in Cave 11 a small hatchet that may have been used by the sectarians to cover their feces. He also identified a large room (locus 51) on the east side of Qumran as a toilet; this was adjacent to a *miqwê*, which would have been used for ritual purification after defecation.

The War Scroll stipulates that at the time of the eschatological combat "there shall be a space between all their camps and the latrine of about two thousand cubits, and no shameful nakedness shall be seen in the environs of all their camps" (1QM VII, 6–7). The Temple Scroll, on the other hand, requires an even greater separation between latrines and the Holy City:

You are to build them a precinct for latrines outside the city. They shall go out there, on the northwest of the city: roofed outhouses with pits inside, into which the excrement will descend so as not to be visible. The outhouses must be three thousand cubits [i.e., four thousand five hundred feet] from any part of the city. (11QT XLVI, 13–16; see Magness 1998)

The rabbinic compilations (the Mishnah, Tosefta, Babylonian Talmud, and Jerusalem Talmud) contain many debates over urination and defecation as well as toilet behavior.

Urine was known as *mê raglayim*, "water of the feet." Rabbi Abbaye forbade a mother from urinating before her child unless she did so sideways (*b. Ber.* 44b). As attempting to suppress urination could lead to physical problems, it was permissible to urinate in public (*b. Bek.* 44b). One was not to urinate in river water (*b. Bek.* 14b.) or on solid ground, lest he contaminate well water (*b. Yoma* 31a).

Whether a man could urinate against a neighbor's wall depended on the composition of that wall (*b. B. Bat.* 19b; cf. *t. B. Bat.* 1:4). One was not to pray or recite the Shema while urinating (*b. Ber.* 25a).

Collected urine that was less than forty days old could be used as a cleansing agent (*b. Šabb.* 89b). Urine that was more than forty days old could be used to counter snake poison (*b. Sanh.* 109b), wasp stings, and scorpion bites (*b. Šabb.* 109b).

According to the Mishnah, excrement does not convey uncleanness nor render anything susceptible to uncleanness (*m. Makš.* 6:7). The Talmud states that one should not resist defecating when it is necessary: "When your pot is boiling, empty it out" (*b. Ber.* 62b). If one disobeys the call of nature, he will emit an offensive odor (*b. Šabb.* 82a). Four things are said to increase excrement: new wine, greens, barley, and black bread. If one is constipated, one should massage the abdomen (*b. Ber.* 62a) or concentrate hard (*b. Šabb.* 82a).

While it was a common practice to urinate and defecate outdoors, and even on streets, there were certain rules of behavior to be observed. The rabbis debated whether one could defecate as long as he could not be seen or as long as the exposed part of his behind could not be seen. According to Rabbi Ulla, "Behind a fence one may ease himself immediately; in an open field, so long as he can break wind without anyone hearing it" (*b. Ber.* 62a).

During the day, Raba used to go as far away into the fields as a mile "to ease himself." But at night he said to his attendant, "Clear me a spot in the street of the town." Rabi Zera also said to his attendant, "See if there is anyone behind the Seminary as I wish to ease myself" (*b. Ber.* 62a). "One should not enter filthy alleyways and recite the Shema" (*t. Ber.* 2:17), as they may have been made filthy by human excrement.

Although dung heaps were ideally not permitted in Jerusalem (*b. B. Qam.* 82b), they were to be found in streets (*b. Ḥul.* 12a) and in courtyards (*b. B. Bat.* 11b), where they gave off an unpleasant odor (*b. Ber.* 25a). A dung heap had to be placed at least three handbreadths away from a neighbor's wall (*b. B. Bat.* 17b).

Children's feces could be used as a remedy for scurvy (*y. Šabb.* 14:14). Pigeon dung and the excrement of a white dog could be used for medical purposes (*b. Giṭ.* 69b). Dog's dung was used for tanning leather (*y. Ber.* 3:5), even for Torah scrolls and for tefillin.

Chamber pots and urine pots were used in the bedrooms (*b. Ber.* 25b; *b. B. Bat.* 89b; *y. Ber.* 3:5). As long as the pot was filled with water, one could stand four cubits (6 ft.) away from it and recite the Shema. Some rabbis held that the pot had to be placed under the bed before such a recitation. According to the Mishnah, "If in pots wherein Israelites and gentiles have made water the greater part was from the clean persons, the whole is clean; if the greater part was from the unclean persons, the whole is unclean; if they were equal, the whole is unclean" (*m. Makš.* 2:3).

A private toilet, *bêt kissēʾ*, "house of the seat," was rare and would have been found only in the wealthiest homes. To the question "Who is wealthy?" "R. Jose said: He who has a privy near his table" (*b. Šabb.* 25b). Latrines were absent from the Hasmonean and Herodian palaces (Netzer, 258).

There was a special toilet for priests in the lower level of the temple in Jerusalem. According to the Mishnah: "There was a fire there and a privy, and this was its seemly use: if he found it locked he knew that some one was there; if open he knew that no one was there" (*m. Tamid* 1:1). As priests were required to immerse themselves after defecating or urinating (*m. Yoma* 3:2), they would immediately cleanse themselves in the nearby Chamber of Immersion.

Even after the temple had been destroyed by the Romans in AD 70, the site of the Temple Mount retained its sanctity, so that it influenced the position of the devout in the orientation of his toilet behavior. According to the Tosefta, "He who covers his feet [to defecate] faces the people. And he who urinates turns his back toward the holy place" (*t. Meg.* 3:26). According to the Talmud: "Our Rabbis taught: One who consults nature in Judea should not do so east and west but north and south. In Galilee he should do so only east and west. R. Jose, however, allows it, since R. Jose said: The prohibition was meant to apply only to one in sight of the Temple" (*b. Ber.* 61b).

The famous Rabbi Akiba (d. AD 135) reported, "Once I went in after R. Joshua to a privy, and I learnt from him three things. I learnt that one does not sit east and west but north and south; I learnt that one evacuates not standing but sitting; and I learnt that it is proper to wipe with the left hand and not with the right" (*b. Ber.* 62a; cf. *y. Ber.* 14c, 9:5). The rabbis discussed various objects that could be used to clean the anus after defecating. They debated over the use of grass or a potsherd (*b. Šabb.* 82a), and over the size of the stones that were permitted (*b. Šabb.* 81a).

The two leading Pharisaic schools of Hillel and of Shammai agreed that one should wash one's hands at meals but disagreed on the exact order of doing this within the time of the meal (*m. Ber.* 8.2–4). According to the Talmud, if one should go out to urinate during the meal he need only wash his right hand. But if he should linger, he should wash both hands with a pitcher after seating himself again at the table (*b. Yoma* 30a).

Multi-seat public latrines were not built in Palestine until the Roman suppression of the Jewish Revolts. Only five (dating to the 3rd–4th c. AD) have been excavated. The best example is the large latrine (14.7 x 12.5 m.) found in the eastern bathhouse at Beth Shean, which had marble seats for fifty-seven patrons. Another latrine was found at the western bathhouse. Both had gutters for rinsing out sponge sticks. These were examples of "luxury" latrines with mosaic floors, marble paneling, and porticoes.

The Jerusalem Talmud mentions public latrines only twice, once with respect to the experience of Rabbi Eleazar. "R. Eleazar went to a privy and sat down. A Roman quartermaster came along and made him get up and sat down in his place. . . . There was a snake in the privy, and it came out and gave [the Roman] a bite on his anus" (*y. Šabb.* 6:9)—whereupon Eleazar gave thanks to God.

The version of this story about Eleazar in the Babylonian Talmud (*b. Ber.* 62b) substitutes a Persian for the rude Roman soldier. But there were no multi-seat public latrines in Sassanid Babylonia, and the Persians had a remarkable reputation down through the centuries for relieving themselves in private, possibly because of the Zoroastrian conviction that anything leaving the body, even spit, was defiling.

The Talmud indicates that when a pious Jew enters a privy he should pray: "Give honour to the God of Israel. Wait for me till I enter and do my deeds, and return to you." And when he leaves the privy, he should thank God by saying: "Blessed is He who has formed man in wisdom and created in him many orifices and many cavities. It is fully known before the throne of Thy glory that if one of them should be (improperly) opened or one of them closed it would be impossible for a man to stand before Thee" (*b. Ber.* 60b).

Jews feared the presence of the *šēd bêt kissēʾ*, "the demon of the privy." According to Rabbi Tanhum, "Whoever behaves modestly in a privy is delivered from three things: from snakes, from scorpions, and from evil spirits [*mazzîqîn*]" (*b. Ber.* 62a). After using a privy, a man was to wait long enough to walk a half mile before having intercourse with his wife, lest the demon of the privy cause a child that might be conceived to become an epileptic (*b. Giṭ.* 70a). This belief was very similar to the belief in the Babylonian demon of the privy, Šulak, who was also believed to cause epilepsy. (See Bamberger.)

F. THE CHRISTIAN WORLD

The spread and eventual "triumph" of Christianity with Constantine's conversion in AD 312 brought relief from persecution, but did little to change various aspects of daily life, such as the use of dung for manure. John Chrysostom (d. AD 407), in his sermon on Philippians, interprets Paul's use of *skybala* in Phil 3:8 as meaning "dung": "For dung comes from wheat, and the strength of the wheat is the dung, I mean, the chaff. But as the dung was useful in its former state, so that we gather it together with the wheat, and had there been no dung, there would have been no wheat, thus too is it with the Law" (*Hom. Phil.* 11).

Clement of Alexandria (d. ca. AD 214), who held a semi-Docetic Christology, maintained that Christ did not experience the digestive processes of other human beings: "He ate and drank in a way individual to himself without excreting his food. Such was his power of self-control that the food was not corrupted within him, since he was not subject to corruption" (*Strom.* 3.7.59; Ferguson, 293). Clement denounced the extravagant tastes in expensive foods of wealthy Christians:

> There is no limit to epicurism among men. For it has driven them to sweet-meats, and honey-cakes, and sugar-plums; inventing a multitude of desserts, hunting after all manner of dishes. A man like this seems to me to be all jaw, and nothing else. Desire not, says the Scripture, rich men's dainties; for they belong to a false and base life. They partake of luxurious dishes, which a little after go to the dunghill. (*Paed.* 2.1.4)

Clement also derided the wealthy for their expensive chamber pots:

> It is a farce, and a thing to make one laugh outright, for men to bring in silver urinals and crystal *vases de nuit*, as they usher in their counsellors, and for silly rich women to get gold receptacles for excrements made; so that being rich, they cannot even ease themselves except in a superb way. I would that in their whole life they deemed gold fit for dung. (*Paed.* 2.3.39)

Clement mocked the Romans for their reliance on deities to protect them from possible harm in the latrines: "The Romans, who ascribed their greatest successes to Fortune, and regarded her as a very great deity, took her statue to the privy, and erected it there, assigning to the goddess as a fitting temple—the necessary" (*Protr.* 4.51).

In 325 Constantine invited 318 bishops to the first ecumenical council at Nicaea. The council condemned Arius for denying the deity of Christ. In 336, just before he was to be pardoned by Constantine, Arius died in a latrine in Constantinople (Sozomen, *Eccl. Hist.* 2.29–30). His arch-critic, Athanasius, the bishop of Alexandria, took this fate as a sign that Arius was divinely judged as one who had not truly repented of his heresy. An inscription at Aphrodisias in southwestern Turkey threatens any person who dumps refuse inside the walls of the city with the curse of the 318 bishops of Nicaea as an enemy of God (Liebeschuetz, 57).

That urban sanitation problems persisted in the fourth century AD may be seen in the vivid sermons of John Chrysostom preached in his native city of Antioch. John's teacher Libanius noted that the open sewers of the city were so noxious that their fumes killed some of those assigned to clean them. In a sermon on the Acts of the Apostles (*Hom. Act.* 7.4), John mentions the practice of throwing "filth" from an upper story on people passing below.

An examination of his sermons reveals that John used the term *kopros*, "excrement," over sixty times and *phorytos*, "refuse," twenty-eight times in them (Leyerle, 337). John chastises obese Christians as choosing to live in a cesspit (*borboros*), compares those who indulge in lust to sewer ditches (*ochetous amaras*), and likens slanderers to dung beetles, who crawl in excrement and carry balls of dung in their mouths (Leyerle, 348–50).

Speaking on Colossians, John describes the making of silver chamber pots for women as madness, when there were poor to be fed (*Hom. Col.* 7.5). In a sermon on Ephesians, John contends that Christians who had engaged in reveling were like chamber pots, no longer fit vessels for the Lord's use:

> Suppose there were a royal vessel, and that always full of royal dainties, and set apart for that purpose, and then that any one of the servants were to take and use it for holding dung. Would he ever venture again, after it had been filled with dung, to store it away with those other vessels, set apart for those other uses? Surely not. (*Hom. Eph.* 14)

The monastic movement began in Egypt in the fourth century. The earliest monasteries were built on the edge of the deserts in Egypt, which made it natural for monks to relieve themselves in the desert, especially at night. A recently published papyrus, which was recovered from the rubbish dump at Oxyrhynchus over a century ago, reads as follows:

> When I was in Oxyrhynchus, some poor people came there on the evening of the Sabbath (i.e., Saturday) so that they might receive charity. They were lying

down, and there was one who had only a little reed mat; half of the mat on top
of him and half the mat underneath. Now it was very cold and going out to
relieve myself I heard him feeling pain from the cold and comforting himself,
saying, "I give thanks to you, O Lord, how many rich persons are in prison
right now wearing irons, and others having their feet fastened to wood are
not able to relieve themselves. But I am as a king stretching out my feet, and
go wherever I wish." As he was saying these things I stood listening. Going in
I related these things to the brethren and when they heard they were edified.
    (Blumell and Wayment, 171)

The continuing sanitary problems in the sixth century may be seen
from some of the laws in Justinian's Digest. The section on public streets
commands the city overseers to require each property owner to keep the
streets before their houses in repair and to clean out the open gutters.
"They are not to allow anyone to fight in the streets, or to fling dung, or to
throw out any dead animals or skins" (*Dig. Just.* XLIII.5; Watson IV.91). In
the section on "Those Who Pour or Throw Things Out of Buildings," the
praetor (judicial official) stipulates: "If anything should be thrown out or
poured out from a building onto a place where people commonly pass and
repass or stand about, I will grant an action to be brought against whoever
lives there for double the damage caused or done as a result" (*Dig. Just.*
IX.3.1; Watson I.293).

BIBLIOGRAPHY: G. P. Antoniou and A. N. Angelakis, "Latrines and
Wastewater Sanitation Technologies in Ancient Greece," in *Sanitation, Latrines and Intestinal Parasites in Past Populations*, ed. P. D. Mitchell (2015),
41–68; L. R. Bailey, "Gehenna: The Topography of Hell," *BA* 49 (1986),
187–91; A. M. Bamberger, "An Akkadian Demon in the Talmud: Between
Šulak and Bar-Širiqa," *JSJ* 44 (2013), 282–87; A. I. Baumgarten, "The
Temple Scroll, Toilet Practices, and the Essenes," *Jewish History* 10 (1996),
9–20; L. H. Blumell and T. A. Wayment, ed., *Christian Oxyrhynchus: Texts,
Documents, and Sources* (2015); D. Boyarin, *The Jewish Gospels: The Story
of Jesus Christ* (2013); B. Brier, *Ancient Egyptian Magic* (1980); J. Cahill et
al., "It Had to Happen—Scientists Examine Remains of Ancient Bathroom,"
BAR 17.3 (1991), 64–69; R. Castleden, *Minoans: Life in Bronze Age Crete*
(1990); R. D'Andria, "The Latrine in Hierapolis of Phrygia," in *Cura
Aquarum in Ephesus*, ed. G. Wiplinger (2006), 2.467–72; R. De Vaux, "Une
hachette Essénienne?" *VT* 9 (1959), 399–407; D. M. Dixon, "Population,
Pollution, and Health in Ancient Egypt," in *Population and Pollution*, ed.
P. R. Cox and J. Peel (1972), 29–36; J. Ferguson, trans., *Stromateis: Books
One to Three* (1991); A. Goldwater, A. O. Koloski-Ostrow, and K. Neudecker,
"Users of the Toilets: Social Differences," in *Roman Toilets*, ed. G. C. M. Jan-
sen, A. O. Koloski-Ostrow, and E. M. Moormann (2011), 131–46; J. W.

Graham, *The Palaces of Crete* (1962); H. F. Gray, "Sewerage in Ancient and Mediaeval Times," *Sewage Works Journal* 12.5 (1940), 939–46; O. Gülbay, "Western Anatolian Public Latrines," in Wiplinger (2006), 2.461–66; S. Harter et al., "Toilet Practices Among Members of the Dead Sea Scrolls Sect at Qumran (100 BC–68 AD)," *RevQ* 21 (2004), 579–84; J. Henderson, *The Maculate Muse: Obscene Language in Attic Comedy* (1991); B. Hobson, *Latrinae et Foricae: Toilets in the Roman World* (2010); V. M. Hope and E. Marshall, ed., *Death and Disease in the Ancient City* (2000); J. Hopkins, "The Cloaca Maxima and the Monumental Manipulation of Water in Archaic Rome," *The Waters of Rome* 4 (2007), 1–15; J. Hopkins, "The 'Sacred Sewer': Tradition and Religion in the Cloaca Maxima," in *Rome, Pollution and Propriety: Dirt, Disease and Hygiene in the Eternal City from Antiquity to Modernity*, ed. M. Bradley and K. Stow (2012), 81–102; G. C. M. Jansen, "Private Toilets at Pompeii: Appearance and Operation," in *Sequence and Space in Pompeii*, ed. S. E. Bon and R. Jones (1997), 121–34; G. C. M. Jansen, "Social Distinctions and Issues of Privacy in the Toilets of Hadrian's Villa," *JRA* 16 (2003), 137–52; G. C. M. Jansen, "Studying Roman Hygiene: The Battle between the 'Optimists' and the 'Pessimists,'" in *Cura Aquarum in Sicilia*, ed. G. C. M. Jansen (2000), 275–79; G. C. M. Jansen, "Systems for the Disposal of Waste and Excreta in Roman Cities. The Situation in Pompeii, Herculaneum and Ostia," in *Sordes Urbis: La Eliminación de Residuos en la Ciudad Romana*, ed. X. D. Raventós and J.-A. Remolà (2000), 37–49; M. Jansen, "Water Supply and Sewage Disposal at Mohenjo-Daro," *World Archaeology* 21.2 (1989), 177–92; R. Jones, ed., *Manure Matters: Historical, Archaeological and Ethnographic Perspectives* (2012); A. O. Koloski-Ostrow, *The Archaeology of Sanitation in Roman Italy: Toilets, Sewers, and Water Systems* (2015); A. O. Koloski-Ostrow, "Finding Social Meaning in the Public Latrines of Pompeii," in *Cura Aquarum in Campania*, ed. N. de Haan and G. C. M. Jansen (1996), 79–86; A. O. Koloski-Ostrow, "Roman Latrines: How the Romans Did Their Business," *ArchOd* 7.3 (2004), 48–55; S. T. Lachs, *A Rabbinic Commentary on the New Testament: The Gospels of Matthew, Mark and Luke* (1987); L. Lambton, *Temples of Convenience and Chambers of Delight* (1996); B. Leyerle, "Refuse, Filth, and Excrement in the Homilies of John Chrysostom," *Journal of Late Antiquity* 2 (2009), 337–56; W. Liebeschuetz, "Rubbish Disposal in Greek and Roman Cities," in Raventós and Remolà (2000), 51–61; C. F. MacDonald and J. M. Driessen, "The Drainage System of the Domestic Quarter in the Palace at Knossos," *Annual of the British School at Athens* 83 (1988), 235–58; J. Magness, *Stone and Dung, Oil and Spit: Jewish Daily Life in the Time of Jesus* (2011); J. Magness, "Two Notes on the Archaeology of Qumran," *BASOR* 312 (1998), 37–44; J. Magness, "What's the Poop on Ancient Toilets and Toilet Habits?" *NEA* 75.2 (2012), 80–87; J. Marcus, *Mark 1–8: A New Translation with In-*

troduction and Commentary (2000); J. C. McKeown, *A Cabinet of Roman Curiosities* (2010); A. McMahon, "Waste Management in Early Urban Southern Mesopotamia," in Mitchell (2015), 19–39; N. Morley, "The Salubriousness of the Roman City," in *Health in Antiquity*, ed. H. King (2005), 192–204; R. Neis, " 'Their Backs toward the Temple, and Their Faces toward the East': The Temple and Toilet Practices in Rabbinic Palestine and Babylonia," *JSJ* 43 (2012), 328–68; E. Netzer, *The Architecture of Herod the Great Builder* (2008); R. Neudecker, *Die Pracht der Latrine* (1994); E. Neufeld, "Hygiene Conditions in Ancient Israel (Iron Age)," *BA* 34.2 (1971), 42–66; V. Nutton, "The Seeds of Disease: An Explanation of Contagion and Infection from the Greeks to the Renaissance," *Medical History* 27 (1983), 1–34; A. L. Oppenheim, *The Interpretation of Dreams in the Ancient Near East* (1956); E. J. Owens, "The *Koprologoi* at Athens in the Fifth and Fourth Centuries B.C.," *CQ* 33 (1983), 44–50; C. Palyvou, *Akrotiri Thera* (2005); J. Rawlinson, "Sanitary Engineering: Sanitation," in *A History of Technology*, ed. C. Singer et al. (1958), 4.504–19; P. Reimers, "Roman Sewers and Sewerage Networks—Neglected Areas of Study," in *Munuscula Romana*, ed. A.-M. Leander Touati, E. Rystedt, and Ö. Wikander (1991), 111–16; U. Z. Rizvi, "Subjectivity and Spatiality in Indus Urban Forms: Mohenjo-Daro, the Body, and the Domestication of Waste," in *The Archaeology of Politics: The Materiality of Political Practice and Action in the Past*, ed. P. G. Johansen and A. M. Bauer (2011), 221–44; P. Roberts, *Life and Death in Pompeii and Herculaneum* (2013); W. Scheidel, "Germs for Rome," in *Rome the Cosmopolis*, ed. C. Edwards and G. Woolf (2003), 158–76; P. Scherrer, "Ephesus Uncovered: From Latrines to Libraries," *ArchOd* 4.2 (2001), 26–37; J. W. Schofer, *Confronting Vulnerability: The Body and the Divine in Rabbinic Ethics* (2010); A. Scobie, "Slums, Sanitation, and Mortality in the Roman World," *Klio* 68 (1986), 399–433; J. Scurlock, *Sourcebook for Ancient Mesopotamian Medicine* (2014); D. E. Smith, " 'Pisser against a Wall': An Echo of Divination in Biblical Hebrew," *CBQ* 72 (2010), 699–717; D. Sperber, *The City in Roman Palestine* (1998); M. Stol, *Epilepsy in Babylonia* (1993); A. Tamburrino, "Water Technology in Ancient Mesopotamia," in *Ancient Water Technologies*, ed. L. W. Mays (2010), 29–51; C. Taylor, "The Disposal of Human Waste: A Comparison Between Ancient Rome and Medieval London," *Past Imperfect* 11 (2005), 53–72; G. Turner, "The State Apartments of Late Assyrian Palaces," *Iraq* 32 (1970), 177–213; J. Van Vaerenbergh, "The Latrines in and near the Roman Baths of Italy: A Nice Compromise with a Bad Smell," in Wiplinger (2006), 2.453–59; P. J. Warnock and K. J. Reinhard, "Methods for Extracting Pollen and Parasite Eggs from Latrine Soils," *Journal of Archaeological Science* 19 (1992), 261–64; A. Watson, trans., *The Digest of Justinian* (4 vols., 1985); D. F. Watson, "Gehenna," *ABD* II.926–28; K.-W. Weeber, *Luxus im alten Rom: Die öffentliche Pracht* (2006);

K. Wheeler, "Theoretical and Methodological Considerations for Excavating Privies," *Historical Archaeology* 34 (2000), 3–19; R. J. White, trans., *The Interpretation of Dreams: Oneirocritica by Artemidorus* (1975); F. A. M. Wiggerman, *Mesopotamian Protective Spirits* (1992); Y. Wilfand, "Did the Rabbis Reject the Roman Public Latrine?" *Babesch Annual Papers on Mediterranean Archaeology* 84 (2009), 183–96; A. Wilson, "Drainage and Sanitation," in *Handbook of Ancient Water Technology*, ed. Ö. Wikander (2000), 151–79; A. Wilson, "Incurring the Wrath of Mars: Sanitation and Hygiene in Roman North Africa," in *Cura Aquarum in Sicilia*, ed. G. C. M. Jansen (2000), 307–12; A. G. Woodhead, "The State Health Service in Ancient Greece," *The Cambridge Historical Journal* 10 (1952), 235–53; R. E. Wycherley, *The Stones of Athens* (1978); E. M. Yamauchi, *The Archaeology of New Testament Cities in Western Asia Minor* (1980); J. E. Zias, J. D. Tabor, and S. Harter-Lailheugue, "Toilets at Qumran, the Essenes, and the Scrolls: New Anthropological Data and Old Theories," *RevQ* 22 (2006), 631–40.

EMY

See also AQUEDUCTS & WATER SUPPLY, BATHS & BATHING, DISEASES & PLAGUES, DOGS, DWELLINGS, HUMAN SACRIFICE, INSECTS, LAUNDRY & FULLERS, and PURITY & IMPURITY.

SEALS

Seals are small engraved objects, most often made of stone or other hard substances, designed to leave distinctive impressions on soft media such as clay or wax. The impression left by a seal is often also referred to as a "seal," though "sealing" is a more accurate term. Stamp seals were the earliest form of seal and were common to many cultures, while cylinder seals, designed to create rolling impressions on clay tablets, were an invention of the Mesopotamians. From Egypt came the distinctive scarab seal design, a stamp seal carved in the shape of a scarab beetle. Almost all forms of seals were commonly worn by their owner, either suspended on a cord or mounted on a ring. The designs of seals, whether iconographic or textual, were usually carved *intaglio*, so that the seal impressions they made would appear in raised relief. Many seals are masterpieces of glyptic art.

Seals served various purposes in ancient daily life, including personal identification, the witness and authentication of documents, and the labeling and securing of personal or institutional property. As markers of personal identity and status, seals often acquired significance beyond their practical functions, and might be displayed as jewelry, kept for generations as heirlooms, or even perceived as magically potent "charms."

A. THE OLD TESTAMENT

Seals (Heb. sing. *ḥôtām*) appear in various OT narratives in personal, official, and economic uses. In Gen 38, Tamar asks Judah for his "seal and its cord" as a means of verifying his identity. Joseph, when appointed as an Egyptian official, receives a signet ring (*ṭabbaʿat*) from the pharaoh (Gen 41:42). The Israelite queen Jezebel writes letters under the name of King Ahab and stamps them with his seal (1 Kgs 21:8). The description of a purchase of land in Jer 32 is illustrative of the use of seals in the documentation of such transactions:

I signed and sealed the deed, had it witnessed, and weighed out the silver on the scales. I took the deed of purchase—the sealed copy containing the terms and conditions, as well as the unsealed copy—and I gave this deed to Baruch son of Neriah, the son of Mahseiah, in the presence of my cousin Hanamel and of the witnesses who had signed the deed and of all the Jews sitting in the courtyard of the guard. (Jer 32:10–12)

The official use of seals is emphasized in the book of Esther (3:12; 8:8–10). The oath of loyalty to God described in Neh 9:38–10:27 is sealed by all the leaders of the people.

The imagery of seals and sealing is used by OT prophets, especially regarding secrecy and divine revelation (Isa 8:16; 29:11; Dan 12:4, 9). The metaphor in Jer 22:24 underscores the importance of a seal: " 'As surely as I live,' declares the LORD, 'even if you, Jehoiachin son of Jehoiakim king of Judah, were a signet ring on my right hand, I would still pull you off.' " Haggai 2:23 is similar: " 'On that day,' declares the LORD Almighty, 'I will take you, my servant Zerubbabel son of Shealtiel,' declares the LORD, 'and I will make you like my signet ring, for I have chosen you,' declares the LORD Almighty." The book of Job makes diverse use of seal imagery: God "seals off the light of the stars" (Job 9:7), Job longs that his offenses might "be sealed up in a bag" (Job 14:17), and at the dawn of day "the earth takes shape like clay under a seal" (Job 38:14). In the Song of Songs seal imagery expresses love: "Place me like a seal over your heart, like a seal on your arm; for love is as strong as death, its jealousy unyielding as the grave" (Song 8:6).

The picture of seals in the world of the OT has been significantly augmented by archaeological finds of seals and seal impressions (both in pottery and in small clay lumps called "bullae") from Iron Age Israel, many containing Hebrew text and some relating directly to biblical persons or place names. (See Mykytiuk 2004; Mykytiuk 2014.) A seal discovered at Megiddo bears an inscription identifying its owner as "Shema, servant of Jeroboam" (*lšmᶜ ᶜbd yrbᶜm*), who is understood to have been an official of King Jeroboam II in the eighth century BC. Another from Tell en-Nasbeh names a "Jaazaniah, servant of the king" (*lyʾznyhw ᶜbd hmlk*), possibly the military commander mentioned in 2 Kgs 25:23 and Jer 40:8. This famous seal, which is dated ca. 600 BC, depicts a rooster, a bird imported from southeast Asia to the Near East for cockfighting (*ANEP*, 85, 280).

A group of hundreds of seal impressions from the region of Judah bearing the text "to the king" (*lmlk*), usually followed by the name of a city, are thought to reflect some sort of taxation or redistribution system, and have been dated to the reign of King Hezekiah. A similarly large corpus of seal impressions on wine jars from the Persian Period bear the name "Judah" (*yhwd*).

A seal impression with the name Gedaliah has been found at Lachish (*lgdlyhw [ʾ]šr ʿl hbyt*); this may possibly be the governor Gedaliah appointed by Nebuchadnezzar in 2 Kgs 25:22–25.

The seal impression of "Baruch the son of Neraiah," which was the name of Jeremiah's scribe, was purchased from an antiquities dealer and published by Nahman Avigad (cf. Shanks). Its authenticity, however, has been challenged (Goren and Arie). In 2005 Eilat Mazar discovered in her excavations at Jerusalem a bulla belonging to Jehukal the son of Shelemiah (*lyhwkl bn šlmyhw*), one of Zedekiah's officials (Jer 37:3). In 2008 she found underneath Nehemiah's northern tower a bulla that belonged to Gedaliah son of Pashhur (*lgdlyhw bn pšḥwr*), another official of the same king (Jer 38:1), who oppressed Jeremiah (see Mazar 2009, 66–67; see Figures 4 and 5 on p. 473).

In 2015 Mazar announced the find of a seal impression belonging to the biblical king Hezekiah (727–698 BC). The seal bears the Hebrew text *lḥz[q]yhw ʾ[ḥ]z mlk yhd*, "Belonging to Hezekiah (son) of Ahaz, King of Judah," along with a winged sun disc and Egyptian *ankh* symbols [see Figure 6 on p. 474]. The seal impression was found during the sifting of soil from an ancient refuse dump located next to the large structures unearthed in the Ophel excavations near the southern wall of the Temple Mount. Although other seal impressions of Hezekiah had previously surfaced on the antiquities market, this is the first seal or seal impression of any biblical king to have been found in a controlled archaeological excavation.

B. THE NEW TESTAMENT

The clearest reference in the NT to actual seal usage is the mention in Matt 27:66 of the sealing of the stone door of the tomb of Jesus. Paul's statement in Rom 15:28 that the offering for the Christians in Jerusalem will be "sealed to them" (*sphragisamenos autois*) may indicate delivery of the money under seal, if the statement is meant literally.

While references to sealing practices in daily life are scarce in the NT, metaphorical usage of the language of seals (sing. *sphragis*) and the act of sealing (*sphragizō*) is common. The Gospel of John uses seal language both of a human's vindication of God (John 3:33) and God's vindication of "the Son of Man" (John 6:27). In Paul's letters circumcision is said to be a "seal of righteousness" for Abraham (Rom 4:11), while for Christians the Holy Spirit is God's "seal of ownership" upon them (2 Cor 1:22; Eph 1:13; 4:30).

By far the most elaborate use of seal imagery in the NT is found in the book of Revelation, which describes an apocalyptic vision of a scroll sealed with seven seals, which only "the Lamb" is worthy to open (Rev 5–8). The opening of each seal unleashes a new element of the vision; after the sixth, one hundred forty-four thousand from the tribes of Israel are each marked with a seal on their foreheads (Rev 7:3–8). In the visions following the opening of the seventh seal, John is told to "seal up" the words spoken by the "seven thunders" (Rev 10:4), but later is commanded not to "seal up the words of the prophecy of this scroll" (Rev 22:10).

C. THE ANCIENT NEAR EAST

Mesopotamia

The use of seals (Sum. sing. KIŠIB, Akk. sing. *kunukku*) in the Near East begins with simple stamp seals. The earliest evidence for them in Anatolia, Mesopotamia, and Syria dates as far back as the seventh millennium BC. By the fourth millennium BC, clay sealings used on containers are extant. Seals were especially used to mark the outside of clay balls containing economic "tokens." This technology is now understood to have led directly to the earliest pictographic forms of Mesopotamian writing on clay tablets, which subsequently evolved into cuneiform script (see Schmandt-Besserat). An important group of seal impressions from the early third millennium BC are the so-called "city seals," which bear only symbols indicating specific Mesopotamian cities. With increased use of seals on clay tablets, the stamp seal was largely replaced with the cylinder seal, a design well suited to use on clay tablets. This became the standard wherever cuneiform writing was employed, for over three millennia. Occasionally both formats were combined in "stamp-cylinders," multipurpose cylinder seals that also had stamp seals carved on their bottom face.

The earliest uses of seals seem to have been administrative and economic, especially to verify the recording of exchanged goods and to prevent tampering with containers or records. Over time their use was extended to a wide range of texts, including legal contracts, political documents, and letters. Seals were most often associated with an individual, and might identify the owner by name if they bore a text, but they could also be associated with a specific government office instead, or even with specific deities.

Cylinder seals were usually made of hard stone. Šimatum, the daughter of king Zimri-Lim of Mari (18th c. BC), requested a seal in lapis lazuli (ARM 10.95). As part of her dowry she already had one in gold (Sasson, 113n227).

So-called "royal seals" were associated with kings or their high officials. Important seals might possess a certain prestige and be kept as heirlooms for long periods of time. A dramatic example of such heirloom seal use is found on the tablets of the Esarhaddon Succession Treaty (ca. 670 BC), which bear the impressions of three seals associated with the deity Aššur. The first, from the reign of Esarhaddon's father Sennacherib, is described by its own text as "The Seal of Destinies," while the other two were already ancient when impressed on these tablets: a seal dating back five centuries to the Middle Assyrian Period, and an Old Assyrian seal that was roughly twelve hundred years old at that time. (See Wiseman, 14–19.)

The loss or theft of a seal created the potential for fraud. A brief Sumerian text used in the Old Babylonian scribal curriculum describes a communal response to the loss of a personal seal: "A seal inscribed with the name of Ur-dun, the merchant, was lost. In accordance with the word of the assembly, the herald has sounded the horn throughout all the streets: no one now has any claim against him" (*ETCSL* t.5.7.a#). The importance and prestige of seals is also reflected in omen literature, where dreams involving the receiving of a seal were positive omens, while dreams of their loss portended the death of a child. Even the Greek historian Herodotus seems to relate an impression of the ubiquity of seals in the Near East when he remarks concerning the Mesopotamians: "every man has a seal and a carven staff" (*Hist.* 1.195).

Egypt

In Egypt, after initial borrowing of the Mesopotamian cylinder seal design, the distinctive scarab seal was developed, which was a type of stamp seal bearing designs and/or hieroglyphic text carved on the underside of an amulet in the shape of a scarab beetle. Although scarab amulets (associated with the Egyptian deity Khepri) had been around for centuries, they seem to have first been used as seals toward the latter periods of the Old Kingdom. Scarab seals (as well as "scaraboid" seals, which retained the same basic shape without the carved beetle design) spread well beyond the borders of Egypt, and were commonly used in the Levant, including in Israel, where many were incised with Hebrew inscriptions.

D. THE GRECO-ROMAN WORLD

Greece

The use of seals in the Greek world dates back to the the Neolithic era, and became common in the Early Bronze Age. In the Middle and Late Bronze Age, the Minoan and Mycenaean cultures used stamp and cylinder seal designs borrowed from the Near East, as well as distinctive lentoid ("lens-shaped") and amygdaloid ("almond-shaped") seals. Beginning in the mid-sixth century BC, island gems such as chalcedony, carnelian, and rock crystal were utilized. Scarab seals also became common in the Archaic Period and in the classical period of Greece's history. Clay, lead, and wax sealing media were used with documents and for securing packaging of goods.

The iconography of Greek seals often depicted specific deities or mythological figures, and at later times even portraits of the owner. Greek cities employed "civic seals" owned by the city itself for use with public documents. It was the president (*epistatēs*) of the executive committee of the *prytaneis* who was charged with the safekeeping of the seal of Athens (Aristotle, *Ath. pol.* 44.1).

Hellenistic-period papyri from Egypt provide intact examples of sealed documents, which often include direct reference to the identity of the person affixing a sealing to the text and a general description of the seal's design.

Greek authors often mention the use of seals in securing personal property around the household. There are numerous references to seals in Greek drama. In Aeschylus's play *Agamemnon*, the reference to Clytemnestra's "having broken no seal" of the storerooms is probably a reminder to the audience that she has already broken the "seal" of her marriage by her affair with Aegisthus (*Ag.* 609). In a play by Sophocles, Electra recognizes her brother Orestes by the fact that he is wearing the signet ring of their father, Agamemnon (*El.* 1222–1224). In a tragic drama by Euripides, Theseus beholds a document sealed by his wife Phaedra's golden seal that falsely accuses the innocent Hippolytus (*Hipp.* 864–865).

Fraudulent seal usage was always a concern. Seal engravers were forbidden by Solon from keeping copies of seals they produced (Diogenes Laertius, *Solon* 57). Diodorus Siculus reports that in Greco-Roman Egypt, "in the case of counterfeiters or falsifiers of measures and weights or imitators of seals . . . both their hands should be cut off" (*Bib. hist.* 1.78).

Various tactics used for circumventing seals on letters and goods are noted. Lucian explains how Alexander "the False Prophet" was able to cleverly open a sealed letter and then replace the seal with a counterfeit one (*Alex.* 21).

Rome

Under the Romans, glass or stone seals (Lat. sing. *signum*) mounted on rings became common. An innovation of the Roman period was the use of seal cases—bronze boxes that encased and protected clay sealings used in commerce.

Seals are mentioned in literary texts, such as the comedies of Plautus (*Cas.* 2.1; *Amph.* 1.1.265). Apuleius relates the tale of a jealous wife who took the signet ring from her husband and sent a servant with it to tell the suspected rival to come to the house for an assignation. She then brutally beat the woman and killed her (Apuleius, *Metam.* 10.24).

When Cicero became one of the two consuls for 63 BC, he discovered and exposed the plot of Catiline and his co-conspirators in a series of speeches in the Senate. Letters of the conspirators were brought into the Senate. During his third speech, Cicero confronted Lentulus with the impression of his seal, which was in the likeness of his illustrious grandfather (Cicero, *Cat.* 3.5; cf. Sallust, *Cat.* 44). The other conspirators were also convicted by the evidence of their seals on the treasonable letters.

Shortly before he committed suicide, Petronius, the author of the *Satyricon* and the arbiter of Nero's tastes, sent the emperor a letter that Tacitus describes as follows:

> Not even in his will did he follow the routine of suicide by flattering Nero or Tigellinus or another of the mighty, but—prefixing the names of the various catamites and women—detailed the imperial debauches . . . and sent the document under seal to Nero. His signet-ring he broke, lest it should render dangerous service later. (*Ann.* 16.20)

E. THE JEWISH WORLD

Jewish literature from the Second Temple period reflects the continued importance of seals in everyday life. The Wisdom of Ben Sira acknowledges the skill of the seal maker's trade: "Those who cut the signets of seals, each is diligent in making a great variety; he sets his heart on painting a lifelike image, and he is careful to finish his work" (Sir 38:27). Tobit mentions the sealing of the marriage contract for Tobias and Sarah by both of Sarah's parents (Tob 7:14), and the sealing of bags of money (Tob 9:5). First Maccabees notes the passing of a signet ring in narrating the succession of Antiochus IV Epiphanes (1 Macc 6:15).

Rabbinic literature provides various details about the use of seals in Jewish contexts. The wearing of seals on rings or on cords is noted, and this activity was regulated on the Sabbath (*m. Šabb* 6:1, 3; *t. Šabb.* 5:8; *b. Šabb.* 58a). The presence or absence of sealings on containers had various implications for customs regarding purity and impurity (*m. Kelim* 13:6; *m. Maʿaś. Š.* 3:12; *m. Parah* 5:5, 7; 11:1; *m. Ṭehar.* 3:5; 7:5–6; 8:1; 10:5; *m. Miqw.* 5:5; *b. ʿAbod. Zar.* 31a). Uses of seals in magical/ritual contexts are also occasionally mentioned (*b. Ber.* 6a; *b. Šabb.* 66b; *b. Giṭ.* 68a). One passage notes the seal emblems used by several rabbis for signing documents, which seem to reflect an avoidance of potentially idolatrous subjects (*b. Giṭ* 36a).

Extant early Jewish seals show that iconographic subjects from Jewish tradition, such as the menorah, were often used in seal designs. Finds from the cave in the Wadi ed-Daliyeh included many sealed Aramaic documents from the fourth century BC. Seal impressions from these show a mixture of seal formats, including Persian-style cylinder seals and Greek signet rings. One of these seals bearing Paleo-Hebrew script mentions an individual who was "son of Sanballat, Governor of Samaria." (See Cross; Lapp and Lapp.)

F. THE CHRISTIAN WORLD

Early Christian writers employed the imagery of sealing for baptism (*Barn.* 9; Basil, *De Spiritu Sancto* 12, 16, 26; Ambrose, *De Spiritu Sancto* 1.6.78–80; 1.14.169; 3.8.48), and the image of the breaking of a seal for apostasy (*2 Clem.* 7.6; 8.6; *Herm. Simil.* 8.6.3).

Clement of Alexandria observed that "if all were well trained, there would be no need of seals, if servants and masters were equally honest" (*Paed.* 3.11). He further noted that the wearing of a seal ring should be for utilitarian purposes only, and that Christians ought to be scrupulous in their selection of seal designs:

> And let our seals be either a dove, or a fish, or a ship scudding before the wind, or a musical lyre . . . or a ship's anchor. . . . For we are not to delineate the faces of idols, we who are prohibited to cleave to them; nor a sword, nor a bow, following as we do, peace; nor drinking-cups, being temperate. (*Paed.* 3.11)

In the Byzantine era, seals carved from hard stones were used to make impressions in a variety of media associated with different functions. Wax and lead sealings were widely used to endorse documents and secure letters, and lead sealings were also commonly used to secure packaging. Because of their durability, tens of thousands of lead sealings survive from antiquity. Silver sealings are also attested, and official state documents of emperors were even affixed with sealings in gold. The inscriptions of Byzantine seals most often named the owner, and his or her office if relevant, but they might also include Christian invocations. Iconography present on Byzantine seals typically depicted Christian motifs, especially Christ, Mary, or various saints. Such images were among those targeted in the iconoclastic movements of the eighth and ninth centuries AD.

BIBLIOGRAPHY: P. Amiet, *La glyptique mésopotamienne archaïque* (1980); N. Avigad, *Bullae and Seals from a Post-Exilic Judean Archive*

(1976); N. Avigad and B. Sass, *Corpus of West Semitic Stamp Seals* (1997); J. Boardman, *Greek Gems and Finger Rings: Early Bronze Age to Late Classical* (rev. ed., 2001); B. Buchanan, *Early Near Eastern Seals in the Yale Babylonian Collection* (1981); D. Collon, *First Impressions: Cylinder Seals in the Ancient Near East* (Rev. ed., 2005); D. Collon, *Near Eastern Seals* (1990); F. M. Cross, "The Discovery of the Samaria Papyri," *BA* 26.4 (1963), 110–21; Dumbarton Oaks, "Online Catalogue of Byzantine Seals," http://www.doaks.org/resources/seals; H. Frankfort, *Cylinder Seals: A Documentary Essay on the Art and Religion of the Ancient Near East* (1939); M. Gibson and R. D. Biggs, ed., *Seals and Sealing in the Ancient Near East* (1978); L. Gorelick and E. Williams-Forte, ed., *Ancient Seals and the Bible* (1983); A. F. Gorton, *Egyptian and Egyptianizing Scarabs: A typology of steatite, faience and paste scarabs from Punic and other Mediterranean Sites* (1996); L. G. Herr, *The Scripts of Ancient Northwest Semitic Seals* (1978); R. Hestrin and M. Dayagi-Mendels, *Inscribed Seals: First Temple Period, Hebrew, Ammonite, Moabite, Phoenician and Aramaic, from the Collections of the Israel Museum and the Israel Department of Antiquities and Museums* (1979); P. W. Lapp and N. L. Lapp, ed., *Wâdī ed-Dâliyeh* (1974); O. Lipschits and D. S. Vanderhooft, *The Yehud Stamp Impressions: A Corpus of Inscribed Impressions from the Persian and Hellenistic Periods in Judah* (2011); A. Lohwasser, ed., *Skarabäen des 1. Jahrtausends: Ein Workshop in Münster am 27. Oktober 2012* (2014); G. T. Martin, *Scarabs, Cylinders and Other Ancient Egyptian Seals: A Checklist of Publications* (1985); E. Mazar, *The Palace of King David: Excavations at the Summit of the City of David: Preliminary Report of Seasons 2005–2007* (2009); L. Mykytiuk, "Archaeology Confirms 50 Real People in the Bible," *BAR* 40.2 (2014), 42–50; L. J. Mykytiuk, *Identifying Biblical Persons in Northwest Semitic Inscriptions of 1200–539 B.C.E.* (2004); D. Nadali, "Neo-Assyrian State Seals: An Allegory of Power," *SAAB* 18 (2009–10), 215–44; N. Oikonomides, *Byzantine Lead Seals* (1985); N. Oikonomides et al., ed., *Studies in Byzantine Sigillography*, vols. 1–11 (1987–2012); H. Pittman, *Ancient Art in Miniature: Near Eastern Seals from the Collection of Martin and Sarah Cherkasky* (1987); H. Pittman, "Cylinder Seals and Scarabs in the Ancient Near East," *CANE* 3.1589–603; D. Plantzos, "Seals and Seal Usage in Antiquity," in idem, *Hellenistic Engraved Gems* (1999), 18–32; E. Porada, *Ancient Art in Seals* (1980); E. Porada, ed., *Corpus of Ancient Near Eastern Seals in North American Collections* (1948); B. A. Porter, "Old Syrian Popular Style Cylinder Seals," Ph.D. diss., Columbia University (2001); I. Regulski, K. Duistermaat, and P. Verkinderen, ed., *Seals and Sealing Practices in the Near East: Developments in Administration and Magic from Prehistory to the Islamic Period* (2012); P. Taylor, ed., *The Iconography of Cylinder Seals* (2006); G. Vikan and J. Nesbitt, *Security in Byzantium: Locking, Sealing, and Weighing* (1980); L. Werr,

Studies in the Chronology and Regional Style of Old Babylonian Cylinder Seals (1988); J. G. Westenholz, ed., *Seals and Sealing in the Ancient Near East* (1995); A. von Wickede, *Prähistorische Stempelglyptic in Vorderasien* (1990); R. H. Wilkinson, *Egyptian Scarabs* (2008); D. J. Wiseman, *The Vassal Treaties of Esarhaddon* (1958).

ALB and RKH

See also ART, COMMUNICATIONS & MESSENGERS, and INHERITANCE.

S̄LAVERY

Slavery is defined as one person's owning another and having almost total control over his or her life. But the border between what is traditionally called chattel slavery and other forms of dependent servitude can blur the distinction between who is a slave and who is free. Historians are aware that there are numerous models that explain the ideology of slavery, and they often disagree as to how much of a contribution slavery made to the economy of any slaveholding society.

A. OLD TESTAMENT

The most common Hebrew term for "slave" is *ᶜebed*, which is related to the verb *ᶜābad*, "to work, serve." The word *ᶜebed* is used both literally and metaphorically in the OT. In addition to denoting the state of being owned by someone else, *ᶜebed* is used to refer to a person of lower status in an asymmetrical relationship. Subjects of a king or a noble may metaphorically refer to themselves as slaves. And worshippers of God may refer to themselves as "slaves of God" (Exod 32:13; Ps 31:16; 1 Sam 3:9). The nations who were defeated by David were referred to as slaves, but may have been subject to periods of forced labor (2 Sam 8:2–14; 1 Chr 18:2, 6, 13). *Naᶜar* and *naᶜărâ* may refer, respectively, to a young male or female slave (2 Kgs 4:25; Neh 4:16, 22, 23); *ʾāmâ* refers to a slave woman (Gen 30:3; Exod 21:20, 26; Lev 25:6). This is used in contrast to *śākîr*, which is often translated "hired servant" (e.g., Exod 12:45; Lev 25:6, 40, 50).

Slavery is a routine part of life in the patriarchal narratives, and slaves are mentioned in inventories along with other valuables (Gen 12:16; 20:14; 24:35; 30:43; 32:5). In Genesis, Sarai has a female Egyptian slave named Hagar, whom she gives to Abram to bear a child, Ishmael (Gen 16:1–3); even after Ishmael is born, Hagar is still referred to as a slave (Gen 21:12). Abraham possesses slaves and circumcises them (Gen 17:23). Both Rachel and Leah provide slaves for Jacob who provide him with children (Gen

30:3, 5–13). Though they bore him children, they are still called slaves (Gen 33:2; cf. 21:12). Joseph's brothers sell him as a slave to Midianite traders (Gen 37:25–28).

The book of Exodus recounts how the Egyptians subjected the Hebrews to forced labor and controlled their population. This made a deep cultural impression on the Israelites, and their slavery in Egypt is a prominent reason given in the OT for why they should regulate servitude among themselves. Non-Hebrews were bought and sold as chattel slaves by Hebrews and had very limited rights and protections. The conquest narratives mention that prisoners of war from conquered cities were taken as chattel slaves (Num 31:42; Deut 20:1–14). These were supplemented by house-born slaves and Hebrews punished for theft (Exod 22:1–3). Hebrew debt slaves were used as temporary labor. Foreign slaves in Israel underwent circumcision and had to keep the Sabbath (Exod 20:10).

The books of Exodus, Leviticus, and Deuteronomy each contain regulations concerning the practice of slavery. Each book limits how long someone could be a slave and is concerned with curbing the abuses slavery could entail, but the regulations vary from each other in significant ways. Exodus 21:1–6 indicates that a man may sell himself, his wife, or his children to settle a debt. But after six years, he is to be freed along with his family with no further obligation. If a man is single when he becomes a slave and gains a wife while serving, she and any children remain with the debt holder. But if he loves his master, wife, and children, he can remain as a permanent bond-slave and keep his family intact (Exod 21:5–6). Exodus 21:7–11 states that if a single woman is placed in servitude, after six years she will not be freed. Female debt slavery was usually in expectation of marriage to the debt holder or one of his sons. Protective clauses allowed for manumission, but only if a woman was treated unfairly or neglected. Female slaves were vulnerable to sexual exploitation.

Leviticus 19:20 is concerned with the case of a man who has had sex with a slave woman betrothed to a free Hebrew. The man is the only guilty party. The woman goes unpunished, as she is a slave and has the status of property. The male must make a sacrifice because he has violated the sanctity of a pending marriage (Lev 19:21–22). There is significant tension in the law codes as they attempt to mediate between family law and property law in cases such as this.

Exodus 21:20–21 states that "Anyone who beats their male or female slave with a rod must be punished if the slave dies as a direct result, but they are not to be punished if the slave recovers after a day or two, since the slave is their property." The verb translated "be punished," *nāqam*, probably refers to the death penalty. If a beating results in the loss of a slave's eye or tooth, the slave is to be set free (Exod 21:26–27). This law seems to have applied to all slaves.

The regulations in Deut 15:12–18, like the ones in Exodus, limit servitude to six years. However, this text states that the debt slave is not only to be set free but is also to be provisioned to start a new life. A male or female debt slave who loves his or her master can go through a ritual and become a permanent bond-slave. Here the law for manumission is the same for males and females. If a Hebrew soldier marries a captive girl and later divorces her, he is not allowed to sell her as a slave. Marriages between Hebrews and slaves were apparently recognized as valid (Deut 21:10–14). Deuteronomy 23:15–16 declares that escaped slaves are to be given refuge and not re-enslaved or returned to their masters. This is unique and contrary to known laws from the ancient Near East.

The laws about debt slavery found in Lev 25 are much different from the earlier sets of regulations found in Exodus and Deuteronomy. Some historians speculate that the two earlier debt slave codes, from Exodus and Deuteronomy, covered small debts and that the Leviticus code covered larger debts tied to land. Others maintain that these codes were modified over time to cover different economic and political circumstances, which resulted in conflicting statues.

Leviticus 25 indicates that the land was to be given its Sabbath rest every seventh year, but no manumission of debt slaves is mentioned (Lev 25:2–7). Leviticus 25:42–43 states concerning Hebrew debt servants: "they must not be sold as slaves. Do not rule over them ruthlessly but fear your God." The word "ruthlessly" (Heb. *perek*) refers to a crushing burden of labor and harks back to the abuse that the Egyptians laid upon the Hebrews when they enslaved them (Exod 1:13–14). Ideally, a Hebrew debt slave received better treatment than a non-Hebrew chattel slave. Non-Hebrew slaves were considered property and could be sold or bequeathed to the owner's heirs (Lev 25:44–46). Perhaps the greatest difference between the treatment of non-Hebrew chattel slaves and Hebrew debt slaves was the intensity of the required labor. While the text maintains that debt servitude is distinct from chattel slavery (Lev 25:39–41), universal manumission is provided for, though it occurred only every fifty years, during the Year of Jubilee. While in service, a debt slave could not be beaten or overworked. A debt slave's term of service could be very short or lifelong. At the Jubilee, a debt slave was to return to his ancestral land. If he had gained children during servitude, they were released with him. There is no mention in the text of his wife being released with him. The possibility exists that the wife was a slave and remained with her master but the children followed the status of the father and were free and left the master's household with him (Lev 25:39–43).

The number of slaves possessed by the Hebrews and later by the Jews is unknown. Israel did not have a slave economy comparable to that of Rome. In Ezra 2:64–65 the entire population of the "assembly" is given at 49,697, of which 7,337 (14 percent) were slaves. But there is no compelling evidence to justify projecting this percentile to earlier periods. These numbers themselves do not correspond with the numbers totaled from the preceding list (Ezra 2:1–63).

The protections afforded Hebrew debt slaves in the law and its revisions, as well as the prohibition against enslaving fellow Hebrews, were often ignored. Second Kings 4:1 describes the plight of a widow of a man belonging to Elisha's prophetic circle whose sons were taken as slaves by a creditor. Jeremiah 34:8–11 and 14–17 indicate that there was widespread enslavement of Hebrews, which was contrary to the law, and a royal decree freeing them met only with temporary compliance. Later, Nehemiah addressed this in one of his significant reforms (Neh 5:1–5). In one of the conflicts between Israel and Judah, a number of Judean captives were about to be enslaved by Israel. But after the Israelites were chastised by the prophet Oded, they cleaned and dressed the captives and returned them to Judean territory (2 Chr 28:8–15).

There are numerous Biblical references that exiles from Judah were made slaves in Babylon until the rise of the kingdom of Persia (2 Chr 36:20; Isa 14:3; 47:6; Ezra 9:9). Lamentations 5:5, 8, and 13 describe hard labor and the conquered Judeans' humiliation now that slaves have become their masters. But this is probably a figurative use of the term "slaves" in the early years of the exile. Evidence from the later Persian period of the exile comes from the Murašhu Archives from Nippur and a series of cuneiform texts dispersed in museums and collections, many of them unpublished, which concern Jews in exile and their legal cases. Preliminary analysis of these texts indicates that Jews under Babylonian and Persian rule in exile were not only free but frequently owned chattel slaves themselves. These slaves were rented out or sold by their Jewish owners, and some evidence indicates that Jews occasionally owned other Jews as chattel slaves. It is apparent that with the Jews in exile, slave ownership was regulated to some extent by Babylonian and Persian laws, as opposed to the laws of the OT. The Jews' living for seventy years under this legal system may explain, in part, the large number of slaves owned by Jews returning to Jerusalem during the time of Ezra and Nehemiah (Ezra 2:64–65) and the difficulties slave owners had in returning to the slave regulations of the law of Moses.

Proverbs warns that debt can result in slavery (Prov 22:7). The subject of slaves not behaving according to their place in society is also discussed in very negative terms (Prov 19:10; 29:19, 21; 30:22 and Eccl 10:7). The OT does not criticize the existence of slavery, but it consistently seeks to curtail the institution's abuses.

B. NEW TESTAMENT

Issues regarding slavery appear numerous times in the NT. The most common Greek word for slave is *doulos*. Less common words include *oiketēs* (a household servant), *pais* ("child, boy, slave"), *therapōn* ("attendant"), and *hypēretēs* ("underling"). There is no legal code regarding slavery in the NT, but several texts address both slaves and masters. Although there is a theme of liberation in some of Paul's writings (Gal 3:28; 1 Cor 12:12–13), in practical matters the Christian household was ordered very much like a Roman household. Rome was a slaveholding society, with many families owning at least one slave. When a family was converted to the Christian faith, slaves remained part of the household.

Jesus's ministry took place in a context in which rural slavery was well established and in which large Roman households had numerous slaves. When Jesus spoke in parables, he often used the example of slaves to teach about the kingdom of God. From these we can glean information about the lives of slaves in Roman Judea. For example, in the Parable of the Dinner Guests (Matt 22:1–14; Luke 14:15–24), slaves are sent to invite first wealthy and elite guests and then lowly guests to a banquet (or wedding feast). The slaves themselves are too low in status to be invited. Agricultural slaves worked hard in the fields and then had to cook the master's meal before eating their own (Luke 17:7–10). However, some slaves had higher status and authority over their master's property, which might include others of the master's slaves. In one parable, a slave manager entrusted with his master's estate abuses other slaves and raids his master's wine and food stores. His lapse of judgment results in demotion and punishment (Matt 24:45–51; Luke 12:42–48).

Slave managers and even cases of slaves owning slaves are known from the Roman period. In most of the parables of Jesus that involve slaves, a slave who fails in his task is demoted, exiled, beaten, or executed (Matt 18:23–35; 21:33–41; 25:14–30). Luke 12:47–48 displays a standard that any Roman master would have been familiar with: "The servant who knows the master's will and does not get ready or does not do what the master wants will be beaten with many blows. But the one who does not know and does things deserving punishment will be beaten with few blows." Slaves who were successful gained more responsibility rather than manumission (Matt 25:14–30). Jesus did not endorse slavery with these stories, but used their familiar content to teach about the kingdom of God.

Throughout the sayings of Jesus and the teachings of Paul, slavery is presented in terms of all its brutal inhumanity, but Jesus also presents it as an ideal that is expressed in his own ministry and that he expects his disciples to follow. Jesus admonishes his disciples, "The greatest among you should be like the youngest, and the one who rules like the one who serves. For who is greater, the one who is at the table or the one who serves? Is it not the one who is at the table? But I am among you as one who serves" (Luke 22:26–27; cf. Mark 10:42–45). Jesus gives strong praise to a gentile, a centurion, who wishes to have his slave (*pais*) healed because he recognizes the authority Jesus had over sickness even if he was not physically present (Luke 7:1–10; cf. Matt 8:5–13; John 4:46–54). Jesus takes the role of a lowly slave when he washes the feet of his disciples (John 13:1–17). His death on the cross was typical of the execution of a rebel slave and his call for his disciple to take up their cross and follow him was radical (Matt 16:24). In the Gospels and in the teachings of Paul, the juxtaposition of the ideal of Christ's disciples as slaves and the complexity and brutality of slavery in the Roman world created a tension for the church that has been evident from the first century to the present.

Paul set an ideal of equality within the church that is both radical and liberating: "for all of you who were baptized into Christ have clothed yourselves with Christ. There is neither Jew nor Gentile, neither slave nor free, nor is there male and female, for you are all one in Christ Jesus" (Gal 3:27–28). And again, "For we were all baptized by one Spirit so as to form one body—whether Jews or Gentiles, slave or free—and we were all given the one Spirit to drink" (1 Cor 12:13). Paul refers to himself as a slave (*doulos*) of Christ (Rom 1:1; Phil 1:1) and builds his doctrine on the slave-like self-sacrifice of Christ as the example to follow and emulate (Phil 2:4–8). According to Paul, all believers have, in a sense, become slaves of God after forsaking their old lives by faith followed by baptism (Rom 6:1–20). But the new faith was spreading in Rome, the greatest slave state of all. The need to deal with the complexity of the social reality of slavery was perhaps, in Paul's mind, lessened initially by his belief in the imminent return of Christ (1 Cor 7:29–31).

Paul advises that everyone remain in the state (*klēsis*) he or she was in upon conversion (1 Cor 7:17, 20, 24). The question of how rigid this advice was meant to be concerning slavery is controversial. The problems of translating 1 Cor 7:21, over which commentators are deeply divided, involve a translation difficulty regarding the Greek phrase *mallon chrēsai* (compare, e.g., NIV, "[although if you can gain your freedom,] do so," and NRSV, "[Even if you can gain your freedom,] make use of your present condition now more than ever"). Many translations assume that Paul is telling slaves to remain slaves even if freedom is offered. Others assume that slaves are to accept their freedom. But manumission was not something a slave could demand in the Roman world. Even the allowance (*peculium*) that sources indicate slaves could save up over the years and use to purchase their freedom was in fact the property of their master and could be taken at any time. When manumitted, a slave was not freed from the many obligations he had to his former master, who was now his new patron. So, however one translates this passage, an obligation remained for the slave.

In Philemon Paul directly engages slavery as his main topic. While in prison, Paul led to faith Onesimus, the slave of Philemon. He then sought to reconcile an unspecified problem between Onesimus and his master, and sent Onesimus home with this letter. Paul desires Onesimus to serve him (*diakonē*) in prison on Philemon's behalf. But the letter raises tantalizing questions with no answers: for example, does Paul want Onesimus to serve him as a freed man or as a slave? Even if freed, Onesimus would still be a client of Philemon and subject to his authority. While some scholars advance the view that Paul wanted Onesimus freed, others claim that Paul want him to remain a slave and that he was asking Philemon to radically Christianize their relationship. The evidence allows for no clear conclusion.

Order in the household appears to be an important concern of other NT writings. Texts referred to by scholars as "house codes" (*Haustafeln*) affirm key roles in the Christian household. Most of the standards found in these texts reflect those of the traditional order in a Greco-Roman household. A well-run household had long been a concern in the classical world (Arist. *Pol.* 1.1.2.3; 1.1.3.1–4; Stobaeus, *Florilegium* 4.85.21). A house out of order, including its slaves, was a disgrace and reflected on the status of the *paterfamilias* as the head of a household.

The house codes in Ephesians and Colossians, in addition to exhorting husbands, wives, and children, address slaves and masters (Eph 6:5–9; Col 3:22–25). Slaves are commanded to live in heartfelt obedience to their masters, fearing the Lord and expecting a reward in heaven. Masters are reminded that they themselves have a master in heaven and are told to treat their slaves justly and fairly and not to threaten them. This moderating advice, reminding masters of their own impending judgment, is not a standard feature of Greco-Roman ideology.

Other house codes seem to go even further in maintaining the master/slave hierarchy. In 1 Timothy, slaves are exhorted to "consider their masters worthy of full respect, so that God's name and our teaching may not be slandered. Those who have believing masters should not show them disrespect just because they are fellow believers. Instead, they should serve them even better because their masters are dear to them as fellow believers and are devoted to the welfare of their slaves" (1 Tim 6:1–2). Titus is exhorted to "teach slaves to be subject to their masters in everything, to try to please them, not to talk back to them, and not to steal from them, but to show that they can be fully trusted, so that in every way they will make the teaching about God our Savior attractive" (Tit 2:9–10).

The house code attributed to Peter goes even further. "Slaves [*oiketai*], in reverent fear of God, submit yourselves to your masters [*despotais*], not only to those who are good and considerate, but also to those who are harsh" (1 Pet 2:18). In this text, the act of suffering for doing right is considered a Christian testimony (1 Pet 2:18–20). It is hard to reconcile these admonitions with the liberating language of Gal 3:28. Some historians speculate that the house codes were written to uphold the rights of slaveholding Christian patrons, or speculate that they were an attempt to accommodate the church's practice of slavery to Rome's to reduce hostility. Others conclude that church leaders believed that any social distinctions among Christians, while necessary social roles, were irrelevant in the light of the doctrine of Jesus's sacrifice. While there is no call for manumission and an end to the institution of slavery in the NT, a number of abuses are addressed.

C. ANCIENT NEAR EAST

Slavery existed in all periods of ancient Near Eastern history, though most labor was performed by free or semi-free people. The states of the ancient Near East often possessed law codes that addressed different aspects of slavery. Occasionally other forms of evidence concerning the institution have survived.

Mesopotamia

Slaves were a feature in every Mesopotamian kingdom, but the institution was not the principal source of labor in any period. Evidence for slavery appears in a number of the major law codes and in a variety of cuneiform documents. Most wealthy households had only one to three slaves, though some prominent families could boast of twenty or more. The number and the sources of slaves varied from kingdom to kingdom in Mesopotamia. The use of slave labor was limited in early Mesopotamia kingdoms. But the numbers of slaves increased through the conquests of the empires of the first millennium BC. Most labor was provided by serfs and dependent laborers. Most prisoners of war were not enslaved but were instead settled in communities with limitations on their movements and with the burden of some forced labor. Generally in the ancient Near East it was too expensive to maintain and control large numbers of slaves when most of the work was agricultural and subject to long periods when slaves in large numbers were not needed. Those who were chattel slaves were able to be recognized by marks (e.g., branding).

The most common Akkadian words for "slave" were *ardu* (*wardum* in OB, as in Hammurabi's Code), "male slave," and *amtu*, "female slave." In the sixth century BC, the terms *qallu* (masc.) and *qallatu* (fem.) were common. The Neo-Babylonian *širku* has often been described as a temple slave, but this word actually denotes a dependent relationship distinct from slavery.

Law codes and records of court cases from the Third Dynasty of Ur (2112–2004 BC) provide some of our earliest information on Mesopotamian slavery. If a man committed a crime and could not pay compensation, he could be sentenced to become the slave of his victim or the victim's family. In one case, a murderer was killed while being apprehended. His wife and daughters were sentenced to be slaves to the relatives of the murder victim. They fled and were recaptured, and the court imposed the sentence (ITT2¹ 2789 = NG 241). Such slaves could be sold, indicating that this status was permanent (MVN 3 102). There is evidence from the Ur III period for self-sale into slavery as well as the sale of children to settle a debt (L 11053 = ZA 5322). Sumerians with greater wealth would pledge slaves, rather than themselves, as security for debts. Slaves could also be rented. In one rental contract from Nippur, a female slave has to swear not to run away (NRVN 1 226). Slaves had access to courts and sometimes successfully contested their status.

Law codes protected the property rights of slave owners rather than the slaves themselves. In the Code of Eshnunna, if a slave girl lost her virginity to a free man, he paid compensation to her master (CE 31). If a female slave was seized illegally by a free man who falsely claimed her to settle a debt, the master was compensated if the woman was killed in this attempt (CE 22–23). The laws in the Code of Eshnunna that applied when a slave was wounded or killed by an ox or a dog are similar to laws found in the Code of Hammurabi and the book of Exodus (CE 53–57; CH 247–252; Exod 21:28–36).

The Code of Hammurabi contains more detailed regulations concerning slaves. Some resemble the laws in the OT. Individuals guilty of crimes and negligence could be condemned to slavery (CH 53–54; cf. Exod 22:1–3). Debt slavery was common to both Babylon and Israel, but in the former service was limited to three years (CH 117). According to the Code of Hammurabi, a debt could be repaid by handing a slave over in lieu of the debt. This slave could be sold by the new owner like any other chattel property. But if the slave was a woman who had borne the previous owner children, he could redeem her for the cost of the debt and she would be returned (CH 117–119). Babylonian law assessed penalties based upon class.

Slaves committing crimes received harsher punishments than other members of society. Slaves victimized by crimes, negligence, assault, or medical incompetence received no compensation. Instead, their owners were compensated (CH 196–201; 202–225; 228–231; 250–252).

Some of the laws in the Code of Hammurabi are concerned with runaways and theft. Even members of the upper class faced the death penalty if they helped a slave escape through the city gates or hid the slave in their home. One who captured a runaway slave but did not return him or her could be fined or executed (CH 15–20). The purchase of slaves who may have been stolen is also addressed (CH 280–282).

The Code of Hammurabi allowed a wife to present her husband with a female slave if she proved to be infertile. As was the case in Egypt and in the book of Genesis, the children born of this union were free. The surrogate mother remained a slave. If the slave did not produce children, she could be sold (CH 144–147). Children of these relationships could become joint heirs with the father's other children (CH 170–171). Childless people in general had the option of adopting a slave to care for them in their old age. Often this was done with the promise of manumission at their deaths.

The Assyrians and the Babylonians took numerous prisoners of war in the first millennium BC and resettled them throughout their empires. Most of these prisoners did not become slaves but were semi-free people with limited rights. As mentioned above, in these societies slavery was never the dominant form of labor. While a small number of captives were enslaved, most were settled in communities or given as offerings to temples. Historians have often described these temple dependents, the *širkū*, as slaves. Their numbers were augmented by slave owners donating slaves as acts of piety, slaves transferred to the temples to settle debts, and by mothers donating children to the temples in time of war and famine. Slaves donated to temples were first manumitted. Once made *širkū*, their status was hereditary. Such individuals differ from slaves on many points. Slaves were known only by a given name and the name of their owner. The *širkū* were known by a given name and their father's name. While *širkū* new to the temple were branded or marked, their subsequent offspring were not. These experienced a normal family life, possessed moveable property, and lived in independent homes. Some historians speculate that temples served as an artificial clan for the dislocated and unconnected (Culbertson). But some *širkū* ran away from forced labor. There is no known legal process by which *širkū* could be released from their dependent status.

Adoption, marriage, and dedication or sale to a temple were possible routes to manumission from chattel slavery (Paulissian). Manumission could be granted by a master in court, a procedure that would be followed by a religious ritual of purification.

Egypt

In Egypt all the land was owned by the pharaoh, and all subjects were considered his servants. The terms most commonly translated "slave," *b3k* and *ḥm*, can denote a number of slave or semi-free relationships.

There is little information for slavery in the Old and Middle Kingdoms. A 5th Dynasty inscription from Neferirkare in Abydos indicates that if priests with temple duties were put to forced labor, those responsible would be sentenced to working in the king's quarry (MFA 03.1896). Forced labor in the king's quarry may be enslavement as a punishment for a crime. The Middle Kingdom Pap. Brooklyn 35.1446 contains the names of seventy-nine servants or slaves associated with a large 13th Dynasty Egyptian household. Forty-eight of these have Semitic names, which a number of scholars consider evidence for the historical reliability of the Joseph saga in Genesis (chs. 37–50).

There is more evidence for slavery in the New Kingdom. During the campaigns of Ahmose I, a commander of an Egyptian ship carried away several slaves awarded to him as spoils. Ahmose I claimed to have carried off prisoners "beyond number" (*ANET*, 233–34), and Tuthmosis III claimed to have taken numerous slaves in his campaigns (*ANET*, 234–38). Tuthmosis IV, Amenhotep III, and Ramesses II used forced labor from Palestine, Libya, and Nubia for their massive building projects. The tradition of the Hebrews being enslaved by Egypt fits into this time period. Papyrological evidence indicates that slaves could be rented (Pap. Berlin 9784:22) or sold by private parties (Pap. Cairo 65739). A slave could also be brought into a family when a wife was unable to conceive children. Nebnefer and his wife Rennefer, for example, purchased a slave girl who bore him three children. All three were adopted and manumitted, and one was married off to Rennefer's younger brother (Pap. Ashmolean Museum 1945.96). In one case, two slaves who were owned by a builder named Wenenamun were entrusted to a merchant named Amenkhau and subsequently disappeared. The court proceeding indicates that such events were not uncommon (Pap. Bankes I = BM Pap. 10302; 75019; 75020). When slaves ran away, they were hunted down in the same manner as serfs fleeing corvée labor (Pap. Brooklyn 35.1446).

Anatolia

Like the Assyrians and Babylonians, the Hittites had laws concerned with slaves. Hittite Laws 1–4 assess the penalties for the deaths of both free citizens and slaves. The compensation for the death of a slave is one-half that of a free person. Other laws are concerned with runaway slaves, the kidnapping of slaves (##20–24, 93), and slave marriage and divorce (##31–36, 175, 194, 196). Other laws discuss crimes of both slaves and free people (##95–101, 132–143), a rebellion of slaves against their master (#173b), and even sorcery (#170). In each case, the penalty for a slave is harsher than that of a free person. Most crimes committed by slaves or upon slaves resulted in the assessment of fines and/or mutilation. Only sorcery and rebellion resulted in the death penalty. Unlike the slave law of Exod 21:26–27, if a Hittite slave lost an eye or teeth in an altercation or beating, compensation was paid by the offending party to the owner but there was no manumission for the injured slave (Hittite Laws 7–8).

D. THE GRECO-ROMAN WORLD

Both Greece and Rome developed slave states. We find slavery among the Mycenaeans, in the worlds of Homer and Hesiod, and as a major feature of Classical Greek society. Evidence for slavery in Rome appears in its first law code, the Twelve Tables, and slavery became especially prominent during Rome's expansion into an empire.

Greece

Slaves appear in inventories of palaces and temples from the Mycenaean world. Slavery reappeared among Greek *polies* ("city-states") during the Archaic Period. The words *dmōs* and *dmōē* were used for male and female slaves, respectively. In Homer's world of warrior elites, slaves were the absolute property of their owners (*Od.* 22:35–41, 462–473). Slaves were beaten (*Od.* 4.244–246) and dressed in degrading clothing (*Od.* 14.324–343; 24.249–150), made to perform a number of menial tasks (*Od.* 1.147; 7.104–109, 340–342; 10.123), were sold or traded (*Il.* 7.472–475), and were aware of their low social value (*Od.* 17.322–325). In the *Iliad*, women captured in battle were enslaved and exploited sexually by their masters (1.12–13; 2.699; 6.654–655).

Hesiod writes about common Greek landowners from a later period. When setting up a farm, he says, the first things to acquire are a house, an ox, and a slave wife (*Op.* 405–409). Slaves were widely used in every farm task (*Op.* 458–461, 469–471, 502–503, 571–573, 597–599). In the Pre-Classical period, it appears that slavery was a significant feature in Greek economy and society. The first slave market is thought to have been on the island of Chios (Ath. *Deipn.* 6.88).

During the seventh century BC, the enslavement of farmers who held small amounts of land became common. This was due to poor harvests, partible inheritance, and the use of human collateral to secure loans. With revolts looming, the aristocracy appointed Solon as archon and chief magistrate. Among his reforms, Solon outlawed debt slavery and human collateral, and he then worked to manumit Athenians enslaved for debt, including those sold abroad (Plu. *Sol.* 13–16).

The number of chattel slaves increased in Classical Athens. *Doulos* was the most common word for slave. Others include *oiketēs* ("house slave") and *pais* and *paidiskē* ("slave boy" and "slave girl," respectively). Slave populations were maintained by war, slave markets, exposure of infants, and piracy. Some wealthy Athenians owned slaves in the hundreds, renting them out to mines for large profits. Xenophon suggested that Athens should own three or four public slaves for every citizen in order to rent them out and bring wealth to the public treasury (*Poroi* 4.14–19). Plato considered a person who owned fifty slaves wealthy (*Resp.* 9.578c). But most Athenian families had only one.

Slaves living conditions and the work they did varied. Working in mines was brutal, while domestic slaves had close bonds with families. Slaves could be punished by flogging, starving, and chaining (Xen. *Mem.* 2.1.6). But harsh treatment could ruin a significant investment, and slaves could not be killed without reason. Masters were compensated for injuries to their slaves. Slaves could be tortured when providing testimony at court. Prostitutes were often slaves (Pseudo-Demosthenes, *Against Neaera* 59.18–23).

The Spartans had both chattel slaves and serfs (the latter of whom were known as helots) (Paus. *Descr.* 3.20.6). The helots were the descendants of Messenians conquered in two major conflicts in the eighth and seventh centuries. Unlike chattel slaves, *helots* could not be sold and were allowed to live in villages. They were subjected to acts of humiliation and brutality (Plut. *Lyc.* 3–7; Athenaeus, *Deipn.* 14.74), but they could be manumitted. Thucydides mentions hoplites fighting for Sparta known as *neodamōdeis* who were manumitted helots (*Hist.* 4.80; 5.34; cf. Athenaeus, *Deipn.* 6.102).

There was little philosophical discussion on the morality of slavery in the Greek world. Most philosophers only discussed slavery as a bridge to other subjects. Plato generalized that slaves are easily influenced and limited by belief (*doxos*), while a free man, he believed, operates with rationality (*logos*). To illustrate this, he provides a comparison between free and slave doctors (*Leg.* 4.720b–e). Elsewhere he comments that the soul of a slave has no soundness in it whatsoever (*Leg.* 6.776e). Aristotle claimed that some people, mainly barbarians, are natural slaves (*Pol.* 1.1252a–b). But this outlook created an ideological dilemma when elite Greeks were taken captive and enslaved (*Pol.* 1.1255a–b). Stoics developed a system of philosophy that recognized the humanity of slaves and warned that slavery could corrupt both the slave and slave owner. They did not seek to abolish slavery, however. Instead, Stoics like Epictetus, himself once a slave, advocated finding contentment in any human circumstance by the consistent exercise of the will (*Disc.* 1.1).

Some Greek slaves were manumitted. Over twelve hundred manumission records from the second century BC are extant from Delphi. Most commemorate a fictitious sale to Pythian Apollo by the owner. In about a third of them, former slaves continued to owe services to their masters that vary from a limited period of several years to the death of their former owners because of a series of obligations (*paramonē* clauses). Manumission did not provide the former slave with citizenship status.

Rome

Rome produced a vast slaveholding empire. Slaves were taken during conquest, and slave numbers were maintained by children born of slaves during times of peace. Other, less plentiful sources included piracy, exposure of unwanted infants, debt slavery of various kinds, and, most infrequently, sale of children by distressed families. There were slave markets in every significant city.

Common Latin words for "slave" were *servus* and *puer* ("boy"); *famulatus* meant "slavery." The words *serva* or *ancilla* referred to female slaves. Once enslaved, slaves' names were discarded. Males were given the *praenomen* of their master, with the suffix *-por* added (for *puer*). Thus, a slave of Marcus Porcius Cato would be Marcipor. Women were often given foreign names. Later, it became common to give slaves Greek or Syrian names, names from mythology, or names that characterized a virtue: hence the names Felix ("Lucky") or Melissa ("Bee").

Roman slaves could be found doing every kind of job. At times, slaves made up 30 percent of the Roman population. Numerous laws were created to manage slavery. While the treatment of slaves was an issue periodically, there was little criticism of the institution. Romans saw slavery as a function of fate and Roman invincibility. Everywhere, Romans saw masters holding *dominium* (absolute mastery) over the conquered and their descendants. Both the jurists Florentinus (2nd c.) and Ulpian (3rd c.) commented that slavery was not part of natural law (*Dig. Just.* 1.5.4.1; 50.17.32), but this did not change any aspect of slaves being managed as property. The Stoic Seneca affirmed the humanity of slaves, but never manumitted his own (*Ep.* 47).

Romans worried about rebellions. There were three slave revolts during the Republic. Two occurred in Sicily, and the third (led by the famous Spartacus) was in Italy. All were crushed by Roman armies, and the third resulted in the crucifixion of six thousand slaves (Diod. Sic. *Bib. hist.* 34/35 2.1–48; 36.1–11; Plut. *Crass.* 8–11). No slave revolts occurred during the Empire, but Seneca notes the common saying that one had as many enemies as slaves (Sen. *Ep.* 47.5).

Slaves formed the lowest class of Roman society, though little separated them from the free poor. A slave could expect food and shelter. Almost every imaginable task was performed by slaves. Perhaps those who received the barest essentials were agricultural workers, who were housed in barracks and chained together to work in fields (Columella, *Rust.* 1.6.9). Such labor was intensive and debilitating, and there was little chance of manumission unless it occurred when the slave was old, sick, and no longer productive. This happened enough to result in laws forbidding the practice (Suet. *Claud.* 25).

Slaves owned by the imperial family often acquired wealth and slaves of their own. Sometimes they were appointed to high offices. Governor Felix of Judea started out as a slave of Emperor Claudius's mother (Jos. *Ant.* 20.7). Roman slaves carried the prestige of their owners. Slaves attached to a household were trained to perform a variety of tasks. The richer the household, the more specialized the tasks the slaves performed. Upper-class Romans often owned businesses, and the workers and managers were frequently slaves. This could include brothels with slave prostitutes (*Dig. Just.* 5.27.1).

Slaves were always in danger of beatings for real or imagined infractions (Martial, *Ep.* 3.94; Seneca, *Ep.* 47.3–5). A slave's life was balanced between the hope of manumission and fear of abuse. Seneca relates that Vedius Pollio fed clumsy slaves to lampreys (Seneca, *Clem.* 1.18; see also Pliny, *Nat.* 9.39). Abuse often resulted in flight, and when slaves escaped owners would post notices with rewards for their return (P. Oxy. LI 3616, 3617). Roman law required a disclosure if an owner sold a slave who had run away, because this reduced the slave's value (*Dig. Just.* 21.1.1.1). Harboring a fugitive slave resulted in large fines. By the second century, the Roman state took a greater role in apprehending fugitive slaves (*Dig. Just.* 11.4.1–3, 8a).

Any slave, male or female, and of any age, was sexually available to his or her male master (Dio Chrys. *Or.* 7. 133–152). Although Romans were traditionally monogamous, sex with slaves had no legal consequence (*Dig. Just.* 48.5.6.1; 48.5.35 [34]). But a Roman matron caught having sex with a slave suffered penalties and dishonor (Livy 1.58). Slaves having sex with each other was of no legal consequence.

Slaves did not have *conubium*, the legal capacity to marry. But slaves often entered into relationships that looked like marriage; such partners were called *contubernales* (lit., "tent companions"). Slave families could be broken up by sales or even bequests. No law prohibited this, but Roman jurists discouraged such practices (*Dig. Just.* 33.7.6–7). Most slaves were able to legally marry after manumission (*Dig. Just.* 23.3.24).

Manumission was the hope that kept Rome's slavery system running smoothly. Slaves could save up an allowance (*peculium*) to purchase their freedom, with their master's permission. Slaves could also be freed on account of a master's will, but this did not end slaves' obligation to their former masters or their families. Freed slaves still owed *opera* ("free labor") for a specified period to their former master or their families. He or she would also become a client, an advantage for which poor free people strived. Once manumitted, former slaves were considered "freed people," and with formal manumission in front of a magistrate, they would gain Roman citizenship. Those manumitted informally became Junian Latins and had limited citizen rights.

E. THE JEWISH WORLD

When the exiles from Babylon returned and built the second temple, they continued the practice of owning slaves (Ezra 2:64–65; Neh 5:1–5). Slaves appear in the Apocrypha, the OT Pseudepigrapha, and rabbinic writings. They were not a major source of labor in any period of Jewish history. Slavery was regulated but not abolished, used as a metaphor for service to God, and subject to occasional moral discourse. The slave codes of Exod 20, Lev 25, and Deut 15 formed the foundation of many rabbinic discussions. Though in the Mishnah these codes have a relatively minor place, they are frequently considered in the longer Tosefta. The primary focus in both the Mishnah's and Tosefta's discussions of slavery was on the practical management of slave owning.

Owning slaves was a symbol of wealth and prosperity. When Tobias returns to his family after his marriage to Sarah, his father-in-law, Raguel, gives Tobias half his wealth, including male and female slaves (Tob 10:10). Slavery is used as a symbol of desolation when Mattathias the priest describes Jerusalem under Antiochus, lamenting, "What nation has not inherited her palaces and has not seized her spoils? All her adornment has been taken away; no longer free, she has become a slave" (1 Macc 2:10–11; 2 Macc 5:24).

Slavery is used metaphorically to indicate the virtues of self-control by the Stoic author of 4 Maccabees, who praises the martyrdom of the seven brothers and their use of pious reason to overcome "slavish" emotion in the face of torture and death (4 Macc 13:1–3). In Jubilees, slavery is portrayed negatively as one of the signs of the depravity and violence of Noah's descendants (*Jub.* 11:1–5).

A unique commentary on slavery is found in Ben Sira: "Do not abuse slaves who work faithfully, or hired laborers who devote themselves to you. Let your soul love intelligent slaves; do not withhold from them their freedom" (Sir 7:20–21). This is one of the few exhortations in early Jewish literature to free slaves based upon their character. For the owner of a single slave, Ben Sira admonishes, "If you have but one slave, treat him like a brother, for you will need him as you need your life. If you ill-treat him, and he leaves you and runs away, which way will you go to seek him?" (Sir 33:31). But Ben Sira also advocates that slaves do hard work and that they be punished for disobedience. He makes it clear that one should not be "ashamed" to beat a "wicked slave" until his "back was bloody" (Sir 42:5). As a whole, his advice is pragmatic rather than moral and resembles the rulings of later rabbinic literature.

More compassionate is the gnomic poem written under the name of Pseudo-Phocylides:

> Provide your slave with the tribute he owes his stomach. Apportion to a slave what is appointed so that he will do as you wish. Do not brand (your) slave, thus insulting him. Do not hurt a slave by slandering (him) to his master. Accept advice also from a judicious slave. (Pseudo-Phocylides 223–227)

Here it is the master, not the slave, who is exhorted to act appropriately. Philo of Alexandria reminds his readers that a Hebrew debt slave is actually a brother and that a master should release his slave joyfully when the six years of servitude end (*Spec.* 2.18). Philo seems to reject the Greek concept of natural slavery when he asserts that both slave and master have the same nature and that this fact should moderate both reckless abuse of a slave and deserved punishment (*Spec.* 3.25). Philo's ideal of the ethical treatment of slaves revolves around the virtues of gentleness and humanity (*Virt.* 24–24). But Philo seems to support the idea of natural slavery when discussing Jacob and Esau. He affirms that slavery is the best circumstance for a fool, because the loss of independence would keep him from transgressing without fear of punishment, and thus improve his character (*Prob.* 57). Philo mentions two Jewish sects that repudiated slavery. The Therapeutae was a Jewish sect that considered slavery contrary to nature (*Contempl.* 1.1–2; 9.69–70), and the Essenes were pacifists who also repudiated slavery (*Prob.* 12.75–87; Jos. *J.W.* 2.119–161).

After the temple was destroyed, Judaism survived by organizing around local synagogues, and it maintained a number of oral traditions of interpreting the Hebrew Scriptures. These traditions were codified in the late second and perhaps late third centuries into the Mishnah (between AD 180–200) and the Tosefta, a commentary on the Mishnah (possibly ca. 300). Later, between the fourth and sixth centuries AD, the Jerusalem and

Babylonian Talmuds (commentaries on the Mishnah and Tosefta) were codified. They regulated Jewish community life. Throughout the period when these documents were codified, most Jews did not possess large-scale wealth and political power, but rather the modest wealth of households centered on the ownership and management of tracts of farm land and pastures. The Mishnah, Tosefta, and Talmuds all assume private ownership of lands and goods, including debt and chattel slaves. In general, the Mishnah makes a number of pronouncements based upon existing oral traditions, while the Tosefta attempts to tie rabbinic teachings to the three slave codes in Exodus, Leviticus, and Deuteronomy. Rabbinic literature frequently discusses slavery but whether their rules were put into common practice is a matter of debate among modern scholars.

Different ideas about slavery are conveyed in rabbinic texts. On the one hand, slaves are likened to cattle and said to be spiritually blind and considered as mere chattel (*Gen. Rab.* 56:2; *t. Mak.* 4:15). But other sources describe slaves as moral, responsible human beings who are capable of understanding right from wrong (*m. Yad.* 4:7; *m. Yad.* 4:7).

Sexual relations were regulated within servile relationships. If a child was born between a free man and a slave woman, the child was a slave (*m. Qidd.* 3:12). If a gentile male slave and a free Jewish woman had sex and produced a child, the baby would not be recognized as a Jew, despite the usual custom of matrilineal descent (*t. Qidd.* 4:16). If a Jewish man had a slave as a lover and freed her, they were not to marry. If they did, however, the marriage would be recognized (*t. Ketub.* 1:3). And if a Hebrew man sold his daughter to settle a debt, she had to be a minor, and would be released from servitude as soon as there was evidence that she had begun experiencing puberty (*m. Qidd.* 1:2; 3:12). This was to reduce the potential for sexual abuse and prostitution.

Slaves frequently made transactions—including handling and moving property—on behalf of their owners. Profits earned by slaves were owned solely by their masters. Slaves could not gain property (*t. B. Qam.* 11:1). Even if a slave found something of value that had been abandoned, he or she could only acquire it on behalf of his or her master (*m. B. Meṣ.* 1:5).

Both Hebrew debt slaves and "Canaanite" (a euphemism for gentile) slaves were disciplined by corporal punishment (*t. B. Qam.* 9:24). A slave could be beaten but not wounded. The distinction is ambiguous, and the legal emphasis is on the damage such injuries caused the community. Slaves were not compensated for any injury (*m. B. Qam.* 8:3). While the Mishnah does not advocate prosecuting an owner for the wounding of a non-Jewish slave, the Tosefta does (*m. B. Qam.* 8:5; *t. B. Qam.* 9:10, 21). If an owner killed a slave, that was a criminal offense, whether the slave died immediately or remained alive for a period of time after the injury. This law was stronger than the provision in Exod 21:20, but an owner could avoid prosecution by transferring ownership of the wounded slave to someone else before the slave's death. The new owner would not be liable (*t. B. Qam.* 9:22).

According to Exod 21:26–27, if in the course of corporal punishment a slave owner blinds a slave's eye or knocks out a slave's tooth, the slave is allowed to go free. The Tosefta imposes a series of limits on manumission based upon the injury of an eye or a tooth. If the only witnesses to the injury were the slave and master, the master could deny the slave's accusation. The Tosefta further specifies that the blow had to be directly on the eye or tooth, not next to them on the face, and there had to be proof that the owner was deliberately targeting an eye or a tooth (*m. Šebu.* 5:5; *t. B. Qam.* 9:26–27). Harsh penalties for false testimony in this specific kind of case discouraged witnesses from testifying (*y. B. Qam.* 8:8, 6c).

Hebrew slaves could expect to be manumitted in their seventh year of service or in a Jubilee year. Hebrew debt slaves could also be freed by the payment of their remaining debt (*m. Qidd.* 1:3; *t. Qidd.* 1:5). The Jubilee year and the Sabbatical Year manumissions were not always enforced, however. Much was left to the piety of the owner. Because a gentile slave could not own anything, self-purchase was impossible. If a third party paid, a gentile slave could be redeemed and manumitted (*m. Qidd.* 1:2). A dying slave owner could free any slaves by an oral or written declaration, and they would be released at his death (*t. B. Bat.* 9:14).

F. THE CHRISTIAN WORLD

As Christianity entered the second century, the institution of slavery continued to be a feature within the early church. Jennifer Glancy summarizes two possible historical interpretations that explain this feature. According to the first, which she calls a story of ascent, the rise of Christianity gradually caused the decline of the institution of slavery. Despite the fact that there is little direct opposition to slavery in the writings of the early church, the ethical teachings of Jesus and his valuing of all human life eroded the institution. The late Empire, under the influence of Christian teaching, modified the laws and ethics of slaveholding. But it took many centuries before the church declared that slaveholding was incompatible with Christian teaching. In the various versions of this narrative, the church gradually triumphed over the values of the surrounding cultures.

The second trajectory is a story of descent. There was a brief period in the lifetime of Paul when Gal 3:28 served to promote equality between men and women, free people and slaves, and Jews and gentiles. In time, however, the church accommodated itself to Roman culture to gain the patronage of influential people and to avoid persecution, and Christians did nothing to threaten the institution of slavery. Glancy describes this as an "evangelical strategy" to position the church to grow in Roman society as opposed to a compromise of Christian values. In this scholarly narrative, traditional Roman values triumphed over the early egalitarian values of the primitive church (Glancy, 145).

There is also a third, more radical approach that has less of an academic following. To explain the long history of slavery in the Christian West, some claim that the church was pro-slavery and that it saw the institution as natural and beneficial. This has been the argument of John Fletcher, the pro-slavery apologist writing before the American Civil War, and of Hector Avalos, in his recent analysis of slavery in the age of the church (see Fletcher; Avalos).

Writings after the apostolic era tend to amplify the advice to slaves and masters found in the house codes of the NT. The *Didache* discusses Christian slaves in a Christian household. It advises that masters not give harsh orders to slaves when angry and that slaves act in modesty and fear. Neither will be judged by God according to their class (*Did.* 4.10–11; cf. *Barn.* 19.7). The *Shepherd of Hermas* uses the example of a slave in a parable to describe the rewards in store for the faithful believer. In his fifth *Similtude*, he writes of a faithful slave who not only fulfills his master's commandment by caring for a vineyard in his absence, but goes beyond this to make the vineyard prosper. His reward is manumission and being made a joint heir with the master's son. According to tradition, Hermas himself had been a slave.

Slaves participated in the church of the second century. In Pliny the Younger's famous letter to Trajan, he reports that as part of his investigation of those denounced as Christians, he tortured two female Christian slaves who were *ministrae* (Pliny, *Ep.* 10.96). This is often translated as deaconesses and may indicate that female slaves held some church offices. Among the acts of selfless love that Clement of Rome praises is the act of Christians selling themselves as slaves, either to free others or to raise money for the poor (*1 Clem.* 55.2). In some cases, at least in Smyrna, slaves were purchased by the church for the purpose of manumitting them. Ignatius was concerned about the practice and warned slaves not to desire freedom but to submit to their masters and not expect to be freed at public (congregational) expense. Ignatius's warning that such desires resulted in them being "slaves of lust" is interesting and may be based upon the desire of a slave to marry legally and have a family with free children (*Eph.* 6.1). When Polycarp was martyred around AD 160, his place of hiding was revealed by one of his two slaves under torture (*Mart. Pol.* 6.1–2). It is apparent from these and other texts that Christians were both slaves and slave owners in the second century.

In his *Apology*, Athenagoras of Athens states that the Christians of his community had slaves, some owning many and others owning few (Athenagoras, *Leg.* 35). Aristides mentions that some members of his Christian community were slave owners, but states that they were kind toward their slaves, leading them and their children to the faith. At their conversion, the slave owners called the slaves brethren, without distinction. There is no mention of manumission, however, and his account sounds very much like the family order idealized in the biblical house codes (Aristides, *Apology* 15).

Slavery was often used as a metaphor in the literature of the early church and beyond. The title "slave of God" is used to describe followers of Christ in the various apocryphal *Acts* (e.g., *Acts John* 23; 45; 106; 111; 151). In a dramatic scene, Jesus sells Thomas to Abbanes as his slave, complete with a bill of sale, because of Thomas's resistance to his mission to India (*Acts Thom.* 1.2). The term "slave" (*doulos*) is used to describe saints (Athanasius, *Vit. Ant.* 52; 53; 85) and martyrs (*Mart. Pol.* 9.3; 20.1) in early hagiographies, as well as clerics and monks (Athanasius, *Letter to the Bishops of Africa* 3; *History of the Arians* 68.2). Basil, who frequently used slave metaphors, required that a bishop consider himself a slave of God (Basil, *Ep.* 190 1). John Chrysostom uses a dramatic metaphor in a discussion of baptism, describing new converts as slaves in a market where prospective masters ask them if they intend to obey and serve if they are purchased; Chrysostom discusses the difference between being a slave to a tyrant and a slave of Christ, but the image is quite vivid (*Baptismal Instructions* 2.50–51). Eusebius likens Constantine, the first Christian emperor, to Moses and describes him, as the Septuagint does Moses, as God's *therapōn*, "servant" (Eus. *Vit. Const.* 1.5, 6). This Greek word can describe a servant who may be either free or a slave.

Slavery to sin, the law, false gods, or the world continued to be a powerful metaphor in the early church. Numerous examples can be found in the writings of Gregory of Nazianzus (*Or.* 1.4; 8.4; 21.6; 30.3, 6, 20; 31.24), as well as in the *Didascalia* (e.g., 6.16). The metaphor of manumission is used to describe salvation from sin, for example, by the Egyptian desert father Macarius, who speaks vividly of both a manumission ritual and the destruction of the bill of sale (*Hymns on the Nativity* 11.10; 44.8). There are many more examples of such metaphors in Christian liturgies, exegetical works, and other patristic writings (see Combes, chs. 5–7). But few of these address the issue of slavery itself; rather, most Christian writers used the metaphor of slavery as a bridge to discussions on sin, salvation, obedience, and piety. The Canons of the Council of Elvira (AD 305) are often used as evidence of disinterest in the life of slaves in favor of the quest for personal morality. Canon Five rules that a woman who beat her slave to death on purpose will be denied communion for seven years. But if she kills the slave unintentionally, she will be denied communion for only five years. Canon Eight, in contrast, states that a woman who commits adultery will be banned from communion for life.

There is no early Christian treatise against slavery. The fourth-century Council of Gangra even condemned Christian leaders who would teach slaves to despise their masters and run away (Canon 3). But some voices criticized the institution for a number of reasons. The Apologist Justin Martyr (2nd c.) condemned the exposing of infants because they would be enslaved and often made prostitutes. He was also concerned that male slaves could prove too big a temptation to free women living in the same household (*1 Apol.* 27; *2 Apol.* 2). As influenced by Stoicism, he noted that yielding to one's passions was the lowest form of slavery, and that ruling over them was the only true liberty (fragment 18, preserved in Antonius Melissa, *Loci Communes*).

Augustine taught that slavery is punishment for man's sin and that it is not part of God's original order (*Civ.* 19.15–16). The famous passage by Gregory of Nyssa in which he describes the "Divine Word" not wishing us to be slaves and sharing in a hope that, like death and illness, slavery will eventually disappear seems to describe an event far off and not a present reality (*Against Eunomius* 10.4). Elsewhere, Gregory comments as follows on the concept of chattel slavery:

> Who can buy a man, who can sell him, when he is made in the likeness of God? . . . He would hardly reduce human beings to slavery. But if God does not enslave what is free, who dares to put his own authority higher that God's?
> (*Homilies on Ecclesiastes* 4)

As liberating as these words may be, Gregory's works received little attention until fairly recently.

Slave law continued in Byzantium long after Rome fell, and the pattern of chattel slavery was gradually changed to other forms of dependent relations, like serfdom. In laws dated to 316 and 323, Constantine allowed clergy to manumit slaves in a public ritual (*manumission in ecclesia*). This eventually became the standard in the eastern and western halves of the Empire. No one was obligated to manumit slaves. Individual clergy as well as the church as an institution continued to hold slaves. A slave could only become a cleric with his master's permission. Though long a feature of Roman slave law, the breaking up of slave families continued to be discouraged under the Theodosian Code (*Cod. Theod.* 2.25.1 [325]). The final codification of Roman law occurred in the sixth century, under the Christian emperor Justinian. It reaffirmed the right to own slaves, as well as earlier and current laws that afforded slaves some protection. Some of Justinian's reforms show Christian influence. A runaway slave who became a monk at a monastery would gain the status of a freedman after three years, provided he remained there (*Corp.* 1.3.37 [38]). The right of a master to grant manumission to a slave in a public ceremony before clergy, rather than magistrates, which dated from the time of Constantine, was reaffirmed (Justinian, *Institutes* 5.1.5). Laws dating to the second century, under Antoninus Pius, that protected slaves from being killed by their masters that were also upheld, and laws that discouraged mistreatment of slaves were affirmed. In short, with a few amendments, the main features of Roman slave law were maintained. Though several bishops and popes started life as slaves, there was no abolition movement within the church until the modern period.

BIBLIOGRAPHY: H. Avalos, *Slavery, Abolitionism, and the Ethics of Biblical Scholarship* (2011); S. S. Bartchy, "Paul Did Not Teach 'Stay in Slavery': The Mistranslation of *Klesis* in 1 Cor. 7:20–21," Paper presented at the Annual Meeting of the Society of Biblical Literature, Boston, MA, 22 November 2008; S. S. Bartchy, "Slavery (Greco-Roman)," *ABD* VI.65–73; E. Bleiberg, "The Economy of Ancient Egypt," *CANE* 3.1373–85; K. R. Bradley, *Slavery and Society at Rome* (1994); K. R. Bradley, *Slaves and Masters in the Roman Empire: A Study in Social Control* (1987); K. Bradley, and P. Cartledge, ed., *The Cambridge World History of Slavery*, vol. 1 (2011); W. W. Buckland, *The Roman Law of Slavery* (1908); D. E. Callender, Jr., "Servants of God(s) and Servants of Kings in Israel and the Ancient Near East," in *Slavery in Text and Interpretation*, ed. A. D. Callahan, R. A. Horsley, and A. Smith (*Semeia* 83/84; 1998), 67–82; I. A. H. Combes, *The Metaphor of Slavery in the Writings of the Early Church* (1998); L. Culbertson, "A Life-Course Approach to Household Slaves in the Late Third Millennium B.C.," in *Slaves and Households in the Near East*, ed. L. Culbertson (2010), 33–48; M. A. Dandamayev, "Slavery (ANE)," *ABD* VI.58–62; M. A. Dandamayev, "Slavery (OT)," *ABD* VI.62–65; C. S. de Vos, "Once a Slave, Always a Slave? Slavery, Manumission and Relational Patterns in Paul's Letter to Philemon," *JSNT* 82 (2001), 89–105; J. Evans-Grubbs, "'Marriage More Shameful than Adultery': Slave-Mistress Relationships, 'Mixed Marriages,' and Late Roman Law," *Phoenix* 47 (1993), 125–54; C. J. Eyre, "The Adoption Papyrus in Social Context," *JEA* 78 (1992), 207–21; J. Fletcher, *Studies on Slavery: In Easy Lessons* (repr. of 1852 edition, 2012); J. F. Gardner, *Women in Roman Law and Society* (1991); Y. Garlan, *Slavery in Ancient Greece*, trans. J. Lloyd (1988); P. Garnsey, *Ideas of Slavery from Aristotle to Augustine* (1996); J. A. Glancy, *Slavery in Early Christianity* (2002); J. K. Goodrich, "From Slaves of Sin to Slaves of God: Reconsidering the Origin of Paul's Slavery Metaphor in Romans 6,"

BBR 23.4 (2013), 509–30; M. A. Harbin, "The Manumission of Slaves in Jubilee and Sabbath Years," *TynBul* 63.1 (2012), 53–74; K. Harper, *Slavery in the Late Roman World, AD 275–425* (2011); J. A. Harrill, *Slaves in the New Testament: Literary, Social, and Moral Dimensions* (2005); E. Harris, *Democracy and the Rule of Law in Classical Athens* (2006); E. Harris, "Homer, Hesiod, and the 'Origins' of Greek Slavery," *Revue des Études anciennes* 114.2 (2012), 1–22; C. Hezser, "Slaves and Slavery in Rabbinic and Roman Law," in *Rabbinic Law in its Roman and Near Eastern Context*, ed. C. Hezser (2003), 133–76; C. Hezser, ed., *The Oxford Handbook of Jewish Daily Life in Roman Palestine* (2010); J. K. Hoffmeier, *Israel in Egypt* (1997); K. Hopkins, *Conquerors and Slaves* (1978); B. S. Jackson, "Biblical Laws of Slavery: A Comparative Approach," in *Slavery and Other Forms of Unfree Labour*, ed. L. J. Archer (1988), 86–101; S. R. Joshel and S. Murnaghan, ed., *Women and Slaves in Greco-Roman Culture* (1998); A. Leahy, "Ethnic Diversity in Ancient Egypt," in *CANE* 1.225–34; N. P. Lemche, "The 'Hebrew Slave,'" *VT* 25 (1975), 129–44; P. López Barja de Quiroga, "Junian Latins: Status and Numbers." *Athenaeum* 86.1 (1998): 133–163; A. Loprieno, "Slaves," in *The Egyptians*, ed. S. Donadoni, trans. R. Bianchi et al. (1997), 185–219; R. MacMullen, "Late Roman Slavery," *Historia* 36 (1987), 359–82; F. R. Magdalene and C. Wunsch, "Slavery between Judah and Babylon: The Exilic Experience," in Culbertson, ed. (2010), 113–34; I. Mendelsohn, *Slavery in the Ancient Near East: A Comparative Study of Slavery in Babylonia, Assyria, Syria, and Palestine, from the Middle of the Third Millennium to the End of the First Millennium* (1978); L. Meskell, *Private Life in New Kingdom Egypt* (2002); S. S. Monoson, "Navigating Race, Class, Polis and Empire: The Place of Empirical Analysis in Aristotle's Account of Natural Slavery," in *Reading Ancient Slavery*, ed. R. Alston, E. Hall, and L. Proffitt (2012), 133–51; H. Neumann, "Slavery in Private Households towards the End of the Third Millennium B.C.," in Culbertson, ed. (2010), 21–32; J. Neusner, *The Mishnah: Social Perspectives* (1999); O. Patterson, "Paul, Slavery and Freedom: Personal and Socio-Historical Reflections," in Callahan, Horsley, and Smith, ed. (1998), 263–79; O. Patterson, *Slavery and Social Death: A Comparative Study* (1982); S. M. Paul, "Exod. 21:10: A Threefold Maintenance Clause," *JNES* 28 (1969), 48–53; R. Paulissian, "Adoption in Ancient Assyria and Babylonia," *Journal of Assyrian Academic Studies* 13.2 (1999), 5–34; N. R. Petersen, *Rediscovering Paul: Philemon and the Sociology of Paul's Narrative World* (1985); J. N. Reid, "Runaways and Fugitive-Catchers during the Third Dynasty of Ur," *JESHO* 58 (2015), 576–605; R. Saller, "Corporal Punishment, Authority, and Obedience in the Roman Household," in *Marriage, Divorce, and Children in Ancient Rome*, ed. B. Rawson (1991), 144–65; A. Seri, "Domestic Female Slaves during the Old Babylonian Period," in Culbertson, ed. (2010), 49–67; C. W. Shelmerdine and J. Bennet, "Mycenaean States A: Economy and Administration," in *The Cambridge Companion to the Aegean Bronze Age*, ed. C. W. Shelmerdine (2008), 289–309; J. D. Sosis, "Manumission with Paramone: Conditional Freedon?" *TAPA* 145 (2015), 325–381; C. W. Tucker, "Women in the Manumission Inscriptions at Delphi," *TAPA* 112 (1982), 225–36; P. R. C. Weaver, *Familia Caesaris: A Social Study of the Emperor's Freedmen and Slaves* (1972); P. R. C. Weaver, "Social Mobility in the Early Roman Empire: The Evidence of the Imperial Freedman and Slaves," *Past and Present* 37 (1967), 2–30; R. Westbrook, "The Female Slave," in *Gender and Law in the Hebrew Bible and the Ancient Near East*, ed. V. H. Matthews, B. M. Levinson, and T. Frymer-Kensky (1998), 214–38; W. L. Westermann, *The Slave Systems of Greek and Roman Antiquity* (1955); T. Wiedemann, ed., *Greek and Roman Slavery* (1981); D. P. Wright, " 'She Shall Not Go Free as Male Slaves Do': Developing Views about Slavery and Gender in the Laws of the Hebrew Bible," in *Beyond Slavery: Overcoming its Religious and Sexual Legacies*, ed. B. J. Brooten (2010), 125–42; E. Yamauchi, "Slaves of God," *BETS* 9.1 (1966), 31–49; E. Yamauchi, "Two Reformers Compared: Solon of Athens and Nehemiah of Jerusalem," in *Bible World: Essays in Honor of Cyrus H. Gordon*, ed. G. Rendsburg et al. (1980), 269–92.

JFD

See also BANKS & LOANS, BEGGARS & ALMS, CITIZENS & ALIENS, EUNUCHS, INFANTICIDE & EXPOSURE, INHERITANCE, MARRIAGE, POLICE & PRISONS, and WEALTH & POVERTY.

SPECTACLES

The term spectacle derives from the Latin *spectaculum* (from the verb *spectare*, "to behold, see"). In the ancient world, spectacles would include anything that attracted a large number of spectators, such as sports and athletic games, dance performances, and drama. Since, however, these categories are covered elsewhere in this dictionary, the present entry will deal with such other spectacles as royal appearances, victory parades, great religious festivals, chariot races, animal acts, and exhibitions of brutality (gladiatorial combat and persecutions in the arena).

A. THE OLD TESTAMENT

Certainly the crossing of the Red (or better, "Reed") Sea by the Israelites escaping Egypt and the drowning of the Egyptian army in pursuit would rank as the greatest spectacle in the OT, unless it would be Joshua's armies marching around Jericho before its conquest. But these are singular events that stood apart from daily life at the time. As in all ancient cultures, victory parades were major spectacles also among the Hebrews. When Saul and David return victorious from battle with the Philistines, they are greeted by the music and dancing of Israelite women who sing, "Saul has slain his thousands, and David his tens of thousands" (1 Sam 18:7). Great events in the OT also prompted festive processions, as when David brought the ark of the covenant into Jerusalem and "was dancing before the Lord with all his might" (2 Sam 6:14), followed by a procession that included singing, shouting, and trumpeting. Yet the dancing David had also made a spectacle of himself, complained his wife Michal (2 Sam 6:16).

The ark figures in another festive procession when the Levites bear it inside Solomon's new temple in Jerusalem and place it inside the holy of holies. Then follows the grand spectacle when Solomon dedicates the temple (1 Kgs 8). After the division of the kingdoms, royal coronations and funerals, whether in Israel or Judah, were often attended by much spectacular pomp. Finally, when the walls of Jerusalem are rebuilt after their destruction by the Babylonians, Nehemiah arranges a great dedicatory celebration, dividing priests and princes into two groups that process along the top of the walls in opposite directions until they meet in praise and thanksgiving along with crowds below. This vast spectacle is accompanied by horn, cymbal, harp, and lyre (Neh 12:27–43).

B. THE NEW TESTAMENT

The most extraordinary spectacle in the NT could be considered that of the angelic hosts speaking over Bethlehem at the nativity. As with such singular events recorded in the OT, however, this was totally atypical of daily life at the time. The word for spectacle in Greek is *theatron*, a flexible term referring not only to a "theater" but also to the audience (i.e., the spectators) and what they see there: drama, performances, shows, and spectacles. The gathering of pilgrims at religious festivals in Jerusalem, such as Passover, Tabernacles, and Pentecost, was spectacular in terms of the numbers of people involved and their far-flung places of origin (Acts 2:5–12). The great ceremonies taking place at the temple on such occasions offered a further spectacle. Jesus's brothers advise him to observe the Feast of Tabernacles in Jerusalem as the place to "go public" with his message in view of the crowds there, though he decides to go secretly instead (John 7).

The two greatest spectacles in Jesus's public ministry were his triumphal parade into Jerusalem on Palm Sunday and his crucifixion, which followed only five days later; both of these were witnessed by large crowds of spectators. After Jesus's ascension—a brief spectacle only seen by his disciples (Acts 1:1–11)—the multilingual crowds at Pentecost experienced the spectacle of uneducated Galileans speaking in their own vernaculars (Acts 2:1–13).

Other NT-era spectacles were secular, such as the elaborate funeral procession for Herod the Great (Jos. *Ant.* 17.193; *J.W.* 1.686) and the appearance of Herod's grandson, Herod Agrippa I, at the theater in Caesarea Maritima, whose refulgent royal garb so astonished the crowd that they hailed him as a god, an event reported both in Acts (12:21–23) and by Josephus (*Ant.* 19.343).

At various points in his writings, Paul shows himself to be totally familiar with Greco-Roman spectacles. In 1 Cor 15:32, he employs a figure from gladiatorial combat: "If I fought with wild beasts in Ephesus with no more than human hopes, what have I gained?" In 1 Cor 4:9, he reflects the Roman *pompa* ("triumph"): "For it seems to me that God has put us apostles on display at the end of the procession, like those condemned to die in the arena. We have been made a spectacle [*theatron*] to the whole universe, to angels as well as to human beings." Elsewhere, however, he describes Christians as victors rather than victims, again with an eye to the spectators. This triumph motif shows up in 2 Cor 2:14: "But thanks be to God, who in Christ always leads us in triumphal procession, and through us spreads in every place the fragrance that comes from knowing him" (NRSV). In the Roman triumphal parade, burning spices were used to sweeten the air at the reception of a victorious general. The image of victory and triumph appears again in Col 2:15: "having disarmed the powers and authorities, he made a public spectacle of them, triumphing over them by the cross."

C. THE NEAR EASTERN WORLD

In Mesopotamia, religious ritual provided a prime occasion for public spectacles. From Sumerian times on, each city-state had its primary deity— not to the exclusion of other gods and goddesses—and the mythology concerning them was passed on to the successive Akkadian, Babylonian, and Assyrian cultures. The year was studded with religious festivals, and when the king presided in his role as high priest, the event became a spectacle indeed. Greatest was the twelve-day Babylonian New Year celebration at the spring equinox, when the Mesopotamian creation epic, the *Enuma Elish*, was recited and even dramatized in mime. Highlights included Marduk's slaying of Tiamat and the establishing of order in creation. Images of other gods were carried into the temple so that the whole Mesopotamian pantheon would recognize Marduk's primacy and participate in a festal banquet as did the deities at the close of the *Enuma Elish*.

Other cities had colorful ceremonies for their own civic deities. At Ur, for example, the Akitu festival honored the god Nanna. Each of these celebrations featured long processions of priests and officials from the political establishment filing into the city temple to do sacrifice and perform rites that were so demanding that one false move could vitiate the entire ceremony. Feasting followed these rites; much of the food was supplied from those portions of the sacrifices not assigned to the priests. Belshazzar's great feast for a thousand of his courtiers (Dan 5), a spectacle in itself, was quite typical, even if the handwriting on the wall was not.

The far-reaching conquests of the Persians in the ancient Near East were also featured in spectacles. While the great Achaemenid king Cyrus II (r. ca. 559–530 BC) was too preoccupied with conquest to indulge in spectacles, his successors more than compensated for this through that great spectacle in stone called Persepolis. Within its extraordinary ruins are many stone panels showing religious processions arriving at the city, bearing gifts from all the countries under Persian control. Edwin Yamauchi and a majority of scholars have concluded that Persepolis was not merely one of the four capitals of the vast Persian Empire, but a religious center that drew delegations of pilgrims from all corners of the Near East, processions that must have been spectacular indeed. (See Yamauchi, ch. 10, "Persepolis.")

In ancient Egypt, where the ruler did not simply represent deity, as in Mesopotamia, but was himself considered a god, an augmentation of spectacles should be expected, and this was in fact the case. Here the colossal, the grandiose, the truly spectacular was the rule, as symbolized by the largest constructions on earth prior to the twentieth century, the pyramids at Giza. Religious processions and rites, the temples in which they were celebrated, public appearances of the pharaoh, his funerary processions and mortuary temples—these were all on a large scale, especially his victory parades. Even non-victories were transformed into triumphs during the New Kingdom period (1540–1075 BC) in Egypt, as is witnessed by the gigantic statuary of Ramesses II (1279–1213 BC) at Abu Simbel on the upper Nile.

As in nearly all ancient cultures, religious festivals controlled the calendar. In Egypt, many were held at the time of Inundation of the Nile— June to September—when the river flooded the fields and the farmers were given some respite from their toil and could participate in celebrations for the gods. The New Year in Egypt began in July. At least annually, the gods and goddesses were brought out of their temples into shrines along the Nile, where they were exposed to the public. Pilgrims on the way to these shrines usually came by boat, singing, piping, dancing, and playing castanets while stopping at various places along the way to involve the townspeople and villagers in celebration. According to Herodotus, the festival at Bubastis drew seven hundred thousand pilgrims, who drank more wine there than they consumed the rest of the year (*Hist.* 2.59–60).

The most famed of the festivals, however, was Amon's "Beautiful Feast of Opet," which was held at Thebes (now Luxor). It fell in the middle of Inundation and lasted ten days during the reign of Tuthmosis III (1479–1425 BC), but twenty-four days by the time of Ramesses II. It commemorated the one annual outing of the god Amon, when he left his temple at Karnak to survey his other temple at Luxor. The procession of priests, monumental in length, preceded the divine images of Amon, his consort Mut, and his son Khonsu, which were carried to the Nile, amid beating tambourines, and reverently seated on thrones aboard a royal barge for each for the brief sail upstream to Luxor. Massive crowds, shouting and singing, lined the banks of the Nile and the roadway to the Luxor temple. Military percussion bands and dancing girls entertained the procession as music filled the air. One record shows the daily consumption of food and drink at the festival: 11,341 extra-large loaves of bread and 385 kegs of extra-strength beer (see Nelson and Holscher, 58). Even the annual celebration of the pharaoh's coronation required less than half that supply. At the close of the festival, the pageantry was simply reversed, as the gods were restored to their regular temple abodes. Many of these details come from images cut into the massive stonework at the temples of Karnak and Luxor.

Aside from royal appearances on state occasions—anniversaries, jubilees, victory parades, and religious festivals—people also came out en masse for royal funeral processions to the west bank of the Nile. The great burial grounds in ancient Egypt at Giza, Saqqara, and Abydos are littered with some seventy-two pyramids of various sizes and thousands of mastaba tombs, while those at the Valleys of the Kings and Queens at western Thebes are honeycombed with tombs deep inside the hills, with their funerary temples dominating the plains. Subjects lining the roadways to these at a pharaonic funeral and what they witnessed offered a spectacle unparalleled in the ancient world.

D. THE GRECO-ROMAN WORLD

Greece

As the culture of the Near East was absorbed by the Greeks and then the Romans, spectacles in sports, dance, drama, and civic/religious festivals were prime features of Greek culture. Since the first three are covered elsewhere in this dictionary, the focus here will be on the fourth. Originally, sacred processions and rites honored the local deities—particularly those that figured prominently in Greek mythology—at many locations in the Greek world, such as at the temples of Apollo at Delphi, Aphrodite at Corinth, Athena at Athens, and Poseidon at Sounion, and the shrine of Demeter and Persephone at Eleusis. In his campaign to make Athens the cultural leader of Greece, Pericles (5th c. BC) enhanced the Panathenaea, which became the greatest religious-cultural-athletic festival in Greece. Held toward the end of *Hekatombaiōn* (July, the New Year month), it celebrated the birth of Athena and presented her with an annual birthday gift of a newly woven *peplos* (robe). This hung on the mast of a parade float in the form of a ship. A great procession carried this up the acropolis to the Parthenon, a scene depicted on one of the Elgin Marbles in the British Museum in London. Every fourth year, the festival was augmented to become the Great Panathenaea, with the addition of contests involving poetry, music, and drama, as well as games that included chariot racing.

Given the competitive nature of Hellenic culture, it is not surprising that the Greeks raced chariots almost from the beginning of their history. Chariots show up on Mycenaean pottery, and Homer tells of chariot races at the funeral games for Patroclus (*Il.* 23.257–699). Horse and chariot racing early became part of the Olympic and other games. As spectacles, they may have had a more limited audience, since only the wealthiest could afford to sponsor them. Two-horse chariots had a 2.5-mile run, while four-horse versions had to go eight.

Rome

When Nero made his notorious athletic and concert tour of Greece in AD 67, one of the extraordinary spectacles of the ancient world took place when he tried to race with a ten-horse team at Olympia but fell out of the cab. The judges stopped the race to let Nero remount, and then resumed the race. Even so, Nero gave up before the end. Still, the judges declared him the winner! Nero was so appreciative that he gave them a large sum of money. Clearly, the judges were no fools—if Nero wanted to play, they would join the play (Suet. *Nero* 24).

Rome, inheriting all the forms of spectacular attraction cited thus far, typically enlarged and expanded them before devising new spectacles of her own, some brutish and cruel. The Etruscans had chariot races, and they were featured attractions throughout the Republic. Rome's principal hippodrome, the Circus Maximus, lay in the valley between the Palatine and Aventine Hills. Julius Caesar enlarged it so that during the period of the Roman Empire (27 BC–AD 476) it held two hundred fifty thousand spectators. Both two- and four-horse races took place there, the latter being the most prestigious. The Romans added a center divider to the Greek hippodrome—the *spina*—and the charioteer no longer held the reins in his hand, as in Greece, but wrapped them around his waist, adding to the danger of the race since, in the event of an accident, he would have to cut the reins or be dragged to death around the track.

Many trappings of modern horse racing were there: starting gates, multiple races per day, wealthy owners of the teams, servant charioteers who became famous with victories, much betting on the winners, and furious partisanship. The major factions were distinguished by the color of the garb worn by the charioteer. The reds and the whites were the earliest, and then came the greens and the blues. Domitian (AD 81–96) added purple and gold, but the greatest subsequent rivalry was between the greens and the blues. This was a very dangerous and bloody spectacle, and those with bloodlust usually took seats around the first U-turn after the starting gates, where accidents were prone to occur as chariots aimed for the inside track. The factions became deeply involved also in political and social issues, as witness the Nike Riots at Constantinople in 532 under the emperor Justinian.

While the hippodrome was the centerpiece of Roman entertainment from the days of the Republic onward, the amphitheater and its gladiatorial combat (*gladiatoria munera*) was not far behind. Whether inherited from the Etruscans or developed in Campania before the Punic Wars, shows involving gladiator pairs in combat began as privately funded displays in memory of one's ancestor (*munera*), but state-sponsored gladiatorial games (*ludi*) developed in the late Republic. Politicians used them to win popularity and votes, as did Julius Caesar, who borrowed money to field 320 gladiatorial pairs, a new record. During the Empire, government-supported gladiatorial spectacles became the norm, along with the dole—*panem et circenses*, "bread and circuses"—until such games were outlawed by Constantine (AD 306–337).

Mortal combat in the amphitheater was often preceded by animal shows—a camel race, a polar bear spectacle, and an elephant walking a tightrope were all recorded in the first century. Wild beast hunts and public executions followed. Slaves, war captives, and criminals often served as gladiators, but there were also volunteers for this bloody sport, and all were trained in gladiatorial schools, such as at Capua. In actual combat, pairs fought either with similar weapons, or, on occasion, in exotic combinations: a net-and-trident gladiator against a swordsman, a pikeman versus a small-shield man, or a woman fighting a dwarf. Gladiators who fought well before being defeated were often given *missio*, or release from death, by the crowds or the emperor, although some shows were advertised "*sine missione*," where defeat meant inescapable death. As with charioteers, some victorious gladiators became famous and wealthy and could retire in honor.

Finally, the grandest spectacle in the ancient world was the Roman Triumph (*pompa*), the victory procession/parade into Rome by a victorious commander or emperor. The parade route led eastward through the Circus Maximus, then northward to the Roman Forum and westward on the Via Sacra through the Forum, until it ended atop the Capitoline Hill. The long cavalcade began with city magistrates marching in front, followed by a corps of trumpeters; next, spoils from the enemy were exhibited on floats, then the king of the conquered country and his top officers in chains. More floats followed with tableaus of scenes from the war, then the staff officers of the victorious army, more musicians, dancing as they played, and finally the great general himself on his war chariot, multitudes on both sides of the route screaming their accolades in an atmosphere made fragrant by the burning of sweet spices.

E. THE JEWISH WORLD

Since so many of the nonbiblical spectacles reported thus far were pagan religious processions and rites that involved images of the gods and goddesses, the rabbis early prohibited Jewish participation in such events—even as a spectator—considering this to be a violation of the first and second commandments (*b. 'Abod. Zar.*18b). As Hellenistic culture infiltrated Judaism, however, especially in the diaspora, Jewish attendance, particularly at secular events, was inevitable. Even in Jerusalem, the center of Jewish orthodoxy, Herod the Great, that Hellenistic monarch, erected a theater and a hippodrome for horse and chariot racing, as well as at Caesarea Maritima, which antagonized the Jewish orthodoxy. Such large structures had to have audiences that were not limited to Gentiles. As for the diaspora, Claudius (AD 41–54) warned the Jews in Alexandria not to agitate for participation in the civic games, which demonstrates that the rabbinic restrictions were not being observed in Egypt, or in Asia Minor, as witnessed by a stone inscription at the excavated theater in Miletus reserving special seating for the Jews. Clearly and inevitably, Jews were also drawn to spectacles.

Yet they became spectacles themselves after the great war with Rome. The famed relief on the southern inside of the Arch of Titus at the Roman Forum shows a triumphal parade of victorious Roman troops with the sacred menorah of the Jerusalem temple as a trophy. Even more graphic is Josephus's portrayal of that triumph toward the close of his *Jewish War*, providing an eyewitness description of one of Rome's grandest spectacles: the *pompa*, or triumphal victory parade, detailed above. Josephus writes of "moving stages" (*J.W.* 7.139), i.e., floats of scenes from the Jewish war with Jews as victims and their leaders executed at the end of the parade (*J.W.* 7.139–157).

F. THE CHRISTIAN WORLD

The early Christian opposition to spectacles that had any connection to pagan religious festivals was similar to that found in Judaism, although in many cases the opposition was even stronger inasmuch as Christian martyrs became spectacles themselves in the Roman persecutions, beginning with that of Nero after the great fire of Rome in AD 64 and continuing sporadically until the time of Constantine, the first Christian emperor. In his *Annals*—the most important passage in pagan literature in support of Christian claims—Tacitus describes the grisly spectacle of how the Christian victims were tortured:

> And derision accompanied their end: they were covered with wild beasts' skins and torn to death by dogs; or they were fastened onto crosses, and, when daylight failed were burned to serve as lamps by night. Nero had offered his Gardens for the spectacle, and gave an exhibition in his hippodrome, mixing with the crowd dressed as a charioteer, or mounted on his cab. (15.44)

Although only three forms of torture are cited in this passage, dozens more are reported by Eusebius in his *Church History*, such as making the martyrs fight wild boars, goaded bulls, panthers, or bears; flogging, cudgeling, or scraping them to death; stretching on the rack; decapitation; butchery by swords; disjointings by pulleys; dragging to death in the streets; starving and strangling; binding and drowning; hanging by the feet over fire to choke on smoke; pouring molten lead into wounds; burning at the stake; tearing victims in half by binding an arm and a leg on one side to a young tree bent over by machine, and the other arm and leg to an adjacent tree bent similarly, then cutting all cords simultaneously. This listing is far from complete.

Such persecutions were even worse in frequency and numbers of victims in Egypt and North Africa, Asia Minor, and as far west as Gaul, where martyrdoms took place in Lyons at the Amphitheatre of the Three Gauls. Many of these were inspired, as in Gaul, not by emperors, but by local pagan priests complaining to provincial governors that Christians were enemies of the state and accusing the governors of failing to uphold the law if they took no action against them.

Christian disgust at gladiatorial combat is equally predictable in view of the commandment against murder in the Decalogue. As in Judaism, some erosion of Christian revulsion at gladiatorial slaughter took place as some were drawn to the spectacles. Tertullian finally had to warn such people that the games were simply murder, the gladiators themselves were agents of pagan human sacrifice, and even witnessing these spectacles was morally and spiritually harmful (*Spec.* 22). A century later, Augustine reprimanded his young friend Alypius for his fascination with gladiatorial spectacles and told him they were hostile to Christian ethics and salvation (*Conf.* 6.8). Alypius heeded his friend's admonition, converting to Christianity and even becoming a bishop. Although Constantine had banned gladiatorial combat in 325, it still survived both at Rome and at scattered locations later in the fourth and even the early fifth centuries; so powerful were the spectacles in antiquity.

BIBLIOGRAPHY: L. and R. A. Adkins, *Handbook to Life in Ancient Greece* (1997); R. Auguet, *Cruelty and Civilization: The Roman Games* (1994); A. Baker, *The Gladiator: The Secret History of Rome's Warrior Slaves* (2000); T. D. Barnes, "The Pre-Decian *Acta Martyrum*," *JTS* 19 (1968), 509–531;

C. A. Barton, "The Scandal of the Arena," *Representations 27* (Summer, 1989), 1–36; S. Bertman, *Handbook to Life in Ancient Mesopotamia* (2003); P. Bienkowski and A. Millard, ed., *Dictionary of the Ancient Near East* (2000); A.C. Bouquet, *Everyday Life in New Testament Times* (1954); M. Bunson, *The Encyclopedia of Ancient Egypt* (1991); M. Bunson, *Encyclopedia of the Roman Empire* (1994); J. Carcopino, *Daily Life in Ancient Rome*, ed. H. T. Rowell, trans. E. O. Lorimer (1980); L. Casson, *Everyday Life in Ancient Egypt* (1975); P. Connolly and H. Dodge, *The Ancient City: Life in Classical Athens and Rome* (2001); G. Contenau, *Everyday Life in Babylon and Assyria* (1959); H. Daniel-Rops, *Daily Life in Palestine at the Time of Christ*, trans. P. O'Brian (1962); R. David, *Handbook to Life in Ancient Egypt* (1998); F. Dupont, *Daily Life in Ancient Rome*, trans. C. Woodall (1994); A. Erman, *Life in Ancient Egypt*, trans. H. M. Tirard (1971); R. Flaceliere, *Daily Life in Greece at the Time of Pericles*, trans. P. Green (1966); D. R. French, "Christian Emperors and Pagan Spectacles: The Secularization of the *LUDI* A.D. 382–525," PhD diss., University of California, Berkeley (1985); Z. Weiss, "Theatres, Hippodrome, Amphitheatres, and Performances,"*OHJDL* 623–40; S. Hornblower and A. Spawforth, ed., *The Oxford Companion to Classical Civilization* (1998); D. G. Kyle, *Spectacles of Death in Rome* (1998); D. G. Kyle, *Sport and Spectacle in the Ancient World* (2007); G. Leick, ed., *The Babylonian World* (2007); B. Mertz, *Red Land, Black Land: Daily Life in Ancient Egypt* (rev. ed., 1978); M. S. and J. L. Miller, *Harper's Encyclopedia of Bible Life* (1973); S. Mitchell, "Festivals, Games, and Civic Life in Roman Asia Minor," *JRS* 80 (1990), 183–93; H. Nelson and U. Holscher, *Work in Western Thebes* (1932); T. G. Parkin and A. J. Pomeroy, ed., *Roman Social History: A Sourcebook* (2007); D. S. Potter, "Martyrdom as Spectacle," in *Theater and Society in the Classical World*, ed. R. Scodel (1993), 53–88; C. Roueché, *Performers and Partisans at Aphrodisias in the Roman and Late Roman Periods* (1993); H. W. F. Saggs, *Everyday Life in Babylonia & Assyria* (1965); J.-A. Shelton, *As the Romans Did: A Sourcebook in Roman Social History* (2nd ed., 1998); T. Stevenson, "The Parthenon Frieze as an Idealized, Contemporary Panathenaic Festival," in *Sport and Festival in the Ancient Greek World*, ed. D. J. Phillips and D. Pritchard (2003), 233–80; K. Szpakowska, *Daily Life in Ancient Egypt* (2008); E. M. Yamauchi, *Persia and the Bible* (1990).

PLM

See also ARMIES, ATHLETICS, DANCE, DRAMA & THEATERS, GAMES & GAMBLING, HORSES, INCENSE, and WILD ANIMALS & HUNTING.

TAXATION

Taxation was a means by which money was raised by a governing authority on citizens under its jurisdiction. Tribute consisted of compulsory contributions by a conquered state to the conquering overlord. Taxes and tribute were paid in the form of goods, services, forced labor, slavery, or in gold or silver. Most taxes in the ancient world were not equitable but regressive, as the bulk of the taxes were extracted from the peasants to support the privileged classes.

A. THE OLD TESTAMENT

In Egypt the Hebrews were subject to forced labor (Exod 1:11), as was the general population. The term *mekes*, "tax," occurs only in Num 31:28–41 and refers to the obligatory donations given to support the Israelite priests. A half-shekel poll tax was required from males (Exod 30:11–16) for the support of the tent of meeting. In Nehemiah's day the tax given to the temple was reduced to a third of a shekel (Neh 10:32).

The advent of the Hebrew monarchy witnessed a dramatic rise in taxes, as predicted by Samuel, who foresaw that a king would demand a tenth of their crops and animals (1 Sam 8:15, 17). Under David and Solomon, the national treasury was enriched by conquests, as well as by the levying of tolls for trade (1 Kgs 10:15).

The victorious Israelites were able to require forced labor from various Canaanite peoples (Josh 16:10; Judg 1:28). Later, Solomon required forced labor from the Israelites themselves (1 Kgs 5:13–18), and he also imposed taxes by setting up a rotation system requiring twelve districts to supply provisions for a month each (1 Kgs 4:7). The intention of Rehoboam to continue Solomon's corvée (Heb. *mas*) system of enforced labor (1 Kgs 12:1–15) and possibly to increase it (cf. 1 Kgs 9:22; 2 Chr 2:17–18) caused the ten northern tribes to rebel (1 Kgs 12:16–20). The revolt against this demand from Rehoboam was led by Jeroboam (1 Kgs 11:28), who had been an overseer of the corvée before he had fled to Egypt.

The Samaria ostraca (8th c. BC), which contain the phrase *lmlk* ("[belonging] to the king"), have been interpreted as records of tax contributions in kind. Scholars have debated whether the names listed on these records were those of land owners, tax officials, or nobles resident at Samaria.

Both Israel and Judah paid tribute to foreign nations: the Assyrians demanded tribute from both Israel and Judah (2 Kgs 15:19; 18:13–16), and, after the northern kingdom came to an end, the Egyptians and Babylonians demanded tribute from Judah (2 Kgs 23:33; 24:1). Prophets such as Amos (5:11) denounced the very high level of taxation and the seizure of land prompted by this requirement.

The Persian king Artaxerxes offered subsidies for the rebuilding of the temple in Jerusalem and tax exemption (Ezra 7:24) because he wished the Jews to pray for them (Ezra 6:10). But the Persians still exacted a king's tax, a land tax in kind, and a poll tax (Ezra 4:13). These proved so burdensome that the Jews had to sell members of their families to borrow money (Neh 5:1–5). Unlike previous governors, Nehemiah, instead of demanding provisions for himself and his staff, paid for these expenses out of his own funds (Neh 5:14–15).

B. THE NEW TESTAMENT

The Greek word *telōnēs* in the Synoptic Gospels is more correctly translated "toll collector" or "tax collector" than "publican." Matthew, also known as Levi (Matt 9:9||Mark 2:14||Luke 5:27), was a toll collector at the key Galilean city of Capernaum, where Jesus saw him sitting at his custom house. Zaccheus, a "chief tax collector," probably supervised other toll collectors in the area of Jericho. John the Baptist advised the tax collectors who came to him, "Don't collect any more than you are required to" (Luke 3:13).

In the NT, tax collectors are linked with "sinners" (Matt 9:10–11; 11:19; Mark 2:15–16; Luke 5:29–30; 7:34; 15:1), "prostitutes" (Matt 21:31), and gentiles (Matt 18:17), and Jesus was criticized by his contemporaries for associating with them (Matt 9:11; 11:19; Mark 2:16; Luke 5:30; 7:34; 15:2). Jesus related a parable in which he contrasts a penitent tax collector with a hypocritical Pharisee (Luke 18:9–14).

The Roman poll tax was at an annual rate of one denarius per person, the average wage for a day's work. In Syria, which included Judea, men from the age of fourteen to sixty-five and women from twelve to sixty-five were liable to pay this poll tax. This tax, which is denoted by the term *kēnsos* (cf. Latin *census*) in the Gospels, had to be paid in coins bearing Caesar's likeness, and this distasteful requirement became a subject of discussion with Jesus (Matt 22:15–22||Mark 12:13–17||Luke 20:20–26, where the term *phoros*, "tribute," is used). To the question of the Pharisees and Herodians as to whether it was right to pay taxes to Caesar, Jesus replied: "Give to Caesar what is Caesar's, and to God what is God's" (Matt 22:21||Mark 12:17||Luke 20:25). Jesus also counseled his followers to accept the forced labor that Roman soldiers often required (Matt 5:41). One of the false charges against Jesus before Pilate was: "He opposes payment of taxes to Caesar" (Luke 23:2).

The Gospel of Matthew relates how Peter was asked if his master paid the *didrachmon*, the equivalent of the half-shekel temple tax, to which Peter replied that he did (Matt 17:24–25). Although Jesus maintained that he and his followers were not required to do so, in order to avoid offense he directed Peter on this occasion to pay the tax with a *statēr* found in a fish, a coin that was enough to pay for both Jesus and Peter (Matt 17:25–27).

Paul advised Christians: "Give to everyone what you owe them: If you owe taxes, pay taxes [*phoros* = direct tax]; if revenue, then revenue [*telos* = indirect tax]; if respect, then respect; if honor, then honor" (Rom 13:7). One of Paul's important converts at Corinth was Erastus, who, as the city's director of public works (*ho oikonomos tēs poleōs*; Rom 16:23), would have been expected to spend some of his wealth on a public project (*leitourgia*). Near the theater in Corinth was found an inscription: *Erastus pro aedilit[at] e s(ua) p(ecunia) stravit*, "Erastus in return for his aedileship laid (the pavement) at his own expense."

C. THE NEAR EASTERN WORLD

Mesopotamia

Around 2500 BC, the Sumerian Uruinimgina (formerly known as Urukagina) of Lagash described how the former prosperity of the state had been dissipated by officials who imposed taxes upon all forms of social activity and who even seized the property of tax delinquents. His rule was marked by the removal of the tax on wool and on all private enterprises, as well as the reduction of death duties by 50 percent.

In the Ur III period, taxes were paid in sheep to the pen at Puzrish-Dagan, near Nippur. Assyrian merchants traveling to Cappadocia during the Old Assyrian period paid taxes on the goods they took from Aššur, and also paid a 10 percent tax on garments they bought at the Cappadocian site of Kanesh (Veenhof and Eidem, 84). From the Kassite Middle Babylonian period we have *kudurrus* (boundary stones) that list exemptions from taxes and obligations for labor on building city walls, clearing canals, and quartering troops. Land given to temples was exempt from taxes, and temple personnel were exempted from the state's corvée demands.

In the Neo-Assyrian period farmers were taxed 25 percent of their grain, 10 percent on straw, and a share of their flocks and herds (Postgate 1979, 205). Taxes were also levied on traders at ferries and town gates. Annals from the reign of Ashurnasirpal II (883–859 BC) show that at this time tribute from foreign lands was more important to the economy than local taxes. During times of weakness in Assyria, vassal kingdoms were disinclined to pay tribute, and this inevitably invited reprisals.

Egypt

In Egypt taxes normally comprised about 10 percent of the crops harvested from estates, private gardens, and non-temple property. When they were received, they were usually either stored in royal granaries or allotted as rations to the military forces. By the Middle Kingdom period, a large bureaucracy was busily engaged in collecting taxes on animals, produce, property, and sailing vessels.

After Egypt invaded Upper Nubia (ca. 1500 BC), the pharaohs appointed a "viceroy of Kush" to collect taxes and extract gold from this area. The tribute for year 38 of Tuthmosis III (1479–1425 BC) included seventy-seven cattle, sixteen slaves, and 2,844 deben of gold (one deben equals 91 grams = 0.2 lb.). (See Adams, 231.) Customs duties were levied at the First Cataract on goods entering Egypt from the south, and at the Delta in the north on goods coming in from the Mediterranean.

In Persia, Darius I (522–486 BC) instituted wide-ranging reforms that included the establishing of satraps in provinces to gather taxes. To secure support, the usurper Smerdis declared "to every nation of his dominions and proclaimed them for three years freed from service and from tribute" (Her. *Hist.* 3.67), before he was killed by Darius. Though some of the Persian nobility may have been exempt from taxes (cf. Her. *Hist.* 3.97), Elamite tablets from Persepolis reveal that farmers from the Persian heartland had to pay one-tenth of their sesame, one-tenth of their wine, one-tenth of their grain, and more, as taxes. Some taxes were paid in weighted silver.

Besides the expected tribute, many nations brought voluntary gifts, The staircase of the Apadana (Audience Hall) at Persepolis depicts a procession of delegations from twenty-three different peoples bringing various gifts to Darius (see Yamauchi 1990, 351–56).

Darius fixed the annual tribute of the various satrapies in talents of silver (Her. *Hist.* 3.89–96). According to Herodotus, Egypt, for example, had to pay seven hundred talents of tribute and one hundred twenty thousand bushels of grain (*Hist.* 3.91), Babylonia had to present one thousand talents of silver and five hundred eunuch boys (*Hist.* 3.92), and Arabia had to provide one thousand talents' worth of frankincense (*Hist.* 3.97). Subjects were also required to furnish corvée labor on demand. From the reign of Darius II we have records of the Murashu family, whose members were given lands for their services in collecting royal taxes and who loaned almost everything for a price. Among two thousand five hundred individuals mentioned in the Murashu records, about seventy borrowers can be identified as Jews.

D. THE GRECO-ROMAN WORLD

Greece

In the Classical Age (5th c. BC), the wealthy were expected to offer *liturgies* ("public duties") for the city-state of Athens, such as paying for ships or sponsoring dramatic choruses. Originally a voluntary matter, such duties became compulsory by the fourth century BC. Key taxes were a 1 percent excise tax on transactions in the agora; 2 percent duties on imports and exports; the *metoikion*, a poll tax on resident aliens at twelve drachmas per person; a 1 to 2 percent tax on auctions; and a tax on brothels called *pornikos telos*. The *hetairai*, non-Athenian women who served as entertainers and companions at banquets, had to pay a tax. The city farmed out the collection of these taxes to contractors (Arist. *Ath. pol.* 47–48), a system later adopted by the Romans. In times of war, the Athenians levied an emergency war tax called the *eisphora*, which amounted to 1 to 2 percent of the value of a citizen's property and possessions.

In the Hellenistic period, cities were subject both to royal taxes that were paid to the monarchs of various kingdoms and to local civic taxation. Some favored individuals received exemption (*ateleia*) from civic taxes. The Seleucids collected one-third of the grain harvest. The Ptolemies allocated the collecting of taxes to the highest bidder. Taxes on salt, which was controlled by a royal monopoly, were very important under the Ptolemies.

The Ptolemies also levied an annual land tax of one *artaba* of grain per *aroura* of land, which amounted to about 10 percent of the harvest. They also collected the *apomoira* tax, which ranged from one-tenth to one-sixth of wine, fruit, and vegetables. The Ptolemies levied very high customs, which ranged from 20 to 59 percent on merchandise, as well as a circulation tax of 5 to 10 percent on sales. To promote Hellenistic culture, Ptolemy II exempted school teachers, actors, athletic coaches, and victors in the games at festivals.

Rome

In Rome, during the early Republic, the state in times of emergency required a *tributum*, which, like the Athenian *eisphora*, was originally a war tax and was originally at a rate of 1 to 3 percent. When the war was over and the treasury was filled, this was sometimes repaid to the citizens. Later, as Rome expanded, Roman citizens and those living in Italy became exempt, although land held by a Roman citizen outside of Italy was subject to taxation. It was the conquered people in the provinces who were expected to pay for the expense of the government and the armies stationed abroad. When the Romans conquered Sicily (3rd c. BC), they took over the tithe that Syracuse had required of farmers. Cicero prosecuted the corrupt governor Verres, who had exacted a triple tithe (Cicero, *Verr.* 2.3.25; cf. Cowles, 68).

After 212 BC, a class of publicans (*ordo publicanorum*) bid for contracts to collect taxes for the Roman government. Members of this group would pay in advance and collect as much as they could, often by extortion, for their profit. These men, who belonged to the equestrian order, also loaned money at exorbitant rates. Gaius Gracchus imposed a tithe on the province of Asia in 123 BC and authorized the *publicani* to collect this.

Julius Caesar entrusted cities and communities to collect taxes, though indirect taxes, such as customs, market dues, and sales taxes, were still farmed out to the publicans to collect. The indirect taxes (*vectigalia*) included customs on exports and imports (*portorium*), usually at the rate of 2.5 percent, taxes on houses and builders, and tolls at bridges and ferries.

Augustus introduced a 5 percent tax on inheritances, except those that passed to a very near relative. He also enacted a 1 percent sales tax and a 4 percent special sales tax on slaves. Augustus granted citizens of Alexandria in Egypt and their slaves exemption from the poll tax. Citizens of the administrative capitals of the nomes, the *metropoleis*, paid a reduced rate. Adult males of the *chōra* ("countryside") who were aged fourteen to sixty-two paid sixteen drachmas a year, whereas metropolites paid half that rate. Taxes on farm lands were assessed at two to five *artaba*s per *aroura*, which would have been about 20 to 50 percent of an average crop. Tax rates on cleruchic land, which had been given to military settlers, was lower, roughly 10 to 20 percent of an average crop.

Tiberius shifted the responsibility of the collection of direct taxes from publicans or tax-farmers to officials called *praktores*, who were nominated by each community. These officials were unpaid and were liable for collecting the taxes expected. Nero exempted the province of Achaea from taxes in gratitude for the reception that the Greeks gave him when he participated in the Panhellenic games at Isthmia. To replenish the treasury that Nero had depleted with his extravagance, Vespasian imposed a tax even on public urinals, in spite of his son Titus's objections (Suet. *Vesp.* 23).

In AD 217 Caracalla made all free inhabitants of the empire Roman citizens in order that they could be liable—with the exception of those resident in Italy—to the inheritance tax introduced by Augustus. Diocletian (AD 284–305) faced an economic crisis because of inflation, which reduced the denarius to about 10 percent of its second-century value. He tried unsuccessfully to fix prices, and required taxes in kind to provide food and materials to support his officials and soldiers. The poll tax, or *capitatio*, was exacted on the rural farmers but not on the urban population. The land tax, or *iugatio*, was fixed in value and had to be paid even when harvests were poor. Those who failed to pay the taxes were threatened with capital punishment. There was no income tax, so lawyers, doctors, and civil servants who gained their living by salaries and fees paid no tax at all.

Throughout the Roman world, municipal magistrates, who were unpaid, were expected to offer *summae honorariae*, including donations for games, civic buildings, and baths. These offices were held by the curial class of landowners. As these so-called "honors" became increasingly burdensome, some abandoned their fields rather than bear the cost of such "liturgical" services.

E. THE JEWISH WORLD

Since in the Pentateuch the requirements of the tithe are expressed in terms of agricultural produce, many of the later urban Jewish population, who earned their livelihood apart from agriculture, felt exempt from the requirement of the tithe, which placed an unfair burden on farmers. When taxes were added to the requisite tithes, the burden might well have equaled 40 percent of a farmer's crops.

Antiochus IV re-imposed a land tax on the Jews after the revolt of Jason. In order to gain the support of the Jews, his successor, Demetrius (162–150 BC), wrote,

> And now I free you and exempt all the Jews from payment of tribute and salt tax and crown levies, and instead of collecting the third of the grain and the half of the fruit of the trees that I should receive, I release them from this day

and henceforth. . . . And let Jerusalem and her environs, her tithes and her revenues be holy and free from tax. (1 Macc 10:29–31; cf. 11:34–35)

Simon stopped paying tribute to the Seleucids in 142 BC (see 1 Macc 13:37–39).

The Tobiad Joseph collected taxes from the Jews for the Ptolemies (Jos. *Ant.* 12.164–180). John Hyrcanus appointed tax collectors who collected tithes by force. Philo's brother in Alexandria served as the *alabarch* responsible for collecting taxes from the Jews for the Romans.

After Pompey's conquest of Palestine in 63 BC, the Jews were required to pay tribute to Rome. Caesar reduced their taxes and exempted the Jews during their sabbatical years, and he also allowed Jews in the diaspora to send their temple tax to Jerusalem. Cicero defended Flaccus, the governor of the province of Asia, who had impounded such funds (*Flac.* 28).

The Romans permitted Herod the Great to collect taxes on property, crops, and transportation. Herod introduced a sales tax on goods purchased or sold, and at Herod's death in 4 BC the people clamored for tax relief (Jos. *Ant.* 17.205). Judea became an imperial province in AD 6 and thereafter land and poll taxes were collected by Roman officials appointed for that purpose. In AD 17 the provinces of Syria and Judea petitioned Tiberius for a reduction of their taxes (Tac. *Ann.* 2.42.7).

In AD 66 Herod Agrippa tried in vain to persuade the Jews not to rebel against the Romans by speaking at length about the overwhelming military might of the Roman legions (*J.W.* 2.161.4). But the Jews refused to pay the taxes claimed by the governor Florus just before the outbreak of their revolt against Rome (Jos. *J.W.* 2.295, 331). This revolt was instigated by the Zealots, who asserted that it was unlawful to pay taxes to Rome.

After the destruction of the temple in AD 70, the Romans added insult to injury by requiring Jews throughout the Empire to keep paying the half-shekel tax that they had paid to the Jerusalem temple and by redirecting it into a special treasury for the temple of Jupiter. Women who had not had to pay the Jewish temple tax were now also obliged to pay the new tax, which was known as the *fiscus Iudaicus*, as were all children from the age of three years on. Dio Cassius specifies that the new tax was imposed on *practicing* Jews (*Hist. Rom.* 66.7.2).

In AD 96 the emperor Nerva minted coins with the inscription FISCI IUDAICI CALUMNIA SUBLATA ("The calumny of the Jewish Tax is removed"), though this does not mean that he canceled this tax but only that he did away with the abuses that had been involved in collecting it. Suetonius recalls that, "As a boy, I remember once attending a crowded court where the procurator had a ninety-year-old man stripped to establish whether or not he had been circumcised" (*Dom.* 12).

Exodus 30:13–14 had stipulated that every Israelite man twenty years and older contribute a half-shekel for the service of the tabernacle. According to one Dead Sea Scroll text (4Q159 1 II, 6–7), a member of the Qumran community had to give a half-shekel tax, only once in his lifetime, rather than annually in contrast to the understanding of most jews at the time (cf. Matt 17:24–27). The temple tax is the subject of an entire tractate in the Mishnah, *Sheqalim*. Priests argued from Lev 6:16 that they were exempt from paying the temple tax, a position opposed by Johanan b. Zakkai (*m. Šeqal.* 1:4).

The rabbinic literature uses the term *môkēs* for a toll collecter, and *gabbay* for a collector of direct taxes. For both individuals, repentance was held to be difficult because compensation for those unfairly oppressed was nearly impossible (*y. B. Mes* 6:4). The Mishnah associates tax collectors and toll collectors with murderers and robbers (*m. Ned.* 3:4). It declares, "If taxgatherers entered a house [all that is within it] becomes unclean" (*m. Ṭ ehar.* 7:6). They could not give testimony in a Jewish court.

Gamaliel II (ca. 100 AD) complained of the Romans: "This empire gnaws at our substance through four things: its tolls, its bath buildings, its theaters, and its taxes in kind" (*'Abot R. Nat.* 28). The Talmud, which is of a later date, considered the tax collector to have a respected profession as long as he did not abuse his authority. A tax collector named Bar Ma'jan was given an honorable funeral because he invited the poor to a banquet when city counselors refused his invitation (*y. Sanh.* 6.23c).

F. THE CHRISTIAN WORLD

Lactantius, a contemporary of Constantine, wrote about the emperor's predecessor, Diocletian: "There began to be fewer men who paid taxes than there were who received wages; so that the means of the husbandmen being exhausted by enormous impositions, the farms were abandoned, cultivated grounds became woodland, and universal dismay prevailed" (*Mort.* 7).

After Constantine converted to Christianity in AD 312, he granted clergy exemption from taxes, and generously gave the church properties, which were exempt from certain taxes. Constantine imposed the *gleba*, or *follis*, a special land tax on senators. He required the *chrysargyron* ("gold and silver") on those who received fees, such as merchants, traders, and even prostitutes. This had to be paid in gold every fourth year. This was so onerous that some had to sell their children into slavery to pay it.

The great increase in imperial bureaucracy and the military required more and more taxes and requisitions from the populace. Themistius reports that between AD 324 and 364 the amount of taxes was doubled (Jones 1959, 39).

The state required tax on land whether it was cultivated or not. The tax burden on landowners became so great that many abandoned their lands. *Anachōris*, or flight into the countryside to avoid the burdens of taxes, may have been a key factor in the growth of the monastic movement in Egypt. One of the designations of the monks, "anchorite," was derived from this word.

Gregory of Nazianzus, a monastic leader in Cappadocia in eastern Turkey, addressed a poem, three letters, and a sermon to Julian, a Christian tax assessor. During an imperial census in AD 374 or 375, Gregory asked his old friend to exempt church property and clergy from taxation.

BIBLIOGRAPHY: W. Y. Adams, *Nubia: The Corridor to Africa* (1984); P. Altmann, "Tithes for the Clergy and Taxes for the King: State and Temple Contributions in Nehemiah," *CBQ* 76 (2014), 215–29; E. Badian, *Publicans and Sinners: Private Enterprise in the Service of the Roman Republic* (1972); P. Briant, *From Cyrus to Alexander: A History of the Persian Empire*, trans. P. T. Daniels (2002); F. F. Bruce, "Render to Caesar," in *Jesus and the Politics of His Day*, ed. E. Bammel and C. F. D. Moule (1984), 249–63; I. A. F. Bruce, "Nerva and the Fiscus Iudaicus," *PEQ* 96 (1964), 34–45; P. A. Brunt, "The Revenues of Rome," *JRS* 71 (1981), 161–72; T. M. Coleman, "Binding Obligations in Romans 13:7: A Semantic Field and Social Context," *TynBul* 48 (1997), 307–27; F. Cowles, *Gaius Verres: An Historical Study* (1917); D. Daube, "Temple Tax," in *Jesus, the Gospels, and the Church*, ed. E. P. Sanders (1987), 121–34; J. D. M. Derrett, "Luke's Perspective on Tribute to Caesar," in *Political Issues in Luke-Acts*, ed. R. J. Cassidy and P. J. Scharper (1983), 38–48; R. Doran, "The Pharisee and the Tax Collector: An Agonistic Story," *CBQ* 69 (2007), 259–70; T. A. Friedrichsen, "The Temple, a Pharisee, a Tax Collector, and the Kingdom of God: Rereading a Jesus Parable (Luke 18:10–14A)," *JBL* 124 (2005), 89–119; S. Harrison, "The Case of the Pharisee and the Tax Collector: Justification and Social Location in Luke's Gospel," *CurTM* 32 (2005), 99–111; F. Herrenbrück, *Jesus und die Zöllner* (1990); S. R. Holman, "Taxing Nazianzus: Gregory and the Other Julian," *StPatr* 37 (2001), 103–9; S. Honigman, *Tales of High Priests and Taxes: The Books of the Maccabees and the Judean Rebellion against Antiochus IV* (2014); A. H. M. Jones, "Over-Taxation and the Decline of the Roman Empire," *Antiq* 33 (1959), 33–42; A. H. M. Jones, *The Roman Economy*, ed. P. A. Brunt (1974); S. R. Llewelyn, "The Development of the System of Liturgies," *NewDocs* 7.93–111; S. R. Llewelyn, "Tax Collection and the τελῶναι of the New Testament," *NewDocs* 8.47–76; S. R. Llewelyn, "Taxes on Donkeys: An Illustration of Indirect Taxation at Work in Roman Egypt," *NewDocs* 8.77–96; S. Mandell, "Who Paid the Temple Tax When the Jews Were under Roman Rule?" *HTR* 77 (1984), 223–32; A. Mittwoch, "Tribute and Land-

Tax in Seleucid Judaea," *Bib* 36 (1955), 352–61; R. A. Oden, "Taxation in Biblical Israel," *JRE* 12 (1984), 162–81; S. E. Orel, ed., *Death and Taxes in the Ancient Near East* (1992); P. Perkins, "Taxes in the New Testament," *JRE* 12 (1984), 182–200; P. W. Pestman, ed., *A Guide to the Zenon Archive (P. L. Bat. 21)* (1981); J. N. Postgate, *Taxation and Conscription in the Assyrian Empire* (1974); J. N. Postgate, "The Economic Structure of the Assyrian Empire," in *Power and Propaganda*, ed. J. T. Larsen (1979), 193–222; A. F. Rainey, "Compulsory Labour Gangs in Ancient Israel," *IEJ* 20 (1970), 191–202; D. Rathbone, "Egypt, Augustus and Roman Taxation," *Cahiers du Centre Gustave Glotz: Revue d'histoire ancienne* 4 (1993), 81–112; A. Samuel et al., *Death and Taxes* (1971); A. Segrè, "Studies in Byzantine Economy: Iugatio and Capitatio," *Traditio* 3 (1945), 101–27; J. S. Ukpong, "Tribute to Caesar, Mark 12:13–17 (Mt 22:15–22; Lk 20:20–26)," *Neot* 33 (1999), 433–44; K. R. Veenhof and J. Eidem, *Mesopotamia: The Old Assyrian Period* (2008); W. O. Walker, "Jesus and the Tax Collectors," *JBL* 97 (1978), 221–38; S. L. Wallace, *Taxation in Egypt from Augustus to Diocletian* (1938); E. Yamauchi, "Two Reformers Compared: Solon of Athens and Nehemiah of Jerusalem," in *The Bible World: Essays in Honor of Cyrus H. Gordon*, ed. G. Rendsburg et al. (1980), 269–92; E. Yamauchi, *Persia and the Bible* (1990); E. Yamauchi, *Africa and the Bible* (2004).

RKH and EMY

See also BANK & LOANS, CENSUS, CITIZENS & ALIENS, MEDIUM OF EXCHANGE, SLAVERY, and WEALTH & POVERTY.

TEXTILES

The word "textile" is derived from the Latin adjective *textilis*, "woven," and thus describes any kind of fabric that has resulted from the process of weaving. This craft is one of the oldest known to humanity, and presupposes the ability to spin yarn from various materials and intertwine it lengthwise and crosswise on a frame. In antiquity, the textile industry was second in importance only to agriculture.

A. THE OLD TESTAMENT

The primary textile in ancient Israel was wool derived from sheep, Hebrew *ṣemer*, a word that occurs sixteen times in the OT. When David encountered the churlish Nabal, the latter was shearing his three thousand sheep at Carmel, south of Hebron (1 Sam 25:4). So valuable was wool as a commodity that it was acceptable as tribute from vassals (Isa 16:1). Mesha, the king of Moab, presented Ahab with one hundred thousand lambs and the wool of one hundred thousand rams (2 Kgs 3:4). The bleached "white wool" (*ṣemer ṣāḥar*) of Damascus was especially costly (Ezek 27:18). Isaiah promises, "Though your sins are like scarlet, they shall be as white as snow; though they are red as crimson, they shall be like wool" (Isa 1:18). Hebrew law forbade wool to be mixed with linen in weaving (Deut 22:11; cf. Lev 19:19).

There is some evidence for the weaving of goat hair (*ʿizîm*) for garments (Num 31:20) and especially for the curtains for the tabernacle (Exod 25:4; 26:7; 35:6, 23, 26; 36:14). Dark, rough, and uncomfortable sackcloth (Heb. *śaq*) made from goat hair was worn as a sign of mourning or repentance (Gen 37:34; 2 Sam 3:31; 1 Kgs 20:31–32; Jonah 3:5).

Linen, denoted by the Hebrew term *bad*, was woven from the fibers of the flax plant, which was grown to a limited extent in Palestine. The Gezer Calendar (ca. 900 BC) refers to a month of flax gathering (March/April). Rahab hid the Israelite spies under the drying flax stalks on top of her roof in Jericho (Josh 2:6). The one OT reference to the flax plant (*pištâ*) concerns its growth in Egypt (Exod 9:31). The best linen was imported from Egypt (Exod 9:31; Prov 7:16; Isa 19:9), and this was worn by royalty, the wealthy, and priests. Spectacular evidence of linen in the ancient Levant has come from the discovery in 1993 of a 7 x 2 meter linen cloth, dated to about 4000 BC, in the so-called "Cave of the Warrior," located northwest of Jericho in the Wadi el-Makkukh.

The OT contains nearly thirty references to priestly linen garments, including linen underwear (Lev 6:10). Linen was valued for its relative lightness. According to Ezekiel, the priests "must not wear anything that makes them perspire" (Ezek 44:18). Angelic messengers are also described as garbed in white linen (Ezek 9:2–3; 10:2, 6–7; Dan 10:5; 12:6–7), and apostates from the worship of Yahweh used linen to clothe their idols (2 Kgs 23:7).

An early Hebrew word for fine linen, *šēš* (a loanword from Egyptian), is used for the new garments Joseph receives when he is elevated by the pharaoh (Gen 41:42), for the priests' garments (Exod 35:25), and for a bride's clothing (Ezek 16:13). In postexilic times, fine linen was referred to by the term *bûṣ* (a loanword from Akkadian through Aramaic) (1 Chr 15:27). In Ezek 16:10, 13, the word *mešî* (which is derived from the verb "to draw" and which is rendered by the Septuagint as *trichapton*, "very fine thread") may mean "fine linen" (NIV), rather than "silk," as it is rendered by most versions (KJV, ESV, NASB, RSV), since Chinese silk is not attested this early. *Karpas*, a word derived from Sanskrit, occurs only in Esth 1:6, in connection with the white curtains hanging in the palace of Ahasuerus (i.e., Xerxes) in Susa. This term is usually translated "linen" but may refer to "cotton."

Embroidery is mentioned several times in the OT. For example, the tabernacle hangings were embroidered; that is, threads of various colors were interwoven to form patterns. God inspired Bezalel (Exod 35:35) and others in this craft. Sisera's mother waited in expectation that her son would bring back as booty "highly embroidered garments for my neck" (Judg 5:30). And the prophet Ezekiel, addressing Tyre, notes that "fine embroidered linen from Egypt was your sail" (Ezek 27:7). The bride of a king (Ps 45:13–14) is said to wear a gown embroidered with gold thread.

The spinning of thread was the work of women, as described in the portrait of the model wife in Proverbs: "She selects wool and flax and works with eager hands" (Prov 31:13) and "In her hand she holds the distaff and grasps the spindle with her fingers" (Prov 31:19). In Judg 16:13 we read that Delilah treacherously wove Samson's hair into a ground loom.

The OT sometimes refers to weaving tools analogically. For example, weapons are compared to the heddle rod of a weaver's loom (1 Sam 17:7; 2 Sam 21:19), and Job complains, "My days are swifter than a weaver's shuttle" (7:6).

In 2016 Erez Ben-Yosef of Tel Aviv University discovered a unique group of textiles dating to the period of the united monarchy (10th c. BC) at the copper mines of Timna in the Arabah south of the Dead Sea. The tiny pieces, which are of varied color and some of which measure only five centimeters square, came from tents, bags, and clothes. They include elaborately decorated fabric that was probably worn by the supervisors of the mines.

B. THE NEW TESTAMENT

Wool, *erion*, is mentioned only twice in the NT: in Heb 9:19, in reference to an act of Moses in which he used scarlet wool and hyssop, and in Rev 1:13, to describe the appearance of one like a son of man whose hairs were "white like wool." Another Greek word for wool, *pokos*, never occurs in the NT. Silk, *sērikon*, a textile from (northwest) China, is mentioned once, in Rev 18:12.

Linen is referred to a number of times in the NT. The wealthy man in one of Jesus's parables wears *byssos*, "fine linen" (Luke 16:19). In the book of Revelation, the bride of the Lamb is pictured as being clothed in fine linen (*byssinos*), which "stands for the righteous acts of the saints" (Rev 19:8). The armies of heaven are also clothed in this material (Rev 19:14), and the harlot city's wearing of *bysinnos* reflects its luxurious lifestyle (Rev 18:16). The word *linon*, which appears only twice in the NT, is used to refer to smoking "flax" (Matt 12:20) and to the dress of angels (Rev 15:6). *Sindōn*, which originally denoted a textile from India, came to mean "fine linen," and is used of the garment covering the young man in the garden of Gethsemane (Mark 14:51–52) and of the burial shroud that is provided for the corpse of Jesus (Matt 27:59; Mark 15:46; Luke 23:53). The *othonion* was a strip of linen used to swathe the dead (John 19:40; 20:5–7).

John the Baptist wears a garment woven from camel's hair (Matt 3:4; Mark 1:6). Camel's hair falls off in clumps as the weather gets warmer. The hair next to the skin is a short, soft fiber, whereas the outer hair is coarse and wiry.

From extrabiblical texts and archaeological evidence we know of the special importance of textiles in the cities of western Asia Minor. Wool from Miletus was famous as far back as the fifth century BC. Laodicea, Colosse, and Hierapolis (Col 4:13) produced fine wools. Hierapolis had guilds of wool washers (*erioplytai*) and purple dyers (*porphyrobaphoi*) and was also noted for its guild of tapestry weavers, as Ephesus was for its towel weavers. Excavations at the terrace houses at Ephesus have yielded sewing needles, loom weights, spindle whorls, and decorated distaffs.

Inscriptions from Thyatira (cf. Rev 1:11; 2:18–29) in Lydia refer to guilds of clothiers, linen workers, wool merchants, and dyers. Working with textiles was one of the most common occupations of Jews in Asia Minor. When Paul preached at Philippi, Lydia, a woman from Thyatira who was a seller of purple cloth, responded positively to Paul's message (Acts 16:14). The guild of dyers at Thyatira was unusually prosperous.

Paul's hometown, Tarsus, was a center of textile production and was famous for its linen weavers (cf. Acts 21:39). Paul also worked with his hands (1 Cor 4:12); he is described as a *skēnopoios*, or "tent-maker." He was probably trained to weave tents from the hair of Cilician goats raised near his hometown. Aquila and Priscilla also made their living by this craft (Acts 18:3). Because fabric made from goat's hair is both heat- and water-resistant, it made excellent material for tents.

C. THE NEAR EASTERN WORLD

Mesopotamia

Though linen may have been the earliest textile, wool was the dominant one in the ancient world, with the exception of Egypt. The best wool came from wethers (castrated male sheep) and ewes. Wool has several positive and some negative characteristics. Wool fibers are crinkly and have scales that interlock easily, creating air pockets with insulating properties and allowing the fiber easily to be spun into thread. Wool fibers can be compacted as waterproof felt, even without weaving. Wool comes in various colors; can be readily dyed, even on the animal itself; and is crease-resistant. One negative property of wool is that when it gathers moisture and dirt, it is difficult to launder.

Around 3500 BC the Sumerians learned how to gather wool and spin it into thread for weaving into cloth. A Protoliterate seal from Choga Mish (3300 BC) depicts a woman spinning. During the next several millennia, the same process and tools were used throughout the ancient world to spin wool into thread. This always involved a spindle, a wooden rod that was four to ten inches long, and a spindle whorl, which acted as a flywheel to maintain the spindle's rotation. The left hand would attach a few wool fibers to the tip of the spindle, and the right hand would give the spindle a vigorous twist and drop the spindle toward the floor as it continued to rotate. In this process the thread, rotating clockwise, develops a so-called "Z-spin," which describes the angle of the thread as descending from the upper right to the lower left when held vertically.

Over time, three types of looms were developed for the weaving of cloth from fibers: the ground loom, the warp-weighted loom, and the vertical two-beam loom. The ground loom consisted of two beams fastened to four pegs pounded into the ground. This was the earliest and the most portable loom, and it was widely used from the Neolithic Age until the middle of the second millennium BC. It is first depicted on seals from Susa from the late fourth millennium BC. Its limitation was that the cloth was restricted to the width of the arm span of the weavers. Three women working together could weave eight to fifteen inches in one day, depending on the type of cloth produced.

Used already in the mid-3rd millennium BC, the warp-weighted loom became widespread in Palestine at the beginning of the Iron Age (ca. 1200 BC), as attested by the widespread presence of doughnut-shaped clay loom weights at Megiddo, Jericho, Gezer, and other sites. From a wooden frame leaning against the wall hung perpendicular warp threads with loom weights in parallel rows. The horizontal thread, known as the weft or woof, would be passed by a shuttle over one thread, then under the next, and at the end would be reversed, forming a selvage at the sides. The simplest type of weaving is known as the "tabby weave," in which the weft passes over and under each alternating warp. More complex weaves included the "twill weave," with two weft threads twining each other as they enclosed warp units. This last procedure was facilitated by the attachment of alternate warp threads by loops to a heddle rod, which could be raised and lowered to form a natural shed (or opening) and then an artificial shed. After a certain number of weft threads had passed through, a "sword beater" would compact these threads. The weaver stood and began at the top of the loom, working downward.

The vertical two-beamed loom was developed in the fifteenth century BC in Syria and then spread to Egypt. This innovation permitted the insertion of colored wool wefts to form patterns, resulting in what is called tapestry weaving.

Large flocks of sheep were gathered during the Babylonian New Year's festival (in the spring) to be either plucked or clipped with a knife. Records indicate that as many as two thousand sheep were shorn in a single day during this festival. Shears are first mentioned in a Neo-Babylonian text. Each sheep produced one to two pounds of wool. To clothe a person required three to seven pounds of wool. As sheep are quite dirty, the wool had to be soaked in an alkaline reagent to remove the wool's natural lanolin oil.

The majority of the more than ten thousand tablets discovered at Ebla (24th c. BC) deal with the site's textile industry. "Some herds owned by the king [of Ebla] could have as many as 67,000 head, a number about one-tenth of the sheep the state owned" (Milano, 1225). One-sixth of all the Ur III tablets at Nippur deal with the wool industry. They record that king

Shulgi had sixty-six thousand sheep and that the temple of Nanna had forty thousand. Sheep were sheared at Nippur once a year for a period of up to three months. Within the temple complex was a separate weaving area. Up to fifteen thousand women, including slaves, worked in the wool industry under supervisors. Wool and woolen garments were given as wages.

During the Old Assyrian period (1850–1700 BC), donkey caravans from Aššur transported Babylonian textiles to trade colonies in Cappadocia in eastern Turkey and returned with gold and silver. These caravans took about six weeks to complete their journey, with each donkey carrying about 150 pounds of textiles, which earned a 300 percent profit when sold. In the international Amarna age (14th c. BC), textiles were presented as royal gifts. Tushratta, the king of Mitanni, sent to the Egyptian court sashes of red wool and a garment and a cap of blue-purple wool (EA 22). From reliefs and the paintings at Til Barsip we see that in the Neo-Assyrian period kings wore special garb embroidered with fine needlework.

The Medes in the reliefs at Persepolis appear to be wearing bowler hats made of felt. Among the presentations depicted on the Apadana stairway reliefs of Darius at Persepolis, the Babylonians, Egyptians, and Arabians bring textiles, and the Ionian Greeks bring skeins of wool.

In the frozen tomb of the Scythian nomads at Pazyryk (ca. 500 BC) in the Altai Mountains (in present-day Mongolia) numerous textile fragments were discovered, including felts, tapestry-woven wool fabrics, and embroidered silks. A patterned pile carpet about two meters square had been hand woven by tying three thousand six hundred knots in a square decimeter (ca. four inches square).

Linen was a relatively rare and expensive textile in Mesopotamia. The sun god Utu promised his sister Inanna: "Sister mine, I will bring you the cultivated flax, Inanna, I will bring you the cultivated flax" (Kramer, 68). Inanna was said to have worn a linen garment. Linen garments are recorded in temple records in the Ur III period, and a linen fabric was found around a copper statuette of Shulgi (2075 BC). Linen was also used to clothe the statues of the gods. Only in the Neo-Babylonian period, however, did linen become an important commercial product.

Before 1500 BC the people of the Indus River civilization (now in Pakistan) developed the process whereby fabric was made from fibers of the cotton plant (*Gossypium herbaceum*, or "Levant cotton"). The ripening of the fruit of the plant causes its long seed hairs to swell out, resembling a snowball. Cotton fibers are short, about an inch in length, and are difficult to spin into thread. Cotton is spun using a small, light, supported (rather than dropped) spindle. According to Herodotus, "There too there grows on wild trees wool more beautiful and excellent than the wool of sheep; these trees supply the Indians with clothing" (*Hist.* 3.106). The first reference to cotton west of India comes in an inscription of Sennacherib, who planted "trees bearing wool" in his garden. There is also evidence of cotton at Ḥorvat ʿUza in the Arad Valley in the seventh century BC, and it appeared in the Aegean in the sixth century BC.

Egypt

Though Egypt had numerous sheep, its wool was inferior, and woolen textiles were not very popular. Narmer (1st Dynasty) claimed that he had captured 1,422,000 sheep and Sahure (5th Dynasty) that he had captured 243,688. Herodotus observed of the Egyptians, "But nothing of wool is brought into temples, or buried with them; that is forbidden" (*Hist.* 2.81). Only rare fragments of woolen garments have been found preserved.

Linen was much more popular. Of more than twenty thousand textiles preserved in Egypt, more than 95 percent are linen. Linen feels cool, is easily washable, and because it is difficult to dye it was almost always sunbleached white. It was therefore the ideal textile for hot and sunny Egypt.

Linen fibers were derived from the flax plant (*Linum usitatissimum*), which grew in the well-watered Delta. Flax was domesticated in Egypt by 4500 BC. The flax plant grows to about a meter. Its blue or white flowers turn into linseed, which can be processed for oil. Flax was sown in the fall, grew quickly, and was harvested in March. When pulled from the ground when the stalks are green, fibers for very fine thread can be produced; when yellow (flaxen colored), strong fibers can be produced. If the stalks are allowed to dry out, tough fibers suitable for mats and sails develop.

The extraction of the fibers from the stalks required a laborious series of processes. The stalks were first dried. They were then "retted," or soaked in water, for two weeks in order to disintegrate the bark and woody core by bacterial action. After the stalks had been "scutched," or beaten with a wooden mallet, they were "hackled," that is, pulled through a series of comb-like devices, yielding single fibers. These were then twisted to form strands that could be woven into thread. Flax fibers are four times as strong as wool. Short fibers, called tow, were used as wicks.

Thanks to numerous paintings and models in tombs, we have detailed information about the manufacture of linen in Egypt. We see a woman who is a splicer taking fibers and rolling them on her right thigh. She wets the fibers with her saliva and then places them on a spindle that is twisted, spun in a counterclockwise motion, and then dropped, forming an "S-twist." The skein of thread is then removed as the spindle reaches the ground. Some scenes show a woman working with two spindles at the same time. The 1st Dynasty tomb of Zer at Abydos contained a linen cloth with a count of 160 x 120 threads per inch.

The oldest representation of the ground loom, which was used for more than two millennia in Egypt, comes from a bowl from Badari (ca. 3400 BC). The warp-weighted loom is seen on a model of a weaver's shop from the tomb of Meket-re (2000 BC). The vertical two-beamed loom was introduced into Egypt during the New Kingdom period. It is first attested in the tomb of Tuth-nefer (ca. 1425 BC). This new loom, with which weavers worked sitting, permitted tapestry weaving, that is, the insertion of colored weft threads to form patterns. The first evidence of linen tapestries dates to the reigns of Tuthmosis III (1504–1450 BC) and Tuthmosis IV (1425–1417 BC).

The Egyptians believed that the goddess Isis created flax and taught women to spin its fibers, and they believed that she herself wove clothes for Osiris. In Egypt the professional weavers were men, however, not women. According to a satire, theirs was not a happy lot: "The weaver in the workshops, he is worse than a woman, with his thighs against his belly. He cannot breathe the (open) air. If he cuts short the day of weaving, he is beaten with fifty thongs. He must give food to the doorkeeper to let him see the light of day" (*ANET*, 433).

Egyptian linen was the finest in the ancient world and was a lucrative export. The Amarna Letters record that all kinds of fine linen cloth were sent by the pharaohs as gifts. In the 3rd Dynasty a position existed called "director of all the flax of the king." When Wenamon returned to Phoenicia from Egypt, he brought with him "garments of royal linen" and "garments of fine linen."

Certain fine-quality linens were reserved for the images of gods, for pharaohs, and for priests. The Coffin Texts specify five types of linen that were not to be used by the living. Hatshepsut's coffin contained numerous linen objects, including eighteen shawls and sheets covering her body and fourteen more sheets in the wrapping, along with eighty bandages and twelve pads of linen.

D. THE GRECO-ROMAN WORLD

Greece

The textile industry in the Greek world is attested from the time of the Mycenaean occupation of Knossos in Crete. Linear B tablets as well as spindles and loom weights provide evidence for the palatial oversight of textile production. Detailed information about the spinning of yarn from wool and the weaving of textiles in Greece comes from numerous illustrations on black-figured and red-figured vases, which depict these operations as the chief activities of women. A woman would place the raw wool on a distaff, called a *gerōn* ("old man") because an old man's face was carved on its upper part, which she would hold under her left arm or stick through her girdle. Then, sitting, she would spin the fibers onto a spindle, creating Z-spun thread. She would prop up her feet on a footstool called an *onos* ("donkey") and use a terra-cotta shield called an *epinētron* to protect the dress covering her knees and thighs from being stained by the unspun wool, which was naturally greasy.

When a baby girl was born, a tuft of wool (*lēnos*) was placed on the doorway of her home to show that another spinner had come into the world. As the essential skill required of a wife was the ability to spin and weave, the *kalathos*, or wool basket, served as a symbol of wifehood. Young marriageable girls were expected to weave their own wedding gowns. Unmarried women who earned their keep by spinning gave us the word "spinster." According to the Gortyn Law Code (5th c. BC), a woman who was widowed or divorced could keep half of what she had woven while married.

Selected young girls called the *arrhēphoroi* lived in seclusion on the acropolis, where they were taught how to weave the myth of the Battle of the Gods into the woolen *peplos* ("robe") that was presented annually to the goddess Athena in the Parthenon. According to the *Iliad* (5.733–737; 14.178–179), Athena was the first to work with wool. The *Moirai*, or "Fates," were three goddesses who determined a person's destiny: Clotho, who spun the thread; Lachesis, who measured how long it should be; and Atropos, who severed it.

Weaving was highly developed in the Aegean by the middle of the third millennium BC. Nearly ten thousand spindle whorls were found at Troy II (ca. 2500 BC). A Minoan Linear A tablet dating to ca. 1500 BC from Hagia Triada, Crete, depicts the warp-weighted loom, which was the only kind of loom used in Greece. At Gordium excavators found two thousand three hundred loom weights dating to ca. 700 BC, which means that Midas could have employed over a hundred women as weavers.

Weaving is a major theme in the Homeric epics, most memorably in the case of Penelope, who fends off suitors in Odysseus's absence by weaving a shroud by day and undoing it at night (*Od.* 2.93–110). King Alcinous has fifty women weaving in his palace (*Od.* 7.103–105). Queens like Helen were able to introduce patterns into the woolen garments they wove (*Il.* 3.125–128). Hera weaves many *daidala*, or "figures," into a veil when she attempts to seduce Zeus (*Il.* 14.179). These references reflect the importation of patterned Assyrian textiles in the Archaic Age (8th–7th c. BC), which also influenced the Orientalizing pottery of that era.

Fine linen (Gk. *linon*) is already attested in the Mycenaean Linear B tablets (*ri-no*). The Mycenaeans used linen cuirasses, which are also mentioned in the *Iliad* (2.529, 830). In the Archaic Age, Phoenician traders brought elaborately decorated linens from Egypt to Greece. Flax was grown in Elis and on the island of Amorgos. Amorgian linen was made into diaphanous, gauze-like material. In Aristophanes's comedy *Lysistrata*, the women are advised to captivate men by appearing "naked" in their Amorgian *chitōnes* (inner garments; see CLOTHING).

In the Hellenistic era, the Ptolemies improved their stock of wool-bearing sheep. Ptolemy II imported Arabian sheep, and the finance minister Apollonius imported a flock of Milesian sheep. They also organized weaving factories staffed by large crews of women. A Zenon papyrus (P. Cairo 59295) contains the following list: "Women working wool according to the declaration of the year 35: At Mouchi 320, at Oxyrhynchus 314, Tebtynis 150, total 784" (Edgar, 2:161).

Alexander introduced cotton (*karpasos*) to the West. The Macedonian soldiers made use of cotton: "From this wool, Nearchus says, finely threaded cloths are woven, and the Macedonians use them for pillows and padding for their saddles" (Str. *Geogr.* 15.1.20). Theophrastus, a disciple of Aristotle and the founder of botany, noted, "They say that the island [Tylos = Bahrain] also produces the 'wool-bearing' tree (cotton-plant) in abundance" (*Hist. plant.* 4.7.7–8). Cotton (Lat. *carbasus*) was introduced to Italy ca. 190 BC.

Chinese silk became known to the Mediterranean area in the late Hellenistic age, though a form of silk was known somewhat earlier. Aristotle was familiar with the silk derived from the wild moth, known as tussah, that was imported from India. He reported, "Some of the women actually unwind the cocoons from these creatures, by reeling the thread off, and then weave a fabric from it" (*Hist. an.* 5.19). This "wild" silk came from the island of Cos and was used to produce "Coan fabric."

In China the secret of silk was discovered, according to legend, in 2640 BC when a cocoon fell into an empress's cup of hot tea. The earliest silk fragment comes from China and dates to ca. 2300 BC. Silk is an amazingly strong and beautiful fiber. It feels cool to the skin and is easily dyed. It became prized as the luxury of luxuries. True silk was derived from the Chinese moth (*Bombyx mori*). Its caterpillar fed only on mulberry leaves, then enveloped itself in a cocoon made of a double filament extruded from a gland on its lower lip. The cocoon was dipped in boiling water to kill the grub and soften the sericin gum. Then young girls reeled as much as a thousand yards of silk fiber from a single cocoon.

Sericulture (the production of silk) in China was a closely guarded state secret, with the penalty of death imposed on anyone exporting silkworms or mulberry seeds. Raw silk was brought to Tyre and Berytus by Persian merchants, and there silk threads were dyed and interwoven with linen. Interwoven silk garments were called *serisērika*; pure silk garments were known as *holosērika*.

In the West, the earliest evidence of silk is found in princely burials of the Hallstatt culture in southern Germany (6th c. BC). Silk has also been preserved in the Kerameikos cemetery in Athens (5th c. BC). The silk trade developed only in the second century BC, when a Chinese emperor of the Han Dynasty fortified a caravan route, "the Silk Road," to the Persian/Bactrian (Afghanistan) frontier. Silk also went by sea from the west coast of India to Alexandria.

Rome

From Pliny the Elder's *Natural History* (8.190–197) it is evident that the Romans were familiar with wool (*lana*) in different colors, including white fleece from Italy, black fleece from Spain, and golden-red fleece from Asia Minor. Some of the best wool came from Tarentum in Apulia in southern Italy. According to Varro, "The treatment is, in general, the same in the case of jacketed sheep—those which, on account of the excellence of the wool, are jacketed with skins . . . to prevent the fleece from being soiled, in which case it cannot be so well dyed, or washed and bleached" (*Rust.* 2.2.18).

Among the Italians sheep were initially plucked. Iron shears reached Rome ca. 300 BC. The root of the soapwort plant (*Saponaria officinalis*) was employed to clean the wool. Wool was then "carded," a word derived from Latin *carduus* ("thistle"), which refers to the thistle heads used in the process of loosening the tangled wool fibers. Wool was dyed before spinning. Tyrian double-dyed wool, which first appeared in 63 BC, fetched one thousand denarii a pound (a denarius was a day's wage).

Matrons, servants, and special spinning girls known as *quasillariae* performed the task of spinning wool into thread. In Rome, as in Greece, the standard loom was warp-weighted, with the weavers working from the top down. It was not until the first century AD that the two-beamed or tubular loom was introduced into the Roman world. This allowed the weavers to sit and work from the bottom up, which made possible the production of a continuous tube of cloth.

According to Suetonius, Augustus wore simple clothing: "Except on special occasions he wore common clothes for the house, made by his sister, wife, daughter or granddaughters" (*Aug.* 71). Columella later complained,

> Nowadays, however, . . . most women so abandon themselves to luxury and idleness that they do not deign to undertake even the superintendence of wool-making and there is a distaste for home-made garments and their perverse desire can only be satisfied by clothing purchased for large sums and almost the whole of their husband's income. (*Rust.* 12, preface, 9)

In Roman society, wool-work was viewed as a symbol of the virtuous matron. In the wedding ceremony, the bride or her attendant carried a distaff and a spindle. The loom was placed in the atrium, where visitors could view the matron of the house weaving. Livy relates the tale of Lucretia, who was judged the most virtuous of the wives, for the officers found that "it was already late at night, but there, in the hall of her house, surrounded by her busy maid-servants, she was still hard at work by lamplight upon her spinning" (*Rom. Hist.* 1.57–58).

Among the highest compliments a husband could pay to his deceased wife was that she had been dutiful in working with wool. One epitaph reads: "She managed the household well. She spun wool (*lanam fecit*).—I have spoken. Go on your way" (*CIL* 1.2.1211). Another inscription states: "Why should I mention your personal virtues—your modesty, obedience, affability, and good nature, your tireless attention to wool working" (*CIL* 6.1527). Frequent symbols on the tombstones of wives were the *quasillum* ("wool basket"), *colus* ("distaff"), and *fusus* ("spindle").

The Romans developed factories, called fulleries (such as those recovered at Pompeii), that cleaned, fulled (that is, preshrunk), and sold wool. A wealthy woman named Eumachia erected a large, two-story building that contained offices and storage spaces on the second floor and facilities for the auction of wool. The establishment of M. Vecilius Verecundus at Pompeii, as the frescoes show, prepared and sold objects of wool and felt. In shops such as those of Verecundus, wool was placed on frames and whitened by the use of sulfur fumes. The weavers lived together in the eleventh district of the city. A screw cloth press has been recovered at Herculaneum.

Pliny devotes a long passage in his *Natural History* to extolling the qualities of flax (*Nat.* 19.1–25). Linen was used for sails and for awnings over theaters and amphitheaters. By the first century AD, linen underwear had replaced woolens. As only a limited amount of linen was produced in Italy itself, during the Empire most linen was imported from Egypt, Cilicia, and Syria.

During the period of the Roman Empire, silk, though still very expensive, was brought west in increasing amounts. In AD 97 Chinese ambassadors were sent west, and in AD 166 Roman merchants reached China. Pure silk garments were quite revealing and scandalous. Seneca praised his mother for never wearing such a garment: "I see clothing of silk [*serica*], if that can be called clothing, which provides nothing that could possibly afford protection for the body, or indeed modesty, so that, when a woman wears it, she can scarcely, with a clear conscience, swear that she is not naked" (*Helv.* 16.4). Lucan credited a silk garment with the seduction of Caesar, as Cleopatra appeared with "her white breasts . . . revealed by the fabric of Sidon, which, close-woven by the shuttle of the Seres, the Egyptian needle-worker pulls out, and loosens the thread by stretching the stuff" (*De bello civili*, 10.141).

Under Tiberius it was decided "that Oriental silks should no longer degrade the male sex" (Tac. *Ann.* 2.33.1). Later, the effete emperor Elagabalus from Syria, who was homosexual, disgraced himself (especially in the eyes of the praetorian guard) by wearing a garment of pure silk (*S.H.A. Elagabalus* 26.1). Other extravagant emperors, such as Nero, wore clothes woven with gold (Suet. *Nero* 6.50). Commodus had "clothes of silk woven with gold thread of remarkable workmanship" (*S.H.A. Pertinax* 8.2–4). Marcus Aurelius raised money for his war efforts on the Danube by selling "his wife's silk and gold clothes" (*S.H.A. Marcus Aurelius* 17.4).

E. THE JEWISH WORLD

In a comprehensive listing of 1727 textiles recovered from Israel from the Roman era (1st c. BC to 3rd c. AD), 60 percent were woolen, 35 percent linen, a very few were made of goat's hair, and even fewer were made of camel hair. "Cotton textiles from the Roman period were not found in the Land of Israel. Silk from the Roman period was not found in the textiles of the Land of Israel, although silk is mentioned in Talmudic sources" (Shamir and Sukenik, 214).

The important study by Shamir and Sukenik has established a notable distinction between the textiles used by the sectarian community at Qumran and other Jews. It can now be shown that all of the textiles found at various sites around Qumran (Cave 1, Cave 8, Cave 11) were exclusively of undecorated, white linen in contrast to the decorated garments of wool worn by the rest of the Jewish population. Some of the linen scroll wrappers were decorated with blue lines.

The multicolored textiles discovered in the "Christmas Cave" located south of Khirbet Qumran, so called because it was discovered by John Marco Allegro on Christmas Day, 1960, were wrongly classified as "Qumran" textiles by the Rockefeller Museum. They came instead from a cave used by Jewish refugees during the Bar Kochba Revolt.

At Masada an embroidered wrapper of blue wool was recovered, as well as remains of woolen tunics that had bands of many colors. A unique linen sock was also found. The most extensive find of textiles came from the Cave of Letters, located in a cliff on the western shore of the Dead Sea, where Jewish rebels attempted in vain to hide from the Romans in AD 135. Among the objects discovered were spindle whorls, skeins of yarn, and woolen textiles in thirty-four colors.

Also discovered in the Cave of Letters were tunics, most of which had been torn apart to be used as shrouds. At a first-century AD cemetery at Khirbet Qazone in Jordan, some of the dead still had such reused textiles wrapped around them. In a contemporary tomb in the Ben Hinnom Valley, the remains of a shroud with a Z-spin indicate that it was imported from Greece or Italy. (See Yadin.)

The Talmud refers to the practice of placing jackets over certain sheep (*kbrnrt*) to produce a whiter and softer wool known as *mylt*. Plucking (*tlš*) of wool from the sheep was allowed on the Sabbath, but not shearing (*gzz*), as this would require the use of implements (*y. Šabb.* 10c).

According to the Mishnah, one of the duties a husband required of his wife was to work in wool. "These are the works which the wife must perform for her husband: ... working in wool. ... R. Eliezer says: Even if she brought him in a hundred bondwomen he should compel her to work in wool, for idleness leads to unchastity" (*m. Ketub.* 5:5). Married women were required to spin indoors and not where their arms could be seen, which was considered grounds for divorce (*m. Ketub.* 7:6). The home-woven linen of the women of Galilee remained theirs after a divorce.

In Mesopotamia, some Jewish men were engaged in spinning (Jos. *Ant.* 18.314). But in Jerusalem, at least, the status of male weavers was despised: "And is it not so that you have no more degraded craft than weaving?" (*t. ʿEd.* 1:3). They were under suspicion as they had frequent contact with women (*t. Qidd.* 5:14; *b. Qidd.* 82a). The wool merchants had their own district (*m. ʿErub.* 10:9; Jos. *J.W.* 5.331), which was the worst section of Jerusalem. Weavers wore a tuft of wool behind their ears as a badge and had their own place in the synagogue at Alexandria.

The village of Kefar Namra was said to have three hundred weaving shops. The villages of Sarepta (Zarephath), Neapolis, Lydda, and Arbela in Galilee were known as centers of weaving. Beth-Shan (Scythopolis) became famous for the fine quality of its linens, so much so that Clement of Alexandria lamented that they were favored over native Egyptian linen.

The use of silk is illustrated by an incident reported in the Babylonian Talmud:

> R. Huna once came before Rab girded with a string. He said to him, "What is the meaning of this?" He replied, "I had no [wine for] sanctification, and I pledged my girdle so as to get some." He said, "May it be the will of heaven that you be [one day] smothered in robes of silk." At the wedding of his son, his daughters and daughters-in-law stripped [clothes] from themselves and threw them on him until he was smothered in silks. (*b. Meg.* 27b)

Philo of Alexandria commented: "The high priest is bidden to put on a similar dress when he enters the inner shrine to offer incense, because its fine linen is not, like wool, the product of creatures subject to death" (*Spec.* 1.84). He further observed that the high priest "puts on another one of linen made from the purest kind . . . , a figure of strong fibre, imperishable-ness, most radiant light" (*Somn.* 1.216–217).

F. THE CHRISTIAN WORLD

It is in the dry climate of Egypt that textiles from the Christian era have been best preserved. Cotton cultivation was introduced from Nubia into Upper Egypt during the Coptic period. Cotton fabric has been recovered from the fourth-century Monastery of Apa Phoebammon. Loom pits have been found in Nubia (4th c. AD), including eight that have been recovered from the Monastery of Epiphanius near Thebes (ca. AD 475–600).

Coptic textiles are divided into three periods: (1) a pre-Coptic phase (before Constantine's conversion in AD 312); (2) the proto-Coptic phase (late 3rd and 4th c. AD); and (3) the High Coptic phase (5th–7th c. AD). In the earlier phases, decorative motifs came from Egyptian mythology and nature. In the last phase symbols like the cross and the fish appeared, and then episodes from the OT and the NT. Coptic Christians also made large wall hangings for their churches that featured Mary as the Theotokos (mother of God; lit. "God-bearer"), drawing the rebuke of the iconoclastic bishop Epiphanius of Salamis (ca. AD 393).

Diocletian's Edict of Prices (AD 301) indicates that purple wool was worth its weight in gold and that purple silk was worth three times its weight in gold. It was not until two monks smuggled silkworm eggs to Byzantium in AD 552 that sericulture was established in the West. According to Procopius,

> About the same time certain monks arrived from the country of the Indians. . . . they had lived, they said, a long time in the country where there were many nations of the Indians, and which goes by the name SERINDA (i.e., western China). When there they had made themselves thoroughly acquainted with the way in which silk might be produced in the Roman territory. . . . they went back again to India and brought a supply of the eggs to Byzantium. Having treated them just as they had said, they succeeded in developing the caterpillars, which they fed upon the mulberry leaves. From this beginning originated the establishment of silk-culture in the Roman territory.
>   (J. Havry, *Procopius, De Bello Gothico*, 4.17; cited in Muthesis, 20)

In his letter to Fabiola, Jerome, commenting on the priestly garments (*Ep.* 64), associates wool garments with earth and death and states that linen is a garment of life. Augustine, commenting in his Sermon 37 on the references to wool and linen in Prov 31:13, was influenced by the fashion of his day, in which undergarments were made of linen and outer garments of wool. For him the exterior, woolen garment represented that which was carnal, whereas the internal, linen garment represented that which was spiritual.

Cyril of Alexandria (d. AD 444) also made the same contrast (commenting on Exod 28:42):

> Now the linen placed upon the parts of the body about the thighs intimates that the cooling of the pleasures of the flesh is most becoming holy men: for linen is cool. . . . But that which is taken from something mortal (I mean from a sheep) is a symbol of a state of death. To be clothed, therefore, in garments of linen, instead of wool, typifies the putting aside of dead works.
> (*Ep.* 64.19; cited in Burghardt, 484)

The so-called Shroud of Turin cannot be authentic, as it is made of linen in a herringbone twill, with thread that was Z-spun. Thread in Palestine was S-spun.

BIBLIOGRAPHY: W. al-Jadir, "Le métier des tisserands à l'époque assyrienne, filage et tissage," *Sumer* 28 (1972), 53–74; E. J. W. Barber, *Prehistoric Textiles* (1993); R. Batigne and L. Bellinger, *The Significance and Technical Analysis of Ancient Textiles as Historical Documents* (1953); H. Baumgarten, *Die textilen Rohstoffe und ihre Verarbeitung* (1950); C. Bier, "Textile Arts in Ancient Western Asia," *CANE* 3.1567–88; W. J. Burghardt, "Cyril of Alexandria on 'Wool and Linen,'" *Traditio* 2 (1944), 484–86; B. Burke, *From Minos to Midas: Ancient Cloth Production in the Aegean and in Anatolia* (2010); M. E. Burkett, "An Early Date for the Origin of Felt," *AnSt* 27 (1977), 111–15; C. M. Carmichael, "Forbidden Mixtures," *VT* 32 (1982), 394–415; D. Cassuto, "Textile Production, Bronze and Iron Age," *OEBA* II.425–29; L. S. Clark, *Textiles and Textile Manufacturing in Ancient Greece* (1984); C. C. Edgar, ed., *The Zenon Papyri* (4 vols.; 1971); R. J. Forbes, *Studies in Ancient Technology IV*: Fibres and Fabrics of Antiquity (1964); A. Geijer, *A History of Textile Art* (1979); C. Gillis and M.-L. B. Nosch, ed., *Ancient Textiles: Production, Craft and Society* (2003); M. Gleba and J. Pásztókai-Szeoke, ed., *Making Textiles in pre-Roman and Roman Times* (2013); R. Hall, *Egyptian Textiles* (1986); N. R. Hollen and J. Saddler, *Textiles* (1955); P. Horn, "Textiles in Biblical Times," *Ciba Review* 2 (1968), 1–37; A. Hurvitz, "The Usage of שׁשׁ and בוץ in the Bible and Its Implication for the Date of P," *HTR* 60 (1967), 117–21; A. H. M. Jones, "The Cloth Industry under the Roman Empire," in *The Roman Economy*, ed. P. A. Brunt (1974), 350–64; L. B. Jørgensen, "A Matter of Material: Changes in Textiles from Roman Sites in Egypt's Eastern Desert," *Antiquité Tardive* 12 (2004), 87–99; S. N. Kramer, *The Sacred Marriage Rite: Aspects of Faith, Myth, and Ritual in Ancient*

Sumer (1969); H. F. Lutz, *Textiles and Costumes among the Peoples of the Ancient Near East* (1923); H. Maguire, "Garments Pleasing to God: The Significance of Domestic Textile Designs in the Early Byzantine Period," *DOP* 44 (1990), 215–24; P. Mayerson, "The Role of Flax in Roman and Fatimid Egypt," *JNES* 56 (1997), 201–7; C. Michel and M. L. Nosch, ed., *Textile Terminologies in the Ancient Near East and Mediterranean from the Third to the First Millennia BC* (2010); L. Milano, "Ebla: A Third-Millennium City-State in Ancient Syria," *CANE* 2.1219–30; W. O. Moeller, *The Wool Trade of Ancient Pompeii* (1976); A. Muthesius, "The Byzantine Silk Industry: Lopez and Beyond," *Journal of Medieval History* 19 (1993), 1–67; M. C. Pantelia, "Spinning and Weaving: Ideas of Domestic Order in Homer," *AJP* 114 (1993), 493–501; F. E. Petzel, *Textiles of Ancient Mesopotamia, Persia, and Egypt* (1987); E. Riefstahl, *Patterned Textiles in Pharaonic Egypt* (1944); C. Rogers et al., *Ancient Coptic Textiles* (1979); P. W. Rogers, L. B. Jørgensen, and A. Rast-Eicher, ed., *The Roman Textile Industry and Its Influence* (2001); H. L. Roth, *Ancient Egyptian and Greek Looms* (2nd ed., 1951); K. S. Rubinson, "The Textiles from Pazyryk," *Exped* 32.1 (1990), 49–61; T. Schick, *The Cave of the Warrior: A Fourth Millennium Burial in the Judean Desert* (1998); T. Schick, "Cordage, Basketry and Fabrics," in *Naḥal Ḥemar Cave*, ed. O. Bar-Yosef and D. Alon ('Atiqot 18; 1988), 31–43; O. Shamir and N. Sukenik, "Qumran Textiles and the Garments of Qumran's Inhabitants," *DSD* 18 (2011), 206–25; A. Sheffer, "Needlework and Sewing in Israel from Prehistoric Times to the Roman Period," in *Fortunate the Eyes That See*, ed. A. B. Beck et al. (1995), 527–59; G. Vogelsang-Eastwood, *Patterns for Ancient Egyptian Clothing* (1992); G. Vogelsang-Eastwood, "Textiles," in *Ancient Egyptian Materials and Technology*, ed. P. T. Nicholson and I. Shaw (2000), 268–98; J. M. Wade and G. L. Mattingly, "Ancient Weavers at Iron Age Mudaybiʿ," *NEA* 66.1–2 (2003), 73–75; D. B. Weisberg, "Wool and Linen Material in Texts from the Time of Nebuchadnezzar," *ErIsr* 16 (1982), *218–26; Y. Yadin, *Bar-Kokhba* (1971).

RKH and EMY

See also ANIMAL HUSBANDRY, CLOTHING, DYEING, LAUNDRY & FULLERS, and TRADE.

THRESHING & WINNOWING

Threshing and winnowing are activities employed in the processing of harvested grain crops. These two processes, the first employing friction and the second employing wind, are used to separate edible grains from the inedible parts of the grassy plants upon which they grow. In antiquity many different grains were cultivated, but varieties of barley and wheat were the most common. Grain heads are comprised of a fibrous stem upon which rows of florets blossom and ears subsequently develop. The growing ears have husks and beards that envelop and protect the kernel. When grasses mature, the plants dry and become brittle. Domesticated grains typically have stems that are less brittle than wild varieties, and their heads hold together better than wild varieties. This quality contributes to greater crop yields as fewer seeds fall to the ground when they are handled. In some species, such as einkorn, emmer, and spelt, the kernels are described as being "hulled" since their tougher husks are difficult to remove; other varieties, like durum wheat, are described as "free-threshing" or "naked" since they are easily separated from their husks. Threshing processes break spikelets of grain from tough stems and remove husks from the seeds. Winnowing processes then take threshed material and separate the seeds of grain from the leaves, stalks, stems, beards, and husks of the plants, as well as any contaminating dust, pebbles, or insects. These processes, well known to ancient people who depended on agriculture, provided metaphors to which they could relate.

A. THE OLD TESTAMENT

Sweat equity is seen as the norm for food acquisition from the time of the fall in the antediluvian period (Gen 3:17–19). Grain processing through threshing and winnowing was labor intensive. The biblical text first mentions grain crops in its account of the patriarchal period (ca. 2150–1850 BC). Harvesting of grains was a significant family activity of Jacob in

Aram-Naharaim (Gen 30:14) and in Canaan (Gen 37:7). From early on, the Hebrews pulled plants out by hand, or cut them low with flint-edged sickles, and gathered them in bound sheaves (ʾălummîm). Shocking (the process of stacking several sheaves upright to dry) indicates that the grain was picked green so as to reduce grain loss. This strategy produced more work when removing straw at the threshing floor (gōren).

The determination that Canaanean blades were employed in the bottom of wooden threshing sledges that were dragged over piles of grain crops heaped on threshing floors confirms the early utilization of these devices throughout the Levant. An early second-millennium BC Sumerian text suggests the possibility of such patriarchal-era threshing sledges. Later, Isaiah alludes to such a sledge: "See, I will make you into a threshing sledge, new and sharp, with many teeth. You will thresh the mountains and crush them, and reduce the hills to chaff" (Isa 41:15). When Jacob's sons and an Egyptian entourage take his body back to Canaan for burial, they mourn for a week at a threshing floor near the frontier at Atad, which came to be known as Abel-Mizraim (Gen 50:10–11).

Grain production and processing is a central part of the background of the sojourn in Egypt (ca. 1850–1450 BC) in the Bible. Threshing and winnowing would have been one of the varieties of hard labor that the Hebrew foreigners were compelled to perform alongside brick-making for which the chaff and straw, by-products of grain processing, were utilized (Exod 5:7). The Mosaic Law associated with the wilderness wanderings anticipates Israelite settlement in the grain-producing land of Canaan, where they would give offerings of the firstfruits of their threshing floors (Num 15:20).

During the period of the judges (ca. 1400–1050 BC), the Israelite tribes engaged in grain production in Canaan. Gideon is introduced as furtively beating out (ḥābaṭ) wheat at a winepress to keep the food from Midianite marauders (Judg 6:11). He probably performed his small-scale threshing operation with a stick. Later, at an open-air threshing floor used as a rallying point, Gideon twice spreads a fleece in order to seek divine reassurance based upon unusual dewfall patterns (Judg 6:36–40). The story of Ruth, which takes place in Bethlehem during the period of the judges, shows the Mosaic system of social justice at work as she gleans and threshes barley from Boaz's fields (Ruth 2:17). She accomplishes her small-scale threshing operation, like Gideon, by beating (ḥābaṭ) grain heads with a stick.

In early Israelite grain production, the stalks of grain were cut in handfuls at the base of plants using flint-edged sickles. Laborers gathered the handfuls of stalks with the heads still attached, which the reapers placed on the ground, tying them together in sheaves. The binders stood the sheaves in the field for further drying until they could be transported to the threshing floor. Threshing floors had a circular shape that allowed tethered animals to move about in a circle while harvested material was placed in their path. At the threshing floor, this material was kept dry and was processed when the urgency of harvesting passed.

When the possibility of gleaning diminishes with the conclusion of the grain-harvesting season, Naomi instructs Ruth how to make her approach to Boaz, who is winnowing barley at the threshing floor in the late afternoon and evening (Ruth 3:1–5). In the hill country of Judah, land and sea breezes blew predictably in the late spring and early summer, at the time of the grain harvest. The method of threshing the harvested material is not mentioned. The people of the tribe of Judah would have employed the hooves of draft animals and flails to break the ears or spikelets from the heads and to knock the hulls from the kernels. In Boaz's winnowing (*zārâ*; Ruth 3:2), threshed material was lofted into the predictably moving air, which blew the broken hulls and other pieces of chaff downwind while the heavier grain fell nearby (cf. Ps 1:4). After finishing the task and seeing the harvest Boaz would have celebrated with his coworkers. In order to guard his interests, the fatigued Boaz sleeps on his pile of body-conforming barleycorns, but he is awakened by Ruth's advance (Ruth 3:7). Boaz's response indicates that he wants Ruth's proposal to remain a secret until he has resolved the potential issue with a kinsman or because reputable women did not stay at night at threshing floors (Ruth 3:14).

Israelite threshing floors located at elevated locations open to the wind were often strategic positions and meeting places. Sometimes threshing floors were located in the open area adjacent to city gates and served as venues for rulers to hold court. This was an old Canaanite custom, attested in Ugaritic texts (*Aqhat* i 5.6–8; iii 1.23–25; *ANET*, 149–55), that continued for centuries (1 Kgs 22:10). The most prominent example of a threshing floor taking on a greater significance is the threshing floor of Araunah at Jebus (Jerusalem), which King David purchases and establishes as the location for a national worship center with an altar (1 Chr 21:18). When David proposes the purchase, Araunah offers his threshing sleds (sing. *môrag*) as fuel and his draft animals as sacrifices (1 Chr 21:23). In texts relating to the period of the united monarchy (1050–930 BC), references to threshing sledges and threshing carts (sing. *ʿăgālâ*) increase.

The Gezer Calendar (10th c. BC) points to April as the month of the barley harvest and May as the month of the wheat harvest and measuring once the grains were processed. Israelites understood along threshing season that lasted until the grape harvest to be a sign of divine approval (Lev 26:5). Weighted threshing sledges pulled by animals and carrying drivers crushed piles of grain. The wheels of threshing carts and teeth of sledges broke the hard stems and crushed the hulls of grains against the floor. Proverbs 20:26 instructs wise kings to winnow out the wicked and crush them with the threshing wheel. Prophetic writers embraced the processes of threshing and winnowing as metaphors both for divine judgment against unfaithful Israelites (Isa 21:10) and for the condemnation of their enemies (Jer 51:2; Mic 4:12–13; Hab 3:12).

During the early divided monarchy, as iron became abundant, the prophet Amos condemned the Arameans of Damascus for having threshed Gilead with iron-toothed sledges (Amos 1:3). While chert flakes, which provided sharp edges, were available in lands rich with limestone, such as the kingdoms of Judah and Israel, iron was useful for making teeth because pieces of recycled iron were more easily driven into the wooden planks of threshing sledges. Amos later refers to the shaking and sifting of grain through a uniform-gauge sieve (*kĕbārâ*) as a part of the winnowing process that the people of the kingdom of Israel would experience (Amos 9:9). This process was long employed in Canaan and is seen in the religious texts of Ugarit (*Baal and Anat*, Tablet H, I AB 2.33; *ANET*, 129–42). In this primary winnowing process, the desired grains would fall through the grid as the sieve was shaken side to side, leaving straw and larger pebbles that might look like cereal grains in the sifter. As grains fell through, some of the remaining hulls were also loosened and blown away before the grain fell into a container below. One of the injustices that Amos condemns is the sale of sweepings with the wheat instead of a pure winnowed product (Amos 8:6). Obtaining a pure product required a secondary winnowing with a fine sieve that allowed the material smaller than a grain kernel to shake out. This left the remaining grains for winnowers to inspect, which would produce a high-quality product.

In the period of Assyrian dominance, prophets considered that oppressing nation to be the "rod of my [God's] anger" (Isa 10:5). While wooden rods could be walking sticks that could serve as weapons, they could also be employed in threshing. Such wooden sticks were used to thresh cumin and caraway since, in these cases, toothed sledges and crushing-wheels were too hard on the spicy seeds and would release their aromatic oils (Isa 28:27). The impact of single-piece wooden rods depended upon their length and diameter and the velocity with which they were used. Two-piece rods joined by a leather thong or chain offered the benefit of increased velocity while reducing the impact on the joints of the worker. Like Isaiah, Hosea predicted the Assyrian domination of the kingdom of Israel. He describes the tribe of Ephraim as a trained heifer that had previously enjoyed the task of trampling out grain but which would soon be put to the more onerous task of plowing (Hos 10:11). Trampling out grain was a preferred task for cattle because they did not have to bear a heavy yoke, and they could eat some of the grain if they were not muzzled, which was a Mosaic commandment (Deut 25:4). Tined implements (sing. *mizrê*) and shovels (sing. *raḥat*) for winnowing were known earlier in the biblical period, but they are rarely mentioned in prophetic texts (Isa 30:24; Jer 15:7).

The OT writers were aware of contemporaneous developments in threshing and winnowing techniques and equipment. When the hard work of processing grain was completed, the Israelites celebrated. The Torah established the Feast of Unleavened Bread in conjunction with Passover. At this time of year, farmers took the first sheaf of their barley harvest to the priests as a wave offering, prior to their consumption of any parched grain or bread made from the new crop (Lev 23:10–11). The next pilgrimage festival, the Feast of Weeks, took place fifty days later and coincided with the main wheat harvest (Exod 23:16). Observant worshippers of Yahweh regularly brought the produce of their threshing and winnowing, after it had been ground into flour, to their religious center to present it as a grain offering, and bread was prepared weekly for the Holy Place (Lev 2:1–10; 24:5–9).

B. THE NEW TESTAMENT

The NT texts continue to assume readers' familiarity with the processes of threshing and winnowing, using them as a metaphor for judgment. John the Baptist uses the images of the winnowing fork/shovel (*ptyon*) and the practice of clearing threshing floors (sing. *halōn*) and burning chaff to preach the coming judgment of the Messiah, in which a separation would be made between the righteous and the wicked (Matt 3:12; Luke 3:17). The sweeping of threshing floors is a possible reflection of Jewish fastidiousness in maintaining an unmixed product, especially given that animals used for threshing often dropped foreign matter on the floor. Jesus alludes frequently to the harvest, including in a scene in his Parable of the Weeds (Matt 13:24–30) in which there is separation of contaminating materials (weeds) from the desired harvest (wheat). But Jesus does not expound on the threshing or winnowing processes in further accounts of his preaching. He addresses Peter, the small-town Galilean, with both warning and reassurance as he tells him in the Upper Room that Satan has wanted "to sift all of you [pl.] as wheat" (Luke 22:31), but that he has prayed for Peter's faith and future leadership (Luke 22:31–32). This shaking in a sieve was an exacting, final winnowing process that occurred before small batches of grains would be ground into flour.

The Apostle Paul, whose ministry was focused on urban settings, speaks in terms meaningful to his audiences, using imagery from the realm of sports, for example, rather than that of grain processing. He does, however, refer to threshing and the benefits of participants in harvests (1 Cor 9:8–11; 1 Tim 5:17–18) when addressing congregations and individuals familiar with the Torah (Deut 25:4), in order to argue for the appropriateness of paying Christian workers.

C. THE NEAR EASTERN WORLD

Grains were a key source of calories in ancient Egypt, Mesopotamia, and Anatolia. Effective grain cultivation, processing, and preservation were crucial for the early development of urbanization and craft specialization. Well-processed grains could be preserved better, were more easily ground into flour, and damaged fewer teeth.

Mesopotamia

Material remains and cuneiform texts testify to the processes by which grain was processed in Mesopotamia. A fragment of a cylinder seal from the Early Bronze age site Malatya in Eastern Anatolia provides the earliest depiction of a threshing sledge. Through microscopic analysis, heavy Canaanean blades have been determined to have been employed as teeth in threshing sledges. Ancient Near Eastern texts include a mid-second-millennium BC "Farmer's Almanac." This Sumerian text concludes with directions for the threshing and winnowing of grains that took place in April and May and that employed advanced techniques. In conjunction with the specified techniques, the text calls for ritual prayers at key stages in the process. The ripened harvested material, which was processed in bulk, was cut by reapers, tied into sheaves by binders, collected by other workers into shocks, and then transported to prepared threshing floors. First, wagon wheels and draft animals trampled down the mountains of harvested material. Second, workers employed threshing sledges that further "opened" the grains. These processes left a heap of still-hulled grains. The hulled grains received a second threshing, being beaten with sticks to remove husks. The grain was then winnowed in the wind and the husk-free grain moved in baskets to storage (*Sumerian Farmer's Almanac* 87–109).

Early Sumerian Laws show that reapers were valued twice as much as winnowers, whose work was less time sensitive (CE 7–9). Hittite laws produced about a millennium later show that, in that culture, reapers, threshers, and winnowers were paid equivalent wages, but women were paid significantly less than their male co-workers who had the same roles (*Hittite Laws*, 158). The Old Babylonian laws of Hammurabi attest to the fact that beyond human laborers, goats, donkeys, and oxen were hired at the ratio of 1:10:20—rates reflective of their perceived contribution to the threshing process (CH, 268–270).

The later dominant civilizations of Neo-Assyria, Neo-Babylonia, and Persia made no significant additions to grain-processing techniques other than using an increased amount of iron. The cultivation of free-threshing species of grain reduced the efforts required for this process. The Neo-Assyrian conqueror Tiglath-Pileser III knew of the metal-toothed threshing sledge and used the image of this machine's capacity to crush and tear apart grain heads to describe the effect of his army on Chaldean opponents in a manner reminiscent of Amos 1:3.

Egypt

Large-scale grain production and processing was key to establishing a large population and pharaonic power. Reliefs of harvesting scenes from the Old Kingdom mastaba tombs of Ty and Mererukaat Saqqara depict males with sickles cutting handfuls of cereal crops at mid-stalk to form sheaves. As a result of this process, considerable straw removal was a part of threshing operations. It appears that in early Egypt there was no market for long straw. In pharaonic Egypt, hulled barley and emmer were the primary grain crops. At circular threshing floors, animals were driven over harvested materials to separate the spikelets of emmer and hulled barley kernels from the heads. Egyptians of the pharaonic period did not use the threshing sledge. Spikelets of emmer and hulled barley that had been trampled out could be stored in their husks. After primary winnowing using the wind and coarse sieves to remove straw, these crops required secondary threshing and winnowing operations. The partially processed crops were beaten with flails, winnowed again, and then sieved using fine sieves that retained the kernels while letting the chaff and dust fall away. Models of granaries found in tombs from the Middle Kingdom (1980–1760 BC) show that grain processing and storage was closely supervised. Contaminated and wet grain from the threshing floor could ruin the grain in a silo.

The tombs of Menna, Nakht, and Sennedjem at Thebes provide vivid images of threshing and winnowing as practiced in the New Kingdom (1540–1075 BC). The grain was cut in the upper stalk, near the head, using sickles, which left little for the gleaners. Laborers carried the harvested material in large hampers to the threshing floors. At the floors, workers moved harvested material with three-tined forks to promote drying and to raise unbroken heads to the top as cattle trampled the grain heads. At the end of the threshing process, workers shoveled the threshed material on the floor into a heap. Teams of male laborers using lightweight wooden winnowing fans then winnowed the threshed material. These fans resembled enlarged hands that came together to lift up a portion of grain high into the air. The grain then passed through the gap opened between the two fans and fell to the ground as the chaff blew downwind. These fans helped to make up for inconsistent winds in Egypt. The move in the New Kingdom to harvesting grain crops at the head of the grain may reflect either a greater desire for efficiency at the threshing floor or the increased value the Egyptians of this period placed upon straw. Later Egyptian wisdom literature encourages individuals to be satisfied with the produce of their own fields and threshing floors rather than seek illicitly gained wealth (*Instruction of Amen-em-Opet* 18).

Egyptian civilization adapted to new techniques over time. While under Assyrian political domination, the Egyptians embraced the use of the threshing sledge. As new free-threshing varieties like durum wheat were cultivated in the Ptolemaic period (332–30 BC), the need for secondary threshing diminished. Processed Egyptian grains were essential for the later burgeoning city of Rome.

D. THE GRECO-ROMAN WORLD

Greek and Roman populations, like their Mediterranean neighbors, depended upon grains for much of their caloric intake, which was in the form of breads and fermented drink. It is therefore not surprising that their authors include discussions of processing grain crops in treatises regarding agriculture. The famous Roman Republican Cato, who had risen from humble rural plebian roots through the *cursus honorum* to the highest political offices, wrote his treatise *On Agriculture* in the first half of the second century BC. This text became a standard followed by Marcus Varro, Lucius Columella, and Rutilius Palladius. These texts show that the Romans not only employed grain-processing techniques and equipment like those used by their contemporaries but also introduced a new mechanical implement that reduced the amount of threshing that was required. In his accounting of the labor investment for various crops, Columella does not include the time required for threshing and winnowing (*Agr.* 2.12.1–7). Threshing rates would have varied with the techniques used for harvesting and the kind of crop.

At harvest time, the Greeks and Romans employed significant animal power in their reaping, threshing, and winnowing operations. Draft animals pulled wagons of harvested materials from the fields to threshing locations. At threshing floors, the Greeks and Romans traditionally drove large domesticated animals over piles of harvested material in order to trample grain from the heads. Later, individual animals or yoked teams pulled drags or threshing sleds around threshing floors across the harvested material.

The Greek and Roman cultures saw an evolution in sickle production. Early on, they employed flint-toothed sickles. These sickles had knapped-flint microliths hafted in curved wooden handles. Memory of such jagged flint-edged harvesting equipment is preserved in Hesiod's colorful story of Cronos's revengeful act of castrating his faithless father, Heaven (*Theog.* 160–190). Reaping sickles (sing. *falx messoria*) made with curved metal blades were a standard piece of Roman farm equipment. They generally had longer and thinner blades than pruning hooks used in grape production (see Cato, *Agr.* 11). A whetstone and a horn of oil kept such sickles effectively sharp and served as standard equipment for reapers (Pliny, *Nat.* 18.67.261). Varro observes that some Romans used wooden-handled sickles with serrated iron blades (*Rust.* 1.50), and Columella notes that some sickles worked like combs, cutting away heads (*Rust.* 2.20.3).

Sickles were used to sever the stalks of grain plants in the field. Varro describes three strategies that were employed. The first, practiced by the Umbrians in central Italy, involved grasping and cutting bunches of grain stalks at the base of the plant and placing them on the ground. These bunches were subsequently picked up and the ears were cut off into baskets to be taken to the threshing floor while the straw was collected in the field. The second approach, used in Picenum in eastern Italy, was to cut away handfuls of heads, leaving the tall straw stalks standing, to be cut later and collected as hay or used for thatching roofs. The third technique, used around Rome, was to grab bunches of grain with the left hand and to cut the stalks in the middle, leaving some to be collected later and some material to be worked through at the threshing floor (Varro, *Rust.* 1.50).

In the first century AD, Pliny described the *vallus*, a mechanical harvester (*Nat.* 18.296). This machine, operating on the same principle as a serrated sickle blade, was a low, two-wheeled cart (*carpentum*) pushed by donkeys. The bed of the cart was open at the side opposite the pushing animal. Along the bottom edge of the open side, sharp, triangularly shaped iron blades were set pointing forward and close together. As the donkeys pushed forward, the stalks of grain were concentrated and pushed along the knife edges back to where adjacent blades came together. There the brittle, dry straw was cut or broken, the heads fell back into the hopper created by the cart bed, and the standing straw passed beneath the cart. This device combed out the grain heads. Palladius (4th c. AD) provides a more complete description of such a harvesting *vehiculum* that had an adjustable-height cutting edge (*Rust.* 7.2.2–3). The Roman mechanical harvester was used for centuries and is depicted in several pieces of artwork. The availability of cheap labor, the expense of investment, and low crop yields limited the adoption of this device.

Greek and Roman threshing floors, like those of other cultures, were deliberately constructed with the objective of being as productive as possible. Hesiod (*Op.* 597, 805) describes the early Greek custom of employing rollers to compact smooth threshing floors (*alōē*).

Temporary threshing sites, described by Columella in the first century, did not receive the investment of more permanent sites (*Rust.* 2.19). Varro identifies the ideal locations as elevated places that were open to the wind and well drained. The circular floor of the threshing installation was to be hard, slightly convex, smooth, and free of vegetation. Soil floors were cleared, tamped, and trampled by animals. Stone drums were rolled to achieve optimum compaction and treated with *amurca*, a concentrated by-product of olive oil processing that was perceived to reduce pests. Stone-cobbled and paved floors were installed at long-term facilities. Such superior floors were more efficient and produced a cleaner product. Threshing facilities in northern Italy, where it was more prone to rain, were roofed. In the sunny, hot south of Italy, threshing floors were open to take full advantage of the wind. Adjacent shelters were constructed for laborers to find respite from the midday sun, to protect the product, and for the stationing of security guards (Varro, *Rust.* 1.51).

Threshing sleds, known as *tribula* to the Romans, may have been introduced prior to the third century BC, through contact with either the grain-producing colonists of Magna Graecia or the Carthaginians. The Punic civilization knew of this implement through its Phoenician connections in the Levant. Traditionally, the Romans had used animals to trample grain from plant stalks. Cato, the Roman traditionalist who fought the forces of Hannibal in Italy, appears to have advocated the old ways and does not mention such foreign innovations, but many Romans embraced the new technology. In the first century BC, Varro describes the use of the simple threshing board made of wood with stone or metal teeth inserted on the bottom side and the "Punic Cart." This wheeled cart was a variation of the threshing sled that produced less friction with the ground. It was comprised of a toothed roller rotating on an axle below a small cart weighed down by a seated animal driver. As the animals pulled the cart, the roller below compressed the grain and the teeth chopped the straw and knocked grains from the hulls (*Rust.* 1.52). Columella, in the first century AD, recognized the use of a sled pulled by a draft animal to be the most convenient method of threshing grain, but he preferred that grain be beaten out with flails, which resulted in a cleaner and higher-quality product (*Rust.* 1.20).

The Greeks and Romans typically looked to take advantage of the wind in separating grain from chaff. After the threshing process, the combined mixture of grain and chaff was piled in the middle of the threshing floor. This helped the material to dry and built a stockpile from which wind from any direction could be used. A variety of implements were used to move the harvested material. Wooden winnowing forks with long handles and broad tines made of wood were easy to manufacture and lightweight. Heavier metal-headed forks were more expensive and harder to lift but were more durable. Both metal and wooden forks enabled workers to loft the initially threshed material filled with longer pieces of straw into the air. Winnowers used shovels at the end of the process to scoop up and loft material from the floor, which allowed the wind to blow smaller particulate matter away. Winnowing with forks and shovels was a very dirty process that left workers covered in dust (Hom. *Il.* 5.499–503).

When there was no wind, the Romans employed gravity to separate the edible grains from chaff and contaminants. Small quantities of processed materials were bounced in lightweight sieves woven from reeds, which had holes that permitted dirt and chaff particulates smaller than the size of the grain to fall away when the material was bounced or agitated. Columella recognized that this technique enabled crops to be preserved that might deteriorate if they were left until an appropriately windy day (*Rust.* 2.20.5). Lightweight woven baskets were employed in transferring grain during and after the threshing and winnowing processes. When threshed material was thrown into the air above baskets, the grain would fall into the baskets and the lighter detritus would be blown away from the threshing floor (Varro, *Rust.* 1.52). The processed grain could then be easily reprocessed to achieve an even cleaner product, and it could be transferred to storage receptacles like silos, ceramic jars, and textile bags. Winnowing fans or scoops were specialty baskets woven in an asymmetrical design, with one side of the shallow basket having a sturdy lip but no side. Workers pushed such baskets into piles of threshed material and lifted the contents. They then lofted the material into the air or allowed it to gradually spill out above a catchment vessel.

The Greeks and Romans found grain processing to be sweaty work. But they also found threshing to be most effective when the sun was hot and the heads most brittle. They employed slaves and large numbers of seasonal laborers for this onerous task (Hes. *Op.* 597). They sang songs, such as the "Lityerses Song" to Demeter, as they winnowed (Theocritus, *Id.* 10.41). A convention employed by the Roman army during the Third Macedonian War was to use their sickles to harvest only the heads of wheat, since they had no need of the straw and this made threshing easier (Livy, *Rom. Hist.* 42.64).

E. THE JEWISH WORLD

In the OT Apocrypha, threshing and winnowing continued to be employed in scenes of judgment (Wis 5:23). In a discussion regarding salvation, 2 Esdras compares the relationship that exists between the essential character of the farmer and the product of his threshing floor with the relationship that exists between a righteous person and his deeds (2 Esd 9:17). The book of Sirach, a wisdom composition from the same era, encourages people to maintain their integrity by advising, "Do not winnow with every wind, nor follow every path" (Sir 5:9). Winnowing with shifting winds created contamination and was counterproductive.

The Mishnah promotes fastidiousness in producing uncontaminated crops. Monoculture was the norm, and the same concern for maintaining pure crops was continued at threshing. Observant Jews swept after the barley threshing and before wheat processing. Workers cleared temporary threshing floors in the fields of disparate crops, and weeds prior to threshing (*m. Kil.* 2:5). Potentially contaminated crops were carefully processed. In fields where workers discovered a grave, they took care to keep the grain from that field separate. They double-sieved it to ensure the removal of any bone fragments (*m. ʾOhol.* 18:2).

Jews took great care to keep grain crops from getting wet and becoming more prone to mildew. The rabbis concluded that the practice of sprinkling threshing floors to allay dust did not involve enough water to constitute a defiling of the grain, which might absorb some moisture as a result (*m. Makš.* 3:5). Another area of possible ritual contamination concerned broken and contaminated tools. The rabbis determined that workers could use and repair wooden winnowing forks that had lost a wooden tine but that they could not continue to use tools with broken metal tines (*m. Kelim* 13:7; 15:5; *m. Ṭ. Yom* 4:6). Worn-out woven basketry employed in winnowing and transporting grain (*m. Kelim* 16:3) and leather gloves used to protect the hands of winnowers as they worked in granaries could also become sources of defilement for the grain (*m. Kelim* 16:6).

The pentateuchal directive that draft animals should not be prevented from eating from the grain that they were employed in threshing was discussed frequently by the rabbis and their contemporaries (Jos. *Ant.* 4.233; Philo, *Virt.* 125–127; *m. Ter.* 9:3, *m. B. Qam.* 5:7). Discouraging animals from eating by putting a thorn in their mouths, for example, or by distracting them was equated by the rabbis with muzzling (*b. B. Meṣ.* 90), which is prohibited by the Torah. The Talmud extrapolates principles underlying this law, which is for animals, and applies them to people. The Jews were concerned to avoid the contamination of their grain by unclean rodents and avoided unclean draft animals, such as the donkey, in threshing operations.

The rabbis developed several laws that related to threshing. In their concern with avoiding contamination, the rabbis specified in the Mishnah that permanent threshing installations had to stand at least fifty cubits from towns and another person's property (*m. B. Bat.* 2:8). The rationale appears to be that this would protect townspeople and their homes from the blowing dust generated by the winnowing process. The use of separate threshing floors for different crops reduced the potential for contamination but multiplied the obligation for wave offerings (*b. Naz.* 56b).

The Mishnah reveals that the Jews of late antiquity continued to bind sheaves in the field for transport to threshing floors. This binding of sheaves reveals that long stalks of straw with heads still attached were still being moved to threshing floors (*m. Pe'ah* 5:7–8). Jewish sheaves were generally uniform in size within a field, but they varied in their production, yielding from one *kab* (a double handful) to two *seahs*, twelve times as much (*m. Pe'ah* 6:1–6). The descriptions of the steps leading from the Court of Women into the Court of Israel (*m. Mid.* 2:5) and of the chamber of the Sanhedrin (*m. Sanh.* 4:3) as being in the shape of "half of a round threshing-floor" indicates that threshing floors continued to be circular installations in which animals walked in a circular pattern while pulling threshing devices.

Talmudic discussion of the threshing sledges (*môriggîm*) offered by Araunah to David (2 Sam 24:22; 1 Chr 21:23) reveals that in later Babylon the Jewish community knew toothed threshing sledges as "turbel beds" and "goats with hooks" (*b. 'Abod. Zar.* 24b; *b. Zebaḥ.* 116b). These are the same devices described in Byzantine literature.

F. THE CHRISTIAN WORLD

The Early Byzantine civilization was rather conservative and adopted few changes in the realm of threshing and winnowing. The Christian world overlapped that of Rome in late antiquity and its clerical writers had little interest in discussing threshing and winnowing unless they related to the explanation of Scripture or served as metaphors in sermons. An example of the latter is found in the following comment by Clement of Alexandria: "We must then often, as in winnowing sieves, shake and toss up this the great mixture of seeds, in order to separate the wheat" (*Strom.* 4. 2). Most references to the subject discuss the Mosaic mandate regarding the muzzling of threshing oxen (Deut 25:4; cf. 1 Cor 9:9; 1 Tim 5:18). Origen, for example, expounds the application of Deut 25:4 in 1 Cor 9:9–10 as follows:

> "Does God take care for oxen? Or says he it altogether for our sakes? For our sakes, no doubt, this is written, that he that ploughs should plough in hope, and he that threshes in hope of partaking of the fruits." By which he manifestly shows that God, who gave the law on our account, i.e., on account of the apostles, says, "You shall not muzzle the mouth of the ox that treads out the grain;" whose care was not for oxen, but for the apostles, who were preaching the Gospel of Christ.
>
> (*Prin.* 2. 4. 2; cf. Chrysostom, *Hom. 1 Cor. 9:9–10; Hom 2 Cor. 7:12*)

John Chrysostom's preaching on Matt 3 reflects the threshing technology of northern Syria known to him when he explains that the saw-toothed wheels of threshing vehicles do not break hard wheat kernels (*Hom. Matt. 3:12*).

The *Geoponika*, a tenth-century compilation of texts on agriculture, stands out among preserved Byzantine literature because of its focus on farming. It discusses the attributes of a good threshing floor and advises that reaped material should be dried at the threshing floor for two days prior to threshing (*Geoponika*, 2.26). Christians used the donkey in their grain-threshing operations, unlike Jews, who considered this animal unclean.

BIBLIOGRAPHY: P. C. Anderson, J. Chabot, and A. van Gijn, "The Functional Riddle of 'Glossy' Canaanean Blades and the Near Eastern Threshing Sledge," *JMA* 17. 1 (2004), 87–130; M. M. Aranov, *The Biblical Threshing-Floor in the Light of the Ancient Near Eastern Evidence: Evolution of an Institution* (1982); O. Borowski, *Agriculture in Iron Age Israel* (1987); L. Cheetham, "Threshing and Winnowing—An Ethnographic Study," *Antiq* 56 (1982),127–30; J. Gray, "The *Goren* at the City Gate: Justice and the Royal Office in the Ugaritic Text 'AQHT," *PEQ* 85 (1953), 118–23; S. Hodel-Hoenes, *Life and Death in Ancient Egypt: Scenes from Private Tombs in New Kingdom Thebes*, trans. D. Warburton (2000); J. W. Humphrey, J. P. Oleson, and A. N. Sherwood, ed., *Greek and Roman Technology: A Sourcebook.* (1998); M. A. Littauer and J. H. Crouwel, "Ceremonial Threshing in the Ancient Near East I: Archaeological Evidence," *Iraq* 52 (1990), 15–19; M. A. Murray, "Cereal Production and Processing," in *Ancient Egyptian Materials and Technology*, ed. P. T. Nicholson and I. Shaw (2000), 505–36; B. D. Shaw, *Bringing in the Sheaves: Economy and Metaphor in the Roman World* (2013); S. Smith, "On the Meaning of Goren," *PEQ* 85 (1953), 42–45; S. Smith, "The Threshing Floor at the City Gate," *PEQ* 78 (1946), 5–14; P. Steinkeller, "Ceremonial Threshing in the Ancient Near East II: Threshing Implements in Ancient Mesopotamia: Cuneiform Sources," *Iraq* 52 (1990), 19–23; K. D. White, *Agricultural Implements of the Roman World* (1967).

RWS and MRW

See also AGRICULTURE and FOOD PRODUCTION.

TIME

Human beings directly experience time only as the present, but their memory of the past and their expectations of the future produce the sensation of time as a continuous flow. Civilizations based on hunting and gathering had little need to mark the passage of time, but when humans began to cultivate crops, they marked the passing of time by the seasons so that they would know when to plant and harvest.

Over the course of history, the need arose to demarcate time into both larger and smaller segments, including eras, centuries, generations, decades, years, seasons, months, weeks, days, watches, hours, and seconds. Only days, months, and years are founded in natural phenomena; the other segmentations of time are inventions of the human mind. Human beings invented calendars, chronologies, and timekeeping devices to track these various segments, and they revised and improved them over time in order to overcome their inherent flaws.

The most immediate and consistent experience of time was the day. Ancient peoples calculated the beginning of the day in different ways, divided it into parts in different segments, and used a variety of terms to describe aspects of time.

A. THE OLD TESTAMENT

The OT uses a variety of terms to describe different aspects of time. The most common Hebrew word for "time" is *ʿēt,* which is used 296 times in the OT. It can refer to a point or period of time, either long or short, and it can indicate an appropriate or suitable time. The Hebrew word *môʿēd,* which is used 223 times, denotes a fixed appointment or designated date. Sometimes, the distinction between *môʿēd* and *ʿēt* is blurred so that they are used synonymously (Jer 8:7; Hos 2:9). *Zĕmān* is used only four times in the Hebrew portions of the OT, but it appears in Aramaic in Ezra and Daniel. Borrowed from Aramaic, this term refers to an appointed time, similar to *môʿēd*. The Hebrew word *ʿōlām*, used 440 times, refers to a long or remote time, in the past or in the future.

The Hebrew word translated "day" is *yôm*, which is the most frequently occurring OT word for a unit of time. In fact, it is the fifth most frequently occurring substantive in the OT. It was used in three ways. First, it referred to the time of daylight, from dawn to dusk, in contrast to night (Gen 1:5, 18; 8:22; Num 11:32). Second, it indicated the return of the sun to the same position in the sky (Gen 7:24; Job 3:6). Third, it described "the period of an action or state of being" (De Vries, 783). For example, the phrase "in the day that" (*bĕyôm*) links two events in time and is usually translated "when" (Gen 2:4; 3:5; 5:1; Lev 14:2; Lam 3:57).

Like the Egyptians, the early Hebrews may have reckoned the civil day from sunrise to sunrise (Gen 19:34; Num 11:32; Judg 19:5–9). There are numerous references in the OT to the order of day and night, but it appears that the Israelites gradually shifted to counting the days from sunset to sunset (Exod 12:18; Lev 23:27, 32; 1 Sam 11:9–11; Ps 55:17; Isa 27:3; 34:10; Dan 8:14, 26; Neh 13:19), perhaps in response to the increasing importance of their lunar festivals.

The OT never refers to the division of days into hours; indeed, biblical Hebrew has no word for "hour," although the Aramaic *šāʿâ* (the word that means "hour" in Modern Hebrew, for example) occurs five times in Daniel in idiomatic expressions typically translated "immediately." The OT does refer to broader divisions of the day such as morning, noon, and evening (Ps 55:17). Parts of the day are also indicated by the customary occupations performed at those times, such as the gathering of animals (Gen 29:7) and the drawing of water (Gen 24:11). Nighttime was divided into watches (Lam 2:19), often three in number (Exod 14:24; Judg 7:19; 1 Sam 11:11; Lam 2:19). The times of the morning and evening sacrifices in the temple could also indicate specific periods of the day (Exod 29:38–45; Num 28:1–8).

The only reference in the OT to a timekeeping device occurs in the parallel passages of 2 Kgs 20:8–11 and Isa 38:7–8. As a sign to Hezekiah that he would be healed of his illness, the Lord made the shadow of the sun go back the ten steps it had gone down on the stairway of Ahaz. Some English translations, such as the KJV and NRSV, have understood *maʿălôt* (lit., "steps") to refer to the degrees of a sundial. This interpretation is found in the Targums and in the Vulgate, the latter of which uses *horologio* to translate the Hebrew word in the phrase "steps of Ahaz" in Isa 38:8. Other ancient authorities, including the LXX, Josephus, and the Qumran Isaiah scroll (1QIsaᵃ), understood this word to refer to stairs connected to the palace of Ahaz. In this case, the steps of a stairway marked the passing of time as the shadow of a nearby object passed over them. R. K. Harrison suggested that "the stairway in question was probably connected with the covered way for the Sabbath, which had been built inside the palace by Ahaz at a time when the outer royal entrance was being removed (2 Kgs 16:18)" (Harrison, 941). An object, perhaps a nearby building in the temple, stood to the west of the east-facing stairs so that the shadow began at the top of the stairs and moved downward as the sun descended.

B. THE NEW TESTAMENT

Two Greek words used in the NT to refer to time are *kairos* and *chronos*. *Kairos* is used 487 times in the LXX and 85 times in the NT. It usually refers to a point in time or a short duration (Matt 11:25; 12:1; 14:1), although it can also refer to a longer period (Acts 17:26). It is often used as a non-specific reference to an occasion or moment of time (Matt 12:1; Luke 21:36; Acts 13:11). It can also denote an appropriate or decisive moment or a fixed time or opportunity (Matt 8:29; 13:30; Luke 19:44; Heb 11:15; Acts 24:25; 2 Cor 6:2).

Chronos appears 54 times in the NT. It refers to a span or duration of time, either long or short (Matt 2:7; 25:19; Acts 18:23; Rev 20:3). Accordingly, it is often modified by the adjectives "little," "long," "many," and "as long as." When it occurs in the plural, it is often translated "ages" to indicate an expanse of time (Luke 23:8; Rom 16:25; 2 Tim 1:9; Titus 1:2; 1 Pet 1:20). In texts written in Classical and Hellenistic Greek, *chronos* is used more frequently than *kairos*, but in the LXX and the NT the opposite is the case. Some interpreters have tried to draw a sharp distinction between *kairos* and *chronos*, but sometimes the terms are used synonymously (1 Thess 5:1).

Another time-related term in the NT is *aiōn*, which appears 122 times and is commonly translated "age" or "world" (Matt 28:20; Mark 4:19; Rom 12:2; 1 Cor 2:6; 2 Cor 4:4). The LXX uses *aiōn* to translate Hebrew *ʿōlam*. It can refer to a long span of time in the past (Luke 1:70; 1 Cor 2:7; Col 1:26) or in the future (John 4:14). Its adjective form, *aiōnios*, is used seventy-one times and is often translated "eternal" (2 Cor 4:18; Heb 9:12, 15). The phrases *eis ton aiōna*, *eis tous aiōnas* (*tōn aiōnōn*), and *eis ton aiōna* (*tou aiōnos*) are typically translated idiomatically as "forever" (Luke 1:55; John 6:51; Rom 1:25; 11:36; 2 Cor 9:9; Heb 1:8).

The Greek word translated "day" is *hēmera*. Like the OT word *yôm*, *hēmera* is used to refer to the period of daylight (Matt 4:2; Acts 20:31), the period of the sun's return to the same position in the sky (Luke 9:37; John 2:12; Acts 9:19; 21:26), and the period of an action or state of being (John 8:56; 2 Cor 6:2; Eph 6:13). In addition to these usages, the NT also uses the word "day," with reference to the period of light, to symbolize salvation and righteousness (John 11:9; Rom 13:12–13; 1 Thess 5:5, 8). The word also refers to the eschatological time of judgment and salvation (Luke 17:24; Phil 1:6, 10; 1 Thess 5:2, 5; Rev 6:17).

References to the beginning of the day reflect the later OT practice of starting and ending the day at sunset (Matt 28:1; Mark 1:32; 4:27; 5:5; Luke 2:37; 4:40; 23:54; John 19:31, 42; Acts 20:7, 31; 26:7; 2 Cor 11:25; 1 Thess 2:9; 3:10; 2 Thess 3:8; 1 Tim 5:5; 2 Tim 1:3). In contrast to the OT, the order of "night and day" is more common than "day and night." Other passages, however, reflect the earlier OT practice of regarding the morning as the beginning of the day (Matt 28:1; Mark 11:11–12; 16:1–2; Luke 24:1; Acts 4:3; 23:32). The book of Revelation refers to "day and night" several times, as does Luke in a couple of places (Rev 4:8; 7:15; 8:12; 12:10; 14:11; 20:10; Luke 18:7; Acts 9:24). The NT does not consistently describe day as beginning at sunrise or at sundown. As in the OT, it appears that both reckonings could be used, even by the same writer.

The Greek word for "hour" is *hōra*. Sometimes *hōra* just refers to a short span of time without specifying its length (Matt 8:13; Luke 2:38; 7:21; 10:21; 12:12; 13:31; 20:19; 24:33; Acts 16:18; 22:13). It can also be used imprecisely to refer to a division of the day, such as evening (Matt 14:15; Mark 6:35; 11:11). *Hōra* also refers to one-twelfth of the period of daylight. For example, John 11:9 refers to twelve hours of daylight, reflecting the practice of the Greeks and Romans, who divided the period from dawn to dusk into twelve equal parts.

Hōra is sometimes used with an ordinal number to indicate the part of the day when an event took place. The most common phrases of this kind in the NT are "third hour," "sixth hour," and "ninth hour." The NT contains one reference to the "seventh hour" (John 4:52), one reference to the "tenth hour" (John 1:39), and two references to the "eleventh hour" (Matt 20:6, 9). At least fifteen different events are indicated in this way.

Commentators often fail to recognize that the Gospel writers divided daylight into twelve equal parts beginning with dawn. For example, they mistakenly interpret the "third hour" in Mark 15:25 as equivalent to 9 a.m. based on the assumption that Mark began counting hours from 6 a.m. However, counting hours beginning at 6 a.m. would happen only two days of the year, when sunlight and night time were equally twelve hours long. Similarly, the "third hour" of Matt 20:3 should not be equated with 9 a.m.; the "seventh hour" of John 4:52 should be not be equated with 1 p.m.; the "ninth hour" of Mark 15:33–34 and Matt 20:5 should not be equated with 3 p.m.; the "tenth hour" of John 1:39 should not be equated with 4 p.m.; and the "eleventh hour" of Matt 20:6 should not be equated with 5 p.m.

John 19:14 places Jesus's death at the "sixth hour," which most commentators interpret to mean noon. However, some interpreters, such as

N. Walker, have tried to reconcile the discrepancy between this text in John and Mark 15:25 by arguing that John was following the Roman custom of beginning the civil day at midnight. In contrast, R. T. Beckwith and R. G. Bratcher reject the theory that the Romans began counting hours at midnight.

The NT refers to hours of the night only in Acts 23:23. Again, interpreters mistakenly interpret the third hour of the night to refer to 9 p.m. on the assumption that night began exactly at 6 p.m. The REB paraphrases the reference correctly as "three hours after sunset."

In contrast to the OT's three watches of the night, the NT divides the night into four watches, as did the Egyptians, Greeks, and Romans (Matt 14:25; Mark 6:48; 13:35; Luke 12:38; Acts 12:4). Terms used for these four watches were evening, midnight, cockcrow, and morning.

C. THE NEAR EASTERN WORLD

Because ancient people thought of time primarily in the present, the day was the fundamental unit of time. Ancient humans could easily track the sun's return to the same point in the sky. The division of day or night into segments called "hours" is a human convention influenced by the passage of the celestial bodies through the sky. When trade and commerce developed, the need arose to divide time into smaller segments.

In ancient Mesopotamia, the day began at dusk. The Babylonians divided the period from sunset to sunset into twelve *bērū* (one *bēru* is roughly the equivalent of two hours). The Babylonians, who followed a number system based on sixty, were responsible for dividing hours into sixty minutes and minutes into sixty seconds. In his *Almagest*, Ptolemy followed the Babylonian practice by dividing the equinoctial hour into sixty minutes.

In contrast to the Babylonians, the Egyptians began their day at dawn. As early as 2100 BC, the Egyptians divided the time from sunrise to sunrise into twenty-four parts. Originally, the Egyptians calculated ten daylight hours, two twilight hours, and twelve night hours, but in 1300 BC this system gave way to the simpler arrangement of twelve hours of day and twelve hours of night.

Beginning around 2000 BC, the Egyptians were able to divide the night into twelve parts by tracking the rise of thirty-six stars or star clusters in the eastern sky. These celestial markers were later called "decans" by the Greeks because they divided the sky into ten-degree segments.

The Egyptians also developed transit instruments to detect when bright stars passed the zenith of the sky. One priest would look toward the north through a slot in a notched palm leaf, called a *bay*, to view a plumb line hanging from an L-shaped scale, called a *merkhet*. Most ancient cultures, however, measured only the hours of sunlight since little activity took place during the night.

The earliest known device for tracking the length and direction of the sun's shadow was an upright stick stuck in the ground. Called "gnomons" (from the Gk. word for "indicator"), these have been found in Egypt and perhaps date from as early as 3500 BC. When the shadow pointed due north and was at its shortest, it was noon.

The primitive gnomon was eventually replaced by a more sophisticated shadow clock, called a *setjat*, that could divide daylight into twelve equal parts. The earliest example, which is now housed in the Egyptian Museum in Berlin, has been dated to 1479–1425 BC. It is a one-foot-long block of green schist on which five holes were inscribed to divide it into six time periods. Shaped like a *merkhet*, the device has a block affixed at a right angle on one end to serve as the gnomon. The gnomon would face east in the morning and west after midday.

Other shadow clocks consisted of a length of wood or ivory, called a "table," and an upright T shape, called a "style." A later version of the *setjat* had the time scale marked on an inclined rule set at an angle based on the latitude of the location.

Shadow clocks divided daylight into twelve hours (referred to as "temporal" or "seasonal" hours), but a summer hour would be longer than a winter hour. On only two days of the year, the vernal and autumnal equinoxes, would the twelve hours of daylight and twelve hours of night be almost equal to each other.

Beginning around 1300 BC in Egypt, sundials consisting of a flat, circular scale with an upright rod were used to track the direction, but not the length, of the sun's shadow. In 2013, a vertical, limestone sundial dating to the thirteenth century BC was found on the floor of a workman's hut in the Valley of the Kings. A portable ivory sundial made in Egypt around the eleventh century BC was discovered at Gezer. A tripartite sundial was discovered at Tell er-Râs on Mt. Gerizim in 1968. Between the sixth and third centuries BC, the sundial was improved by inclining the gnomon at an angle according to the latitude of the place of origin and pointing it toward the North Pole.

During the last five centuries BC, sundials of many varieties were created by the Egyptians, Babylonians, and Greeks to provide the correct hour in any season or month. They were formed in various shapes, including flat disks, sunken hemispheres and cones, cubes, columns, open rings, and open tablets. The marks on the sundials were adjusted to show the correct time for the various seasons and months of the year.

Sundials were useful only outdoors during daylight and only when the sun was shining; consequently, other devices were invented to track hours indoors and on cloudy days and during the night. Water clocks, called "clepsydras" ("water thieves" in Gk.), provided the first accurate method of tracking time through day and night [see Figure 7 on p. 474]. The Mesopotamians may have invented them since they are mentioned in Old Babylonian texts; however, no remains of one have ever been found in that region. The earliest example of a water clock was found in the Temple of Karnak in Egypt and dates to the reign of Amenhotep III (1386–1349 BC).

D. THE GRECO-ROMAN WORLD

The Greeks and Romans divided daylight into twelve equal seasonal hours, which varied in length according to the time of year. At the winter solstice, Rome experienced eight hours and fifty-four minutes of daylight and fifteen hours and six minutes of darkness, yet they would have divided each of those periods into twelve equal parts. The first hour would have begun at 7:33 a.m. and the twelfth hour at 3:42 p.m.

For scientific purposes, they could divide the entire day into twenty-four equal parts, which the astronomer Hipparchus termed "equinoctial hours" because on the two equinoxes both daylight and nighttime can be divided into twelve equal parts each. Ptolemy also distinguished between ordinary and equinoctial hours (*Tetrabiblos* 76), but most people, who relied on sundials, would have observed seasonal hours.

The Greeks had sundials for two centuries before the Romans. Beginning in the fifth century BC, sundials could be found in Athens and other Greek cities, but the earliest existing example dates from the third century BC. Greek astronomers understood how to adjust sundials to work accurately in the latitude where they would be used.

For Greeks, the day began at sunset, but the astronomer Hipparchus of Nicaea (2nd c. BC) reckoned the day from midnight to midnight. He divided the day into twenty-four equinoctial hours for astronomical purposes. For Romans, the day began at dawn, but Pliny the Elder claimed that Roman priests and authorities fixed the official day as the period from midnight to midnight (*Nat.* 2.79.188). The Romans were able to determine when the sun crossed the meridian at midday and when it set, but for many centuries they had no way to divide daylight into hours.

Before the introduction of the sundial, the Romans divided the day into large segments. Through the fourth century BC, they divided the day into only two parts: *ante meridiem* (before midday) and *post meridiem* (after midday). An assistant to the consul announced in the Forum when the sun had passed the meridian. Later, the Romans divided the day more finely into four parts: (1) *mane* (sunrise to the beginning of the third hour); (2) *ad meridiem* (forenoon); (3) *de meridie* (afternoon); and (4) *suprema* (ninth or tenth hour until sunset). Even after sundials became more common, many Romans observed these larger divisions.

According to Pliny the Elder (*Nat.* 7.60), the first sundial was introduced in Rome by M. Valerius Messalla in 263 BC as part of the booty taken from Catania in Sicily during the First Punic War. Because the imported sundial was not calibrated to the latitude of Rome, it gave the incorrect time until 164 BC when the censor Q. Marcius Philippus installed a properly calibrated sundial next to it. Both sundials were placed on pillars behind the Rostra in the Forum, a visible and convenient place for regulating public business.

The introduction of the sundial may have initiated in Rome the custom of dividing daylight hours into twelve equal parts. In Rome, a midwinter hour would have lasted about forty-four minutes, and a midsummer hour would have lasted about seventy-five minutes.

In the second century BC, a character in a Roman comedy written by Aquilius complained that the town was overflowing with sundials, which forced him to eat on a regular schedule rather than at the natural promptings of his stomach. He lamented: "May the gods destroy that man who first discovered hours, the very man who first set up a sundial here, who smashed my day, alas, into fragments" (Shelton, 124).

By the first century BC, every city wanted a sundial. Sundials were installed in public areas, temples, and houses throughout the Roman Empire. For example, excavations at Pompeii have discovered all or part of about thirty stone sundials. Wealthy Romans carried tiny pocket sundials that were a little more than an inch in diameter. Most of the populace, however, did not own sundials and probably paid little attention to them.

Vitruvius reports the existence of thirteen different kinds of sundial. In 1976, S. L. Gibbs published a catalogue of 256 extant examples of Greek and Roman sundials. Not one was a disk-shaped horizontal model. The most popular type was the *scaphe* dial, which typically had a curved bowl shape scooped out of marble with twelve equally divided hour lines scored on its surface. A gnomon was placed parallel to the surface of the earth in a U-shaped hole at the top so that its shadow would point to the correct hour of the day.

In 10 BC, Augustus erected a giant sundial, called the Solarium Augusti, in the Campus Martius to commemorate his victory over Mark Antony and Cleopatra. He transported a seventy-one-foot obelisk from Heliopolis in Egypt and set it in the center of an enormous grid of inlaid lines of bronze on the travertine pavement; this served to mark the hours, months, seasons, and signs of the zodiac.

The Greeks began to use water clocks in the fifth century BC, and the Romans adopted them in the second century BC. According to Petronius and others, water clocks were a status symbol in first-century Rome.

Water clocks were designed in two forms. The earliest form, called the outflow type, allowed water to escape through a hole near the bottom of a bowl so that the descending water level indicated the passing of the hours. The later and more precise form, called the inflow type, had two basins. An upper vessel received a constant flow of water, which streamed out a hole near its bottom at a constant rate into a lower vessel. The second vessel was marked at hourly intervals or equipped with a float so that the rising of the water marked the passing of the hours.

Water clocks of the inflow type sometimes included alarms that would go off when the water reached the top of the vessel. These alarms consisted of metal balls or pebbles that would be dumped or whistles that would blow. Later, elaborate water clocks were equipped with mechanical floats and levers.

Although water clocks could have easily been marked to divide the twenty-four hours of day and night into equal parts, most were calibrated with sundials to mark daylight into twelve equal parts and nighttime into twelve equal parts. The twelve hours of night could be measured by using the daytime calibrations from exactly six months before.

Like other timekeeping devices, water clocks had their limitations. During colder weather, water clocks were unreliable, and in warmer climates the water would evaporate quickly. The rate of flow depended on the head of water in the upper vessel, but this was solved by Ctesibius of Alexandria (ca. 135 BC), who devised a method to keep the head of water at a constant level. Water clocks were not portable, and they were too expensive for all but the wealthy to possess. Even during the Middle Ages, they were found mainly in monasteries.

Greeks used water clocks to tell time by both day and night. One was placed in the marketplace of every important town. Water clocks were used in Greek and Roman law courts to limit the length of speeches. In a speech defending a woman, Demosthenes (4th c. BC) complained, "And when the archon took the case to court, and it was to be tried, the claimants had everything readied for the trial. They even had four times as much water [in the clock] as we did for making speeches" (*Against Macartatus* 8–9; cited in Humphrey, Oleson, and Sherwood, 519).

While he was in Britain, Julius Caesar used water clocks to indicate the night watches for his troops. Aeneas Tacticus observed:

> A water clock is a very useful device for the nighttime guards. Since the nights become longer or shorter, it is constructed in the following manner. It is nec-

essary to smear the inside with wax and when the nights become longer to take out some of the wax so that there is room for more water; when the nights become shorter to mould on more so that it holds less water.
(Fragment 48; cited in Humphrey, Oleson, and Sherwood, 520)

One of the most notable examples of a water clock is the Tower of the Winds in Athens, which is located to the east of the Roman agora and which still stands largely intact. Built in the mid-second century BC by Andronikos of Kyrrhos (although some date it to the 1st c. BC), this octagonal, marble tower has eight winged male figures carved around its top, with radiating lines of a sundial incised beneath each figure. On top of the tower is a bronze Triton holding a rod in his right hand, which functioned as a weather vane. The tower also contained a water clock. The circular chamber outside the tower contained two tanks of water fed by a stream called the Clepsydra. The flow of water from one tank to another would turn an axle, which in turn would move a large metal disk inside the tower in order to indicate the passing of hours, days, and phases of the moon.

In the second century BC, a water clock was placed beside the sundial that Marcius Philippus had installed in Rome. The Romans used water clocks to limit the length of pleas in court, regulate the work of slaves, and mark the length of guard duty at night. In the second century AD, the Greek author Lucian described a bath building in Rome that provided two devices for telling time: a loud water clock and a sundial.

The use of water clocks caused the Romans to equate time with water. "To grant water" (*aquam dare*) meant to allot more time for a lawyer, and "to lose water" (*aquam perdere*) meant to waste time. Timekeeping devices were so imprecise that Seneca remarked that it was as impossible to find agreement among the clocks of Rome as to find agreement among Roman philosophers.

Sandglasses, or hourglasses, may have been invented as early as the thirteenth century BC, although some historians would date their emergence as late as the third century BC. These devices consisted of two conic reservoirs joined at their apexes by a small hole. Sand would flow from the upper reservoir to the bottom reservoir over a set duration of time.

Like water clocks, sandglasses had some inherent limitations and imperfections. They could track only shorter passages of time, which made them useless for measuring nighttime hours. The coarseness of the sand could make a sandglass less precise than a water clock. Friction would eventually make the hole bigger so that the sand would flow faster. To avoid this, higher-quality hourglasses contained ground eggshells rather than actual sand. Unlike the water clock, the hourglass was used in nautical navigation. Mariners could use a thirty-second sandglass to estimate their speed by counting the number of knots in a rope that played out behind the ship during the interval.

E. THE JEWISH WORLD

Like the OT, the intertestamental literature and the Dead Sea Scrolls divided day and night each into three periods (Jdt 12:5; *Jub.* 49:10–12). However, Josephus followed the Roman practice of a fourfold division (*Ant.* 18.9.6). Judaism prescribed prayer three times a day: after daybreak, before sunset, and after dark. The rabbis debated whether nighttime should be divided into three watches or four (*b. Ber.* 3a–b).

Unlike the OT, the intertestamental literature refers to "hours" of the day and night (*Let. Aris.* 303; *T. Jos.* 8:1; *3 Macc.* 5:14). Likewise, Philo (*QE* 1:11) and Josephus (*J.W.* 6.1.7; 6.9.3; *Ant.* 6.14.6; 14.4.4; *Life* 54) refer to hours in a way that suggests the division of the day into twelve parts.

The intertestamental literature and Josephus indicate that the Sabbath and other days began at sundown (2 Macc 8:25–26; *J.W.* 4.9.12; *Ant.* 16.6.2; 16.8.5; *Life* 32). However, the literature sometimes mentions day before night (Tob 10:7; Jdt 11:17; Wis 10:17; Bar 2:25; 2 Macc 3:10).

Although it is not attested at Qumran, the word *zĕmān* is the most common word used for aspects of time in early rabbinic Hebrew and Aramaic, displacing the biblical *ʿēt*. It can refer to specific points in time or finite periods of time but is never used to refer to the dimension of time as a whole. The concept of hour (*šāʿâ*) rarely occurs in early rabbinic writings, which reflects limited access to timekeeping devices.

Early rabbinic literature makes just a few references to sundials and water clocks. In 1954, a limestone roundel was discovered at Qumran. George Hollenback has proposed that the non-penetrating hole in the middle and the enigmatic markings surrounding it indicate that it was an equatorial sundial. Barbara Thiering has proposed that its secondary purpose was to function as an odometer for travelers. In his excavations south of the temple platform in Jerusalem, Benjamin Mazar found a small stone sundial. Furrows radiating from a central groove mark twelve hours. (See Mazar, 143.)

F. THE CHRISTIAN WORLD

By the third century AD, the Romans divided days into quarters, and the third, sixth, and ninth hours were publicly announced. Consequently, Tertullian added to the Jewish practice of prayer three times a day the requirement that Christians pray at the third, sixth, and ninth hours of the day. In the sixth century AD, Saint Benedict of Nursia prescribed seven precise times for prayer during the liturgical day for his monastic order. These prayer times became known as the Canonical Hours, but they still depended on dividing daylight into twelve equal parts.

Until mechanical clocks were invented in the fourteenth century AD, sundials continued to serve as the primary means of tracking temporal (i.e., seasonal) hours. During these centuries, Arabs, who first encountered the sundial in the second century BC in Alexandria, were largely responsible for improvements made in sundials. Their innovations influenced European designs in the Middle Ages. Water clocks also existed in the West from the time of the Roman Empire through the Middle Ages. Arabs also made elaborate improvements to water clocks.

BIBLIOGRAPHY: J. E. Barnett, *Time's Pendulum: The Quest to Capture Time—From Sundials to Atomic Clocks* (1998); J. Barr, *Biblical Words for Time* (2nd rev. ed., 1969); R. T. Beckwith, "The Day, Its Divisions and Its Limits, in Biblical Thought," *EvQ* 43 (1971), 218–27; D. J. Boorstin, *The Discoverers: A History of Man's Search to Know His World and Himself* (1983); R. G. Bratcher, "Reckoning of Time in the Fourth Gospel," *RevExp* 48 (1951), 161–8; J. H. Breasted, "The Beginnings of Time-Measurement and the Origins of Our Calendar," in *Time and Its Mysteries, Series I* (1936), 59–96; R. J. Bull, "A Tripartite Sundial from Tell er Râs on Mt. Gerizim," *BASOR* 219 (1975), 29–37; H. J. Cadbury, "Some Lukan Expressions of Time (Lexical Notes on Luke-Acts VII), *JBL* 82 (1963)," 272–78; J. M. Camp, *The Archaeology of Athens* (2001); G. Delling, "καιρός," *TDNT* III.455–62; G. Delling, "χρόνος," *TDNT* IX.581–93; D. de Solla Price, "Clockwork before the Clock and Timekeepers before Timekeeping," in *The Study of Time*, ed. J. T. Fraser and N. Lawrence (1975), 2.367–80; R. de Vaux, *Ancient Israel: Its Life and Institutions*, trans. J. McHugh (1961); S. J. De Vries, "Day," *IDB* I.783; E. Eynikel and K. Hauspie, "The Use of ΚΑΙΡΟΣ and ΧΡΟΝΟΣ in the Septuagint," *ETL* 73 (1997), 369–85; J. Finegan, *Handbook of Biblical Chronology: Principles of Time Reckoning in the Ancient World and Problems of Chronology in the Bible* (rev. ed., 1998); D. Fléchon, *The Mastery of Time* (2011); S. L. Gibbs, *Greek and Roman Sundials* (1976); J. Guhrt, "αἰών," *NIDNTT* III.826–33; H.-C. Hahn, "καιρός," *NIDNTT* III.833–39; H.-C. Hahn, "χρόνος," *NIDNTT* III.839–45; H.-C. Hahn, "ὥρα," *NIDNTT* III.845–49; W. W. Hallo, *Origins: The Ancient Near Eastern Background of Some Modern Western Institutions* (1996); R. K. Harrison, "Dial of Ahaz," *ISBE* I.941–42; G. F. Hasel, "Day," *ISBE* I.877–78; M. A. Heselton, "Hourglass," in *Encyclopedia of Time: Science, Philosophy, Theology, and Culture*, ed. H J. Birx (2009), II.677–9; G. Hollenback, "The Qumran Roundel: An

Equatorial Sundial?," *Dead Sea Discoveries* 7 (2000), 123–29; J. W. Humphrey, J. P. Oleson, and A. N. Sherwood, ed., *Greek and Roman Technology: A Sourcebook* (1998); E. Jenni, "Time," *IDB* IV.642–49; K. Lippincott et al., *The Story of Time* (1999); H. A. Lloyd, "Timekeepers—An Historical Sketch," in *The Voices of Time*, ed. J. T. Fraser (2nd ed., 1981), 388–400; B. J. Malina, "Christ and Time: Swiss or Mediterranean?," *CBQ* 51 (1989), 1–31; B. Mazar, *The Mountain of the* Lord (1975); H. W. Morisada Rietz, "Time," *NIDB* V.595–600; J. V. Noble and D. J. de Solla Price, "The Water Clock in the Tower of the Winds," *AJA* 72 (1968), 345–55; W. M. O'Neil, *Time and the Calendars* (1975); C. H. Pinnock, "Time," *ISBE* IV.852–53; J. B. Priestley, *Man and Time* (1964); E. G. Richards, *Mapping Time: The Calendar and Its History* (1998); E. Robbins, "Day, OT," *NIDB* II.48; F. Rochberg-Halton, "Babylonian Seasonal Hours," *Centaurus* 32 (1989), 146–70; J.-A. Shelton, ed., *As the Romans Did: A Sourcebook in Roman Social History* (1998); R. W. Sloley, "Primitive Methods of Measuring Time: With Special Reference to Egypt," *JEA* 17 (1931), 166–78; S. Stern, *Time and Process in Ancient Judaism* (2007); H. R. Stroes, "Does the Day Begin in the Evening or Morning? Some Biblical Observations," *VT* 16 (1966), 460–75; B. Thiering, "The Qumran Sundial as an Odometer Using Fixed Lengths of Hours," *Dead Sea Discoveries* 9 (2002), 347–63; N. Walker, "The Reckoning of Hours in the Fourth Gospel," *NovT* 4 (1960), 69–73; G. J. Whitrow, *Time in History: Views of Time from Prehistory to the Present Day* (1988).

GLL

See also ASTROLOGY and CALENDARS.

Tools & Utensils

In a world where survival comes at the expense of "sweat equity" (Gen 3:19), humans have creatively developed equipment that gives them the capacity to engage successfully in tasks otherwise beyond their capacities. In this article, "utensils" refers to equipment employed in domestic applications like food preparation or personal grooming, and "tools" refers to equipment employed in farming and professions through which people made their livelihood. There are many items that may be seen to fit both categories. The basic processes accomplished by such equipment included cutting, moving, shaping, and containing materials. In antiquity, people or harnessed animals powered most equipment. A single use consumed some items of equipment but most were capable of repeated action. Creative persons overcame functional fixedness and used the properties of purposefully shaped equipment for secondary purposes. Hammer stones, for example, could become grinders. Specifically designed instruments that were made of particular materials or multiple pieces and needed by specialists typically commanded higher prices than simple tools employed for common tasks.

People made tools and utensils from available physical materials that had beneficial properties. While aesthetics and traditions played a role, the function and cost of materials were the most important factors in determining forms. Simple, inexpensive, and functional items like stone blades used in harvesting equipment thus continued long after the appearance of potential metal substitutes. The most common inorganic materials used in the manufacture of tools and utensils included stone, clay, metal, and glass. Common organic materials included wood, plant fibers, leather, hair, and bone.

Stone tools and utensils are prominent among those found in early archaeological contexts. Some stones were used with little or no modification, while others required the development of shaping methodologies. A hand-sized rock could become a hammer, for example, and a flat, thin slab of igneous stone could provide a griddle for cooking. Stone tools that were not specifically shaped probably often go unrecognized by archaeologists. Hand implements made of flaked and chipped chert nodules are among the earliest tools found in archaeological contexts. Chert, with its hardness and conchoidal fracturing, provided cores and flakes with extremely sharp edges that people used as borers, knives, axes, projectile points, sickles, and threshing sled teeth. Archaeologists have identified handheld megalithic core tools (i.e., tools formed from a stone core that has been shaped by chipping away unwanted material) as a typological feature of the Paleolithic corpus of artifacts. Over time, greater sophistication is observed with the emergence of bifacial implements and the use of lithic flakes. Smaller microliths hafted in materials like wood and ground stone tools became increasingly common and comprise the bulk of the Neolithic corpus. The adoption of wooden handles provided increased leverage and helped absorb the shock of impact. Hammers and other tools with handles increased productivity. Chipped and ground stone tools and utensils were used throughout antiquity.

Stone materials provided the resources needed for a variety of applications, depending on their specific qualities. People used gemstones, located at the top of the Mohs' Scale for hardness, for engraving softer materials. Igneous stones like basalts are dense, relatively thermal, and shock resistant. People ground basalt into implements such as hammers, axes, querns, mortars and pestles, vessels, saddle querns, and, later, rotary grindstones. Lighter vesicular basalts had the advantage of a texture and lighter weight that made them superior for grindstones. Sedimentary stones like limestone and sandstone are often less dense and shock resistant than basalt, and they produced more grit, but people used them in similar applications when the preferred stone was not available.

Pyrotechnology was fundamental to people of antiquity moving from dependence on stone to the use of ceramic and metal tools and utensils. Fire at the appropriate temperatures transformed shapable, water-soluble clay into a durable, fixed shape. Clay transformed into ceramics with the capacity to endure heat was particularly used around fire, where it was not subject to sharp physical impact (since it is prone to fracturing). Initially, potters made stationary, free-form objects by hand or by pressing clay into baskets or molds. Later, simple plano-convex stone platforms served as rotating working surfaces. A yet later development was pivoting working surfaces that turned on a simple bearing of a conoid projection on one platform that fit into a matching conoid socket in a second platform. These were made of ceramic where appropriate stone was unavailable. Archaeologists refer to these hand-turned platforms as "slow wheels." Hand-turned ceramic vessels were common in the third millennium BC. The "fast wheel," which was driven by the momentum of a heavy kick stone at the base attached to an elevated working head, was adopted by potters in the latter half of the first millennium BC and perfected by the Neo-Assyrians. These pieces of equipment created centrifugal force sufficient to allow potters to throw thin-walled vessels. As earthenware vessels rotated, they could also be scraped with a sharp edge of a shell or a knife, burnished by a smooth stone, or impressed with a repeated design using roulettes. Slips and glazes on pots served utilitarian functions but were usually employed for aesthetic purposes. Unless burnished or specially coated, ceramic vessels were liquid-permeable. People used clay to make earthenware vessels and ovens in domestic applications and, in industrial applications, for the bases of pot bellows, fire-resistant nozzles to blow-pipes, crucibles, and molds.

Pyrotechnology made possible the manufacture of metal tools and utensils. Metals vary in hardness and tensile strength but generally possess a high strength-to-weight ratio and a high resistance to deformation, shock, and corrosion. Metal supplanted stone as a more versatile tool-making material when available materials and technology came together. At sufficient temperatures, fire made native telluric metals and meteoritic metals malleable. Softened by heat, metals could be hammered into desired shapes that could serve as tools and utensils. With additional heat, smiths liberated metal trapped by physical and chemical bonds within ore-bearing stones. Liquefied metals could then be poured into clay and stone molds of desired shapes. Ox-hide and ring-shaped ingots were chosen since they were transportable. The more easily smelted copper alloy bronze was widely embraced in the third millennium BC. Artisans carved depressions in flat-sided, heat-resistant stones to form voids in the shape of ax heads, knives, and other tools. After these voids were filled with molten metal, they cooled and contracted, allowing the metal objects of desired shapes to be freed from the mold. More sophisticated two-piece molds with false cores provided the technology needed to make tools that allowed for superior hafting of handles. The most intricate of shapes could be formed with the embrace of the "lost wax" method of casting metal. The shapes of tools and utensils were subsequently limited largely by the imagination of craftworkers. Through the processes of tempering and quenching, the properties of metal tools made of bronze were modified. The result was that the working edges of metal tools remained sharper longer, thus creating less friction and greater productivity. Ancient workers recognized the superiority of sharp tools and used hard, abrasive stones to sharpen their domestic and professional equipment.

The last inorganic material developed through pyrotechnology and used to make tools and utensils was glass. A naturally occurring glass called obsidian was used to make flaked tools, but it was not widely available.

Manufactured glass formed of silica from quartz, soda, and lime was particularly resistant to corrosion but was also susceptible to fracture. Added chemicals generated decorative colors. Although mold-made glass bowls appeared as luxury items in Egypt in the third millennium BC, the use of glass became common only in the first century BC with the invention, in the Levant, of the technique of blowing glass. When glass could be blown into molds or bent into desired shapes while hot, it became widely embraced. During and after the Roman Empire, glassware was mainly used for making light, leak-proof containers that protected contents during storage from contamination and evaporation.

Ancient societies employed a variety of organic plant materials in the manufacture of tools and utensils. Wood, with its properties of low specific gravity, shock resistance, shapability, water absorption, heat resistance, and flammability, made it the material of choice for handles, mud-brick molds, wheels, and bowls. Carpenters split timbers with wedges, cut wood with saws, trimmed wood with adzes, bent wood using steam and jigs, turned wood on lathes, carved wood with knives and chisels, penetrated wood with drills, and smoothed wood with abrasives. The attachment of pieces of wood with edge and butt joints required precision workmanship.

Ancient people used plant materials such as reeds, palm fronds, and grasses with lightweight, flexible stems to make brooms, woven mats, baskets, and sieves. Basketry required only a few tools, such as knives to cut fibers, awls to make holes, and needles to insert fibers. Textile manufacturing required a more extensive toolbox. After the second century BC, plant fibers like flax, hemp, and cotton were used to spin thread, which could be woven into textiles. Tools employed in spinning thread included spindles and whorls. In weaving, wood was used to make the beams needed for horizontal and vertical looms, as well as to make combs used to compress woven fibers. Flax fibers provided the strong, lightweight, and shock-resistant long fibers for most woven textiles in Egypt, as well as items like sacks and ropes.

Many ancient tools and utensils were made of components from animal products. Leather was lightweight, shock resistant, flexible, durable, and wettable. People used it to make protective clothing, animal harnesses, wineskins, and containers like buckets that would not shatter on the walls of wells cut into bedrock. Animal hair was a renewable commodity that had pliability, durability when exposed to the elements, and the capacity to be dyed. Goat, sheep, and camel hair was spun to make yarn that could be used in ropes and textiles. Animal gut and sinew provided strong, elastic connective materials. Bone, ivory, and horn from animals were carved to make lightweight objects like needles, harpoons, spindles, handles, and containers.

A. THE OLD TESTAMENT

The OT historical texts contain references to many tools and utensils, which are an integral part of accounts from every period. According to Genesis, tool-making originated in the antediluvian period. The metallurgist Tubal-Cain is highlighted as having developed the processes of making metal tools (Gen 4:22). Tools were used to construct the cypress ark (*tēbâ*) built by Noah (Gen 6:14–16) and, after the flood, to fashion the mud-bricks of the Tower of Babel (Gen 11:3–4). In the patriarchal period, skins were used as containers for water (Gen 21:14–15) and digging tools were required for well excavation in the limestone strata of the Negev (cf. Gen 21:25, 30; 26:15, 18–22, 25, 32). Several tools were needed by Abraham as he faced the challenge of his faith at the mountain in the region of Moriah: one for chopping wood, one for carrying fire, rope for binding, and a knife for dispatching the sacrifice (Gen 22:1–19). He later needed scales to determine the measure of silver shekels to be paid for the burial place for his wife in the cave located in the field of Ephron (Gen 23:16).

Agricultural implements were employed in grain harvests like the one about which Joseph dreamed (Gen 37:6–7). In the Egyptian period, a variety of tools would have been employed by the enslaved Hebrews in the various aspects of hard labor. Particularly essential were wooden forms for making uniform mud-bricks (Exod 1:14). A pitch-coated papyrus basket (*tēbâ*) (Exod 2:3) provided sanctuary for the Levite baby the pharaoh's daughter called Moses. In the wilderness period, Moses used a chisel to shape the stone tablets on which the Decalogue was inscribed (Exod 34:1, 4), and artisans like Bezalel and Oholiab used tools to make the sacred objects of metal, textiles, and wood for the tabernacle (Gen 31:1–39:41). The most precious of these objects was the gold-covered acacia wood chest known as the ark (*'ărôn*) (Exod 25:10–22). A source for bronze that was used in creating special objects was recycled bronze mirrors (*mar'ōt*) (Exod 38:8). Hand mills (*rēḥayim*) and mortars (sing. *mĕdōkâ*) were employed in preparing manna for consumption in the wilderness (Num 11:8). Under the Mosaic law, tools by which people made their living, like millstones (*rēḥ ayim*), could not be taken as a guarantee (Deut 24:6). These sets of stones comprised the lower grinding slab, seen as a beast of burden (*pelaḥ taḥ tît*) in Job 41:24 (Heb. 41:16), and the upper hand stone, called the "rider" (*pelaḥ rekeb*), mentioned in Judg 9:53 and 2 Sam 11:21. Flint knives (sing. *ṣōr*), with their sharp edges, were embraced as the instrument employed in effecting circumcisions (Exod 4:25; Josh 5:2).

Tools and utensils appear on a number of occasions in the biblical accounts of the conquest period. The Gibeonites, for example, disguised their identity through the ruse of worn sacks and repaired wineskins (*nō'dôt*)

(Josh 9:4). They were therefore condemned to be woodcutters and water carriers, both of which tasks required the use of tools. During the period of the judges, Shamgar used an ox goad (*malmād*) as his weapon against the Philistines (Judg 3:31). Under Deborah, the Kenite Jael dispatched the Canaanite general Sisera after lulling him to sleep with a bowl of milk from a skin and driving a tent peg (*yātēd*) through his temple with a hammer (*halmût*) (Judg 5:25–26). Gideon's defeat of the Midianites came after jars (*kaddîm*) that had been used to conceal torches (Judg 7:16) were broken as his soldiers attacked the Midianite camp at night. Abimelech's attempt to crush the rebellion against his usurpation of power ended as a woman dropped an upper millstone on his head (Judg 9:53). Samson moved toward revealing his secret to Delilah when he told her to weave his hair into fabric on a loom using a tightening peg (*yātēd*) fixed in the ground (Judg 16:13–14). The later-subdued Samson was humiliated by being blinded and by being forced to grind grain (Judg 16:21), possibly working a saddle quern like a woman, but more probably turning a rotary mill like an animal (see van der Toorn).

Hannah committed her son Samuel to be a Nazirite whose hair was never to be cut with a razor (*môrâ*) (1 Sam 1:11). In the period of the united monarchy, the Philistines possessed metallurgical knowledge that gave them a military and economic advantage over the Israelites, who were dependent upon them for help in manufacturing and maintaining mattocks (sing. *'ēt*), axes (sing. *qardōm*), and sickles (sing. *maḥărēšâ*) (1 Sam 13:20). Samuel anointed Saul as Israel's first king with oil from a flask (*pak*) (1 Sam 10:1). The future king, David, took the sleeping Saul's personal water jug (*ṣappaḥat*) (1 Sam 26:12) to use as evidence that he had spared his pursuer. After defeating the Ammonites, David subjected them to the hard labor of using saws (sing. *mĕgērâ*), iron picks (*ḥărîṣê habbarzel*), and iron axes (*magzĕrōt habbarzel*) (2 Sam 12:31).

During the construction of the Solomonic Temple, masonry was finished away from the building site so as to avoid noise from hammers, chisels, and other iron tools at this location (1 Kgs 6:7). In the period of the divided monarchy, the prophet Elisha miraculously neutralized the poisoned soup in a large cooking pot (*sîr*) (2 Kgs 4:38–41) and made an ax head (*barzel*) float that had been lost in the Jordan (2 Kgs 6:5). In the period of the Babylonian dominance, King Jehoiakim cut the scroll containing Jeremiah's condemning prophecy to pieces with a scribe's knife (*ta'ar*) (Jer 36:23), though this did not change the predicted course of events. Nebuchadnezzar's forces plundered the temple and took away the pots, shovels, wick trimmers (*mĕzammĕrôt*), and dishes used in it (2 Kgs 25:14). Later, just prior to the fall of Babylon, Belshazzar and his party drank from gold goblets (sing. *mā'n*) from this collection (Dan 5:2). In the period of

Persian dominance, King Cyrus returned the precious metal dishes (*'ăgarṭ ālîm*), pans (*maḥălāpîm*), and bowls (*kĕpôrîm*) for use in a reconstructed Jewish temple (Ezra 1:9–10). The best-known utensil referred to in Jewish historiography on the Hellenistic period is the lamp that kept burning in the temple, which provided a basis for the subsequent Festival of Lights.

As with the historical books, the OT prophetic and poetic books make many references to tools used by metalworkers, vinedressers, farmers, and potters. Jeremiah's references to tools at the time when the Assyrians were supplanted by the Neo-Babylonians reflect the tools of that period, as he proclaimed that the sins of his Judean audience were engraved deeply on their hearts with iron tools and flint points (Jer 17:1). He also visited a potter and saw him working clay from a stool at a potter's wheel (*'obnayim*) (Jer 18:3).

B. THE NEW TESTAMENT

Domestic utensils appear frequently in the accounts of the life of Jesus, and they are also referred to on occasion in the other books of the NT. In the Gospels, John the Baptist's head is displayed on a platter (*pinax*) to the vengeful Herodias (Matt 14:8||Mark 6:28); the Samaritan woman at Sychar leaves her water jar (*hydria*) to report to her village about Jesus (John 4:28); and it is mentioned that large measuring bowls (sing. *modios*) could be used to cut off the illumination of burning lamps (Matt 5:15||Mark 4:21||Luke 11:33). Jesus is anointed by a disreputable woman (Luke 7:37–38), and later by Mary, the sister of Lazarus (Matt 26:7||Mark 14:3), with perfume from distinctively shaped alabaster bottles (sing. *alabastros*). The scene of the upper room in Jerusalem where Jesus and his disciples celebrate Passover contains a concentration of references to utensils: A man carrying an earthenware jar (*keramion*) of water (Mark 14:13||Luke 22:10), a task typically carried out by women, is the unusual sign that leads the disciples to the upper room. There, Jesus uses a foot-washing basin (*nipter*) to teach his still proud disciples humility (John 13:5). A small communal bowl of food (*tryblion*) is shared by Jesus and Judas at the Last Supper (Matt 26:23||Mark 14:20), and after Judas departs Jesus takes a cup (*potērion*) and establishes the memorial of his covenant (Matt 26:27–28||Mark 14:23–24||Luke 22:20).

Some Jews of the first century had a heightened concern for purity. This led to the embrace of stone as a preferred material for domestic vessels since it was not deemed susceptible to contamination. Large ceremonial stone jars of water in Cana are the subject of Jesus's first reported miracle (John 2:1–11). The over-scrupulous Pharisaic traditions in regard to purification of utensils like cups, dishes, pitchers, and kettles are challenged by

Jesus (Mark 7:3–4; Luke 11:38–39). Concern regarding the defilement of utensils by non-Jews and "sinners" lies behind the Jews' criticism of Jesus's extended table fellowship. Jesus is never described as using dining utensils. This is because food at that time was prepared in bite-sized portions.

Jesus was reared by his father, a *tektōn* ("carpenter"), and pursued the same craft (Mark 6:3). Jesus would have been familiar with the contemporary suite of wood- and stone-working tools like hammers, saws, and chisels. Tools are part of the context of Jesus's life and teaching. His audiences lived close to the land and understood his references to agricultural tools like the plow (*arotron*) (Luke 9:62), sickle (*drepanon*) (Mark 4:29), winnowing fork (*ptyon*) (Matt 3:12||Luke 3:17), and yoke (*zygos*) (Matt 11:29). Jesus's Galilean disciples, who through their involvement in the fishing industry used such tools as the trammel net (*diktyon*) and the cast net (*amphiblēstron*) (Matt 4:18||Mark 1:16), understood his references to other tools of that trade, such as the dragnet (*sagēnē*) (Matt 13:47) and the handled market basket (*angos*) (Matt 13:48). They were also familiar with tools used in other pursuits, like the millstone (*mylos*) (Matt 18:6||Mark 9:42) and needles (sing. *rhaphis*) (Matt 19:24||Mark 10:25). They knew the difference between the grass- or reed-woven baskets (sing. *kophinos*) used to collect the scraps after the feeding of the five thousand (Matt 14:20||Mark 6:43||Luke 9:17||John 6:13) and the large rope-woven baskets (sing. *spyris*) used to collect the remaining food following the feeding of the four thousand (Matt 15:37||Mark 8:8). The latter type of container was substantial enough to lower Paul over the wall of Damascus (Acts 9:25).

Christians were not restrained from using tools and utensils on the "Lord's Day" by the apostolic teaching in the NT. According to Paul, Lord's Day observances are an area of individual liberty (Rom 14:5–6). The social position of some early Christians as poor artisans and slaves would have made it difficult for them to embrace the day of rest dear to Jewish-Christian traditions.

The Greek word *skeuos* can mean "vessel" or "instrument." At his conversion, Paul is declared by the Lord to be "his chosen instrument" (Acts 9:15). Paul asks rhetorically if the sovereign Lord does not have the right like the potter "to make out of the same lump of clay some pottery [*skeuos*] for special purposes and some for common use" (Rom 9:21). Paul declares to the Corinthians that they have the treasure of the gospel "in jars of clay," which refers to their mortal bodies (2 Cor 4:7). Elsewhere he writes,

> In a large house there are articles [*skeuē*] not only of gold and silver, but also of wood and clay; some are for special purposes and some for common use. Those who cleanse themselves from the latter will be instruments [*skeuos*] for special purposes, made holy, useful to the Master and prepared to do any good work. (2 Tim 2:20–21)

C. THE NEAR EASTERN WORLD

The ancient Mesopotamians recognized the patron deity of craftsmen by the name of Enki (Sumerian) or Ea (Akkadian). The Canaanites knew the patron of toolmakers as Kothar-wa-Ḥasis, and the Egyptians called him Ptah. Ancient Levantine society valued tools and tool-working. The Code of Hammurabi describes the relative values of artisans who brought their tools and knowledge to job sites (CH 274).

Domestic utensils in the ancient Levant were generally simple items made of clay, stone, wood, or bone. Bowls were ubiquitous. Hungry persons who did not want to waste a drop needed these for hot soups, stews, and porridge. Individual plates were virtually unknown since pieces of flat bread served as consumable plates. The Egyptians appear to have been the inventors of spoons and ladles. Egyptian and Mesopotamian domestic earthenware vessels were largely unadorned, and their styles continued for centuries without change. The Canaanites embraced more decorations. The Philistines who migrated into Palestine from the Aegean were most prolific in painting their beer jugs and other vessels with geometric designs and stylized animals. Round-bottomed cooking vessels were supported on open hearths with tripods of similarly sized stones. Containers and drinking vessels hammered into shape from ductile metal proliferated among the cultural elite in the Iron Age. Utensils used for personal adornment that appear in Early Bronze Age Egypt include mirrors and cosmetic applicators. Round, polished metal disks held by handles decorated with shapes like that of the beneficent goddess Hathor or with the protective grimace of the homely god Bes were used as mirrors. The Amarna Letters show that these valued Egyptian utensils were sought by the Kassite king of Babylon Burna-Buriash III (EA 14 ii 75–79).

Ancient Near Eastern tools are well represented as artifacts and in texts and images. The most extensive corpus comes from Egypt. The finest Middle Kingdom portrayal of tools adorns the tomb of Amenemhet at Beni Hasan. The most extensive New Kingdom portrayal of Egyptian tool utilization is on the walls of the tomb of Rekhmire at Thebes. Grave goods and models found in other tombs provide additional insights. Ancient Near Eastern texts are filled with references to tools and utensils. Census lists found at Mari identify approximately 20 percent of the population as being craftspeople such as metal workers, textile weavers, carpenters, masons, leather workers, fullers, jewelers, painters, and perfumers. These trades each developed expertise in the use of specific tools they employed. Although tools and utensils did not change much during the second millennium BC, the craftsman's toolbox evolved in the first millennium BC with the increased use of metal.

Among the assemblages of Mesopotamian, Canaanite, and Egyptian tools, the most fundamental were those used in agriculture and the acquisition of water. On farms, animals pulled plows and threshing sleds. Humans powered hoes, sickles, flails, winnowing equipment, and grinders. Tools that helped with acquiring potable water were important in arid regions where water did not flow at the surface of the land. Workers used hammers and chisels to cut shafts down through limestone to reach the water table. Water carriers could climb down into wide shafts and carry water out in containers. Water was removed from deeper wells that had narrow vertical shafts using ropes tied to containers. Wellheads show that ropes abraded grooves as people pulled heavy containers of water from the depths. An innovation evidenced in the late third millennium BC in southern Mesopotamia and embraced in Middle Kingdom Egypt was the *shaduf*. This device consisted of a long wooden pole laid across a vertical support that acted as a fulcrum. The short end of the pole was weighted, and a leather bucket was attached by rope to the long end. This counterbalanced beam facilitated the lifting of water from shallow wells or from rivers to irrigation canals that watered crops. This tool helped to increase Mesopotamia's and Egypt's dominance as food suppliers and helped sustain large populations. Later, the Neo-Assyrians found that the windlass provided a mechanical advantage in raising water from deep wells.

D. THE GRECO-ROMAN WORLD

Greece

The Classical World embraced the tools and technologies of neighboring regions and developed many innovative, specialized tools and domestic utensils. The Greeks recognized Hephaistos, whom the Romans knew as Vulcan, as the patron deity of artisans. The female patron of crafts was known as Athena by the Greeks and Minerva by the Romans. Knowledge of professions and tools was a valuable legacy passed from one generation to the next. Greek philosophers recognized tools as being of great potential value when placed in the hands of persons who knew how to employ them (Arist. *Pol.* 1.1253; Plato, *Resp.* 2.374). They also recognized the value of standardizing tools and utensils (Plato, *Leg.* 5.746).

Archaeologists know the domestic utensils and manufacturing tools of the Greeks through artifacts, artistic depictions on pottery, and literary references. Early Greeks are seen on pottery decoration to have employed the pestle and mortar to crack their grains, but in the Classical period the Greeks adopted hopper-rubbers and developed varieties of hand-querns (sing. *cheiromylos*). Later Hellenistic cooking and food-related utensils are well represented in Athenaeus's *The Deipnosophists*, for example. Even though their metal technology made it possible for them to have metal items, the Greeks used the cheaper terra-cotta in the manufacture of most domestic food utensils. While thin-walled and artfully decorated Greek fine wares are well known, the majority of utensils were undecorated, thicker-walled coarse wares. The most famous Greek container of antiquity was the amphora, a large vessel with substantial handles, a cone-shaped base, and a small neck. The Greeks adopted the amphora for its portability and its ability to be easily stored, to deliver controlled content, and to minimize evaporation. The dated stamps on the handles of amphorae from wine exporters like Rhodes are important evidence used by archaeologists in determining the dates of the strata of archaeological sites and trade networks. The Greeks employed portable cooking equipment made of ceramics, in contrast to the fixed-location earthenware, stone ovens, and hearths of the Levant. Greek utensils used for personal care included mirrors that, like earlier Egyptian models, might have a handle in the form of a statuette of the goddess Aphrodite.

Rome

The utensils of the Roman home and tools of Rome's craft workers are well known. The sites of Herculaneum and Pompeii provide assemblages of utensils employed in homes from the various strata of society and tools from a variety of trades. Roman domestic utensils are also known through literary references in authors such as the chef Apicius. An inventory of the contents of a commandant's kitchen chest found at Hadrian's Wall includes dishes (*scutulae*), plates (*parapsides*), bowls (*trullae*), vinegar bowls (*acetabula*), cups (*calices*), eggcups (*ovaria*), and bread baskets (*panaria*). The Romans made increasing use of metal utensils as the price for metal dropped. Metal spits, tripods, gridirons, and chains were used in kitchens to hold cooking vessels and food at the ideal distance from the heat sources. *Thermospodia*, metal stoves that contained hot coals, kept food and beverages hot in dining areas. The social elite used decorated utensils made of valuable metals. The Roman Empire saw the introduction of spoons (sing. *cocleare*) and knives at the dining table, as well as the increased use of glass vessels. Colored glass containers blown into molds became popular in the Principate. As blown glass technology proliferated, transparent glass (*vitrum*) vessels decorated with applied glass became the preferred material. Glass started to be used for large mirrors, like one found at Pompeii, but polished metal hand mirrors continued to be the norm until the appearance in the early sixteenth century AD of modern mirrors foliated with a tin amalgam. A distinctly Greek utensil adopted by the Romans, identified initially with athletic activities and moved to use in the public baths and personal hygiene, was the *strigil*, a curved metal blade used to scrape oil and grime from one's skin.

Sets of tools that played a significant role in Roman life were those of the land surveyors (*agrimensores*) and merchants. Civil engineers established field boundaries, plotted roads and aqueducts, and made other famous Roman architectural accomplishments possible. The basic tool was the *groma*, an instrument used to establish angles from a fixed point. Merchants used simple balances and more sophisticated "steelyard" balances for heavier commodities. While a Roman household might have had a small rotating hand mill, the industrial-scale donkey mill was the source of most flour. These "Pompeian mills" were composed of two stones. The upper stone, shaped like an hourglass, had an open center that formed a hopper for grain (*catillus*) and a hollowed-out lower section. The *catillus* was supported on a spindle above a lower, inverted, cone-shaped stone base (*meta*). Spokes inserted into the sides of the upper *catillus* and framework and supported by the spindle provided handles for rotating the mill by either animals or people.

E. THE JEWISH WORLD

The law and its interpretation shaped the Jewish community's use of tools and utensils. The rabbinic opinions contained in the Talmud reference a wide spectrum of domestic utensils. The prohibition against work on the Sabbath (Exod 31:14) was a Jewish distinctive. Rabbinical schools debated the use of industrial tools and domestic utensils on the Sabbath. The School of Shammai initially insisted on the total refraining of using instruments of production on the Sabbath, while the more flexible School of Hillel allowed processes such as textiles soaking in a vat of dye to continue on the Sabbath (*b. Šabb.* 18a–b). Rabbis agreed on the propriety of using domestic utensils and drew a contrast with similar tools used in industrial processes. Thus, on the Sabbath a hammer could be used to crack nuts, a cleaver to chop dried figs, a saw to cut hard cheese, a reed to skewer items, and a pot to carry food without causing offense (*b. Šabb.* 122a–b).

A second Jewish distinctive from the Torah that related to tools and utensils was ritual purity (Lev 11:29–44; 15:12; Num 31:20–24). The rabbis, who were concerned about contamination, engaged in long discussions concerning the ritual defilement of domestic utensils by vermin and unclean animals and persons. Their judgment varied with the shapes of items and their constituent materials. Earthenware items contaminated by corpses of unclean animals and human body emissions were deliberately broken to prevent subsequent useage. Utensils of wood, leather, bone, stone, metal, and glass that were contaminated to a lesser degree could be purified. Purification of utensils perceived to be impermeable was accomplished by washing those that carried cold materials in cold water and those that carried hot contents in boiling water. Metal items like spits and griddles that might have been used for non-kosher meat were purified in fire.

Some scholars have questioned the identification of Qumran as a settlement of the Essene sect. Those who support the Essene identification point toward artifacts such as the great number of carved stone utensils as being consistent with the Essenes' strictures in maintaining the purity of their food and drink (1QS V, 13). Stone containers are also found in other Jewish contexts. Domestic structures like the "Burnt House" in western Jerusalem and a cave on Mount Scopus where limestone vessels were both knife-pared and turned on lathes attest to the variety of stoneware mugs, bowls, and jars.

Jewish individuals embraced religious symbols, such as the menorah, on mold-made oil lamps, which could be used in domestic as well as cultic contexts. Jewish communities included depictions of symbolic utensils in their religious artwork in synagogues. Most common are the lampstand (menorah), lanterns, and, following the destruction of the temple in AD 70, incense shovels. By the sixth century AD, some Jewish communities, such as the one at Beth Alpha in the Beth Shan Valley of Israel, embraced didactic pictorial mosaics that showed the tools used by Abraham at the "Binding of Isaac." The laws of *kashrut* insisted on the use of separate utensils with dairy foods and meat.

F. THE CHRISTIAN WORLD

Christians embraced tools and utensils as instruments that could be used to serve God and people. Like the philosopher Plato, their teachers promoted restraint with regard to possessions and the acquisition of utensils and tools made of precious metals that served as status items more than serving utilitarian purposes. As Clement of Alexandria observed, knives decorated with ivory and silver handles cut no better than those made of wood, and ceramic lamps burn just as bright as those made of gold (*Paed.* 2.3). Augustine similarly attempted to avoid worldly entanglements and ate from earthenware and wooden dishes, although he did employ silver spoons (Possidius, *Vita Aug.* 22). The domestic utensils excavated at the Monastery of Martyrius, which was destroyed by the Persians in the seventh century AD, were made of plain terra-cotta. Christians in Egypt plundered temples of Serapis and recycled precious metals from idols to make vessels and utensils like chalices for use in post-Constantinian church buildings (Theodoret, *Hist. eccl.* 5.16). Christians did not have the same scruples as Jews about acquiring utensils from those who did not share their religion. Glass lamps set in bronze polycandelia hanging on chains and elevated on stands illuminated ecclesiastical structures.

Christians did not typically develop new tools; rather, they adopted many and marked them with Christian symbols when they were dedicated to ritual use. Distinctive bread stamps were used to mark Eucharistic loaves. *Eulogia* vessels like ampullae, lamps, and glass, ceramic, and metal flasks that were decorated with religious symbols served as religious curios carried home by pilgrims.

Although the Apostle Paul had declared Christians to be free from legalistic observance of the Sabbath, the general custom that developed before the reign of Constantine was for Christians to observe a day of rest from their labors on Sundays. According to Eusebius, the concept of such a day was transferred from Judaism (*Comm. Ps.* 92:32). The practice was subsequently retrojected onto the apostles (*Apostolic Constitutions* 1.7.23). In AD 321 Constantine made Sunday observance a matter of civil law, restricting craftworkers from practicing their trades but allowing farmers the freedom to work if the weather was right for planting or harvesting (*Cod. Theod.* 2.8.1). In AD 364 the Council of Laodicea condemned the observance of rest from labor on the seventh day as Judaizing and promoted only the first day of the week as a holy day of rest (Canon 29). In the increasingly Christian-dominated society of the Latin West and Byzantium in the East (*Corp.* 3.12.3), the church pressured urban workers to lay aside their tools on Sundays, thus restricting public and private business, but did grant them freedom to take up their domestic utensils and enjoy the day as a feast day.

BIBLIOGRAPHY: S. Cuomo, *Technology and Culture in Greek and Roman Antiquity* (2007); R. J. Forbes, *Studies in Ancient Technology* (8 vols., 1955–1964); S. Hodel-Hoenes, *Life and Death in Ancient Egypt: Scenes from Private Tombs in New Kingdom Thebes*, trans. D. Warburton (2000); Y. Israeli and D. Mevorah, ed., *Cradle of Christianity*, trans. D. Maisel and E. Goldstein-Leibowitz (2000); J. Magness, *Stone and Dung, Oil and Spit: Jewish Daily Life in the Time of Jesus* (2011); P. R. S. Moorey, *Ancient Mesopotamian Materials and Industries: The Archaeological Evidence* (1999); L. A. Moritz, *Grain-Mills and Flour in Classical Antiquity* (1958); P. T. Nicholson and I. Shaw, ed., *Ancient Egyptian Materials and Technology* (2000); J. P. Oleson, ed., *The Oxford Handbook of Engineering and Technology in the Classical World* (2008); S. A. Rosen, "Lithics" *OEANE* III.369–82; B. A. Sparkes, "The Greek Kitchen," *JHS* 82 (1962), 121–37; K. van der Toorn, "Judges xvi 21 in the Light of the Akkadian Sources," *VT* 36 (1986), 248–53.

RWS

See also BELLOWS & FURNACES, BONE & OBJECTS OF BONE, BOTTLES & GLASS, CERAMICS & POTTERY, FISH & FISHING, FOOD PRODUCTION, IVORY, LEATHER, METALLURGY, PURITY & IMPURITY, TEXTILES, and TREES.

TRADE

Trade refers to the physical exchange of goods and services. An early form of trade that is still practiced is barter. Trade can be done on the domestic or local level between individuals; in local markets; or on a broader level between kings and rulers or regions and nations, though such large-scale trade developed at a much later point in history than the earlier, more local varieties. Trade on a large scale is referred to as commerce. In addition to facilitating the exchange of commodities, trade also has an anthropological function: it is a primary means by which cultures, ideas, and technology merge and spread.

The origin of trade is unknown and little is known about long-distance exchange, how it was organized, and what standards of value existed before the third millennium BC. Karl Polanyi offers three models of economic behavior in ancient societies: exchange, redistribution, and reciprocity. These models functioned beside each other and according to Polanyi are the basic forms of early trade. In later periods trade shifted and began to take on a more commercial role. With the development of coinage and markets, commercial networks developed to allow trade to expand. At this stage, trade was also used for economic gain and profit. The simple subsistence system now worked alongside those whose aim was not to survive but to thrive.

A. THE OLD TESTAMENT

The land of Israel is part of a natural land bridge that joins Africa with Asia Minor and Mesopotamia. Its geography contains a number of natural arteries that run north-south and east-west. The Great Trunk Route, one of the oldest and longest roads used for trade, extends across one of these natural arteries connecting Egypt with Mesopotamia. The location and natural formation of these corridors allowed movement and exchange of goods from the earliest periods of humankind. In the patriarchal narratives, trade is portrayed as a common aspect of everyday life (Gen 23:13–16; 34:10). It is associated with kingdoms and foreigners who come into new lands (Gen 42:34), as in the story of Joseph. These references show that from an early point in biblical history trade was domestic and common, as well as civic and international.

The land of Israel did not contain an abundance of natural resources that could be traded; instead, Israel relied on its agriculture as its main resource for trade and export. During the Iron Age, agriculture expanded, arable land was converted into orchards, and hillsides were terraced for better farming. Wine, olive oil, and produce provided the greatest value for trade. This encouraged farming families to produce goods for market rather than just for their own consumption. By Late Iron II (ca. 700 BC), commercial trade had grown and local urban markets were filled with merchants trading goods and services (Amos 8:4–6; Jer 19:2; 37:21). Weights and scales measured silver pieces as the means of exchange for transactions if no other goods were available for trade (Jer 32:10).

Trade was conducted in and around the city gate, which was the center of commercial, political, and judicial activity (Deut 22:24; Josh 20:4; 2 Sam 15:2; Job 29:7). Near the city gate, traders and merchants were able to set up booths that collectively made up the local market. Excavations at a number of sites have revealed large open areas around city gates, which provided sufficient space for small shops and served as a prime location for business as people moved in and out of the city. Traders who traveled from location to location had easy access to the city gate and could sell their goods there.

Regional and international trade was necessary to obtain goods and unavailable resources. This became a common aspect of business and political relationships, as can be seen in the variety of trading partnerships referenced in the biblical text (the Midianites in Gen 37:28; Egypt, Kue, Syria, the Hittites, the Arabians, and Ophir in 1 Kgs 10:11, 15, 28–29; Tyre in Isa 23:8; Ashur, Eden, Haran, Raamah, Sheba, Tarshish, Tubal, Meshech, Javan, Kilmad, Edom, Judah, Israel, Rhodes, Damascus, Arabia, Kedar, Cyprus, Uzal, Helbon, Chaldea, and Elishah in Ezek 27).

During Solomon's reign, a network of "storage cities" was placed throughout the land to help control the royal commerce (1 Kgs 9:19). This does not mean that goods were necessarily produced at a high volume. The majority of the people who produced goods and resources were pastoralists and subsistence farmers who consumed most of their products and who relied on trade very little. Therefore, the expansion of trade beyond the local market stayed primarily within the realm of the elite and ruling classes.

During the historical periods covered by the OT, the majority of Israel's regional and long-distance trade was done overland because the land of Israel does not have good natural harbors for seafaring. The majority of regional overseas trade would have been conducted through Phoenicia,

Egypt, and Arabia. As a result, the development of regional and long-distance overland trade was vital for Israel. This required the domestication of animals as beasts of burden to carry goods over long distances. The OT mentions a number of animals used for carrying loads (the donkey, camel, horse, mule, and ox). Camels were the primary choice because they can carry over four hundred pounds and travel three to four days without drinking water. It has long been argued that the domestication of camels did not take place until sometime around the tenth century BC and that references in the OT to their use prior to this period are anachronistic. However, iconographic and osteological data provide evidence that camels could have been domesticated (at least on a limited scale) prior to the patriarchal period (see CAMELS). This gives credence to the mention of camels in the patriarchal narratives while also providing strong support for the description in 1 Kgs 10:2 of the Queen of Sheba using camels to bring incense to Solomon.

With the rise of the united monarchy, and into the period of the divided monarchy, the role of trade became essential both economically and diplomatically. Under the kingships of Israel during the Iron Age, OT references to trade transactions between rulers increased. David received cedar trees and carpenters from King Hiram of Tyre in order to build his palace (2 Sam 5:11). Hiram also provided Solomon with cedar, juniper, and gold (1 Kgs 9:11). First Kgs 10:28 records that Solomon's horses were imported from Egypt and Kue (Cilicia) at the "current price." Note that in this passage it is the king's traders who do the work rather than independent merchants. Horses were not a commodity generally desired by independent merchants in the Iron Age, as they were more commonly used in war and state affairs. Therefore, trade of this commodity would have primarily been done by the state.

Diplomatic trade, that is, trade between rulers, was also common; it secured relationships and provided safe passage for merchants and traders as they went through other lands (1 Kgs 10). Solomon's establishment of a seaport and fleet at Ezion Geber near Elath was important for the development of international trade. This port provided Israel with access to the Red Sea trade network (1 Kgs 10:11–12). The fleet was a joint expedition between Solomon and Hiram that sailed out to distant lands every three years (1 Kgs 10:22). It is to this port that Solomon imported a number of objects from Ophir, including large amounts of gold (1 Kgs 9:28; 10:11). Ophir, whose location is unknown, is associated with gold in numerous OT texts. An extrabiblical mention of this place is found in an eighth-century BC ostracon found at Tell Qasile with the text "Ophir gold to Beth-horon 30 shekels." The text on the ostracon has led scholars to place its location in India, Arabia, Africa, or North America. (See Yamauchi 2004, 82–90.)

The account of the Queen of Sheba depicts another of Solomon's diplomatic relationships. Accounts in the OT connecting Sheba with merchants and incense (Isa 45:14; 60:6; Jer 6:20; Ezek 27:22) have led scholars to place Sheba in southwest Arabia (Yemen). The above references, along with classical sources, have convinced many scholars that Sheba was the kingdom of Saba, a place known for growing and exporting frankincense and myrrh. These two commodities were precious, aromatic spices obtained from the exudation of trees that primarily grow in east Africa and southwest Arabia. Established connections between southwest Arabia and Palestine, Egypt, Mesopotamia, and India have a long tradition in which these types of commodities flow.

In 1 Kgs 10:1–3, the Queen of Sheba is described as coming to test Solomon's famed wisdom; however, she also brings gifts and a great retinue. The placement of this text between descriptions of Solomon's Red Sea naval voyages and his revenues from various sources, along with the queen's location in southwest Arabia, indicates that she came with commercial and diplomatic interests in mind. It is possible that the queen wanted to establish a commercial relationship with Solomon because his Red Sea trade might endanger her lucrative land trade route.

In a long lament for the city of Tyre, Ezekiel (ch. 27) describes Tyre as a magnificent ship that is doomed to disaster. The prophet lists her numerous trading partners and the great wealth of the merchandise that they traded with her. Prophetic literature also condemns the merchants of Nineveh for their commercial extravagance and greed that had brought the capital great wealth, which would quickly disappear with the city's fall (Nah 3:16).

Another possible indication of the importance of trade between Arabia and the Mediterranean is seen in Geshem's opposition to Nehemiah (Neh 2:19). A fifth-century BC inscription bearing the name Gashmu, which has been understood to refer to Geshem, places him in Ismaila by the Suez Canal (see Yamauchi 1980). The same inscription refers to Geshem as a king, leading scholars to believe that he controlled this area. If Geshem was in control of this area, it would make sense that he would have been opposed to the formation of an independent kingdom under Nehemiah, as this could have disrupted his trade in frankincense and myrrh.

B. THE NEW TESTAMENT

By NT times, Palestine was a part of the Greco-Roman world, and it played an important role in Rome's trade network in the east. Ancient records indicate that Palestine primarily imported luxury goods (wine from Italy, beer from Media, baskets from Egypt, sandals from Laodicea),

in addition to natural resources such as wood and metal. Exports continued to be primarily agricultural (olive oil, wheat, honey, figs). Despite the
difference in goods, the trade balance was generally in favor of Palestine.
Specific references to trade are limited in the NT, but they attest to the fact
that trade was a part of everyday life.

The use of coinage in trade had become a more common practice in
NT times. Things could be bought or exchanged with the right amount
of coinage, but the value of these coins was still based on the weight of
their metal.

Local urban markets comprised rows of shops lining the edges of colonnaded streets. The shops were in close proximity to each other, and were
arranged by the products they offered. This was convenient for shoppers
and allowed vendors to adjust prices in accordance with market changes.
Many of the merchants working in these shops were also traveling tradesmen who would rent a space temporarily before moving on. Merchant or
trader guilds were common within these markets. Paul's travel to Corinth
reflects this type of guild: he meets people of the same trade and stays and
works with them (Acts 18:1–4).

Local markets within Jewish villages and towns did not follow the pattern of the urban markets. People still specialized in specific products, but
trade was based more on subsistence than economic growth. Galilee had a
large commercial fishing industry in which independent fishermen could
make a living catching and selling or trading fish (Matt 4:18–22; Mark
1:16–20; Luke 5:1–11). Archaeological evidence suggests that there was no
standardized market location, leaving trade to be done out of homes and
in open areas around the village (Mark 6:36, 56). Although coinage would
have been accepted at these markets, it is just as likely that goods were
traded by bartering.

Holy or religious places also became hubs of trade or exchange for
those who were not able to supply their own sacrifice. One of the most
dramatic references to this practice can be found in John 2:16, when Jesus
aggressively cleanses the temple and commands the money changers and
those selling to move out, telling them, "Stop turning my Father's house
into a market!" The temple was a pilgrimage site, and since people traveling
to it would not bring the appropriate animals with them, a temple market
allowed them to obtain their sacrifices. This appears to have been an accepted practice, though the manner in which it was done was offensive to
Jesus. The Synoptic Gospels place such a "cleansing of the temple" at the
end of Jesus's ministry (Matt 21:12–13||Mark 11:15–18||Luke 19:45–47).

The port of Caesarea is mentioned in Acts 9:30 as the place from which
Paul sailed to Tarsus. Although the NT does not give details about the port,
archaeological evidence has shown that it functioned as the primary port

of Palestine in NT times. The port allowed Palestine to directly engage in overseas trade. The port was built under the reign of Herod the Great, and was situated near Herod's palace, which allowed him to monitor commodities (imports and exports) and people going in and out of Palestine.

In a passage that is reminiscent of Ezekiel's condemnation of Tyre for pride in its trade (Ezek 27), John condemns Babylon (i.e., Rome) for its greed and its reliance on its trade of luxury goods:

> The merchants of the earth will weep and mourn over her because no one buys their cargoes anymore—cargoes of gold, silver, precious stones and pearls; fine linen, purple, silk and scarlet cloth; every sort of citron wood, and articles of every kind made of ivory, costly wood, bronze, iron and marble; cargoes of cinnamon and spice, of incense, myrrh and frankincense, of wine and olive oil, of fine flour and wheat; cattle and sheep; horses and carriages; and human beings sold as slaves [Gk. *sōmatōn*, "bodies"]. (Rev 18:11–13)

C. THE NEAR EASTERN WORLD

There are no textual sources that describe the economic principles, towns, traders, goods and services, or markets of the ancient Near East prior to the third millennium BC. Therefore, evidence of early trade is gained primarily through archaeology, anthropology, and a number of other related disciplines.

Trade in the Near East has been traced as far back as 10,000 BC and earlier (the Paleolithic Period), with evidence of variations of worked stone tools and seashells being found hundreds of miles from their sources. This may not be due to trade proper, but it shows evidence of the movement of humans to gather resources from various regions for specific purposes.

The Neolithic Period (ca. 8500–4500 BC) saw numerous changes and innovations, including the development and technological advancement of food production, agriculture, herding, building techniques, and stone and tool work, and the emergence of pottery. It is no surprise that with such developments and the emergence of settlements, strong evidence of trade also begins to appear in the archaeological record. Obsidian (volcanic glass) blades that originated in mountainous regions in Anatolia (modern-day Turkey) have been found in Neolithic village sites in the Near East. Lapis lazuli dating from ca. 5500–3500 BC has been found in southern Mesopotamia, far from its source in modern-day Afghanistan.

During the first half of the Early Bronze Age (3500–2250 BC), Egypt was trading with the town of Byblos along the Lebanese coast. Evidence of this trade relationship has been found in excavations at Byblos, which revealed a number of Egyptian-style objects that date to this period.

It is almost certain that by this period a substantial amount of trade was carried out by both river and sea. Settlement patterns and archaeological evidence suggest that water sources were important for reasons beyond survival. The Nile is a prime example of this: people settled around it were able to use it for drinking, cultivating crops, and travel. Travel up the Nile was possible due to the winds, which blew from north to south. The same pattern is also found in Mesopotamia in the region of Sumer, where a number of city-states (Uruk, Kish, Eridu, and Lagash) were established in close proximity to the Tigris and Euphrates.

Administrative documents (2334–2193 BC) from the city of Umma in southern Mesopotamia reveal that merchants were responsible for at least some of the trade that took place. While it is unclear if these merchants traveled to collect their items, it appears that they traded both for the government and for individuals.

Extensive trade between Mesopotamia and the Indus River Valley civilization to the east (now in Pakistan) took place during the reign of Sargon of Agade (2340–2284 BC). Additional evidence of long-distance trade is found in texts dating to the Ur III period (2112–2004 BC) that list locally produced goods as well as goods from foreign regions. These documents record the goods that merchants sold in order to get silver, in addition to the prices of goods they subsequently bought, stated in weights of silver. These merchants sold fish, grain, wool, leather, and silver. In return, the merchants collected fruits, vegetables, oils, spices, timber, metals, gypsum, alkalis, and other goods. Merchants handled official government business, but not all of their transactions were of this nature. It seems that the line between official and private business was blurred, and merchants were able to handle both simultaneously. These texts reveal that by the end of the Early Bronze Age there was a very specific, well-organized, and dynamic trade industry. Trade was not completely controlled by the government, but government standards were still set for fairness, as seen in Hammurabi's Code.

Long-distance trade continued throughout the Middle Bronze Age (1950–1550 BC) in Mesopotamia. Cities such as Sippar, Ur, Larsa, Babylon, and Mari continued to export leather, produce, and oils, and to transship tin. They imported metals, precious stones, medicinal compounds, perfumes, and copper.

Assyrian trade during the Middle Bronze Age is well documented, with over sixteen thousand surviving cuneiform texts kept by the merchants who traveled to and from eastern Asia Minor. Merchants from northern Mesopotamia exported tin and textiles and imported copper and gold. These merchants were entrusted with money from the Assyrian capital, Ashur, and they moved their goods to an area called Kanesh. They were able to keep one-third of the profit. Three generations of numerous merchant families dating from ca. 1900–1820 BC can be traced in cuneiform texts that detail their travels and merchandise.

Trade dramatically increased during the Late Bronze Age (1550–1200 BC), not only in the Near East but also in the Aegean world. Cuneiform tablets written in Akkadian have been found in the capital city el-Amarna that chronicle connections with Palestine and also detail international trade with Babylon, the Hittite Empire, Mitanni, and Egypt. It appears from the Amarna tablets, correspondence between Amenhotep III and IV and the kings of Mesopotamia and Mitanni, that these empires relied on diplomatic trade.

Cuneiform tablets from Ugarit reveal trade with the Aegean in the Late Bronze Age. A large number of fine goods were being shipped into Ugarit and Cyprus from the Aegean. Copper, found chiefly on the island of Cyprus, also became an important commodity for trade. Ox-hide-shaped ingots of copper have been recovered from shipwrecks.

At the turn of the millennium, the Phoenicians expanded trade as far west as Spain. Their base was along the Lebanese and Syrian coasts, where they established small colonies on islands and coastlines, indicating that their interest was in trade, not in expansion. The Phoenicians were traders par excellence; their goods included wood and purple dye from their homeland (in modern-day Lebanon), as well as wine and oil from Greece and Syria.

Not much is known about the Neo-Assyrian trade system. It is evident that trade took place, as foreign goods have been found in the archaeological record, but no administrative documentation detailing trade has been found. The same problem exists for the Neo-Babylonian period, though we do know, for example, that Nebuchadnezzar II (604–562 BC) had a chief merchant with a Phoenician name. By the sixth century BC the Persians had united most of the Near East, allowing for trade and commerce to expand further than before.

D. THE GRECO-ROMAN WORLD

Greece

Trade and seafaring increased in the Mediterranean under both the Phoenicians and the Greeks. As early as 1300 BC, Mycenaean Greek merchants and traders were bartering and trading throughout the Mediterranean. This expansion of trade continued through the Hellenistic period. With the military campaigns of Alexander, trade increased such that some cities began to depend on imports.

Greek trade was motivated by the acquisition of foreign goods. The Greeks used three main sea routes: a southeast route to Crete, Cyprus, and Egypt; a northeast route to the Black Sea; and a western route to southern Italy. The major imports coming from these routes included timber, slaves, hides, grain, nuts, cheese, fish, raisins, and a number of luxury goods. Greek exports included a range of manufactured goods, such as wine, olive oil, weapons, pottery, and jewelry.

Rome

By the late second century BC, Rome had begun to dominate and control a large portion of the Mediterranean. At the beginning of Rome's expansion, the Mediterranean was populated with a number of independent states and kingdoms that were in constant conflict with each other, fighting over territory, goods, and resources. Over time, Rome exerted control over these kingdoms: Macedonia in 146 BC, western Asia Minor in 133 BC, Seleucid Syria in 64 BC, Judea in 63 BC, Ptolemaic Egypt in 30 BC, Galatia in 25 BC, Cappadocia in AD 18, and Nabataean Arabia in AD 106, along with a number of other smaller states. Rome was also able to remove pirates from the Mediterranean. This had a dramatic impact on the economy linked to the Mediterranean and changed the environment for trade by providing safety for merchant shipping.

During the first two centuries AD, the Roman government supported trade and economic interaction across its empire. The many roads that the government built for its military were also useful for traders and merchants. Roman outposts along these roads ensured safety and allowed direct access to places all across the empire. Rome also placed few restrictions on merchants and kept taxes, tolls, and tariffs low on goods passing from region to region within the empire. Rome's military also needed many supplies and goods. This military market provided great opportunity for merchants and traders all over the empire.

The relative stability of the empire allowed for greater urban development and the expansion of city centers. Urban centers relied on goods and supplies being brought into the city, and this provided a large market for both local and long-distance merchants and traders. Most of the cities depended on their rural surroundings for agricultural needs, and the rural towns depended on the goods that could be found within the city.

Coinage also played a role in the trade market of the Roman Empire. Rome minted its own coins, and this coinage was in use throughout the empire, especially in the military and urban centers. Its fundamental value was in the weight of the metal used to make it. Coins were issued in gold, silver, and bronze, each with their own values. It is unclear how extensive the use of this coinage was in rural regions of the empire. The most common means of exchange for trade other than coins was bartering.

Despite Rome's promotion and encouragement of trade, Roman senators were restricted in their involvement in this occupation, according to the ancient historian Titus Livius. The professions of trader and merchant could be held by slaves, freedmen, equestrians, and foreigners. Because trade and commerce could provide large fortunes, senators and equestrians lured by large profits invested in ships and trading enterprises, through intermediaries.

E. THE JEWISH WORLD

Commercial transactions were organized and heavily regulated in rabbinic Judaism. Rules for ethical transactions and religious purity were to be upheld in the commercial world of trade. Wholesale dealers were required, by the Mishnah, to clean scales and measures once a month, while retailers had to clean them twice a week. Furthermore, the Mishnah required balances to be cleaned after every transaction, and weights had to be cleaned once a week. To keep merchants honest and to reduce spillage or waste in fluids and solids, an extra ounce was added to liquid transactions for every ten pounds of material, with half an ounce added to solid transactions at the same rate.

Rules were set in place to protect both sides involved in a transaction. To protect merchants, rules were set as to how they could sell their goods so that consumers could not cast doubt on transactions. Consumers had the right to contest a transaction they thought was unfair. If they could show they had been cheated, they could return an item or claim the balance owed to them, but only if this claim was made within the time needed to inspect and verify the item's value. Furthermore, a bargain was not finalized until both parties had taken possession of their goods.

Trade or craft guilds were common throughout the Roman Empire. In Palestine these guilds even dictated the days and hours their members were allowed to work. They also protected their members against certain losses, such as of ships or donkeys.

F. THE CHRISTIAN WORLD

Trade during the first three hundred years of Christianity was more or less the same as in the pagan world. The use of coinage had become the standard for doing business, and bartering was a secondary means of exchange.

Trade and trade routes took on a new role during this period inasmuch as they provided a means for the Christian message to spread. The spread of Christianity can be linked to the paths of trade, which allowed Christians to travel easily from city to city. For example, the spread of Christianity to Central Asia can be credited to Nestorian merchants traveling along the Silk Route. The first Nestorian missionaries, led by Alopen, were welcomed to the capital of China at that time, Ch'ang-an, by T'ao-tsung, the second emperor of the T'ang Dynasty (618–907). (See Yamauchi 1996, 114–26.)

Not all Christians were in favor of trade. The church father Tertullian warned of trade and its relation to coveting, concerned that it could lead to idolatry. Others saw trade as a natural part of life, and some (following in the footsteps of Paul) viewed it as a tool for the spread of the gospel.

By the fourth century AD, the entire Mediterranean was politically unified. It had a common system of coinage and laws that regulated trade and commerce, though the economy was not completely unified. The transition of Christianity into the political system and the role the church played in trade and commerce changed the nature of trade. Trade was not just a political or economic matter in which Christians participated; it had also became a religious matter connected to the church. The acquisition of goods and services for the church and their distribution to the people involved both local and international trade.

BIBLIOGRAPHY: L. Adkins and R. Adkins, *Handbook to Life in Ancient Greece* (1997); M. Artzy, "Routes, Trade, Boats and 'Nomads of the Sea'" in *Mediterranean Peoples in Transition: Thirteenth to Early Tenth Centuries BCE*, ed. S. Gitin, A. Mazar, and E. Stern (1998), 439–48; M. M. Austin, "Greek Trade, Industry, and Labor," *CAM* II.723–51; W. Ball, *Rome in the East: The Transformation of an Empire* (2007); R. S. Boraas, "Trade and Transportation," in *The HarperCollins Bible Dictionary*, ed. P. J. Achtemeier (1996), 1165–71; P. A. Cartledge, "Trade, Greek," *OCD*, 1535–37; H. Crawford, "An Early Dynastic Trading Network in North Mesopotamia," in *La circulation des biens, des personnes et des idées dans le Proche-Orient ancien: Actes de la XXXVIIIe Rencontre Assyriologique Internationale (Paris 8–10 juillet 1991)*, ed. D. Charpin and F. Joannès (1992), 77–82; W. Culican, *The First Merchant Venturers: The Ancient Levant in History and Commerce* (1966); A. Edersheim, *Sketches of Jewish Social Life in the Days of Christ* (1970); P. Esler, ed., *The Early Christian World I* (2000); T. J. Figueira, "Karl Polanyi and Ancient Greek Trade: The Port of Trade," *The Ancient World* 10 (1984), 15–30; C. Freeman, *The World of the Romans*, ed. J. F. Drinkwater and A. Drummond (1993); R. Gower, *The New Manners and Customs of Bible Times* (1987); W. W. Hallo, *Origins: The Ancient Near Eastern Background of Some Modern Western Institutions* (1996); D. C. Hopkins, "Trade and Commerce," *EDB* 1323–25; K. Hopkins, "Roman Trade, Industry, and Labor," *CAM* 2.753–77; B. S. J. Isserlin, *The Israelites* (1998); J. S. Jeffers, *The Greco-Roman World of the New Testament Era: Exploring the Background of Early Christianity* (1999); V. Karageorghis and D. Michaelides, ed., *The Development of the Cypriot Economy: From the Prehistoric Period to the Present Day* (1996); N. Kashtan, ed., *Seafaring and the Jews* (2001); P. J. King and L. E. Stager, *Life in Biblical Israel* (2001); M. G. Klingbeil, "Trade and Travel," *DOTHB* 962–67; N. Lewis and M. Reinhold, ed., *Roman Civilization: Selected Readings II: The Empire* (3rd ed., 1990); G. L. Mattingly, "Trade," *DANE* 297–98; G. L. Mattingly, "Transport and Travel," *DANE* 299–300; R. McLaughlin, *Rome and the Distant East: Trade Routes to the Ancient Lands of Arabia, India and China* (2010); J. I. Miller, *The Spice Trade of the Roman Empire, 29 B.C. to A.D. 641* (1969); T. G. Parkin and A. J. Pomeroy, *Roman Social History: A Sourcebook* (2007); J. J. Paterson, "Trade, Roman," *OCD* 1537–38; I. Puskás, "Trade Contacts between India and the Roman Empire," in *India and the Ancient World: History, Trade and Culture before A.D. 650*, ed. G. Pollet (1987), 141–56; N. Rodgers, *Life in Ancient Rome* (2007); H. W. F. Saggs, *Everyday Life in Babylonia and Assyria* (1965); J.-A. Shelton, ed., *As the Romans Did: A Sourcebook in Roman Social History* (2nd ed., 1998); D. C. Snell, ed., *A Companion to the Ancient Near East* (2007); D. C. Snell, *Life in the Ancient Near East: 3100–332 B.C.E.* (1997); D. C. Snell, "Trade and Commerce (ANE)," *ABD* VI.625–29; M. Sugerman, "Trade and Power in Late Bronze Age Canaan," in *Exploring the Longue Durée: Essays in Honor of Lawrence E. Stager*, ed. J. D. Schloen (2009), 439–48; J. A. Thompson, *Handbook of Life in Bible Times* (1986); E. M. Yamauchi, "Abraham and Archaeology: Anachronisms or Adaptations?," in *Perspectives on Our Father Abraham: Essays in Honor of Marvin R. Wilson*, ed. S. A. Hunt (2010), 15–32; E. M. Yamauchi, "Adaptation and Assimilation in Asia," *Stylos* 4 (1996), 103–26; E. M. Yamauchi, *Africa and the Bible* (2004); E. M. Yamauchi, "The Archaeological Background of Nehemiah," *BSac* 137 (1980), 291–309; E. M. Yamauchi, *Persia and the Bible* (1990).

LPG

See also AGRICULTURE, BOATS & SHIPS, CAMELS, DONKEYS & MULES, FISH & FISHING, FOOD PRODUCTION, HARBORS, INCENSE, MEDIUM OF EXCHANGE, METALLURGY, SLAVERY, TAXATION, TEXTILES, and TREES.

TREES

Woody plants include trees, shrubs, and vines. Trees are characteristically more than fifteen feet in height and have a single, well-defined trunk. Shrubs, in contrast, typically have several stems and are less than fifteen feet tall. Woody vines are slender plants that require support. Trees provide shade, wood for fuel and construction, foods, seasonings, resins, and medicines. Many ancient societies considered the tree to symbolize the source of life and produced depictions of a "sacred tree."

A. THE OLD TESTAMENT

The "tree of life" stood in the garden of Eden along with the "tree of the knowledge of good and evil" (Gen 2:9). The "tree of life" appears in several passages in the book of Proverbs (3:18; 11:30; 13:12; 15:4).

The Canaanites worshipped the goddess Asherah, who was symbolized by a wooden pole (Deut 16:21; Judg 6:25). The Asherah (Heb. ʾăšērâ) may originally have been a living tree. According to the ESV translation of Deut 16:21, the Lord proclaims: "You shall not plant any tree as an Asherah beside the altar of the LORD your God that you shall make." The NIV reads "any wooden Asherah pole." Asherah's sacred tree could "be a palm, an oak, a terebinth or a tamarisk" (Hestrin, 223).

The prophet Ezekiel condemns apostate Israelites, declaring:

> And they will know that I am the Lord, when their people lie slain among their idols around their altars, on every high hill and on all the mountaintops, under every spreading tree and every leafy oak—places where they offered fragrant incense to all their idols. (Ezek 6:13)

More than fifteen species of tree are mentioned in the OT. Among the most common are the fig, olive, oak, terebinth, acacia, and cedar. The fig tree (Heb. tĕʾēnâ; *Ficus carica*) is the first fruit tree to be mentioned in the Bible (Gen 3:7), as Adam and Eve cover their nakedness with its leaves. The fig tree and figs are mentioned forty-one times in the OT.

The olive is one of the first trees mentioned in the Bible (Gen 8:11), in the passage in which the dove returns to Noah with an olive branch. The olive (Heb. *zayit*; *Olea europaea*) is the best-known and one of the most important trees of the Mediterranean Basin and Middle East. Olives were highly valued, and the harvesting and pressing out of olives was a significant part of the life of rural families. The pulp contains about 40 percent oil, which was used for lamps, cooking, and medicinal purposes, as well as anointing in religious ceremonies. The psalmist proclaims that he is like an olive tree because he trusts in God's unfailing love (Ps 52:8).

Jericho was known as the City of Palms (Judg 1:16; 3:13). The date palm (Heb. *tāmār*; *Phoenix dactylifera*), though one of the most important trees because of its various useful products, is only mentioned in seven passages in the OT (Exod 15:27; Lev 23:40; Num 33:9; Neh 8:15; Ps 93:12; Song 7:8–9; and Joel 1:12). The trees can grow to a height of one hundred feet. As the trees are unisexual, the female trees were artificially fertilized by using the flowers of a male tree. Palms begin to bear dates only after they are at least twenty years old. Their dates are sweet and can be dried and pressed. The trunks can be used for buildings, and the leaves for ropes and basketry.

The oak tree (*Quercus coccifera*) has spiny-toothed leaves and bears acorns. It is a deciduous tree that can reach a height of sixty feet and an age of five hundred years. Abraham settled by the "oaks [Heb. *ʾēlōnê*] of Mamre" near Hebron (Gen 13:18). The Hebrew word for "oak" is etymologically related to the word for God, *ʾēl*. Deborah, Rebekah's nurse, was buried under the oak outside Bethel (Gen 35:8), a site that was henceforth called Allon Bakuth, "the Oak of Weeping." Absalom, David's rebellious son, was caught by his long hair in the branches of the *ʾēlâ* tree (2 Sam 18:9–14), after which he was speared by Joab. The tree name here is rendered "oak" by most English versions, but the ESV marginal note suggests "terebinth" (see Stager and King, 110).

The Lord declares, "But as the terebinth and oak leave stumps when they are cut down, so the holy seed will be the stump in the land" (Isa 6:13). The terebinth (*Pistacia palaestina*), which can grow up to thirty feet tall, produces pistachio nuts (Heb. *boṭnîm*; Gen 43:11).

The sycamore fig (Heb. *šiqmâ*; *Ficus sycomorus*) bore fruits that were inferior to true figs. The trees could reach a height of sixty feet. The prophet Amos of Tekoa worked with sycamore figs, pricking them at a certain stage to make them edible (Amos 7:14).

The acacia (Heb. *šiṭṭâ*), a desert tree, was a member of the Mimosa family. This tree grows nine to eighteen feet high and has spiny branches that bear yellow flowers. Its wood was used for various parts of the tabernacle, including the ark (Exod 25–27, 30).

Seeds of the pomegranate (Heb. *rimmôn*; *Punica granatum*), which was indigenous to Persia and north India, have been found at Early Bronze Age sites in Israel. The pomegranate is a large shrub or small tree with orange flowers and reddish fruits. The pulp surrounds individual seeds inside a spongy, inedible rind. Its numerous seeds made it a symbol of fertility. Images of pomegranates adorned Aaron's priestly robe (Exod 28:33–34) and also the temple of Solomon (1 Kgs 7:18, 20, 42). In addition to a large cluster of grapes, the twelve spies brought back pomegranates from the Valley of Eshkol in Canaan (Num 13:23).

The tamarisk (Heb. *'ēšel*; *Tamarix aphylla* or *syriaca*), with fine scale-like leaves, is a flowering plant rather than a gymnosperm (coniferous tree). This large shrub or small tree, which was distributed widely in dry regions of the Old World, has very deep roots and provided welcome shade in these areas (1 Sam 22:6). Abraham planted a tamarisk in the desert area in Beersheba (Gen 21:33). The bones of Saul and his sons were buried under a tamarisk tree at Jabesh (1 Sam 31:13). The sweet, dried, flake-like exudates of the twigs have been suggested by some scholars as a candidate for the OT manna.

The "cedar of Lebanon" (Heb. *'erez*; *Cedrus libani*) is the best-known gymnosperm of the Middle East. It is a mountain species, and its silhouette graces the modern flag of the country of Lebanon. Its leaves form a pyramid shape, and its wood emits a pleasant odor and resists rotting and infestation by insects. Some cedars live up to five hundred years. There are more than seventy references to this tree in the OT. Solomon obtained cedars from Phoenicia (Lebanon) for his temple (1 Kgs 5:6–10; 2 Chr 2:8–9). He employed crews of ten thousand men in three shifts to cut down trees from the forests. Later, Zerubbabel also obtained cedar logs from the same area, for the rebuilding of the temple (Ezra 3:7).

In cooperation with Hiram of Tyre, Solomon sent fleets from his Red Sea port of Ezion Geber to a distant land called Ophir, which has been variously placed in Arabia, Africa, and India. From Ophir he obtained gold and exotic animals, such as monkeys (or peacocks; see Yamauchi 2004, 84). Some scholars have identified the import *'almuggîm/'algûmmîm* (1 Kgs 10:11–12; 2 Chr 2:7; 9:10–11) as sandalwood. But as it is mentioned with trees from Lebanon, it should more probably be identified as the juniper tree (*Juniperus phoenicea excelsa*). Juniper produced a fragrant red wood, which was often confused with cedar. Some scholars believe that the "cedars of Lebanon" were actually junipers. (See Adams.)

When Nehemiah went to Jersualem from Susa to supervise the rebuilding of the city, he obtained from Artaxerxes I an official warrant to use timbers from Asaph, the official in charge of the royal forest (Heb. *pardēs*; Neh 2:8). The Solomonic figure in Ecclesiastes boasts: "I made gardens and parks [*pardēsîm*] and planted all kinds of fruit trees in them" (Eccl 2:5).

The word *pardēs* occurs in only one other OT passage, Song 4:13, where it is translated "orchard." *Pardēs* is a Persian loanword (Yamauchi 1990, 332–34). The Greek transliteration *paradeisos* is used in the Septuagint for the garden of Eden (Gen 2–3).

The Lord declares:

> I myself will take a shoot from the very top of a cedar and plant it; I will break off a tender sprig from its topmost shoots and plant it on a high and lofty mountain. On the mountain heights of Israel I will plant it; it will produce branches and bear fruit and become a splendid cedar. Birds of every kind will nest in it; they will find shelter in the shade of its branches. All the trees of the forest will know that I the LORD bring down the tall tree and make the low tree grow tall. I dry up the green tree and make the dry tree flourish.
> (Ezek 17:22–24)

In addition to logs of cedar, Hiram supplied Solomon with logs of juniper (Heb. *běrôš*; *Juniperus excelsa*), a conifer that resembles the cedar tree (1 Kgs 5:22, 24). God himself declares: "I am like a flourishing juniper; your fruitfulness comes from me" (Hos 14:8b).

Among the trees that made up "the glory of Lebanon" (Isa 60:13) was the cypress (Heb. *tě'aššûr*; *Cupressus sempervirens*). The Hebrew word for this tree occurs elsewhere only in Isa 41:19. The cypress is a slender evergreen that grows up to fifty feet high.

The almond tree (*Amygdalus communis*) is noteworthy for its white or pink flowers, which blossom as early as January. The Hebrew name *šāqēd* signifies "wakefulness" (cf. Jer 1:11–12).

Incense from frankincense, myrrh, and other resins is mentioned 159 times in twenty-two books of the OT (Herrera). Instructions for making incense included these provisions: "And the LORD said to Moses, 'Take sweet spices, stacte, and onycha, and galbanum, sweet spices with pure frankincense (of each shall there be an equal part), and make an incense . . .'" (Exod 30:34–35, RSV). Stacte is possibly from the storax tree (*Styrax officinalis*), the identity of onycha is uncertain, and galbanum is the resin of *Ferula galbaniflua*, a relative of fennel and parsley.

The oldest and most prized incenses are produced from the gum resins of certain short trees that grow only in east Africa and southern Arabia. The well-known frankincense is obtained from the short trees of the genus *Boswellia* (family Burseraceae), which grow on the coast of Sudan in east Africa (which the ancient Egyptians knew as the land of Punt) and in the southern area of Arabia, such as in Yemen and Oman. Though some species of this tree also grow in India and Pakistan, the Arabian area was the source of this incense (along with myrrh) in antiquity. Harvesting in this area continues to the present day.

Myrrh, another well-known incense, is an oleoresin made from gum resin obtained from two species of small trees of the genus *Commiphora* (also family Burseraceae). The principal species are *Commiphora myrrha*, which grows in Ethiopia, Arabia, and Somalia, and *Centaurium erythraea*, from Arabia. The resins from these two species are sometimes differentiated as herabol and bisabol, respectively.

The poplar (Heb. *ʿărābâ*; *Populus euphratica*) was a tall tree that grew on the banks of streams (Job 40:22; Isa 44:4). The Jewish exiles in Babylonia lamented their removal from their homeland: "By the rivers of Babylon we sat and wept when we remembered Zion. There on the poplars we hung our harps" (Ps 137:2).

The value of fruit trees is attested in the prohibition against cutting them down while besieging a city in Canaan (Deut 20:19). When the kings of Israel and Judah besieged the king of Moab, they cut down "every good tree" at the word of the prophet Elisha. M. Hasel explains this apparent contradiction by pointing out that Moab lay outside the land promised to the children of Israel (Hasel, 206).

Although pine trees, such as the Aleppo pine (*Pinus halepensis*), must have been numerous at the lower elevations, their wood was not strong. The word *ʾōren*, which is translated "pine" in the NIV, occurs only once in the OT (Isa 44:14).

B. THE NEW TESTAMENT

The NT has fewer references to plant life than the OT, perhaps reflecting writing in a more urban setting. Jesus's childhood with his father, Joseph, who was a carpenter or craftsman (Gk. *tektōn*), would have involved woodworking. Jesus taught in the Sermon on the Mount that "every good tree bears good fruit, but a bad tree bears bad fruit" (Matt 7:17).

The fig tree has large leaves that afford a pleasant shade (John 1:48; cf. Zech 3:10). Early figs ripen in June, the late ones (Gk. sing. *olynthos*, a word that occurs only in Rev 6:13) in August. The Parable of the Barren Fig Tree (Luke 13:6–9) is one of the more enigmatic passages in the NT.

The fig-mulberry tree (Gk. *sykomorea*) is mentioned by Luke (19:4) as the tree climbed by Zacchaeus, the tax collector, who wished to get a better look at the passing Jesus. This tree, which is sometimes translated as "sycamore-fig," is to be distinguished from a related tree, the black mulberry (Gk. *sycaminos*; *Morus nigra*), which appears in Jesus's statement, "If you have faith as small as a mustard seed, you can say to this mulberry tree, 'Be uprooted and planted in the sea,' and it will obey you" (Luke 17:6).

The carob tree (*Ceratonia siliqua*) produces a "horn-like" pod containing beans. The carob has been harvested from the wild and also cultivated in the Near East for thousands of years. Its fruits have long been used to feed livestock. These were the pods that the prodigal son fed to pigs (Gk. sing. *keration*, "little horn"; Luke 15:16).

The Mount of Olives loomed to the east of the Jerusalem temple. This was the setting of many events in the life of Jesus, including his ascension from Bethany (Luke 24:50). At the base of the mount was the garden (Gk. *kēpos*) of Gethsemane (Matt 26:36||Mark 14:33||Luke 22:40||John 18:1), where Jesus prayed and where he was betrayed. The name Gethsemane (Gk. *gethsēmani*) reflects the Aramaic *gat šĕmānê*, "olive press."

According to Paul, "Christ redeemed us from the curse of the law by becoming a curse for us—for it is written, 'Cursed is everyone who is hanged on a tree [*xylon*]'" (Gal 3:13, ESV; cf. also 1 Pet 2:24, ESV). The OT had proclaimed that one hung on a "tree" was accursed:

> And if a man has committed a crime punishable by death and he is put to death, and you hang him on a tree, his body shall not remain all night on the tree, but you shall bury him the same day, for a hanged man is cursed by God. You shall not defile your land that the Lord your God is giving you for an inheritance. (Deut 21:22–23, ESV)

The crucifixion thus was a huge stumbling block to Jews.

Paul uses the symbolism of the olive tree to explain the scattering and gathering of Israel, comparing the Jews to a cultivated olive tree and the gentiles to a wild olive branch (Rom 11:16–24). Jude likens the godless to "autumn trees, without fruit and uprooted—twice dead" (Jude 12).

In the final book of the NT, the Lord promises: "To the one who is victorious, I will give the right to eat from the tree of life, which is in the paradise of God" (Rev 2:7). The angels are "told that they should not hurt the grass of the earth, nor any green thing, nor any tree, but only the men who do not have the seal of God on their foreheads" (Rev 9:4, NASB). In the New Jerusalem, as John describes it, "On each side of the river stood the tree of life, bearing twelve crops of fruit, yielding its fruit every month. And the leaves of the tree are for the healing of the nations" (Rev 22:2).

C. THE NEAR EASTERN WORLD

Mesopotamia

The concept of sacred trees and sacred forests or landscapes appears in numerous religious traditions. A text from the library of Ashurbanipal at

Nineveh describes a *giš-kin* tree that grew in Eridu. Shining like lapis-lazuli, it rises from the *apsu*, the underground water, and "is filled with abundance." J. Walton describes it as a "cosmic tree" (Walton, 121).

A ubiquitous symbol in Assyrian palaces was the so-called "Assyrian sacred tree," which most regard as a stylized palm tree. This object may have originally represented the god Aššur. The palm tree was also associated with Ishtar. Some scholars have concluded that it was not a "tree of life" but rather a symbol of prosperity (see Giovino). Synonyms for the date palm are "tree of abundance" (Akk. *iṣ mašrî*) and "tree of riches" (Akk. *iṣ rašê*).

This tree symbol achieved its greatest prominence during the reign of Assurnasirpal II (883–859 BC) in his palace at Nimrud (ancient Kalḫu, Calah), where it is depicted ninety-six times. Many scenes depict the tree in the middle of two genii, winged figures with birds' heads. The genii are holding buckets and reaching out with oval objects toward the tree. E. B. Tylor first interpreted the scene, in 1890, as the ritual fertilization of the date palm, an interpretation that has been rejected by many scholars but has recently been affirmed by B. N. Porter, who regards the buckets as holding the water that would have been used in the process of applying the male pollen to the female flowers (Porter, 14–15). What is striking about this appropriation of such a symbol of fertility is the fact that date palms did not grow in Assyria, but rather farther south, in Babylonia.

Dates (Akk. *suluppū*) are the fruit of the date palm (Akk. *gišimmarum*), which was cultivated in Mesopotamia since Sumerian times (4000–3000 BC). The trees must be well watered, by irrigation or natural oases, to produce a good crop. Shu-Sin of the Ur III Dynasty refers to a well-watered palm plantation that was divided into eight sections. The trees in each section were numbered in batches, and designated as fruiting and immature trees (see Contenau, 73–74). It takes twenty years for a female tree to bear dates. Once mature, a productive tree could yield one hundred pounds of fruit for a century.

The date palm thrives in hot, dry climates. The fruit is classified as a drupe and has a hard pit containing a single seed. The dried fruits contain 30 to 80 percent sugar, depending on the variety. The dates could also be processed to produce a sweet syrup (Akk. *dišpu*). The palm heart (Akk. *uqūru*) was also eaten. The wood was employed for construction, including roofing, and the fibers for ropes.

The value of a single tree is highlighted by the Code of Hammurabi (18th c. BC). Law 59 declares: "If a seignior cut down a tree in a(nother) seignior's orchard without the consent of the owner, he shall pay one-half mina of silver" (*ANET*, 169). Since a mina equals sixty shekels, and a shekel of silver was the average wage for a month's work, a single tree was worth two-and-a-half years' worth of wages! By the Neo-Babylonian era (6th c. BC), a tree was worth a full mina, more than the price of a male slave.

Fruit trees were grown in orchards by kings under the care of palace gardeners. Many fruit trees are mentioned in the Mari texts (18th c. BC). The most common fruit tree grown by kings was the fig (Akk. *tittu*). Other fruit trees included the pomegranate (Akk. *nurmû*), the apple (Akk. *ḫašḫūru*; *Malus pumila*), and the pear (Akk. *kamiššaru*; *Pyrus communis*). The olive (Akk. *serdu*; *Olea europaea*) was known but did not flourish in Mesopotamia. Instead of olive oil, the Mesopotamians relied upon sesame oil.

Cornel trees are found along the banks of the Khabur River, a tributary of the Euphrates in northwestern Mesopotamia. In northeastern Mesopotamia, trees such as the ash, oak, and elm were available on the slopes of the Zagros mountains. Also found in that region was the terebinth (Akk. *buṭnu*), which yielded pistachio nuts.

In southern Mesopotamia, the most popular trees were, in addition to the palm trees, the willow (Akk. *ḫilēpu*; *Salix acmophylla*) and the poplar (Akk. *ṣarbatu*; *Populus euphratica*). The poplar, which has a straight trunk, was highly valued for building puposes. Tamarisk (Akk. *ṭarpaʾu*; *Tamarix pentandra*) and willow trunks were used in roofs.

During the Old Babylonian period, schools used lexical lists for their students. The first of six in a series known as Urra contained a list of trees and wooden objects. A Mesopotamian literary genre was the dispute between two rivals; an Akkadian text narrates the dispute between a date palm and the tamarisk:

> [The tamarisk boasts:]
> All he has, the farmer has cut from the crooks of me . . .
> He makes his spade from my trunk and with the spade made from me
> He opens the irrigation canal so the field gets water.
> [The date palm responds:]
> The king cannot make a libation anywhere where I am not present . . .
> Rites are performed with me, my leaves heaped upon the ground
> The orphan girl, the widow, the poor man . . .
> Eat without stint my sweet dates . . .
> You, tamarisk, are a useless tree.
> What are your branches? Only wood without any fruit at all!
>   (*ANESTP*, 592–93)

The *Epic of Gilgamesh* features the Cedar Forest, a sacred realm of the gods not meant for mortals. Gilgamesh declares that he will kill the monster Huwawa:

> I will conquer him in the Cedar Forest! . . .
> My hand I will poise and will fell the cedars,
> A name that endures I will make for me! (*ANET*, 80)

From the earliest periods, Mesopotamian rulers cast their covetous eyes on the "cedars" (Akk. sing. *erēnu*) and other coniferous trees of Lebanon and of the Amanus mountains in southeastern Anatolia. Sargon of Agade (23rd c. BC) extended his influence as far as the Cedar Forest. According to an inscription, the god Nergal opened up the path for his grandson Naram-Sin and "gave him Arman and Ibla, he presented him (also) with the Amanus, the Cedar Mountain and (with) the Upper Sea" (*ANET*, 268). Gudea, the ruler of Lagash, proclaimed that "in (lit.: from) the Amanus, the Cedar Mountain, he formed into rafts cedar [Sum. ^{GIŠ}ERIN] logs 60 cubits long . . . and brought them (thus) out of the mountain" (*ANET*, 269). These logs were floated down the Euphrates nearly a thousand miles to southern Mesopotamia (cf. 1 Kgs 5:8–9).

Beginning in the Middle Assyrian era, the Assyrian kings began aggressive campaigns of expansion. Along with other booty, the Assyrians gathered all kinds of exotic fauna and flora for their zoos and orchards. Tiglath-pileser I (1114–1076 BC) boasted:

> I took cedar, box-tree, Kanish oak from the lands over which I had gained dominion—such trees which none among previous kings, my forefathers, had ever planted—and I planted (them) in the orchards of my land. I took rare orchard fruit which is not found in my land (and therewith) filled the orchards of Assyria. (Grayson, 17)

At the dedication of his new palace at Nimrud (Kalhu, Calah) in Assyria, Assurnasirpal II set up a stela that gives us a complete list of the forty-two varieties of tree planted in his royal orchards:

> All kinds of fruits and vines I planted and the best of them I offered to Aššur my lord and to the temples of my land. . . . From the lands in which I had travelled and the mountains which I had passed, trees and seeds which I saw: cedar, cypress, box (?), pine . . . juniper, *lammu*-oak, date-palm, *ušu*-willow, mulberry, bitter almonds, . . . oak, tamarisk, . . . pistachio, and laurel, poplar, . . . pomegranate, medlar, fir, loquat (?), pear, quince, fig, . . . plum . . . sycamore fig, frankincense. . . . (Wiseman 1952, 30)

Sargon II (8th c. BC) had a variety of trees at his palace at Khorsabad. Nebuchadnezzar's famous Hanging Gardens included cypress and juniper (Akk. *burāšu*) groves.

Imported woods included *sissoo* wood (Pakistani rosewood) from the Indo-Iranian highlands. Ebony (Akk. *ṣulmu*) is listed in the Mari texts. A little over a pound was worth twenty shekels of silver.

As early as the reign of Šulgi, king of Ur (ca. 2000 BC), the destruction of an enemy's trees is attested as a military tactic. He boasted:

I will uproot its small trees,
I will destroy its wide and large trees (with) the axe,
I will tear down its "trees of riches" by their crown,
In its orchards and gardens, where the "honey" of fig trees had been
produced, (I will) make weeds grow.
   (Šulgi D, lines 223–226; Klein, 81)

In their military campaigns, the Assyrians systematically destroyed the orchards of their enemies. In 866 BC Assurnasirpal II cut down the orchards of his enemy while fighting in the Upper Tigris region. In 847 BC Shalmaneser III besieged Damascus and cut down the orchards of the city. Over a century later, in 733, Tiglath-pileser III besieged Damascus again and cut down its orchards. In 710 Sargon II cut down the orchards of the Chaldean Merodach-baladan while suppressing his revolt.

Egypt

The date palm (Egy. *bnrt*) was not indigenous to Egypt. It was probably introduced from the area of the Persian Gulf, perhaps during the Middle Kingdom. A native Egyptian palm was the dom (or doum) palm (*Hyphaene thebaica*), which grew in Upper (i.e., southern) Egypt upriver from Abydos. It was characterized by two trunks that forked at the height of twenty-five to thirty feet. It bore shiny, brown, fist-sized fruits, which were used for medicinal purposes. In contrast to the wood from the date palm, the wood of the dom palm is very hard and compact, and it was used for the construction of rafts. Its fan-shaped leaves were woven into mats and baskets.

The Nile acacia (Egy. *šnd.t*; *Acacia nilotica*) was used in many ways. Leaves and pods were used as cattle fodder. Its long seed pods contained an agent useful in tanning leather. Its wood was used for boats, furniture, and coffins, and also processed for charcoal.

The Nile tamarisk (Egy. *isr*; *Tamarix nilotica*) could grow as either a shrub or a tree. Its wood was processed for charcoal, and its tannin-rich bark was used for medicine and tanning. A grove of tamarisk trees once grew in front of the temple of Mentuhotep.

Only female willow trees (Egy. *trt*; *Salix mucronata*) grew in Egypt, so they were propagated by cuttings. The leaves of the willow were used for funeral garlands, including some that were preserved in the tomb of Tutankhamun. Willow withes were used for basketry. The salicine material of the willow (now used in aspirin) was used for medicinal purposes.

The stylized tree in paintings of gardens represents the sycamore fig (Egy. *nh.t*), which was also known as the wild fig. The sycamore fig trees were planted around pools and gardens, as indicated by the miniature wooden gardens found in the 11th Dynasty tomb of Mentuhotep at Deir el-Bahri by H. E. Winlock. This tree was prized for the shade its dense foliage provided. Its figs were small and sweet, but they had to be cut open before they ripened fully and before the gall wasps by which they were pollinated developed inside the fruits.

The sycamore fig tree was revered by some Egyptians as a tree deity, and was celebrated in literary texts. A love song recorded on one of the Chester Beatty Papyri declares:

> The sycamore fig sends forth its voice.
> Its foliage (?) speaks (thusly)
> The little sycamore (that) she planted with her hand
> sends forth its (voice) to speak:
> The flowers (?) (are like) liquid of honey.
> It is beautiful; its branches are lovely,
> greener than [the grass].
> It is loaded with the abundance of notched sycamore-figs.
>   (White, 186)

An inscription from the tomb of Apoui at Thebes records the wish "that each day I may walk unceasingly on the banks of my water, that my soul may repose on the branches of the trees which I planted, that I may refresh myself under the shadow of my sycamore" (cited by Gallery, 44).

Harkhuf (ca. 2300 BC) was sent on several expeditions to the areas south of Egypt to recover many precious objects, including ivory and ebony. It is possible that the Egyptian word *hbny*, translated "ebony," referred to African blackwood (*Dalbergia melanoxylon*). This was highly prized for its use in furniture.

Furniture decorated with ebony was sent as a gift by Amenhotep IV (Akhenaten) to Kadašman-Enlil, the Kassite king of Babylonia (ca. 1350 BC). Among other objects, the list of gifts included: "1 bed of ebony overlaid with ivory and gold; 3 beds of ebony, overlaid with gold; . . . 1 lar[ge] chair [o]f ebony, overlaid with gold . . . 10 footrests of ebony" (Moran, 11).

Beginning in the Old Kingdom, the Egyptians sent ships to Byblos (Gebal) in Lebanon to obtain cedar logs. The Palermo Stone reports that as early as the reign of Sneferu (ca. 2650 BC) such timbers were being imported: "Bringing forty ships filled (with) cedar logs. Shipbuilding (of) cedarwood, one 'Praise-of-the-Two-Lands' ship, 100 cubits (long) and (of) *meru*-wood, two ships, 100 cubits (long)" (*ANET*, 227).

The funerary boats buried by the Great Pyramid of Khufu (Cheops) (ca. 2600 BC) were made of cedar wood imported from Phoenicia. One of the disassembled funeral barges, which consisted of one thousand two hundred pieces of cedar wood, was reassembled in modern times after a decade of work. It is 144 feet long, with a shallow draft of less than six feet. (See Lipke.)

The trade with Lebanon continued throughout Egyptian history. The Barkal stela of Tuthmosis III (ca. 1450 BC) reports: "Every year there is hewed [for me in Dja]hi genuine cedar of Lebanon, which is brought to the Court—life, prosperity, health!" (*ANET*, 240). Amenhotep III (ca. 1400 BC) boasted, "I made another monument for him who begot me, Amon-Re, . . . making for him a great barque upon the river . . . of new cedar which his majesty cut on the country of God's Land, dragged from the mountains of Retenu by the princes of all foreign countries" (*ANET*, 375). A relief from Seti I (ca. 1300 BC) depicts Phoenician chieftains felling cedar trees and offering their obeisance to Egyptian officials (*ANEP*, 110; fig. 331).

This trade is dramatically illustrated by the entertaining *Tale of Wenamun* (ca. 1100 BC). Wenamun sails to Byblos to obtain timber for the Amun Userhet, the sacred barque of Amun, the god of Thebes. This special boat was carried by priests between the temples of Luxor and Karnak during the feast of Opet. Wenamun, who has his gold stolen by Tjekker during his stop at Dor, is rebuffed by the ruler of Byblos, who says rather dismissively: "I am not your servant! I am not the servant of him who sent you either! If I cry out to the Lebanon, the heavens open up, and the logs are here lying (on) the shore of the sea!" (*ANET*, 27). He is evidently referring to the rains that would fill the streams so the logs could be floated down the mountains to the seashore.

Hatshepsut (ca. 1500 BC) sent expeditions down the Red Sea to the fabled country of Punt, which scholars had previously located on the coast of Somalia, but which has now been located farther north on the east coast of Sudan. Hatshepsut had this expedition depicted on reliefs on the walls of her mortuary temple at Deir el-Bahri. According to her inscription, "Thirty-one fresh myrrh trees, brought as marvels of Punt for the majesty of this god, Amon, lord of Thebes; never was seen the like since the beginning" (*ARE* 2.112).

With the imperial expansion of Egypt during the New Kingdom, many new plants were introduced into Egypt, including the almond, apple, olive, peach, bay, and caster berry trees. Objects made of various kinds of imported wood have been preserved in 18th Dynasty tombs, including the ash (*Fraxinus excelsior*), beech (*Fagus sylvatica*), box (*Buxus sempervirens*), maple (*Acer campestre*), oak (*Quercus cerris*), pine (*Pinus halepensis*), yew (*Taxus baccata*), and plum (*Prunus domesticus*).

Among the numerous offerings presented to temples by Ramesses III (ca. 1160 BC), the Papyrus Harris lists:

Dom-palm fruit: clusters	2,548
Palm leaves: bundles	46,040
. . .	
Cedar wood: various logs	336
. . .	
Palm-fiber: various ropes	355,084
. . .	
Tamarisk and reed-grass: bundles	7,860

        (*ARE* 4.189–90, 196)

Persia

It was the Persians who were noted for their development of "paradises," or royal parks, full of trees and wild game for hunting. The Greek word *paradeisos* is a loanword from the Median word *paridaiza* (Old Pers. *paridaida*, Avestan *pairidaēza*, Elam. *partetaš*). It literally meant "beyond the wall," hence an "enclosure" or "park." In a Socratic dialogue, Xenophon writes: "Then it is of course necessary, Socrates, to take care that these paradises in which the king spends his time shall contain a fine stock of trees and all other beautiful things that the soil produces" (*Oec.* 4.14).

The Old Persian foundation inscription of Darius I (ca. 520 BC) describes the building of his palace at Susa: "The cedar timber, this—a mountain by name Lebanon—from there was brought. The Assyrian [i.e., Syrian] people, it brought it to Babylon, from Babylon the Carians and the Ionians brought it to Susa. The *yakā*-timber was brought from Gandhara and from Carmania" (DSf; Kent, 144). The Old Persian word *yakā* is rendered by the Akkadian version as *musukkannu*, which has been identified as the *Dalbergia sissoo* tree, which grew in Oman, southern Iran, and Pakistan.

The reliefs of the well-preserved eastern staircase of Darius's Apadana (audience hall) at Persepolis depict twenty-three delegations bearing gifts. Each group is separated by a relief of a cypress tree.

Peaches were domesticated in China ca. 2000 BC and reached Persia by 300 BC and Rome by AD 100. The Romans called the walnut "the Persian nut."

D. THE GRECO-ROMAN WORLD

Greece

Sacred trees figured prominently in Minoan art, with numerous seals depicting a goddess or a priestess sitting under a tree. Leto was believed to have given birth to Apollo while leaning on a palm tree on the island of Delos. Apollo was often depicted with a palm tree on vase paintings. The rustling of the trees of a sacred oak at Dodona was revered as an oracle of Zeus. The olive tree was sacred to Athena. According to Greek mythology, the goddess Ge transformed her son Sykeus into a fig tree to save him from Zeus. Dionysus, the god of the vine, was also associated with the fig tree. Two of his epithets were *Endendros*, "He who is in the tree," and *Dendritēs*, "The one of the tree."

For the Minoan (2000–1500 BC) and the Mycenaean (1500–1200 BC) eras, we have frescoes of only the olive, palm, and pomegranate trees. But excavations have yielded evidence of the almond, fig, oak, olive, pear, and plum trees (Vermeule, Appendix I; cf. Ventris and Chadwick, 129).

The Mycenaean Linear B tablets from Knossos, Pylos, and other sites, which were deciphered by Michael Ventris, offer additional evidence. Ideograms represent olives and figs (Linear B *su-za*; Gk. sing. *sykea*), which are listed in great quantities. One tablet lists 1,770 fig trees and 405 olive trees (Ventris and Chadwick, 273), and another lists 9,000 liters of figs and 5,520 liters of olives (Ventris and Chadwick, 219).

The word *po-ni-ke(-qe)* (Gk. *phoinikei*) may indicate "with a palm tree" (Ventris and Chadwick, 573). "Timbers specified on the 'chariot' and 'furniture' tablets include *pe-te-re-wa* (boxwood), *e-ri-ka* (willow), *ki-da-pa* (?), *ku-te-so* (ebony?), *mi-ra$_2$* (yew?), *pu-ko-so* (boxwood) and *ku-pa-ri-se-ja* (adj., cypress)" (Ventris and Chadwick, 135).

A wide variety of trees are mentioned in both Homeric epics. Fruit trees include the apple, fig, olive, pear, and pomegranate. Other trees include the alder, ash, boxwood, cedar, cornel, cypress, elm, fir, laurel, oak, pine, plane, poplar, tamarisk, and willow. (See Vermeule, Appendix I.)

To flatter the princess Nausicaa, the shipwrecked Odysseus declares: "Of a truth in Delos once I saw such a thing, a young shoot of a palm [*phoinikos*] springing up beside the altar of Apollo . . . And in like manner, lady, do I marvel at thee" (*Od.* 162–169).

The most common tree in ancient Greece was the oak (Gk. *drys, phēgos*), which was sacred to Zeus. Its acorns were fed to pigs. At one time the oak was the most widely distributed tree in western, central, and southern Greece up to an elevation of ca. eight hundred meters. Spears were made from the ash tree because its wood was both strong and flexible. The cornel, which was later regarded as a superior wood for spears, is mentioned once in the Homeric epics. Oak and ash wood were used for thresholds. The poplar was frequently associated with areas of water, where it grew.

Among the evergreens, fir (Gk. *elatē*) was the most prominent. Calypso gives Odysseus fir trees for the building of his boat. Fir was the wood used most frequently by the ancient Greeks for oars. Cypress is mentioned only twice in the epics, once as growing on Calypso's island and once as used for the doorposts of Odysseus's palace. The pine (Gk. *pitys*) is relatively rare in the epics. The *thyrsos*, a wand associated with Dionysos, was topped with a pinecone. The box (Gk. *pyxos*) is mentioned only once, as the wood used for a yoke of mules. In Priam's palace at Troy, there was a cedar chest for clothes. Calypso burns cedar logs and also citrus wood (Gk. *thyon*), which came from North Africa.

Homer uses the cutting down of trees as a simile for the fall of a warrior, for example, for the death of Simoïs, who is speared by Ajax:

> He fell to the ground in the dust like a poplar-tree that hath grown up in the bottom-land of a great marsh, smooth of stem, but from the top thereof branches grow: this hath some wainwright felled with the gleaming iron that he might bend him a felloe for a beauteous chariot, and it lieth drying by a river's banks. (*Il.* 4.482–487; cf. 13.289–291)

Elsewhere Homer compares the clash of the Greeks and the Trojans to a conflict of the East and South Winds in "a wood of beech and ash and smooth-barked cornel" (*Il.* 16.780–781).

Homer describes the four-acre orchard of the Pheacians as follows: "Therein grow trees, tall and luxuriant, pears and pomegranates and apple-trees with their bright fruit, and sweet figs, and luxuriant olives" (*Od.* 7.113–116). When the disguised Odysseus returns to Ithaca after twenty years abroad, he finds his father working in the orchard, and addresses him as follows: "Old man, no lack of skill hast thou to tend a garden; nay, thy care is good, and there is naught whatsoever, either plant or fig tree, or vine, nay, or olive, or pear, or garden-plot in all the field that lacks care" (*Od.* 24.244–248).

Olive trees grew on Crete even before the development of the Minoan civilization (2000–1500 BC), and they are listed in the Mycenaean Linear B tablets from Pylos and Knossos (1500–1200 BC), but they were not widely cultivated on the Greek mainland until the Archaic era (800–600 BC). By the sixth century BC Athens had become an exporter of olive oil. In addition to the olive, the Greeks also had orchards where apples, pears, plums, pomegranates, figs, almonds, and quinces were grown. The citron, a citrus from the Near East, was known among the Greeks as "the Persian apple."

Greece originally had some excellent forests, but already by the Classical era (5th c. BC) these had been cut down. Timber had to be imported from Magna Graecia (Greek colonies in southern Italy), Macedonia, and Thrace (Bulgaria). The bulk of the timber used for the construction of the Athenian fleet came from Thrace.

Though not the first natural scientist, Aristotle was the first to bring critical empiricism to the study of the natural world. He classified plants by morphological form (trees, shrubs, undershrubs, herbs). His student

Theophrastus, "the father of botany," followed this approach. He noted that the cultivated olive must be propagated by cuttings, and that plants grown from seeds give rise to thorny, wild-type olives (*On the Causes of Plants* 1.16.10). He reported that the cultivated olive can be grafted on the wild olive, for which the Greeks had a separate name, *kotinos*.

Theophrastus described the cedars of Lebanon as follows: "For in Syria and on its mountains the cedars grow to a surpassing height and thickness: they are sometimes so large that three men cannot embrace the tree. And in the parks they are even larger and finer"(*Hist. Plant.* 5.8.1). In 315 BC Antigonus employed eight thousand men and one thousand yoke of oxen to drag timbers down from the mountains of Lebanon (Diod. Sic. *Bib. hist.* 19.58).

Of the dom palm of Egypt, Theophrastus remarked:

> This tree is fair to look upon, and its fruit in shape, size and flavour differs from the date, being rounder, larger and pleasanter to the taste, though not so luscious. It ripens in three years, so that there is always fruit on the tree, as the new fruit overtakes that of last year. (*Hist. plant.* 2.6.6)

Cyprus

The island of Cyprus in the eastern Mediterranean was the major source of copper. Copper's name in Latin, *cuprum*, is derived from Greek *Kypros*, the name of the island. Copper was found in abundance in the Troodos Mountains and was extracted as early as the eighteenth century BC. More than forty slag heaps totaling over four million tons have been identified. It has been estimated that over a period of three thousand years, two hundred million trees were consumed to provide the charcoal needed to smelt these vast amounts of copper.

Cyprus was originally heavily covered with such conifers as the Brutus pine (*Pinus brutia*), the Troodos pine (*Pinus nigra*), the Mediterranean cypress (*Cupressus sempervirens*), and the Cyprus cedar (*Cedrus brevifolia*). Broad-leaved trees included the Oriental plane tree (*Platanus orientalis*), the Oriental alder (*Alnus orientalis*), and the golden oak (*Quercus alnifolia*). Eratosthenes (3rd c. BC) described the gradual stripping of these forests for shipbuilding and for the production of charcoal (Strabo, *Geogr.* 14.6.5).

Rome

At the beginning of his essay on "Trees," Columella writes:

> We too, like Vergil, think proper, then, to divide growing trees into two classes, those which come into being of their own accord and those which are the

result of human care. The former class, which does not come up by the help of man, is better suited for timber, the latter, on which labour is expended, is adapted to the production of fruit. (*Arb.* 1.1)

Elsewhere Columella declares:

> The olive occupies first place among all trees, and it is far more economical than any other plant. Although it normally bears fruit every other year rather than annually, it is still exceptionally well regarded because only modest cultivation is needed to support it and virtually no expense is involved when it is not bearing. (*Rust.* 5.8)

Columella stipulates that olive (Lat. *olea*) trees should be planted sixty feet apart (*Arb.* 173).

As to fig (Lat. *ficus*) trees, he advises: "But if you wish to make a fig-tree ripen late, though it does not naturally do so, shake down the fruit while the little figs are small; it will then produce a second crop and put off its ripening until late winter" (*Arb.* 20.1). He suggests: "You should plant the almond-tree [Lat. *nux Graeca*], since it is the first nut-tree to blossom, when the constellation of the Bear rises on about Feb. 1st" (*Arb.* 22.1). And: "Plant pear-trees [Lat. sing. *pirum*] in the autumn before mid-winter, so that at least twenty-five days remain before mid-winter" (*Arb.* 24.1).

He recommends:

> Plant the willow [Lat. *salix*] and the broom [Lat. *genista*] when the moon is waxing about March 1st. The willow requires a damp situation, the broom one which is dry; both, however, can be conveniently planted round a vineyard, because they produce bands suitable for tying up vine-shoots. (*Arb.* 29.1)

Frescoes from the houses of Pompeii and Herculaneum depict various fruits (apples, peaches, pears, plums, and lemons) and nuts (walnuts, chestnuts, hazelnuts, and almonds). Archaeological excavations at Pompeii have revealed the presence of the lemon, oleander, and wild strawberry trees, which were prized for their flowers and their fruits, which attracted birds. Other trees favored for gardens included the pitch-pine, box, and cypress, which were valued for the ease with which they could be trimmed (Pliny, *Nat.* 16.60.139–140). The yew, however, was not used because of its highly poisonous nature.

With Rome's expansion to the southern end of the Italian peninsula, the Romans gained the forests of Sila. According to Dionysius of Halicarnassus:

> The Bruttians, after submitting willingly to the Romans, delivered up to them one-half of their mountainous district, called Sila, which is full of timber suitable for the building of houses and ships and every other kind of construction. For much fir grows there, towering to the sky, much black poplar, much pitch

pine, beech, stone pine, wide-spreading oak, ash trees enriched by the streams flowing through their midst. (*Ant. rom.* 20.15.5)

According to Varro, the favorite trees for marking the borders of estates were pines, cypresses, and elms (*Rust.* 1.15). Cedar and cypress were the favorite woods for monumental doors. Cypress twigs were displayed at doors as a sign of mourning. Vitruvius discusses the various timbers used for construction. The wood of the poplar, lime, and willow were regarded as suitable for carving, and the alder for use as pilings for a foundation. The most common woods for the building of ships were oak, pine, elm, fir, cypress, and cedar. Scipio cut down fir trees in the forests north of Rome to build his ships for his attack against Hannibal in North Africa before his victory at Zama in 201 BC.

Figs were an important source of calories during the winter. Dates were imported from the east. The Romans called the almond "the Greek nut" and the hazelnut "the Pontic nut," that is, from Pontus in northern Turkey (Pliny, *Nat.* 15.24.87–90). Wealthy Romans like Cicero had villas with gardens shaded by giant elms. The rural villa at Boscoreale had fig, peach, and apricot trees. At Pompeii, carbonized cherries (*Prunus cerasus*) were recovered.

Virgil (*Georg.* 2.9–72) mentions more than a dozen tree species (including the chestnut, myrtle, beech, oak, olive, ash, and mountain-ash). Grafting and other aspects of plant cultivation are included in his praise of country life.

Pliny the Elder (*Nat.*, esp. books 12–16) lists numerous indigenous plants, including the following woody types: apples, pears, mistletoe, figs, cherries, and myrtle. He also notes products of imported species: myrrh, frankincense, cinnamon, cassia, and black pepper. He discusses the growing of plants, as well as of orchards and vineyards, at great length.

Pliny reports: "Before the victory of Lucius Lucullus in the war against Mithridates [that is down to 74 BC], there were no cherry-trees in Italy. Lucullus first imported them from Pontus, and in 120 years they have crossed the ocean and got as far as Britain" (*Nat.* 15.30.1). The peach (Lat. *malum persicum*), which was native to China, was unknown to Varro (1st c. BC) and was still rare in Columella's time (1st c. AD). By the time of Pliny, who died in the eruption of Vesuvius in AD 79, the Romans knew of thirty-six types of apples.

In 46 BC Julius Caesar made observations of plant life in his reports to the Roman Senate. He noted that chestnuts, which were common in Italy, were absent in Britain. In the time of Emperor Augustus (26–24 BC), Aelius Gallus, prefect of Egypt, sent a military expedition to the Arabian Peninsula with the goal of controlling the source of myrrh and frankincense there, which was located in what today is Yemen. The mission failed, although Mecca and Medina were briefly occupied. Emperors such as Hadrian have left their inscriptions in the cedar forests of Lebanon.

E. THE JEWISH WORLD

In Sirach, the personified Wisdom declares: "I grew tall like a cedar in Lebanon, and like a cypress on the heights of Hermon. I grew tall like a palm tree in En-gedi, and like rose plants in Jericho; like a beautiful olive tree in the field, and like a plane tree I grew tall" (Sir 24:13–14). Sirach describes the high priest Simon, the son of Onias, as one "like an olive tree putting forth its fruit, and like a cypress towering in the clouds" (Sir 50:10).

In the book of Susanna, the virtuous heroine is falsely accused by two lecherous elders of engaging in immorality with a young man. When Daniel questions both of the elders separately, he asks under which tree the lovers were intimate. One elder replies, "under a mastic tree" (Sus 54), but the other elder answers, "under an evergreen oak" (Sus 58). They are then convicted of bearing false witness and condemned to death (Sus 60–62).

Enoch is transported by Raphael on a soaring flight from which he sees many wonders. He reports:

> I saw seven mountains full of excellent nard, fragrant trees, cinnamon trees, and pepper. . . . And I came to the garden of righteousness and saw beyond those trees many (other) large (ones) growing there—their fragrance sweet, large ones, with much elegance, and glorious. And the tree of wisdom, of which one eats and knows great wisdom, (was among them). It looked like the colors of the carob tree, its fruit like very beautiful grape clusters, and the fragrance of this tree travels and reaches afar. (*1 En.* 32:1–5)

The angel explains that this is the very tree from which Adam and Eve ate. Another description by Enoch reads:

> And they placed me in the midst of Paradise. And that place has an appearance of pleasantness that has never been seen. Every tree was in full flower. Every fruit was ripe, every food was in yield profusely; every fragrance was pleasant. . . . And the tree of life is in that place, under which the Lord takes a rest when the Lord takes a walk in Paradise. And that tree is indescribable for pleasantness of fragrance. (*2 En.* 8:1–3 [A])

According to the *Psalms of Solomon*,

> The Lord's paradise, the trees of life, are his devout ones.
> Their planting is firmly rooted forever;
> they shall not be uprooted as long as the heavens shall last.
>   (*Pss. Sol.* 14:3–5)

Philo describes the creation of trees as follows:

> But in the first creation of the universe . . . God produced the whole race of trees out of the earth in full perfection, having their fruit not incomplete but in a state of entire ripeness, to be ready for the immediate and undelayed use and enjoyment of the animals which were about immediately to be born.
> (*Opif.* 13.42)

In his allegorical interpretation of Genesis, Philo regards the "tree of life" (Gk. *xylon tēs zōēs*) as "virtue" (Gk. *aretē*) (*Leg.* 1.18). As to the "tree of knowing [Gk. *gnōseōs*] the science of good and evil," Philo declares that this is "prudence" (Gk. *phronēsis*), "through which good and beautiful things and bad and ugly things are distinguished" (*QG* 1.11).

Josephus mentions that the balsam groves of Jericho, which Antony had given to Cleopatra, were leased from her by Herod the Great: "This country bears balsam, which is the most precious thing there and grows there alone, and also palm trees, which are both numerous and excellent" (*Ant.* 15.96). The best balsam was made from the sap produced by cutting the tree; inferior balsam was made from its foliage and branches.

The abundance of date palms at Jericho was observed by Alexander the Great and later by the Roman general Pompey. Pliny describes the date palms of Jericho (*Nat.* 13.26–49). The Jerusalem Talmud mentions the export of dates from Palestine to Rome (*y. Maʿaś. Š.* 4:1).

Herod the Great had gardens at his winter palace at Jericho that contained not only shrubs and flowers but perhaps also balsam trees (Jos. *J.W.* 5.177–183). In his palace at Jerusalem, Herod had "groves of various trees intersected by long walks, which were bordered by deep canals, and ponds everywhere" (Jos. *J.W.* 5.181). Excavations at Herod's palace at Masada revealed that much of the timber used there had been imported from the Judean hills, the Transjordan, and even Lebanon.

The Mishnah lists the trees that are subject to the OT rule about leaving a "corner" for the poor in order to give a portion of the fruit to them: "Among trees, sumach, carob, walnut trees, almond trees, vines, pomegranate trees, olive trees, and palm trees are subject to the law of *Peah*" (*m. Peʾah* 1:5).

The Talmud calls for this blessing in regard to trees: "If one goes abroad in the days of Nisan (spring time) and sees trees sprouting, he should say, 'Blessed be He who hath not left His world lacking in anything and has created in it goodly creatures and goodly trees for the enjoyment of mankind'" (*b. Ber.* 43b).

The original list of the "four species" to be used to celebrate the Feast of Tabernacles is as follows:

And you shall take on the first day the fruit of splendid trees [Heb. *ʿēṣ hādār*], branches of palm trees [Heb. *tĕmārîm*] and boughs of leafy trees [Heb. *ʿēṣ-ʿābōt*] and willows of the brook [Heb. *ʿarbê-nāḥal*], and you shall rejoice before the LORD your God seven days. (Lev 23:40, ESV)

The rabbis interpreted the four species to refer to a citrus fruit (*ʾetrôg*), a green branch from the palm tree, a branch from the myrtle, and a branch from the willow.

The bundle of palm, myrtle, and willow branches came to be known as the *lûlāb*. Pilgrims carried this bundle from the Gihon spring in a procession up to the temple. The *lûlāb* became a prominent Jewish symbol on coins, including those of Simon Maccabeus and Bar Kochba. According to the Talmud, the *ʾetrôg* was considered an aphrodisiac, so the high priest was forbidden to eat one on the eve of Yom Kippur, lest he have a nocturnal emission, which would disqualify him from serving (*b. Yoma* 18a–b). The fruit of the tree of knowledge eaten by Adam and Eve was considered to be the *ʾetrôg* by R. Abba but the fig by R. Jose (*Gen. Rab.* 15:7).

The palm tree and palm branches are very prominent on Jewish coins, such as those of John Hyrcanus I and Herod Antipas. They appeared on coins of the First Jewish Revolt (AD 66–73). And after the Romans crushed this revolt, the palm tree with a woman representing a desolate Judea appeared on the *Judea Capta* commemorative coins of Vespasian and Titus. The palm then reappeared on the coins of Bar Kochba during the Second Jewish Revolt (AD 132–35).

It was believed that Noah took fig cakes as food for humans and animals (*Gen. Rab.* 31:14). Dried figs were distributed to the poor, especially at times of famine (*y. ʿErub.* 4:8). The size of a dried fig was the measure of many halakic (legal) matters as to what did or did not convey impurity (e.g., *b. Šabb.* 76a–b). There are no rabbinic references to fig orchards, only to single fig trees. According to the Talmud,

> R. Zadok observed fasts for forty years in order that Jerusalem might not be destroyed, [and he became so thin that] when he ate anything the food could be seen [as it passed through his throat.] When he wanted to restore himself, they used to bring him a fig, and he used to suck the juice and throw the rest away. (*b. Giṭ.* 56a)

The pomegranate tree was one of the trees from which some fruits must be left for the poor (*y. Peʾah* 1:4). A pomegranate fruit was the accepted measure of size for certain matters concerning what did or did not convey impurity (*b. Ber.* 41b). The reference to pomegranates in Song of Solomon 6:7 was interpreted to mean that the merits of even the most unworthy Jews were as plentiful as the seeds of a pomegranate (*b. Meg.* 6a; *b. Sanh.* 37a).

Olive trees were important in Palestine but not in Babylonia. The Mishnah mentions that the first pressing resulted in the best "virgin" oil; later pressings yielded inferior oil (*m. Menaḥ.* 8:4). Josephus describes how his archenemy, John of Gischala, made enormous profits by gaining a monopoly on Galilean olive oil, which he was able to sell to the Jews in Caesarea and in Syria, as they were reluctant to buy oil from gentiles (*J.W.* 2.591–593; *Life* 74–76).

Archaeological evidence indicates the great increase of oil production for export from Palestine after the beginning of the Byzantine era (4th c. AD on). The strict rules against buying oil from gentiles seem to have been relaxed by the Jerusalem Talmud (*y. ʿAbod. Zar.* 2:8).

Over twenty different kinds of trees are mentioned in rabbinic literature. The Jews considered the cedar the tallest and the hyssop the smallest tree (*Num. Rab.* 19:3; *Exod. Rab.* 17:2). In Palestine, pears and peaches were grown in Upper Galilee. The carob tree provided food for animals and the poor (*m. Šabb.* 24:2; *m. Maʿaś.* 3:4).

Myrtle branches were one of the four species used at Sukkoth (*b. Sukkah* 33a). The myrtle tree has a pleasant aroma. Guests danced before a bride with myrtle branches, and canopies for marriage ceremonies were made with myrtle twigs (*b. Ketub.* 17a–b). Myrtle branches were also put on coffins (*b. Beṣah* 6a).

The tree mentioned most frequently in the Babylonian Talmud is the date palm. R. Aha makes reference to grafting: "a male branch was grafted on to a female palm tree" (*b. Pesaḥ.* 56a). A distinction was made between the superior Persian palm and the inferior Aramean palm. It was maintained that dates of the former could not be handled on the Sabbath, whereas the dates of the latter, which were used for animal food, could be handled on the Sabbath (*b. Šabb.* 143a).

While on a journey R. Joseph came across a palm tree that produced enough dates to pay the poll tax for its owner for a year (*b. ʿErub.* 51a). Husbands were advised to invest their wives' money in houses, date palms, other fruit trees, and vines. Guardians of orphans were also advised to invest in date palms for the child. R. Huna said, "He should buy with it [the funds the child inherited] a date tree, of which the child can eat the fruit" (*b. B. Bat.* 52a).

Debates arose over the possibility that an owner could sell a date palm to one man and the ground it grew on to another (*b. B. Bat.* 37b). In the case of a tree whose branchess extended onto the field of a neighbor, the latter was permitted to cut the branches to clear the way for him to plow his field (*b. B. Bat.* 82b).

Nuts, especially hazelnuts, were considered harmful to patients recovering from illness (*b. Ber.* 57b). It was observed that it took twenty-one days from the flowering of an almond tree until the almond nuts developed (*b. Bek.* 8a). An apple tree was observed to give fruit sixty days after it blossomed (*b. Bek.* 8a). As to why the Israelites were compared to an apple tree in the Song of Solomon, a rabbi replied: "To teach you: just as the fruit of the apple tree precedes its leaves, so did the Israelites give precedence to 'we will do' over 'we will hearken' " (*b. Šabb.* 88a).

The Israelites are compared to fruit trees in a midrash:

> R. Samuel b. Nahman said: [God is] like a king who had an orchard in which he planted rows of nut-trees and apple-trees and pomegranates, and which he then handed over to the care of his son. So long as the son did his duty, the king used to look out for good shoots wherever he could find one, and take it up and bring it and plant it in the orchard. But when the son did not do his duty, the king used to look out for the best plant in the orchard and take it up. So when Israel (sic) do their duty to God, He looks out for any righteous person among the other nations, like Jethro or Rahab, and brings them and attaches them to Israel. (*Song Rab.* 6:2)

F. THE CHRISTIAN WORLD

In an infancy gospel, as the Holy Family flees to Egypt, Joseph and Mary become very hungry and thirsty. Resting in the shade of a palm tree laden with dates, Mary expresses the wish that there might be someone who could fetch the fruit for them. The infant Jesus, who is sitting in her lap, commands: "Bend down your branches, O tree, and refresh my mother with your fruit." Also at his behest water gushes out from the base of the tree. As the family departs, Jesus declares:

> O palm, I give you this privilege, that one of your branches be carried by my angels and be planted in the paradise of my Father. This blessing I will confer on you, that to all who shall be victorious in a contest it shall be said: "you have won the palm of victory." (*Pseudo-Matthew* 20–21)

According to Irenaeus, "as through a man death received the palm (of victory) against us, so again by a man we may receive the palm against death" (*Haer.* 5.21.1). The palm became a symbol associated with martyrs. The palm tree appears on Christian sarcophagi, in one example with lambs in a scene where Christ gives the law (Goodenough, VIII.116).

Origen rejected a literal interpretation of the trees in the Garden of Eden for a figurative interpretation, writing as follows:

> And who is found so ignorant as to suppose that God, as if He had been a husbandman, planted trees in paradise, in Eden towards the east, and a tree

of life in it, i.e., a visible and palpable tree of wood, so that anyone eating of it with bodily teeth should obtain life, and, eating again of another tree, should come to the knowledge of good and evil? No one, I think, can doubt that the statement that God walked in the afternoon in paradise, and that Adam lay hid under a tree, is related figuratively in Scripture, that some mystical meaning may be indicated by it. (*Prin.* 4.16)

In a homily in his *Hexaemeron*, a work on the six days of creation, Basil comments on a problem in Gen 1:11, which reads: "Let the land produce vegetation: seed-bearing plants and trees on the land that bear fruit with seed in it, according to their various kinds." He writes:

But, they say, the earth has received the command to produce trees yielding fruit whose seed was in itself, and we see many trees which have neither fruit, nor seed. What shall we reply? First, that only the more important trees are mentioned; and then, that a careful examination will show us that every tree has seed, or some property which takes the place of it. The black poplar, the willow, the elm, the white poplar, all the trees of this family, do not produce any apparent fruit; however, an attentive observer finds seed in each of them. (*Hex. Homily* 5)

In his *History of Copres and Petarpemotis*, Jerome recounts how Petarpemotis had a dream as follows: "I saw Paradise with the eyes of this body, and could not describe, and that could not be uttered thereby. . . . I saw there the multitudes of the saints, and I tasted the fruits of Paradise." As a proof of the reality of this vision, Petarpemotis "gave his disciples to eat (of the fruit of) a great, and marvelous, and extraordinarily large fig-tree, which possessed an odour that was different from any other smell in the world." Copres testified:

I have seen in my youth (portions) of that fig-tree in the hands of his disciples, and kissed them, and wonder at the odour thereof laid hold upon me; and the tree remained with his disciples for many years as a manifestation (of the truth of his words) unto many. For it was great beyond measure, and it had such wonderful properties that any sick person who inhaled its odour was straightway healed of his sickness. (cited in Budge, 369)

Ephrem the Syrian (d. 373) composed a series of Hymns on Paradise, one of which includes this stanza:

At its boundary I saw
figs, growing in a sheltered place,
from which crowns were made that adorned
the brows of the guilty pair,
while their leaves blushed, as it were,

for him who was stripped naked:
their leaves were required for those two
who had lost their garments;
although they covered Adam,
still they made him blush with shame and repent,
because in a place of such splendor,
a man who is naked is filled with shame. (cited in Brock, 87)

Another Syriac hymn proclaims that Christ himself is the tree of life:

Our Saviour typified his body in the tree,
The one from which Adam did not taste because he sinned. . . .
The tree of life which was hidden in paradise
grew up in Marjam (Mary) and sprang forth from her,
and in its shade creation hath repose,
and it spreadeth its fruits over those far and near.
      (cited in Goodenough, VIII, 120)

The depiction of the tree of the knowledge of good and evil in the Garden of Eden as an apple stems from the similarity of the Latin words for "evil," *malus*, and "apple," *malum* (see Apostolos-Cappadona, 37).

BIBLIOGRAPHY: R. P. Adams, *Junipers of the World: The Genus Juniperus* (4th ed., 2014); D. Apostolos-Cappadona, *Dictionary of Christian Art* (1995); G. Bare, *Plants and Animals of the Bible* (1969); P. Briant, *From Cyrus to Alexander: A History of the Persian Empire*, trans. P. T. Daniels (2002); S. P. Brock, trans., *Hymns on Paradise* (1990); J. P. Brown, *Ancient Israel and Ancient Greece: Religion, Politics, and Culture* (2003); J. P. Brown, *The Lebanon and Phoenicia 1: The Physical Setting and the Forest* (1969); E. A. W. Budge, *The Paradise or Garden of the Holy Fathers* (1907); S. W. Cole, "The Destruction of Orchards in Assyrian Warfare," in *Assyria 1995*, ed. S. Parpola and R. M. Whiting (1997), 29–40; G. Contenau, *Everyday Life in Babylon and Assyria*, trans. K. R. Maxwell-Hysop and A. R. Maxwell-Hysop (1959); A. Dafni, S. Levy, and E. Lev, "The Ethnobotany of Christ's Thorn Jujube (*Ziziphus spina-christi*) in Israel," *Journal of Ethnobiology and Ethnomedicine* 1.8 (2005); H. Danthine, *Le Palmier-dattier et les arbres sacrés dans l'iconographie de l'Asie occidentale ancienne* (1937); T. Dejene, M. Lemenih, and F. Bongers, "Manage or Convert Boswellia Woodlands? Can Frankincense Production Pay Off?" *Journal of Arid Environments* 89 (2013), 77–83; D. Eitam and M. Heltzer, ed., *Olive Oil in Antiquity: Israel and Neighbouring Countries from the Neolithic to the Early Arab Period* (1996); J. Feliks, *The Plants and Animals of the Mishnah* (1983) (in Hebrew); R. Gale et al., "Wood," in *Ancient Egyptian Materials and Technology*, ed. P. T. Nicholson and I. Shaw (2000), 334–71; L. M. Gallery, "The Garden of Ancient Egypt," in *Immortal Egypt*, ed. D. Schmandt-Besserat (1978), 43–49; A. S. Gilbert, "The Flora and Fauna of the Ancient Near East," *CANE* 1.153–74; M. Giovino, *The Assyrian Sacred Tree: A History of Interpretations* (2007); E. R. Goodenough, *Jewish Symbols in the Greco-Roman Period 7–8: Pagan Symbols in Judaism* (1958); A. K. Grayson, trans., *Assyrian Royal Inscriptions 2: From Tiglath-pileser I to Ashurnasir-apli II* (1976); J. C. Greenfield and M. Mayrhofer, "The ʾalgummīm/ʾalmuggīm-Problem Reexamined," in *Hebräische Wortforschung: Festschrift zum 80. Geburtstag von Walter Baumgartner*, ed. B. Hartmann et al. (1967), 83–89; N. Groom, *Frankincense and Myrrh: A Study of the Arabian Incense Trade* (1981); M. G. Hasel, "The Destruction of Trees in the Moabite Campaign of 2 Kings 3:4–27: A Study in the Laws of Warfare," *AUSS* 40 (2002), 197–206; M. Herrera, "Holy Smoke—The Use of Incense in the Catholic Church," *Adoremus Bulletin* 27 (2002); R. Hestrin, "The Lachish Ewer and the ʾAsherah," *IEJ* 37 (1987), 212–23; I. Jacob and W. Jacob, "Flora," *ABD* 2.803–17; R. G. Kent, *Old Persian* (rev. ed., 1953); P. J. King and L. E. Stager, *Life in Biblical Israel* (2001); J. Klein, *Three Šulgi Hymns* (1981); S. N. Kramer, *History Begins at Sumer* (1959); W. G. Lambert, "The Background of the Neo-Assyrian Sacred Tree," in *Sex and Gender in the Ancient Near East*, ed. S. Parpola and R. M. Whiting (2002), 321–26; W. G. Lambert, "Trees, Snakes and Gods in Ancient Syria and Anatolia," *BSOAS* 48 (1985), 435–51; C. Linnaeus, *Genera Plantarum* (1753); E. Lipke, *The Royal Ship of Cheops* (1984); A. Lucas and J. R. Harris, *Ancient Egyptian Materials and Industries* (repr. of 1962 edition, 1999); N. MacDonald, *What Did the Ancient Israelites Eat?* (2008); W. A. Maier III, *ʾAšerah: Extrabiblical Evidence* (1986); G. A. Maloney, *Gold, Frankincense, and Myrrh: An Introduction to Eastern Christian Spirituality* (1997); R. Meiggs, *Trees and Timber in the Ancient Mediterranean World* (1982); M. W. Mikesell, "The Deforestation of Mount Lebanon," *The Geographical Review* 59 (1969), 1–28; P. R. S. Moorey, *Ancient Mesopotamian Materials and Industry* (1994); W. L. Moran, trans. and ed., *The Amarna Letters* (1992); P. Murray and L. Murray, *The Oxford Companion to Christian Art and Architecture* (1998); A. C. Myers, "Asherah," *EDB*, 112–13; J. Newman, *The Agricultural Life of the Jews in Babylonia between the Years 200 C.E. and 500 C.E.* (1932); S. Parpola, "The Assyrian Tree of Life: Tracing the Origins of Jewish Monotheism and Greek Philosophy," *JNES* 52 (1993), 161–208; N. Perrot, *Les représentations de l'arbre sacré sur les monuments de Mésopotamie et d'Elam* (1937); B. N. Porter, *Trees, Kings, and Politics: Studies in Assyrian Iconography* (2003); J. N. Postgate and M. A. Powell, ed., *Trees and Timber in Mesopotamia* (1992); M. B. Rowton, "The Woodlands of Ancient Western Asia," *JNES* 26 (1967), 261–77; L. Ryken, J. C. Wilhoit, and T. Longman III, ed., *Dictionary of Biblical Imagery* (1998); Z. Safrai, "Agriculture and Farming," *OHJDL*, 246–63;

R. Sallares, *The Ecology of the Ancient Greek World* (1991); J. M. Sasson, trans. and ed., *From the Mari Archives: An Anthology of Old Babylonian Letters* (2015); G. F. Snyder, *Ante Pacem: Archaeological Evidence of Church Life before Constantine* (1985); J. V. Thirgood, *Cyprus: A Chronicle of Its Forests, Land, and People* (1987); J. V. Thirgood, *Man and the Mediterranean Forest* (1981); A. O. Tucker, "Frankincense and Myrrh," *Economic Botany* 40 (1986), 425–33; United Bible Societies, *Fauna and Flora of the Bible* (1972); J. G. Vaughan and C. Geissler, *The New Oxford Book of Food Plants* (1997); M. Ventris and J. Chadwick, *Documents in Mycenaean Greek* (2nd ed., 1973); E. Vermeule, *Greece in the Bronze Age* (1972); S. Wachsmann, *Seagoing Ships & Seamanship in the Bronze Age Levant* (1998); Y. Waisal, *Trees of the Land of Israel* (1980); J. H. Walton, *The Lost World of Adam and Eve: Genesis 2–3 and the Human Origins Debate* (2015); W. G. E. Watson, "A Botanical Snapshot of Ugarit. Trees, Fruit, Plants and Herbs in the Cuneiform Texts," *Aula Orientalis* 22 (2004), 107–55; J. B. White, *A Study of the Language of Love in the Song of Songs and Ancient Egyptian Poetry* (1978); D. J. Wiseman, *Nebuchadrezzar and Babylon* (1985); D. J. Wiseman, "A New Stela of Aššur-naṣir-pal II," *Iraq* 14 (1952), 24–44; M. Zohary, *Plants of the Bible* (1982).

GCT

See also BOATS & SHIPS, DWELLINGS, FOOD PRODUCTION, FURNITURE, INCENSE, and PLANTS & FLOWERS.

VIRGINS & VIRGINITY

A virgin is one who has not experienced sexual intercourse. Families in antiquity were accustomed to having their young daughters given in marriage as soon as they were able to bear children, as brides were expected to be virgins at the time of their marriage.

A. THE OLD TESTAMENT

The Bible lays great stress on the importance of the family. The stories in Genesis and the laws in Deuteronomy indicate that in an Israelite family generation superseded gender. Although wives were subordinate to husbands and girls might be under the supervision or even control of their brothers, both sons and daughters in a family were subordinate to both mother and father (Frymer-Kensky, 96). Father and mother were both to be given respect in the home, as shown by Prov 1:8: "Listen, my son, to your father's instruction and do not forsake your mother's teaching."

Stories in the OT show that families expected their sons to act properly, to use the family wealth responsibly, and above all to bring honor and not shame to the family. Daughters, likewise, were to act with propriety; they had the special responsibility of remaining virgins until marriage (Frymer-Kensky, 96).

The Hebrew word that has been translated "virgin," *bĕtûlâ*, occurs fifty times in the OT. The KJV translates *bĕtûlâ* and its plural as "virgin(s)" thirty-seven times, as "maid(s)" six times, and as "maiden(s)" five times. Commenting on these translations, Miller writes that "it is obvious, therefore, that the connotation of virginity is not inherent in this word, although it can be demonstrated that the word does sometimes specifically connote a virgin" (Miller, 243). For example, the word *bĕtûlâ* specifically means "virgin" in Lev 21:13, which forbids a priest from marrying a widow, divorcée, or one defiled, and commands him to marry only a virgin.

The Hebrew word *bĕtûlâ* is often clarified by an additional phrase. In Gen 24 Abraham's servant is sent to find a bride for Isaac and sees Rebekah, who is described as "very beautiful, a virgin; no man had ever lain with her" (Gen 24:16). The double reference makes it clear that she had never had a sexual encounter. A similar phrase is found in the quest for wives for the Benjamites. The four hundred young women are described by means of the word *bĕtûlâ*, and again there is the restated emphasis that they were "young women who had never slept with a man" (Judg 21:11–12).

It would therefore seem that in present-day English the term "virgin" has a different connotation than does the Hebrew word *bĕtûlâ* in the OT: whereas in present-day English the word "virgin" indicates someone who has not experienced sexual intercourse, the Hebrew word *bĕtûlâ* in the OT would seem to indicate a young woman who had not yet married. However, in Joel 1:8, the context may indicate a woman who already had a husband (Schmitt, 853). Indeed, there may be more of an emphasis on the concept of youth and youthfulness with the word *bĕtûlâ*, especially when it is paired with the word for "young man," *bāḥûr*, as it is twelve times (Schmitt, 853).

Deuteronomy 22:13–21 is an interesting text covering marriage, virginity, slander, and honor. It sheds light on the importance of virginity to a family. The text addresses this scenario: A man marries a woman; later he dislikes her and makes the very serious accusation that she was not a virgin when he married her. He fans this accusation and it becomes public gossip, thereby placing the woman and her family under great pressure: the father's honor is at stake, because such an assertion claims that he cannot control his family or protect its members. If the parents can prove their daughter's virginity, then they gain one hundred shekels; if they cannot prove it, they will be publicly shamed and lose standing in the community. Their chances of marrying off the rest of their children in profitable ways would diminish (Frymer-Kensky, 93).

This text instructs the parents of the woman to bring the wedding sheets to the elders at the city gate in order to prove that defloration had occurred (Deut 22:15). The father is to declare that his daughter's husband has not loved her and has slandered her by his accusation. If the accusation is untrue, the elders beat the man and fine him one hundred shekels of silver (which goes to the father) "because this man has given an Israelite virgin a bad name" (Deut 22:19). Furthermore, the accusing husband can never divorce the woman. While this law provides in this way for the woman's lifelong provision, it does not ensure a happy marriage. However, this law did prevent Israelite men from easily ridding themselves of unwanted wives (Frymer-Kensky, 94).

If the charge against the woman holds, "she shall be brought to the door of her father's house and there the men of her town shall stone her to death. She has done an outrageous thing in Israel by being promiscuous while still in her father's house. You must purge the evil from among you" (Deut 22:21).

Sometimes the word *bětûlâ* refers to a nation (Jer 18:13; 31:4, 21; Amos 5:2). Miller argues that in such cases the word does not carry "the idea of virginity from a sexual standpoint" (Miller, 244). Perhaps the designation of a nation as a "virgin" carried a reference to the idea of a father's protection over a young woman (Schmitt, 853–54).

The two other Hebrew words that refer to a "young woman" are *naʿărâ*, which occurs eighty times in the OT, and *ʿalmâ*, which occurs nine times. The word *ʿalmâ*, which can mean "virgin" or have the generic meaning of "young woman" (translations also sometimes use "maiden" or "girl"), is well-known for its appearance in Isa 7:14. Using the NIV as an example, Miller concludes that "the newest of the standard translations concurs in the judgment of former translators that the word *ʿalmâ* does not inherently refer to a virgin" (Miller, 245).

The Septuagint translates *ʿalmâ* as *parthenos*, "virgin," in Isa 7:14, the familiar text cited by Matthew (Matt 1:23). Blomberg comments that in the light of Isa 9:1–7 the promised child was to be "born to a young woman of marriageable age, . . . to a woman who also was a virgin at the time of conception" (Blomberg, 5; cf. Keener, 87).

The virgin daughters of Israelite fathers could be sold by their fathers to other Israelites to pay for debts (Exod 21:7–11). Exodus 21:10 implies that the owner would have conjugal relations with the woman. Consequently, the daughter could not be released after six years of service, the way a male Israelite sold for debt purposes could be. If the owner agreed to terminate the arrangement, the female Israelite could be redeemed in the sense that her freedom could be purchased by payment of the debt (Exod 21:7–11).

Jephthah makes a foolish vow to God, saying that if God gives him victory over the Ammonites he will sacrifice whatever comes out of his door to greet him (Judg 11:30–31). His virgin daughter, his only child, comes dancing to the sound of tambourines to greet him as he arrives home from battle. She bravely tells him to keep his vow but asks for two months to wander the hills with her friends and to mourn the fact that she will never marry (Judg 11:36–39a). The sad tale ends with these words from the narrator: "And she was a virgin" (v. 39b). The narrator thereby confirms that she never married and never bore children.

B. THE NEW TESTAMENT

The Greek word for "virgin," *parthenos*, occurs fifteen times in the NT. The NT emphasizes that Mary was a virgin at the time of the conception of Jesus, as well as throughout her pregnancy, until Jesus was born. An important feature of the traditional doctrine of Christology is the belief that

Mary became pregnant with Jesus, the Son of God, by the Holy Spirit, that is, by "the creative agency of God" (Pazdan, 585).

The account in Matthew of Mary's virginity and pregnancy states that before Mary and her betrothed, Joseph, "came together"—that is, before they had sexual intercourse—"she was found to be pregnant through the Holy Spirit" (Matt 1:18). Joseph considered divorcing her quietly (Matt 1:19), but an angel reassured Joseph in a dream that "what is conceived in her is from the Holy Spirit" (Matt 1:20). When Matthew quotes Isa 7:14, he uses the Septuagint version, which has the Greek word *parthenos*, "virgin" (Matt 1:23). Joseph takes Mary home with him as his wife (Matt 1:24), "but he did not consummate their marriage until she gave birth to a son" (Matt 1:25). (On the Matthean birth account, see Brown, 122–64; Keener, 83–87; Lincoln, 68–98.)

The Lukan account of the annunciation to Mary and the conception of Jesus stresses Mary's virginity in both narrative and direct speech (Luke 1:27, 34). As in Matthew, her pregnancy is the result of the power of the Holy Spirit and not sexual intercourse. The angel Gabriel explains to Mary that the Holy Spirit will come upon her and overshadow her (Luke 1:35). (On the Lukan birth account, see Brown, 298–308; Marshall, 64–65; Lincoln, 99–124.)

Some scholars note that the textual emphasis on Mary's virginity before the birth of Jesus "neither affirms nor denies a sexual relationship with Joseph afterward" (Pazdan, 585). However, the Gospels mention the fact that Jesus had sisters and brothers, "James, Joseph, Judas and Simon" (Matt 13:55–56; Mark 6:3), which many interpreters consider to be evidence that Mary did not remain a virgin throughout her life.

In the parable traditionally called the Parable of the Ten Virgins (Matt 25:1–13), Jesus does not emphasize the virginity of these individual women. Indeed, various scholars and translators refer to the ten as "girls" or "maidens" (Schmitt, 854). The parable stresses the need to be ready for the Lord's return rather than these women's condition of never having had sexual intercourse.

The NT remains silent on the marital status of John the Baptist, Jesus, and Paul. As there is no mention of their wives, the presumption is that they were celibate.

Paul affirms, "An unmarried woman or virgin is concerned about the Lord's affairs" (1 Cor 7:34). In 1 Cor 7:36–38 Paul addresses the issue of a man who is concerned "that he might not be acting honorably toward the virgin [*parthenon*] he is engaged to." In the main text of the NIV, the man is understood to be the fiancé and the "virgin" his betrothed; the NIV marginal note presents the alternative view that the man is the father and the girl is his daughter. (See Schmitt, 854.) Paul also uses the Greek term for virgin to refer to the Corinthian church community, which he has betrothed to Christ (2 Cor 11:2).

Scholars generally view the one hundred forty-four thousand "who did not defile themselves with women, for they remained virgins [*parthenoi*]" symbolically (Rev 14:3–4). This probably does not literally mean that this number—all men—are virgins. A more probable contextual reading indicates that the one hundred forty-four thousand are those in the Greco-Roman culture who did not defile themselves with worshipping the gods and goddesses of the empire (Schmitt, 854; see also Beale, 738–40; Mounce, 269–71).

C. THE NEAR EASTERN WORLD

Mesopotamia

In Akkadian the words *batultu* and *ardatu* designate adolescent girls; the latter word is confined to literary texts. Neither word in itself necessarily denotes a "virgin," although the normal assumption would have been that such a girl was one. According to Cooper, "The basic meaning of *batultu* remains 'unmarried adolescent,' but because such girls are assumed to be virgins, the word can be used specifically in that sense, as it surely is in the Neo-Babylonian marriage agreements" (Cooper 2002, 93).

A girl who died prematurely, without experiencing sex, was believed to become a *lilith* (cf. Lat. *succubus*), who has sexual relations with men in their sleep (the original meaning of "nightmare"). Her poignant fate is described in an incantation:

> A maiden who has never had intercourse like a woman,
> A maiden who has never been deflowered like a woman,
> A maiden who has never felt sensuality in her husband's lap,
> A maiden who has never stripped off her clothes in her husband's lap,
> A maiden whose (garment-)pin no handsome lad has loosened,
> A maiden in whose breasts there was never milk—bitter liquid came forth.
>   (Cooper 2002, 92)

A letter from Mari (ARM 26.488) contains the protestation of the wife of Sin-iddinam as reported by Buqaqum, a diplomat, to king Zimri-Lim:

> Before Sin-iddinam could marry me, I agreed with father and son, so that whenever Sin-iddinam left his home, the son of Asqudum would notify me, "I want to have you!" He kissed my lips and touched my vagina; but his penis did not penetrate my vagina, for I thought, I will not sin against Sin-iddinam

who has not sinned against me. I have not done in my own house what I am not to do. (Sasson, 293)

As Cooper observes, this text cannot be used "as evidence for a physical sign of virginity" (Cooper 2002, 96). As she negotiated her own marriage, this woman was not a young adolescent.

Egypt

Janet Johnson notes that "there is no evidence in Egyptian documentary or literary materials of any concern with virginity. It is not even easy to find a word in Egyptian which means 'virgin'" (Johnson 155). The Egyptian word *rnn.t* (pl. *rnn.wt*) is better translated "young woman" than "virgin." The word *h.wn.t*, which is used of the goddesses Hathor, Nephthys, and Isis, does not refer to a "virgin" but to a sexually mature woman. The office of "God's Wife," that is, the high priestess of Amon at Thebes, was held by a celibate daughter of the pharaoh, and was especially important in the transition from the 25th Dynasty to the 26th Dynasty (see Yamauchi, 144–46).

D. THE GRECO-ROMAN WORLD

Greece

The Greek word *parthenos*, translated "virgin," designated a young adolescent girl who was preparing for marriage by learning domestic skills. According to Giulia Sissa, "the Greek word *parthenos* does not unambiguously signify the perfect integrity implicit in our word *virgin*" (Sissa, 76). But texts describing the role of girls performing in a ceremony to the virgin goddess Artemis Hymnia at Mantineia require that the *parthenoi* who are to participate were chaste. In contrast to the possible ambiguity of the word *parthenos*, the Greek word *parthenia* unambiguously means "virginity" (Sissa, 77–78).

The Pythia, the mantic priestess of Apollo's oracle at Delphi, was an older woman dressed as a young unmarried woman. A myth recorded by Plutarch explains that the priestesses had originally been chosen from among virgins, but that one had been raped. According to Plutarch, "It is for these reasons that they guard the chastity of the priestess, and keep her life free from all association and contact with strangers" (*Def. orac.* 438c).

At Sikyon, only a *neōkoros*, "guardian," who abstained from intercourse with his wife and a *loutrophoros*, "bath-bearer," who was a virgin, could enter the sanctuary of Aphrodite. The *neōkoros*, a word that originally meant "temple sweeper," was the warden of the temple.

In the Greek pantheon of gods, Athena, a virgin goddess, was the patron of wisdom and of Athens. After their victorious repulse of the Persian invasion of 480–479 BC, the Athenians erected the Parthenon on the acropolis to house Athena's gold-and-ivory statue. The famous caryatid statues on the Erechtheion, another temple on the Athenian acropolis, portray young virgin followers of the goddess. During the Panathenaic festival, which took place once every four years in Athens, young girls served as *arrēphoroi*, who helped in the weaving of Athena's *peplos* ("garment"), or as *kanēphoroi*, "basket bearers."

The Greek terms *parthenios* and *parthenia* ("child of an unmarried woman") were used for children (masculine and feminine, respectively) whose fathers were unknown or believed to be divine. This name was famously given to a generation of Spartan children who were born while the Spartans were away fighting. These children were then exiled. An example of someone given this name on account of having a divine father is found in the myth of Zeus impregnating Danaë, who gives birth to Perseus. Certain outstanding figures, such as Plato, were given divine as well as human paternity. Ariston, Plato's father, was said to have had a dream that Apollo had impregnated his wife Perectione. According to a poem reported by Diogenes Laertius, "If Phoebus [Apollo] did not father Plato in Greece, how did Plato heal the souls of mortals with words?" (*Vit. Phil.* 3).

Greek culture segregated the sexes, and women had little contact with men outside their family. Wives and daughters were under the protection of husbands and fathers, partly because they were not trusted to remain chaste and partly to guard them from other men (Cole, 97). In early Greek culture, laws and beliefs about virginity focused on the "integrity" of the woman (G. Clark, 73–74).

In general, however, the Greco-Roman world saw sexual intercourse and pregnancy as beneficial to women's health. Pregnancy and sexual intercourse were believed to be necessary to keep the uterus moist. The Hippocratic texts viewed pregnancy as well as sexual intercourse as not only a cure for many female illnesses but also as essential for maintaining a woman's good health.

The Greek Hippocratic treatise *Peri Partheniōn* ("On Virgins") discusses the problems young girls suffer during their menarche, or first period. The author criticizes the ancient Greek custom of making offerings of clothes to the virgin goddess Artemis to seek a cure, since the problem in his opinion stems from an excess of blood.

Rome

Galen of Pergamon, a prominent Roman physician who transmitted Greek Hippocratic views to the Roman world, considered celibacy to be a health risk for both men and women because the men would retain the male seeds and the women the female seeds (G. Clark, 76). However, Soranus of Ephesus, a Greek physician of the Roman period (2nd c. AD) who wrote the most important ancient work on gynecology, argued that life-long virginity was more healthful for women than was childbearing. He declared, "We, however, contend that permanent virginity is healthful, because intercourse is harmful in itself as has been shown in more length in the book 'On Hygiene' " (*Gyn.* 1.32; Temkin, 29). His opinions went against the prevailing cultural views of the time.

Plutarch shares the Romans' customs and attitude toward virginity when he writes that the Romans gave their daughters "away at twelve and even younger, for thus the body and the moral character (of the girl) might be clean and untouched for the husband" (*Num.* 26.2). By the time of Augustus, the minimum age for the marriage of girls was set at twelve; girls who were espoused before that age became legitimate wives when they turned twelve.

The regulations governing the Vestal Virgins, special Roman priestesses dedicated to Vesta, the goddes of the hearth, were established by Numa, the second king of Rome. According to Plutarch: "It was ordained by the king that the sacred virgins should vow themselves to chastity for thirty years. ... Then the thirty years being now passed, any one who wishes has liberty to marry" (*Num.* 10.1–2). These women had extraordinary honors and privileges. The wills of rulers, such as that of Julius Caesar, were deposited to their care. They were given seats of honor at public events. For minor violations of the regulations, a Vestal could be scourged by the Pontifex Maximus. A violation of her vows of chastity would result in a Vestal's being buried alive.

E. THE JEWISH WORLD

The Jewish sect of the Therapeutae described by Philo was unusual in celebrating celibacy. He writes that the community's feast "is shared by women also, most of them aged virgins, who have kept their chastity not under compulsion, like some of the Greek priestesses, but on their own free will in their ardent yearning for wisdom" (*Contempl.* 68).

In ancient Jewish thought, virginity had economic implications. *Ben Sira* makes it plain that a father's main concern about his daughter was her virginity: "Do you have daughters? Be concerned for their chastity, and do not show yourself too indulgent with them" (Sir 7:24). This reflects the biological fact that although a woman could be certain that a child was hers, the paternity of a child could not be verified in antiquity. The chastity of the bride before marriage was necessary to ensure the family's honor and the child's legitimacy and right to inheritance.

A fragmentary text from Qumran (4Q159) is based on Deut 22:13–21, which concerns the test of a bride's virginity:

> If a man brings an accusation against a virgin of Israel, if [it is at the time] he marries her, let him speak and they shall investigate her trustworthiness [n'mnwt]. If he has not lied about her, she shall be put to death, but if he has testified f[alse]ly against her, he shall be fined two minas [and] he may [not] divorce her all of his life.

On the basis of parallels from Jewish and Near Eastern customs and from an unpublished fragment of the Damascus Document, J. Tigay has made a persuasive case that we should restore before the word n'mnwt the word nšym, "women." That is, the virginity of the bride was to be examined by "trustworthy women."

In the Mishnah, we find that a husband's claim that his bride was not a virgin could be countered by her claim that she had been raped:

> If a man married a woman and *found not in her the tokens of virginity*, and she said, "After thou didst betroth me I was forced and thy field was laid waste," and he said, "Not so, but [it befell] before I betrothed thee and my bargain was a bargain made in error," Rabban Gamaliel and R. Eliezer say: She may be believed. But R. Joshua says: We may not rely on her word; but she must be presumed to have suffered intercourse before she was betrothed and to have deceived her husband unless she can bring proof for her words.
> (*m. Ketub.* 1:6)

The Talmud (*b. Ketub.* 10a) records a series of six stories in which husbands approach R. Nahman claiming that their brides were not virgins in order to divorce their wives without paying them their *ketubah* (divorce settlement). In every case, the rabbi denies these claims; in one case he orders the husband to be beaten.

The rabbis identified the onset of puberty on the basis of "two pubic hairs," at about the age of twelve to twelve and a half. The rabbis held that a *bōgeret*, that is, a girl who had reached that age, was no longer subject to the virginity test of a bloody sheet, because they did not believe she would bleed upon the penetration of her hymen (*t. Ketub.* 1:3; *y. Ketub.* 1:1; Kulp, 46). Thus, claims of the non-virginity of brides based on their lack of bleeding were difficult to prove.

The Mishnah contains an interesting story that sets a halakic precedent regarding the dictum that the high priest could only marry a virgin. The priest Joshua b. Gamla had married the widow Martha (*m. Yebam.* 6:4). Problems arose when Joshua was appointed high priest. A high priest was halakically prohibited from marrying a widow. Yet Joshua remained firm in his resolve and kept Martha as his wife.

There was a contentious debate over four centuries between Jews and Christians concerning Isa 7:14, which the Gospel of Matthew cites as a prophecy of Jesus's birth from a virgin (*parthenos* in the Septuagint version quoted by Matthew). The later Greek versions of the OT produced by Jewish translators (Aquila, Symmachus, and Theodotion) use the word *neanis*, "young woman," in Isa 7:14.

This dispute is first attested in Justin Martyr (*Dial.* 43.8; 67.1; 71.3; 84.3). It also appears in Irenaeus (*Haer.* 3.21.1), Tertullian (*Mart.* 3.13.4–5; *Adv. Jud.* 9.8), and Eusebius (*Ecl. proph.* 4.4). The church fathers argued that if the reference had been simply to a "young woman," it would not have been a "sign." They also pointed out that in certain passages of the Septuagint (e.g., Deut 22:23–29) the words *parthenos* and *neanis* are used interchangeably. Jerome was the only church father whose knowledge of Hebrew enabled him to use the etymological argument of taking the root of ʿ*almâ*, ʿ-*l-m*, to state, in a typically rabbinic way, that the word meant "the hidden one." (See Kamesar, 62–75.)

According to Origen, Celsus, an anti-Christian critic, relied on a Jewish informant who contested Jesus's claims: "first, because *he fabricated the story of his birth from a virgin. . . .* He says that *she was driven out by her husband, who was a carpenter by trade*" (*Cels.* 1.28; Chadwick, 28). Elsewhere Celsus charged that Mary "*had been convicted of adultery and had a child by a certain soldier named Panthera*" (*Cels.* 1.32; Chadwick, 31).

Aphrahat (ca. 280–345) was a church leader in northeastern Mesopotamia who wrote in Syriac. In his *Demonstration against the Jews* (18), he responded to their criticisms of the Christians' exaltation of celibacy and virginity. According to Aphrahat, the Jews charged:

> But you do a thing which was not commanded by God, for you have received a curse and have multiplied barrenness. You have prohibited procreation, the blessing of righteous men. You do not take wives, and you do not become wives for husbands. You hate procreation, a blessing given by God.
> (Neusner, 77)

In opposition to a Christian, a Jew proclaimed: "You are unclean [*tame'in*], for you do not take wives. But we are holy [*kadishin*] and excellent, who procreate and increase seed in the world" (Neusner, 82; see also Koltun-Fromm).

F. THE CHRISTIAN WORLD

The Christian church developed out of Jewish roots. A Jewish woman was duty-bound to bear legitimate children to her husband. Barrenness was considered a curse, as seen in the longing of Elizabeth for a child (Luke 1:7, 25). The interactions of Jesus with women and Paul's teaching that all are one in Christ (Gal 3:28) fostered a healthy spiritual and intellectual relationship between men and women by encouraging women to participate in worship services and to serve in various ministries. The early church provided an improved level of intellectual and social equality between the sexes. The Letters of Pliny the Younger (early 2nd c.) attest that slave women were serving as *ministrae* "deaconnesses" (*Ep.* 10.96).

The difference of opinion between the Jews and early Christians regarding marriage, virginity, and celibacy was especially pronounced regarding the enjoyment of sexual intercourse and the command to procreate. The Jews have traditionally interpreted Gen 1:28, "be fruitful and multiply," as the very first of God's commandments. The Christian response has been more nuanced, allowing for the gift of celibacy and the choice of remaining a virgin. Some early Christian writers believed that the command to "be fruitful and multiply" had been superseded by the possibility of living "like angels in heaven" (Matt 22:30) through virginity (cf. Tertullian, *Exh. cast.* 6).

The debate concerning marriage versus celibacy and virginity was open and vigorous in the early church. The church fathers agreed with Paul that it is better to marry than to burn with sexual passion (1 Cor 7:9). They recognized that choosing celibacy and virginity could constitute self-denial, a concept popular at the time, but they also recognized that marriage likewise offered many opportunities for self-denial. The church fathers pointed out that a virgin could become preoccupied with herself, whereas one who took on the cares of having and raising a family had many opportunities to put others first.

While earlier writers such as Tertullian and Clement (2nd–3rd c.) had praised marriage, all the great leaders of the church in the 4th–5th centuries, including those writing in Latin such as Ambrose, Augustine, and Jerome, and those writing in Greek as Athanasius, Basil, Gregory of Nyssa, Gregory Nazianzus, and John Chrysostom, valued virginity and celibacy as a more spiritual state than marriage. All except Ambrose came from monastic backgrounds. Jovinian and Vigilantius, who thought otherwise, were denounced by Jerome and other Christians as heretics.

According to the early apologists, when Christians were being persecuted, sexual purity seemed to many believers to be the best way to present their commitment to Christ to the non-believing public. With the conversion

of Constantine and the end of persecution, a new ascetic movement emphasized celibacy and virginity as ways to demonstrate devotion to Christ.

In his letter to the Smyrnaeans, Ignatius, bishop of Antioch, greets "virgins called widows" (*tas parthenous tas legoumenas chēras*) (*Smyrn.* 13.1).
Some scholars, such as J. B. Lightfoot, take this to refer to widows who
were regarded as virgins, but most believe that the order of "widows" that
existed in the early church had by Ignatius's time been opened up to virgins,
especially older women who had no other means of support (Schoedel,
252–53). Ignatius also wrote to Polycarp, "If anyone is able to remain chaste
to the honor of the flesh of the Lord, let him so remain without boasting. If
he boasts, he is lost" (*Pol.* 5.2).

When Christianity was a marginal cult, a girl's choice to remain a virgin could be financially detrimental to her household. "Oppressive families and fiancés, who call in the local governor to force a reluctant heroine
into marriage, are a favourite theme of Christian romance," writes Clark
(G. Clark, 52). The apocryphal *Acts of Thecla* (see below) tells one such
story. But when Christianity became the prevailing religion of the land, the
emphasis of the problem shifted to maintaining support for the choice of
celibacy while deferring to fathers (ibid.).

An early source regarding the practice of virginity and asceticism
among Christian women is the *Apocryphal Acts of the Apostles*, a set of
narratives that documents the attraction of Christian asceticism for some
women in the second and third centuries.

The Acts of Thecla, an important part of the apocryphal *Acts of Paul*,
was exceedingly popular in the early church, as we have about eighty extant Greek manuscripts of this text. This text can be dated by an important
reference from Tertullian in his treatise on the theme of baptism (17.5),
dated ca. AD 200. Tertullian denounces the *Acts of Paul* as the work of
a demoted presbyter of Asia Minor, and claims that it was used by some
women to support their right to teach and to baptize. It was therefore composed probably between AD 170 and 180 (Klauck, 50), or between AD 185
and 195 (Hennecke and Schneemelcher, 351).

In the *Acts of Thecla*, the Apostle Paul comes to the house of Onesi-
phorus in Iconium (modern Konya) in south central Asia Minor, and proclaims a series of beatitudes:

> Blessed are they who have kept the flesh pure [*hagnē*], for they shall become
> a temple of God.

> Blessed are the continent, for to them will God speak. . . .

> Blessed are they who have wives as if they had them not, for they shall inherit
> God. . . .

Blessed are the bodies of the virgins [*makaria ta sōmata tōn parthenōn*], for they shall be well pleasing to God, and shall not lose the reward of their purity. (*Acts of Thecla* 6)

Listening intently from the window of a house next door is Thecla, a daughter of Theocleia who is betrothed to Thamyris. When Thecla is convinced by Paul's teachings to renounce her betrothal, Thamyris accuses Paul before the Roman governor Castellius, who has Paul scourged and expelled from the city. Thecla is denounced by her own mother and brought naked into the arena to be burned on a pyre, but is miraculously saved by an outpouring of rain and hail. She travels all the way to Myra in northwestern Asia Minor and finds Paul, who had been praying for her. She vows to follow him and declares: "I will cut my hair short and follow thee wherever thou goest" (*Acts of Thecla* 25).

Hair-cutting was a mark that designated the early women ascetics. Thecla, who was held up as a model of virginity for generations of ascetic women, not only cut her hair but also wore men's clothing. Mygdonia, yet another example of an ascetic woman in the *Apocryphal Acts*, showed that she had renounced the world by cutting her hair; Syncletica of Alexandria is likewise reported to have cut her hair as an outward sign of her renunciation of the world. These ascetic women dressed in men's clothing and are said to have lost female bodily characteristics; this was followed "by a negation of sexuality altogether" (Castelli, 76).

Tertullian outlines three degrees of virginity through which Christians might be sanctified: (1) to remain virgins from birth; (2) to remain virgins from the time of a second birth (Christian baptism); and (3) for husbands and wives to practice continence, and for widows and widowers not to remarry (*Exh. cast.* 1.1). Tertullian also held that virgins were wedded to Christ (*Virg.* 16.4).

Although Tertullian does not condemn marriage as evil, as did some, he reminds his readers that there will be no marriage in heaven. He writes eloquently on the pull of worldly desires and the bliss of life in heaven in this manner:

How many men, therefore, and how many women, in Ecclesiastical Orders, owe their position to continence, who have preferred to be wedded to God; who have restored the honour of their flesh, and who have already dedicated themselves as sons of that (future) age, by slaying in themselves the concupiscence of lust, and that whole (propensity) which could not be admitted within Paradise! Whence it is presumable that such as shall wish to be received within Paradise, ought at last to begin to cease from that thing from which Paradise is intact. (*Exh. cast.* 1.13)

Cyprian of Carthage writes that those who keep sexual purity are "the flower of the tree that is the Church, the beauty and adornment of spiritual grace, the image of God reflecting the godliness of the Lord, the more illustrious part of Christ's flock" (*Hab. virg.* 5). Cyprian cautions virgins not to adorn themselves in order to display their charms or to give glory to their bodies "since there is no struggle greater than that against the flesh" (ibid.). Cyprian counsels virgins not to paint their eyes or accent them with cosmetics or "to change their hair by false colors" (*Hab. virg.* 14).

There is evidence that large numbers of men and women were attracted to lives of asceticism, chastity, and community. One tradition reports that Maria, the sister of Pachomius, the founder of cenobitic (communal) monasticism, came to visit her brother in his community in Egypt. He refused to see her but had a hut built nearby so that she could follow the ascetic life. Maria agreed and became the leader of one of the two women's monasteries that remained after the death of Pachomius. Together this brother and sister left a lasting impact on Christianity in Egypt. Maria's influence on virgins and women monastics became widespread. Theodoret reports that by the beginning of the fifth century communities of virgins had been established in Palestine, Egypt, Asia, Pontus, and Europe (Castelli, 78–79).

The *Apophthegmata Patrum*, a collection of sayings attributed to the monks of Egypt, also includes sayings from the "Desert Mothers" Theodora, Sara, and Syncletica, who were known as holy women (Castelli, 64).

Though Athanasius, bishop of Alexandria, promoted monastic ideals, especially through his influential biography of St. Anthony, he condemned the learned Coptic monk Hieracas, who insisted that only celibate men and virgins could receive salvation. Athanasius advised virgins to abandon a womanly mindset, because women who please God will be elevated to male ranks (Castelli, 75).

By the fourth century, so-called "spiritual marriages" had become widespread in the church. This was an arrangement whereby "virgins" lived together with celibate priests for mutual benefits—that is, the woman did the household chores and provided companionship in exchange for room and board. But it soon became clear that such arrangements could easily lead to temptations. The Council of Ancyra in AD 314 issued a canon prohibiting women from living together with men as "sisters." The third canon of the Council of Nicaea in AD 325 condemned all clerics who lived with women who were not their relatives.

The three great Cappadocians—Basil, his brother Gregory of Nyssa, and their friend, Gregory of Nazianzus—were leaders in the monastic movement. In his *On the True Purity of Virginity*, Basil not only urges virgins to forego makeup and jewelry but also encourages them to obscure their natural beauty and make their appearance and voice masculine so as not to attract men (Shaw, 166).

By Basil's time, virgins constituted an official order (*tagma*) in the church. They were supported by the church even when they lived with their families, so that some families had an incentive to enroll their daughters as "virgins." The young girls who vowed virginity wore a special habit, fasted until evening, and did not visit churches alone.

Basil advised that the choice to remain a virgin should not be made until the age of sixteen or seventeen. His sister, Macrina, however, chose at the age of twelve to remain a virgin after her fiancé died (Basil, *Ep.* 199.18; Clark, 52). Basil writes of families who dedicated a daughter to virginity simply to save for themselves what would have been her dowry.

Between AD 374 and 375 Basil exchanged lengthy letters on matters of church governance with Amphilochius, bishop of Iconium. Some sixty years before, a council at Ancyra had dealt with the case of virgins who had not kept their vows. They were condemned to one year's penance. But Basil's judgment is more severe. According to him, a fallen virgin was to be excommunicated for fifteen years (*Ep.* 188).

Although monasticism was gaining popularity, some writers of this time were careful not to praise virginity at the expense of the married state. Instead, some acknowledged that both marriage and virginity were acceptable ways of life for Christians. In his funeral oration for his married sister Gorgonia, Gregory of Nazianzus declares:

> In modesty she so greatly excelled, and so far surpassed, those of her own day, to say nothing of those of old time who have been illustrious for modesty, that, in regard to the two divisions of the life of all, that is, the married and the unmarried state, the latter being higher and more divine, though more difficult and dangerous, while the former is more humble and more safe, she was able to avoid the disadvantages of each, and to select and combine all that is best in both, namely, the elevation of the one and the security of the other, thus becoming modest without pride, blending the excellence of the married with that of the unmarried state, and proving that neither of them absolutely binds us to, or separates us from, God or the world. (*Oration* 8.8)

John Chrysostom, who wrote a treatise on virginity, condemned the Encratites, a sect that rejected marriage. He also criticized the widespread practice of the *subintroductae*, the later Latin term for *parthenoi syneisaktoi*, or "virgins brought in" to live with monks in so-called "spiritual marriages." (See E. A. Clark.)

The concepts of virginity and asceticism came to be associated with a Greek term borrowed from Stoicism, *andreia*. While the word may mean "manliness," it also carries the notion of courage. For instance, John

Chrysostom many times makes reference to the *andreia* of the deaconness Olympias (Castelli, 77). Olympias was a wealthy widow who refused the order of the emperor Theodosius to remarry. She had been married at the age of sixteen and her husband had died two years later. When John Chrysostom became the archbishop of Constantinople, Olympias, who as chief deaconness supervised the nuns in the city, became his close confidant.

Jerome was a learned monk who produced a new Latin Bible (later known as the Vulgate) by translating the OT from Hebrew and the NT from Greek. While in Rome and later from his monastery in Bethlehem, Jerome enouraged girls and women to pursue a life of virginity and asceticism. According to Jerome, virginity was the original state of human beings; intercourse came into existence only after the fall. According to him, marriage was only necessary for providing children who would become celibates or virgins.

Eustochium, the daughter of Paula, Jerome's close friend, dedicated herself to virginity as a child of twelve. Jerome claimed that she was the first young woman of noble birth to embrace virginity. At Jerome's urging, she stayed in her room, ate little, neglected her appearance, avoided baths, and wore shabby clothes. She attended Bible classes and sang the psalms in Hebrew. Her days and nights were spent in prayer.

In his famous Letter 22, written to Eustochium ca. AD 384, Jerome states: "Death came through Eve, but life has come through Mary. And thus the gift of virginity has been bestowed most richly upon women, seeing that it has had its beginning from a woman" (*Ep.* 22.21). Jerome wrote in opposition to Jovinian, who had claimed that virgins and celibates are in no way superior to married couples. In response, Jerome declared:

> Virginity is to marriage what fruit is to the tree, or grain to the straw. Although the hundred-fold, the sixty-fold, and the thirty-fold spring from one earth and from one sowing, yet there is a great difference in respect of number. The thirty-fold has reference to marriage. . . . The sixty-fold applies to widow . . . while one-hundred-fold . . . expresses the crown of virginity. (*Jov.* 1.3)

During the fourth century there was a significant movement among Christian women to renounce marriage and to embrace a life of asceticism. This renunciation offered women "the possibility of moving outside the constraints of socially and sexually conventional roles, of exercising power, and of experiencing a sense of worth which was often unavailable to them with the traditional setting of marriage" (Castelli, 61).

It would seem that women who chose virginity and asceticism achieved an elevated status in their communities. The decision to renounce marriage and the world and to remain a virgin gave some wealthy women the chance for a lifetime of study. This kind of life was attractive to some aristocratic women. Consider these examples given by Castelli: Blesilla received praise from Jerome for her excellence in Greek and Hebrew; and Melania the Younger became so astute in theology that women from the senatorial class as well as other people in high places sought her counsel in matters of theology (Castelli, 82).

But Castelli notes with sadness that texts written by ascetic women and virgins themselves are lacking. For instance, although the letters of Jerome to Paula, Marcella, Eustochium, and other literate and learned women have been preserved, their letters to him have not. The same is true, Castelli observes, of the letters of Olympias to John Chrysostom. Also noteworthy is the fact that Macrina, the sister of Gregory of Nyssa and Basil, was influential in the conversion of Basil, yet she is not mentioned in any of Basil's 366 letters. Macrina is celebrated, however, in a famous eulogy by Gregory of Nyssa.

Castelli asks these questions about the lack of extant records about women:

> How many women lost their places in the written record of the church because no one chose to write their biographies and because the men whose lives they influenced omitted any mention of them? How many exceptional women may have been only mentioned and been otherwise lost without a trace? How many "ordinary" virgins are absent from the record altogether? (Castelli, 63)

Ambrose of Milan (d. 397) wrote four treatises on the topic of virginity: *De virginibus*, *De virginitate*, *De institutione virginis*, and *Exhortatio virginitatis*. He held that marriage is honorable but that virginity is more honorable. Ambrose writes to his disciples exhorting them to make their lives resemble that of Mary: "Let, then, the life of Mary be as it were virginity itself, set forth in a likeness, from which, as from a mirror, the appearance of chastity and the form of virtue is reflected" (*Virg.* 2.6).

In large part, the culture in which the early church grew was unfavorable to women. Ambrose acknowledged this and saw the dilemma many women faced because the marriage market demeaned them. Ambrose states that a woman of marriageable age is in a pitiable situation:

> But how wretched a position, that she who is marriageable is in a species of sale 'put up as it were to auction to be bid for, so that he who offers the highest price purchases her. Slaves are sold on more tolerable conditions, for they often choose their masters; if a maiden chooses it is an offense, if not it is an insult. (*Virg.* 1.10.56)

Augustine, while praising Soranus as the greatest medical authority of his day, did not endorse his view that lifelong virginity was more healthy for women than marriage. Augustine states instead that virginity in no way makes life easier and should not be chosen for the reason that it would ensure better health. Augustine also writes that the church does not honor virgins for their pure, virginal flesh but instead because such women had consecrated their virginity to God. He affirms, "no one keeps modesty in the body, unless chastity have been before implanted in the spirit" (Augustine, *Virginit.* 8).

Celibacy and virginity became so popular that Augustine cautioned that too many in the culture were choosing virginity because of selfish motives like pride. Indeed, some who chose virginity may have prided themselves on being superior to those who chose marriage (Augustine, *Bon. conj.* 35).

The concept of virginity also figured in the debate between Augustine and Pelagius on the doctrine of sin. Augustine argued that sin is perpetuated from generation to generation; only Jesus was exempt from sin and this was because of Mary's virginity. Pelagius argued that a person could reach a sinless perfection by virtue of his or her own efforts. For Pelagius, Augustine's theory of original sin meant that procreation and marriage were evil. Augustine's theory that sin is somehow inherited or original became the commonly accepted orthodox view.

All orthodox Christians have believed in the virginal conception of Jesus through the agency of the Holy Spirit and in his birth from the Virgin Mary (Matt 1:18). The NT's reference to Jesus as Mary's "firstborn" son (Luke 2:7) suggests that there were other children from her union with Joseph. Indeed, the NT mentions four named brothers of Jesus (James, Jude [also known as Judas], Simon, and Joseph) and unnamed sisters (Matt 13:55–56; Mark 6:3).

Both the Orthodox churches and the Catholic Church, however, affirm that Mary remained a virgin both before and after giving birth to Jesus. They hold this based on two different interpretations of Jesus's reputed siblings. The Orthodox believe that Jesus's so-called siblings were stepbrothers and stepsisters from an earlier marriage of Joseph, who was a widower when he wed Mary. The Catholic Church has accepted Jerome's interpretation that these *adelphoi* (Lat. *fratres*) were actually "cousins."

The first explanation is found in the *Protevangelium of James*, the earliest (2nd c. AD) and most important of the apocryphal infancy gospels. This text names Mary's parents as Anna and Joachim. According to the text, when Mary was three years old she was dedicated to live in the temple (*Prot. Jas.* 7). But when she became twelve years old, the priests became concerned that her menstruation might pollute the temple (*Prot. Jas.* 8), so they called for a gathering of the widowers of the land. The sign of a dove designated Joseph as the prospective bridegroom for Mary, but he protested: "I (already) have sons and am old, but she is a girl." Reassured by the priests that this was God's will, Joseph took Mary as his wife. She became pregnant by the Holy Spirit when she was sixteen years old (*Prot. Jas.* 12).

The *Protevangelium of James* is also the source of the tradition that Mary remained a virgin (*virginitas in partu*) even while delivering Jesus. According to the story, a disbelieving midwife named Salome declared, "As the Lord my God lives, unless I put (forward) my finger and test her condition, I will not believe that a virgin has brought forth" (*Prot. Jas.* 19.3). When she did so, her hand withered as punishment for her unbelief. Clement of Alexandria appears to be referring to this story when he remarks:

> But, as appears, many even down to our own time regard Mary, on account of the birth of her child, as having been in the puerperal state, although she was not. For some say that, after she brought forth, she was found, when examined, to be a virgin. (*Strom.* 7.16)

The Syriac *Odes of Solomon* (2nd c. AD) describe Mary's birth process as unlike that of other mothers: "And she labored and bore the Son but without pain, because it did not occur without purpose" (*Odes* 19.8).

Tertullian, however, who was attempting to counter the docetic Christology of Marcion, stressed the birth travail of Mary as indeed a very human process:

> Come now, beginning from the nativity itself, declaim against the uncleanness of the generative elements within the womb, the filthy concretion of fluid and blood, of the growth of the flesh for nine months long out of that very mire. Describe the womb as it enlarges from day to day, heavy, troublesome, restless even in sleep, changeful in its feelings of dislike and desire. Inveigh now likewise against the shame itself of a woman in travail which, however, ought rather to be honoured in consideration of that peril, or to be held sacred in respect of (the mystery of) nature. (*Carn.* 4)

Helvidius (fl. AD 380s) was one of the very few in the fourth century to criticize Jerome's arguments for Mary's perpetual virginity and his elevation of celibacy and virginity above marriage. Another critic of the prevailing view was Jovinian (d. ca. AD 405), who contended that Mary must have lost her virginity in the process of bearing Jesus, otherwise he was not truly human. Their criticisms were refuted by Jerome, Ambrose, and Augustine. Both Helvidius and Jovinian were condemned. However, Jerome did not maintain that Mary remained unaffected by the process of giving birth.

The view of Mary's *virginitas in partu* was championed by Ambrose and became the accepted view in the West. In the East, the virginity of Mary was celebrated in the lyrical hymns of Ephrem the Syrian.

How much more they slandered the mother of the Son!
By water ordeals and by cloths
He taught them, so that when the Lord of conceptions
came to them, and they slandered that womb
in which He dwelt, pure evidence of virginity (*btwlwt*)
concerning her conception would convince us about it.
    (Hymn 14.13–14; McVey, 143)

BIBLIOGRAPHY: P. R. Amidon, trans., *The Panarion of St. Epiphanius, Bishop of Salamis* (1990); I. Balla, *Ben Sira on Family, Gender, and Sexuality* (2011); R. Bauckham, *Jude and the Relatives of Jesus in the Early Church* (1990); G. K. Beale, *The Book of Revelation: A Commentary on the Greek Text* (1999); M. Beard, "The Sexual Status of Vestal Virgins," *JRS* 70 (1980), 12–27; R. M. Berchman, *Porphyry Against the Christians* (2005); C. L. Blomberg, "Matthew," in *Commentary on the New Testament Use of the Old Testament*, ed. G. K. Beale and D. A. Carson (2007), 1–109; R. E. Brown, *The Birth of the Messiah* (1977); G. Carey, "Virgin, Apocalypse of the," *EDB*, 1359; H. L. Carrigan, Jr., "Virgin Birth," *EDB*, 1359; E. Castelli, "Virginity and Its Meaning for Women's Sexuality in Early Christianity," *Journal of Feminist Studies in Religion* 2 (1986), 61–88; H. Chadwick, trans., *Contra Celsus* (1980); E. A. Clark, "John Chrysostom and the *Subintroductae*," *CH* 46 (1977), 171–85; G. Clark, *Women in Late Antiquity: Pagan and Christian Life-styles* (1993); S. G. Cole, "Greek Sanctions against Sexual Assault," *CP* 79 (1984), 97–113; J. G. Cook, *The Interpretation of the New Testament in Greco-Roman Paganism* (2000); J. S. Cooper, "Virginity in Ancient Mesopotamia," in *Sex and Gender in the Ancient Near East*, ed. S. Parpola and R. M. Whiting (2002), 1.91–112; P. L. Day, "Virgin," *EDB*, 1358–59; J. J. Devault, "The Concept of Virginity in Judaism," *Marian Studies* 13 (1962), 23–40; M. Dillon, *Girls and Women in Classical Greek Religion* (2001); W. J. Dooley, *Marriage according to St. Ambrose* (1948); S. Elm, '*Virgins of God': The Making of Asceticism in Late Antiquity* (1994); L. M. Epstein, *Sex Laws and Customs in Judaism* (1967); M. J. Evans, "Women," in *DOTP* 897–904; R. S. Evans, *Sex and Salvation: Virginity as a Soteriological Paradigm in Ancient Christianity* (2003); M. F. Foskett, *A Virgin Conceived: Mary and Classical Representations of Virginity* (2002); T. Frymer-Kensky, "Virginity in the Bible," in *Gender and Law in the Hebrew Bible and the Ancient Near East*, ed. V. H. Matthews, B. M. Levinson, and T. Frymer-Kensky, (2004), 79–96; L. S. M. Gambero, *Mary and the Fathers of the Church: The Blessed Virgin Mary in Patristic Thought*, trans. T. Buffer (1999); E. Hennecke and W. Schneemelcher, *New Testament Apocrypha II: Writings Relating to the Apostles, Apocalypses and Related Subjects*, trans. R. M. Wilson (1964); A. Hughes, "The Legacy of the Feminine in the Christology of Origen of Alexandria, Methodius of Olympus, and Gregory of Nyssa," *VC* 69 (2015): 1–26; D. G. Hunter, "Helvidius, Jovinian, and the Virginity of Mary in Late Fourth-Century Rome," *JECS* 1 (1993), 47–71; D. G. Hunter, *Marriage, Celibacy and Heresy in Ancient Christianity* (2007); K. H. Jobes and M. Silva, *Invitation to the Septuagint* (2000); J. H. Johnson, "Sex and Marriage in Ancient Egypt," in *Hommages à Fayza Haikal*, ed. N. Grimal, A. Kamal, and C. May-Sheikholeslami (2003), 149–59; S. E. Johnson, *The Life and Miracles of Thekla* (2006); P. S. Johnston, "Life, Disease and Death," in *DOTP* 532–36; A. Kamesar, "The Virgin of Isaiah 7:14: The Philological Argument from the Second to the Fifth Century," *JTS* 41 (1990), 51–75; C. S. Keener, *A Commentary on the Gospel of Matthew* (1999); J. N. D. Kelly, *Golden Mouth: The Story of John Chrysostom: Ascetic, Preacher, Bishop* (1995); J. N. D. Kelly, *Jerome: His Life, Writings, and Controversies* (1975); H.-J. Klauck, *The Apocryphal Acts of the Apostles*, trans. B. McNeil (2008); N. Koltun-Fromm, "Sexuality and Holiness: Semitic Christian and Jewish Conceptualization of Sexual Behavior," *VC* 54 (2000), 375–95; J. Kulp, "'Go Enjoy Your Acquisition': Virginity Claims in Rabbinic Literature Reexamined," *HUCA* 77 (2006), 33–65; J. K. Lillis, "Paradox *in Partu*: Verifying Virginity in the *Protevangelium of James*," *JECS* 24 (2016), 1–28; A. T. Lincoln, *Born of a Virgin? Reconceiving Jesus in the Bible, Tradition, and Theology* (2013); J. G. Machen, *The Virgin Birth of Christ* (2011); D. Marcus, *Jephthah and His Vow* (1986); I. H. Marshall, *The Gospel of Luke: A Commentary on the Greek Text* (1978); K. E. McVey, trans., *Ephrem the Syrian: Hymns* (1989); C. M. Miller, "Maidenhood and Virginity in Ancient Israel," *ResQ* 22.4 (1979), 242–46; D. Montserrat, ed., *Changing Bodies, Changing Meanings* (1995); R. H. Mounce, *The Book of Revelation* (1977); J. Neusner, *Aphrahat and Judaism: The Christian-Jewish Argument in Fourth-Century Iran* (1971); M. M. Pazdan, "Mary, Mother of Jesus," *ABD* IV.584–86; C. Pharr, trans., *The Theodosian Code and Novels, and the Sirmondian Constitutions* (repr. of the 2001 ed., 2012); J. R. Pinault, "The Medical Case for Virginity in the Early Second Century C.E.: Soranus of Ephesus, *Gynecology* 1.32," *Helios* 19 (1992), 123–39; R. O. Rigsby, "Judah," in *DOTP* 480–84; J. M. Sasson, trans. and ed., *From the Mari Archives: An Anthology of Old Babylonian Letters* (2015); M. L. Satlow, "'Texts of Terror': Rabbinic Texts, Speech Acts, and the Control of Mores," *Association for Jewish Studies Review* 21 (1996), 273–97; J. J. Schmitt, "Virgin," *ABD* VI.853–54; W. R. Schoedel, *Ignatius of Antioch* (1985); T. M. Shaw, "Creation, Virginity and Diet in Fourth-Century Christianity: Basil of Ancyra's *On the True Purity of Virginity*," in *Gender and the Body in the Ancient Mediterranean*, ed. M. Wyke (1998), 155–72; G. Sissa, *Greek Virginity*, trans. A. Goldhammer (1990); J. Stiebert, *Fathers & Daughters in the Hebrew Bible* (2013); O. Temkin, trans., *Soranus' Gynecology* (1956); J. H. Tigay, "Examination of the Accused Bride in

4Q159: Forensic Medicine at Qumran," *JANES* 22 (1993), 129–34; M. O. Wise, M. G. Abegg, Jr., and E. M. Cook, trans., *The Dead Sea Scrolls* (Rev. ed., 2005); B. Witherington III, *Women in the Earliest Churches* (1988); E. M. Yamauchi, *Africa and the Bible* (2004).

RGB

See also CELIBACY, HAIR, MARRIAGE, MENSTRUATION, and RAPE.

Viticulture

The cultivation of grapevines, or viticulture (Lat. *viti(s)*, "vine"), was an important agricultural process in most societies of the ancient world, including those of Mesopotamia, Egypt, and other regions around the Mediterranean Sea. The Eurasian grape (*Vinis vinifera* L. subsp. *sylvestris*) appears to have originated in the region bordered by the Caucasus, eastern Turkey, and the Zagros range (Isaac, 69). Traces of wine were identified in the residue of terebinth resin found in pottery dating to ca. 6000 BC from the Neolithic village of Hajji Firuz in the northern Zagros Mountains in Iran (Unwin, 6).

A. OLD TESTAMENT

In the OT, the common grapevine (*Vitis vinifera*) is usually designated by the Hebrew *gepen*. The Hebrew terms *śōrēq* and *śĕrēqâ*, "choice vine" (Gen 49:11; Isa 5:2; Jer 2:21), apparently refer to a superlative grapevine that yielded smaller berries of a deep red hue. The term "vineyard" (Heb *kerem*) usually implies a group or plantation of grapevines (cf. 1 Kgs 21:1–7).

According to biblical tradition, Noah was the first to plant a vineyard and drink of its wine (Gen 9:20–21). Other OT vintners include Isaac (Gen 27:28, 37), Nabal (1 Sam 25), and David (1 Chr 27:27). The land of Canaan was known for its vineyards (Num 16:14; Deut 8:8; Josh 24:13). Melchizedek, the Canaanite king of Salem, offered wine to Abraham as a token of hospitality and friendship (Gen 14:18). Vineyards were located in the fertile plain of Jezreel (1 Kgs 21:1–7), in the Jordan Valley, and along the Dead Sea at En Gedi (Song 1:14), as the warmer climate permitted grapes to ripen faster than in other areas. Other biblical locations known for their vineyards are Shiloh in Ephraim (Judg 21:19–21); Helbon, north of Damascus (Ezek 27:18); and Sibmah, east of the Jordan (Isa 16:8; Jer 48:32).

The spies brought back large clusters of grapes from the Valley of Esh-col in the area of Hebron (Num 13:22–24). According to the Mosaic law, a person who had planted a vineyard and had not begun to enjoy its fruits was exempt from military service (Deut 20:6). The law also indicated that where vines were planted, no other seeds were to be sown (Deut 22:9), which may reflect repugnance toward Egyptian horticultural practices. Vineyards were to remain unpruned and unharvested in the Sabbath year (Lev 25:3–5). One could eat freely of the grapes of the vineyard of one's neighbor but could carry none away in a basket (Deut 23:24). At harvest, which took place in September and October, the owner of a vineyard was not permitted to go over his vineyard a second time or to pick up grapes that had fallen. What remained was to be left for the alien, the father-less, and the widow (Lev 19:10; Deut 24:21). One who voluntarily took the Nazirite vow was forbidden to consume anything that comes from the grapevine (Num 6:3–4).

In the time of the monarchy (10th c. BC), private royal vineyards were established. The king took a tenth of the vintage (1 Sam 8:15) that came from the personal produce of the populace. David put Shimei the Ramathite in charge of his royal vineyards and Zabdi the Shiphmite in charge of the produce of the vineyards for the wine vats (1 Chr 27:27). At the instigation of his wife Jezebel, Ahab seized the vineyard of his neighbor Naboth, which was a valued heirloom in his family (1 Kgs 21).

The prophets assumed that their audiences understood viticultural processes (Isa 16:10; 37:30; 65:21; Jer 31:5; 48:32; Ezek 28:26; Amos 4:9; 5:11; 9:14; Zeph 1:13). Isaiah's "Song of the Vineyard" (5:1–7) reflects a vine grower's daily concerns and the practical procedures in which he en-gaged. Ezekiel indicates that the grapes harvested in the late summer were often sour and set the teeth on edge (18:2).

Several texts reflect the fact that the winepress, a central component of viticulture, was an administrative center (Joel 3:13; Lam 1:15; Isa 63:2; Neh 13:5). The harvesting of grapes was a time of rejoicing and feasting that represented divine blessing (Judg 9:27; Isa 16:10; Jer 48:33). During the Babylonian captivity (6th c. BC), the poorest people of the land were left to do the pruning and other viticultural chores (2 Kgs 25:12).

In the OT, the vine, grape, and vineyard at times symbolize the Hebrew nation (Jer 12:10; Ezek 17:6–8), and viticultural images can represent God's provision and blessings. According to Hosea, when the Lord found Israel "it was like finding grapes in the desert" (9:10). The Psalms and Isaiah state that God's elect were brought as a vine from Egypt and planted by their loved one's hand in a carefully prepared vineyard (Ps 80:8–16; Isa 5:1–7). When, however, this choice vine of reliable stock turned into a wild vine (Jer 2:21) and yielded bad grapes (Isa 5:4), it became subject to the Lord's pruning hand of correction (Isa 5:5–6). Likewise, the image of treading the winepress is used to describe God's judgment on the nations (Isa 63:2–6).

Solomon's reign is described as a time when the Israelites "lived in safety, everyone under their own vine and under their own fig tree" (1 Kgs 4:25), and Amos envisages the future blessing of the Lord upon his people in terms of a viticultural paradise (Amos 9:13–14; cf. Mic 4:4). On the other hand, Habakkuk describes the impending invasion of an enemy and national calamity as a time when "there are no grapes on the vines" (Hab 3:17).

B. THE NEW TESTAMENT

Jesus refers to vines and vineyards in his teachings. A vineyard is the scene for four of his parables: "The Parable of the Workers in the Vineyard" (Matt 20:1–16), "The Parable of the Two Sons" (Matt 21:28–32), "The Parable of the Tenants" (Matt 21:33–46; Mark 12:1–12; Luke 20:9–19), and "The Vineyard and the Unfruitful Fig Tree" (Luke 13:6–9). As these parables reflect, vineyards required careful stewardship.

Jesus describes his relationship to his followers in his discourse on the vine and the branches (John 15:1–17), declaring that he is the "true vine" and that his Father is the "gardener" (v. 1). True believers, like branches, must remain in the vine in order to bear fruit (vs. 4–5).

Viticultural production at times required the establishment of a wall, which during the NT period would have been constructed of heavy stones and briars, as well as watchtowers to protect the vineyard (Matt 21:33; Mark 12:1). Proper maintenance of the vines included pruning dead and fruitless branches, which was essential to a productive vineyard (John 15:2; cf. Luke 13:6, 7). These pruned branches were then dried and used as fuel (John 15:6).

The owner of a vineyard often hired laborers to care for and harvest his grapes. These workers may have received daily wages for their work (Matt 20:1–16). A landowner might also rent his vineyard to tenants, who would give him a share of the crop at harvest time (Matt 20:9–16; Mark 12:1–9; Luke 20:9–19).

Addressing the church in Corinth, Paul contends for his rights as an apostle to support his ministry by comparing his role to that of a vineyard planter who is justified in consuming the fruits of his labor (1 Cor 9:7).

Employing language and imagery from the OT, the book of Revelation portrays the eschatological judgment in terms of an angel harvesting the ripe "grapes from the earth's vine," which are then deposited in the "great winepress of God's wrath," where they are trodden underfoot (14:18–20).

C. THE NEAR EASTERN WORLD

Viticulture was a key feature in the development of agriculture in the civilizations that emerged in the region known as the Fertile Crescent. Vines came to symbolize peace, security, and prosperity, features that were necessary for the cultivation of vineyards.

Mesopotamia

According to Mesopotamian tradition, viticulture existed before the flood. In the *Epic of Gilgamesh*, the hero comes upon clusters of black grapes, described as "lapis," in his travels (Tab IX.5.156). The presence of vineyards and wine in the story not only attests to the significance of viticulture in this region but also symbolizes fertility and divine blessing (Tab IX).

Soil conditions made grape cultivation difficult in southern Mesopotamia, so wine was an imported luxury, whereas beer was a locally produced commodity (Matthews, 21). Although small vineyards were being cultivated by the Sumerians as early as the third millennium BC, these were generally not for wine but for raisins (Unwin, 64).

A number of Old Babylonian letters refer to grapes and wine. An official (probably located at Saggaratum, near the confluence of the Khabur and the Euphrates in the north) wrote to Yasmaḥ-Addu as follows: "My lord wrote me as follows, 'Grapes must not be harvested until I send you controllers/inspectors (*ebbūtum*).' The time to harvest grapes has come or (the crop) will turn *overripe*. My lord should send me controllers so grapes are harvested" (*Florilegium marianum* 11.188; Sasson, 57).

Zimri-Lim, the king of Mari (18th c. BC), wrote to his wife as follows:

> Hammurabi, king of Babylon, has written me for wine. I am now conveying to you a cylinder-seal in a (metal) mounting. Open up the wine stockroom with Ṣidqummaṣ standing by, let him purify his hands, then select 11 jars of red (*sāmum*) wine of good quality that I drink. . . . (The merchant) Kutkutum has brought me 60 jars of second-quality wine. Another matter: Do convey via the Babylonian messengers first-rate wine. (ARM 10.133; Sasson, 157–58).

Later, with the ascendency of the Assyrians (c. 900–612 BC), power shifted further north into regions more suited for the establishment of vineyards. Viticulture could be used to project political power. For example, Ashurnasirpal II (883–859 BC) served ten thousand skins of wine to nearly seventy thousand guests at the inauguration of Nimrud (*ANESTP*, 558–60). A famous relief of Ashurbanipal (668–627 BC) depicts the king reclining on a couch and his queen seated on a chair before him (*ANEP*,

155, fig. 451). They are under a bower of vines and are drinking a beverage that is likely wine (Unwin, 67, fig. 12). Eventually, viticultural practices spread beyond Mesopotamia and northern territories along trade routes into the Levant and other neighboring regions.

Syria and Palestine

Grape cultivation was widely practiced in Syria and Palestine, a region that, in contrast with Mesopotamia and Egypt, provided the ideal climate and topography for viticulture. Excavations at Jericho and Lachish have uncovered grape seeds from the Early Bronze Age (ca. 3100–2000 BC). The hills of the region were perfectly suited for the planting of vineyards (cf. Gen 49:8–12; Isa 5:1; Jer 31:5) with gentle slopes where the vines could take root and benefit from the heavy dews that fell overnight in the dry summers.

The Gezer calendar (10th c. BC), one of the earliest extant inscriptions written in a Northwest Semitic language, indicates that grapes were a principal agricultural product in ancient Israel. The Samaria Ostraca, a collection of inscribed potsherds from the eighth century BC, record extensive wine and oil deliveries made to the northern kingdom, probably by clans who were responsible for cultivating vineyards (Chavalas, 398–99).

Textual evidence such as this is supported by the discovery of numerous rock-hewn winepresses at Iron Age sites (McGovern, 217). Harvesters would bring grapes to these presses, which had vats in which barefoot workers trod the grapes, keeping time with festive songs. While there were large vineyards, the keeping of vines was a ubiquitous practice in Palestine: even poor families would have had a few vines.

Egypt

Grapes were cultivated in Egypt from an early period. According to Egyptian mythology, the god Osiris, judge of the dead, first imparted to the world the skill of viticulture. The Egyptians were engaged in viticulture by the time of the 1st Dynasty (ca. 3000 BC), although vineyards were often part of private gardens belonging to the king, priests, or other high officials. From this period there is evidence of seals and clay stoppers from royal vineyards. The images from royal tombs provide examples of viticultural processes. The tomb of Khaemwese at Thebes (ca. 1450 BC) featured images of workers picking grapes and placing them in wicker baskets for transfer to the presses. There the grapes are shown being pressed underfoot by laborers supporting themselves by a network of overhead ropes.

During the New Kingdom, Semitic prisoners tended royal vineyards. The Egyptians were also known to dedicate vineyards to their gods. Ramesses III, for example, gave numerous vineyards to the god Amun; he also equipped them with workers responsible for making wine.

The Delta region of northern Egypt was famed for its vineyards and the quality of its grapes that were made into wine, so much so that ancient wine jars were labeled as coming from this region (Brier and Hobbs, 105). Egypt was involved in the regional trade of grapes, including from Palestine. The *Story of Sinuhe* (ca. 2000 B.C.) narrates how an official returned to Egypt from Canaan with descriptions of the abundance of grapes and wine there (*ANET*, 18–22). An imported Syrian wine jar found in the tomb of Tutankhamun provides further evidence of the quality of wine from Palestine, and also reflects the vitality of wine trade (McGovern, 139, fig. 6.5).

D. THE GRECO-ROMAN WORLD

Greece

Viticulture, alongside the production of wheat and olives, was a central part of ancient Greek agriculture. The Minoans were cultivating grapevines by the fifteenth century BC, as is evidenced by a winepress at Palaikastro on Crete (Unwin, 77). Archaeological evidence of grapes has been found at major Minoan and Mycenaean sites (Ventris and Chadwick, 129). The ideogram for wine occurs on the Linear B tablets (1400–1200 BC) as well as on sealings from the wine magazine at Pylos (Ventris and Chadwick, 412). The word *wo-no* (apparently *oinos*, "wine") appears on one tablet (PY 250).

The *Iliad* and the *Odyssey* mention Dionysus, the god who was the source of viticulture and wine. Among the marvelous scenes fashioned by Hephaistos on the "Shield of Achilles" is the following: "Therein he set also a vineyard heavily laden with clusters, a vineyard fair and wrought of gold; black were the grapes, and the vines were set up throughout on silver poles" (*Il.* 18.561–563).

After twenty years away from home, Odysseus returns to Ithaca in disguise and seeks out his father, Laertes. In a poignant scene, he finds the former king working as a gardener in the vineyard:

> Odysseus drew near to the fruitful vineyard to make his test. Now he did not find Dolius as he went down into the great orchard, nor any of his slaves or of his sons, but as it chanced they had gone to gather stones for the vineyard wall. . . . But he found his father alone in the well-ordered vineyard, digging about a plant. (*Od.* 24.220–226)

Hesiod's *Works and Days* records the daily tasks involved in cultivating vines for wine production (*Op.* 609–617). Silver coins depicting grapes or vines from Mende, Naxos, Thebes, Corcyca, Chios, and Thasos (among others) indicate the vitality of Greek wine production and trade.

With the emergence of the polis, or city-state, vine cultivation was expanded to ensure that the inhabitants were fed. The use of slaves was fundamental to the success of vineyards in Greek society (Unwin, 96). While the full extent of viticulture in Greece is unknown, by the eighth century BC it was practiced throughout the ancient Greek mainland, and it spread further with the establishment of colonies around the Mediterranean. It was through the Greek colony of Massalia (Marseille) on the Mediterranean coast that viticulture was introduced into France.

Vine cultivation produced wine both for trade and for local consumption. Wine was widely used in Greek culture, particularly in drinking parties (*symposia*), banquets for men that featured various entertainments, such as performances from flute-girls and dancing. It was also central to the Dionysiac cultic rituals that were an important part of Greek culture (Unwin, 131).

Rome

Viticulture spread from Greece to Italy first in the south, which became known as *Oenotria*, "the land of wine." Wine became an essential part of Roman agriculture and the Roman economy (Pliny, *Nat.* 14.87). The beverage was consumed widely by the Roman populace, especially as part of the worship of Bacchus, the god of wine. The festivals of Vinalia Priora and Vinalia Rustica celebrated viticultural activity in the spring and summer, respectively. Roman landowners considered vineyards to be more profitable ventures than the cultivation of grain (Columella, *Rust.* 3.3.2–10), so much so that eventually viticulture had to be curbed, and more attention given to the production of grain, because of food shortages (Suet., *Dom.* 7.2; 14.2).

A number of sources have survived that provide insights into Roman viticultural processes and techniques. Cato's *De agricultura* (4, 11, 17, 33, 40, 41, 47, 49) and Varro's *De re rustica* (8, 26, 40), both from the second century BC, give practical advice on establishing and maintaining a vineyard. Columella, in his first-century AD work *De re Rustica* (3–5, 12), provides detailed descriptions of viticultural processes, such as the need for the vine cultivator to control the luxuriant growth of the grapes in order to achieve the ideal number for each plant (*Rust.* 3.3.2) and the correct way to prune the vine after it has blossomed (*Rust.* 4.9, 23).

Pliny the Elder (*Nat.* 14, 17) discusses not only grape cultivation but also the quality of wines produced in various regions. He provides at least five methods for training vines: allowing them to trail on the ground, using a small bush, using regular stakes, using stakes with single crossbars, and using trellises with rectangular frames. Roman sources also provide information on various press installations, including the screw press, that were used for extracting the grape juice so that it could be made into wine (*Nat.* 14.10.77).

E. THE JEWISH WORLD

Viticulture was important for Jewish communities, as wine was an important part of celebrations and festivals. A vine or bunches of grapes were symbolically displayed on Maccabean coins and as decorations on lamps, lintels, and places of burial. Wine motifs are found on coins of Herod Archelaus, who reigned from 4 BC–AD 6, as well as on lamps and ossuaries of Greco-Roman period (Goodenough, V.99–111). Large storage facilities were used to store wine at the Jewish fortress of Masada.

In Ecclesiasticus (Ben Sira), wisdom is likened to a vine who invites people to eat her fruit and drink her wine (24:17–21). In *4 Ezra*, Israel is called the "one vine" special to God (5:23). Philo explains that Noah's planting of a vineyard was a sign of security, as wine was a "superfluous pleasure," not a critical resource only God can provide (*QG* 2.67). The Qumran community referred to itself as a well-watered, eternal "plantation" (1QH^a XIV, 15).

Josephus notes that golden vines with grape clusters decorated the most sacred part of the temple in Jerusalem (*J.W.* 5.210). A golden vine stood over the entrance of the sanctuary in Herod's temple. According to Josephus, this vine, from which hung clusters of grapes, was "a marvel of size and artistry to all who saw with what costliness of material it had been constructed" (*Ant.* 15.395). Because the vine was so heavy, on one occasion three hundred priests were appointed in order to clear the vine of its golden leaves, berries, and clusters that worshippers had brought to be hung there (*m. Mid.* 3:8).

The Mishnah stipulates that wine used for the temple should come from grapes grown on a vine trailing on the ground (*m. Menaḥ.* 8:6). Rabbinic guidelines about the settlement of grievances indicate the value of vineyards as personal property (*b. B. Qam.* 7a).

Blameless individuals were compared to grape clusters (*m. Soṭah* 9:9; *y. Soṭah* 9:10), and marrying one's daughter to a learned man was compared to grafting one grapevine upon another (*b. Pesaḥ.* 49a–b).

F. THE CHRISTIAN WORLD

Viticulture was a source for a number of Christian symbols, in part because Jesus had described himself as the "true vine" and his followers as the branches growing from this vine (John 15).

The author of *2 Clement* writes that the church, like a vine that must have sour grapes before sweeter ones take their place, must endure hardships before experiencing better times (11.3). A vineyard is featured in a parable in the *Shepherd of Hermas* in which a master entrusts a servant to care for his property and makes him co-heir with his son (*Herm. Simil.* 5.2.2–3). This same work describes God's people as vines in a healthy vineyard from which the weeds are removed (*Herm. Simil.* 5.2.5; 10.26.3–4).

The cultivation of grapes continued during the Byzantine period, as wine played a critical role in the Christian ritual of the Eucharist. The wine trade continued to flourish in the eastern empire. Monasteries became repositories of viticultural knowledge inherited from the classical world. The number and variety of winepresses were extensive and diverse in the Byzantine era, especially in Palestine, where viticulture thrived (Frankel, 84). A massive press has been discovered at Akhziv, along with many other presses found throughout the Negev region (Leibner, 288).

The symbolism of the vine can be found in Byzantine art and architecture. In the eastern province, at al-Mukhayyat in Jordan, images depicting grapes being harvested, transported, and crushed by an apparent screw press adorned the Church of Sts. Lot and Procopius. The Temple of Clitumnus in Umbria in Italy depicts the Christian cross entwined with bunches of grapes, and the fourth-century Church of Santa Costanza in Rome is decorated with mosaic images of viticultural production, including grape clusters being cut with small knives to be loaded onto ox carts for the treading mill (Unwin, 142).

BIBLIOGRAPHY: P. Albenda, "Grapevines in Ashurbanipal's Garden," *BASOR* 215 (1974), 5–17; P. Bienkowski and A. Millard, "Wine," *DANE* 319; O. Borowski, *Agriculture in Iron Age Israel* (1987); B. Brier and H. Hobbs, *Daily Life of the Ancient Egyptians* (1999); J. P. Brown, "The Mediterranean Vocabulary of the Vine," *VT* 19 (1969), 146–70; M. W. Chavalas ed., *The Ancient Near East: Historical Sources in Translation* (2006); J. Daniélou, *Primitive Christian Symbols*, trans. D. Attwater (1961); G. Edelstein and S. Gibson, "Ancient Jerusalem's Rural Food Basket: The 'New' Archaeology Looks for an Urban Center's Agricultural Base," *BAR* 8.4 (1982), 46–54; A. Erman, *Life in Ancient Egypt* (repr. of 1921 edition, 1971); R. Frankel, *Wine and Oil Production in Antiquity in Israel and Other Mediterranean Countries* (1999); E. R. Goodenough, *Jewish Symbols in the Greco-Roman Period*

V–VI: Fish, Bread, and Wine (1956); A. Goor, "The History of the Grape-Vine in the Holy Land," *Economic Botany* 20 (1966), 46–64; E. Hyams, *Dionysus: A Social History of the Wine Vine* (1965); E. Isaac, *Geography of Domestication* (1970); W. F. Jashemski, "The Discovery of a Large Vineyard at Pompeii: University of Maryland Excavations, 1970," *AJA* 77 (1973), 27–41; W. F. Jashemski, "A Vineyard at Pompeii: Part I: Discovery," *Archaeology* 25 (1972), 48–56; W. F. Jashemski, "A Vineyard at Pompeii: Part II: The Vineyard Complex," *Arch* 25 (1972), 132–39; H. Johnson, *Vintage: The Story of Wine* (1989); U. Leibner, "Arts and Crafts, Manufacture and Production," *OHJDL*, 264–96; L. H. Lesko, *King Tut's Wine Cellar* (1977); H. F. Lutz, *Viticulture and Brewing in the Ancient Orient* (1922); V. Matthews, "Treading the Winepress: Actual and Metaphorical Viticulture in the Ancient Near East," in *Semeia* 86 (1999), 19–32; P. E. McGovern, *Ancient Wine* (2003); B. Mertz, *Red Land, Black Land: Daily Life in Ancient Egypt* (1978); H. N. Moldenke and A. L. Moldenke, *Plants of the Bible* (1952); N. Purcell, "Wine and Wealth in Ancient Italy," *JRS* 75 (1985), 1–19; J. Robinson, *Vines, Grapes, and Wines* (1986); J. M. Sasson, trans. and ed., *From the Mari Archives: An Anthology of Old Babylonian Letters* (2015); J. Scarborough, *Facets of Hellenic Life* (1976); W. Schottroff, "Das Weinberglied Jesajas (Jes 5 1–7): Ein Beitrag zur Geschichte der Parabel," *ZAW* 82 (1970), 68–91; J. A. H. Seely, "The Fruit of the Vine: Wine at Masada and in the New Testament," in *Masada and the World of the New Testament*, ed. J. F. Hall and J. W. Welch (1997), 207–27; T. Unwin, *Wine and the Vine* (1991); M. Ventris and J. Chadwick, *Documents in Mycenaean Greek* (2nd ed., 1973); F. H. Wight, *Manners and Customs of Bible Lands* (1953), 187–95; J. T. Willis, "The Genre of Isaiah 5:1–7," *JBL* 96 (1977) 337–62.

ACC

See also AGRICULTURE, ALCOHOLIC BEVERAGES, BANQUETS, FOOD CONSUMPTION, PLANTS & FLOWERS, and TRADE.

WEALTH & POVERTY

Wealth and poverty are multifaceted and entwined concepts involving social status, power, and security in terms of goods, food sources, and shelter. In the ancient world wealth typically included land, servants and slaves, cattle and livestock, and an assured supply of material goods. The wealthy were generally powerful, while poverty meant a lack of material goods, power, and security. The poor were marginalized, lacked influence, and were often the objects of shame. The rich enjoyed influence, received honor, and actively engaged in the society in which they lived.

Ancient societies generally provided some amount of aid to the poor, but the amount and the reasons for doing so varied greatly depending on the society's religious and ethical values. These societies also held differing opinions on the accumulation of wealth—specifically with regard to the manner in which it was accumulated and the amount that any one person should amass.

A. THE OLD TESTAMENT

The biblical model for handling wealth and dealing with the poor differed from that of other cultures in the ancient world. The biblical worldview is that God, as creator, is the true owner of all and gives liberally (Deut 8:18; Pss 24:1; 50:10; 145:9, 15–17; Hag 2:8). The eighth commandment forbids stealing, and the tenth commandment forbids coveting anything that belongs to one's neighbor (Exod 20:15, 17). Wealth and riches acquired by greed, trickery, and deceit are not considered blessings but will bring on God's wrath.

In the biblical tradition, spiritual wealth and poverty are sometimes contrasted with material wealth and poverty, and the true value of material wealth may be different from its apparent value. A person can lack the material trappings of wealth and yet be rich in terms of spiritual matters. For example, in Gen 37:12–36, Joseph, the favorite son of Jacob, is sold to

Midianite merchants by his jealous brothers. He becomes a slave in Poti-phar's household, is soon thereafter falsely accused of accosting Potiphar's wife, and is then jailed. Yet, the story contains this observation: "The LORD was with Joseph so that he prospered" (Gen 39:2, 23). This bracketing state-ment, which is repeated twice in Gen 39, shows that although Joseph's cir-cumstances changed, the Lord's favor on his life did not. The Lord made him successful, even prosperous, in difficult and impoverished circumstances.

Two broad ideas form the biblical idea of wealth and poverty in the OT. In some passages wealth is seen as a sign of God's blessing and poverty is seen as a sign of God's curse or as the result of a pattern of unwise behavior (see Deut 28 and the book of Proverbs, e.g., 10:4, 22). But in other passages it is understood that wealth is achieved at the expense of the poor, since wealth is finite and goods are limited. To counteract this, measures ensuring social justice had to be in place for the poor. In addition, while it seems that abundance and wealth are considered good gifts from the Lord throughout the Bible, the dangerous effects of wealth are also a common motif. After they have been given wealth, some recipients trust in their fortunes or in themselves and not in the Lord. This attitude brings on his judgment.

Wealth

The first reference to wealth in the OT describes God's blessings upon Abraham: "Abram had become very wealthy in livestock and in silver and gold" (Gen 13:2; cf. 24:35). Isaac was similarly blessed by God and became wealthy (Gen 26:12–13). The references to "wealth" in Gen 31:1, 16 are to the livestock of his father-in-law Laban, which Jacob took with him when he fled with Rachel and Leah to his father, Isaac.

Moses warns the Israelites against claiming that they have produced their wealth by their own hand (Deut 8:10–17). They are to "remember the LORD your God, for it is he who gives you the ability to produce wealth" (Deut 8:18a). Moses then immediately links wealth with a confirmation of the covenant (8:18b).

Boaz, who was a relative of Naomi and was therefore eligible to be a kinsman-redeemer for her widowed daughter-in-law Ruth, is described in Ruth 2:1 as "a prominent rich man" (NRSV) or "a man of standing" (NIV). Both translations reflect nuances of the noun *ḥayil*, which can be trans-lated "wealth."

God answers Solomon's prayer for wisdom by also giving him wealth, riches, and honor (2 Chr 1:11–12). The way in which God's answer is ex-pressed indicates the value of wisdom over all else.

At a time of great prosperity in the northern kingdom, Pul (Tiglath-pileser III), king of Assyria, invaded Israel (ca. 740 BC). In order to make him withdraw, King Menahem of Israel decreed that "every wealthy person had to contribute fifty shekels of silver to be given to the king of Assyria" (2 Kgs 15:20; cf. *ANET*, 283).

In commands against intermarriage with neighboring peoples who worshipped other gods, Ezra warns the Jews not to give their daughters to the sons of their neighbors, nor to take the daughters of these neighbors for their sons. Joined with this command is the admonition not to take their neighbors' wealth (Ezra 9:12).

The OT often presents wealth neutrally, as a gift from the Lord that can be used for good or ill and that can be taken away and restored again by the Lord. The book of Job begins with an assessment of Job's character (he was blameless and upright) and an itemization of his wealth (Job 1:1–3). Job owns sheep, camels, oxen, servants, and slaves. In one day, he loses his wealth and his ten sons and daughters. Job suffers greatly over a long period of time. However, God restores his wealth by doubling it and by providing Job with ten more children (Job 42:12–13).

Psalm 49 discusses the concepts of wealth and false trust. The wicked not only trust in their wealth but also boast of their great riches (vs. 6). The psalm also examines another principle found in wisdom literature, namely, that the wise, foolish, and senseless all die and leave their wealth to others (vss. 10, 17–19). The psalm advises against being overawed by or envying a man who grows rich during his lifetime and flaunts his wealth with trappings, like a splendid house, for riches by themselves do not indicate understanding (vss. 16, 20).

Proverbs details the many consequences of adultery, one being the loss of wealth (5:10). It contrasts wealth and poverty by saying that the "wealth of the rich is their fortified city, but poverty is the ruin of the poor" (Prov 10:15). In other words, while wealth protects the rich, the poor have no such protection. In Proverbs, Lady Wisdom gives riches and honor, and the blessing of the Lord brings wealth (Prov 8:18; 10:22). A good man leaves his inheritance to multiple generations, but the wealth of a sinner "is stored up for the righteous" (Prov 13:22). Moreover, wealth brings friendship (Prov 19:4).

The book of Ecclesiastes examines the paradoxes of the lives of wealthy individuals. For one man, wealth, which is a gift from God, comes with a sense of enjoyment, an acceptance of his lot in life, and happiness in his work (Eccl 5:19). God gives other persons wealth, possessions, and honor in such measure that they lack nothing, but "God does not grant them the ability to enjoy them, and strangers enjoy them instead." The writer of Ecclesiastes concludes that this paradox is both "meaningless" and "a grievous evil" (Eccl 6:2).

The prophets decry both economic disparity between the wealthy and the poor and the tendency of the wealthy to oppress the poor. Amos 4:1–3 delivers a strong reprimand to Israel's wealthy women who, according to the prophet, oppress the poor, crush the needy, and order their husbands around. Amos warns that they will be led away with hooks and fishhooks. According to Amos, the people of Israel condemned here had grown to view amassing wealth at the expense of others as their right—greed had become normal. They had forgotten that wealth comes from the Lord and that he commands Israel to act like him in all areas of life (Lev 19:2).

Prophetic literature speaks of a coming time when wealth will be redistributed. In an apocalyptic prophecy, Zechariah speaks of a great battle at Jerusalem that will end with "the wealth of all the surrounding nations" being collected (Zech 14:14).

Poverty

The first reference to poverty in the OT is in the context of Joseph's promise to take care of his brothers and their families because he knows that there are five years of famine coming and he does not want them to "become destitute" (Gen 45:11).

Yahweh is seen as one who defends poor individuals, such as widows and orphans, and he commands Israel to do the same (e.g., Lev 25:35–55; Deut 14:29; 15:11, 14; Ps 68:5; Isa 1:17). Furthermore, Yahweh contends with those who oppress and mock the poor; he is personally affronted by these actions as if they were done contemptuously to him (Prov 14:31; 17:5).

Proverbs advocates taking a middle way through life, one that avoids the extremes of poverty and riches (Prov 30:8–9). This advice is typical of biblical wisdom literature. According to Proverbs, poverty is a condition to avoid primarily because "poverty is the ruin of the poor" (Prov 10:15). One paradox noted by Proverbs is that the person who "gives freely ... gains even more," but the one who withholds without reason "comes to poverty" (Prov 11:24). The person who refuses to accept instruction "comes to poverty and shame," but the one who accepts correction comes to honor (Prov 13:18). Strong drink should be given to one who is ready to perish because it will help him forget his misery and poverty (Prov 31:6–7).

In the Psalms, those who were poor represented the Lord's faithful and humble people, the ones who could anticipate his vindication concerning the injustices they experienced (see Pss 86:1–4; 147:6; 149:4). God defends the poor and saves "the poor from those too strong for them, the poor and needy from those who rob them" (Ps 35:10).

The legal, prophetic, wisdom, and liturgical traditions of the OT "all see poverty as a matter of grave significance to the community" (Pleins, 413). Throughout the OT, Israel is commanded not to "oppress the widow or the fatherless, the foreigner or the poor" (Zech 7:10; cf. Job 31:16–23).

In wisdom literature, the concept emerged that a poor person's cause was championed by the Lord himself. It is in this context that Proverbs asserts that the person who is kind lends to the Lord and that the Lord will reward the person for what he has done (Prov 19:17).

B. THE NEW TESTAMENT

Wealth

The NT describes wealth and poverty in metaphorical and practical terms. For example, Paul, James, and John refer to those who are "rich in faith" (Jas 2:5; see also 1 Cor 4:8; 2 Cor 6:10; 8:9).

The NT also continues the OT's warnings against being controlled by wealth. In the Sermon on the Mount, Jesus warns against storing up treasures on earth, which are prone to damage and loss from moths, rust, and thieves. Instead, he encourages his audience to store up treasures in heaven and have a heart that seeks heavenly treasures (Matt 6:19–21). He also warned: "No man can serve two masters: for either he will hate the one, and love the other; or else he will hold to the one, and despise the other. Ye cannot serve God and mammon [Gk. *mamōnas*]" (Matt 6:24, KJV). The Aramaic word *māmôn* meant "wealth, possessions, money." The NIV renders it in this verse as "money."

Jesus challenges the rich young ruler to sell what he possesses and to give the proceeds to the poor—actions that would put his treasure firmly in heaven and make him a follower of Jesus (Mark 10:21). But the price was too steep for the young man. He could not do it "because he had great wealth," and he turned away from Jesus sad and crestfallen (Mark 10:22). Jesus comments that it is very hard for the rich to enter the kingdom of God (Mark 10:23), but encourages his audience that "all things are possible with God" (Mark 10:27).

Writing to Timothy, Paul does not condemn money itself, but advises that "the love of money is a root of all kinds of evil" (1 Tim 6:10; cf. Eccl 5:10). He cautions Timothy that people "who want to get rich fall into temptation and a trap and into many foolish and harmful desires that plunge them into ruin and destruction" (1 Tim 6:9). While Paul acknowledges the pitfalls of wealth (attitudes of arrogance and a trust in riches), he also asserts that wealth, when used properly, can be a way that God provides for our enjoyment (1 Tim 6:17–19; cf. Eccl 5:19).

According to Revelation, the church at Laodicea was so wealthy that it thought it needed nothing. The book's warning to the Laodicean church was that its real condition was "wretched, pitiful, poor, blind, and naked"

(Rev 3:17). In Revelation, Jesus counsels the church there to buy "gold re-
fined in the fire" from him so that it can indeed become rich (Rev 3:18).

Poverty

In Matt 5:3, Jesus praises those who are "poor in spirit, for theirs is the
kingdom of heaven," while the parallel passage in Luke mentions only "you
who are poor" (Luke 6:20). Jesus (Luke 9:58), the disciples (Matt 19:27;
Mark 2:23), and John the Baptist (Mark 1:6) all embraced lives of poverty.

In the ancient Mediterranean world, with its multiple religions, what
might now be considered humanitarian benefits were not generally bestowed for selfless motives, but instead were given to increase a benefactor's
honor and standing. A benefactor entered the relationship for long-term
benefits for himself, and the beneficiary was expected to show an appropriate gratitude in reciprocation.

The teachings of Jesus stand in marked contrast to this "reciprocity" or
quid pro quo mentality. Indeed, those who had nothing to give in return
were seen as worthy to receive gifts and services. Furthermore, the recipients were under no moral obligation to return the services or try to balance
gifts in terms of reciprocity. Christians were taught to give without expecting anything in return and to give to others as if giving to Christ himself (cf.
Matt 25:40). They were taught that Christ eventually would reward them
for the gifts they gave to others.

Jesus did not show favoritism to either the rich or the poor when approached for healing. On the one hand, he raised the daughter of a wealthy
synagogue ruler, Jairus, from the dead. On the other hand, he healed a
woman who had spent all of her wealth on doctors in a vain attempt to
stop a flow of blood (Mark 5:21–43). On other occasions, Jesus healed the
blind beggar Bartimaeus (Mark 10:46–52) and a man born blind who was
known as a beggar (John 9:1–12).

Writing to the Corinthians, Paul stresses the need to make all members
of a diverse congregation, and not just the rich, feel welcome (1 Cor 12:12–
26). Using the parts of a body as an allegory, he writes that those parts
that are unpresentable—perhaps meaning the poor—are to be treated with
special honor. Those parts that are prominent, like the head and the eye—
perhaps meaning the rich—should not disdain the other parts by saying "I
don't need you!" (1 Cor 12:21).

Paul notes the example of the overflowing joy of the Macedonian believers, who sent him a liberal financial gift in spite of their deep poverty. He
sees evidence of the grace of God in their lives (2 Cor 8:1–2). Paul reminds
the Corinthian believers that Jesus "became poor, so that you through his
poverty might become rich" (2 Cor 8:9).

The Epistle to the Hebrews concludes its "Heroes of the Faith" chapter with a description of righteous believers who endured stoning, destitution, persecution, and homelessness, and who wore shabby clothing like sheepskins and goatskins (Heb 11:37–38). Some of the new converts addressed in the letter to the Hebrews may have faced impoverishment, as they may have been threatened with the confiscation of their property (Heb 10:34).

The Epistle of James, like the writings of the OT prophets, warns against the rich who are godless and greedy. James considers earthly riches to be as ephemeral as wildflowers (Jas 1:10). James rebukes Christians who would show favoritism in seating a well-dressed visitor with a gold ring, and in dismissing a shabbily dressed visitor to a lesser place (Jas 2:1–5). James also reminds them not to show favoritism to the rich, since God has chosen the poor who are rich in faith. Favoritism toward the rich is against the "royal law" of love that Jesus advocated (Jas 2:8–9). In a diatribe against the rich, James writes that they should be weeping and wailing because of their coming misery. Their clothes will become motheaten, and even their gold and silver will be corroded. The wages they fail to pay their workmen cry out against them. As their wealth earned them power, they condemned and murdered innocent men who did not oppose them (Jas 5:1–6).

The Epistle of First Peter is written to the scattered and strangers of the diaspora who nonetheless are God's elect (1 Pet 1:1). Although this description probably implies poverty, Peter encouragingly calls them a chosen people, a royal priesthood, a holy nation, a people who belong to God and who are called to declare his praises (1 Pet 2:9).

In the book of Revelation, John is instructed to write to the church at Smyrna that the risen Lord Jesus knows the church's affliction and poverty, and he encourages the church not to be afraid for what it is about to suffer (Rev 2:9–10).

C. THE NEAR EASTERN WORLD

Mesopotamia

Our knowledge about the lives of both the rich and the poor in ancient Sumer is based on archaeological evidence as well as literary texts from the period. Archaeological evidence from Kish, Lagash, Ur, and Nippur suggests that the cities were similar. The structures were made of mud-brick. The major streets, which were straight and wide, led to the center of the town, which contained public buildings, temples, and the homes of the elite. The homes of the wealthy were built on the main streets and around courts. The shops and dwellings of craftsmen, like jewelry-makers, potters, and carpenters, were in other areas of the city. The poorer inhabitants lived in areas with narrow alleys.

The primary clues revealing aspects of Sumerian life come from tombs because they preserved the objects that were buried with the dead for use in the afterlife. Tombs from the fourth and third millennia BC indicate that people were buried with goods that were intended to make life better for them in the afterlife. Tombs contained clothes, food, ornaments, tools, weapons, musical instruments, and games.

A Sumerian poem entitled "The Death of Ur-Nammu and His Descent into the Netherworld" describes the elaborate funeral of Ur-Nammu, one of the great kings of Sumer, who was beloved for his military leadership and his temple-building projects. It is possible that the expensive presents described in the poem were intended for the lords of the underworld. A number of tombs at Tepe Gawra contained prestige goods like lapis lazuli, gold, and carnelian, indicating that the ruling elite possessed a considerable degree of wealth.

The amassing of wealth by the king and his courtiers by taxing the poor for military and palatial expenses is illustrated by the dire situation found in the city-state of Lagash when the world's "first reformer," Uruinimgina (formerly spelled Urukagina), came to the throne ca. 2350 BC. Not only had previous kings of his dynasty acquired temple properties, they also had seized the property of citizens and imposed innumerable taxes. Those who were unable to pay were thrown into prison. "If sheep were brought, the (influential) man used to carry off the best of these sheep for himself. . . . If the son of a poor man laid out a fish pond, the (influential) man would take away its fish, (and) that man went unpunished" (Kramer 1963, 321). The reforms of the king, which are preserved in six inscriptions, declared: "A citizen of Lagash living in debt, (or) who had been condemned to its prison for impost, hunger, robbery, (or) murder—their freedom he established. Uru-inimgina made a compact with the divine Nin-Girsu that the powerful man would not oppress the orphan (or) widow" (*COS* 2.152:408).

One of the intentions of the Code of Hammurabi (r. 1792–1750 BC) was to bring about justice in the land so "that the strong might not oppress the weak" (prologue, line 36; *ANET*, 164; see also the epilogue, lines 58–60; *ANET*, 178). Such protection of the less fortunate was viewed as a virtue of both gods and kings in Mesopotamia.

A humorous tale of a poor man's revenge upon a powerful figure is "The Tale of the Poor Man of Nippur," which was preserved in Akkadian in tablets found at Sultantepe in southeastern Turkey. The story begins:

> There was a man of Nippur, poor and humble, Gimil-Ninurta was his name, a
> miserable man. In his city Nippur wearily he sat. He had no silver, the pride of

his people, he possessed no gold, the pride of mankind. His store-room thirsts for the pure grain. With craving for bread his liver was *oppressed*, with craving for meat and beer his face was disfigured. Daily for lack of food he used to lie hungry. He was clad in garments for which he had no change.
   (Gurney 1956, 151)

He then buys a goat and brings it to the mayor as a gift, but this is misinterpreted as a bribe. The mayor declares, "Give him, the citizen of Nippur, a bone and a sinew, give him a drink of 'one-third' [beer] from what you can, send him away and show him out of the gate!" (Gurney 1956, 153). As Gimil-Ninurta exits, he vows to the gate-keeper that he will wreak a threefold vengeance for this insulting treatment. When the mayor hears this, he laughs.

Gimil-Ninurta somehow manages to borrow a chariot from the king on the promise of a mina (pound) of red gold. Dressed in finery, he is mistaken by the mayor for a wealthy official who has brought a box of gold. After lulling the mayor to sleep, Gimil-Ninurta displays an empty box, accuses the mayor of theft, and beats him. He receives two minas of red gold from the mayor.

He then returns in the guise of a physician to heal the mayor's wounds, and lures him into a dark room and beats him again. He finally hires a man to claim that he was the one who beat the mayor. While all pursue this imposter, Gimil-Ninurta, who waits under a bridge, assaults the mayor a third time. He then flees the country, while the mayor returns to the city more dead than alive.

This remarkable tale, written on tablets dated to 701 BC, was repeated over the centuries in various versions, including as a story in the Arabian Nights (Gurney 1972).

Egypt

Ancient Egyptian culture centered on the dead and the needs of the gods. Egypt's economy was closely tied to all aspects of religion. The country produced food for the gods as offerings placed in temples and for the wealthy dead as they began their journey in the afterlife. Egyptian traders went to Punt for incense and Byblos for timber for coffins.

The economic structure of Egypt concentrated on building religious monuments, temples, and tombs. Quarrying, stoneworking, mining, metalworking, and carpentry skills thrived. The temples became industrial monopolies, for they owned both the mines and the metalworking industries. In this, Egypt differed from other Mediterranean countries, for its emphasis was on the gods and the royal and wealthy dead even more than on the living.

The wealth of the Egyptian pharaohs may best be seen in the unlooted tomb of Tutankhamun, with its wealth of gold objects, including his dazzling gold funeral mask. (See Desroches-Noblecourt.) By its conquest of Kush (Sudan), Egypt acquired the gold mines that made it the richest nation in antiquity. This gold was mined by slaves and prisoners, many of whom paid with their lives in the harsh desert conditions. (See Yamauchi 2004, 51–53.)

We also have some evidence about the lives of the poor in ancient Egypt. One story from ancient Egypt lauds an unexpected person, a common man, and makes him a hero. *The Protests of the Eloquent Peasant* details the adventures of Khun-anup. Khun-anup and his donkey come to the lands of Rensi, a nobleman and son of Meru. A wicked overseer tricks Khun-anup to cross the lands in such a way that his donkey eats Rensi's crops. The overseer then confiscates the donkey. Khun-anup searches for Rensi and delivers an eloquent speech protesting his innocence. Impressed, Rensi considers the peasant's words, but delays in delivering justice. Khun-anup insults Rensi and earns a beating for this, but ultimately receives the overseer's property and job. No doubt the story was popular with Egypt's poor, for the overseer ends up as poor as Khun-anup had been at the story's beginning. (See *ANET*, 407–10.)

Egyptian wisdom texts contain numerous statements on wealth and poverty that are similar to the biblical proverbs. *The Instruction of Ani* advises: "Thou shouldst not eat bread when another is waiting and thou dost not stretch forth thy hand to the food *for him. It is here* forever. A man is nothing. The one is rich; another is poor, while bread continues—*can he pass it by?*" (*ANET*, 421).

The *Instruction of Amen-em-Opet*, which has been compared with Prov 22–24, contains these sayings: "Better is poverty in the hand of the god than riches in a storehouse; better is bread, when the heart is happy, than riches with sorrow" (*ANET*, 422). "If thou findest a large debt against a poor man, make it into three parts, forgive two, and let one stand" (*ANET*, 423). "God desires respect for the poor more than the honoring of the exalted" (*ANET*, 424).

D. THE GRECO-ROMAN WORLD

Greece

The poets, playwrights, and philosophers of ancient Greece wrote eloquently about the condition of the masses. Greek attitudes about wealth varied with the times. The Greeks saw the rich as potentially hubristic, extravagant, profiteering, and soft.

The vast majority of the population in ancient Greece was poor. The poet Hesiod expresses a sentiment prevalent in the ancient world: "Give to him who gives and do not give to him who does not give" (*Op.* 354). Overall, the poor received little sympathy and garnered no pity throughout the Greco-Roman world.

Coinage, which was invented by the Lydian king Gyges (7th c. BC), was adopted by the Athenians, who had rich silver mines at Laurion. Money in the form of portable coins made extreme wealth possible for some. The Greek lyric poets of the sixth century BC wrote frequently about the new infatuation with money. Theognis of Megara wrote: "For the multitude of mankind there is only one virtue: Money" (Lattimore, 30). Alcaeus of Mytilene commented, "'Money's the man.' It's true. There's no poor man who's known as good or valued much" (Lattimore, 44).

Solon of Athens declared:

> But money, there is no end of its making in human endeavor. Those among us who have already the biggest estates try to get twice as much as they have. Who can satisfy all of them? Money, when a man makes it, is the gift of the gods, but disaster can grow out of money, and when retribution comes at the sending of Zeus, none can tell where it will light. (Lattimore, 20)

Solon was not only a poet but also a political reformer. He was elected archon at Athens in 594 BC, when the city faced a grave economic and social crisis. Many tenant farmers, who had to pay one-sixth of their produce to landowners, were in arrears, and some were sold into debt slavery. Solon's *seisachtheia* (lit., "shaking off of burdens") abolished the use of one's person as security and canceled all debts. Solon also tried to buy back Athenians who had been sold abroad as debt slaves. (See Yamauchi 1980.)

The alliance of the Athenians and the Spartans defeated the Persian invasion of Greece under Xerxes in 480 BC. After the final battle of Plataea in 479 BC, Pausanias, the leader of the Spartans, proclaimed that no one should touch the Persian spoil, which consisted of many gold and silver objects. He remarked, "Men of Hellas, I have brought you hither because I desired to show you the foolishness of the leader of the Medes, who, with such provision for life as you see, came hither to take away from us ours, that is so pitiful" (Her. *Hist.* 9.82). The sight of such wealth, however, eventually corrupted the Spartan leader, who entered into treasonable negotiations with the Persian king.

In 388 BC Aristophanes produced his play *Wealth* (Gk. *Ploutos*; Lat. *Plutus*). At the beginning of the play, a character named Blepsidemus states the problem: "There's nothing sound or honest in the world, the love of money overcomes us all" (*Plut.* 362–363).

In *Wealth*, Chremylos, a poor elderly Athenian, has been advised by the Delphic Oracle to follow the first man he meets and to invite him home. This person turns out to be the god Wealth, who is personified as a blind beggar. Chremylos believes that if only his guest's sight can be restored at the shrine of Asclepius, Wealth will share his gifts not randomly but by bestowing them upon the just. Chremylos states: "For if Wealth should attain to his eyesight again, nor amongst us so aimlessly roam, to the dwellings I know of the good he would go, nor ever depart from their home" (*Plut.* 494–95). But when Wealth receives his sight, everyone attends to him and neglects the gods, incurring their anger.

In the play, a character named Penia, who personifies poverty, argues that poverty is necessary. She comments,

> Tis a beggar [*ptōchos*] alone who has nought of his own, nor even an obol possesses. My poor [*penētos*] man, 'tis true, has to scrape and to screw and his work he must never be slack in; there'll be no superfluity found in his cot; but then there will nothing be lacking. (*Plut.* 552–554)

Certain Greek philosophers also criticized the pursuit of wealth. The Epicureans, who followed the teachings of the Greek philosopher Epicurus (ca. 300 BC), took a moderate approach to life. Epicurus thought that to live rationally was to live naturally, and he lived primarily on bread and water. He believed that anyone who wants to live a free life cannot acquire many possessions (*Vatican Sayings* 67; Malherbe 2010, 396). An ideal Epicurean shuns selfishness and shares with others. Epicurus associated sharing with wisdom, for when it becomes necessary to share, the wise person already has established a pattern of self-sufficiency (*Vatican Sayings* 44; Malherbe 2010, 396). Thus, he further advised that if many possessions, a sign of wealth, come to a person, then that person, because he has learned to treasure self-sufficiency, "would easily distribute them so as to obtain the good will of neighbors" (*Vatican Sayings* 67; Malherbe 2010, 396).

Another Greek school of thought that criticized wealth was Cynicism. The name "Cynic" comes from the Greek word for "dog," *kyōn*. Diogenes Laertius wrote that Cynics advocated living simply, eating only as much food as one needs, and wearing one single garment. They despised wealth, noble birth, and fame. The most well-known Cynic of all was Diogenes of Sinope (404–323 BC), who lived in a tub (*pithos*). He possessed only a cloak, a wallet, and a cup. When he saw a child cupping his hands to drink water, he threw away his cup. Diogenes defied all the conventions of his day, copulating and defecating in public. But Diogenes had a ready wit, and was popular with some. When Plato defined man as a bipedal and featherless animal, Diogenes plucked a fowl and brought it into the lecture room with the words, "Here is Plato's man" (Diogenes Laertius, *Lives of Eminent*

Philosophers, 6.40). When Alexander the Great encountered Diogenes at Corinth, the Cynic was not awed by his famous visitor. Later Alexander, impressed by Diogenes's fierce independence, was reported to have said: "Had I not been Alexander, I should have liked to be Diogenes" (Diogenes Laertius, *Lives of Eminent Philosophers*, 6.32).

Rome

In the early history of the Roman Republic (509–133 BC), there was a long struggle between the Orders, or classes, as plebeians sought more and more rights from the dominant Patricians. After the unification of Italy, Roman armies conquered lands to the east and the west. While generals and soldiers profited from wars against Macedonia, bringing home numerous captives and objects, Rome's war against Numantia in Spain created a social and economic crisis. The long deployment of the army drove many plebeian farms into bankruptcy, after which they were bought up by the wealthy owners of *latifundia*, large estates that were farmed by slaves. The dispossessed veterans became a landless proletariat that flocked to Rome. Moved by their plight, the Gracchi brothers, Tiberius (tribune in 133 BC) and Gaius (tribune in 123 BC), proposed measures such as allowing the veterans a grant of land from the *ager publicus*, which the wealthy had been using for pasturing their flocks. The reaction of the optimates (members of the aristocratic class) led to the assassination of both brothers.

The establishment by Gaius Gracchus of the *annona* (the dole), which provided grain at subsidized prices, proved to be a long-lasting reform; at its height, the dole had three hundred thousand citizens on its rolls. As there was no maximum wealth limit, all citizens were eligible. This subsidy did not help those who were very poor, as the recipients of grain still needed to pay to have the grain milled into flour and then have the flour baked into bread. It was not until the third century AD that the *annona* was transformed into a dole for all the poor, including non-citizens.

As the Roman Empire expanded, the opulence of Roman entertainment and feasts expanded, too. Attitudes changed from the early days of Rome. The wealthy sought to outdo both earlier generations and their contemporary rivals in ostentatious displays.

For a Roman who aspired to a political career, the cost of entering and staying in politics was steep, and politicians frequently went into deep debt. If he survived the life-and-death intrigues he would face over decades in the political sphere, a proconsul might receive a province as a hefty reward. As governor or magistrate of a province in Gaul, Sicily, Spain, Asia Minor, or Africa, he would burden his new subjects with taxes and look for ways to start a war or pillage a nearby town. Caesar may have had this mindset when, as proconsul of the Gauls, he waged war against some Helvetians who were trying to escape from their native country (modern Switzerland) as they were being pursued by a hostile tribe.

During the period of the Empire, the wealthy sought funds from many sources. For example, the need for money spurred Marcus Licinius Crassus to desperate measures. Although born into the nobility, he lacked the means to enter politics and stay in it. Crassus, who was known for his ambition and many scams, took advantage of the frequent fires in Rome. He even paid arsonists to set fire to homes he wanted to buy. He would then stay nearby with a hired team of firefighters and wait for the home-owner to arrive. He would then offer to put out the fire if the owner agreed to sell him the building. If the owner refused, Crassus would prevent the fire from being extinguished. Crassus became one of the richest men in the history of Rome. (See Plu. *Crassus* 2.)

Wealthy Romans like Cicero and Pliny the Younger spent much of their time at their villas outside the city. The Bay of Naples proved especially popular. There, wealthy Romans could go to relax and escape from the crowded city of Rome. While luxury villas were not uncommon, a more common abode was the working villa, an agricultural unit that developed on a piece of property over generations. These working villas combined living spaces, storehouses, and buildings for livestock around a central courtyard. As a farmer became more prosperous, he might expand the complex by building a separate dwelling for himself and his family. As time went on, another building might be added for the servants' quarters. The ideal arrangement was to have the owner's home as far away as possible from the working areas, or at least facing away from them.

Romans invested their wealth in land, for it was on the whole a fairly secure investment. A laborer's daily wage was four sesterces, an amount sufficient to buy grain for a family of four for three days. In order to qualify as a senator, a man needed one million sesterces. Many Romans exceeded this. Careful management of land and resources meant that these vast fortunes were reasonably secure. However, one of Augustus's admirals lost one hundred million sesterces because he chose the wrong crops for his estates. Pliny the Younger was estimated to be worth twenty million sesterces.

Seneca, who was a Stoic philosopher and the young Nero's tutor, was worth three hundred million sesterces. He accumulated this wealth despite the fact that his Stoic philosophy detailed the miseries associated with being wealthy. He taught that money brings tears and toils. Greed, he observed, leads to the possession of riches, and this escalates to "even greater agony of spirit than the acquisition of riches" (*Ep.* 115.16).

Horace (*Carm.* 3.24) and Livy (*Rom. Hist.* 1.10–12) stated that poverty had made Rome great, but that wealth and luxury would ruin her. This criticism of Rome's apparent decline from the moderation of the Republic period became a common theme throughout the latter period of the Roman Empire.

According to the Roman author Sallust (86 BC–ca. 35 BC),

[W]hen our country had grown strong through toil and the practice of justice, when great kings had been vanquished in war, savage tribes and mighty peoples subdued by force of arms, when Carthage, the rival of Rome's dominion, had perished root and branch, and all seas and lands lay open, then Fortune began to be savage and to throw all into confusion. Those who had easily endured toil, dangers, uncertain and difficult undertakings, found leisure and wealth, desirable under other circumstances, a burden and a curse. Hence a craving first for money, then for power, increased; these were, as it were, the root of all evils. (*Bell. Cat.* 10)

Traditional wealth was held in land by the aristocratic families, who belonged to the senatorial class. In the Empire, enterprising members of the equestrian class, which was one level below the senatorial rank, could make fortunes by taking on tax-collecting contracts. Some freedmen (former slaves) also became wealthy. The classic example in fiction is the character Trimalchio in Petronius's *Satyricon*, who boasts before the guests at his spectacular dinner that he made millions by outfitting ships.

Some leaders in Rome sponsored legislation and encouraged public sentiment that tried to curtail the rush toward wealth. Politicians earned public goodwill by sponsoring games, handing out food, and building baths and temples.

An overwhelming majority of the population in the Greco-Roman world consisted of the poor, including beggars and the working poor. The working classes possessed scant savings and owned little property. Some slaves, who were guaranteed food and minimal clothing, probably fared better than some poor citizens. The working poor, however, did have personal freedom. The poor faced a constant daily struggle for survival and were looked down upon by many with disgust. For example, Cicero did not consider the impoverished to be true citizens. According to him, only those released from the grind of daily survival and the struggle for provision could practice the virtue of being good citizens by supporting friends and the state.

Romans considered wealth an essential requirement of a virtuous life. They believed that only the rich could afford to be honest—and hence virtuous. Since being poor meant a day-to-day struggle for existence, the poor did what it took to survive. The poor sometimes suffered a double indignity. According to Juvenal, a poor man is accused, after being beaten, of starting the altercation:

They beat you up just the same and then, still angry, they sue for assault. This is a poor man's freedom: when he's been beaten and treated like a punchbag, he can beg and plead to be allowed to go home with a few teeth left.
(*Sat.* 3.298–301)

The poor had to work their land or hire themselves out to work the land of the rich, and the wealthy viewed this with disdain. Cicero states, "Unbecoming to a gentleman, too, and vulgar are the means of livelihood of all hired workmen whom we pay for mere manual labour, not for artistic skill; for in their case the very wage they receive is a pledge of their slavery" (*Off.* 1.150).

In the later Roman world, the emperor became known as the *curator*, or caretaker, of the people. Expressions of this care were seen in imperial acts, as when Trajan provided funds for grain for all the children of citizens of Italy. Because of similar actions by other emperors and leading Roman citizens, some have thought that few citizens went hungry in Rome because of the dole, which provided them with subsidized grain. By Nero's reign, one hundred and fifty thousand tons of wheat were being imported to Rome annually. The amount of grain allotted to each citizen would have been enough to feed him but not his family. And from time to time there would have been a food shortage caused by poor harvests abroad, such as one that nearly caused a riot against the emperor Claudius (AD 41–54).

People were more inclined to assist those who had recently lost economic resources than those who were beggars. Some philosophers addressed the ongoing concerns of the poor and those trapped in poverty. In general, giving to the poor was viewed as good, but one had to give wisely. Seneca puts it this way:

> Whoever believes that giving is an easy matter, makes a mistake; it is a matter of very great difficulty, provided that gifts are made with wisdom, and are not scattered at haphazard and by caprice. To this man I do a service, to that one make return; this one I succour, this one I pity; I supply this other one because he does not deserve to be dragged down by poverty and have it engross him; to some I shall not give although they are in need, because, even if I should give, they would still be in need. (*Vit. beat.* 24.1)

Plutarch writes that giving to the poor only perpetuates their condition (*Mor.* 235e).

Juvenal, the satirist, describes the status of the poor:

> Though you swear an oath on the altars of the Samothracian and Roman gods, a poor man [*pauper*] is thought to disregard the divine lightning bolts, with the acquiescence of the gods themselves. Then what do you make of this, that this same man provides everyone with material and substance for amusement

if his cloak is dirty and torn, if his toga's rather mucky and one shoe's gaping open where the leather is split, or if several scars display their coarse new thread where a gash has been sewn up? There's nothing harder about unfortunate poverty than the way it makes people ridiculous. (*Sat.* 6.145–153)

E. THE JEWISH WORLD

The Dead Sea Scrolls and literature of the Second Temple period investigate the disparity between the rich and the poor and discuss its theological implications. *First Enoch* defends the poor and attacks the rich for unjustly oppressing them (*1 En.* 92–105). The rich in *1 Enoch* are consistently seen as the wicked oppressors of the righteous (*1 En.* 96:4–8; 97:7–9). The author speaks of retributive justice in a future time in which there will be a major social and economic reversal that will reestablish the correct relationship between righteousness and justice.

Ben Sira explores more nuances of the interaction of wealth and poverty. He sees wealth and poverty as a part of God's created order that operates under his control (11:14). He sees wealth as both a good thing (if rightly earned) and as functionally neutral. Wealth should be enjoyed if earned in a right way (14:3–19). Despite the prosperity that well-earned wealth can bring, it is still no substitute for good health (30:14–16), friendship (7:18–19), and godly wisdom (1:16–17; 40:25–27). Ben Sira also sees that it is possible to be both poor and righteous, especially if the righteous person is being tested (2:1–9) or his justice has been delayed (11:20–28). While awaiting justice, the righteous poor receive honor (10:19–11:6)—in particular, the honor associated with a good name (41:6–13).

During the Second Temple period, the theology expressed by Ben Sira led to the view that almsgiving, or giving to the poor, helped the giver by depositing the good deed "in one's heavenly treasury" (Gregory, 1335). A triangular theological relationship was thought to entwine God, the giver, and the poor in practical ways. Tobit and Ben Sira credit this deposit, so to speak, with providing for the giver's future deliverance from trouble or death (Tob 4:5–11; Sir 29:8–13). Almsgiving becomes a substitute for sacrifice in Tobit and Ben Sira, (Tob 4:11; Sir 3:30). The Hebrew and Aramaic term for "righteousness," *ṣĕdāqâ*, was used to mean "almsgiving" as well.

The Qumran *War Scroll* asserts that God will avenge the poor (1QM XI, 13; XIII, 12–14). The people of Qumran called themselves the "congregation of the poor ones" (Gregory, 1335) in a pesher on Ps 37 (4QpPs[a] I, 1–10; II, 10).

Portions of Leviticus required the Israelites to act with charity toward the poor and the alien in their midst. The Israelites were to have an attitude of sharing, even of being open-handed toward each other and the strangers among them. Leviticus 19:10 stipulates that a vineyard is not to be stripped bare and that all of the fallen grapes are not to be gathered. The Israelites were instructed to leave these items for the poor and the alien to glean. The explanation given is: "I am the LORD your God." In the same manner, at harvest time, the Israelites were not to harvest to the very edges of the field, but were to leave some of the produce on purpose for the poor and the alien—the reason given remained the same: "I am the LORD your God" (Lev 23:22).

Building on this OT foundation, the mishnaic tractate *Pe'ah*, also known as "The Corner-Offering for the Poor" (Brooks, 1), describes how poor people are to be supported in the land of Israel. Israelite farmers are to give them a portion of all the crops that grow on their land—the amount being determined in "accord with the size of the field and the number of the poor and the yield [of the harvest]" (*m. Pe'ah* 1:2). The tractate asserts that the poor make up a special group that is prevented by adverse circumstances from owning some of their own land. In a similar way, the priests of Israel likewise form a special group, one prevented by Scripture from owning land. The tractate reasons that in the same way that the priests deserve a portion of the land's produce, the poor do as well. "This is because God has promised that all Israelites will share equally in the bounty of the Land of Israel" (Brooks, 1). The tractate reflects the overall concerns of the Mishnah's authors. Compiled around AD 200, after the fall of Jerusalem and the destruction of the Jewish armies, the Mishnah advanced a view of the world in which God, not Rome, ruled over the land of Israel and demanded that the people support those who needed his special care, namely the poor. "Far from being mere subjects of the Roman Empire, Mishnah's [*sic*] authors asserted, ordinary farmers must take responsibility for the welfare of others" (Brooks, 1).

Tosefta *Pe'ah* addresses questions that arose from specific circumstances. For instance, if a poor person lodges overnight, the host is to give him provisions for lodging, plus oil and beans. If the person is known to the host, the host must also clothe him. On the Sabbath, the poor person is to be given enough for three meals, and one of these meals must include a small fish (*t. Pe'ah* 4:8).

The Jews were viewed by the Romans as being poor. Martial wrote that Jewish mothers taught their children to beg (*Ep.* 12.57.13). Juvenal also comments: "A palsied Jewish woman will abandon her hay-lined chest and start begging into [a wealthy woman's] private ear" (*Sat.* 6.542–543).

Among the Jews, God's blessings were associated with riches, and demons were sometimes linked to poverty (*b. Pesaḥ.* 111b; *b. Ḥul.* 105b). The Jews recognized that poverty was not preferable, but also recognized that

God is faithful to the poor and that God requires the covenant people to help the poor. The rabbis believed that poverty should not hinder one from the study of the Torah (*b. Yoma* 35b). Both the poor and the rich were created by God "that one might be sustained by the other" (*Pesiq. Rab.* 191b; Montefiore and Loewe, 439).

The Jews were known for their efforts to care for their own poor. In general the Jews did not receive assistance from the gentiles, although they could offer aid to foreigners (cf. *y. Demai* 4:6). Although some Jews despised professional beggars, to refuse to give them alms was considered as bad as participating in idolatry (*Sifre Deut*, 116–117). There is little evidence of starvation among the Jews. Tacitus wrote that the Jews were generally loyal and compassionate to one another (*Hist.* 5.5). However, the Jews of Qumran charged the Jerusalem hierarchy with mistreating the poor (1QpHab XII, 2–10). This sect favored self-imposed poverty in a framework of communal living (1QS I, 12; V, 3–4; VI, 19–22).

Many in the Jewish community did have wealth. Tacitus describes the Jewish communal wealth in Jerusalem (*Hist.* 5.5). The Tosefta tells of a "vestry of secret givers" in every city to assist those who had recently encountered financial hardship (*t. Šeqal.* 2:1; cf. *m. Šeqal.* 5:6; see also *m. Peʾah* 8:7). As mentioned above, almsgiving became an important religious duty during the Second Temple period (Tob 4:6–11, 16; Sir 3:30). After the destruction of the Second Temple in AD 70, Johanan b. Zakkai claimed that charitable acts would replace sacrifices in securing forgiveness of sins (*ʾAbot de Rabbi Nathan* 4), an idea based on Hos 6:6: "For I [the Lord] desire mercy, not sacrifice, and acknowledgment of God rather than burnt offerings." The Talmud states that "Charity is equivalent to all the other religious precepts combined" (*b. B. Bat.* 9a).

F. THE CHRISTIAN WORLD

Jesus's "royal law" of love—loving your neighbor as yourself (Mark 12:31; Jas 2:8)—became a hallmark of the early church. The earliest reference to the Christian community's care for others comes from the NT: Acts 6 describes the community's ministry to the widows of both Greek- and Aramaic-speaking Jews in Jerusalem. The Roman Empire eventually recognized that ministering to the poor and needy was one of the most important aspects of the new religion called Christianity. Over the centuries, compassion for the needs of the poor led to the spread of the gospel and the expansion of the church in the Roman Empire.

In addition to caring for the poor, the early church experienced a lively debate that, although sensitive to prevailing cultural norms, boldly forged a theology of wealth and poverty that ran counter to the culture of Greco-Roman world. This theology built on the view of wealth that is reflected in the NT, even going so far as to identify Christ with the poor people of the day.

In addition to what would come to be recognized as the NT, the writings of Ignatius of Antioch, Clement of Alexandria, Cyprian of Carthage, and the *Acts of Thomas* are among the documents that formed the basis of Christian ethics during early centuries of the church's existence. These writings warned against the dangers of wealth, endorsed generosity, and maintained a place for ascetic minimalism without making such minimalism incumbent on all Christians.

Clement of Alexandria preached a sermon called "Who Is the Rich Man That Shall Be Saved?" (*Quis dives salvetur*), which addressed the issue of wealth. He maintained:

> Riches, then, which benefit also our neighbours, are not to be thrown away. For they are possessions, inasmuch as they are possessed, and goods, inasmuch as they are useful and provided by God for the use of men; and they lie to our hand, and are put under our power, as material and instruments which are for good use to those who know the instrument. (*Quis div.* 14)

Clement also warned:

> But he who carries his riches in his soul, and instead of God's Spirit bears in his heart gold or land, and is always acquiring possessions without end, and is perpetually on the outlook for more, bending downwards and fettered in the toils of the world, being earth and destined to depart to earth—whence can he be able to desire and to mind the kingdom of heaven—a man who carries not a heart, but land or metal, who must perforce be found in the midst of the objects he has chosen? (*Quis div.* 17)

Concerning the Parable of the Good Samaritan, Clement concluded:

> Well, first let the point of the parable, which is evident, and the reason why it is spoken, be presented. Let it teach the prosperous that they are not to neglect their own salvation, as if they had been already fore-doomed, nor, on the other hand, to cast wealth into the sea, or condemn it as a traitor and an enemy to life, but learn in what way and how to use wealth and obtain life. (*Quis div.* 27)

Justin Martyr describes the celebration of the Sunday Eucharist as including a time of giving, so that those who were prosperous could give as they wished; the collection was deposited with the presider. According to him, the presider aided the orphans and widows, those who were diseased, in prison, and foreigners, and acted as a guardian to those in need (*1 Apol.* 67).

North African Christians were kidnapped by barbarians and money was raised for their release. In a letter to the bishops of Numidia, Cyprian expresses support for the brethren who experienced captivity. Cyprian writes that their captivity, grief, and suffering are to be reckoned as shared by all the brethren (*Epistle* 59). Elsewhere, Cyprian states that almsgiving atones for sin committed after baptism:

> Nor would the infirmity of human frailty have any resource to do anything unless the divine mercy, coming once more in aid, should open some way to obtain salvation by pointing out the works of justice and mercy, so that by almsgiving we may wash away whatever pollutions we later contract.
> (*Eleem.* 1.116; cited in Phan, 86)

In addition to its discussions about how and in what measure to serve the poor, the early church debated the organizational structure it should have. Ignatius of Antioch argued strongly for a model that was prevalent in the Greco-Roman world and widely seen in the management of luxury villas and working villas. In these working enterprises, Christ, the Master of the House (*oikodespotēs*; Ign. *Eph.* 6.2) was absent, but left detailed instructions for his steward (the bishop) to follow.

Polycarp, the bishop of Smyrna and a contemporary of Ignatius, wrote to the Philippians as follows:

> The presbyters, for their part, must be compassionate, merciful to all, . . . visiting all the sick, not neglecting a widow, orphan, or poor person . . . They must avoid all anger, partiality, unjust judgment, staying far away from all love of money. (Pol. *Phil.* 6.1–5)

The early church distinguished between the voluntary, ascetic poor and those made poor by birth or economic circumstance. Those belonging to the former category had a high status in the church and were judged "the most deserving, the most to be honored, the most Christ-like" (Winslow, 326). The concept of voluntary poverty was embraced by the monastic movement, which provided most of the dynamic leaders of the church in the fourth and fifth centuries, such as the three great Cappadocians (Basil, his brother Gregory of Nyssa, and their friend Gregory of Nazianzus), John Chrysostom in the Greek church, and Jerome and Augustine in the Latin church.

In his eulogy for Basil, Gregory of Nazianzus urged the grieving congregation to go outside Caesarea, capital of the province of Cappadocia, to see what their beloved bishop had done. Basil not only possessed great learning, but was also a man of deep spirituality and great foresight. He built what Gregory called "a new city" (*Or. Bas.* 63). That is, he transformed the city of Caesarea in Cappadocia in eastern Anatolia into a new community. He organized philanthropic foundations like hospitals, hostels for poor travelers, homes for the aged, orphanages, and leprosaria.

In his homily on "Tearing Down My Barns," Basil proclaimed:

> When someone strips a man of his clothes we call him a thief. And one who might clothe the naked and does not—should not he be given the same name? The bread in your board belongs to the hungry: the cloak in your wardrobe belongs to the naked, the shoes you let rot belong to the barefoot; the money in your vaults belongs to the destitute. All you might help and do not—to all these you are doing wrong. (cited in Phan, 117)

Writing to the rich, Gregory of Nyssa reminds those with wealth that they must recognize the special role the poor have in the Christian community of believers and acknowledge the special dignity the poor possess. He tells the rich:

> Do not despise these [poor] men in their abjection, do not think them of no account. . . . they have taken upon them the person of our Savior. . . . The poor are the treasures of the good things that we look for, the keepers of the gates of the kingdom [of God], opening them to the merciful and shutting them on the harsh and uncharitable. (*Love of the Poor*; cited in Phan, 132)

John Chrysostom likewise identifies the poor with Christ. He encourages the rich to see the poor as Christ and to consider their own actions toward him. For example, the rich eat in excess, but Christ (a poor person) does not have enough to eat. A rich person chooses between cakes, but Christ (a poor person) lacks even a piece of dried bread. A rich person acquires the resources of Christ (a poor person) and consumes them without thought. Chrysostom emphasizes that a time of accountability is coming (*Hom. Matt.* 48.8). He urges the rich to remember that when they are decorating the church with silk wall hangings, they are not to neglect the naked Christ (the poor person) outside who is perishing from cold and nakedness (*Hom. Matt.* 50.4).

Chrysostom draws a vivid contrast between a poor beggar and a wealthy Christian in one of his sermons:

> For how is [the beggar] to sleep after all, with pangs of the belly, restless famine besetting him, and that often while it is freezing, and the rain coming down on him? And while thou, having washed, returnest home from the bath, in a glow with soft raiment, merry of heart and rejoicing, and hastening unto a banquet prepared and costly: he, driven every where about the market place by cold and hunger, takes his round, stooping low and stretching out his hands; nor has he even spirit without trembling to make his suit for his

necessary food to one so full fed and so bent on taking his ease; nay, often he
has to retire with insult. When therefore you have returned home, when you
lie down on your couch, when the lights round your house shine bright, when
the table is prepared and plentiful, at that time call to rememberance that
poor miserable man wandering about, like the dogs in the alleys, in darkness
and in mire; except indeed when, as is often the case, he has to depart thence,
not unto house, nor wife, nor bed, but unto a pallet of straw; even as we see
the dogs baying all through the night. And thou, if you see but a little drop
falling from the roof, throwest the whole house into confusion, calling your
slaves and disturbing every thing: while he, laid in rags, and straw, and dirt,
has to bear all the cold. (*Hom. 1 Cor.* 11.10)

After his dramatic conversion in Milan, Augustine returned to his home
town in Thagaste in North Africa, sold his property, and gave the proceeds
to the poor. When he became bishop of Hippo, he provided clothing for the
poor. He admonished the wealthy that riches could be as much a burden
as poverty. He reminded his audience that in heaven, Christ is at the right
hand of the Father interceding for those on earth and is rich; yet, Christ is
present with the poor on the earth (*Sermons on the New Testament* 73.4).

Augustine preached as follows on 1 John 3:17:

Lo, whence charity begins withal! If you are not yet equal to the dying for your
brother, be even now equal to the giving of your means to your brother. Even
now let charity smite your bowels, that not of vainglory you should do it, but
of the innermost marrow of mercy; that you consider him, now in want. For
if your superfluities you can not give to your brother, can you lay down your
life for your brother? There lies your money in your bosom, which thieves
may take from you; and though thieves do not take it, by dying you will leave
it, even if it leave not you while living: what will you do with it? Your brother
hungers, he is in necessity: belike he is in suspense, is distressed by his creditor: he is your brother, alike you are bought, one is the price paid for you, you
are both redeemed by the blood of Christ: see whether you have mercy, if you
have this world's means. (*Homily 5* on First John)

Archaeologists have found beautiful mosaics in Hippo, the city of Augustine. The elaborate floors attest to the wealth of the city in late antiquity. Peasants and craftsmen were poorly paid for their labor, while the
rich enjoyed a high standard of living. Augustine writes on the social tension this economic differentiation produced (*Enarrat. Ps.* 39.7). He writes
about a corrupt official who reduced many people, especially tradesmen,
shopkeepers, and craftsmen, to ruin because of his embezzlements. When
some of the corrupt man's victims pursued him, he took refuge in a church.
But the rioters forced him to leave and then lynched him in the street. The
parishioners approached Augustine and asked him to meet with the pro-

consul of Africa in their defense and to seek to obtain mercy for their actions (*Sermon* 302.12–13).

The church fathers stressed care for the poor as an important way of attaining communion with God. Consequently, what came to sharply distinguish the early church from the existing governmental practices and the cultural mores of the time regarding wealth and poverty was the church's welcome of the downtrodden, destitute, sick, and others unable to help themselves. The church sought to comfort those whom society cast aside: prostitutes, lepers, aged slaves, shipwrecked sailors, those waylaid by bandits, and those exiled to the mines. Christians sought such people out and offered them whatever they could to meet their needs. This practice of *agapē*-love was founded on the belief that the stranger "was a potential representation of Christ" (Herrin, 152).

The Roman emperor Julian the Apostate (r. AD 361–363) railed against the "Galileans," but admitted in a letter to a pagan priest in Galatia that the Jews and the Christians provided a model for benevolence to the poor: "For it is disgraceful that, when no Jew ever has to beg, and the impious Galilaeans support not only their own poor but ours as well, all men see that our people lack aid from us" (*Letter 22* to Arsacius, 130d).

Among the early Christian sects were the Ebionites (lit., "poor ones"). They are referred to in the writings of Irenaeus, Tertullian, and Origen. This ascetic group apparently emphasized poverty and retained certain Jewish practices in their way of life (see Klijn and Reinink).

BIBLIOGRAPHY: L. Adkins and R. A. Adkins, *Handbook to Life in Ancient Greece* (1997); G. A. Anderson, *Charity: The Place of the Poor in the Biblical Tradition* (2013); D. L. Baker, *Tight Fists or Open Hands? Wealth and Poverty in Old Testament Law* (2009); R. G. Branch, "Handling a Crisis via a Combination of Human Initiative and Godly Direction: Insights from the Book of Ruth," *In die Skriflig/In Luce Verbi* 46 (2012); R. G. Branch, "Proverbs 31:10–31: A passage containing wisdom principles for a successful marriage/Spreuke 31:10–31: 'n Gedeelte met wysheidsbeginsels vir 'n suksesvolle huwelik," *Koers* 77 (2012); R. G. Branch, "A Study of the Woman in the Crowd and Her Desperate Courage (Mark 5:21–43)" *In die Skriflig/In Luce Verbi* 47 (2013); R. G. Branch, "Teaching the Old Testament Book of Proverbs via a Play" *Christian Higher Education* 4 (2005), 57–69; R. Brooks, *Support for the Poor in the Mishnaic Law of Agriculture: Tractate Peah* (1983); K.-K. Chan, "The Organization of the Caritative Ministry in the Early Church," *The East Asia Journal of Theology* 2 (1984), 103–15; G. C. Chirichigno, *Debt-Slavery in Israel and the Ancient Near East* (1993); E. Clapsis, "Wealth and Poverty in Christian Tradition," *GOTR* 54 (2009), 169–87; D. J. Constantelos, "Basil the Great's Social Thought and Involvement," *GOTR* 26 (1981), 81–86; H. Crawford, *Sumer and the Sumerians* (2nd ed.; 2004); R. David, *Handbook to Life in Ancient Egypt* (1998); J. K. Davies, "Wealth, Attitudes to," OCCS, 774–75; C. Desroches-Noblecourt, *Tutankhamen* (1963); G. D. Dunn, "Augustine's Homily on Almsgiving," *Journal of Early Christian History* 3 (2013), 3–16; F. C. Grant, "The Economic Background of the New Testament," in *The Background of the New Testament and its Eschatology*, ed. W. D. Davies and D. Daube (1964), 96–114; B. Gregory, "Wealth and Poverty," *EDEJ* 1334–36; O. R. Gurney, "The Sultantepe Tablets V. The Tale of the Poor Man of Nippur," *AS* 6 (1956), 145–64; O. R. Gurney, "The Tale of the Poor Man at Nippur and Its Folktale Parallels," *AnSt* 22 (1972), 149–58; G. Hamel, *Poverty and Charity in Roman Palestine* (1990); C. M. Hays, "Resumptions of Radical-ism: Christian Wealth Ethics in the Second and Third Centuries," *ZNW* 102 (2011), 261–82; J. Herrin, "Ideals of Charity, Realities of Welfare: The Philanthropic Activity of the Byzantine Church," in *Church and People in Byzantium*, ed. R. Morris (1990), 151–64; G. G. Hoag, *Wealth in Ancient Ephesus and the First Letter to Timothy* (2015); S. J. Joubert, "Reciprocity and the Poor among the First Followers of Jesus in Jerusalem," in *Life and Culture in the Ancient Near East*, ed. R. E. Averbeck, M. W. Chavalas, and D. B. Weisberg (2003), 371–88; L. E. Keck, "The Poor among the Saints in Jewish Christianity and Qumran," *ZNW* 57 (1966), 54–78; L. E. Keck, "The Poor among the Saints in the New Testament," *ZNW* 56 (1965), 100–29; A. F. J. Klijn and G. J. Reinink, *Patristic Evidence for Jewish-Christian Sects* (1973); S. N. Kramer, *The Sumerians: Their History, Culture, and Character* (1963); S. N. Kramer, "The Death of Ur-Nammu," in *Near Eastern Studies: Dedicated to H. I. H. Prince Takahito Mikasa on the Occasion of His Seventy-Fifth Birthday*, ed. M. Mori, H. Ogawa, and M. Yoshikawa (1991), 193–214; R. Lattimore, trans., *Greek Lyrics* (1955); C. Lepelley, "Facing Wealth and Poverty: Defining Augustine's Social Doctrine," *Augustinian Studies* 38 (2007), 1–17; N. Lohfink, "Poverty in the Laws of the Ancient Near East and of the Bible," *TS* 52 (1991), 34–50; B. W. Longenecker, *Remember the Poor: Paul, Poverty, and the Greco-Roman World* (2010); A. J. Malherbe, ed., *Moral Exhortation, A Greco-Roman Sourcebook* (1986); A. J. Malherbe, "Godliness, Self-Sufficiency, Greed, and the Enjoyment of Wealth: 1 Timo-thy 6:3–19: Part 1" *NovT* 52 (2010), 376–405; P. J. Martin, "Wealth," *EDB* 1371; P. C. Phan, ed., *Message of the Fathers of the Church 20: Social Thought* (1984); W. Mayer, *Poverty and Generosity toward the Poor in the Time of John Chrysostom* (2008); C. G. Montefiore and H. Loewe, *A Rabbinic Anthology* (1938); J. D. Pleins, "Poor, Poverty (OT)," *ABD* V.402–14; H. Rhee, *Loving the Poor, Saving the Rich: Wealth, Poverty, and Early Christian Formation* (2012); D. Schmandt-Besserat and S. M. Alexander, *The First Civilization: The Legacy of Sumer* (1975); V. D. Verbrugge and K. R. Krell, *Paul & Money*

(2015); K. Ward, "Porters to Heaven: Wealth, the Poor and Moral Agency in Augustine," *JRE* 42 (2014), 216–42; K. H. Weaver, "Wealth and Poverty in the Early Church," *Int* 41.4 (1987), 368–81; R. H. Williams, "Bishops as Brokers of Heavenly Goods: Ignatius to the Ephesians" in *Proceedings: EGL & MWBS* 19 (1999), 119–28; Y. Wilfand, *Poverty, Charity and the Image of the Poor in Rabbinic Texts from the Land of Israel* (2014); D. F. Winslow, "Poverty and Riches: An Embarrassment for the Early Church," StPatr 18.2 (1989), 317–328; J. L. Womer, ed., *Morality and Ethics in Early Christianity* (1987); E. M. Yamauchi, "Two Reformers Compared: Solon of Athens and Nehemiah of Jerusalem" in *The Bible World: Essays in Honor of Cyrus H. Gordon*, ed. G. Rendsburg, R. Adler, M. Arfa, and N. H. Winter (1980), 269–92; E. M. Yamauchi, *Africa and the Bible* (2004); G. A. Yee, "The Bible, the Economy, and the Poor," *Journal of Religion & Society*, Supplement 10 (2014), 4–19.

RGB and EBP

See also BANKS & LOANS, BEGGARS & ALMS, BRIBERY, DWELLINGS, JEWELRY, MEDIUM OF EXCHANGE, PALACES, TAXATION, and WIDOWS & ORPHANS.

WEAPONS

Numerous weapons and their uses are mentioned in the Bible but few of them are described in any detail. However, the types and uses of weapons mentioned in Scripture accord well with known data from archaeology and written records. This article will focus on the offensive weapons and defensive equipment carried and worn by individual soldiers in antiquity.

The development of weapons followed the development of the ability to create and manipulate various metals. The earliest weapons, which were used both for hunting and in battle, were made of stone. Shortly after 4500 BC copper came into use. This gave warriors greater weapon options. With the development of bronze (an alloy of copper and tin) in the third millennium BC, weapons gained more durability and designs became more sophisticated. Starting in the thirteenth century BC, iron weapons provided maximum durability, and iron continued to be used through the Roman era and beyond. However, bronze also continued in use, and sometimes both metals were used in the same weapon.

It can be helpful to classify weapons based on their effective range: short-range weapons are those used in hand-to-hand combat, long-range weapons are those used to hit a distant target, and mid-range weapons fall between these two extremes. In antiquity, short-range weapons included swords, daggers, battle axes, clubs, and maces. Mid-range weapons included spears, javelins (smaller versions of spear that were thrown at the enemy), and lances (extremely long spears). Long-range weapons included bows and arrows as well as slings and sling stones. A fourth category that will be discussed below is defensive equipment.

A. THE OLD TESTAMENT

In its descriptions of the time of the patriarchs, the OT refers to only two weapons: the sword (a short-range weapon) and the bow (a long-range weapon). The first military assault and counter-assault recorded in the

Bible is found in Gen 14, when Abraham has to rescue Lot, but there are no weapons mentioned in that chapter. However, later it is recorded that Ishmael grew to be an archer (Gen 21:20) and that Jacob and Esau used swords (Gen 27:40; 48:22) and bows (Gen 27:3; 48:22), so both of these weapons were probably also used by Abraham and his men. Swords and bows are also mentioned in the accounts of Jacob's twelve sons (34:25–26; 49:24). The only piece of defensive equipment found in the narratives describing this period is mentioned in Gen 15:1, where God tells Abram, "I am your shield."

During the time of the exodus and conquest, swords and bows continued to be used, and the first mid-range weapon is also mentioned: the spear. The biblical text mentions swords being used by the Israelites (Exod 17:13; 32:27; Num 21:24; 31:8; Josh 5:13; 6:21; 8:24; 10:11), the Egyptians (Exod 5:21; 15:9; 18:4), the Canaanites (Num 14:43), and the Edomites (Num 20:18). It has been suggested that the phrase "to strike with the edge of the sword" (e.g., Josh 8:24, ESV; 10:35) is evidence that at this time the Israelites used the sickle sword, a weapon that inflicted damage by hitting and cutting, as opposed to stabbing, the enemy. This is supported by the fact that most of the occurrences of this phrase are found in narratives describing the periods of the conquest, the judges, and the early monarchy, when sickle swords are dominant in the archaeological record.

The only clear reference to a mid-range weapon used during this time is in Num 25:7–8, where Phinehas uses a spear to kill an Israelite man and a Midianite woman. Although this is the only occurrence of a spear in the biblical texts related to this period, it is probably safe to assume that spears were part of the arsenal of weapons used by Israelite warriors during the wilderness wanderings and the conquest. (Although *kîdôn* in Josh 8:18 and 26 is usually translated as "javelin," which would make it an additional mid-range weapon, the meaning of this term is uncertain; it could refer to a double-edged sword instead.) There is only one mention of a bow during this period, in Josh 24:12, but this verse implies that the bow was in common use by the Israelites as a weapon at the time of Joshua. Arrows are also mentioned in poetic passages from this period (Num 24:8; Deut 32:23, 42), which indicates that they were well known to the Israelites. The only piece of defensive equipment mentioned during this period is a shield, and this reference too is found in a poetic context (Deut 33:29).

It seems that the quality and variety of the Israelites' weapons declined during the time of the judges. The sword was still a common short-range weapon. It was used in conflicts during the times of Ehud, Barak, Gideon, and Abimelek (Judg 3:16, 21–22; 4:15–16; 7:22; 8:20); by the Danites in their attack on Laish (Judg 18:27); and by all the tribes during the civil war against Benjamin (Judg 20:2, 15, 17, 25, 35, 37, 46, 48).

Swords were worn in a "sheath" (ta'ar, 1 Sam 17:51), which was normally worn on the left side. Ehud, a left-handed man, was able to conceal his weapon in his girdle on the right side. He made for himself a short sword with a small hilt, with which he was able to assassinate Eglon, the king of Moab (Judg 3:15–22). Ehud's double-edged weapon was one cubit long and can be defined as a short sword or a long dagger. It seems to have had an unusual size and shape for the period since the author of Judges describes it in such detail (Judg 3:16).

Another possible short-range weapon, the ax, is mentioned for the first time in a military context in Judg 9:48, but in this text the ax is used only to cut down branches to be used in attacking a tower. There is no clear indication that the Israelites used axes against their enemies in battle, as other nations did.

Unconventional short-range weapons were also used during this period. Shamgar killed six hundred Philistines with an oxgoad (Judg 3:31), and Samson used a donkey's jawbone against a thousand Philistines in a single day (Judg 15:15–17).

Regarding long-range weapons, there is only one reference to a bow in this period. In 1 Sam 2:4, Hannah sings, "The bows of the warriors are broken." Based on this reference, it is clear that the bow continued to be a familiar weapon to the Israelites during the time of the judges. Another long-range weapon is introduced in this period: the sling and sling stone. Judges 20:16 states that the Benjamites had seven hundred left-handed slingers, "each of whom could sling a stone at a hair and not miss." Judges 5:8 provides the only biblical information we have on mid-range weapons and defensive equipment for this period, stating that spears and shields were not common during the time of Deborah and Barak. However, a cache of inscribed javelin heads from this period was found near Bethlehem.

During the time of the united monarchy (11th and 10th c. BC), Israel organized a standing army for the first time, and the weaponry gradually improved. Saul was made king during a time when Israelite weaponry was at an all-time low since the Philistines were preventing the Israelites from making swords or spears (1 Sam 13:19, 22), but the Philistines themselves continued to use these weapons (1 Sam 14:20; 17:45, 51). However, later in Saul's reign swords (1 Sam 15:8; 22:19; 25:13; 31:4) and spears (1 Chr 12:8, 24, 34) were common once again, and this continued into the reign of David (2 Kgs 11:10; 1 Chr 12:8, 24, 34). The term ḥereb, which is usually translated "sword," can refer to either a long sword (such as Goliath's, 1 Sam 17:51) or a short sword (Judg 3:16), or even a dagger (2 Sam 2:16; 20:8–10). Sometimes the context helps one decide on the best translation, but it seems that there was a variety of blades used by the Israelites and their enemies, so the exact kind of weapon being described is not always clear.

Another short-range weapon mentioned in narratives describing this time is the staff or rod used by Benaiah while fighting an Egyptian (2 Sam 23:21; 1 Chr 11:23; cf. Prov 25:18); Benaiah won the day, however, by snatching his opponent's spear and killing him with it. Although Saul owned a sword (1 Sam 13:22; 17:39; 31:4), his spear plays a more prominent role in the biblical storyline (1 Sam 18:10–11; 19:9–10; 20:33; 22:6; 26:7–22; 2 Sam 1:6), which may indicate that it was his weapon of choice.

As far as long-range weapons from this period are concerned, Jonathan used a bow (1 Sam 18:4; 20:20–22, 36–38; 2 Sam 1:22), and Saul was injured by Philistine archers (1 Sam 31:3). Upon the death of Saul and Jonathan, David ordered the "lament of the bow" to be taught to the people of Judah (2 Sam 1:17–27). A contingent of Benjamite archers served David (1 Chr 12:2). Thus the bow continued to be used by the Israelites and their neighbors. Even flaming arrows seem to have been used in David's day (Ps 7:13; cf. Prov 26:18). An analysis of arrowheads and possible javelin heads found at various sites throughout the southern Levant from the Iron I period indicates that bronze was used predominantly and that elliptic, lanceolate, and oblanceolate shapes were preferred. The sling also continued to be used. The mention of David's use of the sling in his battle with Goliath is complemented by references to slingers in 1 Chr 12:2 and 2 Chr 26:14. So although David learned to use the sling as a shepherd, there are clear examples of warriors from this period who were trained to use the sling in warfare.

Regarding defensive equipment, Saul and Jonathan both used armor (1 Sam 17:38–39; 18:4; 1 Chr 10:9–10), and Saul is known to have owned a bronze helmet (1 Sam 17:38) and a shield (2 Sam 1:21). Shields were also used by warriors under David's command (2 Kgs 11:10; 1 Chr 12:8, 24, 34).

Goliath's weapons and defensive equipment have been a topic of much study and debate. His three weapons are mentioned in 1 Sam 17:45 and are typically translated as "a sword [ḥereb], a spear [ḥănît], and a javelin [kîdôn]." The definition of the first term is clear, but the translations of the second and third terms are debated. The comment that Goliath's "spear shaft was like a weaver's rod" (1 Sam 17:7; cf. 2 Sam 21:19; 1 Chr 11:23) is most likely a reference to a looped cord wrapped around it that would have provided him with the ability to throw it farther than he could throw it merely by hand. Such looped javelins are known to have been used in the Aegean in antiquity. This indicates that the term ḥănît should most likely be translated as "javelin" in this context. Regarding the third term, there is good evidence for translating the term kîdôn, which, as mentioned above, is typically translated as "javelin," as "sword" instead. For example, 1 Sam 17:6 describes Goliath's kîdôn as being "slung between his shoulders" (ESV). On the reliefs at Medinet Habu in Thebes, which date to about a century before Goliath, a few of the Sea Peoples (including the Philistines) are depicted as having double-edged swords slung between their shoulders. Thus it is possible that Goliath carried a javelin (*ḥănît*) and two types of swords (a *ḥereb* and a *kîdôn*). A tapering double-edged sword and a curved sickle sword were both common in the eleventh century and make good candidates.

Goliath's defensive equipment is listed as a bronze helmet, scale armor, bronze greaves, and a shield (1 Sam 17:5–7). The bronze greaves (vs. 6), or shin guards, were a distinctively Aegean form of defensive armor, as is known from Mycenaean discoveries and depictions. Homeric heroes were regularly described as *chalkoknēmides*, "bronze-greaved." (See Yamauchi 2004, 76.) This accords well with the Aegean origin of the Philistines.

In the period of the divided monarchy, a full arsenal of weapons and defensive equipment were used by Israel, Judah, and their enemies. Swords (2 Kgs 3:26; 6:22; 2 Chr 36:17; Isa 3:25; 21:15) and spears (2 Chr 11:12; 14:8; 25:5; 26:14; Isa 2:4; Jer 46:4; Mic 4:3; Nah 3:3; Joel 3:10) continued to be common items used in warfare. Axes were carried by the Babylonian army (Ps 74:5–6; Jer 46:22–23).

Bows and arrows were also used throughout this period (1 Kgs 22:34; 2 Kgs 6:22; 9:24; 13:15–16; 19:32; 2 Chr 14:8; 17:17; 18:33; 26:14–15; 35:23). An analysis of arrowheads and possible javelin heads found at various sites throughout the southern Levant from the Iron II period indicates that iron was predominantly used at this time but that bronze heads were still pro- duced, and occasionally heads of bone as well. These heads have a wide va- riety of shapes, with elliptic, lanceolate, and pointed ovate shapes being the most common. The trilobite arrowhead also begins to appear during this period. Sling stones are mentioned in 2 Chr 26:14 as one of the military supplies prepared by Uzziah, and slingers made up part of the coalition forces of Israel, Judah, and Edom in 2 Kgs 3:25.

Defensive equipment included helmets (2 Chr 26:14; Jer 46:4; Ezek 23:24), shields (2 Kgs 11:10; 19:32; 2 Chr 11:12; 14:8; 17:17; 25:5; 32:5; Isa 22:6; Jer 46:3, 9; Ezek 23:24), and armor (1 Kgs 20:11; 22:34; 2 Kgs 3:21; 20:13; 2 Chr 26:14; Jer 46:4; 51:3.). The shields were made of wood with a leather covering that needed to be oiled, a process that is referred to in Isa 21:5. It seems that different types of shields were used by different divisions of troops: 2 Chr 14:8 notes that spearmen used one type of shield (*ṣinnâ*) while bowmen used another (*māgēn*); these terms perhaps denoted large and small shields, respectively.

A summary list of equipment for war is found in 2 Chr 26:14: "Uzziah provided shields, spears, helmets, coats of armor, bows and slingstones for the entire army." Yet helmets and armor do not seem to have been common through most of the monarchy period. Sennacherib's relief of his battle at

Lachish in 701 BC portrays some Judean weapons and defensive equipment from this period: gently curved swords with rounded pommels, elliptical short swords (or daggers), spears, bows, arrows, quivers, slings, sling stones, round shields, a few helmets, and head wraps with flaps hanging over the ears and neck.

Nehemiah provides us with some details about the weaponry and defensive equipment used by the Jews who lived during the period of the Persian Empire. The defenders of Jerusalem used swords, spears, bows, and shields (Neh. 4:13, 16, 18, 21). As was typical in earlier periods (Exod 32:27; Neh 4:18; cf. Ps 45:3), a Jewish warrior of this time would carry his sword on his side (Neh 4:18), probably encased in a sheath (1 Sam 17:51; 2 Sam 20:8; cf. 1 Chr 21:27; Jer 47:6) and attached to a belt (2 Sam 20:8; cf. 1 Sam 25:13).

The last three Hebrew words of Neh 4:23 (Heb. 17), *ʾîš šilḥô hammāyim* (lit., "each man his weapon the water") have puzzled interpreters. The Septuagint omits this phrase altogether. The Vulgate understands the word *šilḥô* not in the sense of "his weapon" but as a verb meaning "he stripped himself." This sense was followed by the KJV: "every one put them off for washing." Some scholars emend the word *hammāyim*, "water," to *bîmînô*, "in his right hand"; cf. the NEB's "each keeping his right hand on his weapon." The NIV's rendering "each had his weapon, even when he went for water" would recall the vigilance of Gideon's chosen band, who had their weapons at hand as they drank water (Judg 7:5–8).

The most striking metaphorical use of the word *ḥereb*, "sword," occurs in Ezek 21, which contains a vivid description of the "sword of Yahweh" at work as an instrument of his judgment. In verses 1–7 [Heb. 6–12] we see his sword unsheathed for action. Then in the furious "Song of the Sword" (vss. 8–17 [Heb. 13–22]), we see the sword polished, then brandished, and even addressed as a living object (vs. 6 [Heb. 21]). Though it is the king of Babylon who wields the sword against Judah and Ammon (vss. 18–27 [Heb. 23–32]), it is actually Yahweh himself who wields his sword in divine judgment (vs. 7 [Heb. 22]).

Hebrew *ḥereb* is the most commonly used word referring to a weapon in the OT. The LXX translates it 195 times as *rhomphaia*, "sword," 165 times as *machaira*, "short sword," eight times as *xiphos*, "straight sword," and four times as *encheiridion*, "dagger."

B. THE NEW TESTAMENT

The NT is not as detailed as the OT in its description of the weapons used during the time it depicts, since physical warfare was not a focus of the NT writers. However, the following facts can be gleaned from the text.

The sword is the most frequently mentioned weapon in the NT. The Greek word used in most passages is *machaira*. The rarer word *romphaia* is used only in Luke 2:35 and in Revelation (1:16; 2:12, 16; 6:8; 19:15, 21). In classical texts, this word signifies a broad sword used by barbarians, but in the LXX and the NT it simply signifies "sword."

The word "sword" is used metaphorically in the NT (Matt 10:34; Luke 2:35; Eph 6:17) but also in reference to actual swords used by the Romans (Luke 21:24), the Philippian jailer (Acts 16:27), a mob (Matt 26:47; Mark 14:43; Luke 22:52), and even by the apostles (Matt 26:51–52; Mark 14:47; Luke 22:38, 49–50; John 18:10–11). There are a few references in the NT to a double-edged sword (Heb 4:12; Rev 1:16; 2:12), which was the typical sword used by Roman soldiers. Another short-range weapon mentioned in the NT is the club (*xylon*, lit., "wood"), which was used by the mob that came to arrest Jesus (Matt 26:47; Mark 14:43; Luke 22:52).

The only mid-range weapon mentioned in the NT is the spear (*lonchē*) that was used to pierce Jesus's side as he hung on the cross (John 19:34). There is no mention of the sling in the NT, so the only long-range weapons referred to are the bow (*toxon*; Rev 6:2) and arrows (sing. *belos*; Eph 6:16; KJV "darts"). The defensive equipment mentioned in the NT includes the helmet (*perikephalaia*; Eph 6:17; 1 Thess 5:8), the shield (*thyreos*; Eph 6:16), and the breastplate (*thōrax*; Eph 6:14; 1 Thess 5:8; Rev 9:9, 17).

It is significant that many of these references to weapons in the NT are metaphorical. Swords, spears, helmets, shields, and breastplates were all used by Roman soldiers throughout the empire, so these items would have been familiar to everyone in the Roman world. Thus the authors of the NT were able to use them as powerful illustrations of spiritual truths. Paul in particular capitalizes on this as he encourages Christians to "be strong in the Lord" (Eph 6:10). Ephesians 6:11 and 13 refer to the "full armor [*panoplia*] of God," and the following verses use the Roman soldier's belt, breastplate, shoes, shield, helmet, and sword as symbols for spiritual resources available to the Christian.

When Paul was taken into custody after the Jews rioted because of the false rumor that he was introducing a gentile into the sanctuary area, the Roman officer asked him, "Aren't you the Egyptian who started a revolt and led four thousand terrorists out into the wilderness some time ago?" (Acts 21:38). The Greek word that the NIV translates as "terrorists" (KJV "murderers"; RSV and ESV "Assassins") is a form of *sikarios*, which comes from the Latin *sicarius*, which in turn is derived from *sica*, "a dagger." According to Josephus, these were the most violent of the Zealots, who surreptitiously mingled with crowds and killed pro-Roman collaborators, including the high priest: "The so-called *sicarii*—these are brigands—were particularly numerous at that time. They employed daggers, in size resembling the scimitars of the Persians, but curved and more like the weapons called by the Romans *sicae*, from which these brigands took their name because they slew so many in this way" (*Ant.* 20.186; cf. *J.W.* 2.254–257). It was the Sicarii who seized the Herodian fortress of Masada. Before it fell to the Romans in AD 74, almost a thousand of them, including women and children, killed themselves.

C. THE NEAR EASTERN WORLD

Mesopotamia

The earliest civilizations in Mesopotamia had surprisingly developed forms of weapons and defensive equipment. The short-range weapons of the fourth and third millennia BC included the mace, the ax, the dagger, and the sickle sword. Stone and copper mace heads from the fourth millennium have been found in the ancient Near East, but primarily from Egypt and the Levant. The Sumerian ax contained a narrow blade, which was intended for piercing the protective equipment of the enemy. The ax head was made of copper and was attached to the shaft by means of a socket. A second type of ax that developed in Mesopotamia in this period contained a broad, curved blade that was attached to the shaft by means of three tangs, giving it a shape like the Greek letter epsilon. This type of weapon would have been used for cutting the enemy instead of piercing. A third type of ax, which had a smaller blade on the back side of the weapon, developed in Anatolia. Daggers were also used in this period. Due to technological obstacles, the blades of this period were typically short and were used primarily for stabbing the enemy, so they are best described as daggers rather than as swords. But by the end of this period, curved sickle swords are clearly depicted in illustrations.

The mid-range weapons of the fourth and third millennia included both spears and javelins. In fact, in the third millennium, the Sumerians had already developed a phalanx formation strikingly similar to the formation used in the first millennium by the Greeks, as depicted in the "Vulture Stele" of Eannatum of Lagash (ca. 2400 BC). The soldiers marched in close rows with their shields forming a wall and their spears sticking out in front of them to engage the enemy. (See *ANEP*, fig. 300.) Sumerian chariots were equipped with javelins that the driver could throw at the enemy.

Regarding long-range weapons, it does not appear that the Sumerians used the bow, but other Mesopotamian civilizations did. The Warka stela, which dates from the late fourth millennium, shows what appears to be a simple or perhaps reinforced bow. Later, the stela of Naram-Sin (23rd c.

BC) depicts a double-convex bow of relatively small size with arms that parallel the string, all of which indicates a composite bow. (See *ANEP*, fig. 309.) Such bows were made of strips of horn placed in a groove in a wooden frame, with the outer side covered with flexible sinews. So already by the end of the third millennium, the expensive and difficult-to-produce composite bow was in use. Such bows had a much longer range than simple bows. At least some of the arrows of this period appear to have forked arrowheads.

Defensive equipment used in Mesopotamia in the third and fourth millennia included helmets, capes, and shields. The Standard of Ur, from the mid-third millennium, depicts soldiers with protective capes and tight-fitting helmets that covered the ears. A ceremonial helmet of this type was found in the tomb of Mes-kalam-dug, a prince of Ur. It is a single piece of electrum, hammered out into the correct shape, and was originally inlaid with cloth. (See *ANEP*, fig. 160.) The use of the helmet so early in Mesopotamia explains why the mace was not common there: the helmet rendered the mace ineffective. Capes were draped around the shoulders, fastened across the chest, and extended down to the warrior's knees. They are dotted with small circles and were most likely made of leather. It has been suggested that the circles were small metal disks sewn on the outside of the cape to provide extra protection, possibly as a primitive form of scale armor, but they could also have been merely decorations. The shields used by these soldiers were rectangular and large, extending from the soldier's neck to his ankles. Significantly, the only shields depicted in Sumerian artwork are the ones used in the phalanx; the caped warriors carry no shields.

It seems that during the Middle Bronze period the mace fell out of use in this region, so short-range weapons were limited to the ax and the sword. In the Levant, a socketed, curved ax head developed with holes that looked like two eyes, resulting in a shape that looks like a duckbill. Later in the Middle Bronze Age, an extremely narrow ax head was used. Curved sickle swords also were widely used at this time. It has been suggested that the shape of the sickle sword was derived from the shape of the battle ax of the previous period. The dagger also continued to be used during this period.

As far as mid-range weapons are concerned, the spear and javelin also continued to be used during the Middle Bronze period. The spearheads continued to be tanged (not socketed), but the end of the tang was bent to prevent the head from splitting the wood on impact. For long-range weapons, there is some evidence from illustrations from Beni-Hasan in Egypt that the simple, double-convex bow was used in the Levant during this period.

In the Late Bronze period, the ax, sword, spear, and bow continued to be used. Tanged ax heads from Anatolia with narrow blades were used during this period, as were socketed ax heads with decorative prongs off the back. The sickle sword continued to be used, but its blade section was lengthened. The double-edged dagger also continued to be used, but eventually a long, straight sword also became common. The composite bow finally came into widespread use.

Defensive equipment from this period included shields, armor, and helmets. The Late Bronze Age boasted a wide variety of shapes and sizes of shields. The style of shield varied from culture to culture. Canaanites are depicted in Egyptian art as carrying relatively small rectangular shields. The Sea Peoples are depicted with round shields. The Hittites preferred a shield that was similar in shape to a figure eight, with wide sections at the top and bottom tapering to a narrow section in the middle, where the handle was positioned. The decorations of one of the chariots of Tuthmosis IV depict some Canaanites warriors as wearing helmets and scale armor. Depictions of scale armor from this period, as well as actual artifacts, show that the size of the scales varied from one garment to the next, and they also varied within the same garment, based on where they were positioned. (See *ANEP*, fig. 161.) Such defensive equipment was costly to manufacture, so it was typically reserved for archers and charioteers, who could not defend themselves by holding a shield.

Our knowledge of the weapons used in the Neo-Assyrian empire is extensive due to the numerous reliefs that have been discovered. Short-range weapons included swords, axes, and maces. The typical Neo-Assyrian sword had a long, straight blade and a hilt with a rounded pommel. It was carried in a sheath that was attached to the soldier's belt and to a strap that extended over one shoulder. The sword served as a secondary weapon for all Assyrian soldiers, no matter what their primary weapon was. Curved swords are also depicted on the reliefs, but only as used by foreigners (such as the Judeans). Daggers are also depicted on many of the reliefs, either tucked in the belt of the king or being used on the field by soldiers. Socketed axes with narrow blades are another type of short-range weapon depicted on the reliefs. This type of ax was part of the standard equipment carried in a chariot during the time of Ashurnasirpal and Sennacherib. The Neo-Assyrian reliefs show axes being used by soldiers to injure enemies or cut down trees. A final short-range weapon from this period that can be mentioned is the mace. Maces are commonly portrayed on the Neo-Assyrian reliefs, but it seems they primarily served a ceremonial function, since they are only rarely seen used in battle. The mace heads depicted on the reliefs have a variety of decorative shapes, including a simple sphere, a rosette, and a flower bud.

Mid-range weapons used by Neo-Assyrian soldiers included the spear and javelin. Spears were carried by infantry, by cavalry, and on the back of chariots. They were used not only to attack the enemy but also to break up city walls. (Instances of swords and daggers being used in this way can also be found.) The reliefs and the artifacts indicate that socketed spearheads were preferred during this time, usually with a lanceolate head. Examples of both extremely short and extremely long spears can be seen in the reliefs of Sargon II (721–705 BC), so there seems to have been much variety in length during this period. Typically, an Assyrian spearman is depicted as attacking by holding the spear above his head and thrusting it at the enemy. There is also some evidence of the use of the javelin by Assyrian troops.

Long-range weapons included bows, arrows, slings, and sling stones. The typical bow depicted on the Assyrian reliefs had a somewhat angular shape when it was at rest and was segment-shaped when it was drawn. Often the bows were decorated with a bird's head on each tip. The string was typically tied to the beak, passed over the bird's head, extended to the back of the bird's head at the other end of the bow, and tied to the beak of that bird's head. Some Judean bows depicted on the reliefs of Sennacherib contained a similar curved shape on their tips, but the picture is not detailed enough to tell us if they too were shaped like a bird's head. An additional Judean bow from this period is depicted in a seal that was found in Jerusalem: an archer is shown with a drawn bow that has flaring tips. The typical bow of this period was a composite bow, but there is at least one example in the Assyrian reliefs of a simple bow being used by a foreign soldier. One relief from the time of Ashurbanipal (7th c. BC) shows a bow being strung by two soldiers: one leans into the center of the bow with his knee and bends the limbs with his hands while the other soldier attaches the string. The arrows seen on the Assyrian reliefs had arrowheads and feathered vanes of a wide variety of shapes. Soldiers equipped with slings are less frequent in the reliefs. They only appear during the reigns of Sennacherib and Ashurbanipal (7th c. BC).

Sennacherib's reliefs of his attack on Lachish in 701 BC, which are now in the British Museum, depict squads of slingers standing behind the archers. Based on the angle of the slings, these slingers appear to be moving their arms in a vertical motion as they launch their projectiles. Usually a pile of sling stones is depicted next to the slinger, and numerous sling stones have been recovered at Lachish. These stones were spherical with an average diameter of approximately six centimeters, which is typical for the region in the Iron Age. The sling stones from Lachish are made of flint, however basalt, chert, and quartz examples are also known from this region and period.

Defensive equipment used by Neo-Assyrian soldiers included helmets, scale armor, and shields. The helmets and shields came in a wide variety of shapes and sizes. The most common helmets had a conical shape or had a decorative crest at the top the head. The excavations at Lachish recovered the crest of a bronze helmet (see *ANEP*, fig. 175). Assyrian scale armor was composed of hundreds of metal scales that overlapped one another. Such armor was costly to produce and was usually reserved for the archers, charioteers, and cavalry, who needed their hands free to operate their equipment and could not hold a shield. Sometimes the scale armor would reach all the way down to the soldier's knees or feet, but at other times it extended only down to the waist. During the time of Ashurnasirpal II, there are a few examples in the reliefs of scale armor being attached to the bottom of the soldier's helmet and covering the bottom part of his face and his neck. Shields ranged from small, circular ones held in the hand to full-length rectangular ones that rested on the ground, with other variations in between these extremes. Some shields appear to have been made of wood, leather, and metal, while others seem to have been made of a thick wickerwork.

There is not much detailed evidence for the types of weapon used by the Babylonians, although the biblical writers mention swords, axes, bows, arrows, spears, helmets, armor, and shields.

Egypt

In the Predynastic period, the Archaic Era, and the Old Kingdom, the short-range weapons used by the Egyptians were the mace and the ax. Since the Egyptians' enemies did not wear armor or helmets during this period, the mace and a broad-bladed ax were effective weapons. The mace heads of this period were typically oblong or round, and the base of the shaft flared out to prevent the weapon from accidentally being thrown. The Egyptian ax head of this period came in two varieties: one with either a long, gentle curve or one that was semicircular. The Egyptians would attach an ax head by tying it to the shaft by means of a tang, holes in the ax head, or both.

The Hunter's Palette from the Predynastic period shows that the spear was in use at this time in Egypt, but there is not much other evidence for the use of the spear in this early period of Egypt's history. The Predynastic and Old Kingdom Egyptians used the bow as their long-range weapon. The bows depicted on the monuments from this period have tips that curve in toward the string, showing that the Egyptians were using a simple or perhaps reinforced bow at this time. The only defensive equipment that was possibly used by the Egyptians during this period was the shield, but there is scant evidence for its use.

It seems that during the Middle Kingdom the mace fell out of use in Egypt, as it did elsewhere. The Egyptian ax of this period had a wide, gently curved blade that was attached to the shaft with three tangs. It is known as the "epsilon axe" and was first developed in Mesopotamia, but by this time it was obsolete in its place of origin. The Egyptians also used double-edged short swords or daggers during this period.

For mid-range weapons in the Middle Kingdom, the Egyptians used throw sticks, spears, and javelins. As for long-range weapons, the simple bow continued to be used. The Egyptians enlisted squadrons of the *Medjay*, a tribe from Kush (the Sudan) to serve as archers [see Figure 8 on p. 475; *ANEP*, fig. 179]. There is also some evidence of the sling being used as a weapon of war during this period.

Some Egyptian shields from the Middle Kingdom were very large and covered the soldier's whole body; others were relatively small, protecting only his face and chest. These shields were flat on the bottom and tapered to a pointed or rounded top. The large shield quickly fell out of use, probably because it was not easy to carry into battle. The smaller shield was used for a thousand years. These shields were made from leather stretched over a wooden frame, and sometimes the color pattern from the animal's hair is depicted on the monuments. It appears that the Egyptians did not use helmets during most of the Middle Bronze period.

Egyptians in the New Kingdom period started to carry sickle swords, but Egyptian soldiers with tapering double-edged swords can also be found in the reliefs. Axes also continued to be used, but their blades changed shape. The ax heads became longer and narrower so that they could penetrate the defensive coverings of the enemy. A relief from the time of Ramesses III shows axes with narrow blades being used by soldiers for cutting trees and breaking through a city gate. Blunt wooden weapons, such as single-sticks, clubs, boomerangs, and throw sticks, were found in the tomb of Tutankhamun (14th c. BC), and examples of similar weapons being used in a battle can be seen on the Medinet Habu reliefs of the twelfth century BC. As in the Middle Kingdom, in the New Kingdom the mace seems to have mostly fallen out of use. Mid-range weapons used by the Egyptians during this period included spears, javelins, and throw sticks.

Long-range weapons during the New Kingdom included bows and (to a limited extent) slings. The bows depicted on artistic works in the tomb of Tutankhamun (14th c. BC) had a triangular shape when they were at rest and a segmented shape when they were drawn. Bows depicted on the reliefs of Ramesses III (12th c. BC) follow the same pattern. At least seventeen bows were found in the tomb of Tutankhamun (14th c. BC), ranging from forty-four to forty-nine centimeters in length. Many of these bows were lavishly decorated with gold and intricate patterns. The tips of one bow were decorated with carvings of captives, with the string attached to the captive's neck. The typical arrow in the reliefs of Tutankhamun and Ramesses III had an angled, lanceolate head and feathered tails. One of the reliefs of Ramesses III show a U-shaped notch at the back of the arrow.

The excavators of Tutankhamun's tomb found 278 arrows inside, with a wide variety of shapes and sizes. Each arrow was composed of a reed shaft, feathered vanes, and an arrowhead. A short section of hardwood was typically found between the reed shaft and the arrowhead, which was made of bronze, ivory, wood, or glass.

The remains of two slings were found in the tomb of Tutankhamun. These were made of plaited linen thread and were designed with a diamond-shaped pouch in the middle, with thin strings attached to either end of the pouch and a loop at one end of the strings for the slinger to insert a finger and secure the sling to the hand. Given their provenance, these were likely luxury items and may not be indicative of the typical sling used in this period. It is presumed that slings made from leather or textiles were used throughout antiquity by commoners. Egyptian slingers from the time of Ramesses III are depicted as standing in the crow's nests of warships, twirling their slings in a horizontal motion over their heads.

Defensive equipment used by the Egyptians in the New Kingdom period included helmets, scale armor, and shields. Helmets and scale armor were new developments for the Egyptians in this period, and their use spread from the officers to the soldiers over the course of the period. Some helmets appear to be made of metal, while others were probably merely made of cloth or leather. The typical shield of this period had a flat base that tapered to a rounded top. The size varied from the full height of a man to half his height. One shield found in the tomb of Tutankhamun was comprised of leather stretched across a wooden frame.

The Philistines and other Sea Peoples are also depicted on reliefs at Medinet Habu (12th c. BC). The Philistines who attacked Egypt are depicted with long, tapering double-edged swords with a central ridge and a flared pommel. It is likely that Goliath carried such a sword. Philistines also are depicted carrying spears with lanceolate heads. With the exception of a possible quiver at the back of a Philistine chariot, the Philistines are not depicted with any long-range weapons on the reliefs. However, arrowheads have been found at Philistine sites, and the Bible records that the Philistines had archers in the battle at Mount Gilboa (1 Sam 31:3; 1 Chr 10:3). For defensive equipment, the Philistines were well supplied. Their heads were protected by what appear to be feathered, leather headdresses with chinstraps; their torsos were protected with armor in the form of leather or metal strips; and they carried small, round shields with a handle in the center.

Persia

We have considerable evidence for Persian weapons, both from artistic representations and from Greek texts, primarily Herodotus. From Susa comes a brightly colored glazed brick relief of a royal guard holding a long spear before him and carrying a curved bow over his left shoulder and a large quiver on his back. From Persepolis come numerous stone reliefs, now bereft of their original colors, with Persians and Medes (or Persians wearing Median garb) in a very similar pose, with long spears before them, and bows and quivers; a few carry round shields. The weapon bearer who stands behind the seated Darius in the Treasury Relief holds a battle ax in his right hand (see Wilber, 90–91).

Many of the twenty-three delegations depicted on the eastern stairway of the Apadana at Persepolis bring weapons as gifts: the Medes bring bows, daggers, and a sword; the Elamites bring daggers and bows; Gandharians bring lances and a shield; Sogdians bring axes and a sword; Indians bring axes; Thracians bring spears and shields; and a group identified as Drangians, Hyrcanians, or Parthians bring a lance and a shield. (See Yamauchi 1990, 351–56.)

In his idealized "Education of Cyrus," Xenophon writes: "Those who go [with the king] must take bow and arrows and, in addition to the quiver, a sabre or bill in its scabbard; they carry along also a light shield and two spears, one to throw, the other to use in case of necessity in a hand-to-hand encounter" (*Cyr.* 1.2.9).

Herodotus gives details of the weapons carried by the various contingents in the vast army of Xerxes that invaded Greece in 480 BC. For example, the Persians wore "scales of iron like in appearance to the scales of fish . . . for shields they had wicker bucklers, their quivers hanging beneath these; they carried short spears, long bows, and arrows of reed, and daggers withal that hung from the girdle by the right thigh" (*Hist.* 7.61).

The primary offensive weapon of the Persians was the bow and arrow. At the battle of Marathon in 490 BC, Miltiades, the commander of the ten thousand Athenians, ordered his hoplites to attack the Persians at a run in order to minimize their exposure to the Persian archers (*Hist.* 6.112). This gained them a great victory. At the narrow pass at Thermopylae in 480 BC, three hundred Spartans withstood furious Persian frontal attacks. When the Spartans were forewarned that Persian arrows would darken the skies, one Spartan quipped: "If the Medes hide the sun we shall fight them in the shade and not in the sunshine" (*Hist.* 7.226). Unfortunately, a local traitor showed the Persians a back route over the mountains, and all the Spartans were killed.

D. THE GRECO-ROMAN WORLD

Greece

The archaeological evidence from this region can be subdivided into the time of the Mycenaean culture (16th–13th c. BC) and of the Greek culture (8th–4th c. BC). The Mycenaean Linear B tablets from Knossos list a number of weapons. One tablet lists fifty *pa-ka-na* (Gk. *phasgana*), "swords." Another lists forty-two [e]-*ke-a ka-ke-re-a* (Gk. *enchea chalkarea*), "bronze-tipped spears." (See Ventris and Chadwick, 360–61.)

In the Mycenaean culture, short-range weapons consisted of swords and daggers. In the sixteenth century, a double-edged rapier was used, as evidenced by finds in the royal Shaft Tombs at Mycenae. This was a narrow sword that was over a meter long. The blade was attached to the handle by means of a tang, which indicates that it was used primarily for thrusting instead of striking. Starting in the fourteenth century, a different type of double-edged sword was used. The blade was about 0.75 meters long (30 in.), and was made in one piece with the handle, which meant it could be used for thrusting or striking. This is the type of sword depicted in the hands of the Philistines on the twelfth-century BC Medinet Habu reliefs from Egypt. Ornately decorated bronze daggers from the Mycenaean culture have also been found. Gold inlays depicting lions and warriors adorned the blade of this type of weapon.

For mid-range weapons, spears and javelins were used in the Mycenaean culture. Homer (writing centuries later) typically describes the heroes of this period as equipped with a spear as their primary weapon, and this is confirmed by artistic representations of warriors that date to this period. The men on the Warrior's Vase (13th c.) carried long spears with elliptical heads. Javelins with looped cords (similar to the one used by Goliath, discussed above) and throwing spears were also used.

For long-range weapons, there is some evidence that the sling and the composite bow were used in the Mycenaean period. Obsidian and bronze arrowheads have been found in the archaeological record, and at least one inlayed dagger depicts an archer.

The defensive equipment that the Mycenaeans developed set them apart from others. The most unique item was the boar's tusk helmet. This type of helmet was composed of a leather or felt cap with rows of boar tusk sewn onto it. Each helmet used sixty to eighty pieces of tusk, so it is probable that this type of helmet was used only by the elite. Cheek guards protected the warrior's face. One example of a boar's tusk helmet was found in a tomb at Dendra near Mycenae, along with bronze armor. The armor comprised a breastplate and backplate. Above this cuirass were plates protecting the neck and shoulders, and below it were metal bands that protected the waist and thighs. Greaves and arm guards completed the ensemble. The finds from this tomb at Dendra date to ca. 1400 BC. Due to the immense weight and cumbersome nature of this armor, it is unlikely that it was used for very long or by very many warriors.

The thirteenth-centeury BC "Warrior's Vase" depicts soldiers wearing helmets. The helmets have cheek guards, a flared crest, a limp plume trailing out of the top, and what appears to be a horn projecting from the front. The helmets are dark but are covered with white dots, which has caused some to suggest that the vase depicts leather helmets on which metal discs were sewn. These warriors are also wearing long-sleeved shirts, a fringed kilt (with white dots similar to those on the helmets), leg coverings that go from the top of the knee to the ankles, and some sort of protective covering on their feet.

The shields on the Warrior's Vase, which were round with a curved section cut out of the bottom, were intended to protect the torso only. Other types of shield from this period were longer and protected the whole body. On a single dagger from this period with an inlay depicting a lion hunt, two types of full-body shields can be seen: one is shaped like a figure eight and the other is rectangular with a curved top. Both types of shield were carried by means of a strap that hung over the warrior's shoulder, freeing the warrior's hands to wield his spear. One of the figure-eight shields is depicted as curving outward, and the front of it is white with black patches, which probably indicates that it was covered with animal hide.

Numerous weapons are mentioned in the Homeric epics. There are three words for "sword" used in the epics: *xiphos*, which perhaps describes a narrow, rapier-like weapon; *phasganon*, which refers to a broader slashing sword; and *aor*, which refers to a sword slung from the shoulder by a baldric. In arming scenes, Paris and Achilles each take up a single spear (*enchos*), while Agamemnon and Patrolus take a pair of spears (*doure*).

In the *Iliad*, the bow (*toxon*) is associated with Teucer, the brother of Ajax, with Pandaros, a Lycian, and with Paris, the Trojan. Odysseus's bow plays a major role in the *Odyssey*. While Odysseus has been away for twenty years and presumed dead, many suitors have come to his home in Ithaca to seek the hand of Penelope. She finally brings out his bow and agrees to marry the suitor who can string his bow and shoot an arrow through the holes of twelve ax handles aligned in a row. None, however, can do this except Odysseus, who comes disguised as a beggar:

> So without effort did Odysseus string the great bow. . . . and he took up a swift arrow . . . and drew the notched arrow even from the chair where he sat, and let fly the shaft with sure aim, and did not miss the end of the handle of one of the axes, but clean through and out at the end passed the arrow weighted with bronze. (*Od.* 21.409–423)

The adjective *euknēmides*, "well-greaved," is the most frequent epithet of the Greeks, occurring thirty-one times in the *Iliad* and five times in the

Odyssey. The adjective *chalkoknēmides,* "bronze-greaved," occurs once (*Il.* 7.41). The heroes wear a *thōrax,* "cuirass." The Linear B texts depict this armament with an ideogram. There are two words for shields: *aspis,* which describes a shield that is round and bossed, and *sakos,* which described a shield that is large and stout. The god Hephaistos fashions a marvelous shield for Achilles (*Il.* 18.598–606).

Four words for helmet are used in the epics: *korys* (forty-six times), *kyneē* (twenty-eight times), *tryphaleia* (fifteen times), and *pēlēx* (ten times). We cannot be certain of what kinds of helmets these represented. The epithet *chalkērēs* indicates that the helmets were made of bronze. Hector's helmet, which frightened his baby son (*Il.* 6.469), had a *lophos hippiochaitēs,* "crest of horse-hair." Meriones gave Odysseus a helmet made of boar's tusks (*Il.* 10.261–65).

Earlier scholars regarded Homer's references to bronze swords, weapons, breastplates, and greaves as anachronistic. But recent discoveries have confirmed that these reflect traditions passed on orally from the Mycenaean age, rather than weapons from Homer's age (8th c. BC). According to Anthony Snodgrass,

> His exclusive use of bronze, for every sword and every spearhead mentioned in both poems, is the point of the greatest significance; for these are the two supreme weapons of the Epic. There is no period of Greek history or prehistory, later than the first half of the eleventh century B.C., of which such a picture would be representative. (Snodgrass, 122)

There is a gap of a few centuries from which we do not have much archaeological evidence from the Aegean regarding weapons. When the next period begins, in the eighth century BC, it is clear that the Mycenaean culture left a legacy to the Greeks but that there were some changes as well.

For short-range weapons, the Greek hoplite warrior relied on a short thrusting sword. Another type of sword was the single-edged, curved *kopis,* which was introduced in the fifth century BC and which lasted until the time of Alexander. This was a smiting weapon. Warriors using this sword are typically depicted as raising it above their head to bring it down on their enemy.

The Greeks, however, only used the sword as a secondary weapon. Like the Mycenaeans, the Greeks preferred the spear as their primary weapon. The hoplite warrior used a long thrusting spear that was about 1.8 to 2.4 meters (six to eight ft.) long. The spearhead could be made of iron or bronze, and a metal spear butt was common. The shaft would be wrapped in leather to assure a firm grip. Later in Greek history, Philip II of Macedon and Alexander the Great perfected the art of the phalanx and equipped their soldiers with a longer spear called a *sarisa.* This type of lance was 5.5 to 7.5

meters (eighteen to twenty-five ft.) long and was wielded with both hands. It was made extremely long so that the spear tips of all the men in the phalanx would protrude out the front of the formation. Supporting the phalanx would be soldiers equipped with smaller and lighter spears that were thrown as javelins. Often a looped cord would be attached to the javelin, similar to what was seen in the Mycenaean period. Although there is some evidence for long-range weapons in the Myceneaean period, typically the Greeks would hire mercenaries to wield the bow and the sling to supplement their short-range and mid-range weapons. In the Classical period, slingers from Crete and Rhodes were hired. In contrast to the use of stone missiles in the ancient Near East, these slingers used lead missiles, which provided greater range. The Greeks are known to have used a simple bow, but again, their archers typically came from elsewhere. Archers from Crete were hired as mercenary soldiers, and Scythian mercenaries were used from the seventh century onward. The Scythian bow was a meter in length, and each arm of the bow curved out from the grip. It was a composite bow made of horn, wood, and sinew. The Scythians' arrowheads were made of bronze and were attached to the shaft by means of a socket. The shapes of the arrowheads can be divided into three types, distinguished by their cross-sections: one type had a triangular cross-section, one type was tri-bladed, and the last was relatively flat with only two blades. The Scythians were known for using a unique case, called a *gōrytos*, that doubled as a quiver and a bowcase. Each one could hold two to three hundred arrows. A type of crossbow called a *gastraphetēs*, which was developed at the beginning in the fourth century BC, is decribed by Hero of Alexandria in his first-century AD work *Belopoeica*.

For defense, the Greeks used a wide variety of helmets, armor, and shields. In the eighth century BC, the *dipylon* shield was common. This shield was oval-shaped with two round sections removed from the right and left sides, making it similar to the figure-eight shields of the Mycenaean period. Like the Mycenaean shields, it was strapped to the warrior's shoulder. A round shield is also known to have been used in this century. In the seventh century BC, the *dipylon* shield was replaced by the Argive shield, or *hoplon*. This was a round shield, 0.8 to 1 meter (thirty to forty in.) in diameter. The shield was convex and was carried by means of straps on the inside through which the soldier could slip his arm to distribute the shield's weight. It is estimated to have weighed seven kilograms (fifteen lbs.) It was comprised of wood overlaid with leather or bronze, and had a bronze rim to strengthen the edge. This type of shield was used effectively for several centuries, until the fourth century BC. With the development of the phalanx formation, a new type of shield developed that was smaller and lighter. As the *sarisa* spear needed two hands to operate, this shield included a neck strap that would free the hands of the soldier.

Various types of metal helmets were also common throughout the Greek period. In the eighth century BC, the Kegelhelm and Corinthian helmets were used. The Kegelhelm helmet was cone-shaped with a horseshoe-shaped crest. It included cheek plates but no nose piece. It seems that the Kegelhelm helmet evolved into the Insular and Illyrian helmets in the seventh century BC. The Insular helmet, which is known from Crete, had a rounded top with a crest and extended down in the front to protect the cheeks. The Illyrian helmet was similar but did not include a crest, and it sometimes extended in the back to cover the neck.

The Corinthian helmet was introduced in the eighth century BC and evolved until the fifth century. The earliest versions were dome-topped cylinders that covered the entire head, with the exception of a T-shaped hole in the front for the eyes and mouth. A short, narrow extension came down between the eyes to help protect the top of the nose. Later versions of the Corinthian helmet were shaped to match the contours of the head, had an extended noseguard, and were extended in the back to protect the neck. The Chalcidian helmet (early 6th to 4th c.) was derived from the Corinthian helmet. It differed in that it had an opening for the ears and a larger opening for the face. Tiny holes on the bottom edge of some helmets indicate that the inside of the helmet was lined with leather or cloth that was stitched to the metal.

In the fifth century, other types of helmets developed independently from the Kegelhelm and Corinthian helmets. The Bell helmet was merely a cap of metal with no protection for the face and neck. The Boeotian helmet was similar but included a visor and remnants of cheek plates. The Thracian helmet was somewhat cone-shaped and could include a facemask.

The armor used by the Greeks went through various stages of development as soldiers tried to strike a balance between protection and flexibility. In the eighth century BC, a bell-shaped, bronze cuirass was used that was molded to the contours of the human body. This is the type of armor used by the hoplites. In the middle of the sixth century, the muscled cuirass, which was shaped to match the muscles and chest of the male torso, came into use. Bronze greaves that went from the knee to the ankle were used to protect the legs in the seventh and sixth centuries. Later in the sixth century and continuing into the fifth, warriors wore a type of linen armor, as we know from depictions on pottery: a linen girdle was wrapped around the body, rectangular shoulder pieces (made of metal or leather) were attached at the top, and a series of overlapping leather strips comprised a protective kilt. There is some evidence that metal scales or plates were sewn on the linen. This type of covering would naturally make the warrior more agile, but would provide less protection than the heavier metal cuirass. In the fifth century, plate armor was further developed.

In 1977 Manolis Andronikos made the spectacular discovery of an unlooted royal Macedonian tomb at the site of Aegae (near modern Vergina). Andronikos has plausibly identified as the tomb of Philip II, who was assassinated in 336 BC and who was the father of Alexander the Great. Buried under a huge tumulus were two chambers containing two golden chests with the remains of cremated individuals, which had been wrapped in purple cloth. In addition to jewelry, such as a magnificent crown of gold oak leaves, a number of weapons were found.

In the smaller antechamber, which contained the remains of a queen, were found bronze greaves and a splendid gold *gōrytos* (combination bow-case and quiver) with bronze arrows. The *gōrytos*, which is similar to ones that have been found in royal Scythian burials, depicts scenes of a siege, perhaps that of Troy.

The main chamber contained a complete suit of Macedonian armor, including: the hilt of an iron sword decorated with gold; the remains of a shield, including ivory and gold decorations; a cuirass of iron decorated with bands of gold; a helmet with a large crest and cheek pieces, the first of its kind to be recovered; and a pair of unequal gilded bronze greaves. The left greave is 3.5 centimeters shorter than the right one, which would accord with the fact that Philip was lame. A small ivory portrait of the king depicts one of his eyes, which had also been damaged in battle.

Rome

In their use of weapons and defensive equipment, the Romans were influenced heavily by the Greeks and the Celts. For short-range fighting, Roman soldiers were equipped with a straight double-edged sword known as a *gladius*. The blade was about 0.5 meters (1.6 ft) long. This weapon originated in Spain, and the Romans probably first encountered it in the third century BC as they fought the Spanish troops who were assisting Hannibal. According to Vegetius (5th c. AD), a properly trained Roman soldier would use this weapon primarily by thrusting with the point and not striking with the edge. But Roman artwork shows the sword also being used for striking, and not just piercing. Around AD 200, the *spatha* replaced the *gladius*. It was a long sabre sword, about 0.7 meters (2.3 ft) in length. A dagger (*pugio*) was also used in various periods of Roman history. Although an ax is listed among the equipment of the Roman soldier (Jos. *J.W.* 3.95), it appears that this weapon was not employed in battle but was merely used as a tool.

For mid-range weapons, the Romans were equipped with three-meter long javelins (sing. *pilum*; pl. *pila*). They would be thrown at the enemy at the beginning of the attack, a maneuver that was followed by an assault with swords. The *pilum* existed in various forms throughout the Roman

period. In the second century BC, there was a version with a long, socketed head and another version with a short, tanged head. Later, Marius and
Caesar modified the *pilum* so that the weapon would be rendered useless
after impact. Marius switched out a metal rivet with a wooden one so that
it would break on impact. Caesar made the shaft of the *pilum* softer than
the tip so that the metal would bend upon impact, making it difficult for
the enemy to extract it from their shields. These types of *pila* were used
in the first and second centuries AD. The javelin continued to be used by
Roman soldiers in later centuries, but it also continued to evolve in various
ways. In the fifth century AD, Vegetius noted that every soldier carried five
javelins. Long lances, called *hastae*, were also used by the Romans. Early
in their history, the Romans adopted the Greek phalanx style of fighting,
but that strategy was abandoned after 370 BC, when it failed them in their
battles with the Celts.

For long-range weapons, Roman soldiers were trained to use a bow.
They also are known to have used slings. In addition to using their slings
to fire stones, the Romans fashioned small lead pellets in the shape of almonds. Such a projectile would have some advantages over a sling stone
since it could be fired at a faster speed and could penetrate the flesh.

Defensive equipment for a Roman soldier included a helmet, armor,
and a shield. The Roman helmet followed the pattern of the Greek Thracian helmet with a metal cap and cheek pieces. The Romans also adopted
Greek armor, specifically the muscled cuirass, which had a breastplate and
backplate. This metal armor was used by the officers, but the troops were
protected with leather and sometimes metal strips. Mail armor, comprised
of small metal rings, was invented by the Celts and was used by wealthier
Roman soldiers in the third and second centuries BC. It could weigh fifteen kilograms (thirty-three lbs.). In the second century AD, the *lorica
segmentata* began to be used. This was an armor suit that had metal plates
covering the upper torso (one in front and one in back) and horizontal
strips of metal arranged over the lower torso. It could weigh nine kilograms (twenty lbs.), so it had the advantage of being much lighter than
the mail armor. Eventually, this evolved into armor comprised entirely of
metal strips.

At first, the Romans used a small, round shield known as a *clipeus*. In
the fourth century BC, this changed to the large, oval-shaped *scutum*. This
kind of shield was constructed from thin panels of wood that were glued
together; these were then covered with leather and sections of metal, including an iron rim. The *scutum* was larger than the *clipeus*, measuring
about 1.2 meters (four ft.) long and about seventy-five centimeters (2.5 ft.)
wide. This oval-shaped *scutum* lasted until the first century BC, when it
became rectangular. Later in Roman history, a variety of shapes were used.

E. THE JEWISH WORLD

The weapons and defensive equipment used by the Jews in the Hellenistic and Roman periods were not significantly different from those used by their neighbors. The OT Apocrypha mentions swords (Jdt 7:14; 1 Macc 5:51), spears (Jdt 7:10), slingers (Jdt 6:12), arrows (shot by angelic beings, 2 Macc 10:30), and armor (worn by angelic beings, 2 Macc 10:30). Philo mentions various offensive and defensive weapons in his writings, sometimes using them as metaphors. The Talmud mentions the sword in passing from time to time (e.g., b. ʿAbod. Zar. 25b), and b. Kelim 10.8 discusses the ability of various pieces of military equipment to be unclean; in this context helmets, cheek-pieces, javelins, spears, greaves, and breastplates are specifically mentioned.

The most extended treatment of weapons in early Jewish writings comes from one of the Dead Sea Scrolls. The War Scroll describes the weapons of the "Sons of Light" in minute detail, and essentially describes military equipment that was common in the Roman army. For short-range fighting, the soldiers would be armed with a straight, double-edged sword with a blade 1.5 cubits long. (As in the case of Goliath's weapons, the War Scroll refers to this sword as a *kîdôn*.) For mid-range fighting, they would have javelins and spears. Slings, bows, and arrows are also mentioned in the War Scroll. Defensively, the soldiers would be equipped with helmets, greaves, and shields that were rectangular and curved. Since the War Scroll describes the idealized battle between the "Sons of Light" and the "Sons of Darkness," there is no evidence that Jewish warriors were ever equipped in such a fashion. However, the scroll does provide us with a window into what a Jew who lived during this period imagined the ideal set of military equipment might be.

F. THE CHRISTIAN WORLD

Having been commanded by Jesus to love their enemies and to pray for their persecutors (Matt 5:44), the early Christian leaders were generally pacifists, though there is evidence of Christians in the Roman armies, including some who were martyred. We have, for example, the narrative of the Christians in the "Thundering Legion" of Marcus Aurelius, who claimed that it was their prayers that brought an end to a dangerous drought—a claim also made by the pagans. (See DeFelice.) There is also the riveting testimony of Julius, who served for twenty-seven years and fought in seven campaigns and who was martyred in 304 at Durostorum (see Musurillo, 261–63).

To be sure, the early Christians were more often the victims of the sword than the wielders of it. While Tertullian noted that there were Christians in the army camps (*Apol.* 37, 42), he advised Christians not to serve as soldiers in the Roman army, basing some of his arguments on Jesus's teaching that "all who draw the sword will die by the sword" (Matt 26:52) and on the fact that the Christian would be using the same type of spear that had pierced Jesus (*Cor.* 11). He argued, "But how will a *Christian man* war, nay, how will he serve even in peace, without a sword, which the Lord has taken away?" (*Idol.* 19).

Constantine's conversion in 312 was inspired by either a dream (according to Lactantius) or a vision (according to Eusebius) that he had on the eve of the battle against Maxentius at the Milvian Bridge outside of Rome. Constantine is reported to have seen the cross-shaped letter X, with its top bent over—that is, a monogram combining the first two Greek letters of the name of Christ, *chi* and *rho*. After his victory, he emblazoned this monogram on his *labarum*, or military banner, and had it affixed on the helmets of his soldiers, as is displayed on his coins.

Canon 3 of the Council of Arles (AD 314) decreed that a soldier who threw down his weapon in a time of peace should abstain from communion. The council also forbade soldiers who had become Christians from leaving the service. On the other hand, Christian soldiers were told that they could not use their weapons to kill. After his conversion, Martin of Tours (ca. 316–397) remained in the army and continued "to wear his sword, yet when an actual battle was imminent he refused to use it but volunteered to rebuke the charge of cowardice by standing unarmed in the front ranks" (Dörries, 113).

BIBLIOGRAPHY: L. Adkins and R. A. Adkins, *Handbook to Life in Ancient Greece* (1997); L. Adkins and R. A. Adkins, *Handbook to Life in Ancient Rome* (1994); M. Andronikos, "The Royal Tombs at Aigai (Vergina)," in *Philip of Macedon*, ed. M. B. Hatzopoulos and L. D. Loukopolos, trans. D. Hardy (1980), 188–231; M. Andronikos and M. Fotiadis, "The Royal Tomb of Philip II," *Arch* 31.5 (1978), 33–41; H. Carter and A. C. Mace, *The Tomb of Tut-ankh-Amen* (3 vols., 1923–33); F. M. Cross, Jr. and J. T. Milik, "A Typological Study of the El Khadr Javelin- and Arrow-Heads," *ADAJ* 3 (1956), 15–23; J. DeFelice, "The Rain Miracle of Marcus Aurelius," *FiHi* 26 (1994), 23–35; H. Dörries, *Constantine the Great*, trans. R. H. Bainton (1972); A. Eitan, "Vered Yeriḥo," in *The New Encyclopedia of Archaeological Excavations in the Holy Land*, ed. E. Stern (2008), V.2067–68; M. J. Fretz, "Weapons and Implements of Warfare," *ABD* VI.893–95; R. Gabriel and K. Metz, *From Sumer to Rome* (1991); R. Gonen, *Weapons of the Ancient World* (1975); M. Heltzer, "Akkadian *katinnu* and Hebrew *kīdōn*, 'Sword,'" *JCS* 41 (1989), 65–68; P. King and L. Stager, *Life in Biblical Israel* (2001); T. A. Madhloom, *The Chronology of Neo-Assyrian Art* (1970); M. E. L. Mallowan, *Nimrud and Its Remains* (1966); V. H. Matthews, *Manners and Customs in the Bible* (1988); W. E. McLeod, "An Unpublished Egyptian Composite Bow in the Brooklyn Museum," *AJA* 62 (1958), 397–401; J. T. Milik and F. M. Cross, Jr., "Inscribed Javelin-Heads from the Period of the Judges: A Recent Discovery in Palestine," *BASOR* 134 (1954), 5–15; A. Millard, "The Armor of Goliath," in *Exploring the Longue Durée: Essays in Honor of Lawrence E. Stager*, ed. by J. D. Schloen (2009), 337–43; J. D. Muhly, "How Iron Technology Changed the Ancient World and Gave the Philistines a Military Edge," *BAR* 8.6 (1982), 40–54; H. Musurillo, trans., *The Acts of the Christian Martyrs* (1972); H. H. Nelson, "The Epigraphic Survey, 1928–31," in *Medinet Habu Reports* (1931), 1–48; H. H. Nelson, "The Epigraphic Survey of the Great Temple of Medinet Habu (Seasons 1924–25 to 1927–28)," in *Medinet Habu, 1924–28* (1929), 1–36; H. Nelson, "The Naval Battle Pictured at Medinet Habu," *JNES* 2 (1943), 40–55; N. Pollard, "Weapons and Equipment, Roman," in *The Oxford Encyclopedia of Ancient Greece and Rome*, ed. M. Gagarin and E. Fantham (2010), VII.223–25; M. Quinn, "Weapons and Equipment, Greek," in Gagarin and Fantham (2010), VII.220–23; G. Rausing, *The Bow: Some Notes on Its Origin and Development* (2nd ed., 1997); S. Rodriquez, "The Arsenal of the Hebrew Kings and Their Neighbors," Ph.D. diss., The Southern Baptist Theological Seminary (2010); J. Russell, *Sennacherib's Palace Without Rival at Nineveh* (1991); J. M. Russell, *The Final Sack of Nineveh* (1998); B. V. Seevers, *Old Testament Warfare: The Organization, Weapons, and Tactics of Ancient Near Eastern Armies* (2013); O. R. Sellers, "Sling Stones of Biblical Times," *BA* 2 (1939), 41–44; A. M. Snodgrass, "An Historical Homeric Society?," *JHS* 94 (1974), 114–25; F. H. Stubbings, "Arms and Armour," in *A Companion to Homer*, ed. A. J. B. Wace and F. H. Stubbings (1962), 504–22; D. Ussishkin, *The Conquest of Lachish by Sennacherib* (1982); M. Ventris and J. Chadwick, *Documents in Mycenaean Greek* (2nd ed., 1973); J. W. Wevers, "Weapons and Implements of War," *IDB* IV.820–25; D. N. Wilber, *Persepolis* (rev. ed., 1989); Y. Yadin, *The Art of Warfare in Biblical Lands* (1963); Y. Yadin, "Goliath's Javelin and the מנור ארגים," *PEQ* 87 (1955), 58–69; Y. Yadin, ed., *The Scroll of the War of the Sons of Light Against the Sons of Darkness* (1962); E. Yamauchi, *Foes from the Northern Frontier: Invading Hordes from the Russian Steppes* (1982); E. Yamauchi, "Homer and Archaeology: Minimalists and Maximalists in Classical Context," in *The Future of Biblical Archaeology*, ed. J. K. Hoffmeier and A. Millard (2004), 69–90; E. Yamauchi, *Persia and the Bible* (1990).

SMR

See also ARMIES, METALLURGY, MILITARY TECHNOLOGY & TACTICS, TOOLS & UTENSILS, and WILD ANIMALS & HUNTING.

WIDOWS & ORPHANS

Widows and orphans, along with the poor and "strangers," were the most vulnerable to destitution in ancient societies. Because ancient societies placed many of the responsibilities for providing financial and physical security in the hands of adult men, women and children who lacked support from men were left to fend for themselves. Women were at risk for widowhood primarily because their husbands tended to be ten or so years their seniors or because their husbands engaged in the hazards of war. As for children, even if the mother was still alive, they could be considered orphans if they lost their father because they would have no male adult to provide for them. Children could lose their mother for many reasons, particularly due to the hazards of childbearing, since many women died in childbearing before age forty. In the Greco-Roman world the word "orphan" (Gk. *orphanos*, Lat. *orbus*) referred to a child who had lost his or her father. It was only in the Byzantine era that the word came to designate a child who had lost both parents.

There were many ways in which widows and orphans could be aided by their societies. In many cultures, widows were encouraged to remarry and orphans were assigned another male guardian. Both were also the recipients of almsgiving.

A. THE OLD TESTAMENT

The Hebrew word for widow, ʾalmānâ, refers to a woman with no husband, son, or means of financial support. It can also refer to a woman who was denied the support of her father-in-law because of his death or because his economic support was withdrawn, as in the case of Tamar. For Tamar, the first referenced widow in the OT, having her support withdrawn and being classified as a widow was tantamount to a curse. She was commanded by her father-in-law, Judah, to live as a widow in her father's house until Judah's third son, Shelah, grew up (Gen 38:11). Tamar had already been the wife of Er and Onan, Judah's older sons, but had no children by them (Gen 38:6–10). Sons were supposed to care for a widow in her old age, a responsibility that is included under the commandment to honor one's parents (Exod 20:12). But since some did not do so, widows were often left without support from their families. This is why in these cases the oaths of widows were considered binding without male sanction, as was the case for divorced women (Num 30:9).

According to the Mosaic law, "If brothers are living together and one of them dies without a son, his widow must not marry outside the family. Her husband's brother shall take her and marry her and fulfill the duty of a brother-in-law to her" (Deut 25:5). This provision, known as the levirate law, was not binding if the brother refused, though in this case he would be dishonored before the elders by the widowed woman (Deut 25:7–10). If a widow could not marry her brother-in-law, she was still free to marry again, except she could not marry a high priest, who was only allowed to marry a virgin (Lev 21:14).

The levirate law benefited widows because it allowed them to gain access to landed property and providers (their new husband and any sons they would have), who functioned as their means of support. The brother or other kinsman (the levirate law applied to next of kin as well) was therefore considered a kinsman-redeemer (gōʾēl) for the widow he would marry. Such was the case for Ruth, who was redeemed from a life of destitution by Boaz, a relative of her deceased husband, Mahlon. Though Boaz was not the next of kin to Mahlon, he did convince the man who was not to marry Ruth, since the latter feared that this would endanger his estate (Ruth 4:1–12). Not only did Boaz provide support for Ruth, but also it was anticipated that their son would, when he got older, provide support for Naomi, Ruth's widowed mother-in-law. When Obed was born, the women of Bethlehem said to Naomi, "'Praise be to the LORD, who this day has not left you without a guardian-redeemer. May he [Obed] become famous throughout Israel! He will renew your life and sustain you in your old age. For your daughter-in-law, who loves you and who is better to you than seven sons, has given him birth'" (Ruth 4:14b–15).

The Hebrew word for orphan, yātôm, comes from a root meaning to be deprived and alone and occurs over forty times in the OT. The term does not always imply that the child has lost both parents, although this is the case, for example, with Esther (Esth 2:7). Job 24:9 identifies a child as an orphan even though he or she has a mother and is "snatched from the breast." Moreover, the people of Jerusalem conquered by the Babylonians in 586 BC reflected their destitution and desperation by claiming that they had become fatherless and that their mothers had become widows (Lam 5:3). Whether an orphan lost both parents or just his or her father, the child was without protection and probably destitute.

In keeping with their belief that God cares for the oppressed and disenfranchised (Ps 10:14, 18), the ancient Israelites considered God to be the defender of the cause of the widow and the fatherless (the two are often linked in biblical and ancient Near Eastern texts), "giving them food and clothing" (Deut 10:18; see also Ps 68:5; Prov 23:10–11). God showed his care for the plight of the widow and the orphan by admonishing the Israelites about their social responsibility to those in their midst. Specifically, the Israelites were not to take advantage of widows or orphans; if they did and a widow or an orphan cried out to him, the Lord promised that he would turn the wives and children of those who took advantage into widows and orphans themselves (Exod 22:22–24). In Deut 24:17–18, God commands, "Do not deprive the foreigner or the fatherless of justice, or take the cloak of the widow as a pledge. Remember that you were slaves in Egypt and the LORD your God redeemed you from there. That is why I command you to do this." Indeed, whoever deprived the widow, alien, or fatherless of justice was subject to the curses pronounced by Moses upon the tribes gathered on Mount Ebal (Deut 27:19). The Lord repeatedly reminded Israel of the minimum requirements for living in the land he had given them—the Israelites were not to oppress the alien, the fatherless, or the widow, nor were they to shed innocent blood or follow after other gods (Jer 7:6–7; see Isa 1:17; Zech 7:10). However, he also made it clear that he would withdraw his pity from the fatherless and the widows of a godless nation (Isa 9:17). On the other hand, the Lord promised Zion that in the future she would "remember no more the reproach" of her widowhood (Isa 54:4). According to Jeremiah, God's protection even extended to Edomite orphans and widows, despite the destruction that the Lord promised would come upon this people (Jer 49:11).

During harvest time, grain, olives, and grapes were to be left for the fatherless and the widow (Deut 24:19–21). Along with Levites and aliens, orphans and widows were to receive a part of the tithe on the produce gathered and stored in towns every third year (Deut 14:28–29). These groups were to "eat . . . and be satisfied" (Deut 26:12).

Prophetic texts indicate that Israel and Judah did not always obey these admonitions to be generous to the downtrodden. Ezekiel 22:6–7 recounts Israel's sins, especially those of their princes, which included mistreating the fatherless and the widow. Malachi also recounts the Lord's anger and displeasure against Israel. He states, "So I will come to put you on trial. I will be quick to testify against sorcerers, adulterers and perjurers, against those who defraud laborers of their wages, who oppress the widows and the fatherless, and deprive the foreigners among you of justice, but do not fear me" (Mal 3:5). Lamentations opens with Jerusalem, destroyed and destitute, portrayed as a widow in mourning, a woman who once was a "queen among the provinces" but now is shamed internationally as a slave (Lam 1:1–2).

A reason for Job's sufferings, Eliphaz charges, is that Job sent widows away empty-handed and broke the strength of the fatherless (Job 22:9). Job contrasts himself, however, with the wicked who snatch suckling children who have no fathers and sell them into a life of slavery, and with those who seize a child of the poor for debt (Job 24:9). He later cites his actions of rescuing the poor when they cried for help and assisting the fatherless when no one else came to their aid as examples of his righteousness (Job 29:11–17). Additionally, Job replies that from his youth he treated the fatherless as a father would treat his own child and that he "guided the widow" (Job 31:17–18).

B. THE NEW TESTAMENT

The Sadducees came to Jesus with a question involving levirate marriage, widowhood, and childlessness. They told a story in which a man died without having had children and his widow was subsequently married to each of his six brothers, each of whom also died, one by one. None had children by the woman. Finally, the woman herself died (Matt 22:23–27). The Sadducees asked Jesus, "at the resurrection, whose wife will she be of the seven, since all of them were married to her?" (Matt 22:28). Jesus replied with a new teaching that, at the resurrection, no one will marry but all "will be like the angels in heaven" (vs. 30).

Widows are featured several times in the Gospels, often as women distinguished by their faithfulness. Anna, a prophetess and a member of the tribe of Asher, had been a widow for decades. She lived in the temple area and came upon Mary, Joseph, and the baby Jesus when he was forty days old and being presented to the Lord (Luke 2:26–38). Anna talked about the child Jesus "to all who were looking forward to the redemption of Jerusalem" (Luke 2:38). One time, when Jesus was watching as people put money in the temple treasury, he saw the rich throwing in large amounts and a poor widow putting in two very small copper coins (Mark 12:41–42). Jesus pointed this out to his disciples and told them that she gave more than the rich with all their wealth because "she, out of her poverty, put in everything—all she had to live on" (Mark 12:44). Jesus tells a story about a widow who persistently and vociferously pesters a judge for her rights, and presents this as a model for prayer (Luke 18:1–8). Her public cries for justice against an adversary may reflect a well-known pattern of abuse in ancient Israel—the oppression of the rich regarding economic matters pertaining to women who lacked the protection of male family members.

The ministry of giving to the needy, a hallmark of the early Christians, started with widows as the recipients. Both the Hebraic and Hellenistic widows were supposed to receive a distribution of food on a daily basis, but the Hellenistic widows were being neglected. The apostles saw this discrepancy and appointed seven men, including Stephen, to ensure that all the widows would be provided for (Acts 6:1–6).

Paul speaks extensively about widows in 1 Tim 5:3–16. He distinguishes between widows who have family members, especially children and grandchildren (who, Paul says, should provide for them), and those who do not have families who can support them. Paul strongly condemns those who do not take care of widows who belong to their own families, noting that a person who acts in this way "has denied the faith and is worse than an unbeliever" (1 Tim 5:8). His reasoning is that Christian families were being called upon to help care for widows in the believing community in order to free up the church financially to care for the widows who were without relatives.

Paul goes on to refer to the fact that in the early church some women were put on a list so that they could receive financial aid from the church. To make the list as a "real widow," a woman had to meet the following requirements: she had to be over sixty, faithful to her late husband, and well known for her good deeds. These good deeds included bringing up children, showing hospitality, washing the feet of the Lord's people, and helping those in trouble (1 Tim 5:9–10). These pious widows, like virgins, later acquired a recognized status in the church, though they did not have to be ordained nor were they required to take special vows. As for widows under sixty years of age, Paul recommends that they remarry in order to bear children and manage households (1 Tim 5:14). His commands concerning widows here would later be the basis for an order of widows in the early church.

The term *orphanos* appears twice in the NT. Jesus assures his disciples that he will not leave them as orphans—that is, abandoned, destitute, and helpless (John 14:18). James 1:27 states that the hallmark of "pure and faultless" religion is looking after widows and orphans.

C. THE NEAR EASTERN WORLD

Mesopotamia

The strong defense of widows and orphans that was legislated in Hebrew society was part of an ancient Near Eastern tradition traceable to the third millennium BC. The earliest mention of concern for orphans comes from Sumer. Uruinimgina (formerly known as Urukagina), the last king of Lagash (ca. 2351–2342 BC), set forth the first legal reforms in Mesopotamia. Because of the political situation of warring city-states, the wealthy had been oppressing the poor (see Kramer, 80–83). In an inscription dedicated to the god of Lagash, the king declared: "Uru-inimgina made a compact with the divine Nin-Girsu that the powerful man would not oppress the orphan (or) widow" (*COS* 2.152:408).

The prologue to the legal code of Ur-Nammu (ca. 2050 BC), founder of the Sumerian Third Dynasty of Ur, refers to the positive treatment that widows and orphans were afforded during his reign: "The orphan was not delivered up to the rich man; the widow was not delivered up to the mighty man; the man of one shekel was not delivered up to the man of one mina" (lines 162–168; *ANET*, 524).

The Code of Hammurabi (18th c. BC) likewise emphasizes the need to protect the helpless. On the stela that contains these laws, Hammurabi, one of the kings of the First Dynasty of Babylon, is depicted in bas-relief as the defender of the helpless. He receives the command to inscribe laws from Shamash, the sun god of justice; the king was believed to be the earthly representative of this deity. Law 177 reads,

> If a widow, whose children are minors, has made up her mind to enter the house of another, she may not enter without the consent of the judges; when she wishes to enter the house of another, the judges shall investigate the condition of her former husband's estate and they shall entrust her former husband's estate to her later husband and that woman and they shall have them deposit a tablet (to the effect that) they will look after the estate and also rear the young (children), without ever selling the household goods, since the purchaser who purchases the household goods of a widow's children shall forfeit his money, with the goods reverting to their owner. (*ANET*, 174)

Moreover, a widow was generally entitled to have gifts be set aside from her late husband's possessions (CH 172). In the epilogue of the Code, Hammurabi calls himself "the king of justice" and declares that he shelters his people so "that the strong might not oppress the weak, [and] that justice might be dealt the orphan (and) the widow" (col. 24, lines 59–61, 68; *ANET*, 178).

Egypt

Though there are numerous references to laws, including the reforms of Horemheb (1343–1315 BC), the last ruler of the 18th Dynasty (see *ARE* 2.31–33), and a reference to the codification of Egyptian laws under the Persian king Darius (522–486 BC), no law codes similar to those of

Mesopotamia have been preserved in Egypt. Therefore, our knowledge of widows and orphans in Egypt comes from literary sources.

As in other societies, in ancient Egypt widows and orphans were disadvantaged groups. Some widows remarried, some returned to their father's home, and some joined households of other relatives.

The two Egyptian words for orphan are *tfn(.t)* and *nmḥw*. Since orphans in Egyptian society were generally poor and helpless, kings and rulers felt an obligation to respond to their cries for help.

The sun god Re was viewed as a judge who protected the powerless segments of society. The king was seen as carrying out the will of Re and the other gods on earth. In *The Instruction for King Meri-ka-Re*, the king's father commands him to do the following: "Do justice whilst thou endurest upon earth. Quiet the weeper; do not oppress the widow; supplant no man in the property of his father" (*ANET*, 415). Similarly, in *The Instruction of King Amen-em-het*, the first pharaoh of the 12th Dynasty, the king tells his son and successor, "I gave to the destitute and brought up the orphan" (*ANET*, 418).

D. THE GRECO-ROMAN WORLD

Greece

In ancient Greek marriages, the bride's family was expected to pay a dowry for the bride. The dowry defrayed the expenses the groom's family would incur for the couple's new living arrangements and for the bride's clothes. Marriage and divorce were private matters. Marriage was simply the decision of two families mutually consenting that the new bride and groom be married, and divorce was a withdrawal of that consent. Among members of the upper classes, couples were married for political and financial reasons and divorced for the same. In a divorce, the bride's family often demanded a return of her dowry.

Upon the death of her husband, a widow could return to her father's house or remain in her husband's house if she had any sons. Once her sons came of age, the widow would be under their supervision. If her children were underage, she would be under the tutelage of their *kyrios*, their "master." That is, at all times, both women and children were dependent upon an adult male relative, who was the head of their family. A widow could take her dowry back to her father's home if she chose to do so, but her children would remain in her husband's household. This returning of a dowry to the widow's father meant the legal severance of her relationship with her dead husband's household. It was also not uncommon for a woman to be ejected from her husband's house at his death. A wealthy woman had more security in this situation because of her dowry, which stayed in her name and could be reused in the likely event of another marriage.

In ancient Greece, young widows were expected to remarry. A childless widow likewise was expected to remarry quickly. Dowries were given to widows who remarried. A dying husband might promise his wife to another man, as the story of Demosthenes's father illustrates (*In Aphobum* 1.4–6). Greek law stipulated that if a widow so chose, she could remarry and keep her own property and anything her former husband gave her, as long as there was an agreement written in the presence of three witnesses who were adults and free. However, if she took things belonging to her children, that was grounds for a trial.

If her husband died without giving her children, a widow was to keep the property she had brought to the marriage and half of whatever she had woven in the house. The lawful heirs likewise were to receive their portions. The widow could also take whatever her husband had given her, as long as there was a written agreement. If she took anything additional, though, it was grounds for a trial.

In legal documents, especially those from the Hellenistic era (4th–2nd c. BC), women and widows sometimes mentioned their vulnerability and pleaded with the head of the legal structure, the prefect, for mediation.

In the Greek public sphere, women "had no political rights and could take no part whatsoever in governments; they had no more rights than slaves" (Adkins and Adkins, 408). A woman's life was largely segregated from men outside her family and was confined to the home. While she had no rights in the public sphere, she had total control over the household and its slaves, and supervised the cooking, cleaning, the care of the sick, and the making of clothes. Widows, older women, and the women of Sparta had more freedom in general than younger women and women in other Greek city-states. Poor widows often had to work if they had no financial support after their husbands died.

The *Iliad* presents a chilling look into the lives of Greek war widows and orphans. The Trojan woman Andromache, when she learns of her husband Hector's death, laments for her infant son Astyanax,

> The day of orphanhood cuts a child off from the friends of his youth; ever is his head bowed low, and his cheeks are bathed in tears, and in his need the child goes up to his father's friends, plucking one by the cloak and another by the tunic; and of them that are touched with pity, one holds out his cup for a moment: his lips he wets, but his palate he wets not. And one whose father and mother still live thrusts him from the feast striking him with his hand, and reproaches him with reviling words: "Off with you, quick! No father of yours feasts in our company." (*Il.* 22.490–498)

In Euripides's play *Alcestis*, the wife, Alcestis, decides to lay down her life for her husband, not out of love but because she prefers death to the prospect of raising fatherless children (287–289).

The frequent wars in Greece left many orphans. In the time of Pericles, the city-state of Athens sought to support the orphans of soldiers who fell in battle by assuming responsibility for the education of these children until they could take responsibility for their own estates as adults. The support lasted until they came of age (cf. Thucydides, *Hist.* 2.46). At that time, during the Greater Dionysia, a citywide ceremony held in March, the grown children were honored as described in this proclamation:

> These young men, whose fathers died fighting like the brave warriors they were, have been supported by the State until now, when they come of age: so today the State puts this armour [*panoplion*] upon them, and sends them forth into life, wishing them all good fortune, and invites them to seats of honour in the theatre (*proedria*). (Flacelière, 269)

While the ceremony represented a rite of passage, it also honored the deeds of the orphans' fathers, who had died in earlier wars.

The care of widows and orphans in both Greece and Rome was a private affair and was linked to charity for the poor. In Greece and Rome, the term "orphan" applied only to the offspring of freeborn citizens, who were quite likely heirs of land. Orphans received a guardianship, often by a civil judge. However, fathers sometimes stipulated a specific guardian in their wills, for example, a close relative. This guardian was called an *epitropos* in Greek and a *curator* in Latin.

A guardian took responsibility for providing an orphan with his or her living essentials and education. A guardian likewise served as trustee for the orphan's estate until he or she came of age. Guardianship was considered a virtuous responsibility. Throughout his works, Plato emphasizes the important role the state played in the protection of orphans' rights of property and inheritance (*Leg.* 927). Aristotle writes that the Athenian chief magistrate, known as the archon,

> also supervises orphans and heiresses and women professing to be with child after the husband's death, and he has absolute power to fine offenders against them or to bring them before the Jury-court. He grants leases of houses belonging to orphans and heiresses until they are fourteen years of age, and receives the rents, and he exacts maintenance for children from guardians who fail to supply it. (*Ath. pol.* 56.7)

In Athens, a concerned citizen could prosecute a guardian for misconduct concerning an orphan's inheritance before the *boulē*, the Council.

The Greeks seem to have viewed childhood as merely a preparatory stage in life, and children had few legal rights. Even male children, who might be heirs, resembled women and slaves in Greek society in that they had no legal rights before they became of age. Boys eventually received full integration within society, but girls lacked a similar enlargement of their social status or identity upon maturity. A girl who was an orphan was quite vulnerable, for she was dependent on the integrity of her guardian. However, a male orphan could claim his inheritance at age eighteen. Scholars think that while the lives of many orphans were bleak, the strength of the family unit was such that orphans were rarely destitute.

Even if a young woman had already married, if she became an orphan she could be taken from her husband by her father's relatives. This is addressed by the Attic orator Isaeus, who writes,

> The law ordains that daughters who have been given in marriage by their father and are living with their husbands—and who can judge better than a father what is to his daughter's interest?—in spite of the fact that they are thus married, shall, if their father dies without leaving them legitimate brothers, pass into the legal power of their next-of-kin; and indeed it has frequently happened that husbands have been thus deprived of their own wives. (3.64–65)

Plutarch tells of the two daughters of Aristides. After his death, they were awarded by Athens a pension of three obols per day (worth half a drachma, which was a typical day's wages). This was subsequently increased to one drachma on the recommendation of Demetrios of Phaleron (*Arist.* 27). Quite likely the increase was in recognition of their father's fine services to his *polis*, or city-state.

Rome

For a Roman woman, widowhood meant a drastic change in status. If she had the title of mother of the family (*mater familias*), she lost this title when her husband died, unless she had living sons. The wording specifically was this: "Nor can a widow be called by this title [*mater familias*] who has no sons" (Festus, *De verborum significatu* 112.29 L; Sebesta, 50). Widowhood also mandated a change of dress. Instead of wearing a *palla*, a traditional mantle, a widow covered her head with a *ricinium*. Olson comments: "A few ancient literary sources indicate that the Roman widow also had a special head covering or mantle. Usually called the *ricinium* or *recinium* by modern authors, it seems to have been a mantle worn over the shoulders and head, assumed in place of the *palla*" (Olson, 42). Explaining that the word *ricinium* comes from *reicere*, "to throw back" (Sebesta, 50),

Varro (116–27 BC) had provided these insights: "It is so called from the fact that women use it double-folded, that is, they throw backward half of it" (*De lingua latina* 5.132).

According to Roman funerary laws, a husband should be mourned for ten months, and a close relative for eight months. Parents and children over age six should be mourned for a year. Those in mourning in the Roman Empire were to refrain from going to dinner parties and from wearing fine clothing and jewelry. Widows were also prohibited from remarrying during the period of mourning to ensure that they were not pregnant, but widowers could remarry immediately. However, under Augustus women were also penalized if they did not remarry within a year (Justinian, *Corp.* 2.11.15), as stipulated in Augustus's *Lex Julia de maritandis ordinibus* (18 BC); this deadline was later lengthened to two years in a revision of these laws concerning marriage, the *Lex Papia Poppaea* (AD 9). However, if a widow decided not to remarry, she was respected for remaining celibate as an *univira*, meaning "the wife of one man only" (Sebesta, 50), until her own death. Whether she wore the *ricinium* as part of her daily attire past the single year of mourning or for the rest of her life is not addressed in historical sources.

Husbands frequently made provision in their wills for their widows and heirs. For example, an heir might be required to give the widow annual support during her lifetime. Sometimes, a young widow with children was left the usufruct, or right to use property, of the estate (*Dig. Just.* 33.1.5; 1.21.2; 2.22; 2.32.2; 10.2). Scholars posit that widowhood may indeed have offered an established, wealthy matron much freedom, or at least more freedom than she had during other seasons of her life. Some widows were mistresses of their own houses and their own patrimonies. They could be proud and even imperious, receiving interest from suitors vying for their inheritances. Having the opportunity to take lovers, some did so openly.

According to A. R. Hands,

> the provisions relating to orphans . . . , in both the Greek and Roman worlds, dealt mainly with the protection of property-rights and so concerned only orphans of the propertied class; they had little or nothing to do with the welfare of orphans as such, except in the case of war-orphans. (Hands, 73–74)

We have evidence from papyri from Egypt during the Roman era (1st–4th c. AD) of the appeals of orphans to officials complaining of the mismanagement of their inheritance by their guardians. In the papyri the word *orphanos* primarily refers to children who had lost their fathers; it was not until the age of Justinian that the word came to refer to children who had lost both parents (Kotsifou, 346).

A papyrus dated to AD 297 records the plea of an orphan named Didyme: "After some time, my mother also died, while I was still under-age and already an orphan. . . . In the meantime, my mother's brothers from the same mother plotted together with useless and foolish stupidity, intending to cheat me" (P. Oxy. 34 2713; cited in Kotsifou, 358).

From the archives of a farmer who lived in Theadelphia near the Faiyum area of Egypt (ca. AD 300), we learn about a certain Sakaon who defrauded a widow. When one of his shepherds died, even before he was buried, Sakaon came and stole his sheep and goats. The widow protested in vain to the authorities for redress (Pap. Sakaon 36; Horsley 1983, 20).

E. THE JEWISH WORLD

A Jewish widow could continue to live in her deceased husband's house, or she could return to her father's house. She was to be supported by the estate of her deceased husband, and generally her claims for support outweighed those of his creditors. If she remained in her late husband's household, another man, possibly her son, was appointed to manage its affairs. On the other hand, if she did return to her father's house, the legal relationship to her late husband's household was ended. During the Hellenistic period, a wife was permitted a portion of her own property during her marriage, and she could keep a part of her dowry if she was widowed.

The minimum *ketubah* (the contract detailing the woman's rights during and after marriage) payment of two hundred *zûzîn* was about equal to eight months of wages for a day-laborer (*m. Ketub.* 5:1). It was generally not enough to support a widow; consequently, if she had only the minimum, she had to return to her father's house and would probably seek to remarry. However, if her husband had added to her *ketubah*, or if she had inherited wealth, she probably would have preferred not to remarry, because she would have had enough means to live independently. However, just as Paul had done, rabbinic teachers encouraged widows to remarry during their fertile years. Yet, if a woman became a widow while she was nursing, she could not remarry until the child was twenty-four months old (*b. Ketub.* 60a–b).

A widow was to be maintained by her deceased husband's heirs, and her handiwork was theirs (*b. Ketub.* 43a, 80a). They were also responsible to provide for medical treatment, which was considered maintenance, if she needed it. If the treatment was of a limited liability, it could be deducted from her *ketubah*, but a treatment that did not have a limited liability was regarded as maintenance (*b. Ketub.* 52b). A widow could continue to sell land for her maintenance until only the estate equal to the value of her *ketubah* remained (*b. Ketub.* 97a). Her orphaned children could not sell her dwelling, but it was not their responsibility to rebuild it if it collapsed (*b. Ketub.* 103a). It was the duty of the widow's heirs who inherited her *ketubah* to bury her (*b. Ketub.* 81a). Levirate marriages were practiced, as is assumed in the Mishnaic tractate *Yebamot.* Concerning them Josephus writes,

> for this will at once be profitable to the public welfare, houses not dying out and property remaining with the relatives, and it will moreover bring the women an alleviation of their misfortune to live with the nearest kinsman of their former husbands. (*Ant.* 4.254–255)

As Deut 25:7–10 stipulates, if the brother of the late husband refuses to marry his brother's widow, she has to bring him before the elders, and if he continues to refuse to marry her, she is to pull off his sandal, spit in his face, and speak shameful words. The rabbis called this situation *ḥalitzah.* Josephus adds that the *ḥalitzah* is to be performed whether the reasons for the refusal are "slight or serious" (*Ant.* 4.255) and that the brother has outraged the memory of the deceased; furthermore, the woman is free to remarry. While Lev 21:14 forbids a high priest from marrying a widow, rabbinic law maintains that if the appointment as high priest should occur after the marriage, the priest may keep the woman as his wife (*b. Yebam.* 59a). When a father passed away, his estate would be inherited by his orphaned children. He could even leave instructions that his wife not be buried at the expense of his orphaned children's estate upon her passing (*b. Ketub.* 48a).

The apocryphal book of Judith provides a picture of a beautiful and wealthy woman, Judith, who decides to remain celibate all her life after her husband's death at a young age. Her husband provided her with gold, silver, slaves, cattle, and fields—an estate she maintains well. She is widely respected for her beauty, wealth, wisdom, and virtue. She is a descendant of Simeon and has been a widow for three years and four months when the story opens. The text tells us that she spends her widowhood dressed in widows' clothing of sackcloth; she fasts regularly except for on the Sabbath and its preceding day, as well as on the new moon and its preceding day (Jdt 8:1–8). She is described as shapely and beautiful, so much so that Israelite and Assyrian men equally "admired her beauty" (Jdt 10:7; see also vs. 14). In the story, Nebuchadnezzar, king of Assyria, seeks to conquer the world (Jdt 1–2). His general, Holofernes, is very successful and meets virtually no opposition until he reaches Bethulia, a town at the gateway to the corridor leading to Jerusalem. Holofernes cuts off Bethulia's water supply and waits. The town slowly runs out of water. The townspeople decide to surrender in three days if the Lord does not intervene. Judith secretly asks the leaders for permission to leave the city with her maid, stating that she has a secret plan to save Bethulia. The city leaders let them leave. Judith successfully saves her town, the temple, and her nation by beheading Holofernes in his own tent after a banquet. Despite the fact that many men desire Judith, she remains celibate and chaste throughout her long life and dies at age 105 (Jdt 16:22–23).

Ben Sira urges those blessed with affluence to beware of exploiting the powerless of society, including widows, orphans, the poor, and the oppressed (Sir 35:14–20). The Lord has a special love for these people. God cannot be bribed by expensive offerings. Especially loathsome are offerings that come from extortion of the weak and disadvantaged (vs. 12). Furthermore, Ben Sira asks, "Do not the tears of the widow run down her cheek as she cries out against him who has caused them to fall?" (Sir 35:15). Likewise, the book of 2 Esdras insists on justice for the widow and protection of the orphan (2 Esd 2:20). Second Maccabees states that Judah the Maccabee shared some spoils of war with orphans and widows (2 Macc 8:28, 30).

Philo declares:

> Lowliness and weakness are attributes of the widow, the orphan and the incomer [epēlytos, i.e., "proselyte"]. It is to these that the supreme king who is invested with the government of all should administer justice. . . . For when the Revealer has hymned the excellences of the Self-existent in this manner "God the great and powerful . . . ," he proceeds to say for whom the judgement is executed—not for satraps and despots and men invested with power by land and sea, but for the "incomer, for orphan and widow." (*Spec.* 4.176–177)

F. THE CHRISTIAN WORLD

In keeping with Paul's commands in 1 Tim 5, early Christian social ethics included a concern for the needs of any widow within the believer's family, even if one had no legally binding obligation to support her. In the early church, piety worked both ways. The widow was to be known for a lifetime of pious deeds, and those ministering to her and providing for her had an opportunity to support her and therefore practice piety as well.

As mentioned above, Paul's commands became the basis for an official order of widows in the early church. Guidelines for entrance into the order are given by Paul in various letters. If a widow who has been supported by the church remarries, her support from the church ends (1 Tim 5:11–14). If a widow decides to remarry, she may do so without blame, "but he [her new husband] must belong to the Lord," Paul writes (1 Cor 7:39). It may have been the case that when churches met in houses, women may sometimes have exercised leadership (e.g., Lydia in Acts 16), but when churches acquired their own buildings, women's leadership became more controversial. After the NT era, an order of ministering widows emerged (see Thurston; cf. Spencer).

In general, the teachings of the Christian church enhanced the value of women and their place in societies throughout the Mediterranean world. (See Witherington.) The church condemned divorce, incest, infanticide, and adultery, and its stance on these issues made the position of women throughout the Mediterranean world more secure. The church had a high view of widowhood and did not, unlike Augustus, force widows into remarrying or fine them if they did not find new husbands. Moreover, Augustus's laws that promoted remarriage for widows were abolished by Constantine.

The church took the fifth commandment of honoring one's parents very seriously by honoring the widow (see Winter 1994, 75). If a woman was deemed "a real widow," then the church would "come to the rescue by providing benefactions for the 'widow of God'" (Winter, 75). The *Shepherd of Hermas* states that "good deeds" include "helping widows, [and] looking after orphans and the needy" (*Herm. Mand.* 8). The Shepherd writes that widows and orphans should be cared for and not despised (*Herm. Simil.* 1). He warns that there are deacons who rob widows and orphans of their livelihood and thus wrongly administer their office (*Herm. Simil.* 9.26). He also instructs his Christian audience to combine fasting and charity by tallying up the money they would otherwise have spent on food and giving it to a widow, an orphan, or someone likewise destitute (*Herm. Simil.* 5.3).

Ignatius, bishop of Antioch, and Polycarp, bishop of Smyrna, indicate that an order of widows existed in the early church according to the Pauline instructions (Ign. *Smyrn.* 13; Pol. *Phil.* 4:3). Over the course of time, it seems to have merged into the order of deaconesses or into an order of virgins. In Archelais, Cappadocia, the tombstone of the *diakonos* Maria, which dates to the sixth century or possibly earlier, reads as follows:

> Here lies Maria the deacon, of pious and blessed memory, who in accordance with the statement of the apostle reared children, practised hospitality, washed the feet of the saints, distributed her bread to the afflicted. Remember her, Lord, when you come in your kingdom. (Horsley 1982, 194)

Note that many of the good deeds attributed to her are those mentioned by Paul in 1 Tim 5:10 concerning widows.

Tertullian as a concession maintained that it was better for a widow or a widower to remarry if either could not keep continence (*Mon.* 3). In one of his treatises Tertullian advised a fellow Christian, recently widowed and concerned that he needed "a consort in domestic works," to look among the widows for a new "spiritual wife" (*Exh. cast.* 12). Tertullian described such a woman as "one fair in faith, dowered with poverty, sealed with age" (ibid.).

But to his own wife Tertullian advised against her remarrying if he should die first. "Therefore when, through the will of God, the husband is deceased, the marriage likewise, by the will of God, deceases. Why should *you* restore what God has put an end to?" (*Ux.* 1.7). Tertullian warned those who were spiritual against remarrying, because then one would have two spouses, "one in spirit, one in flesh" (*Exh. cast.* 11). As he embraced the teachings of the rigorist Montanist sect (ca. AD 205), he became more rigid in his opposition to digamy, i.e., remarriage after a spouse's death. (See Le Saint.)

Aristides, a second-century AD apologist and philosopher, defended his fellow Christians before the emperor Hadrian (AD 76–138) by saying that "they love one another, and from widows they do not turn away their esteem; and they deliver the orphan from him who treats him harshly" (*Apology of Aristides* 15). The *Letter of Barnabas* states that those walking in the "way of darkness" "attend not with just judgment to the widow and orphan" (20). Records show that by AD 248, the Church of Rome, then under bishop Cornelius, had a staff of 155 clergy who supported and were in charge of one thousand five hundred widows and poor plus the regular congregation.

By the second century AD, the role of widows in the church involved actively engaging in prayer and charitable deeds. The Syrian document *Didascalia Apostolorum* (*Teaching of the Apostles*), which dates from the third century AD, highlights the intercessory role of widows in this manner: "A widow who wishes to please God sits within her house and meditates night and day, offering prayer and intercession with purity of heart before the Lord. And she obtains whatever she asks, since her prayer is pure, and her mind is fixed on this alone" (15.6; Stewart-Sykes, 187). According to Hippolytus (AD 160–235), widows were not ordained by the laying on of hands, since this feature of ordination was reserved for those administering the Eucharist and baptism; instead, widows were simply appointed by name (*Trad. ap.* 10).

Canon 100 of *Statuta Ecclesiae Antiqua* (5th c. AD) reads:

> Widows or nuns who are chosen for the ministry of baptising women should be trained for that responsibility in such a way that they are able to explain in clear and sensible language to uneducated peasant women at the time of their baptism how they should reply to the questions of the person baptizing them and how they should live after they have received baptism. (Lee, 263)

John Chrysostom points out that the widow of Zarephath

> gave more to hospitality, than our father Abraham. For she 'ran' not 'unto the herd,' as he [Gen 18:17], but by that 'handful' [1 Kgs 17:12] outstripped all that have been renowned for hospitality. For in this was his excellence, that he set himself to do that office; but hers, in that for the sake of the stranger she spared not her children even, and that too, though she looked not for the things to come. (*Hom. 2 Cor.* 19.4)

Chrysostom encourages his parishioners to safeguard their riches by giving them to the poor. According to him, the best way to manage one's wealth is to turn it over to widows, orphans, the sick, and prisoners (*Exp. Ps.* 48.3).

The so-called *Apostolic Constitutions* (4th c. AD) decreed that those who have no children should adopt orphans and take them into their care as their own children:

> When any Christian becomes an orphan, whether it be a young man or a maid, it is good that some one of the brethren who is without a child should take the young man, and esteem him in the place of a son; and he that has a son about the same age, and that is marriageable, should marry the maid to him: for they which do so perform a great work, and become fathers to the orphans, and shall receive the reward of this charity from the Lord God. (4.1)

The document continues:

> Do you therefore, O bishops, be solicitous about their [that is, the orphans'] maintenance, being in nothing wanting to them; exhibiting to the orphans the care of parents; to the widows the care of husbands. . . . have a greater care of the orphans, that nothing may be wanting to them; and that as to the maiden, till she arrives at the age of marriage, and you give her in marriage to a brother: to the young man assistance, that he may learn a trade. (4.2)

Gregory of Nazianzus (ca. AD 330–390) expressed his concern for orphans in his letters. He appealed to a Christian magistrate as follows:

> All the other favours which I have received I know to be due to your kindness; and may God reward you for them with His own mercies; and may one of these be, that you may discharge your office of prefect with good fame and splendour from beginning to end. In what I now ask I come rather to give than to receive, if it is not arrogant to say so. I personally introduce poor Philumena to you, to entreat your justice, and to move you to the tears with which she afflicts my soul. She herself will explain to you in what and by whom she has been wronged, for it would not be right for me to bring accusations against any one. But this much it is necessary for me to say, that widowhood and orphanhood have a right to the assistance of all right-minded men, and especially of those who have wife and children, those great pledges of pity, since we—ourselves only men—are set to judge men. (*Ep.* 104)

Although the word for orphanage does not appear in the Egyptian papyri, monasteries in Egypt served as de facto orphanages. The first officially named *orphanotropheion* was established in Constantinople ca. AD 350 by Zotikos. As such institutions developed in the Byzantine world, some even accepted non-Christian orphans.

It is notable that there are no laws applying to orphans in the great Theodosian Code (AD 439). Only with the great Byzantine emperor Justinian (d. AD 565) was it decreed:

> The superintendents of orphan asylums [shall] discharge the duties of guardians and curators to the extent that they can sue and be sued with reference to the property belonging to their establishments, or to the orphans as individuals, without being obliged to furnish security. They shall receive property belonging to said orphans, or the establishments to which they are attached, in the presence of the public registrars, or by means of documents drawn up in this Royal City [Constantinople] . . . and if the superintendents should deem it necessary to alienate such property, they must keep the purchase-money for the orphans, or employ it for their benefit in the purchase of other things, and they shall not be obliged to render any accounts of guardianship or curatorship. (*Nov.* 131.15; Scott, 136)

BIBLIOGRAPHY: L. Adkins and R. A. Adkins, *Handbook to Life in Ancient Greece* (1997); R. G. Branch, "Biblical Views: Biblical Widows—Groveling Grannies or Teaching Tools?" *BAR* 39.1 (2013), 28, 71; K. M. Campbell, *Marriage and Family in the Biblical World* (2003); A. L. Connolly, "'The weaker sex,'" *NewDocs* 4 (1987), 131–33; C. Fensham, "Widow, Orphan, and the Poor in Ancient Near Eastern Legal and Wisdom Literature," *JNES* 21 (1962), 129–39; R. Flacelière, *Daily Life in Greece at the Time of Pericles*, trans. P. Green (1966); G. W. Forell, *History of Christian Ethics* (1979); J. F. Gardner and T. Wiedemann, ed., *The Roman Household: A Sourcebook* (1991); R. Garland, *The Greek Way of Life* (1993); L. Guy, *Introducing Early Christianity: A Topical Survey of Its Life, Beliefs and Practices* (2011); A. R. Hands, *Charities and Social Aid in Greece and Rome* (1968); G. H. R. Horsley, "Maria the *diakonos*," *NewDocs* 2 (1982), 193–95; G. H. R. Horsley, "A widow's plight," *NewDocs* 3 (1983), 20; C. Kotsifou, "Papyrological Perspectives on Orphans in the World of Late Ancient Christianity," in *Children in Late Ancient Christianity*, ed. C. R. Horn and R. R. Phenix (2009), 339–73; S. N. Kramer, *The Sumerians* (1963); A. D. Lee, *Pagans & Christians in Late Antiquity: A Sourcebook* (2000); M. R. Lefkowitz and M. B. Fant, *Women's Life in Greece and Rome: A Source Book in Translation* (3rd ed., 2005); W. Le Saint, trans. and ed., *Tertullian: Treatises on Marriage and Remarriage* (1951); T. A. J. McGinn, "Widows, Orphans, and Social History," *JRA* 12 (1999), 617–32; T. S. Miller, *The Orphans of Byzantium: Child Welfare in the Christian Empire* (2003); K. S. Nash, "Orphan," *EDB* 994; K. S. Nash, "Widow," *EDB* 1377–78; J. Neusner and W. S. Green, ed., "Widow," in *Dictionary of Judaism in the Biblical Period: 450 B.C.E. to 600 C.E.* (1999), 670–71; K. Olson, *Dress and the Roman Woman* (2008); R. D.

Patterson, "The Widow, Orphan, and the Poor in the Old Testament and the Extra-Biblical Literature," *BSac* 130 (1973), 223–34; H. Ringgren, "יָתוֹם *yāṯôm*," *TDOT* VI.477–81; S. P. Scott, trans., *Justinian: New Constitutions* (2 vols.; 2014 repr. of 1932 ed.); J. L. Sebesta, "Symbolism in the Costume of the Roman Woman," in *The World of Roman Costume*, ed. J. L. Sebesta and L. Bonfante (1994), 46–53; J.-A. Shelton, *As the Romans Did: A Sourcebook in Roman Social History* (1998); A. B. Spencer, *Beyond the Curse: Women Called to Ministry* (1985); A. Stewart-Sykes, *The Didascalia apostolorum: An English Version with Introduction and Annotation* (2009); D. T. Thornton, "'Saying What They Should Not Say': Reassessing the Gravity of the Problem of the Younger Widows (1 Tim 5:11–15)," *JETS* 59 (2016), 119–29; B. B. Thurston, *The Widows: A Women's Ministry in the Early Church* (1989); K. J. Torjesen, "Clergy and Laity," in *The Oxford Handbook of Early Christian Studies* (2008), 389–405; P. Veyne, ed., *A History of Private Life I: From Pagan Rome to Byzantium*, trans. A. Goldhammer (1987); B. W. Winter, *Seek the Welfare of the City: Christians as Benefactors and Citizens* (1994); B. Witherington III, *Women in the Earliest Churches* (1991).

RGB and MRW

See also ABORTION, ADOPTION, CHILDBIRTH & CHILDREN, DEATH, DIVORCE, INFANTICIDE & EXPOSURE, INHERITANCE, MARRIAGE, NURSES & WET NURSES, VIRGINS & VIRGINITY, and WEALTH & POVERTY.

WILD ANIMALS & HUNTING

Hunting has a very early history in the biblical world. Literary materials and archaeological remains have shed considerable light on this activity, which was carried on for subsistence, sport, and the protection of human life. Wild animals such as lions, wolves, bears, foxes, and wild dogs continued to pose a danger to humans and their domesticated animals. Lions in particular became the object of hunts by kings in the Near East, while boars challenged the Greeks. The Romans captured, imported, displayed, and killed thousands of wild beasts as spectacles.

A. THE OLD TESTAMENT

In the tradition of the Israelites, hunting is traced to the pre-Abrahamic character Nimrod (Gen 10:8–9). Hunting (Heb. *ṣayid*; cf. *ṣayyād*, "hunter") during the patriarchal period was undertaken primarily for the acquiring of food, clothing, and implements. It is mentioned a number of times in the patriarchal narratives. Ishmael, a desert-dweller, became an archer (Gen 21:20). Isaac, who had a taste for wild game, favored Esau, a "skillful hunter" (Gen 25:27, 28).

After the account of Israel's settlement in Canaan, the Bible contains little direct information about hunting as a means of supporting life. No longer a seminomadic people, the Israelites turned mainly, though not exclusively, to agricultural pursuits. In regard to hunting, the Law of Moses specifies that if an animal or bird is to be killed and eaten it must be of the "clean" variety (Lev 11:1–47; Deut 14:1–21) and its blood must be drained and covered with earth (Lev 17:13). Acceptable wild game included "the deer, the gazelle, the roe deer, the wild goat, the ibex, the antelope and the mountain sheep" (Deut 14:5). Solomon may have maintained hunters to secure daily provisions of deer, gazelles, roebucks, and choice fowl for all his household (1 Kgs 4:23).

Perhaps such an activity is reflected in the name Pokereth-Hazzebaim (lit., "the gazelle hunter"), one of the descendants of the servants of Solomon (Ezra 2:57). Some individuals were named after wild animals, such as Zibiah, "gazelle of Yahweh" (2 Kgs 12:1||2 Chr 24:1) and Shaphan, "hyrax" or "rock badger" (2 Kgs 22:3). One individual is named Ariel, "lion of God" (Ezra 8:16).

During OT times, people encountered wild animals in a variety of places; some situations revealed human bravery, but others led to a deadly attack by the beast. David states he "killed both the lion and the bear" that had carried off sheep from his father's flock (1 Sam 17:34–36). Samson tore a young lion apart that suddenly came roaring toward him (Judg 14:5–6). Benaiah, a "valiant fighter," went down into a pit and killed a lion (2 Sam 23:20). However, sometimes lions killed people (1 Kgs 13:24; 20:36). The dense thicket area along the Jordan River provided an excellent habitat for wild beasts such as lions (Jer 49:19). Other animals were also feared, including bears (2 Sam 17:8; 2 Kgs 2:24), leopards, wolves, jackals, foxes, and other beasts who might endanger the security of the community.

Hunting methods varied. In situations of self protection, animals were sometimes killed by a sling (1 Sam 17:40), a club (Ps 23:4), or even with the bare hands (Judg 14:6). Normally, however, in animal hunts either bows and arrows (Gen 27:3), nets (Job 19:6; Isa 51:20), or camouflaged pits (Ps 35:7; Ezek 19:8) were used.

Snaring of animals (cf. Sir 27:20), sometimes using a noose of rope (Job 18:10), was another common hunting method. Samson used some kind of trapping device to catch three hundred foxes (Judg 15:4). Spears and swords may also have played a part in dispatching certain animals. Occasionally animals were driven by beaters into confined areas, pits, or traps (cf. Jer 16:16). Archaeologists have discovered the remains of mass-hunting game traps, which funneled herds into restricted areas with walls of stones, around En Gedi and in the Negev (Bar-Oz; Hadas et al.).

Numerous species of birds migrated north-south through Syro-Palestine in the fall and spring since their wings were not strong enough to support them across the Mediterranean Sea. Birds were usually trapped by nets (Pss 124:7; 140:5; Jer 5:26; Amos 3:5), although sticks or stones were also used occasionally. (See the section on Egypt below.) Captured birds were sometimes put in cages (Jer 5:27). The partridge is the only bird specifically mentioned in Scripture as an object of hunting (1 Sam 26:20). It is likely that the reason the Israelites were able to gather such a large number of quails in the wilderness was because of the migratory fatigue of the flocks (see Exod 16:13; Num 11:31–33).

Job 40:15–41:34 is a poetic description of two huge beasts, the "behemoth" (40:15) and the "leviathan" (41:1), which are thought by some scholars to be the hippopotamus and the crocodile. Though there are numerous references to ivory in the OT (see IVORY), the elephant is not mentioned.

The lion pit into which Daniel was cast (Dan 6:7) may reflect the presence of a royal zoo during Nebuchadnezzar's reign (6th c. BC). Daniel interprets two of the king's dreams as presaging the succession of four kingdoms. In Dan 2, Nebuchadnezzar sees a composite statue made of four materials, and in his second dream (Dan 7) he sees four beasts: one like a lion (7:4), one like a bear (7:5), one like a leopard (7:6), and a fourth beast that has ten horns (7:7). The first kingdom is explicitly identified as Babylon. Those who believe that the book of Daniel is a pseudonymous composition from the second century BC identify the other three kingdoms as Persian, Median, and Hellenistic. Others, who hold that Daniel is an authentic prophecy from the sixth century BC, identify the three kingdoms as Medo-Persian, Hellenistic, and Roman.

B. THE NEW TESTAMENT

There are no direct references to hunting in the NT, and only a few uses of words related to hunting, as, for example, when the Pharisees seek "to trap" (*pagideusōsin*) Jesus (Matt 22:15). Paul quotes Ps 69:22, which contains David's wish that the table of his enemies might become "a snare and a trap" (Rom 11:9). He warns that those who want to get rich fall into "temptation and a trap" (1 Tim 6:9).

The NT does, however, contain a number of references to wild animals, in reference to their being both dangerous and symbols of danger. The Marcan account of Jesus's forty days of trial in the wilderness (but not the Matthean or Lucan accounts) reports that "he was with the wild animals" (Mark 1:13). Jesus notes that in contrast to foxes, who have holes, and birds, who have nests, he has nowhere to lay his head (Matt 8:20||Luke 9:58). He addresses Herod Antipas, the ruler of Galilee, as "that fox" (Luke 13:32).

Jesus declares that he is sending his disciples as sheep among wolves (Matt 10:16; cf. Luke 10:3). He warns of false prophets who will appear as wolves in sheep's clothing (Matt 7:15).

Paul issues a similar warning upon his departure from Asia Minor (Acts 20:29). He harshly describes his opponents at Philippi as (wild) "dogs" (Phil 3:2). Peter uses a proverbial saying about a dog returning to its vomit to denounce false teachers (2 Pet 2:22). Evildoers who are described as "dogs" are to be excluded from the Sacred City (Rev 22:15).

Paul speaks figuratively of fighting "with wild beasts at Ephesus," at the end of his long discourse on the resurrection (1 Cor 15:32). In his final letter, Paul declares that he was "delivered from the lion's mouth" (2 Tim 4:17), probably an allusion to his deliverance from a trial before Nero at Rome. Peter declares that the devil "prowls around like a roaring lion, looking for someone to devour" (1 Pet 5:8). Some of the heroes listed in Heb 11 were able to shut "the mouths of lions" by faith (Heb 11:33).

The bear is mentioned only once in the NT (Rev 13:2). In the book of Revelation, one of the four "living creatures" who surround the throne of God is described as having an appearance "like a lion" (Rev 4:7), the infernal locusts have teeth like those of lions (Rev 9:8), and the deadly horses have heads like lions (Rev 9:17). A mighty angel utters a shout that is like "the roar of a lion" (Rev 10:3). The trimphant Christ is described as "the Lion of the tribe of Judah" (Rev 5:5).

C. THE NEAR EASTERN WORLD

Mesopotamia

A stela that dates to the end of the fourth millennium BC depicts a king killing a lion with a spear. Mesilim, the king of Kish (ca. 2500 BC), had a mace head adorned with the face of a lion.

In a self-laudatory hymn, Shulgi (ca. 2094–2047 BC), a king of the Ur III Dynasty, boasts that he is like a "panting lion" and like a "raging lion" (Klein, 73).

The kingdom of Mari on the Euphrates flourished during the Old Babylonian era. Excavations have yielded a vast archive, including dispatches from officials to king Zimri-Lim about lions. One patrol reported:

> Just before nighttime, 2 lions lay down by the fence of the main gate. The farmers of Abullatum (by Mari) and troops from hither and yon gathered, but they could (not) chase them away. We sent out nomads . . . for protection. These nomads killed one lion; one was driven out. (ARM 26.106; Sasson, 165)

Another official reported as follows:

> A lioness was caught at night in a loft at Bit-Akkaka. The next day, when I was notified, I made my way (there). In order not to allow (anyone) to strike this lion [sic], I am remaining in Bit-Akkaka all day. I thought to myself, "I want to have it reach my lord in full health." So I threw him a [dog and] a pig, and he killed them. I left them (there), but he would not take them for food. I have myself written to Biddaḫ (a village) to have a wooden cage brought here. While the cage was being hauled, on the morrow, the lion died. I inspected this lioness [sic]: she was old and was injured. (ARM 14.1; Sasson, 130)

Hammurabi (r. 1792–1750 BC), the king of Babylon, destroyed the kingdom of Mari. In his extensive code of laws, he addresses the danger of lions in paragraph 244: "If a seignior hired an ox or an ass and a lion has killed it in the open, (the loss) shall be its owner's" (*ANET*, 176).

Bas-reliefs and inscriptions from Assyrian palaces reveal that hunting was a favorite royal sport. Beginning in the time of Tiglath-pileser I (r. 1115–1077 BC), a number of Assyrian rulers collected wild animals from Mesopotamia, and sometimes from surrounding countries, to place in special zoological parks as game reserves. The animals were used mainly for public viewing and royal hunts.

Tiglath-pileser I boasted that in a single hunt he killed four wild bulls, ten elephants, and 920 lions (eight hundred from a chariot and 120 on foot) (Bienkowski, 149). He brought back hides and tusks as trophies. He also collected live wild animals for the zoological park at Ashur, the first one of its kind attested in the Near East. These included wild bulls, elephants, lions, monkeys, wild asses, gazelles, deer, bears, cheetahs, a rhinoceros, and a crocodile. (See *ARAB* 1.85–87.)

King Ashurnasirpal II (883–859 BC) boasted:

> I slew 450 mighty lions, and 350 wild bulls I slew . . . I cut (down) 200 ostriches like caged birds and 30 elephants I cast in the pit. 50 live wild bulls, 140 live ostriches, 20 mighty lions with my weapon . . . I captured. Of bulls, lions and ostriches, apes male and female, I collected their herds and caused them to bring forth their increase. (Wiseman, 31)

This king also had his hunters capture gazelles, who were then fattened with barley. Gazelle meat was included on the menu for his famous banquet at Nimrud.

During the Neo-Assyrian period, trained birds were sometimes used for hunting. An eighth-century BC relief from Sargon's capital of Khorsabad depicts a falconer accompanying an archer on a hunt.

As in other lands in the ancient Near East, in Assyria many animals and birds were hunted with nets. A relief of Ashurbanipal (r. ca. 669–627 BC) depicts wild asses hunted with lassos. Arrows, spears, javelins, and darts were other weapons commonly used. Hunting dogs and chariots were employed in the royal chase. The boast of several Assyrian monarchs that they fought on foot and seized wild beasts, including lions, with their own hands appears largely to be rhetoric meant to enhance the popular image and heroic mystique of the ruler.

The Neo-Assyrian monarchs, unlike most rulers who preceded them, seemed to relish the sport of lion hunting, which required skill and daring. Most hunts were held in an enclosed section of a game reserve. In preparation for the hunt, lions were caught and caged. When the hunt began, the lions were released and driven by beaters and hounds toward the royal hunters. The king shot arrows from his chariot, sometimes hastening the dispatch of a wounded lion with his hunting spear. Before servants cleared the hunting field of the dead lions, the king poured a libation over them to atone for the injury he had inflicted on them. The Assyrians believed that the angry spirit of a slain beast might later come and seek vengeance upon the hunter if it was not pacified (Contenau, 135).

Ashurbanipal's reliefs of the lion hunt in his North Palace at Nineveh are masterpieces of Assyrian art. They depict in minute detail attacking and dying lions [see Figures 9 and 10 on p. 476]. They also include figures of huge hunting dogs who are restrained by their handlers. The hunt took place before an audience of men and women. The motif of the lion hunt became the central image of the king's seal. In early sixth-century BC Babylon, during the reign of Nebuchadnezzar, more than a hundred images of lifesize lions adorned the Processional Way leading to the Temple of Marduk.

Persia

We have only a small corpus of texts (Old Persian, Akkadian, Elamite) from the Achaemenid kings who ruled the Persian Empire from its founding under Cyrus the Great (r. 559–530 BC) until its conquest by Alexander the Great. But glyptic art, such as a noted seal impression of Darius I (r. 522–486 BC) now in the British Museum, indicates that the Persian kings were the heirs of the Assyrian ideology of lion hunts. In this seal Darius is shown standing in a chariot along with his driver shooting arrows at an enormous lion who stands upright with arrows in his face and another lion underneath the chariot (Yamauchi, 181). We also have many classical sources that attest to the popularity of the hunt among the later Achaemenid royalty.

Like the Assyrians and Babylonians before them, the Persians maintained enclosed parks with trees and game for hunting, which they referred to by the term *paridaida*, "beyond the wall," which was transliterated into Greek as *paradeisos*.

From the reign of Artaxerxes I (r. 464–424 BC) we learn about the extraordinary career of Megabyzus (Yamauchi, 250). He earned great distinction in defeating the Egyptian revolt aided by the Athenians, but then fell out of favor through a breach of royal etiquette. As related by Ctesias, a Greek physician who had served at the royal Persian court:

The king went hunting and a lion attacked him. As soon as the beast leapt, Megabyzus struck him with a javelin and brought him down. The king was angry because Megabyzus had struck the beast before he could touch it himself; he ordered Megabyzus's head cut off, but, on the pleas of Amestris, Amytis, and others, Megabyzus escaped death by being exiled on the coast of the Red Sea (Persian Gulf), at Kyrta. (Ctesias, *Persica* §40; cited in Briant, 320)

A somewhat similar incident is related by Diodorus Siculus about the intervention of Tiribazus, an official of Artaxerxes II (r. 404–358 BC):

Once during a hunt, while the King was riding in a chariot, two lions came at him, tore to pieces two of the four horses belonging to the chariot, and then charged upon the King himself; but at that very moment Tiribazus appeared, slew the lions, and rescued the King from the danger. (*Bib. hist.* 15.10.3)

In this case the monarch was grateful, until Tiribazus became emboldened to ask for the king's daughter in marriage.

Xenophon, a disciple of Socrates, accompanied the expedition of the so-called "ten thousand" Greek mercenaries who were hired by Cyrus the Younger to overthrow his brother Artaxerxes II. Xenophon wrote a stirring account, called the *Anabasis* ("March Up Country"), about the Greeks' desperate journey to the Black Sea after the death of Cyrus the Younger at Cunaxa in 401 BC. He also wrote the *Cyropaedia* ("The Education of Cyrus (the Great)"), which was inspired by his admiration for Cyrus the Younger.

In the first work, Xenophon relates this incident about his hero: "On one occasion, when a bear charged upon him, he did not take to flight, but grappled with her and was dragged from his horse; he received some injuries, the scars of which he retained, but in the end he killed the bear" (*Anab.* 1.9.6). In the treatise on the education of the Persian king, Xenophon wrote that "he would himself hunt the animals that were kept in the parks. . . . The result of all this constant training was that he and his associates greatly excelled in all the manly exercises" (*Cyr.* 1.38–39).

The Persians' love of hunting was maintained by the later Parthians (247 BC–AD 224) and Sassanians (AD 224–651), as manifested in their magnificent art depicting horsemen hunting lions, boars, and deer (see Ghirshman, 106, 194–96, 207).

When the historian Ammianus Marcelinus accompanied Julian in a campaign against the Sassanians in AD 363, they found a dwelling "displaying in every part of the house, after the custom of that nation, paintings representing the king killing wild beasts in various kinds of hunting" (*Res G.* 24.6.3).

Egypt

The Nile Valley and its adjacent deserts provided the Egyptians with rich hunting grounds for animals and birds. The hieroglyphic script, a pictographic form of writing, illustrates in its many signs some of the wide variety of game available to hunters.

Rock carvings (ca. 4000 BC) in deserts on either side of the Nile depict hunts of ostriches, giraffes, aurochs, ibexes, antelopes, elephants, rhinoceroses, hippopotamuses, and crocodiles.

Among the most informative Pre-Dynastic (before 3200 BC) works of art are slate palettes in which malachite and turquoise were ground to create powder for use as eye shadow. The Hunter's Palette presents a series of animals including the lion, gazelle, deer, fox, and rabbit. One of the human figures has lassoed a gazelle, while another avoids the attention of a wounded lion.

Literary texts and tomb drawings and other artwork indicate that a number of hunting methods were utilized. The bow and arrow were widely used, as was the net. In addition, animals such as the gazelle, the antelope, and the wild ox were sometimes ambushed, lassoed with a noose, and brought back alive. If desired, the animal could then be fattened by hand. Among other animals the Egyptians hunted were the ostrich, wild goat, hyena, leopard, wolf, fox, porcupine, and hare. Hounds were frequently used to chase game. Cats were used for hunting in the thickets. On occasion, tame lions that had been specially trained were used by Egyptian monarchs to pursue game.

Hunting was a favorite sport of royalty. It was both a pleasurable diversion and a continual test of the prowess of the kings. The oldest image of a king as a standing archer shooting at fenced-in game is that of Sahure (5th Dynasty, 2506–2492 BC). This motif is continued down through the Middle Kingdom (ca. 2000–1700 BC) (see Hoffmeier 1975, 1980). An inscription of Amenemhet I (12th Dynasty, 1991–1962 BC) declares: "I captured lions, I took crocodiles" (*ARE* 1.232).

The *Story of Sinuhe* (ca. 2000 BC), which narrates the adventures of an official who fled from Egypt, describes the provisions of the Canaanite chief who had welcomed him: "meat and roast fowl, beside the wild beasts of the desert, for they hunted for me and laid before me, beside the catch of my (own) hounds" (lines 89–90; *ANET*, 20).

The 18th Dynasty kings succeeded in expelling the invading Hyksos and then proceeded to establish the New Kingdom, or Empire, extending Egypt's control eastwards toward Palestine and Syria. The introduction of the chariot and the composite bow at this time made it possible for pharaohs to hunt game from their chariots with bows and arrows.

Tuthmosis III (r. 1504–1452 BC) was the greatest warrior pharaoh, launching nearly a score of annual expeditions into Palestine and Syria, even reaching the Euphrates River. At a site called Niy, where the river passes through two cliffs, Tuthmosis had a nearly fatal encounter with elephants. Though the king awarded gold medals of valor in the forms of lions and flies, while boasting about his elephant hunt he failed to mention the key action of his servant Amenemhab, who saved his life. As Amenemhab recounted in his own tomb inscription:

> He hunted 120 elephants, for the sake of their tusks. . . . I engaged the largest which was among them, which fought against his majesty; I cut off his hand [i.e., its trunk] while he was alive [before] his majesty, while I stood in the water between two rocks. Then my lord rewarded me with gold. (*ARE* 2.233)

Tuthmosis III also claimed to have shot a rhinoceros with an arrow, which was quite a unique occurrence, in Nubia (Sudan).

In his Sphinx Stela, Tuthmosis IV (1419–1410 BC) related the following about an expedition of his:

> Behold, he [i.e., I] did a thing that gave him pleasure upon the highlands of the Memphite nome, upon its southern and northern road, shooting at a target with copper bolts, hunting lions and wild goats, coursing in his chariot, his horses being swifter than the wind; together with two of his followers, while not a soul knew it. (*ARE* 2.322)

Amenhotep III (r. 1410–1372 BC) was an avid hunter who plied his skill both near and far. To publicize his achievements he issued huge (8.3 x 0.57 cm.) commemorative scarab seals, declaring: "Statement of lions which his majesty brought down with his own arrows from year 1 to year 10: fierce lions, 102" (*ARE* 1.347). He also proclaimed that he had spent four days hunting wild bulls in the desert near Faiyum, killing forty of them and capturing fifty-six.

Tutankhamun (r. 1355–1346 BC) was a hunter. The discovery of his intact tomb in 1922 by Howard Carter provided a cornucopia of evidence for hunting. The lid and sides of a chest from his tomb are painted with scenes of war and hunting. One section of the lid depicts him standing in his horse-drawn chariot, bow in hand, rushing violently forward as antelopes, ostriches, and hyenas are trying to escape the pursuit of the royal hounds (Desroches-Noblecourt, 80–81). A statue of Tutankhamun depicts him as ready to hurl a harpoon, presumably at a hippopotamus. Among the wealth of objects discovered in the tomb were: chariots, boomerangs, throw sticks, slings, arrows, quivers, bow strings, three composite bows, and a fourteen-inch child's bow. (See El-Habashi.)

A number of pharaohs had tame lions that accompanied their chariots, including Ramesses II (r. 1304–1237 BC) and Ramesses III (r. 1198–1166 BC) (*ARE* 4.67, 71, 196). In his long list of offerings to temples preserved in the Papyrus Harris, Ramesses III includes among other offerings oryxes and gazelles (*ARE* 4.138). He furthermore declared that he had appointed three "hunting archers" to capture white oryxes as offerings to the gods (*ARE* 4.146). Ramesses III is depicted on bas-reliefs in his mortuary temple at Medinet-Habu hunting lions, wild bulls, and antelopes.

One of the earliest historical documents, the Palermo Stone, records an event it calls "Shooting of the Hippopotamus" (*ARE* 1.60). This was a very dangerous sport, as crews of hunters stood on papyrus skiffs as they prepared to harpoon the animal. The male hippopotamus (Gk., "river horse") was regarded as a symbol of chaos and evil. On the other hand, a standing pregnant hippopotamus represented the beneficent deity Tauret, who watched over childbirth.

Greek visitors to Egypt, such as Herodotus, were astonished that the Egyptians venerated not only domesticated animals as incarnations of their deities, such as the cow, which was considered to be the manifestation of Hathor, the goddess of love, but also wild animals. The latter included the baboon, representing Thoth, the god of wisdom; the jackal, representing Anubis, the god who presided over mummification; the lioness, representing Sekhmet, the goddess of vengeance; and the crocodile, representing Sebek, the god over the area of the Faiyum. (See Smelik and Hemelrijk.)

Herodotus describes the habits of the crocodile and the hippopotamus (*Hist.* 2.58–71), two river animals that posed a special challenge to hunters. The crocodile was often caught in the river by using a hook baited with pork, which the animal swallowed. The line was pulled to shore and the crocodile was subdued (by smearing its eyes with mud) and then killed. The first Greek reference to an elephant does not come until Herodotus (*Hist.* 4.191), who heard about this animal but did not see it when he traveled upstream to the Elephantine Island near Aswan (see Scullard, 32).

Fowling was also a very popular activity in Egypt. Ducks, geese, quail, and other varieties of birds were hunted, sometimes with throw sticks or arrows, but more often with nets or traps. Decoys were sometimes used to lure the birds. One method, used in marshes, involved suddenly lowering a net over a flock of ducks. The birds were trapped when the net was closed by a rope pulled by several of the fowlers. The clap-trap or clap-net was another device often used in fowling (cf. Jer 5:26). It consisted of two wooden frames covered with a net placed on the ground. When the hunter pulled a rope attached to the frames, the trap would clap shut. Other types of traps sprang shut automatically when the bird touched the bait attached to the trigger.

D. THE GRECO-ROMAN WORLD

Greece

Artemis was the Greek goddess of the hunt and the patron of wild animals. A famous myth describes the *hybris*, that is, arrogance, of a hunter named Actaion, who according to one version boasted that he was a better hunter than the goddess, and according to another version viewed the nude goddess as she bathed. In any event, the infuriated Artemis caused the hunter's own hounds to attack and kill him. This is one of the most popular scenes depicted on Greek pottery.

In Greco-Roman mythology, four of the twelve "Labors of Heracles (Hercules)" involved the overcoming of wild creatures: the killing of the lion of Nemea, a city north of Mycenae; the catching of the swift Ceryneian hind; the capture of the Erymanthian boar; and the submission of a bull from Crete, which he brought to Greece. Later Theseus would kill this bull at Marathon.

According to myth, a hybrid monster known as the Minotaur, who had the head of a bull and the body of a man, lived in a labyrinth on Crete. Every year, the Minotaur devoured youth from Greece, until the Athenian hero Theseus killed him and escaped, with the aid of Ariadne, the daughter of King Minos.

When Arthur Evans found a palace at the site of Knossos in north-central Crete in 1900, he named it "The Palace of Minos." Unique bull-leaping feats were performed in the palace's large central courtyard, and probably at the courtyards of the palaces of Mallia and Phaistos as well. A fresco from Knossos (ca. 1500 BC) illustrates a young acrobat somehow avoiding the bull's charge by leaping and somersaulting over its back (Pendlebury, pl. XIII).

The capture of bulls is illustrated on two marvelous gold cups found at Vapheio near Sparta. The bulls are lured by a tethered heifer and then trapped by a net. In one scene a bull kicks violently in a vain attempt to escape, and in another a bull tramples over some hunters.

Heinrich Schliemann excavated Grave Circle A (ca. 1500 BC) within the citadel at Mycenae, just inside the monumental entrance, which features scuptured reliefs of two lions flanking a pillar. Among the great treasures he discovered were daggers decorated with inlays of gold and niello. One depicts several hunters armed with shields, spears, and bows and arrows facing a rampaging lion as he leaps over a fallen hunter. The stela over Grave Alpha has a worn relief that George Mylonas interprets as depicting a man with a spear and a bull, both attacking a lion, who has bitten the neck of a cow (Mylonas, 422). Other images of lions can be found in small figurines and seals from the Mycenaean era.

Seals from this period also depict scenes of boar hunting. From the palace at Tiryns, the site traditionally considered to be the home of Her-acles, wall fresco fragments of a boar hunt depict hounds leaping after a boar. Examples of helmets, each one of which was made from the tusks of thirty to forty boars, have been recovered. Such a helmet was a prized heirloom (Hom. *Il.* 10.261–265).

The syllabic Linear B texts from Knossos and Pylos were deciphered by Michael Ventris in 1952 as the earliest written form of Greek. The lion *re-wo* (Gk. *leōn*) appears, but only as the decorative motif of furniture in-laid with ivory *e-re-pa* (Gk. *elephas*), a type of furniture also described by Homer (*Od.* 19.53–62). (See Ventris and Chadwick, 545, 580.) The ivory was probably imported from Syria.

In the *Iliad*, Homer uses numerous references to wild beasts in similes to describe the Greek and Trojan warriors, who, he says, fought like wolves (*Il.* 16.156), lions (*Il.* 5.161; 10.485), boars (*Il.* 12.126; 13.473–475), and hunters of boars (*Il.* 11.414–418). On the new shield that Hephaistos cre-ates for Achilles, one of the many scenes depicted is one of hunters and dogs holding back in fear in the face of two lions who have killed a bull and are devouring its flesh (*Il.* 18.577–587).

In the *Odyssey*, Homer gives a vivid description of a boar hunt on Mount Parnassus that Odysseus undertakes with Autolycus and his sons:

> Now thereby a great wild boar was lying in a thick lair . . . Then about the boar there came the noise of the feet of men and dogs as they pressed on in the chase, and forth from his lair he came against them with bristling back and eyes flashing fire, and stood there at bay close before them. Then first of all Odysseus rushed on, holding his long spear on high in his stout hand, eager to smite him; but the boar was too quick for him and struck him above the knee, charging upon him sideways, and with his tusk tore a long gash in the flesh, but did not reach the bone of the man. But Odysseus with sure aim smote him on the right shoulder, and clear through went the point of the bright spear, and the boar fell in the dust with a cry, and his life flew from him.
> (*Od.* 19.439–454)

After an absence of twenty years fighting the Trojans and suffering numer-ous adventures on his way back to Ithaca, Odysseus arrives at his home dis-guised as a beggar. His nurse, while bathing his leg, recognizes her master from the wound he received during the boar hunt (*Od.* 19.388–395). The only other to recognize Odysseus is his faithful hunting dog, who lay in a dung heap:

Yet even now, when he marked Odysseus standing near, he wagged his tail and dropped both his ears, but nearer to his master he had no longer strength to move. Then Odysseus looked aside and wiped away a tear. (*Od.* 17.296–304)

Odysseus's dog was named *Argos*, "swift-foot." We have four hundred different Greek names for dogs, such as *Psychē*, "soul," *Chara*, "joy," and *Lailaps*, "whirlwind" (cf. Xen. *Cyr.* 7.5).

In the early history of Greece, hunting was an important source of meat. Game was not sacrificed to gods. Hunting was also an important means of protecting the flocks from predatory animals. But by the fifth century BC, lions were no longer found in Greece. Lions who attacked the camels of the Persians were encountered by Xerxes's army as they traveled from Thrace (Bulgaria) to Macedonia north of Greece (Her. *Hist.* 7.125).

In the Archaic Age (8th–6th c. BC), hunting became primarily a pleasurable diversion for the upper classes. It was also seen as an important preparation for military duties, especially among the Spartans. (See David.) Spartan boys were taken from their families and subjected to rigorous physical discipline. They stole to supplement their meager diet, but were publicly flogged if they were caught stealing. Plutarch relates the incident of a boy "who was carrying concealed under his cloak a young fox which he had stolen, [who] suffered the animal to tear out his bowels with its teeth and claws, and died rather than have his theft detected" (*Lyc.* 18.1). One of the rites of passage for a Spartan youth was the *krypteia*, the hunting and killing of one of the helots, conquered peoples who worked the land for the Spartans.

Among the Athenians, hunting became primarily a prestige activity for the aristocrats, as demonstrated by the hunting scenes depicted on 121 black-figured vases and cups from the sixth and early fifth century BC catalogued by J. Barringer (65–69). With the growth of democracy, hunting received less prominence on the later red-figured ware (after 530 BC). The urbanized region of Attica around Athens was a relatively poor area for the hunting of wild animals. The vases depict hunters with javelins on horseback. In Greek hunts, red deer, boar, and hare were among the species most commonly bagged. Hunters used spears, javelins, traps, and nets, the latter attended by net-keepers. Sometimes hunters pursued game and made the kill directly. At other times, beaters with dogs drove animals into nets where hunters waited to stab their ensnared prey.

Plato, who greatly admired the Spartans, made hunting an essential part of his program for the education of boys. He disdained the hunting of animals with nets and traps. He concluded that the only kind left for all, and the best kind, is the hunting of quadrupeds with horses and dogs and the hunter's own limbs, when men hunt in person, and subdue all the creatures by means of their own running, striking and shooting. (*Leg.* 7.824a–b)

Xenophon not only admired the Spartans, he chose to reside in Sparta after undergoing the harrowing adventures he recounts in his *Anabasis.* Xenophon states in the opening of his discourse *Cynegeticus,* "The Hunter" (lit., "The Leader of Dogs"), that "game and hounds are the invention of gods, of Apollo and Artemis" (*Cyn.* 1.1). *Cynegeticus* goes on to instruct the novice on the breeding and training of hunting dogs and in the art of hunting. Hunting dogs portrayed on Greek vases have pointed ears and narrow muzzles.

Xenophon concentrates on the hunting of hares and deer. Those hunting hares would start at dawn setting up traps in various places (*Cyn.* 6.4). One means of attracting the doe was to use her fawn as bait (*Cyn.* 9.5–9). Xenophon stresses that hunting should be done on foot. Elsewhere, however, he alludes to the use of horses. Xenophon states in his work *The Art of Horsemanship* (8.10) that one should practice the use of weapons on horseback by hunting, where the country is suitable. He suggests that hunters leave an offering of some of their game to Artemis, the goddess of hunting and wildlife (*Cyn.* 5.14).

Hunting played a major role among the Macedonians. A rite of passage for young Macedonian men was to kill a boar without the use of a net. The spectacular unlooted royal tombs at Vergina were excavated by M. Andronikos in 1977. He has plausibly assigned one of the tombs to Philip II, the father of Alexander. There is a hunting scene with three mounted hunters and six on foot depicted over the facade of the entrance to Tomb II (Hatzopoulos and Loukopoulos, 210–11). They kill two deer, a boar, a lion, and a bear.

On his long military campaign to overthrow the Persian Empire, Alexander resorted to hunting as a distraction: "Often, too, for diversion, he would hunt foxes or birds, as may be gathered from his journal" (Plu. *Alex.* 22.3).

Alexander confronted lions on three occasions. On the first of these, in Syria in 332 BC, Craterus came to his assistance. Later Craterus commissioned the leading sculptors of his day, Lysippus and Leochares, to make a huge statue of himself and Alexander to be set up at Delphi (Plu., *Alex.* 40.4). A mosaic floor from the House of Dionysus at Pella, the Macedonian capital, depicts two nude young men on either side of a lion, the one on the left wielding a spear and the one on the right about to strike with his sword. The figure on the left has been identified as Alexander and the figure on the right as Craterus.

When Lysimachus attempted to spear a lion before Alexander in Sog-
diana in 328, he was rebuked for his temerity. On a boar hunt in Bactria
(Afghanistan),

> a wild boar charged Alexander and that Hermolaus hastened to pierce the
> boar, which indeed fell from the stroke; but Alexander, too late for his chance,
> was angry with Hermolaus and in his passion ordered him to be whipped in
> the presence of his fellow-pages and took his horse from him.
> (Arrian, *Anab.* 4.13.2)

The young page was so humiliated that he enlisted other pages in an unsuccessful attempt to assassinate Alexander.

The artistic motif of a lion hunt was first introduced in Greek art on a
frieze decorating the monumental funeral pyre at Babylon for Alexander's
close friend Hephaistion, who passed away at Ecbatana (modern Hamadan in northwest Iran). A Hellenistic lion sculpture, probably erected by
Alexander, now decorates a hill in Hamadan (see Yamauchi, 312–13).

There are magnificent military and hunting scenes on the so-called
"Alexander Sarcophagus" of King Abdalonymos of Sidon, now in Istanbul
(see Barringer, 186–87).

After the battle against Porus at the Hydaspes in the Punjab area of the
Indus River Valley, all of Alexander's generals were determined to acquire
elephants for their armies. After Alexander's death, his general Ptolemy
seized control of Egypt. Ptolemy II (r. 285–246 BC) established the great
library at Alexandria. He was also interested in acquiring all kinds of animals for his zoo (*paradeisos*). According to Diodorus Siculus:

> The second Ptolemy, who was passionately fond of the hunting of elephants
> and gave great rewards to those who succeeded in capturing against odds the
> most valiant of these beasts, expending on this hobby great sums of money,
> not only collected great herds of war elephants, but also brought to the knowl-
> edge of the Greeks other kinds of animals which had never before been seen
> and were the objects of amazement. (*Bib. hist.* 3.36.3)

About 275 BC, Ptolemy II sponsored at Alexandria probably the most
extravagant *pompē*, "procession," ever witnessed in antiquity. The spectacle
involved multitudes of custumed participants, floats with a gold statue
of Alexander and giant images of gods, thousands of troops, and also a
large number of exotic animals. Athenaeus listed these as follows: ninety-
six elephants, twenty-four Saiga antelopes (from north of the Black Sea),
fourteen oryxes, thirty hartebeests, sixteen ostriches, fourteen *onelaphoi*
(wild asses), one large white bear, fourteen leopards, sixteen cheetahs, four
lynxes, twenty-four lions, one giraffe, one rhinoceros, and two thousand
four hundred hunting dogs from various regions (*Deipn.* 5.197a-202f)!

Rome

Diana, originally an Italian goddess and the protectress of women, was identified with Artemis, and by assimilation became the Roman goddess of wild animals and the hunt. But it is not true, as some scholars have asserted (e.g., Anderson, 83), that the Romans did not pursue hunting until after the conquest of Greece in 168 BC. As C. M. C. Green has demonstrated through texts and archaeology, there is abundance evidence that the pre-Roman populations as well as the early Romans engaged in hunting both for protection from predators and for food, and also as an aristocratic sport.

To the north, the pre-Roman Villanovans and Etruscans hunted, as shown by images in their works of art, such as painted pottery, jewelry, and tomb paintings. The Etruscan "Tomb of the Hunter" at Tarquinia (530–510 BC) contains a frieze depicting animals and hunters.

Bones of game animals have been excavated in pre-Roman Latium. The percentage of wild animal bones varies from 2 to 3 percent of the animal bones. At Ficana, a Latin site between Rome and Ostia, 22 percent of the animal bones were from deer (Green, 234). Virgil assumed that the early Latins hunted (*Aen.* 7.651; 11.573–584). Virgil has Aeneas, the Trojan progenitor of the Romans, hunting with Dido while he stayed with her in Carthage (*Aen.* 4.129–170).

According to legend, the founders of Rome (753 BC) were twin brothers, Romulus and Remus. They were born to a Vestal Virgin, who claimed that she had been raped by the god Mars. The boys were sent adrift on the Tiber River. When they washed up on the shore near Rome, they were suckled by a she-wolf. Livy describes the twins hunting animals in the woods before they founded the city of Rome (*Rom. Hist.* 1.4.8–9).

The Republic was established by the overthrow of the last Etruscan king in 509 BC. Early in its military history, the Roman army established as one of the legionary emblems the wild boar, which was associated with the war god Mars.

After Rome's conquest of Carthage (201 BC), its armies were directed eastwards against Macedonia, whose king, Philip V, had unwisely allied himself with Hannibal. The Roman legions defeated the Greek phalanxes in a decisive battle at Pydna (168 BC). It was there that Aemilianus, taking advantage of the Macedonian game parks, acquired his enthusiasm for the chase, which he brought back with him to Rome, according to his friend, the Greek hostage and historian Polybius (*Hist.* 31.29.1–12).

Most ambitious young Roman elites at this time (2nd c. BC) chose to seek prestige in the law courts and not in such physical endeavors as hunting. In his diatribe against Catiline (*Bellum catalinae* 4.1), Sallust (86–ca. 35 BC) goes so far as to link hunting with agriculture as a task fit only for Roman slaves. Yet in his work on Jugurtha, the king of Numidia in North Africa, he describes the king's hunting lions as impressive (*Bellum jugurthinum* 6.1).

Virgil describes the care of hunting dogs used to hunt hare, deer, wild asses, and boars (*Georg.* 3.404–413). Pliny the Elder discusses the hunting of hedgehogs, deer, and bears (*Nat.* 109–134).

The word *venatio* referred to the pursuit of animals. The plural *venationes* came to denote spectacles in which wild animals fought with other wild animals, hunters killed wild animals, and wild animals attacked prisoners. Those who fought these wild beasts were known as *venatores* or *bestiarii*. Unlike the gladiators, who were recruited from among prisoners and slaves, these men were free men who formed their own associations (Roueché, 74).

These animal spectacles began in the second century BC. They were presented in the morning, before the gladiatorial fights in the afternoon. They became a wildly popular form of entertainment. The dictator Sulla (d. 78 BC) was supplied with one hundred lions by King Bocchus of Mauretania in northwest Africa. In 55 BC, at Pompey's games, four hundred leopards and six hundred lions were killed. Julius Caesar (d. 44 BC) built the first wooden amphitheater for such an exhibition.

Such spectacles were sponsored by politicians and candidates for office. When Cicero was the governor of Cilicia in southeastern Anatolia, his friend Caelius, who was running for the office of *aedile*, wrote numerous letters to Cicero, asking for leopards he could exhibit. Finally, the exasperated Cicero wrote that there were few leopards left, as they had decided to leave Cilicia (*Fam.* 2.1.2).

Cicero is about the only Roman intellectual who offered an even half-hearted criticism of these spectacles:

> But what pleasure can a cultivated man get out of seeing a weak human being torn to pieces by a powerful animal or a splendid animal transfixed by a hunting spear? Anyhow, if these sights are worth seeing, you have seen them often; and we spectators saw nothing new. (*Fam.* 24.7.1)

Pliny the Younger took a rather nonchalant attitude toward hunting. He wrote to his friend the historian Tacitus about how on one occasion, after he had set the traps for a boar hunt, he set to writing rather than actively hunting the animals:

> I know you will think it a good joke, as indeed you may, when I tell you that your old friend has caught three boars, very fine ones too. Yes, I really did, and without even changing any of my lazy holiday habits. I was sitting by the hunting nets with writing materials by my side instead of hunting spears, thinking something out and making notes, so that even if I came home emptyhanded I should at least have my notebooks filled. (*Ep.* 1.6)

Only a few of the emperors were themselves personally engaged in hunting; these included Domitian, Marcus Aurelius, Commodus, Septimius Severus, and Caracalla. Hadrian (r. AD 117–138) was addicted to hunting. While hunting for boars on horseback, Hadrian fell and broke his collar bone (Cassius Dio, *Hist. rom.* 69.10.2).

The emperors used their vast resources, including military personnel who were assigned for this purpose, to capture and transport wild animals from Anatolia, the Near East, Egypt, and Africa to Rome. (See Epplett.) In the wilds of the provinces, a network of professional hunters, land transporters, and shippers delivered thousands of captured animals to Rome and other major cities. These included leopards, panthers, bears, lions, tigers, and elephants, as well as numerous ostriches, gazelles, and deer, to be used as prey for hunting dogs or other wild animals. Crocodiles, hippopotamuses, and rhinoceroses were shipped from Egypt. Such an enormous depletion of wild animals throughout the Roman world left a variety of species extinct, or threatened with extinction, by the early Christian centuries.

The first emperor, Augustus (27 BC–AD 14), boasted, "I gave beast-hunts of African beasts in my own name or in that of my sons and grandsons in the circus or forum or amphitheatre on twenty-six occasions, on which about 3,500 beasts were destroyed" (*Res G.* 22; Brunt and Moore, 31). Augustus acquired three thousand five hundred beasts in a fifteen-year period, including six hundred panthers, four hundred tigers, and 260 lions (Auguet, 112).

In AD 80, at the dedication of the Flavian Amphitheater (today known as the Colosseum) by Emperor Titus, nine thousand animals were killed in a hundred days (Suet. *Titus* 7.3). To celebrate his victory over Dacia (Roumania), Trajan (r. AD 98–117) had eleven thousand beasts killed over the course of 123 days (Cassius Dio, *Hist. rom.* 68.15).

On the occasion of the millennium since the founding of Rome (AD 248), Philip the Arab (r. AD 244–249) displayed thirty-two elephants, ten elk, ten tigers, sixty tame lions, thirty tame leopards, ten hyenas, a hippopotamus, and a rhinoceros (*S.H.A. Gordian* 33). Probus (r. 276–282) displayed one thousand ostriches, one thousand stags, and one thousand boars. He displayed and killed one hundred African leopards, one hundred Syrian leopards, one hundred lionesses, and three hundred bears (*S.H.A. Probus* 19).

The human victims in the *venationes* were criminals or prisoners who had been given the sentence *damnatio ad bestias*. This practice began under Augustus. The victims would sometimes be dressed in costume to represent a mythical character. At other times they would be naked. They would be led into the arena by chains or ropes around their necks, then tied to posts or placed on wheeled platforms to be moved into place. Handlers with whips or firebrands would drive the beasts toward the victims. To make sure that the victims were dead, a *confector* went about to slit the throats of the bodies lying on the arena.

The most vivid illustrations of both hunting and the *venationes* come from floor mosaics, often laid in dining halls, from Roman North Africa dating to the Late Roman Empire (3rd–4th c. AD).

The greatest hunting mosaic comes from the Piazza Armerina in central Sicily, which was probably the hunting villa of Maximian, who ruled with Diocletian (r. AD 286–305). Among the vast three thousand five hundred square meters of preserved mosaic is "the Great Hunt," which adorns a corridor that was probably used for dining. It is 15 feet (4.5 m.) wide and 197 feet (60 m.) long. Among the many vivid scenes are ones depicting hounds leaping after a fox, a wounded lioness biting the shield of a fallen hunter, a raging boar stopped from attacking a hunter on the ground by the intervention of another hunter with a spear, the master of the hunt preparing to sacrifice the boar to Diana, and servants carrying two ostriches onto a boat. (See Gentili.)

From Smirat (Tunisia) we have a mosaic showing a group of hunters fighting leopards, with a long inscription praising the generosity of a certain Magerius, who was pressured by the crowd at the amphitheater to donate the gold for acquiring the animals and for rewarding the hunters. Another mosaic, from Sicca Veneria (Tunisia), displays hunters leading hounds who attack ostriches and gazelles.

A famous floor mosaic from the villa at Zliten (Libya) illustrates various events at a spectacle along its perimeter: dogs attack ostriches, gazelles, and stags; a bull and a boar are chained together; a naked man is whipped toward a charging lion; and a victim tied to a stake is pushed on a cart toward a lioness. (See Auguet, 113.)

Aulus Gellius (*Noct. Att.* 5.114) relates the tale of "Androcles and the Lion." Androcles, a fugitive slave, takes refuge in what turns out to be a lion's den. He removes a thorn from the lion's paw. After being recaptured, he is thrown into the arena before the emperor Gaius Caligula (r. AD 37–41). The lion who is to devour him recognizes his friend and lies down before him. When the emperor hears about the story, he releases both Androcles and the lion, who becomes Androcles's pet.

E. THE JEWISH WORLD

Ben Sira observes: "Wild asses in the wilderness are the prey of lions; likewise the poor are pastures for the rich" (Sir 13:19). About David he comments: "He played with lions as with young goats, and with bears as with lambs of the flock" (Sir 47:3). He advises, "Pursue wisdom like a hunter, and lie in wait on her paths" (Sir 14:22).

Though the king of the Jews, Herod the Great (r. 37–4 BC) was a Roman in temperament and culture, and in his activities and interests. Josephus states that Herod was not only a formidable fighter, but also a great hunter: "Always foremost in the chase, in which he distinguished himself above all by his skill in horsemanship, he on one occasion brought down forty wild beasts in a single day; for the country breeds boars and, in greater abundance, stags and wild asses" (*J. W.* 1.429).

When Herod discovered that he had unjustly executed his beloved wife Mariamne, he "went off to the wilderness, where under the pretext of hunting he gave way to his suffering" (Jos. *Ant.* 15.244). Two of his bodyguards, who were arrested, confessed under torture that they had considered killing the king "when he would be pursuing a wild animal in the chase" (Jos. *Ant.* 16.316).

The rabbis did not approve of hunting for mere sport, but they did approve of it for procuring food and for gaining protection from predators. The School of Shammai was stricter than the School of Hillel as to hunting on the eve of the Sabbath: "The School of Shammai say: Nets may not be spread for wild animals, birds, or fishes unless there is time for them to be caught the same day. And the School of Hillel permit it" (*m. Šabb.* 1:6).

Rabbis argued over whether a man was guilty of breaking the Sabbath if he hunted a bird and drove it into a tower trap, or drove a gazelle into a house. Rabban Simeon declared: "This is the general rule: if it must still be hunted he [that pens it in on the Sabbath] is not culpable; but if it no longer needs to be hunted he is culpable" (*m. Šabb.* 13:5). In the Talmudic commentary on this Mishnaic passage, the rabbis taught that on the Sabbath, "if one catches a deer that is blind or asleep, he is culpable; a deer that is lame, aged or sick, he is exempt. . . . The former try to escape; the latter do not try to escape" (*b. Šabb.* 106b). The Talmud adds: "If one catches a lion on the Sabbath he is not culpable unless he entices it into its cage" (*b. Šabb.* 106b).

After the unsuccessful Bar Kochba Revolt (AD 132–135), the Romans forbade the teaching, studying, and practice of the Torah. Rabbi Akiva, who had hailed Bar Kochba as the messiah, defied this injunction. When his disciples asked whether he was afraid, he responded with a fable:

> A fox was once walking alongside of a river, and he saw fishes going in swarms from one place to another. He said to them: From what are you fleeing? They replied: From the nets cast for us by men. He said to them: Would you like to come up on to the dry land so that you and I can live together in the way

that my ancestors lived with your ancestors? They replied: Art thou the one that they call the cleverest of animals? Thou art not clever but foolish. If we are afraid in the element in which we live, how much more in the element in which we would die! So it is with us. If such is our condition when we sit and study the Torah, of which it is written, For that is thy life and the length of thy days, if we go and neglect it how much worse off we shall be! (*b. Ber.* 61b)

Rabbi Akiva was arrested and martyred by the Romans in AD 135.

F. THE CHRISTIAN WORLD

The first persecutions against Christians were unleashed by Nero, who sought to deflect the widespread suspicion that he himself had started the fire that devastated much of Rome in AD 65. While he did not "fiddle while Rome burned," he donned a performer's costume and sang a poem about the fall of Troy while the flames burned. In a passage that contains the most significant non-Christian testimony about the Jesus movement, the historian Tacitus relates:

Therefore to scotch the rumour, Nero substituted as culprits, men, loathed for their vices, whom the crowd styled Christians. . . . And derision accompanied their end: they were covered with wild beasts' skins and torn to death by dogs; or they were fastened on crosses, and, when daylight failed were burned to serve as lamps by night. (*Ann.* 15.44; cf. Suet. *Nero* 16)

Ignatius, the bishop of Antioch, was arrested in Antioch and martyred in Rome during the reign of Trajan (r. AD 98–117). In seven letters that he wrote along the way to various churches and to Polycarp, the bishop of Smyrna, Ignatius warns against false teachers, whom he calls "wild beasts," "mad dogs," and "specious wolves." Speaking of the ten Roman soldiers who took him to Rome, the bishop declares: "From Syria all the way to Rome I am fighting with wild beasts, on land and sea, by night and day, chained amidst ten leopards (that is, a company of soldiers) who only get worse when they are well treated" (Ign. *Rom.* 5.1). In memorable language, Ignatius eagerly welcomes martyrdom, as he writes to the Roman Christians:

I am writing to all the churches and am insisting to everyone that I die for God of my own free will—unless you hinder me. I implore you: do not be unseasonably kind to me. Let me be food for the wild beasts, through whom I can reach God. I am God's wheat, and I am being ground by the teeth of the wild beasts, so that I may prove to be pure bread. Better yet, coax the wild beasts, so that they may become my tomb and leave nothing of my body behind, lest I become a burden to anyone once I have fallen asleep. (*Rom.* 4.1)

In AD 177, during the reign of Marcus Aurelius, numerous Christians were arrested in Lugdunum (Lyon, France) and offered as victims in the amphitheater. The account of the martyrdoms is contained in a letter written to the church in Asia Minor, whence many of the Christians, including the bishop Irenaeus, had come. One of the most striking martyrs was the woman Blandina, about whom Eusebius writes. At first, when she was hung on a stake, none of the wild beasts would touch her:

> And, after the scourging, after the wild beasts, after the roasting seat, she was finally enclosed in a net, and thrown before a bull. And having been tossed about by the animal, on account of her hope and firm hold upon what had been entrusted to her, and her communion with Christ, she also was sacrificed. And the heathen themselves confessed that never among them had a woman endured so many and such terrible tortures. (*Hist. eccl.* 5.1.56)

Another courageous martyr was the noblewoman Perpetua, who was killed in Carthage in AD 203. Perpetua was a nursing mother and her maid, Felicitas, gave birth in prison. The young women were placed in nets and tossed to a wild heifer. "First the heifer tossed Perpetua and she fell on her back. Then sitting up she pulled down the tunic that was ripped along the side so that it covered her thighs, thinking more of her modesty than of her pain" (*Passio Sanctarum Perpetua et Felicitatis* 20; Musurillo, 129). Other Christians were exposed to leopards, bears, and wild boars. Those, like Perpetua, who were not killed by the beasts had their throats slit by a gladiator.

In the apocryphal *Acts of Paul and Thecla* (composed ca. AD 190 in Asia Minor), Paul is saved from the wild beasts by a baptized lion. Thecla is protected by a fierce lioness that fights off a bear. She is placed on a bull that has red-hot irons placed beneath its belly, but the ropes are burned by the heat, and the governor finally spares Thecla.

In the apocryphal *Acts of Philip* (4th c. AD), Philip is accompanied by Bartholomew and Mariamne, who is dressed as a man. They are joined in their journey by a leopard and a kid, who can stand upright and pray in human voices. (See Spittler.)

In AD 326, Constantine passed a law sending criminals who would have been condemned *ad bestias* to the mines instead. His attempt to abolish the gladiatorial combats had little effect, and he subsequently allowed a town in Italy to sponsor such games. In 357 his son Constantius II forbade officials and soldiers from participating in such games. But it was not until 404, when a monk was killed trying to intervene between gladiators, that Honorius succeeded in stopping these games. (See R. Grant, 122–23.)

But the chariot races and the animal games continued into the early Byzantine era. A law of 425 forbade their performances on Sundays and on certain church feast days. In 499, Anastasius forbade games in which humans were killed by beasts. In a decree of 536, the great Byzantine emperor Justinian decreed:

> If this (a consular display) has been devised in order that spectacles be held for the pleasure of the people, and these also are established by us for horse-racing and for the display and slaughter of wild-beasts, and for the delights of acting and the stage, our people will not be deprived of these things.
> (*Nov.* 105.1)

BIBLIOGRAPHY: G. C. Aalders, "The Fishers and the Hunters," *EvQ* 30 (1958), 133–39; P. Albenda, "Assyrian Royal Hunts: Antlered and Horned Animals from Distant Lands," *BASOR* 349 (2008), 61–78; R. L. Alexander, "The Royal Hunt," *Arch* 16 (1963), 243–50; H. Altenmüller, *Darstellungen der Jagd im alten Ägypten,* (1967); J. K. Anderson, "Hunting," *OEANE* III.122–24; J. K. Anderson, *Hunting in the Ancient World* (1985); R. Auguet, *Cruelty and Civilization: The Roman Games* (1972); J. Aymard, *Essai sur les chasses romaines* (1951); R. D. Barnett, *Sculptures from the North Palace of Ashurbanipal at Nineveh (668–627 B.C.)* (1976); G. Bar-Oz et al., "Mass Hunting Game Traps in the Southern Levant: The Negev and Arabah 'Desert Kites,'" *NEA* 74 (2011), 208–15; J. M. Barringer, *The Hunt in Ancient Greece* (2001); P. Bienkowski, "Hunting," *DANE* 149–50; F. S. Bodenheimer, *Animals and Man in Bible Lands* (2 vols., 1960, 1972); O. Borowski, *Every Living Thing: Daily Use of Animals in Ancient Israel* (1998); D. Brewer, "Hunting, Animal Husbandry and Diet in Ancient Egypt," in *A History of the Animal World in the Ancient Near East,* ed. B. J. Collins (2002), 427–56; P. Briant, *From Cyrus to Alexander: A History of the Persian Empire,* trans. P. T. Daniels (2002); S. Brown, "Death as Decoration: Scenes from the Arena on Roman Domestic Mosaics," in *Pornography and Representation in Greece and Rome,* ed. A. Richlin (1992), 180–211; P. A. Brunt and J. M. Moore, trans., *Res Gestae Divi Augusti* (1967); H.-G. Buchholz, G. Jöhrens, and I. Maull, *Jagd und Fischfang* (1973); K. Butz, "Bemerkungen zu Jagdtieren in Mesopotamien," *Bibliotheca Orientalis* 34 (1977), 282–90; G. L. Campbell, ed., *The Oxford Handbook of Animals in Classical Thought and Life* (2014); G. S. Cansdale, *All the Animals of the Bible Lands* (1970); J. Clutton-Brock and C. Grigson, ed., *Animals and Archaeology* (1983); D. Collon, "Hunting and Shooting," *AnSt* 33 (1983), 51–56; G. Conteneau, *Everyday Life in Babylon and Assyria,* trans. K. R. Maxwell-Hysop and A. R. Maxwell-Hysop (1954), 133–35; I. Cornelius, "Animals in the Art of Ugarit," *Journal for Semitics* 16 (2007), 605–23; M. Cultraro, "Exercise of Dominance. Boar Hunting in Mycenaean Religion and Hittite Royal Rituals," in *Offizielle Religion, lokale Kulte und individuelle Religiosität,* ed. M. Hutter and S. Hutter-Braunsar (2004), 117–35; E. David, "Hunting in Spartan Society and Consciousness," Échos du monde classique n.s. 12 (1993), 393–413; W. Decker, *Die physische Leistung Pharaos* (1971); C. Desroches-Noblecourt, *Tutankhamen: Life and Death of a Pharaoh* (1963); M. B. Dick, "The Neo-Assyrian Royal Lion Hunt and Yahweh's Answer to Job," *JBL* 125 (2006), 243–70; Z. El-Habashi, *Tutankhamun and the Sporting Tradition* (1992); C. Epplett, "The Capture of Animals by the Roman Military," *GR* 48 (2001), 210–22; R. L. Fox, "Ancient Hunting: From Homer to Polybius," in *Human Landscapes in Classical Antiquity: Environment and Culture*, ed. G. Shipley and J. Salmon (1996),119–53; G. V. Gentili, *Mosaics of Piazza Armerina: The Hunting Scenes* (1964); G. Gerleman, *Contributions to the Old Testament Terminology of the Chase* (1946); R. Ghirshman, *Iran: Parthians and Sassanians*, trans. S. Gilbert and J. Emmons (1962); I. S. Gilhus, *Animals, Gods and Humans: Changing Attitudes to Animals in Greek, Roman and Early Christian Ideas* (2006); B. L. Goddard, *Animals of the Bible* (1963); R. M. Grant, *Early Christians and Animals* (1999); G. B. Gray, "Crocodiles in Palestine," *PEQ* 52 (1920), 167–76; J. Gray, "The Desert Sojourn of the Hebrews and the Sinai-Horeb Tradition," *VT* 4 (1954), 148–54; C. M. C. Green, "Did the Romans Hunt?" *Classical Antiquity* 15 (1996), 222–60; M. Greenberg, "Two New Hunting Terms in Psalm 140:12," *HAR* 1 (1977), 149–53; G. Hadas, "Hunting Traps around the Oasis of ʿEn Gedi," *IEJ* 61 (2011), 2–11; M. B. Hatzopoulos and L. D. Loukopoulos, ed., *Philip of Macedon* (1980); W. Heimpel and L. Trümpelmann, "Jagd," *Reallexikon der Assyriologie und Vorderasiatischen Archäologie* (1980), V.234–38; M. Herb, "Der Jäger der Wüste. Zur kulturgeschichtlichen Entwicklung der Jagd im Alten Ägypten," *Nikephoros: Zeitschrift für Sport und Kultur im Altertum* 18 (2005), 21–37; R. Higgins, *Minoan and Mycenaean Art* (1967); S. B. Hoenig, "The Sport of Hunting: A Humane Game?" *Tradition* 11.3 (1970), 13–21; J. K. Hoffmeier, "Comments on an Unusual Hunt Scene from the New Kingdom," *Journal of the Society for the Study of Egyptian Antiquities* 9.3 (1980), 195–200; J. K. Hoffmeier, "Hunting Desert Game with the Bow: A Brief Examination," *Society for the Study of Egyptian Antiquities Newsletter* 6.2 (1975), 8–13; J. D. Hughes, "Hunting in the Ancient Mediterranean World," in *A Cultural History of Animals in Antiquity*, ed. L. Kalof (2007), 1.47–70; D. B. Hull, *Hounds and Hunting in Ancient Greece* (1964); G. Jennison, *Animals for Show and Pleasure in Ancient Rome* (1937); M. Jones, "The Royal Lion-Hunt Scarab of Amenophis III in the Grosvenor Museum, Chester (Chester 429.F./1930)," *JEA* 65 (1979), 165–66; J. Klein, *Three Šulgi Hymns* (1981); D. G. Kyle, *Sport and Spectacle in the Ancient World* (2007); B. Leyerle, "Monks and Other Animals," in *The Cultural Turn in Late Ancient Studies*, ed. D. B. Martin and P. C. Miller (2005), 150–71; S. H. Lonsdale, "Attitudes towards Animals in Ancient Greece," *GR* 26 (1979), 146–59; W. C. McDermott, *The Ape in Antiquity* (1938); J. V. S. Megaw, *Hunters,*

Gatherers, and First Farmers beyond Europe (1977); Z. Meshel, "New Data about the 'Desert Kites,'" *TA* 1 (1974), 129–43; H. Musurillo, trans., *The Acts of the Christian Martyrs* (1972); G. Mylonas, "The Lion in Mycenaean Times," *Athens Annals of Archaeology* 3 (1970), 421–25; S. T. Newmyer, ed., *Animals in Greek and Roman Thought: A Sourcebook* (2011); E. Otto, "An Ancient Egyptian Hunting Ritual," *JNES* 9 (1950), 164–77; O. Palagia, "Hephaestion's Pyre and the Royal Hunt of Alexander," in *Alexander the Great in Fact and Fiction*, ed. A. B. Bosworth and E. J. Baynham (2000), 167–206; A. Parrot, *The Arts of Assyria*, trans. S. Gilbert and J. Emmons (1961); J. D. S. Pendlebury, *A Handbook to the Palace of Minos: Knossos* (rev. ed., 1966); D. Petrovich, "Identifying Nimrod of Genesis 10 with Sargon of Akkad by Exegetical and Archaeological Means," *JETS* 56 (2013), 273–305; H. W. Pleket, "Sport and Spectacle in the Ancient World," *Mnemosyne* 62.2 (2009), 344–46; D. S. Potter, "Martyrdom as Spectacle," in *Theater and Society in the Classical World*, ed. R. Scodel (1993), 53–88; C. Roueché, *Performers and Partisans at Aphrodisias in the Roman and Late Roman Periods* (1993); E. Ruprecht, "Das Nilpferd im Hiobbuch," *VT* 21 (1971), 209–31; A. Salonen, *Jagd und Jagdtiere im alten Mesopotamien* (1976); J. M. Sasson, *From the Archives of Mari: An Anthology of Old Babylonian Letters* (2015); T. Säve-Söderbergh, *On Egyptian Representations of Hippopotamus Hunting as a Religious Motive* (1953); C. Schmidt-Colinet, "Die Löwenjagd am assyrischen Neujahrsfest 672 v. Chr.: Beobachtungen an den Jagdreliefs in Raum C im Nordpalast von Nineveh," *Rivista di Archeologia* 36 (2001), 103–18; E. J. Schochet, *Animal Life in Jewish Tradition: Attitudes and Relationships* (1984); A. Scott, "Zoological Marvel and Exegetical Method in Origen and the *Physiologus*," in *Reading in Christian Communities*, ed. C. A. Bobertz and D. Brakke (2002), 80–89; H. H. Scullard, *The Elephant in the Greek and Roman World* (1974); A. E.-D. M. Shaheen, "Royal Hunting Scenes on Scarabs," *Discussions in Egyptology* 30 (1994), 147–72; K. A. D. Smelik and E. A. Hemelrijk, "'Who knows not what monsters demented Egypt worships?' Opinions on Egyptian Animal Worship in Antiquity as Part of the Ancient Conception of Egypt," *ANRW* II.17.4.1852–2000; J. E. Spittler, *Animals in the Apocryphal Acts of the Apostles* (2008); W. E. Sweet, *Sport and Recreation in Ancient Greece* (1987); A. D. Touny and S. Wenig, *Sport in Ancient Egypt* (1969); J. M. C. Toynbee, *Animals in Roman Life & Art* (repr. of 1973 edition, 2013); United Bible Societies, *Fauna and Flora of the Bible* (2nd ed., 1980); A. van der Kooij, "'Nimrod, a Mighty Hunter Before the Lord!' Assyrian Royal Ideology as Perceived in the Hebrew Bible," *Journal for Semitics* 21 (2012), 1–27; M. Ventris and J. Chadwick, *Documents in Mycenaean Greek* (2nd ed., 1973); P. Vidal-Naquet, "The Black Hunter and the Origin of the Athenian Ephebeia," *Proceedings of the Cambridge Philological Society* 14 (1968), 49–64; P. Villard, "Le chien dans la documentation néo-Assyrienne," *Topoi*, Suppl. 2 (2000), 235–49; A. J. B. Wace and F. H. Stubbings, ed., *A Companion to Homer* (1962); D. S. Wallace-Hadrill, *The Greek Patristic View of Nature* (1968); C. E. Watanabe, *Animal Symbolism in Mesopotamia* (2002); C. E. Watanabe, "Mythological Associations Implied in the Assyrian Royal Bull Hunt," in *Studi sul Vicino Oriente antico dedicati alla memoria di Luigi Cagni*, ed. S. Graziani (2000), 2.1149–61; C. E. Watanabe, "Symbolism of the Royal Lion Hunt in Assyria," in *Intellectual Life of the Ancient Near East*, ed. J. Prosecký (1998), 439–50; E. Weissert, "Royal Hunt and Royal Triumph in a Prism Fragment of Ashurbanipal (82-5-22,2)," in *Assyria 1995*, ed. S. Parpola and R. M. Whiting (1997), 339–58; D. J. Wiseman, "A New Stela of Aššur-naṣir-pal II," *Iraq* 14 (1952), 24–44; W. Wreszinski, *Löwenjagd im alten Ägypten* (1932); E. Yamauchi, *Persia and the Bible* (1990).

MRW and EMY

See also ANIMAL HUSBANDRY, ART, ATHLETICS, BIRDS, BONE & OBJECTS OF BONE, BUTCHERS & MEAT, DOGS, FISH & FISHING, FOOD PRODUCTION, HORSES, IVORY, LEATHER, SPECTACLES, and WEAPONS.

SELECT BIBLIOGRAPHY

A. THE BIBLICAL WORLD

Achtemeier, P. J., ed. *The HarperCollins Bible Dictionary*. San Francisco: HarperSanFrancisco, 1996.

Barton, J., ed. *The Biblical World*. 2 vols. London: Routledge, 2002.

Blaiklock, E. M. and R. K. Harrison, ed. *The New International Dictionary of Biblical Archaeology*. Grand Rapids: Zondervan, 1983.

Bromiley, G. W., ed. *The International Standard Bible Encyclopedia*. 4 vols. Rev. ed. Grand Rapids: Eerdmans, 1979–1988.

Buttrick, G. A., ed. *The Interpreter's Dictionary of the Bible*. 4 vols. New York: Abingdon Press, 1962.

Crim, K., ed. *The Interpreter's Dictionary of the Bible: Supplementary Volume*. Nashville: Abingdon Press, 1976.

Douglas, J. D. and N. Hillyer, ed. *The Illustrated Bible Dictionary*. 3 vols. Leicester: Inter-Varsity Press, 1980.

Freedman, D. N., ed. *Anchor Bible Dictionary*. 6 vols. New York: Doubleday, 1992.

Freedman, D. N., ed. *Eerdmans Dictionary of the Bible*. Grand Rapids: Eerdmans, 2000.

Gower, R. *The New Manners and Customs of Bible Times*. Chicago: Moody Press, 1987.

Master, D. M., ed. *The Oxford Encyclopedia of the Bible and Archaeology*. 2 vols. Oxford: Oxford University Press, 2013.

Matthews, V. H. *Manners and Customs in the Bible*. Peabody, MA: Hendrickson, 1988.

Pfeiffer, C. F., ed. *The Biblical World: A Dictionary of Biblical Archaeology*. Grand Rapids: Baker Book House, 1966.

Ryken, L., J. C. Wilhoit, and T. Longman III, ed. *Dictionary of Biblical Imagery*. Downers Grove: InterVarsity Press, 1998.

Sakenfeld, K. D., ed. *The New Interpreter's Dictionary of the Bible*. 5 vols. Nashville: Abingdon, 2006–2009.

Thompson, J. A. *Handbook of Life in Bible Times*. Leicester: Inter-Varsity Press, 1986.

Toorn, K. van der, B. Becking, and P. van der Horst, ed. *Dictionary of Deities and Demons in the Bible*. 2nd ed. Leiden: Brill; Grand Rapids: Eerdmans, 1999.

The Old Testament

Arnold, B. T. and H. G. M. Williamson, ed. *Dictionary of the Old Testament: Historical Books*. Downers Grove: InterVarsity Press, 2005.

Avi-Yonah, M., ed. *Encyclopedia of Archaeological Excavations in the Holy Land*. 4 vols. London: Oxford University Press, 1975–1978.

Borowski, O. *Daily Life in Biblical Times*. Atlanta: Society of Biblical Literature, 2003.

Borowski, O. *Every Living Thing: Daily Use of Animals in Ancient Israel*. Walnut Creek, CA: Altamira Press, 1998.

Botterweck, G. J. and H. Ringgren, ed. *Theological Dictionary of the Old Testament*. 15 vols. Grand Rapids: Eerdmans, 1974–2008.

De Vaux, R. *Ancient Israel: Its Life and Institutions*. Trans. John McHugh. New York: McGraw-Hill Book Co., 1961.

Dever, W. G. *The Lives of Ordinary People in Ancient Israel*. Grand Rapids: Eerdmans, 2012.

Ebeling, J. R. *Women's Lives in Biblical Times*. London: T & T Clark, 2010.

Harris, R. L., G. L. Archer, and B. K. Waltke, ed. *Theological Wordbook of the Old Testament*. 2 vols. Chicago: Moody Press, 1980.

Hoerth, A. J., G. L. Mattingly, and E. M. Yamauchi, ed. *Peoples of the Old Testament World*. Grand Rapids: Baker Books, 1994.

Isserlin, B .S. J. *The Israelites*. London: Thames and Hudson, 1998.

King, P. J. and L. E. Stager. *Life in Biblical Israel*. Louisville: Westminster John Knox Press, 2001.

Matthews, V. H. and D. C. Benjamin. *Social World of Ancient Israel: 1250–587 BCE*. Peabody: Hendrickson, 1993.

Stern, E., ed. *The New Encyclopedia of Archaeological Excavations in the Holy Land V: Supplementary Volume*. Jerusalem: Israel Exploration Society; Washington, DC: Biblical Archaeological Society, 2008.

VanGemeren, W. A., ed. *New International Dictionary of Old Testament Theology & Exegesis*. 5 vols. Grand Rapids: Zondervan, 1997.

Walton, J. H. *Ancient Near Eastern Thought and the Old Testament*. Grand Rapids: Baker Academic, 2006.

Wiseman, D. J., ed. *Peoples of Old Testament Times*. Oxford: Clarendon Press, 1973.

The New Testament

Bell, A. A. *Exploring the New Testament World*. Nashville: Thomas Nelson, 1998.

Bouquet, A. C. *Everyday Life in New Testament Times*. New York: Charles Scribner's Sons, 1954.

Charlesworth, J. H., ed. *Jesus and Archaeology*. Grand Rapids: Eerdmans, 2006.

Daniel-Rops, H. *Daily Life in Palestine at the Time of Christ*. London: Phoenix Press, 1962.

Deissmann, A. *Light from the Ancient East: The New Testament Illustrated by Recently Discovered Texts of the Graeco-Roman World*. Grand Rapids: Baker Book House, 1965 repr.

Evans, C. and S. E. Porter, ed. *Dictionary of New Testament Background*. Downers Grove: InterVarsity Press, 2000.

Green, J. B. and L. M. McDonald, ed. *The World of the New Testament: Cultural, Social, and Historical Contexts*. Grand Rapids: Baker Academic, 2013.

Hall, J. F. and J. W. Welch, ed. *Masada and the World of the New Testament*. Provo: Brigham Young University Press, 1997.

Hawthorne, G. F., R. P. Martin, and D. G. Reid, ed. *Dictionary of Paul and His Letters*. Downers Grove: InterVarsity Press, 1993.

Jeffers, J. S. *Greco-Roman World of the New Testament Era*. Downers Grove: InterVarsity Press, 1999.

Kittel, G., ed. *Theological Dictionary of the New Testament*. 10 vols. Grand Rapids: Eerdmans, 1964.

Rousseau, J. J. and R. Arav. *Jesus & His World: An Archaeological and Cultural Dictionary*. Minneapolis: Fortress Press, 1995.

Tenney, M. C. *New Testament Times*. Grand Rapids: Eerdmans, 1965.

Yamauchi, E. M. *Harper's World of the New Testament*. San Francisco: Harper & Row, 1981.

B. THE NEAR EASTERN WORLD

Averbeck, R. E., M. W. Chavalas, and D. B. Weisberg, ed. *Life and Culture in the Ancient Near East*. Bethesda: CDL Press, 2003.

Collins, B. J., ed. *A History of the Animal World in the Ancient Near East*. Leiden: Brill, 2002.

Gates, C. *Ancient Cities: The Archaeology of Urban Life in the Ancient Near East and Egypt, Greece and Rome.* 2nd ed. London: Routledge, 2011.

Meyers, E. M., ed. *The Oxford Encyclopedia of Archaeology in the Near East.* 5 vols. New York: Oxford University Press, 1997.

Pritchard, J. B., ed. *The Ancient Near East in Pictures Relating to the Old Testament.* Princeton: Princeton University Press, 1954.

Pritchard, J. B., ed. *Ancient Near Eastern Texts Relating to the Old Testament.* 3rd ed. Princeton: Princeton University Press, 1969.

Pritchard, J. B., ed. *The Ancient Near East: Supplementary Texts and Pictures Relating to the Old Testament.* Princeton: Princeton University Press, 1969.

Sasson, J., ed. *Civilizations of the Ancient Near East.* 4 vols. New York: Charles Scribners, 1995; repr. 2 vols. Peabody: Hendrickson, 2000.

Mesopotamia

Bertman, S. *Handbook to Life in Ancient Mesopotamia.* New York: Facts On File, 2003.

Bienkowski, P. and A. Millard, ed. *Dictionary of the Ancient Near East.* Philadelphia: University of Pennsylvania Press, 2000.

Bottéro, J. *Everyday Life in Ancient Mesopotamia.* Baltimore: Johns Hopkins University Press, 2001.

Gelb, I. J. et al., ed. *The Assyrian Dictionary of the Oriental Institute of the University of Chicago.* 20 vols. Chicago: University of Chicago Press, 1956–2010.

Hallo, W. W. *Origins: The Ancient Near Eastern Background of Some Modern Western Institutions.* Leiden: Brill, 1996.

Leick, G., ed. *The Babylonian World.* New York: Routledge, 2007.

Nemet-Nejat, K. R. *Daily Life in Ancient Mesopotamia.* Westport: Greenwood Press, 1998.

Saggs, H. W. F. *Everyday Life in Babylonia & Assyria.* New York: Dorset Press, 1965.

Sasson, J. M. *From the Archives of Mari: An Anthology of Old Babylonian Letters.* Winona Lake: Eisenbrauns, 2015.

Snell, D. C., ed. *A Companion to the Ancient Near East.* Oxford: Blackwell Pub., 2007.

Snell, D. C. *Life in the Ancient Near East.* New Haven: Yale University Press, 1997.

Egypt

Brier, B. and H. Hobbs. *Ancient Egypt: Everyday Life in the Land of the Nile.* New York: Sterling, 2009.

Bunson, M. *A Dictionary of Ancient Egypt.* New York: Oxford University Press, 1991.

Casson, L. *Everyday Life in Ancient Egypt.* Baltimore: Johns Hopkins University Press, 1975.

David, R. *Handbook to Life in Ancient Egypt.* Oxford: Oxford University Press, 1998.

Erman, A. *Life in Ancient Egypt.* London: Macmillan & Co., 1894; repr. New York: Dover Publications, 1971.

Freed, R. E., ed. *Egypt's Golden Age: The Art of Living in the New Kingdom, 1558–1085 B.C.* Boston: Museum of Fine Arts, 1982.

Lucas, A. and J. R. Harris. *Ancient Egyptian Materials and Industries.* Mineola: Dover Publications, 1999 repr.

Mertz, B. *Red Land, Black Land: Daily Life in Ancient Egypt.* New York: Harper, 1978.

Montet, P. *Everyday Life in Egypt in the Days of Ramesses the Great.* London: Edward Arnold, 1958.

Nicholson, P. T., and I. Shaw, ed. *Ancient Egyptian Materials and Technology.* Cambridge: Cambridge University Press, 2000.

Redford, D. B., ed. *The Oxford Encyclopedia of Ancient Egypt.* Oxford: Oxford University Press, 2001.

Silverman, D. P., ed. *Ancient Egypt.* London: Piatkus, 1997.

Szpakowska, K. *Daily Life in Ancient Egypt.* Oxford: Blackwell Publishing, 2008.

Wilkinson, T., ed. *The Egyptian World.* London: Routledge, 2007.

C. THE GRECO-ROMAN WORLD

Aldrete, G. S. and A. *The Long Shadow of Antiquity: What Have the Greeks and Romans Done for Us?* London: Continuum, 2012.

Avi-Yonah, M. and I. Shatzman, ed. *Illustrated Encyclopaedia of the Classical World.* New York: Harper & Row, 1975.

Campbell, G. L., ed. *The Oxford Handbook of Animals in Classical Thought and Life.* Oxford: Oxford University Press, 2014.

Cary, M. and T. J. Haarhoff, ed. *Life and Thought in the Greek and Roman World.* London: Methuen & Co., 1963 repr.

Connolly, P. and H. Dodge. *The Ancient City: Life in Classical Athens & Rome.* Oxford: Oxford University Press, 2001.

Gates, C. *Ancient Cities: The Archaeology of Urban Life in the Ancient Near East and Egypt, Greece and Rome.* 2nd ed. London: Routledge, 2011.

Grant, M. and R. Kitzinger, ed. *Civilizations of the Ancient Mediterranean.* 3 vols. New York: Charles Scribner's Sons, 1988.

Hornblower, S. and A. Spawforth, ed. *The Oxford Classical Dictionary.* Oxford: Oxford University Press, 1996.

Hornblower, S. and A. Spawforth, ed. *The Oxford Companion to Classical Civilization.* Oxford: Oxford University Press, 1998.

Humphrey, J. W., J. P. Oleson, and A. N. Sherwood, ed. *Greek and Roman Technology: A Sourcebook.* London: Routledge, 1998.

Lefkowitz, M. R., and M. B. Fant, ed. *Women's Life in Greece and Rome: A Source Book in Translation.* 3rd ed. Baltimore: Johns Hopkins University Press, 2005.

Greece

Adkins, L. and R. A. *Handbook to Life in Ancient Greece.* New York: Facts On File, 1994.

Devambez, P., R. Flacelière, P.-M. Schuhl, and R. Martin, ed. *The Praeger Encyclopedia of Ancient Greek Civilization.* New York: Frederick A. Praeger, 1966.

Flacelière, R. *Daily Life in Greece at the Time of Pericles.* New York: Macmillan Company, 1966.

Garland, R. *The Greek Way of Life.* Ithaca: Cornell University Press, 1993.

Hooper, F. *Greek Realities: Life and Thought in Ancient Greece.* New York: Charles Scribner's Sons, 1967.

Powell, A., ed. *The Greek World.* London: Routledge, 1995.

Sacks, D. *Encyclopedia of the Ancient Greek World.* New York: Facts On File, 1995.

Scarborough, J. *Facets of Hellenic Life.* Boston: Houghton Mifflin, 1976.

Wace, A. J. B., and F. H. Stubbings. ed. *A Companion to Homer.* London: MacMillan & Co., 1962.

Rome

Adkins, L. and R. A. *Handbook to Life in Ancient Rome.* New York: Oxford University Press, 1997.

Bunson, M., ed. *Encyclopedia of the Roman Empire.* New York: Facts On File, 1994.

Carcopino, J. *Daily Life in Ancient Rome.* New Haven: Yale University Press, 1960.

Casson, L. *Everyday Life in Ancient Rome.* Rev. ed. Baltimore: Johns Hopkins University, 1998.

Dobbins, J. J. and P. W. Foss, ed. *The World of Pompeii.* London: Routledge, 2008.

Dupont, F. *Daily Life in Ancient Rome.* Oxford: Blackwell, 1994.

Freeman, C. *The World of the Romans*. New York: Oxford University Press, 1993.

Gardner, J. F. and T. Wiedemann, ed. *The Roman Household: A Sourcebook*. London: Routledge, 1991.

Levick, B., ed. *The Government of the Roman Empire: A Sourcebook*. 2nd ed. London: Routledge, 2000.

Lewis, N. and M. Reinhold, ed. *Roman Civilization I: The Republic and the Augustan Age*. 3rd ed. New York: Columbia University Press, 1990.

Lewis, N. and M. Reinhold, ed. *Roman Civilization II: The Empire*. 3rd ed. New York: Columbia University Press, 1990.

Parkin, T. G. and A. J. Pomeroy. *Roman Social History: A Sourcebook*. London: Routledge, 2007.

Rodgers, N. *Life in Ancient Rome*. London: Southwater, 2008.

Shelton, J., ed. *As the Romans Did: A Sourcebook in Roman Social History*. 2nd ed. New York: Oxford University Press, 1998.

D. THE JEWISH WORLD

Ausubel, N. *The Book of Jewish Knowledge*. New York: Crown Publishers, 1964.

Collins, J. J. and D. C. Harlow, ed. *The Eerdmans Dictionary of Early Judaism*. Grand Rapids: Eerdmans, 2010.

Hezser, C., ed. *The Oxford Handbook of Jewish Daily Life in Roman Palestine*. Oxford: Oxford University Press, 2010.

Jacobs, J., ed. *The Jewish Encyclopedia*. 12 vols. New York: Funk & Wagnalls, 1901–2006.

Magness, J. *Stone and Dung, Oil and Spit: Jewish Daily Life in the Time of Jesus*. Grand Rapids: Eerdmans, 2011.

Neusner, J. and W. S. Green, ed. *Dictionary of Judaism in the Biblical Period*. Peabody: Hendrickson, 1999.

Schürer, E. *The History of the Jewish People in the Age of Jesus Christ (175 B.C.–A.D. 135)*, rev. and ed. G. Vermes and F. Millar. 3 vols. Edinburgh: T. & T. Clark, 1973–1987.

Skolnik, F., ed. *Encyclopaedia Judaica*. 16 vols. New York: Macmillan, 1971–1972.

E. THE CHRISTIAN WORLD

Blumell, L. H. and T. A. Wayment, ed. *Christian Oxyrhynchus: Texts, Documents, and Sources*. Waco: Baylor University Press, 2015.

Bowersock, W., P. Brown, and O. Grabar, ed. *Late Antiquity: A Guide to the Postclassical World*. Cambridge: Belknap Press, 1999.

Cohick, L. H. *Women in the World of the Earliest Christians*. Grand Rapids: Baker Academic, 2009.

Cross, F. L. and E. A. Livingstone, ed. *The Oxford Dictionary of the Christian Church*. Oxford: Oxford University Press, 1997.

Daniélou, J. *Primitive Christian Symbols*. Baltimore: Helicon Press, 1961.

Di Berardino, A., ed. *Encyclopedia of Ancient Christianity*. 3 vols. Downers Grove: IVP Academic, 2014.

Ermatinger, J. W. *Daily Life of Christians in Ancient Rome*. Westport: Greenwood Press, 2007.

Esler, P. F., ed. *The Early Christian World*. 2 vols. London: Routledge, 2000.

Ferguson, E., ed. *Encyclopedia of Early Christianity*. New York: Garland Publishing, 1990.

Forell, G. W. *History of Christian Ethics I: From the New Testament to Augustine*. Minneapolis: Augsburg Publishing House, 1979.

Guy, L. *Introducing Early Christianity: A Topical Survey of Its Life, Beliefs & Practices*. Downers Grove: InterVarsity Press, 2004.

Lee, A. D., ed. *Pagans and Christians in Late Antiquity: A Sourcebook*. London: Routledge, 2000.

MacMullen, R. and E. N. Lane, ed. *Paganism and Christianity 100–425 C.E.: A Sourcebook*. Minneapolis: Fortress Press, 1992.

Mitchell, M. M. and F. M. Young, ed. *The Cambridge History of Christianity I: Origins to Constantine*. Cambridge: Cambridge University Press, 2006.

Robinson, T. A. *The Early Church: An Annotated Bibliography of Literature in English*. Metuchen: Scarecrow Press, 1993.

Stevenson, J., ed. *A New Eusebius: Documents Illustrative of the History of the Church to A.D. 337*. London: S.P.C.K., 1960.

Thomson, B. *A Bibliography of Christian Worship*. Metuchen: Scarecrow Press, 1989.

Veyne, P., ed. *A History of Private Life I: From Pagan Rome to Byzantium*. Cambridge: Harvard University Press, 1987.

Volz, C. A. *Faith and Practice in the Early Church*. Minneapolis: Augsburg Publishing House, 1983.

Young, F., L. Ayres, and A. Louth, ed. *The Cambridge History of Early Christian Literature*. Cambridge; Cambridge University Press, 2004.

Figure 1 [Sanitation]. A multi-seat latrine associated with a public bath at Ostia, a port city near the mouth of the Tiber River, which flourished in the 1st–2nd c. AD. There were two other similar latrines in the city. Courtesy of William L. Krewson/BiblePlaces.com.

Figure 2 [Sanitation]. This is an illustration of a military latrine. Note the sponge-stick, which was used to clean the anus after defecation, and the shallow gutter of water at the feet, which was used to rinse out the sponge-stick. Photo: akg-images / Peter Connolly.

Figure 3 [Sanitation]. A multi-seat public latrine from the Scholastica
Baths near the Library of Celsus at Ephesus. Seats were arranged around
three sides of the room. This is an example of a "luxury latrine" developed
in the 2nd c. AD with mosaic floors, marble paneling, and provision
for air and light. Courtesy of Steven H. Sanchez/BiblePlaces.com.

Figure 4 [Seals]. A seal impression of Jehukal son of Shelemiah (*lyhwkl bn šlmyhw*), one of Zedekiah's officials (Jer 37:3), discovered by Eilat Mazar in her excavations in Jerusalem in 2005. Photo: Gabi Laron, Institute of Archeology, Hebrew University. Courtesy of Eilat Mazar.

Figure 5 [Seals]. A seal impression of Gedaliah son of Pashhur (*lgdlyhw bn pšḥwr*), another official of Zedekiah (Jer 38:1), discovered by Eilat Mazar in her excavations in Jerusalem in 2008. Photo: Gabi Laron, Institute of Archeology, Hebrew University. Courtesy of Eilat Mazar.

Figure 6 [Seals]. A seal impression of Hezekiah bearing the Hebrew text *lḥz[q]yhw ʾ[ḥ]z mlk yhd*, "Belonging to Hezekiah (son) of Ahaz, King of Judah," discovered by Eilat Mazar in her excavations in Jerusalem in 2015. Photo: Ouria Tadmor, © Eilat Mazar.

Figure 7 [Time]. A limestone clepsydra, or "water clock," from Memphis, Egypt (ca. 3rd c. BC). The interior had twelve vertical rows of holes, which let the water flow out at a known rate of time. Courtesy of the Oriental Institute of the University of Chicago.

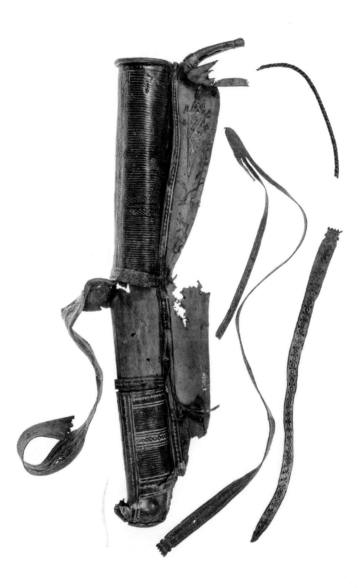

Figure 8 [Weapons]. This quiver was discovered at Qustul in the Sudan near the Second
Cataract of the Nile River and was from the Ballana (formerly called the X-Group)
Culture, ca. 4th–5th c. AD. The warriors of this region (ancient Kush, later known
as Nubia) were famed from the second millennium BC down through the centuries
as expert archers. Courtesy of the Oriental Institute of the University of Chicago.

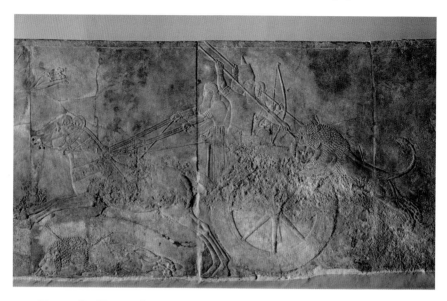

Figure 9 [Wild Animals & Hunting]. Ashurbanipal, the last great Neo-Assyrian king (7th c. BC), celebrated his prowess by hunting lions from a chariot. The lions had been captured, caged, and released in a restricted area where an audience could watch. Photo © The Trustees of the British Museum.

Figure 10 [Wild Animals & Hunting]. With exquisite detail the Assyrian sculptors depicted numerous lions and lionesses who were struck with arrows and spears in various stages of dying. As ancient sculptures were originally painted, the flow of blood gushing out of the lion's mouth would have been colored red. Photo © The Trustees of the British Museum.